The Cambridge Economic History of Modern Britain

Volume II: Economic Maturity, 1860–1939

The Cambridge Economic History of Modern Britain provides a readable and comprehensive survey of the economic history of Britain since industrialisation, based on the most up-to-date research into the subject. Roderick Floud and Paul Johnson have assembled a team of fifty leading scholars from around the world to produce a set of volumes which are both a lucid textbook for undergraduate and postgraduate students and an authoritative guide to the subject. The text pays particular attention to the explanation of quantitative and theory-based enquiry, but all forms of historical research are used to provide a comprehensive account of the development of the British economy. Volume I covers the period 1700–1860 when Britain led the world in the process of industrialisation. Volume II examines the period 1860–1939 when British economic power was at its height. The focus of volume III is 1939–2000, when Britain adjusted to a decline in manufacturing, an expansion of the service economy and a repositioning of external economic activity towards Europe. The books provide an invaluable guide for undergraduate and postgraduate students in history, economics and other social sciences.

RODERICK FLOUD is Vice-Chancellor of London Metropolitan University, a Fellow of the British Academy, an Academician of the Social Sciences and a Fellow of the City and Guilds of London Institute. His publications include *An Introduction to Quantitative Methods for Historians* and (with D. McCloskey) *The Economic History of Britain since 1700.*

PAUL JOHNSON is Professor of Economic History at the London School of Economics and an Academician of the Social Sciences. He has authored or edited seven books and over fifty articles and chapters on various aspects of the economic, social and legal history of modern Britain, and on the economics of ageing and pensions. Publications include *Saving and Spending: The Working-Class Economy in Britain 1870–1939*, *Ageing and Economic Welfare* and *Old Age: From Antiquity to Post-Modernity.*

The Cambridge Economic History of Modern Britain

Volume II: Economic Maturity, 1860–1939

Edited by Roderick Floud
London Metropolitan University

and Paul Johnson
London School of Economics

CAMBRIDGE
UNIVERSITY PRESS

PUBLISHED BY THE PRESS SYNDICATE OF THE UNIVERSITY OF CAMBRIDGE
The Pitt Building, Trumpington Street, Cambridge, United Kingdom

CAMBRIDGE UNIVERSITY PRESS
The Edinburgh Building, Cambridge CB2 2RU, UK
40 West 20th Street, New York, NY 10011–4211, USA
477 Williamstown Road, Port Melbourne, VIC 3207, Australia
Ruiz de Alarcón 13, 28014 Madrid, Spain
Dock House, The Waterfront, Cape Town 8001, South Africa

http://www.cambridge.org

First published 2003

Printed in the United Kingdom at the University Press, Cambridge

Typeface Swift 9.5/12.5 pt. and Formata *System* LaTeX 2ε [TB]

A catalogue record for this book is available from the British Library

ISBN 0 521 82037 5
ISBN 0 521 52737 6

To Louisa and Oriana

Contents

Figures

Tables

Contributors

DUDLEY BAINES is Reader in Economic History at the London School of Economics

SUE BOWDEN is Professor of Economics at the University of Sheffield

GEORGE R. BOYER is Professor of Labor Economics at the School of Industrial and Labor Relations, Cornell University

STEPHEN BROADBERRY is Professor of Economic History at the University of Warwick

P. L. COTTRELL is Professor of Financial History at the University of Leicester

NICHOLAS CRAFTS is Professor of Economic History at the London School of Economics

MICHAEL EDELSTEIN is Professor of Economics at Queen's College and the Graduate School at City University of New York

BARRY EICHENGREEN is Professor of Economics and Political Science at the University of California at Berkeley

RODERICK FLOUD is Vice-Chancellor of London Metropolitan University

C. KNICK HARLEY is Professor of Economics at the University of Western Ontario

TIMOTHY J. HATTON is Professor of Economics at the University of Essex

DAVID M. HIGGINS is Lecturer in Economics at the University of Sheffield

PAUL JOHNSON is Professor of Economic History at the London School of Economics

CLIVE H. LEE is Professor of Historical Economics at the University of Aberdeen

GARY B. MAGEE is Senior Lecturer in Economics at the University of Melbourne

ROGER MIDDLETON is Reader in the History of Political Economy at the University of Bristol

TOM NICHOLAS is Visiting Assistant Professor, Strategy and International Management Group, MIT Sloan School of Management

DUNCAN M. ROSS is Lecturer in Economic History at the University of Glasgow

MARK THOMAS is Associate Professor of History at the University of Virginia

MICHAEL TURNER is Professor of Economic History at the University of Hull

ROBERT WOODS is Professor of Geography at the University of Liverpool

Preface

In their gloomier moments, academics are prone to predict the demise of their subject. As the tastes of students change, as the economy waxes and wanes, as the number of academic jobs fluctuates and the average age of academics increases, so it is easy to discern a long-term decline in the attractiveness of any subject.

Economic historians, above all, ought to be wary of such speculation. After all, if there is one single thing which is taught by study of the subject of economic history, it is that change is continuous and usually slow. As economists put it, 'change is at the margin'; it proceeds by tiny increments or decrements and the end, or even the direction, is rarely to be seen by those who are living through the changes. But change is always with us, a lesson which needs to be learned by each generation. It should be learned particularly by those eminent economic commentators who, at each stage of the business cycle, confidently predict that that stage, whether of boom or bust, will go on forever. But it must be learned also by those who predict that an academic subject is in terminal decline.

On the evidence of the three volumes of *The Cambridge Economic History of Modern Britain*, reports of the death of economic history are clearly premature and probably mistaken. The volumes demonstrate a vibrant subject, reaching out into new areas of research and using new techniques to explore new and old problems. Economic history, as revealed in these pages, is a true interdisciplinary subject, a point emphasised also by the contributors to *Living Economic and Social History* (Hudson 2001) which was published to celebrate the 75th anniversary of the Economic History Society, the guardian of the subject in the United Kingdom.

As Pat Hudson emphasises, the subject has certainly changed. The rotund phrases of Ephraim Lipson, the beautifully crafted analyses of John Clapham, have given way to equations, to the quantitative analysis of bizarre sources such as human skeletal remains and to the increasing emphasis on the study of national economic histories within their global environment. Yet the essence of the subject remains: in the words which are used each Sunday to advertise the *News of the World*, 'all human life is here'. Economic history is about the behaviour of human beings in an uncertain world, as they struggle to earn a living, as they decide when to have a child, as they band together in a common cause or, all too often, fall out and resort to conflict or war.

The economic history of modern Britain, the subject of these volumes, has seen all these and billions more human acts, collective and individual. In most cases, economic history is about collective behaviour. There are few 'great men' (and even fewer 'great women') in British economic history, mainly because economic change can very rarely be attributed to a single person. Even if, on occasion, economic historians identify one person as an inventor who has changed the world, other historians will usually jump in to claim the credit for another, or at the extreme will claim that, counter-factually, the invention really did not make much difference. This alone is enough to keep the subject changing. But also, because we cannot directly observe collective behaviour or describe myriad individual acts, the subject has to theorise as well as describe. Only through theory can we hope to make sense of the economic past.

Some academic subjects, in such circumstances, turn in on themselves and allow theory to predominate. Often, they become the preserve of the favoured few, writing and publishing for each other, theorising in increasingly arcane language. New technologies of academe, the email and the working paper, abet these tendencies as the results of research are circulated within an inner circle and only emerge, months or years later, to inform a wider audience.

The Cambridge Economic History of Modern Britain, by contrast, belongs to a tradition which believes that research and scholarship have no purpose if they are not used, if they are not disseminated as soon as possible to as wide an audience as possible. In other words, its editors and authors have a mission to explain. This certainly does not obviate the use of the most ingenious and complex techniques to tease out the mysteries of the past; it does demand, however, that the techniques and the results that stem from them are explained clearly, concisely and in language which anyone interested in the topic can understand. This was the aspiration which lay, for example, behind *The Economic History of Britain since 1700* (Floud and McCloskey 1981, 1994) and it still animates these volumes. They belong to an academic tradition exemplified by Lord Rutherford, the great Cambridge scientist, who believed (in somewhat antiquated parlance) that 'The good scientist should be able to explain his results to the charlady in his lab.'

These volumes, therefore, are textbooks, in the best sense of books which explain their subject. They are written by leading researchers, drawn from many countries around the world, who have themselves recently contributed to our understanding of British economic history; usually with pleasure, they accept the obligation to tell students and others with an interest in their subjects about the results of academic enquiry by themselves and others in the field. It is not always possible, of course, to be sure of the background knowledge which each reader will possess; most of the techniques and technical terms have been explained as they are used in the chapters which follow, but some readers – if they are puzzled – may need to consult a dictionary or a dictionary of economics.

All authors need critics. A phrase which seems limpidly clear to one person may baffle another and only an informed critic can help the author to express complex notions in a comprehensible way. For this reason, all the drafts of the chapters which follow were discussed, not only by the editors, but by all the other authors within each volume and by a number of invited commentators who gathered together at a conference held in London Guildhall University. The editors are grateful to those commentators: Martin Daunton, Tim Leunig, Richard Smith, Emmett Sullivan, Barry Supple, Rick Trainor and Peter Wardley. Our grateful thanks go also to the Economic and Social Research Council, the British Academy, the Gatsby Foundation and Cambridge University Press for their support for the conference and the production of these volumes. Richard Fisher, Elizabeth Howard and Helen Barton at Cambridge University Press have encouraged us throughout the process of publication and we have also had the invaluable support of an exemplary research assistant, Claudia Edwards.

Roderick Floud and Paul Johnson

1 Long-run growth

NICHOLAS CRAFTS

Contents

INTRODUCTION

This chapter reviews UK economic growth performance from mid-Victorian times to the end of the interwar period. It aims to place this experience in the context both of initial British pre-eminence and subsequent relative economic decline and of new ideas in growth economics. A growth accounting framework is used to establish the proximate sources of growth and to compare UK experience with that of Germany and the United States. Against this background, special attention is given to two controversies, namely, whether the British economy 'failed' in the late Victorian and Edwardian period and whether the interwar period and, especially the 1930s, saw a successful regeneration of the economy's growth potential. Finally, in so far as the UK underperformed during these years, it is important to examine the incentive structures which informed decisions to invest and to innovate and the roles played by market and/or government failure.

AN OVERVIEW OF GROWTH

Britain was the first industrial nation but by the end of the twentieth century had become just another OECD[1] economy with an income level below that of North America, most of western Europe and parts of East Asia. This relative economic decline is sometimes regarded as a continuous process that started around 1870 and had already alarmed contemporaries in the late nineteenth century as Germany and the United States emerged as powerful economic rivals. Its dimensions are, however, not well understood by many commentators. This section sets out a basic quantitative framework within which debates about UK growth performance can be placed.

Table 1.1 reports estimates of income levels and growth rates of real GDP per person for western European economies and for Japan and the United States in the period 1870–1938. The units of measurement are 'purchasing power adjusted' dollars of 1990 so that account has been taken of differences in internal price levels in the assessment of the relative standing of different countries. While these estimates are subject to a number of health warnings in terms of both the imperfect nature of the underlying economic data and the difficulties of solving the 'index number problems' of tracking real output through time, the broad picture in Table 1.1 is reliable enough to make the following points. First, the UK was a clear leader in terms of income per head in 1870 but was overtaken by the USA around the start of the twentieth century and by Switzerland in the interwar period. Nevertheless, the UK continued through to the end of the 1930s to have an income level well ahead of that of both France and Germany – overtaking by these continental European rivals took place during the 'golden age' of European growth after the Second World War. Second, over the whole period 1870–1938 several European countries were catching up through faster growth that enabled them to reduce the income gap with the UK; these included Denmark, Germany and Sweden, while the majority of European countries had faster growth rates than did the UK. Third, in general, growth rates in these years were modest relative to the achievements of the 'golden age' of the 1950s and 1960s when growth of per capita income between 3 and 6 per cent per year was the rule and they were also somewhat below the late twentieth-century experience of these countries (Maddison 2001).

Table 1.2 reports on productivity rather than real income per person. Here the data are more problematic and the table is restricted to comparisons with Germany and the United States where the data are relatively good. The table reports both labour productivity and total factor productivity (TFP). The former is defined as output per worker whereas the

[1] The Organisation for Economic Co-operation and Development, a group of leading developed nations.

Table 1.1 Levels and rates of growth of real GDP/person, 1870, 1913 and 1938 (measured in $1990 international and % per year)

1870		1913		1938	
UK	3,191	UK	4,921	Switzerland	6,390
Netherlands	2,753	Switzerland	4,266	UK	5,851
Belgium	2,697	Belgium	4,220	Denmark	5,762
Switzerland	2,202	Netherlands	4,049	Netherlands	5,250
Denmark	2,003	Denmark	3,912	Germany	5,126
Germany	1,913	Germany	3,833	Belgium	4,833
France	1,876	France	3,485	Sweden	4,725
Austria	1,863	Austria	3,465	France	4,466
Ireland	1,775	Sweden	3,096	Norway	4,337
Sweden	1,664	Ireland	2,736	Finland	3,590
Italy	1,499	Italy	2,564	Austria	3,559
Norway	1,432	Norway	2,501	Italy	3,318
Spain	1,376	Spain	2,255	Ireland	3,119
Finland	1,140	Finland	2,111	Greece	2,678
Portugal	997	Greece	1,592	Spain	2,022
Greece	913	Portugal	1,244	Portugal	1,568
Japan	737	Japan	1,385	Japan	2,449
USA	2,445	USA	5,301	USA	6,126
1870–1913		1913–38			
UK	1.0	UK	0.7		
Netherlands	0.9	Switzerland	1.6		
Belgium	1.0	Belgium	0.6		
Switzerland	1.6	Netherlands	1.0		
Denmark	1.6	Denmark	1.6		
Germany	1.6	Germany	1.2		
France	1.4	France	1.0		
Austria	1.4	Austria	0.1		
Ireland	1.0	Sweden	1.7		
Sweden	1.5	Ireland	0.5		
Italy	1.3	Italy	1.0		
Norway	1.3	Norway	2.2		
Spain	1.2	Spain	−0.4		
Finland	1.4	Finland	2.1		
Portugal	0.5	Greece	2.1		
Greece	1.3	Portugal	0.9		
Japan	1.5	Japan	2.3		
USA	1.8	USA	0.6		

Sources: Maddison 1995, 2001.

Table 1.2 Structural change and relative productivity levels, 1871–1973

	Employment shares			Labour productivity		TFP	
	UK	Germany	USA	Germany/UK	US/UK	Germany/UK	US/UK
1871							
Agriculture	22.2	49.5	50.0	55.7	86.9	58.3	98.4
Industry	42.4	29.1	24.8	86.2	153.6	86.0	153.8
Services	35.4	21.4	25.2	66.1	85.8	69.7	86.3
GDP	100.0	100.0	100.0	59.5	89.8	61.6	95.1
1911							
Agriculture	11.8	34.5	32.0	67.3	103.2	71.4	117.8
Industry	44.1	37.9	31.8	122.0	193.5	102.6	151.1
Services	44.1	27.6	36.2	81.3	107.3	83.2	71.7
GDP	100.0	100.0	100.0	75.5	117.7	75.3	90.5
1937							
Agriculture	6.2	29.9	17.9	57.2	103.3	59.7	118.8
Industry	44.5	38.2	31.6	99.1	190.6	97.1	161.1
Services	49.3	31.9	50.5	85.7	120.0	89.6	89.1
GDP	100.0	100.0	100.0	75.7	132.6	78.3	105.9
1950							
Agriculture	5.1	24.3	11.0	41.2	126.0	44.6	132.5
Industry	46.5	42.1	32.9	95.8	243.9	93.3	218.0
Services	48.4	33.6	56.1	83.1	140.8	89.2	110.2
GDP	100.0	100.0	100.0	74.4	166.9	76.2	138.1
1973							
Agriculture	2.9	7.2	3.7	50.8	131.2	48.1	127.2
Industry	41.8	47.3	28.9	128.9	215.1	112.4	202.4
Services	55.3	45.5	67.4	111.0	137.3	118.0	120.6
GDP	100.0	100.0	100.0	114.0	152.3	108.2	137.5

Note: Employment shares are in percentages. For the productivity levels comparisons in each year the UK level is normalised to 100. For Germany/UK comparison the year is 1935 not 1937.

Source: Broadberry 2003.

latter is a weighted average of output per worker and output per unit of capital and, if well measured, will reflect differences in technology and in the efficiency with which labour and capital were used. TFP estimates are a very important way of benchmarking a country's productivity performance. Unfortunately, in this period they are not altogether reliable, especially for Germany. The economy-wide comparisons of labour productivity in Table 1.2 are not too surprising given the estimates reported in Table 1.1. The United States took the lead before the First World War, had a sizeable lead in 1937 when its labour productivity exceeded that of the UK by almost a third and extended this to two-thirds by 1950. Germany narrowed the gap appreciably between 1871 and 1911 but remained distinctly behind the UK in 1937 and did not overtake the UK until the 1960s.

At the whole economy level, the level of TFP in Germany relative to the UK followed a broadly similar path to that of labour productivity. With regard to the United States, things were a little different as the UK retained its lead until after the First World War and there was only a small American lead in 1937. After the Second World War, however, a large TFP gap was apparent but even so this was appreciably lower than that in labour productivity. Throughout the twentieth century the American economy operated at a much greater level of capital intensity than the UK.

At the sectoral level, the picture is more complex. The USA already had a substantial lead over the UK in labour productivity in industry in 1871; this had grown substantially by 1950 but then the UK caught up a bit. In agriculture and services, American labour productivity was below that in the UK in 1870 but by 1911 this deficit had been turned into a small lead which was also sustained through 1937 and then extended after the Second World War, although productivity gaps in these sectors were always much lower than in industry. Interestingly, the United States did not extend its TFP lead in industry between 1871 and 1911 and the subsequent gains made relative to the UK before 1929 were not sustained during the 1930s but by 1950 the gap was much wider than in 1871. In services the UK TFP level was not overtaken by the United States until the 1940s.

Turning to Germany, where TFP and labour productivity comparisons are fairly similar, the most notable feature is the contrast between agriculture and industry. In industry, Germany overtook the UK in the early twentieth century and had established a lead of over 20 per cent by 1911 which was not, however, maintained between the wars but was re-established during the golden age after the Second World War. In agriculture, however, Germany persistently lagged far behind British levels of labour productivity. In services, Germany reduced Britain's lead during the early part of the period but did not surpass British productivity levels until the 1960s.

Table 1.2 also displays estimates of the sectoral composition of employment. Here the striking feature is that in 1871 the UK had a much smaller agricultural and a good deal larger industrial sector than either of the other two countries. Indeed, the UK was a major outlier in nineteenth-century Europe with regard to the small size of its agricultural sector which derived both from an early embrace of capitalist farming and from free-trade policies. Over time, these discrepancies in economic structure were considerably reduced, as Table 1.2 shows.

Two important points follow from this, as Broadberry (1998) has stressed. First, American overtaking of Britain was based to a considerable extent on relative trends in productivity in services combined with a large shift of labour into that sector rather than simply resulting from the development of higher labour productivity in industry. Second, the

Table 1.3 Aspects of economic growth in the long run, 1780–1973

	1780	1820	1870	1913	1937	1973
GDP/person ($1990 int.)	1,806	2,121	3,191	4,921	5,806	12,022
GDP growth (% p.a.)	1.0	1.9	2.4	1.4	2.2	2.8
TFP growth (% p.a.)	0.05	0.40	0.75	0.45	0.60	2.20
Life expectancy (e_0)	34.7	39.2	41.3	53.4	58.5	72.0
Adult literacy (%)	50	54	76	96	99	99
Primary enrolment (%)		36	76	100	100	100
Secondary enrolment (%)			1.7	5.5	9.9	73
R&D/GDP (%)				0.02	0.5	2.2
Non-residential investment/GDP (%)	4.8	5.3	7.4	7.4	6.0	14.6
Agricultural employment (%)	45	35	22.7	11.8	6.2	2.9

Note: Growth and investment rates are period averages.

Source: Updated from Crafts 1998.

explanation for Germany's relatively weak performance in real gross domestic product (GDP) per person and overall labour productivity (notwithstanding its industrial challenge to Britain) is seen to have resulted largely from a relatively large and low-productivity agriculture. Protectionist German trade policies are seen to have been costly in these terms.

Table 1.3 puts growth after 1870 in the context of experience during the earlier industrial revolution period. The feature that stands out in this table is that Britain was *never* a fast-growing economy prior to the Second World War. Indeed, from today's vantage point, the economy of the industrial revolution period can be seen as having relatively limited growth potential. This assessment is informed by several aspects reported in Table 1.3. Industrial revolution Britain was an economy which had very modest levels of investment in human and physical capital. Despite famous breakthroughs in textiles technology and more generally in the use of steam power, TFP growth in the classical period of the industrial revolution was unimpressive by post-First World War standards; the economy was characterised by weak technological capabilities and by substantial disincentives to innovative activity judged by later rather than contemporary standards (Crafts 1995). To sustain its early lead into and through the twentieth century, Britain would have had to progress very considerably beyond its industrial revolution capabilities. In fact, by the late nineteenth/early twentieth century considerable strides had been made in this direction (see chapters 3 and 4 below). A higher proportion of GDP was devoted to capital accumulation while rapid expansion of educational provision represented a big step forward in investment in people (Sanderson 1999) and the first industrial research and development laboratories were set up (Edgerton and Horrocks 1994). It should be noted, however, that all of these growth-promoting efforts were distinctly modest relative to what would come along after the Second World War and that, as we shall see, they did not entirely match the progress made in other countries.

In every respect, the 'golden age' economy after 1945 had a much higher growth potential than had been the case either during the industrial revolution or in the early twentieth century. Many more resources were devoted to physical investment, human capital formation and research and development (R&D) while TFP growth was far in excess of earlier times. The third quarter of the twentieth century was undoubtedly the period when economic decline relative to other European economies was at its most pronounced (Crafts 2002). Table 1.3 reminds us that this was not because absolute growth performance in the UK had diminished but rather because other countries had adapted better to the enhanced opportunities after the Second World War.

KEY IDEAS FROM GROWTH ECONOMICS

For many years the traditional neoclassical economic growth model ruled the roost. This viewed the sources of economic growth as being growth in the physical capital stock and the labour force and improvements in technology which raised the productivity of these factor inputs. This model has two key assumptions. First, capital accumulation is subject to diminishing returns. Second, technological progress is exogenous and universally available – in a famous phrase it is 'manna from heaven'. These assumptions are fundamental to two well-known long-run predictions of the neoclassical model, namely, that policy and institutions do not influence the rate of steady-state growth and that all countries converge to the same income level with initially poorer countries growing faster as they eliminate initial shortfalls of capital per worker. A variant on the neoclassical model is the so-called Augmented-Solow model which embodies a broader concept of capital including both physical and human capital but comes to the same conclusions albeit with less severely diminishing returns to investment.

Although some insights from this model found favour and an empirical technique derived from it, growth accounting, has been widely used in economic history, it is probably fair to say that the pure neoclassical model has generally been regarded by economic historians as unhelpful in most circumstances. In particular, the notions of universal technology and long-run income convergence have probably seemed far-fetched to historians accustomed to thinking in terms of, say, the new institutional economic history with its emphasis on the importance of institutions and political economy considerations to growth outcomes. Moreover, this model cannot really cope with the leading economy being overtaken and, after all, this is at the heart of Britain's relative economic decline.

Recent developments in growth economics offer more attractive features. These include the acceptance that institutions and policy can promote divergence in growth outcomes and, associated with this, the recognition that catch-up is not automatic. The central ideas concern the microeconomic foundations of growth and the concept of endogenous growth. These have come together most fruitfully in models that analyse the role of endogenous innovation in the growth process, i.e., that consider the rate of technological advance to be influenced by economic incentives. In effect, these models drop the assumption that technology, and the efficiency with which it is used, are universal. Carefully deployed, these ideas can inform a reappraisal of controversies surrounding British growth performance.

Endogenous growth occurs when long-run growth outcomes are determined by economic forces. This requires either that a mechanism is found to eliminate diminishing returns to capital accumulation or that the rate of technological progress is responsive to additional innovative effort without being undermined by diminishing returns to R&D. In such cases, good (bad) policy can permanently raise (lower) the growth rate of income per head, in the former case by leading to a higher investment rate and in the latter case by encouraging more resources into innovative activity.

The hypothesis of endogenous growth is highly controversial. The evidence does not support the claim that there are non-diminishing returns to investment in either narrow or broad capital. Second, the jury is still out on the claim that the steady-state growth rate of the leading economy can be increased by more R&D, but the experience of the late twentieth century is not very encouraging. For this reason, models that embody endogenous innovation do not all have this property (Jones 1995, 1999). Evidence of the impact of incentive structures on the rate of innovation is plentiful; for example, it is clear that the ability to appropriate returns, market size and demand growth all influence innovative effort (Jaffe 1988) and there is strong evidence for post-war Britain that intensification of competitive pressures on firms stimulates innovation (Aghion *et al.* 2002). The theoretical investigation of endogenous innovation has the potential to yield important insights into failures to exploit technological opportunities to the full and thus into long-run divergence of income levels and growth rates.

Broadly speaking, new growth economics suggests that there are two important aspects of the incentive structures that influence decisions to innovate and invest which matter for growth outcomes, namely their impact on expected returns and on agency problems (Aghion and Howitt 1998). Thus, institutions and policies that reduce the supply price of capital or research inputs or reduce fears of expropriation can increase innovative effort, speed up technology transfer and enhance the chances of rapid catch-up growth. Since effective and timely adoption of new technologies tends to be costly to managers of firms in terms of the effort required, it is also important that they are incentivised to work hard on behalf of the owners – when this is not the case we speak of performance being jeopardised by principal-agent problems. Unless there are large external shareholders who can internalise the benefits of effective monitoring of management, strong (though less than perfect) product market competition tends to be important in underpinning productivity performance (Nickell 1996).

Finally, these ideas resonate with economic historians' discussions of the international diffusion of technology. In particular, there is an obvious connection with the idea of 'social capability' used by Abramovitz and David (1996 and see below). But it should also be noted that in another departure from the assumption that technology is universal these authors stress the importance also of 'technological congruence' in catching up or falling behind. Here the point is that the cost-effectiveness of a technology may vary across countries where market size or cost conditions or availability of complementary factors of production are not the same and thus decisions whether or not to adopt it based on profit-maximisation can differ.

A GROWTH ACCOUNTING PERSPECTIVE

Growth accounting is a useful technique, much employed by economic historians, with which to examine long-run growth. It is well explained and put in the context of modern growth theory in Barro (1999). Despite problems that are discussed below, it provides a method of benchmarking growth performance and the estimates of TFP that result from its use are an important diagnostic in international comparisons. Growth accounting was central to the highly influential interpretation of the long-run development of the British economy by Matthews *et al.* (1982).

Growth accounting seeks to attribute growth to its proximate sources in terms of factor inputs and TFP. TFP is the weighted average of the growth of productivity of the individual factor inputs. The basic formula used in growth accounting is the following:

$$\Delta Y/Y = \alpha \Delta K/K + \beta \Delta L/L + \Delta A/A$$

where the growth rate ($\Delta Y/Y$) of output (Y) is accounted for in terms of the contribution of the capital stock ($\Delta K/K$) times the elasticity of output with respect to capital (α), the contribution of the labour force ($\Delta L/L$) times the elasticity of output with respect to labour (β) and the growth of TFP ($\Delta A/A$).

In practice, α and β are approximated by the shares of profits and wages, respectively, in national income, and TFP is found as a residual when estimates of all the other components have been entered into the formula. Capital stocks are estimated using the perpetual inventory method of adding up past investment flows and assuming a lifetime for capital assets, while labour inputs are usually measured in hours worked adjusted for the educational composition of the labour force. This formula would be exactly right if, as in traditional neoclassical growth theory, the economy could be thought of as an aggregate Cobb–Douglas production function, $Y = AK^{\alpha}L^{\beta}$ operating under conditions of perfect competition and constant returns to scale. The parameter A would reflect the state of technology and TFP growth would measure exogenous technological change ('manna from heaven').

Caution is required, however, before assuming that residual TFP growth really measures the contribution of technological change to economic growth. Technological change may be less than TFP growth if there are scale economies or improvements in the efficiency with which resources are used, or if improvements in the quality of factors of production are underestimated, for example owing to unmeasured human capital accumulation (Abramovitz 1993). By contrast, if the elasticity of substitution between factors of production is less than 1 and technological progress has a (Hicksian) labour-saving bias, as many analysts think is often the case, then conventional TFP growth underestimates the contribution of technological change and the mismeasurement increases with the growth in the capital to labour ratio, the degree of labour-saving bias, and the inelasticity of substitution (Rodrik 1997).

Since faster technological change raises the steady-state rate of growth of the capital stock in a traditional neoclassical growth model, part of its impact on growth compared with the counterfactual of no technological change shows up in capital's measured contribution. The advent of endogenous growth theory strengthens this kind of reason to believe that the contribution of technological change exceeds TFP growth. Thus, in models which envisage endogenous innovation driving growth through expanding varieties of capital inputs, a fraction of the contribution of the growth in varieties of capital facilitated by R&D accrues to capital and is not measured by TFP. The undermeasurement will be greater the larger is the endogenous component in technological progress (Barro 1999).

Table 1.4 reports a growth accounting decomposition of the sources of growth for the British economy from the onset of the industrial revolution to the end of the interwar period. These estimates are quite crude in that labour quality is not accounted for in labour's contribution but is part of the TFP residual (although an indication is given of the possible contribution of education) and prior to 1873 labour input is measured by numbers of workers rather than hours worked. The overall picture is one of accelerating growth from the mid-eighteenth to the mid-nineteenth century based on increased contributions from all three sources of growth. After 1873 growth was slower and all three sources of growth, notably including TFP growth, show decreased contributions. In

Table 1.4 Growth accounting estimates, 1760–1973 (% per year)

	Output growth	Capital contribution	Labour contribution	TFP growth	Education
1760–80	0.6	0.25	0.35	0.00	0.0
1780–1831	1.7	0.60	0.80	0.30	0.0
1831–73	2.4	0.90	0.75	0.75	0.3
1873–1913	1.8	0.80	0.55	0.45	0.3
1924–37	2.2	0.55	1.05	0.60	0.3
1951–73	2.8	0.95	−0.35	2.20	0.3

Note: A conventional growth accounting equation is used such that TFP growth $= \Delta Y/Y - \alpha\Delta K/K - \beta\Delta L/L$ where $\alpha = 0.4$ and $\beta = 0.6$ before 1913 and $\alpha = 0.3$ and $\beta = 0.7$ after 1913. Contributions are rounded to nearest 0.05. A crude estimate of the contribution of education which would be added to labour inputs and deducted from TFP if inputs are quality-adjusted is obtained by assuming in line with modern evidence that earnings represent a good estimate of the contribution of schooling to labour quality (Krueger and Lindahl 2000) and that a year's extras schooling raises earnings by 8 per cent (Cohen and Soto 2001). Schooling estimates based on Matthews *et al.* 1982; Maddison 1996; and Mitch 1999.

Sources: Crafts 1995 and Matthews *et al.* 1982.

the interwar period capital's contribution was relatively weak while after the Second World War hours worked per member of the labour force fell sharply and growth was based especially on much stronger TFP growth. Indeed, perhaps the most striking feature of Table 1.4 is how much greater was the contribution of TFP growth after the Second World War than in the industrial revolution or at any time in the nineteenth century. This contrast probably does reflect real changes in the contribution of technological change to growth, but may well exaggerate the magnitude. It seems likely that the bias of nineteenth-century technological change was more labour saving than that in the twentieth century and together with much faster growth in the capital to labour ratio in the latter period this may well mean that the conventional (Cobb–Douglas) assumptions imposed in growth accounting understate technological change before as opposed to after post-Second World War (Abramovitz 1993). The slowdown in TFP growth in the later nineteenth and early twentieth centuries deserves a closer look (see below).

DID VICTORIAN BRITAIN FAIL?

The heading of this section is also the title of a famous article written by McCloskey. In it he claimed that in the pre-First World War period the British economy was 'growing as rapidly as permitted by the growth of its resources and the effective exploitation of the available technology' (1970: 451). This conclusion was based on three very neoclassical arguments. First, using the insights of a traditional growth model, it was argued that devoting more resources to home investment would have run into diminishing returns. Second, it was claimed that the technical choices made by British firms were efficient and that the highly competitive market environment ensured that there would be no serious and persistent errors at the industry level while the capital market operated to equalise returns to different types of investment at the margin. Third, it was maintained that British productivity growth could not have been any higher which in effect rules out the possibility that the UK could have anticipated the American move to faster technological change.

This assessment has, of course, proved highly controversial and allegations that a number of serious failures inhibited economic growth continue. One of the most celebrated of these claims has been 'entrepreneurial failure', perhaps the best-known proponent being Landes (1969) who recently reasserted his view as follows: 'one is inclined to define the British disease as a case of hard tardiness; entrepreneurial constipation' (Landes 1998: 455). Another well-known hypothesis is that the capital market unduly favoured foreign investment and had institutional failures that undermined the flotation of new businesses and slowed down structural change in the economy (Kennedy 1987). Yet another criticism is that the British education system exhibited a number of weaknesses and that technical training was lacking both on the shop floor and in the boardroom with adverse effects on technological progress (Sanderson 1988). Finally, overreliance on 'self-regulating' markets and a regrettable lack of state intervention aimed at modernisation of the economy was the charge levelled by Elbaum and Lazonick (1986).

These arguments are re-examined below (and in more detail in chapter 4) in the light both of the subsequent accumulation of evidence and of new ideas from growth economics. Before this, however, it is necessary to confront the suggestion that there was a climacteric in British growth prior to the First World War. The notion of a climacteric is of a sharp reduction in trend growth and, as proposed by Feinstein *et al.* (1982), a cessation of TFP growth between 1899 and 1913. It is this hypothesis that will be addressed here rather than the earlier literature on an alleged climacteric in the 1870s, a survey of which can be found in Saul (1985).

It should be accepted that the existence or otherwise of a climacteric is not decisive with regard to the growth failure hypothesis. For example, if it is argued that technological revolutions come along at discrete intervals then a growth slowdown accompanied by a hiatus in TFP growth in between the first (steam and steel) and second (electricity and cars) 'industrial revolutions' may be quite understandable and not indicative of underperformance (Phelps-Brown and Handfield-Jones 1952). On the other hand, a constant trend growth rate could represent a failure if opportunities for faster technological change were taken up more vigorously in other countries whose growth consequently accelerated as was noted by Crafts *et al.* (1989). Nevertheless, on balance, establishing that there was a climacteric in TFP growth would strengthen the hand of those arguing for a growth failure. So was there a late Victorian/Edwardian climacteric?

Table 1.5 Growth of GDP and TFP: alternative estimates, 1856–1913 (% per year)

	Output	Income	Expenditure	Compromise	Balanced
GDP					
1856–73	2.0	2.3		2.2	
1873–82	1.8	1.7	2.3	1.9	1.7
1882–9	1.9	2.7	2.0	2.2	1.6
1889–99	1.9	2.3	2.3	2.2	2.2
1899–1907	1.7	1.2	0.9	1.2	1.4
1907–13	1.7	1.4	1.8	1.6	1.7
1924–9	2.3	3.1	2.3	2.6	2.4
1929–37	2.2	1.9	1.7	2.0	2.0
TFP					
1856–73	0.6	0.9		0.8	
1873–82	0.5	0.4	1.0	0.6	0.4
1882–9	0.6	1.4	0.7	0.9	0.2
1889–99	0.5	0.9	0.9	0.8	0.8
1899–1907	0.2	−0.3	−0.6	−0.3	−0.1
1907–13	0.5	0.2	0.6	0.4	0.5
1924–9	0.9	1.7	0.9	1.2	1.0
1929–37	0.8	0.5	0.3	0.6	0.6

Sources: 1856–1913: from Feinstein *et al.* 1982 except final column from Solomou and Weale 1991 where the periods are 1874–83 and 1883–9 rather than 1873–82 and 1882–9. The Feinstein *et al.* income estimates have been adjusted slightly to accommodate the revisions suggested in Feinstein 1990d. 1924–37: from Matthews *et al.* 1982 except final column from Sefton and Weale 1995.

Table 1.5 displays the statistical evidence from which a post-1899 climacteric was inferred. Feinstein *et al.* emphasised the so-called compromise measure of GDP which is a geometric mean of the expenditure, income and output measures. Using this estimate, real GDP growth fell from 2.1 per cent per year in 1873–99 to 1.4 per cent per year in 1899–1913 while TFP growth fell from 0.7 per cent per year to 0.0 per cent (1983: 175). If this were interpreted as a change in trend, then suggestions that the economy experienced a growth failure in the years before the First World War would attain greater credibility. However, Table 1.5 reveals that there are difficulties with the climacteric hypothesis. First, it is apparent that there are problems with the data since if these were perfect there should be no discrepancy between the expenditure, income and output measures of GDP. The reduction in TFP growth after 1899 is much less in the output than the income series. Solomou and Weale (1991) argued in favour of weighting the variants according to reliability rather than equally as in the compromise series and their results, also shown in Table 1.5, reduce the impact of the post-1899 slowdown. Second, the 1899–1907 business cycle stands out as a period of relatively weak TFP growth in all columns of Table 1.5 with the years following 1907 showing a bounce back. Almost all the differences are statistically insignificant – the only exception is that growth in the cycle of the 1890s is found to have been unusually strong – and the 1899–1913 growth is not unusually weak relative to the period as a whole (Crafts *et al.*, 1989). A more sophisticated statistical model estimated by the same authors resulted in a decline in trend growth after 1899 but only of about 0.1 percentage points per year.[2]

The claim that the UK suffered a serious climacteric in its economic growth in the period 1899–1913 seems highly doubtful. This does not, of course, dispose of arguments that the UK experienced a growth failure in the sense that growth could have been higher and, in particular, that the UK should not have fallen so far behind the United States in the early twentieth century.

McCloskey's argument that British growth could not have been any faster is best understood in the framework of a traditional neoclassical growth model. In this case the steady-state growth rate is exogenous and with a Cobb–Douglas production function equals

$$\Delta Y/Y = \Delta L/L + (\Delta A/A)/(1 - \alpha)$$

that is the growth rate is determined by the growth of the labour force and of TFP. In this model, McCloskey's assertion was that these could not have been increased.

The plausibility of this claim would be enhanced if the UK could be shown to have levels of TFP and human capital per worker at least as great as those in other leading economies. This seems to have been the case at the level of the economy as a whole as is shown in Table 1.2 and in chapter 3 below. Faster TFP growth in Germany in the period 1871–1911 could be seen as catching up from initial backwardness rather than British failure. And Thomas (1988) noted that there was little opportunity to increase output by reallocating resources across sectors since the structure of factor endowments, especially skilled labour, was a binding constraint.

Quantitative research at the microeconomic level has generally supported the suggestion that when British managers did not adopt American methods their decisions were rational in British conditions in which labour was less expensive, natural resources were more expensive and demand was less standardised than in the United States. As Pollard concluded: 'British industry was an open, highly competitive world. Entrepreneurial failure would imply the simultaneous failure of thousands of individuals . . . plus the failures of thousands more who were eagerly awaiting to take their places if they failed. Such a development

[2] Readers who are well versed in time-series econometrics will realise that this discussion is only valid if the GDP series does not contain a unit root but is (segmented) trend stationary. This does in fact seem to be the case and the basic conception of the economy as one where shocks cause the economy briefly to depart from but then revert to a pre-existing trend which underlies the Feinstein *et al.* (1982) methodology is probably acceptable (Crafts and Mills 1996a), although some caution on this point is urged by Greasley and Oxley (1995).

would surely strain credulity beyond reason' (1994: 79; see also chapter 9 below). Similarly, the use of a high proportion of British savings to finance foreign investment has been shown to have been economically justified in terms of rates of return while the ex post rate of return on the allegedly unjustly neglected new industries did not match that on traditional activities (Edelstein 1976, and chapter 8 below).

To this extent, McCloskey's position has been vindicated. Yet, it relies fundamentally on the proposition that TFP growth was exogenous. The advent of new growth models in which TFP growth is endogenous means that assessment of the possibility that there was a growth failure in late Victorian/Edwardian Britain has become more complicated than hitherto. And the failure of the Anglo-American wage gap to narrow between 1870 and 1913 despite mass transatlantic migration and a steep fall in transport costs (O'Rourke 1996; see also chapter 2 below) provides a strong indication that the simple neoclassical approach is inadequate. Moreover, in the 1910s and 1920s the United States moved well ahead of Britain so that in 1929 before the difficulties of the depression, TFP levels in the whole economy, industry and manufacturing were, respectively, 12.7, 87.8 and 127 per cent above those in the UK (Broadberry 1998, 2003).

The suggestion that TFP growth should be treated as endogenous has in fact been implicit in a 'Schumpeterian' reaction to claims that there was no entrepreneurial failure in late Victorian Britain. In this view, the role of the entrepreneur is not simply to maximise profits subject to constraints but to innovate constraints away (Payne 1990). The review of UK performance in invention and innovation provided in chapter 4 below is much less favourable to the British entrepreneur in highlighting the relative decline of British patenting and in concluding that 'Britain was not at the forefront of the new wave of technologies breaking at the end of the nineteenth century'. It is clear that by the interwar period levels of R&D spending in the United States were much higher than those in Britain and Germany (Edgerton and Horrocks 1994).

Accepting the notion of endogenous innovation therefore has ambiguous implications for the evaluation of British growth performance. In an era when technology was relatively hard to transfer between countries and networks of cumulative technological learning were primarily national an economic environment that encouraged a greater volume of innovative activity could also underpin divergence in economic growth (Nelson and Wright 1992). On the one hand, this may be a route to additional ways to rebut the suggestion that the American overtaking of the early twentieth century was avoidable. On the other hand, the possibility is opened up that successful policy interventions might have raised the long-run rate of growth.

In the early twentieth century the United States had several obvious features that new growth theorists might suppose were conducive to greater innovative activity than in the UK. These include a much greater domestic market which would allow the fixed costs of R&D to be spread across higher expected sales volumes and a greater availability of engineers and science/technology graduates (Crafts 1998). More subtly, the opportunity to exploit much larger standardised markets gave American employers in many industries much greater economic incentives to undermine trade unionism and craft control of the shop floor (Haydu 1988). The implication was that by the early twentieth century UK employers had less control of levels of work effort than their American counterparts and were more exposed to 'hold-up' problems that impeded technical change that involved high sunk cost investments. Accordingly, in industries like motor vehicles where the sunk cost technology of the assembly line proved important, the British could not readily emulate Henry Ford and potential economies of scale were not achieved (Lewchuk 1987).

Other aspects of the American economy outside the compass of the neoclassical model contributed to higher TFP in industry in particular but do not connote British failure. These include the localised technological learning triggered off by American factor endowments, notably including cheap energy and industrial raw materials, which was identified by David (1975) in his rehabilitation of the Habakkuk (1962) hypothesis. Unlike the endogenous innovation processes envisaged by new growth theory, the factor endowment effect is seen as resulting from unplanned learning resulting from myopic choices of technique although it should be recognised that the abundance of natural resources in late nineteenth-century America itself reflected successful institutions (David and Wright 1997).

American natural resources were a magnet for international flows both of capital and of labour during the half-century before the First World War. As the American economy became bigger, transport costs fell and power became cheaper in large urban areas, it was able to take advantage of both internal and external economies of scale especially in manufacturing (Pred 1977; James 1983). In the way envisaged by the 'new economic geography', agglomeration benefits accrued which facilitated a switch in comparative advantage toward manufacturing and underwrote both factor rewards and further factor flows (Crafts and Venables 2001).

Although thinking in terms of endogenous TFP growth provides some further lines of defence of the performance of the pre-1914 economy, it also offers ammunition to the critics. In particular, it highlights areas where a more proactive stance by government might have promoted faster growth. Two aspects are particularly apparent, in the realms of education and company law.

A long tradition in the literature has criticised related weaknesses in technical education, research and development and in university level science and technology (Landes 1969). Since market failures may lead to sub-optimal investment in these activities this might easily suggest that greater government expenditure was required and an appeal to endogenous innovation theory might enhance such arguments. Although this is not an unappealing argument, its importance should not be exaggerated. Recent discussions of trends in British education have tended to stress that such criticisms are much less valid by 1914 than they had been in 1890 given the vigorous expansion of scientific and technical education in the intervening years – the litany of earlier complaints prompted corrective action and any shortfall may be primarily the result of low demand by the private sector (Sanderson 1999).

It has also been suggested that external finance was particularly important for the new, science-based, industries like chemicals and electrical engineering; critics have argued that the British capital market was handicapped in mobilising resources for innovative new activities, although the extent of this has been disputed by Michie (1988). Critics highlight problems relating to issues of asymmetric information, which, in the absence of adequate legislation on auditing and disclosure of information, stood in the way of new company flotation and typically meant that growth stocks were much less highly valued in the late Victorian capital market than in recent decades. Kennedy (2000) underlined the very high-risk premium that the market attached to the shares of Brunner, Mond despite its impressive track record. In principle, these problems could and should have been addressed by reform of company law, as many later Victorians realised, but attempts at reform were consistently thwarted in parliament by vested interests (Cottrell 1980, and chapter 10 below).

There was another downside to the ability of directors to manipulate accounts at will, namely that shareholders were unable effectively to monitor the management of companies and that there was no hostile takeover mechanism to provide discipline (Hannah 1974). Not until the Companies Act of 1948 was this situation effectively remedied. This implied that the economy was heavily dependent on competition both between domestic producers and from actual or potential imports to enforce sufficient managerial effort in innovation. Not surprisingly, the best-documented case of failure to adopt a cost-effective new technique, namely, the soda manufacturers' neglect of the Solvay process occurred in a heavily cartelised industry not exposed to foreign competition (Lindert and Trace 1971). But this example was the exception rather than the rule; in general, competition could be relied upon to prevent persistent failure in most sectors of the late Victorian economy.

Overall, it seems reasonable to conclude that the general thrust of McCloskey's conclusions is broadly correct. There was no massive failure in the pre-1914 economy, any decline in the trend growth rate was slight and American overtaking was unavoidable. The argument does, however, need to be modernised and taken beyond its original confines of traditional neoclassical economics.

DID THE INTERWAR ECONOMY SUCCEED?

It would be easy to imagine that in an era of sustained high unemployment punctuated by the world depression of the early 1930s economic growth must have been very weak. In general, the empirical evidence is that macroeconomic instability is associated with slower growth, although the reason for this is not entirely clear. Using the econometric estimates reported by Martin and Rogers (2000) and the standard deviation of unemployment rates in chapter 13 below, it can be inferred that, had the lower labour market volatility of the pre-First World War economy been maintained between the wars, growth might have been almost 1 per cent per year higher.

Nevertheless, between the peak years of 1924 and 1937 both output and labour inputs grew more rapidly and labour productivity only marginally more slowly than between 1873 and 1913 (Matthews *et al.* 1982: 208). Indeed, after a lengthy discussion of the quantitative data had taken place, textbook accounts became quite optimistic: 'The view that after a poor performance in the 1920s, the 1930s saw a genuine breakthrough is indeed widespread and finds support not only in the output statistics but also in the quality of the modern investment and the structuring of British industry towards the growth-oriented sectors in the second phase' (Pollard 1983: 53). This relatively favourable interpretation appears to be echoed by the emphasis placed by Matthews *et al.* (1982: 506–7) on a U-shaped pattern in TFP growth in the British economy with a low in the first quarter of the twentieth century followed by revival in the interwar period leading on to the all-time high after the Second World War (cf. Tables 1.4 and 1.5).

The interwar economy also witnessed a major shift in supply-side policy away from Victorian orthodoxy. Prompted initially by high unemployment and the travails of the old staple industries and given considerable impetus by the world economic crisis, governments became more willing to intervene in the market economy. Among the innovations of this period were the beginnings of industrial policy in the 1920s, the general tariff of 1932, the encouragement of cartels and the imposition of controls on foreign investment in the 1930s. These changes were complemented by exit from the gold standard and cheap money so that Britain in the 1930s has been described as a 'managed economy' (Booth 1987).

Two questions immediately arise. First, how much did trend growth performance improve in the interwar period? Second, did the change in policy stance improve long-run growth potential? These issues are the main concern of this section but an important preliminary to engaging with them is to examine interwar productivity performance more closely.

In postulating a U-shape for British trend growth performance, Matthews *et al.* (1982) were claiming both that there was an Edwardian

Table 1.6 Labour productivity and TFP growth in manufacturing, 1871/1913 and 1924/37 (% per year)

	Pre-First World War			
	UK 1873–1913	Germany 1871–1911	USA 1869–1909	
Labour productivity	1.2	1.7	1.6	
TFP	0.6	0.7	0.4	
	Interwar			
	UK 1924–37	Germany 1925–37	USA 1919–29	USA 1929–37
Labour productivity	1.8	2.6	5.6	1.8
TFP	1.9	2.3	5.2	1.9

Note: $\alpha = 0.35$, $\beta = 0.65$ pre-First World War and $\alpha = 0.25$, $\beta = 0.75$ for interwar period. Labour input growth based on hours worked, except for Germany where it is persons employed. No explicit account is taken of education.

Sources: UK from Matthews *et al.* 1982; Germany derived from worksheets underlying Broadberry 1998; USA from Kendrick 1961.

climacteric and that the interwar period saw a return to growth rates both of factor inputs and of TFP on a par with those prior to 1899. Although the notion of a climacteric seems to have been overplayed by these authors, Tables 1.4 and 1.5 do suggest stronger TFP growth in the interwar period, notably in the late 1920s. Table 1.3 suggests that this may have been underpinned in part by more investment in R&D. On the other hand, non-residential investment as a share of GDP fell somewhat compared with the pre-1914 economy and, as Table 1.2 shows, both labour productivity and TFP levels were noticeably lower relative to the United States (though not Germany) in 1937 than they had been in 1911. Table 1.5 also suggests that TFP growth in the 1930s did not compare favourably with that of the 1920s, although, once again, discrepancies between the different ways of measuring GDP muddy the waters somewhat.

Table 1.6 presents estimates of productivity growth in the manufacturing sector which has been the focal point of claims of better performance. Here there is much clearer evidence of a breakthrough in labour productivity growth and, especially, TFP growth which rose from 0.6 per cent per year in 1873–1913 to 1.9 per cent per year in 1924–37. However, this is by no means outstanding relative to what was achieved elsewhere, as Table 1.6 also shows. In particular, at no time did UK manufacturing productivity performance match the surge experienced by the USA when electrification transformed the American factory in the 1920s (David and Wright 1999). If the economy was regenerated between the wars, it might seem natural to expect structural change to have played a large part and this was central to the influential interpretation put forward by Richardson (1967). This need not be the case, however, if productivity improvement took place primarily within sectors rather than being based on the

Table 1.7 Contributions to manufacturing labour productivity growth (%)

	Growth	1924 Weight	Share	1935 Weight	Share
New industries					
Motor and cycle	4.6	3.8	10.11	5.1	12.67
Silk and artificial silk	8.7	0.9	4.53	1.1	5.17
Chemicals	2.4	2.8	3.89	3.9	5.12
Rubber	7.6	1.0	4.43	1.2	4.96
Paper and printing	1.7	4.2	3.75	4.4	4.01
Electrical engineering	0.9	2.8	1.52	4.6	2.34
Aircraft	3.4	0.2	0.40	0.7	1.30
Scientific instruments	3.0	0.4	0.70	0.5	0.82
Aluminium, lead, tin	1.5	0.5	0.43	0.8	0.64
Petroleum	4.3	0.2	0.56	0.2	0.50
Total	*3.1*	*17.0*	*30.32*	*22.5*	*37.51*
Old staples					
Mechanical engineering	1.4	7.3	5.93	7.7	5.83
Iron and steel	1.8	5.5	6.05	5.7	5.57
Clothing	1.1	8.0	5.74	7.9	4.90
Woollens and worsted	1.9	4.5	5.01	3.5	3.64
Cotton spinning and weaving	1.6	7.1	6.91	3.2	2.79
Other textiles	1.2	4.1	3.46	3.0	1.89
Timber	1.3	0.8	0.61	1.1	0.79
Furniture	0.7	1.2	0.51	1.6	0.63
Leather etc.	1.0	1.0	0.54	0.8	0.42
China & earthenware	0.5	0.9	0.28	0.7	0.19
Rope, twine and net	1.6	0.2	0.19	0.2	0.17
Shipbuilding	0.1	2.1	0.13	1.2	0.07
Railway carriage	0.2	0.5	0.05	0.4	0.04
Total	*1.3*	*43.4*	*35.41*	*37.0*	*26.93*

Source: Broadberry and Crafts 1990c.

movement of resources from low to high productivity sectors or if accelerated productivity growth resulted from a new general purpose technology such as electricity which could underpin a very broad advance in productivity.

Table 1.7 reports on the extent to which 'new industries' were responsible for the growth of labour productivity between the *Census of Production* years of 1924 and 1935 using the widest available definition of the term. The table shows that, first, the relative contribution of 'new industries' in productivity growth depends partly on which year's weights are used since their relative importance in economic activity was rising over time. Second, it shows that, on average but not in all cases, 'new industries' experienced substantially faster productivity growth than the 'old staples'. This result is consistent with the suggestion that 'new industries' were important in the interwar period through their impact on intrasectoral manufacturing productivity growth. On the other hand, a calculation of their impact through structural change does not add greatly to their impact. This is because labour productivity growth took place overwhelmingly within sectors and structural change was slow.[3]

Finally, the productivity performance of the new industries can be put in an international perspective. Here two points stand out. First, in most cases labour productivity was further behind the United States than the average for UK manufacturing. Thus while labour productivity in 1935/7 in all US manufacturing was 2.18 times the UK level, in cars the ratio was 2.94, in aircraft 3.15, in radios 3.47 and in chemicals 2.27; in the old staples, on the other hand, productivity gaps were generally lower than the average, for example textiles and clothing a ratio of 1.45 and in shipbuilding 1.54 (Broadberry 1997c). Second, the 'new industries' did not generally establish a strong position in terms of revealed comparative advantage in exporting where the most notable feature of the late 1930s was the persistence of the old staples as the UK's strongest export sectors (Crafts 1989).

Clearly, 'new industries' more than punched their weight and accounted for a substantial fraction of interwar manufacturing labour productivity growth. There is, however, no reason to believe that this contribution was particularly special. In any dynamic economy, it is normal for newer industries to grow relatively quickly as they become established. And, in this case where on average they accounted for about 6 per cent of total employment, their impact in raising the rate of growth of GDP per hour worked could not have been large. The failure of 'new industries' to establish a strong position in international trade argues against seeing their development as representing a renaissance of the British economy.

The inference drawn by optimistic assessments of the interwar economy is that the UK went through a regeneration that was an integral part of the transformation of the Victorian economy with its relatively

[3] Following Nordhaus (1972) a standard decomposition of productivity growth is obtained as follows:

$$\Delta A_O = \Sigma S_i \Delta A_i + \Sigma A_i \Delta S_i$$

where A_O is aggregate labour productivity which equals $\Sigma A_i S_i$ where A_i is labour productivity in the ith industry and S_i is the ith industry's share in employment. Thus:

$$\Delta A_O / A_O = \Sigma S_i (\Delta A_i / A_i)(A_i / A_O) + \Sigma (A_i / A_O) \Delta S_i$$

where the first term is the intrasectoral contribution (which is an employment-weighted average of within-sector productivity growth) and the second term is the structural change effect (which is changes in employment shares multiplied by their relative productivity levels).

Evaluation of this formula for 1924–35 shows that labour productivity growth was overwhelmingly intrasectoral with the second term accounting for only 0.02 (0.02) percentage points out of 1.72 (1.85) with 1924 (1935) weights (Broadberry and Crafts 1990c). This result is not very surprising: throughout the period 1907–68 labour productivity growth was overwhelmingly an intrasectoral phenomenon (von Tunzelmann 1982) and structural change was actually relatively slow in the interwar years (Matthews *et al.* 1982).

limited growth potential to an economy which could take advantage of the opportunities for faster growth after the Second World War. Looking at the British economy in isolation gives this view some plausibility but international comparisons are less kind to it since other European countries experienced much faster growth, notably in TFP, after the Second World War and overtook the UK during the golden age (Maddison 1996).

This suggests that it may also be useful to consider the interwar economy in terms of its 'social capability', i.e., what was happening to the incentive structures that affect the rate of endogenous innovation. Here the picture is decidedly more pessimistic. Three aspects of the economy give particular cause for concern in this regard, namely, capital markets, competition in product markets and industrial relations.

The weakness of outside shareholders continued in what was 'a golden era of directorial power' (Hannah 1974: 77). The Royal Mail case in 1931 where the use of secret reserves effectively to falsify trading returns was not found to be illegal highlighted the continuing deficiencies of company law (Edwards 1989). Managers continued to be immune from hostile takeover threats. Even after the 1948 Companies Act the diffuse nature of shareholding in the typical British company meant that free-rider problems allowed weak discipline and monitoring of managers by shareholders to continue to be the order of the day.

Competition is crucial to innovation and to productivity performance, as post-war evidence shows (Nickell *et al.* 1997; Aghion *et al.* 2002). Yet competition was already much weaker in the 1930s than at the turn of the century and the trend continued strongly in that direction into the 1950s. The merger boom of the 1920s helped to create a situation where across manufacturing the average share of the top three firms in an industry's output rose to 23.9 per cent by 1935 and the top 100 firms accounted for 25 per cent of all manufacturing output (Leak and Maizels 1945; Hannah 1983). By the mid-1930s, cartels, which were encouraged by government, accounted for about 30 per cent of manufacturing output (Mercer 1995) while the introduction of widespread tariff protection in 1932 reduced competition still further. At the microeconomic level, weaknesses in competition were clearly related to poor productivity outcomes in the 1930s (Broadberry and Crafts 1992a). And, given the difficulty of tackling agency problems within the firm, it is not surprising that business historians point to the 'cosy amateurishness' of large companies (Gourvish 1987) and many examples of inadequate strategic vision among large companies (Hannah 1983).

Finally, the Victorian structure of industrial relations continued with no significant reform. Broadly speaking, it entailed a decentralized system of collective bargaining with a substantial incidence of multiple unionism. This contrasted with the moves towards greater co-ordination in some other European countries which underpinned post-war 'social contracts' geared to wage moderation and high investment (Crouch 1993;

Eichengreen 1996). In conditions where, in general, the bargaining power of workers was undermined by low levels of economic activity and where the scope for introducing American technology was limited, this may not have been a serious handicap but it was to become one in the 1950s and 1960s (Bean and Crafts, 1996).

This analysis as a whole indicates that the new policy stance that had come into being by the 1930s was unfortunate for long-run productivity performance, however understandable it may have been as a political response to the shocks to which the UK was subjected. Interwar economic policy was, of course, strongly affected by the persistent unemployment of the time and in the 1930s by attempts to restore the profitability of industry and the employability of labour in the face of price declines in the tradable goods sector that raised real wages given the stickiness of money wages. This helps to make sense of what otherwise would seem an incoherent package of measures adopted in the 1930s (Booth 1987).

In some respects, policy was successful in the short term. For example, Kitson and Solomou (1990) found that newly protected industries experienced a sharp increase in output and productivity growth in the years 1930–5 compared with 1924–30 while this was not the case for non-newly protected industries. Nevertheless, they saw this essentially as a Keynesian policy that reduced the extent of underutilization of productive resources and accepted that it probably slowed down the regeneration of the economy. In the case of the steel industry, additional tariff protection was given to facilitate rationalisation. While this stemmed contraction in the short run, since the removal of protection was politically unthinkable given the industry's location in high unemployment areas, the policy was ineffective in promoting productivity improvement but merely sheltered inefficent vested interests (Tolliday 1987).

In effect, there was a conflict between short-run employment objectives and the promotion of long-run productivity performance particularly since, once in place, policies that reduced competitive pressures on British business would prove hard to rescind. This has always been recognised in the literature. The advent of new growth economics and the recognition that post-war British innovation and productivity performance has been seriously undermined by agency problems within firms (Broadberry and Crafts 2001) suggests that the downside was considerably more serious than used to be supposed.

Overall, it seems that the optimism about economic growth in the 1930s expressed by writers like Pollard is not really warranted. There was no marked and sustained improvement in TFP growth above the levels that the UK in the second half of the nineteenth century could normally achieve and the increasing contribution of the 'new industries' should not be regarded as a major breakthrough. Relative to the pre-First World War period, manufacturing productivity growth accelerated but still compared less well with other leading economies. Especially during the 1930s, developments in supply-side policy were generally adverse to long-run productivity growth prospects in that they weakened management incentives to adopt innovations rapidly and to pursue cost reductions energetically. It should be recognised, however, that growth might have been appreciably higher if the macroeconomic environment had been more stable.

POSTSCRIPT: MARKET FAILURE OR GOVERNMENT FAILURE?

Allegations that the pre-1914 economy failed are, at bottom, claims of market failure – either that markets failed to achieve a restructuring of the economy that would have had a positive social rate of return or failed to enforce the efficient management of business enterprises through market discipline or failed to achieve optimal levels of investment in cases where there were positive externalities on offer. The critics assert that government intervention to correct market failures would have been desirable (Elbaum and Lazonick 1986). In this sense, the problem also becomes one of government failure.

Government failure can also, however, come in the form of badly designed interventions and/or policies that seek votes rather than promote economic efficiency. A classic example is protectionism which rewards well-organised producer groups at the expense of small losses per person to large numbers of disparate consumers and which tends to operate therefore to slow down restructuring of economies in the face of technological change or shifts in comparative advantage. The post-1945 history of British industrial policy is a good example of this (Crafts 2002) which, of itself, calls into question the claim that more state intervention would have improved the economic efficiency of late Victorian Britain.

Our review of the interwar economy suggests, however, that for the UK economy the problem has been potentially more serious. If it is the case that there has been a persistent, and distinctly British, weakness in shareholders' ability to control the management of firms, then productivity performance would have been enhanced by stronger competition policies but weakened by moves to industrial policies which entailed subsidies that cushioned management from the need to innovate and to control costs (Aghion *et al.* 1997). Yet, as the problems of the British economy intensified, political pressures pointed in the opposite direction and the role played by competition in preventing egregious failure in the Victorian economy was undervalued. By the golden age period after the Second World War, unfortunately, industrial policy rather than competition policy was to be entrusted with stimulating economic growth.

2 Population and regional development

DUDLEY BAINES AND ROBERT WOODS

Contents

INTRODUCTION: POPULATION GROWTH IN THE LONG TERM

Population growth (or in rare cases decline) occurs for one of three reasons: changes in the number of births, changes in the number of deaths and changes in the migration balance. However, simple birth, death and migration rates (e.g. deaths per 1,000 people) are rather crude measures. For example, it is possible for the overall death rate to be rising while deaths at each age are falling. This could occur if the population was ageing – i.e., the number in the older age groups was rising. In this case, improvements caused, say, by improved nutrition, would be masked. Demographers therefore prefer to talk about mortality and fertility, which are defined below and which measure deaths and births holding age structure constant. (The measurement of migration poses some particular problems, which are discussed below.)

The main features of population change between the 1840s and the 1940s are as follows. The population of Great Britain increased by nearly two and half times from 18.5 to 45.8 million. Most of the growth occurred in the cities and suburbs, especially London and the great cities of the north and Midlands. There was considerable migration from the countryside and the more remote the area the more likely that it would be depopulated. Many people left Britain for overseas destinations. Most of them went to the new Europe overseas – countries with a low population density (and high resource/population ratio). These countries were also attracting emigrants from many other parts of Europe. Further, there was a rather smaller flow of immigrants from continental Europe and Ireland into Britain. There were also important changes in the characteristics of the British population. People began to live longer and to have fewer children. (In fact, by the 1930s, falling fertility led to a view that the population was not replacing itself, and would eventually fall.) This chapter discusses the causes of the demographic changes and their effects, for example, on the size of the labour force, its structure and regional distribution.

By the 1740s, the population of Great Britain had probably reached a little over 7 million having been around 6.4 million in 1701. The rate of population growth began to accelerate in the late eighteenth century and achieved a peak at around 1.5 per cent per year in the early nineteenth century. Population growth then slowed and in the 1930s reached its lowest rate before the late twentieth century. The system of regular census taking only began in Great Britain in 1801 and civil registration of vital events (births, deaths and marriages) only in 1837 in England and Wales and in 1855 in Scotland. This means that even the crudest indices of births and deaths cannot be calculated directly until the second half of the nineteenth century. Before 1801, we are obliged to rely on estimates for the denominator (the population, or those at risk of dying, giving birth, marrying or migrating), and before 1837 can only estimate the numerator (the number of vital events themselves). However, through the work of the Cambridge Group for the History of Population and Social Structure we now have both denominator and numerator estimates for England back to the 1540s, based on the ecclesiastical registration of baptisms and burials (Wrigley and Schofield 1981; Wrigley *et al.* 1997).

It was thought for a long time that population growth in England followed the classic demographic transition model – i.e., that population growth in the late eighteenth and early nineteenth centuries was caused by a long-run decline of mortality and that after a lag of several decades, fertility also began a long-run decline. This meant that, initially, the gap between birth and death rates widened so that population growth increased, after which it narrowed so that the rate of population growth fell. The question was: what caused the mortality decline which initiated the phase of rapid population growth? This familiar account (which ultimately was based on estimates by Brownlee in 1916) has now largely been undermined by the statistical work of the Cambridge Group and the associated ecological theory of demographic regulation which owes a considerable debt to T. R. Malthus's *Essay on the Principle of Population* of 1803 (Wrigley 1988).

MODELS OF DEMOGRAPHIC CHANGE

Demographic models come in several forms. Perhaps the most famous, the Malthusian demographic system, is fundamentally stable because it is self-equilibrating. The model depends on a close positive relationship between population growth and the price of food. If the latter rises, real income will fall. If real income falls, either (a) mortality will increase (this is the positive check linked to misery and vice by Malthus in his first *Essay* of 1798) or (b) fertility will be reduced as a consequence of reduced nuptiality (the preventive check involving moral restraint and favoured by Malthus in his second *Essay* of 1803). Both increased mortality or reduced fertility will depress the rate of population growth and the relationship between population and food supply will return to some form of balance. It is a system dominated by negative feedback, checks and balances – homeostasis in the jargon. This model has proved an extremely effective device for explaining the regulation of population growth in England before 1800.

However, after 1800, there is little sign of such a closed, self-equilibrating system. The amount of food per person rose because of improvements in agricultural productivity and, in time, because of access to cheap imports. Population could therefore grow without having an adverse effect on the price of food (Wrigley 1988). Individual mortality was still related to real income, but in the nineteenth century, this was more likely to be a consequence of social class differences than annual variation in the price of food. There could also still be a marriage squeeze when economic conditions meant that marriage among young people was postponed. But, after 1800, the balance between economic conditions and population growth had been broken. Other powerful forces were at work on mortality, fertility and migration patterns (Smout 1986; Woods 1995, 2000; Anderson 1996).

The demographic and epidemiological transition models provide us with valuable insights into the process of demographic change during the nineteenth and twentieth centuries. In the demographic transition model, mortality decline was caused by the cumulative impact of the

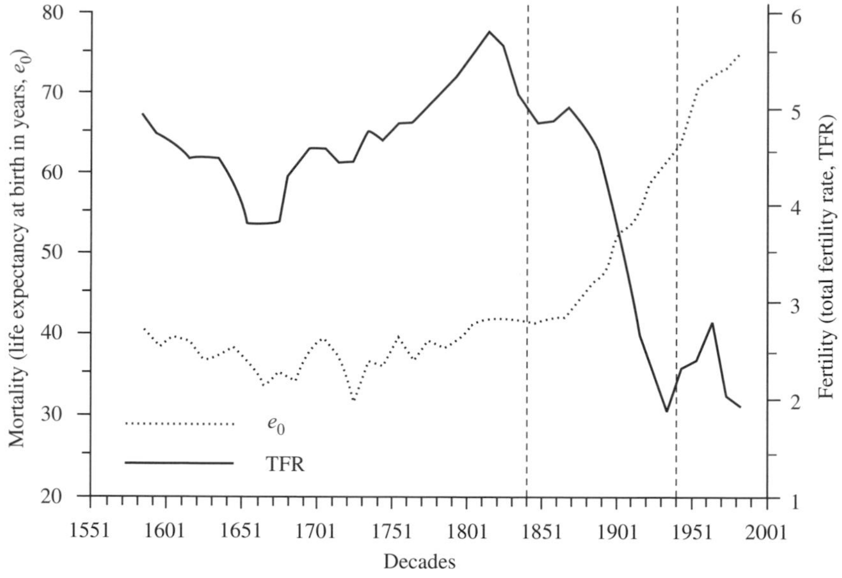

Figure 2.1 Long-run trends in mortality and fertility in England and Wales, 1580s–1990s

Source: Woods 2000: 6.

agricultural, industrial and sanitary revolutions. After a time lag, fertility (which was largely births within marriage) fell as a consequence of individualism, urbanisation and the adoption of family planning practices (Notestein 1945). In the epidemiological transition model, deaths from infectious diseases, including water- and food-borne diseases, childhood infections and pulmonary tuberculosis, fell first. This reduced mortality among relatively young people. But deaths from chronic diseases (cancers and heart disease, for example) did not fall significantly and remained the principal causes of death. This meant that the mortality of the over 50s fell less than that of young adults (Oman 1971). But, as we shall see, there were exceptions to this pattern, not least, through the impact of the First World War.

Figure 2.1 shows the long-run trends in mortality and fertility in England and Wales from the sixteenth to the end of the twentieth century. Mortality is measured by life expectancy at birth in years (e_0) and fertility by the total fertility rate (TFR) which measures the average number of live births a woman was likely to have had on completing her reproductive period (roughly ages 15 to 50). Note that these measures hold age structure constant (see above). TFR and e_0 are modern indices, which have to be estimated for the early part of the period. The trends shown in Figure 2.1 are striking. In the 1840s, life expectancy at birth was in the low 40s. By the mid-1940s, it had risen to the mid-60s. Most of the improvement occurred in the twentieth century. The total fertility rate was about 5 in the 1840s. It fell to something less than 2 in the 1930s. In other words, life expectancy improved by 60 per cent and fertility halved. This was by far the most important transformation to date.

THE DECLINE OF FERTILITY

Figure 2.1 helps us to picture the sequence of changes that influenced the long-term trend in fertility. In the late eighteenth and early nineteenth centuries, the increase in fertility was largely caused by changes in nuptiality – in the main, in the timing of marriage rather than in the number of people who married (Wrigley 1983, 1998). But the post-1870 decline was largely caused by changes in fertility within marriage. Figure 2.2 illustrates this and some important regional variations.[1]

The figure shows the marital fertility decline in London, in Scotland as a whole, in County Durham (a mining and heavy engineering county) and in Sutherland (a remote rural Scottish county). All experienced a substantial fall in marital fertility, but for different reasons. For example, overall fertility (If) in Sutherland was already low in the 1860s (0.25), despite high marital fertility, because only a small proportion of women married (Im). On the other hand, County Durham in the 1860s had the same marital fertility as Sutherland, but much higher fertility overall because a higher proportion of women married. (Interestingly, the proportion married was about the same in the 1930s as in the 1860s, in both counties.) Three of the examples had marital fertility (Ig) above 0.6 for most of the nineteenth century, indicating very little parity-specific birth control. But, by the 1930s, the small family had arrived. A woman born in the 1860s, 1870s or 1880s would have had five, six or more siblings, but she would herself only have four, three or two children. London was a major exception. In mid-century, marital fertility (Ig) was only 0.6, and, moreover, it declined from the 1870s. However, even London contained some very diverse economic, social and demographic worlds. For example, nuptiality tended to be low where the proportion of domestic servants was high.

What caused marital fertility to decline? The simple answer is that we do not fully understand the shift in motivations and behaviour that

[1] Figure 2.2 also shows some important regional variations based on data from the Princeton University European Fertility Project directed by Ansley J. Coale. The project estimated the decline of fertility in virtually every European province/county etc., many of which had poor data. Hence, a new set of fertility indices had to be devised. The measures were; overall fertility (If), the proportion married (Im), marital fertility (Ig), non-marital fertility (Ih). (Where Ih was small, then $Im \times Ig = If$) The indices were expressed as a proportion of Hutterite fertility in the 1920s, which is one of the highest ever observed. (The Hutterites were a fundamentalist community in the USA and Canada, in which the average number of children per marriage was nearly twelve. Hence, an Ig of 0.6 implied about seven children (Coale and Cotts Watkins 1986).) Figure 2.2 shows the contribution of nuptiality (Im) and marital fertility (Ig), to overall fertility (If) which is on the curved isolines. A population with Ig greater than 0.6 is unlikely to be deliberately controlling its fertility. (More correctly, controlling its parity-specific fertility – married couples will not, in general, be changing their behaviour (using contraceptives or reducing coital frequency) in line with the number children already born.) But if levels of Ig increasingly lower than 0.6 are observed, it is likely that a substantial and growing proportion of married couples were deciding on a particular family size, and were trying to avoid further births.

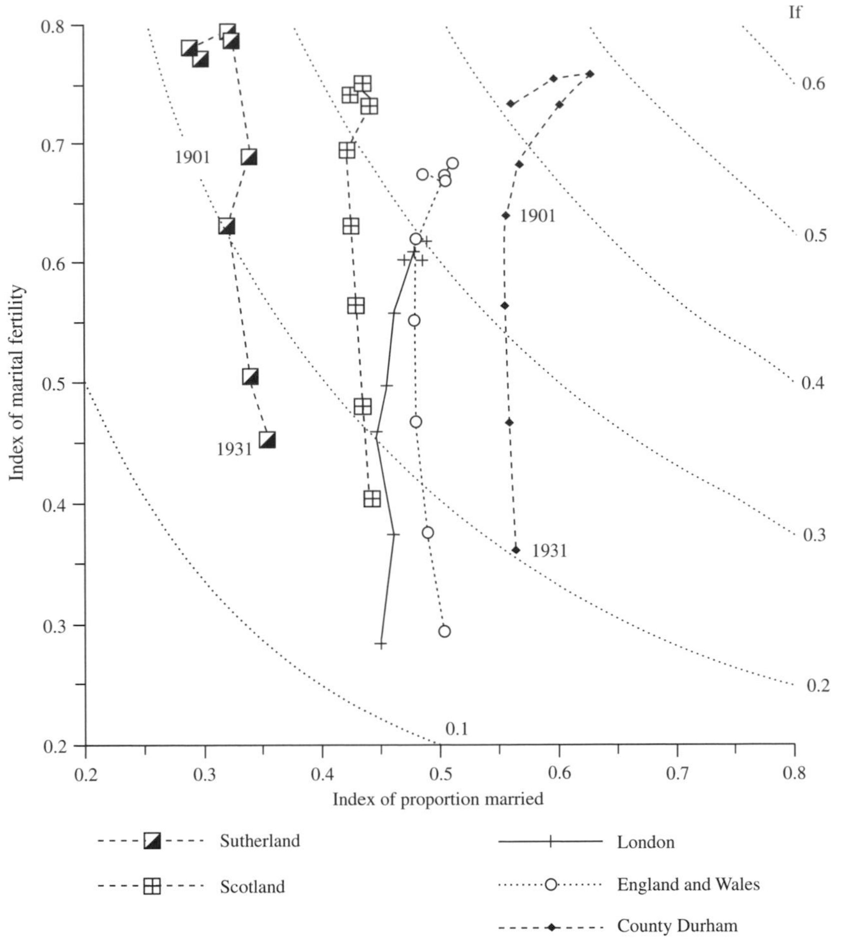

Figure 2.2 Examples of regional variations in the time paths for marital fertility (Ig) and nuptiality (Im), Scotland, 1861–1931, England and Wales, 1851–1931

Source: Woods 2000: 85.

caused one of the most important social phenomena of modern times (Woods 2000: 110–69). However, some important points can be made. First, the secular decline in marital fertility occurred among a substantial proportion of the European population (and among Europeans overseas) at roughly the same time (plus or minus a couple of decades). Even in France, where the decline in marital fertility was apparent in some areas as early as the mid-eighteenth century, there was still a marked downturn in the late nineteenth century (E. A. Wrigley 1987: 270–321). There is, therefore, little point in searching for uniquely British reasons for fertility decline. Second, it is very unlikely that birth control appliances were responsible for initiating the decline, since effective and affordable contraceptives – condoms and IUDs – were not widely available until after the First World War. Third, it is likely that fertility was related to infant and child mortality, which was falling. Fertility remained high until child mortality was low enough to reassure parents that those children they did have were likely to survive. (As we shall see, it was childhood mortality (ages 1–9) that declined from mid-century; for infants, the decline was much later.) Fourth, if we consider the findings of fertility studies in present-day developing countries, their single most important finding is that improved levels of female autonomy (expressed in the forms of education, literacy and bargaining power) reduce completed family size. The association is so clear that it is tempting to read the relationship in reverse: low and/or declining fertility indicates higher and/or increasing levels of female autonomy.

It is therefore likely that fertility in Britain declined between the 1860s and the 1930s for the following reasons. The small family of two to three children became the socially accepted norm. This was a new and critically important departure from past practice in which the timing of marriage and the proportion marrying might have been controlled, but fertility in marriage was biologically determined, subject to coital frequency and the ability to have children (fecundability). Why this change occurred in a few decades before the First World War remains obscure, but lower child mortality, improved female literacy (and education), rising living standards and social aspirations among the urban middle classes would all have pushed in the same direction. Economists often describe this process as the substitution of small numbers of high-quality children born and reared 'for their own sake' instead of larger numbers of lower-quality children born to assist the family wage economy or to provide some security for their parents in old age. But the fall in fertility was essentially a social transformation, not the invention and diffusion of new economic rationality. There was a new-found desire to cheat biology, to plan and control, rather than letting nature take its course. But in the absence of surveys of sexual attitudes and behaviour it is difficult to see how this change in mass action came about. Did Darwin play an unintended part? Did the propaganda associated with the Bradlaugh–Besant trials of the 1870s or Marie Stopes (1918) in later decades raise consciousness, challenge convention and change behaviour? Quite possibly, but we cannot be sure.

WHY MORTALITY BEGAN TO FALL

It is easier to account for the decline in mortality in Britain than for the fall in fertility. There is an exceptional wealth of detailed material on Victorian mortality, its age, gender and geographical variations, but above all stemming from the registration of death (Woods and Shelton 1997). There are many unresolved issues, however. Figure 2.3 shows changes in the age profile of mortality in England and Wales from 1838 to 1913 in four age groups, and, hence, the sequence of mortality decline – falling adult mortality set the pace, then child and finally old age. The figure shows that, in the 15–19 age group, mortality started a sustained decline in the 1850s, which continued beyond the First World War. The decline in young adult (25–34) mortality was similar, but started in the 1870s.

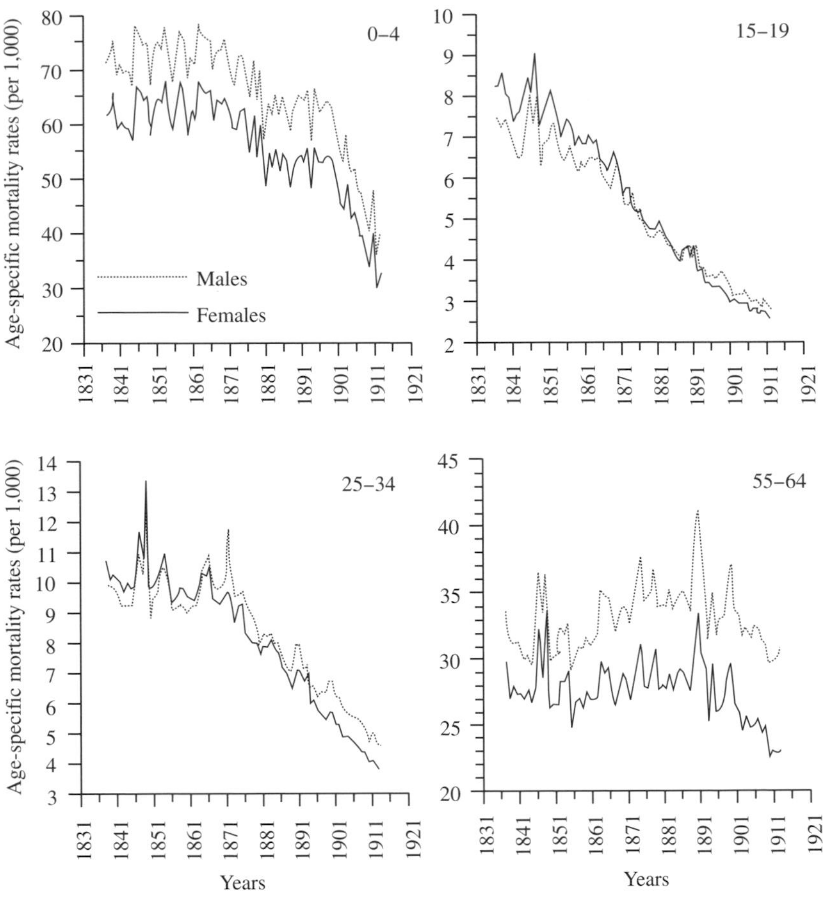

Figure 2.3 Trends in selected annual age-specific mortality rates (ages 0–4, 15–19, 25–34, 55–64), England and Wales, 1838–1913

Source: Woods 2000: 186.

On the other hand, child mortality remained high until the early twentieth century but then declined rapidly. (Infant mortality remained high.) Figure 2.3 also shows gender differences. In the 15–19 age group, female mortality was initially relatively high, but by the early twentieth century it was the same as male. In the 25–34 age group, female mortality was also relatively high but, as the decline set in, it fell below male. On the other hand, among children and the older adults, there was always excess male mortality.

The cumulative impact on overall life expectancy of the mortality fall may be seen in Figure 2.1. The greatest impact came from falling mortality in infancy and childhood. Figure 2.4 shows the childhood mortality rate (CMR) from the mid-sixteenth to the mid-twentieth century and the relationship of infant (first twelve months) to early childhood mortality (1–4). Initially, infant mortality declined with the CMR, but in the 1820s, it suffered a precipitous rise relative to child mortality. This suggests that infant mortality rose and then fell during the nineteenth and twentieth centuries (Woods 2000: 247–309).

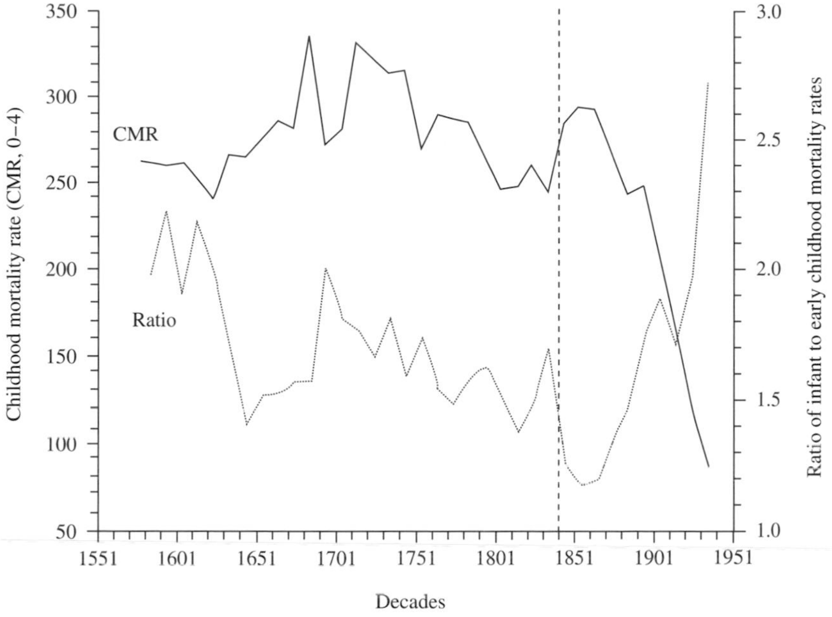

Figure 2.4
Approximate trends in the childhood mortality rate (ages 0–4) and the ratio of infant (age 0 in completed years) to early childhood mortality (ages 1–4), England and Wales, 1580s to 1940s

Source: Woods 2000: 252.

Although there are still some uncertainties in our interpretation of infant mortality trends there is a growing consensus that, once again, stresses the role of women (Millward and Bell 2001). Figure 2.3 shows that female mortality in the reproductive years declined from the 1870s, although deaths in childbirth did not decline until the late 1930s. Since fertility was also falling we may be sure that a major factor was that healthier women were having fewer, healthier children – i.e., a virtuous circle.

The mortality fall may be approached in a different way, using the cause of death data. There are many factors that may have affected causes of death. They include sanitary improvements, autonomous changes in the aetiology (i.e., virulence) of certain diseases, the improvements in living standards and their implication for nutritional status, and the role of medical interventions, including hospitalisation and therapeutic measures. This approach to mortality is usually associated with the name of Thomas McKeown (1976). Although McKeown's generalisations are no longer treated with awe, there is still a considerable attraction in his explanations. The prevailing consensus is that:

(a) Changes in the autonomous fatality rate of certain infectious diseases of childhood (most notably scarlet fever) led to the decline of early childhood mortality in the second half of the nineteenth century.
(b) The sanitary revolution had a beneficial effect on mortality in the largest urban centres by reducing deaths due to water- and food-borne diseases (especially diarrhoea and typhoid), but that the main effect did not come until the early twentieth century (Szreter and Hardy 2000).

(c) The effect of rising living standards (i.e., on nutrition, housing, leisure time) was to improve mortality, but the mechanisms are difficult to judge with any precision. (For example, it was thought that increased living standards largely caused the decline in deaths from pulmonary tuberculosis, but this is now thought to be questionable.)
(d) Advances in medical science had some impact in a few areas in the nineteenth and early twentieth centuries, particularly smallpox vaccination and the isolation of tuberculosis sufferers. But their most important impact was very late – from the 1930s and 1940s.

In short, the doubling of life expectancy at birth from 40 to 80 in only 150 years occurred because of a series of beneficial and cumulative developments – some administrative, some fortuitous, some scientific (Riley 2001). It is also important to remember that the quality of life – e.g., an individual's health – may be as, or even more important, to them than their life expectancy. This is suggested, for example, by the very large sums of money that individuals are prepared to pay for health care in rich countries in the later twentieth century.

UNRESOLVED DEMOGRAPHIC PROBLEMS

There are still aspects of the demographic revolution between the 1840s and the 1940s which we find difficult fully to explain. In this section we shall briefly consider two particular problem areas: the role of social class and the demographic consequences of urbanisation.

Social class and demographic variations

The social classification of occupations, especially male occupations, has proved such a convenient device for examining demographic change that it is difficult to imagine Britain without officially defined social classes. For example, we expect that the higher the social class the lower the level of mortality at all ages and the lower the level of fertility. We also expect the higher social classes to have been early adopters of new medical knowledge and contraceptives. However, Szreter (1984, 1996) has shown that the first social classification of occupations, undertaken by the Registrar General in 1911, owed much to contemporary perceptions of what the social distribution of fertility and mortality *should* look like (Table 2.1). There is, therefore, some circularity at work.

Recent research has examined trends in the 1890s and 1900s (Garrett *et al.* 2001). This work shows that mortality varied considerably within social classes, particularly if the environment was unhealthy. It also shows that local environment could be more important than social class in the decision to limit family size, perhaps because of imitation of local

Table 2.1 Examples of definitions of social classes used by the Registrar General

Social class	Example occupations
I Professional	accountants, engineers, doctors
II Managerial and technical	marketing and sales managers, teachers, journalists, nurses
III N Skilled non-manual	clerks, shop assistants, cashiers
III M Skilled manual	carpenters, goods van drivers, joiners, cooks
IV Semi-skilled	security guards, machine tool operators, farm workers
V Unskilled	building labourers, general labourers, cleaners
Also defined in 1911	Separated from I–V above
VI Textile workers	
VII Miners	
VIII Agricultural labourers	

reference points. The importance of these analytical subtleties may be lost on those who have grown up with the Registrar General's five or six official social classes. The classification has provided such a powerful conceptual and comparative tool that it is unlikely to be given up easily (Goldthorpe 2000).

Figure 2.5 shows mortality of adult males by social class in the first half of the twentieth century. It uses the standardised mortality ratio (SMR); that is, it shows the relation between the mortality of each social class (using the 1911 classification) and average mortality (the base of 100). In 1911, for example, agricultural labourers (class VIII) had substantially lower mortality than members of classes I and II, while class V mortality was significantly higher than III, IV, VI and VII. (The difference between V and VIII was probably related to their working conditions.) By the 1950s, however, relative mortality simply reflected the (now five) classes of the 1951 classification. In fact, there were signs of increasing inequality as classes I–II pulled away from III–IV, and a trailing class V re-emerged. Interestingly in 1931, class inequalities in health, at least as measured by adult male mortality, were at their lowest in the period, raising some interesting questions (Stevenson 1977; Jones 1994). There is evidence that unemployment in the 1920s and 1930s contributed to the deterioration in health of both the unemployed themselves and their children via a worsening diet (Winter 1979; Harris 1988; Eichengreen 1994: 313). But there was little sign of the social health divides of the late twentieth century.

Urbanisation and its demographic effects

Urbanisation in Britain came relatively early. By 1851, half of the population lived in urban areas. This has led to a debate about the effect of urbanisation on mortality, and, most important, how health should be

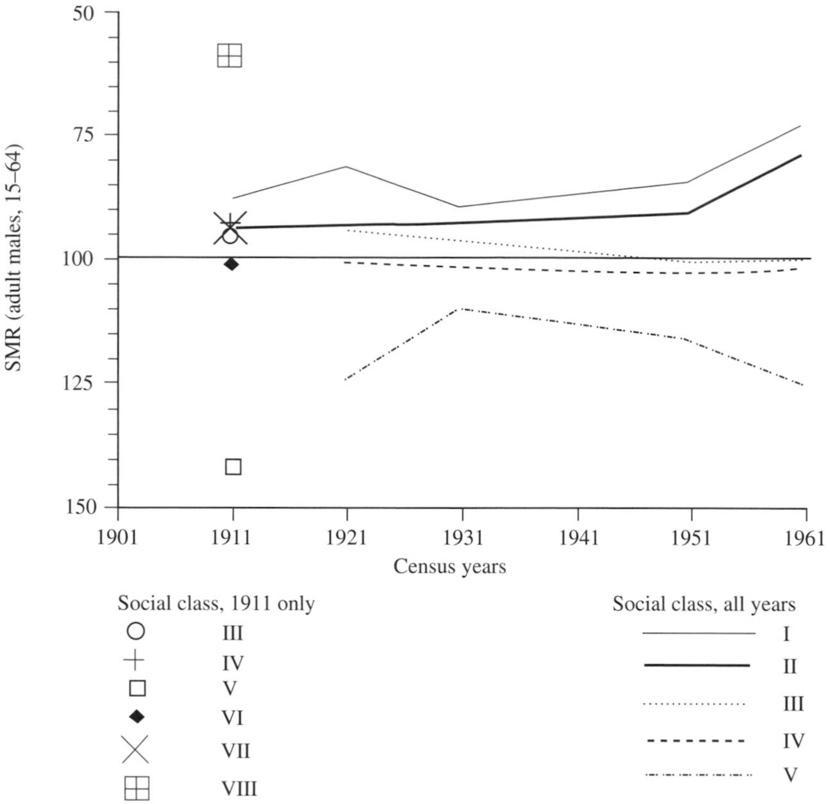

Figure 2.5 Post-1911 trends in social class mortality differentials among adult males (aged 15–64) in England and Wales measured by the standardised mortality ratio (SMR). Social classes as defined in Table 2.1.

Source: new estimates by Woods based on vital registration data for England and Wales.

incorporated in considerations of living standards (Woods and Woodward 1984; Williamson 1990; see also chapter 11 below). The debate may be summarised as follows. Woods (1985, 2000: 360–80) emphasised the effect of population redistribution between lower mortality rural areas and higher mortality urban areas on the relative stagnation in national mortality as measured by life expectancy. Szreter and Mooney (1998) argued that urbanisation in general was not the problem, but rather that worsening health conditions were largely confined to the larger British cities (over 100,000) during the second quarter of the nineteenth century. A second question is whether rising mortality is evidence of declining living standards, as Szreter argued and Woods doubted.

Figure 2.6 illustrates some of the mortality estimates currently available. It shows life expectancy at birth in years for England and Wales together with series for London; Birmingham, post-1851; Glasgow, 1821–61 (Flinn 1977: 376–9); Liverpool in 1841; as well as series for the large towns by Szreter (Szreter and Mooney 1998: 104) and Woods (2000: 369). There appears to be a divergence between the experiences of London and other cities. If Farr's estimates for 1841 are correct, then life expectancy in London at birth was ten years higher than in Liverpool, for example.

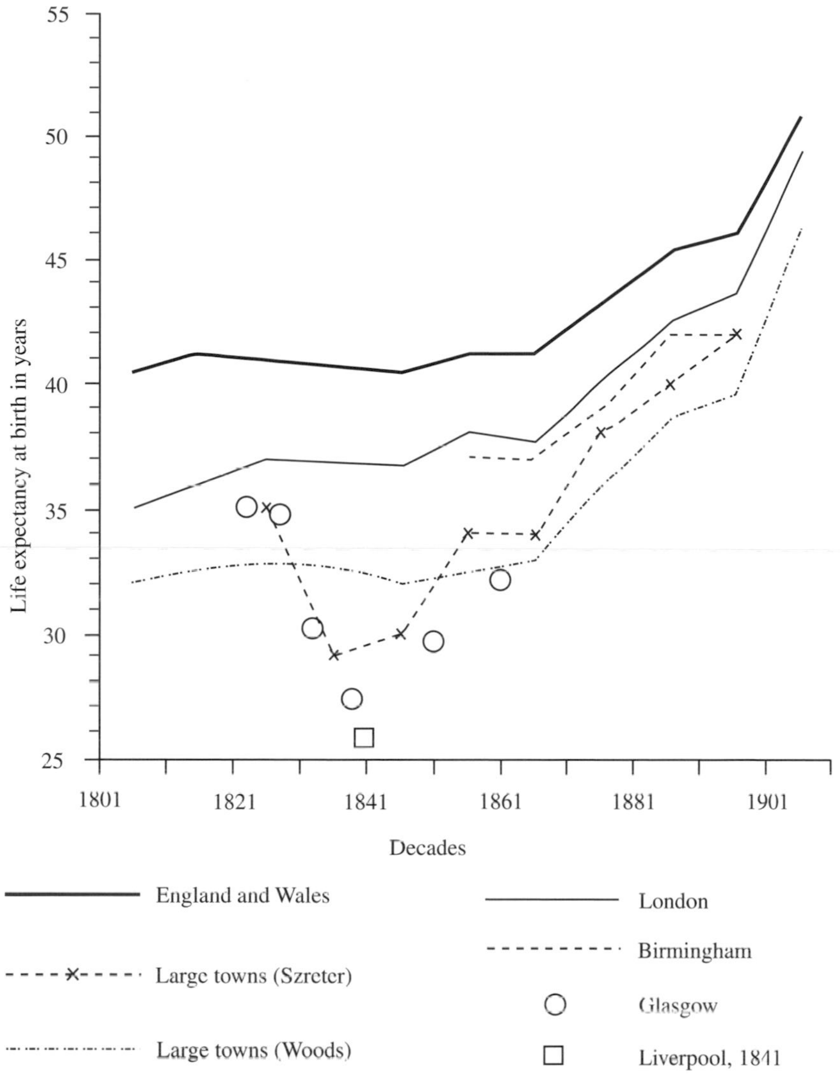

Figure 2.6 Estimates of life expectancy at birth for England and Wales and large towns, 1801–1901

Source: Woods 2000: 369.

There is good reason to believe that some of the other large towns did not have rising mortality and that the view that large cities had rising mortality in the 1830s and 1840s rests on only a limited number of examples.

Despite our best efforts, the decades before the 1850s conceal many hazards for the quantitative historian. Did mortality really increase in the large towns outside London, but not in London itself? Was mortality at this time much more sensitive to the tricks of epidemiology than to fluctuations in real wages? Is life expectancy a poor teacher of economics? As Armstrong (1981: 109) observed more than twenty years ago: 'If particular weight is attached to the course of mortality in discussions of the standard of living, then by the same token we should have to infer massive social improvements in third world countries since the Second World War, which would be a conclusion uncongenial to many pessimists.'

MIGRATION

Compared with mortality and fertility the third demographic component, migration, is relatively difficult to define and, hence, to measure. Migration involves the crossing of state, regional or city boundaries and a change of permanent residence for a minimum period of time – a year, five years, since birth. In addition, unlike birth and death, migration is a selective process: it occurs non-randomly in terms of age, gender, education, places of origin and destination, etc. Most who migrate have made that decision for themselves, but there will also be others who feel obliged to move, who are forced out or taken; most important, there will be many more who might have wished to become migrants had circumstances permitted.

Migration models

Migration is often explained in one of two complementary ways: as a balance of push-pull factors and as a reflection of information flows. A standard formulation of the push-pull model relates migration to the difference between the income which an individual can expect to earn if he or she remains where they are (Ii) and the expected income in a new place of residence (Ij), discounting for the cost of making the move from i to j, including cost of transport and the psychological costs of social disruption. This human capital formulation is especially useful in dealing with labour migrants and can be thought of as analogous to making an educational investment, which will enhance future employment and income prospects. A key feature is that Mij (the migration flow from place i to place j) reflects the combined effects of push in i and pull from j – i.e., one differential might attract one person, but not another. Implicit in the model is that there is a regular flow of information between j and i. Migration may also involve steps (a number of intervening staging posts), returns and circulatory migration (often temporary). The effect on relatives and friends generated by the pioneer leading migrants, who initiate the flow, is critically important. Factors that facilitate information flows include literacy, the post and telegraph, the press, photography, transport links, railways, steamships. Technological advances drive up the quantity and quality of information available whilst driving down the direct costs and social costs of making a move.

The two models which focus, respectively, on economic differentials and information flows have been applied to both internal and external migration. But there are some important differences. Internal migrants

Table 2.2 Destinations of British emigrants (outward bound passengers) other than Europe, 1853–1930 (000s and %)

	USA	Canada	Australia/NZ	All
1853–1900	3,117 [55.9]	735 [13.2]	1,133 [20.3]	5,571 [100]
1900–30	1,528 [27.1]	2,122 [37.7]	970 [17.1]	5,638 [100]
1853–1930	4,644 [41.4]	2,857 [25.5]	2,102 [18.7]	11,209 [100]

Source: Calculated from Carrier and Jeffrey 1953: 95–7.

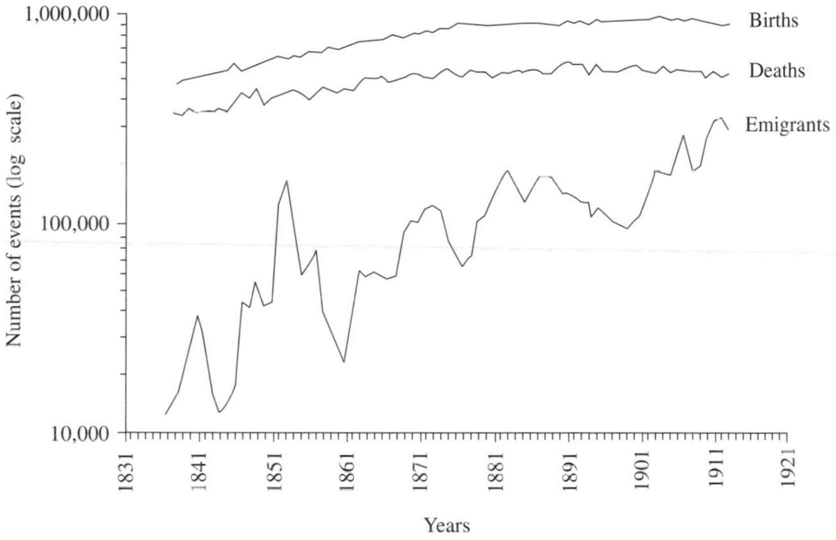

Figure 2.7 Number of births and deaths in, and emigrants from, England and Wales per year before the First World War

Source: Woods 2000: 48.

found information easier to obtain and it was a simpler matter to move within the country than to emigrate. There is also a possibility that internal and external migration were functionally related.

Emigration

About 20 per cent (more than 11 million) of all European emigrants between 1815 and 1930 came from Britain. Only three countries (Ireland, Italy and Norway) had higher emigration rates over any substantial (forty-year) period (Baines 1991: 9–11, 1994; Hatton and Williamson, 1998). The United States was the main destination for British emigrants in the nineteenth century, but by the early twentieth century, Empire migration dominated. Canada became the most important and Australia was the other important destination (Table 2.2).

Emigration from Britain was discontinuous and the same discontinuities occurred in most other European countries, suggesting the same causation. Figure 2.7 shows the estimated number of emigrants per year from England and Wales. The discontinuities correlate with fluctuations in the economies of the United States, Canada and the other destinations. This has an important implication. If many emigrants timed their move to coincide with favourable labour market conditions overseas, it confirms that they must have had access to information about those conditions. The main source of information in Britain was letters and, increasingly, the experience of previous emigrants who had returned. Return migration rates to Britain were high from the 1870s, which was the first decade when emigrants were able to travel by steamship. It has been estimated that, from the 1870s, at least 40 per cent of British emigrants returned (Baines 1985: 128–35).

For a long time it was assumed that British emigration could be entirely explained by a version of the push-pull model, that is, by the problems of the countryside and to a lesser extent by the problems of redundant industries, including the decline of some craft skills (Jones 1973). In other words, the emigrants were assumed to have come from areas of the country lagging behind in terms of economic change. Cornwall is a well-known example. The county had the highest emigration rates in England (1861–1900), which was apparently related to its dependence on agriculture and the collapse of its only significant industries – copper and tin mining (Rowe 1953: 326, 378; Baines 1985: 159). If the push-pull explanation can be generalised to the whole of Britain, the majority of emigrants should have come from counties with problems similar to those of Cornwall, counties that were peripheral to the economy. Moreover, emigration from Britain should have fallen as the country became more urban and industrial.

In fact, as Figure 2.7 illustrates, the emigration rate rose up to the First World War. Serious doubts about the origins of British emigrants were first raised in a classic article by Charlotte Erickson. Using data which enumerated the passengers on ships entering United States ports she showed, *inter alia*, that, by the 1880s, British emigrants were close to a representative sample of the population. In other words, they came primarily from urban areas, not predominantly from the periphery and were mainly unskilled. And when emigration was high the proportion of urban workers increased (Erickson 1972: 370).

In a comprehensive study of English and Welsh emigration, 1861–1900, Baines showed that a third of English and Welsh emigrants had been born in London, Lancashire or the West Midlands and another third had been born in other highly urbanised counties, which could not be considered peripheral. There remained the possibility that many of the emigrants had come from the rural parts of the urban counties or that they had originally been born in the rural areas, and had migrated to the towns before emigrating – so-called rural–urban step migration. (Step migration has been identified in many European countries, particularly in Scandinavia.) If this were the case, the majority of emigrants could still have been from peripheral parts of the economy. But Baines' estimates also showed that at least 45 per cent of the emigrants must have been truly urban (born in urban areas, emigrated from urban areas) and that

33 per cent must have been rural (born in rural areas, emigrated from rural areas). Hence, no more than 22 per cent of the emigrants could have been people who had previously moved to the towns from a rural area. In other words, about half of English and Welsh emigrants were likely to have been both born and brought up in an urban environment, defined in this study as a town of 20,000 people. (Moreover, if we include step migrants, urban emigration rates exceeded rural.) Hence, emigrants were more likely to have come from the centre of economic change than from the periphery, which is more consistent with the information than with the push-pull model (Baines 1985: 145–7, 254, 264–5).

The urban character of British emigration may have been related to the high rate of return to Britain, which was the highest for any European country during a comparable period. In other words, British emigration moved into a high return phase in advance of other European countries. It was to be expected. Britain had industrialised earlier and had superior transport links. In some cases the labour markets in a British and an overseas city (e.g. New York and London) may have overlapped. This is really another way of saying that the information flow to Britain was superior.

Before the First World War few British emigrants travelled with a subsidy. A few subsidies came from private philanthropists and landowners in the early part of the period, but they mainly came from Empire governments towards the end of the period. The purpose of such government subsidies was to channel emigrants towards an Empire country if it was expensive to reach (i.e., Australia), or was close to a more developed competing destination (i.e., Canada). It is unlikely that subsidies significantly increased the emigration rate, rather than diverting people who had already decided to emigrate to the United States to Empire destinations. There was more assisted emigration after the First World War. Among Empire emigrants, 36 per cent (i.e., 15 per cent of all emigrants) were assisted and, for the first time, some of the assistance came from the UK government through the Empire Settlement Act of 1922 (Constantine 1990: 16). Assistance prioritised agricultural labourers, children and domestic servants. Unfortunately the prospects for agricultural settlement in the White Dominions, which was the aim, were poor. The schemes collapsed in the international depression of the 1930s and for the first time in over 200 years Britain had a positive migration balance.

Emigration had demographic effects. Hatton and Williamson estimated that without emigration between 1871 and the First World War, British population would have been 16 per cent larger than it actually was (this includes the effect of the emigrants' unborn children) and the labour force would have been 11 per cent larger (Hatton and Williamson 1999: 208, 213). This is a considerable number and, other things being equal, would have affected wage levels. The development of emigration from a particular country may be divided into three phases. In the first, the bulk of the population could benefit from emigration, but emigration rates are constrained by lack of information or poverty, that is, the inability to finance emigration. In the second phase, information becomes more abundant. Emigration rates are increasingly determined by income differentials in origin and destination countries. In the third phase, incomes rise in the origin country relative to incomes in the destination country. (This is partly caused by the effect of migration on labour supply in the two countries.) Hence, the emigration rate falls.

We may assume that British emigration was no longer in the first phase in the later nineteenth century. Emigrants were leaving from all parts of the country. Emigration rates were rising up to the First World War. But why was Britain still in the second stage? Recent estimates show that, in 1870, real wages in the USA, for example, were, on average, 72 per cent higher than in Britain. In 1910, US real wages were still 72 per cent higher. There had been no convergence (O'Rourke and Williamson 1999: 17). This is particularly puzzling because of a process which economists call 'factor price equalisation'. British labour was moving from a labour abundant, resource scarce, economy to labour scarce, resource abundant economies. This should have increased returns to labour (i.e., real wages) in Britain and reduced it in the overseas economies. One possible explanation concerns countervailing capital movements. British overseas investment reduced the rate of capital accumulation in Britain and increased it in the USA, thus reducing the returns to labour in Britain (Hatton and Williamson 1998: 29, 219). A more likely explanation is that in the early twentieth century European countries were unable to copy American productivity. Fundamentally, this was because the US economy could derive advantages from its resource base which were unavailable to European countries. This meant that the return to both capital and labour in Britain was lower than in the USA (Nelson and Wright 1992). Hence, with existing technology, convergence would not occur and emigration would not reduce wage differentials.

Interregional migration

Despite measurement problems, we may be reasonably confident that internal migration rates were high during the nineteenth century, as they were in the period before industrialisation (Southall 1986; Anderson 1990: 13; Pooley and Turnbull 1998). There may be many reasons why people moved, including marriage, seasonal employment and the tramping of skilled workers from one job to another. (It might also include fleeing from creditors, such as landlords.) Many things that inhibit migration in the early twenty-first century were of little consequence in the nineteenth, such as the location of good schools or elderly relatives. Most important, the housing market must have been more open than today when, for example, salaries in the south-east of Britain do not compensate for the much higher cost of housing there. The exact volume of inter-regional movement is, however, difficult to assess. Most historical data were gathered at particular points in time, such as during a census enumeration. These show only the effect of a period of migration (how many migrants are present) not the number of moves the migrants had made since the last enumeration. To measure intervening moves would have required a continuous register of each change of address, as the Netherlands has had since the mid-nineteenth century. (Modern British censuses enumerate the place of residence one or five years previously, but even this is insufficient to capture the extent of total mobility.) Contemporary estimates for migration into Prussian cities showed that in 1881, 11 per cent of the population left the city each year and 14 per cent entered. In 1912, the rates were 16 per cent and 18 per cent respectively. The inability historically to measure total mobility has an important consequence. Since there are more short-distance than long-distance moves, a measure of net migration, as in a census enumeration, will be higher in localities with a small population than in localities with large populations. In other words, net migration rates to the cities will tend to be lower than net migration rates from the countryside. This is what we observe in the nineteenth century. But this does not prove that the rural population was more mobile than urban. It may simply mean that the urban population was more transient – i.e., the return migration was greater (Daunton 2000).

The next issue is whether we can discern patterns of migration from the large amount of random movement. Anderson drew a 2 per cent sample from the 1851 census. This showed that 54 per cent of the population were living more than 2 kilometres from their place of birth, but there was a significant difference between rural and urban areas. Although people enumerated in the urban and rural areas were equally likely to have been migrants, those who had moved to a rural area had moved a shorter distance: 66 per cent of the rural migrants had moved less than 26 kilometres compared with fewer than 40 per cent of those who had gone to the cities. Most important, migrants to London, on average, had been born even further away – only 20 per cent from within 26 kilometres (Anderson 1990: 8, 11). This and similar studies show two patterns. A large proportion of migration was only for a short distance, but the important urban labour markets, like London, attracted relatively more migrants from long distances (Boyer 1997; Boyer and Hatton 1997).

The most important characteristic of the net migration pattern in the second half of the nineteenth and early twentieth centuries is clear. It is a continuous net outflow from nearly all the rural areas and a continuous net inflow into a limited number of large towns, London, Liverpool, Manchester, Leeds, Sheffield, Glasgow, Birmingham and Newcastle, and the coalfields and heavy industrial areas (Table 2.3). On the other hand,

Table 2.3 Population growth and migration, England and Wales, 1841–1911 (000s)

	Population 1841	Population 1911	Natural increase	Net migration	Mig. × 100 / NI	1911 × 100 / 1841
Greater London	2,262	7,315	3,802	+1,251	32.9%	324
Eight largest northern towns	1,551	5,192	2,747	+893	32.5%	335
Coalfields	1,320	5,334	3,363	+650	19.3%	404
Rural areas	6,166	6,961	5,302	−4,507	−85.0%	113
England and Wales	15,914	36,070	21,366	−1,210	−5.7%	227

Note: Manchester, Liverpool, Birmingham, Leeds, Sheffield, Leicester, Hull, Nottingham. 'Urban' areas are very strictly defined, and include all continuously built-up areas.

Source: Adapted from Cairncross 1953: 82–6.

emigrants came from both rural and urban areas. There was also immigration from Ireland, and a smaller amount from eastern Europe towards the turn of century.

Table 2.3 shows that the countryside (defined as everywhere that did not contain a built-up area of 2,000 persons) lost more than 4.5 million people between 1841 and 1911. Most parts of the countryside experienced out-migration for most of this period. Hence there cannot have been a single cause. For example, if the migration had been caused by the large growth of grain imports in the 1870s, then we would expect exceptional migration rates from the arable counties which were most affected by imports. But there was little difference in net out-migration between arable and livestock counties, where livestock farmers benefited from imports, after 1870. The key point is that the decline in the agricultural labour force was only one of many causes of migration (Friedlander 1992). We may estimate that less than half of the out-migrants from the countryside were agricultural workers and their dependants (1.5 million out of 4.5 million). The other key factor was the change in industrial location. Heavy industry, for example, developed only on the coalfields, since, in the nineteenth century, coal was the key source of energy. Specialisation in the economy increased, induced by improvements in transport, notably railways. Most manufacturing shifted to the urban-industrial areas, increasing labour demand there, but the rural industries, lace making or furniture manufacturing declined (Baines 1985: 239–41, 247–8).

The decline in rural non-agricultural employment tended to affect women more than men and it is not surprising that women were, in the main, more likely to leave the countryside, at least as measured by net migration. The most important occupational destination for young women was domestic service. The growth of domestic service is an example of the importance of the demand for labour, derived in this case from the growth of middle-class occupations particularly in London. Hence, the position of domestic servants in the labour market was relatively strong and, despite migration, the wages of domestic servants rose faster than the national average for most of the period. By 1900 relatively high female migration meant that the female surplus in the countryside had almost disappeared. In 1901, for example, there were 106.8 females per 100 males in England and Wales (one reason being that men were more likely to emigrate), but in the rural districts there were only 101 females per 100 males (Saville 1957: 33; Redford 1964).

Rural out-migration rates declined in the 1880s and fell markedly in the early twentieth century. There is no single reason. Since migration rates were higher among young people, the rural population was ageing, but age-specific migration rates were also falling. Hence, the ageing rural population is not a sufficient explanation. There is also the statistical effect of suburbanisation, towns spreading into the countryside. Out-migration from the rural areas reduced the growth rate of the rural population to almost zero (Table 2.3). In some areas, including rural Wales and the Borders, southern Scotland and the Highlands, the population actually fell. But the main reason for urban population growth was natural increase rather than migration. Natural increase accounted for 75 per cent of the growth of the main cities (1841–1911). Migration into the cities did have an effect on age structure, but allowing for the effect would reduce the natural growth component only to about 60 per cent.[2] In the colliery districts, which had higher fertility, natural increase accounted for 84 per cent of all growth, or 65 per cent discounting for age structure. This calculation is rather arbitrary, however, since the effect of migration was to change the location where children were born. For example, some of the new industrial districts, such as the Rhondda Valley or Middlesbrough, would hardly have existed at all without immigration. Hence, later nineteenth-century British cities were comparable to late twentieth-century cities in developing countries, both growing mainly by natural increase. (Although mortality is relatively much lower in cities in developing countries.) Recent estimates show that as early as the first half of the nineteenth century in-migration accounted for less than a half of urban growth (Williamson 1990: 28).

A major component of the migration pattern in Britain was Irish immigration. Strictly, this was internal migration, since Britain and Ireland had been part of the same country since 1802. Irish immigration was about 600,000 (net of returns) between 1841 and 1861, plus a further 400,000 by 1911. In the 1850s, 3.5 per cent of the British population were Irish. By 1911 the proportion of the British population actually born in Ireland had fallen to 1.6 per cent, but there were many more of Irish

[2] Natural increase depends on the number of births and deaths in the population. Among young adults the death rate is lower than the average for the population as a whole, while the fertility rate is higher. Since the proportion of young adults is normally high among migrants, in-migration will reduce the number of deaths in the population and increase the number of births. In this specific case, migrants increased the urban population directly by 25 per cent, and indirectly by 15 per cent because of their effect on the age structure. Hence, natural increase accounted for the remaining 60 per cent of urban population growth.

extraction. The timing of Irish immigration was related to the famine of 1846–8 but the Irish, sometimes as seasonal workers, had been a part of the British labour market since the early nineteenth century (O'Grada 1999).

The Irish population was very concentrated. In both 1851 and 1901, about a half were living in London, Manchester, Glasgow and Liverpool. As we have seen, these cities were also the main destinations of rural migrants. The effect of Irish immigration on the British labour market depends, therefore, on whether the Irish were paid lower wages than British-born workers and the extent to which they replaced them. We may assume that Irish immigration did replace rural–urban migrants. In other words, without Irish immigration the movement to the British cities could have been greater. However, British emigration far exceeded Irish immigration throughout the period. For example, at the Irish immigration peak between 1841 and 1861, about 1 million British left (Baines 1985: 48–50, 218). This flow would have been lower without Irish immigration. There is no evidence that the Irish were paid lower wages for the same work than natives were. This is not surprising, for why would an employer pay different wages according to place of birth? Of course, most of the Irish entered the labour market at the bottom, as nearly all unskilled immigrants had to do. The Irish lived and worked in the centre of towns where they were very visible, but this does not mean that they were paid less than native workers (Hunt 1973: 298–9, 1981; Lees 1979: 247; Williamson 1990).

The only other quantitatively important immigrants in the period were eastern European Jews. About 120,000 entered before the First World War, especially between 1882 and 1905. The Jewish population, even more so than the Irish, was highly concentrated; in 1911, three-quarters of it was in London. Unlike the Irish, the most important Jewish occupation was, in effect, a new industry – mass-produced clothing. Their apparent poverty was also visible, although in the Jewish case it was partly because there were economic benefits of the extreme concentration of the East End clothing industry (Gartner 1960; Marks 1994). We might ask why immigration into Britain was not greater. Germany, for example, had net immigration from the 1890s when Britain had net emigration. The natural population growth rate was not very different. The simple answer is that the growth of gross domestic product (GDP) was lower in Britain, and, hence, the demand for labour was lower.

THE EFFECTS OF DEMOGRAPHIC CHANGE: DEPENDENCY, EMPLOYMENT, SKILLS

The most important effect of the demographic changes came through changes in age distribution (Figure 2.8). Assuming no migration, the age

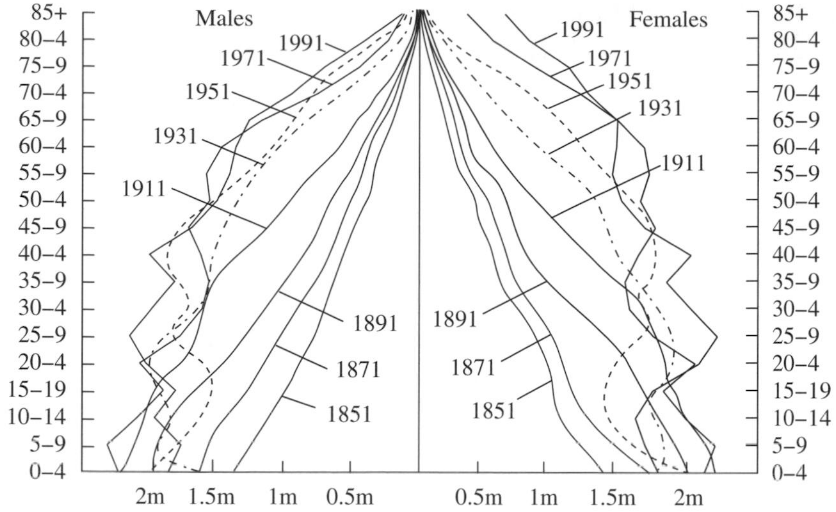

Figure 2.8 Age distribution of the British population in five-year age groups, 1851–1991

Source: 1851–1951: Mitchell and Deane 1962; 1971 and 1991: HMSO 2001.

structure of a population changes through the effect of current fertility and mortality on each age group, the size of which depends on previous fertility and mortality. In this period, the dominant cause of changes in age structure was fertility. Fertility is the only demographic event that affects a single age. A shortfall in births in year 1 means a shortfall of 10-year olds in year 10. This can be seen in Figure 2.8, which shows, among other things, the marked effect of the wars on fertility. The dominance of fertility was transient. In the late twentieth century, mortality has become a more important component in age structure because fertility is low and relatively unchanging, while the mortality of some of the older age groups is falling.

Figure 2.8 shows how the shape of the age-sex pyramid began to change between 1891 and 1911. The diamond-shaped age distribution, seen in 1851 and 1871, is characteristic of countries with high mortality and fertility, that is, with high wastage at each age. Many developing countries today have a similar age distribution, but with lower mortality and even higher fertility. This means that the slope of the pyramid is steeper, showing that they have faster population growth than in nineteenth-century Britain, which never exceeded 1.5 per cent per year, whereas late twentieth-century Kenya, for example, has experienced growth rates in excess of 3 per cent. The characteristic age structure of twentieth-century industrial societies starts to appear in 1911. Each age group is a little smaller than the previous one and population growth is slower. But the effect of falling fertility before 1911 was muted because of the large number of young people, the survivors of previous higher fertility, in the population. In the 1930s, the picture changed. There was still a large young adult population but age-specific fertility had fallen to such a low level that most demographers predicted that the population would actually

Table 2.4 Employment and the labour force, UK, 1920–38 (000,000s)

	Working population	Employment	Unemployment
1920	20.7	20.3	0.4
1921	20.1	17.9	2.2
1938	23.6	21.4	2.2

Source: Adapted from Feinstein: 1976: T127.

begin to decline, leading to fears about the effect on the economy and stimulating eugenic concerns (Glass 1938; Teitelbaum and Winter 1985). In fact, the situation was reversed during and after the Second World War. The population projections proved to be ill founded and the accompanying social and political scares misplaced. The rise in the proportion of the population aged 15–64 meant that, other things being equal (a large assumption), in the interwar period, the number of 'producers' rose relative to the number of dependants. In 1931, 68 per cent of men were aged 15–64 compared with 63 per cent in 1911 and 59 per cent in 1861. In the 1930s and before, the main problem was child dependence – the age group 0–14. By the later twentieth century, by contrast, the problem had become age dependence. Age structure also has welfare implications. For example, non-contributory old age pensions were introduced at a time (1909) when the proportion of old people in the population was small. There were similar age structure effects in education. Before the First World War, the cost of education fell on a relatively small number of producers, which was one reason (but only one) why education was poor. After the war, the number of children was declining. Hence, schools took fewer new entrants each year, which allowed an improvement in the quantity and quality of education. The high level of unemployment in the interwar period was also affected by age structure, since the labour force (defined as those looking for work) increased relative to the total population. Table 2.4 shows that about 2.4 million jobs were lost in the post-war collapse (1920–1), but that 3.5 million jobs were created between the low point of 1921 and 1938, a creditable performance. At the same time, however, the labour force increased by 3.5 million, which meant that unemployment in 1938 (2.2 million) was as high as in 1921. Of course, the crude data require some explanation. It is reasonable to assume that most adult males were looking for work, and, hence, that the size of the male labour force was demographically determined. Female participation is more complicated. Before the 1914–18 war most young single women were employed, but in a relatively limited number of sectors (typically, textiles, clothing and domestic service). Married women, and particularly those with children, were rarely part of the paid labour force. But after the First World War, there was a change in female employment. Domestic service began to decline and jobs in shops and offices to increase. Married women's participation also began to increase (Glucksmann 1990).

Table 2.5 shows that the labour force was ageing. This had implication for skills, i.e., the human capital stock. Most skills were learned by doing, that is, on the job. Other things being equal, an older labour force would be expected to have a high average skill level. But in the interwar period, other things were not equal. The economy was considerably restructured, following the decline of the staple industries, so that old skills became obsolete. Hence, retraining became more important – possibly from coal miner to production line worker. Hence, the fact that the labour force was ageing was not necessarily an advantage.

Table 2.5 Age distribution of male labour force, 1901, 1931 and 1951 (%)

Age group	1901	1931	1951
<25	32	25	18
25–44	43	41	45
>45	25	34	37

Note: Children could be counted as 'occupied' at 10 years in 1901, at 14 in 1931 and 15 in 1951. 3–4 per cent of the labour force was over 65 at each census.

Source: Calculated from Mitchell and Deane 1962: 15–18.

Declining fertility meant that family size became less varied. In a high-fertility regime, chance meant that there was great variation in the number of children per marriage. In the 1870s marriage cohort there were about as many families with ten children, or five children, as there were families with no children (Anderson 1985: 80). The number of children often determined whether the family lived in poverty or not, a factor recognised by social investigators like Charles Booth and Seebohm Rowntree (see chapter 11 below). By the 1930s, the variation in family size had declined markedly. For example, 65 per cent of the 1925 marriage cohort had two children or fewer.

Falling fertility also reduced the reproductive span of the average woman. In the 1870s many women bore children well into their 40s, which meant that many still had young children at 60 when their daughters may also have had children. By this time their own parents would probably have died. By the interwar period, the situation was quite different. Although it became easier for married women to re-enter the paid labour force, a large rise in married women's participation depended on demand as well as supply. Demand was only to rise marginally in peacetime until the 1950s when there was, for the first time, a shortage of male labour (Anderson 1985: 73).

The First World War and its impact

War deaths in England and Wales were 634,000 (722,000 in the United Kingdom), or 6.8 per cent of males aged 15–39 in 1911. The 20–4 age group was depleted by 16.1 per cent and the 25–9 age group by 9.9 per cent (Wall and Winter 1988: 82). The issue of a lost generation, which, among other things, was supposed to have affected female marriage chances, was much debated in the 1920s. In fact, the demographic effects of the war were surprisingly small. The most important effect was probably the permanent birth deficit of some 670,000 (Winter 1985: 253). But, as we know, unemployment was high in the post-war period. Hence, it is difficult to see population size *per se* as a problem. The effect of the war on civilian health was largely neutral. Infant and adult mortality continued to fall (Wall and Winter 1988: 14), as was to be expected, since the war had many positive effects on civilians. It led to full employment, the narrowing of skill differentials and (eventually) price controls and rationing, all of which disproportionately benefited poorer people. But the war did have a serious effect on the housing stock, which was to the detriment of the less well off.

The effect of the war on age structure was limited because it interrupted a period of heavy emigration. Net outflow was probably of the order of 150,000 per year in the three years before 1914 but only 75,000 per year in 1920–1. In other words, it is likely that if there had been no war, emigration would have been higher. Nor is it true that the marriage chances of a generation of women were ruined. Naturally, there was an increase in the number of widows, but a higher proportion of women were married in 1921 than had been the case in 1911 in every age group except one (30–4). It was not necessary for the British to adopt the post-war French pattern, where men married at a younger and women at an older age. France (where in any event there was no cushion of emigration) lost in the war proportionately more than twice as many men as Britain (Wall and Winter 1988: 68, 72). In Britain, there was no lost generation in the population as a whole.

Regional variations in employment

The growth of heavy industry in the nineteenth century was concentrated on the coalfields. Other important sectors, for example, commercial services were also highly concentrated but in cities that were remote from the coalfields, notably London (36 per cent of the increase in employment in commercial services between 1851 and 1911 was in London.) By 1900, industries and occupations in Britain were probably more localised than at any other time before or since (Brown 1972).

In the nineteenth century there were wide differentials in the wages paid for the same job. Some of the differentials reflected capital-output ratios (and hence, productivity). But in the nineteenth century, there were regional differences in wages in occupations where there was no mechanisation or where technology in the regions was the same. Table 2.6 shows the wages of agricultural labourers, which are a good proxy for the wages of unskilled labourers as a whole. It is obvious that wages were highest close to the cities. This was not because urban prices were higher than rural. Living costs in the cities, except for rents, were normally lower than in the countryside (the cheapest food was imported, for example). Hence, real wages were higher. Unions were weak in the nineteenth century, and government interference non-existent. The table shows, however, that regional differentials in unskilled wages narrowed in the nineteenth century. This must have been largely a consequence of migration. It is certainly the case that if labour had not left the land, agricultural productivity would have been lower, for example, and this

Table 2.6 Wages of agricultural labourers, 1867–1907 (shillings and pence per week)

	1867–70	[a]	1907	[a]
London and Home Counties	16/6	115	18/7	102
Primarily industrial				
South Wales	12/8	88	18/2	100
Lancs, Cheshire, Yorks/West Riding	17/1	119	19/7	107
East and West Midlands	14/1	98	18/5	101
Central Scotland	14/4	100	20/4	111
Northumberland, Durham	18/9	131	21/6	118
Primarily rural				
South-west England	12/5	87	16/10	92
South-east England	14/5	101	16/5	90
Lincoln, East and West Ridings	17/1	119	18/10	103
Cumberland/Westmorland	18/6	129	19/2	105
Rural Wales	13/-	91	17/8	97
Southern Scotland	15/-	105	19/4	106
Highlands of Scotland	13/2	92	17/7	96
Britain (unweighted mean)	14/4	100	18/7	100

[a] = index relative to GB mean.

Source: Based on Hunt 1973: 127–96.

would have affected unskilled wages in non-agricultural occupations in the rural areas. During and after the First World War, there was a considerable growth in trade union power leading to an increase in national pay bargaining. Other things being equal, regional wage differentials should have been reduced. But the post-war economy was different. The growth of trade union power and unemployment insurance in the interwar period meant that, in some industries, quite high wage levels could coexist with high unemployment rates. This did not (i.e., could not) have happened in the nineteenth century. In the nineteenth century, the variation in regional incomes was more likely to have been determined by the variation in income for the same occupations. In the interwar period, regional incomes were more likely to have been determined by the distribution of industry – whether the industries in a particular region offered a large or small number of high-wage occupations. The variation in regional unemployment rates was greater after the First World War than it had been before. Significantly, these differences persisted until after the outbreak of the Second World War. Interwar participation rates showed the same pattern. The more prosperous regions tended to have more workers per family. Hence, regional differences in family income tended to be larger than differences in unemployment rates.

The experience of depressed areas in the interwar period raises many questions. These include: was the problem in fact regional? What was the role of migration? That is, did regional unemployment differentials

Table 2.7 Employment growth in Greater London, Lancashire and Clydeside, 1841–1911 [000s]

	Greater London	Lancs	Clydeside
Males			
1841	432	479	256
1911	1,735	1,539	716
Increase	1,303 [302%]	1,060 [221%]	460 [180%]
Females			
1841	203	218	109
1911	913	792	263
Increase	710 [329%]	574 [263%]	154 [141%]
All			
1841	635	697	365
1911	2,648	2,331	979
Increase	2,013 [317%]	634 [235%]	614 [169%]

Note: 'Greater London' = London proper + Middlesex; 'Clydeside' = Strathclyde.

Source: Calculated from Lee 1979.

persist because, for some reason, labour did not move from areas of high to areas of low unemployment? Or was the economy as a whole unable to create full employment? These issues are discussed in detail elsewhere in this volume, but it is appropriate to make a few observations. It is possible to view the relations between regions as, in some respects, analogous to the relation between economies. Regions exported goods to other regions (and overseas), in exchange for imports. Services (many of which could not be exported) developed around the export industries of each region. In the interwar period, simple observation shows that the regions with the more diversified industrial structures were more prosperous than those that were less diversified. (This showed that the latter had attracted relatively less new investment.) Virtually all the new employment in the interwar period was created in the south-east and the Midlands, the majority in services (Law 1980: 88–9). The regions based on the great (overseas) export industries of the nineteenth century – textiles, shipbuilding, coal mining and heavy engineering (South Wales, Clydeside, the north-east and the north-west) – were heavily specialised in those industries. Regional income depended on their ability to export. When exports declined after the First World War they suffered a severe squeeze on their income. In other words, in the nineteenth century, when the staple industries were at the forefront of the British economy, these regions were not attracting other industries and services of sufficient importance to protect them from the collapse of exports after the First World War.

Table 2.7 illustrates this. It compares employment growth between 1841 and 1911 in Greater London and in two of the important staple industry regions, Lancashire (textiles, coal, engineering) and Clydeside (shipbuilding, engineering). The analysis of nineteenth-century employment data presents difficulties, but the main trends are clear. Even in the period when these regions should have had the greatest advantage, employment growth in Greater London was faster. Total employment rose by about 317 per cent in London compared with 235 per cent in Lancashire and only 169 per cent on Clydeside. In fact, in the heyday of the staple industries, a third of all new employment was created in Greater London (Lee 1979). These data are surprising because workers in both Lancashire and Clydeside had relatively high incomes. Hence, local demand should have encouraged the growth of consumer services and industries. What seems to have happened is that a larger proportion of their income was spent on imports, for example, from London, than the Londoners spent on imports from the rest of Britain. In other words, the employment multiplier was larger in London, and, on average, expenditure leaked out of Clydeside and Lancashire (and the other regions). This meant that the London economy diversified faster than the regional economies. This returns us to the question of the determinants of the location of industry.

A distinction is often made between absolute and comparative advantage. Since coal was the dominant source of power, the regions with large coal deposits had an absolute advantage in coal and a comparative advantage in the heavy industries. London, with a few other areas, had a comparative advantage in other (mainly consumer) industries and particularly in services (national and international). The latter were an extremely important component of economic growth during the twentieth century (Lee 1986). There was no overwhelming reason for consumer industries and services to develop in London (i.e., there was no absolute advantage); yet in the nineteenth century it was relatively more profitable to invest in these industries in London, because many complementary industries and services were already there, leading to 'positive externalities'. In addition, London was still the seat of government, the most important port and the home of the richest people. We could say that the effect of industrialisation was to reduce the dominance of London in the economy, but not to replace it with the dominance of anywhere else. After the First World War, the old industrial regions still had an absolute advantage over London, but the relative decline of international trade relatively reduced their income. Moreover, changes in the cost and quality of transport after the First World War favoured London (now including parts of the south-east). The motor vehicle made it possible for the new consumer industries to be located almost anywhere. In theory this could have led to a wider geographical distribution of industry, but in a country as small as Britain it meant that the new industries could be located where the greatest comparative advantage then lay.

Because the differences in regional unemployment rates persisted through the interwar period, it could be argued that labour may have been relatively immobile. In the nineteenth century there were few institutional barriers to mobility as workers moved from high to low unemployment regions and forced their way into the bottom of the labour market by accepting the going (and often low) wage. After the war, several factors would have tended to reduce mobility, notably, a less free housing market, stronger trade unions and unemployment benefits.

But was labour less mobile in an economic sense? The simplest measure of net migration is obtained by summing net population gains and losses. By this measure mobility after the war was less than in some decades in the late nineteenth century. (Mobility after the Second World War was even lower, by this measure.) However, it is possible that after the

First World War the observed migration was a lower proportion of the migration that actually occurred. The two main migration flows which had a high proportion of non-returning moves (emigration and rural–urban migration) were less important than they had been in the nineteenth century. In other words, the evidence for lower mobility is doubtful. It may also be inappropriate to use regional unemployment rates as a device for judging whether a labour force was mobile or immobile. The relevant variable should be the number of jobs (employment vacancies) that were on offer in a region. We do know that there was a great deal of movement, for example of South Wales miners to the new motor industry in Oxford. We do not know if additional migrants would have found additional jobs. In fact the majority of new jobs in the south-east were usually taken by people from within the region (Scott 1990: 339). The labour supply was abundant, partly because of the exceptional number of school leavers. In other words, it is difficult to say that labour was immobile if no part of the country had a tight labour market. People may have been perfectly willing and able to move, but there would be no point in moving if vacancies were few. Unemployment rates in the regions would only fall when the number of jobs created in the economy as a whole exceeded the number of people searching for them.

CONCLUSION: BRITAIN'S NEW DEMOGRAPHY

Since the Second World War Britain, like the rest of western Europe, has experienced the emergence of new and often unstable demographic structures. Mortality is now at a low, and probably stable, level – life expectancy at birth is unlikely to rise much beyond 90 years. Fertility is at an extremely low level, below replacement in several countries. Those children who are born tend either to be the consequence of accidental conceptions (out of stable sexual partnerships) or they are the result of precise calculations and timings intended to maximise female labour force participation whilst satisfying the emotional need for children. Induced abortion is now an important form of birth control alongside the oral contraceptive. Cohabitation has become a popular form of living arrangement. On the other hand, single-person households have become far more important among young adults and the elderly. More than a third of marriages end in divorce, but serial monogamy is still the dominant cultural norm. In terms of labour migration and regional development, many of the cities of Britain have lost population, but their wider regions are still the dominant economic, residential and cultural areas. The metropolitan regions in particular, especially London, continue to dominate. And their size has increased because of long-distance commuting. So-called 'counter-urbanisation' in the rural periphery appears to have been a short-lived affair. Finally, British cities, even the provincial ones, have become far more culturally diverse, but also more divided in terms of material conditions.

Some of this new demography reflects recent social, economic and technological changes but some changes may be traced back to the late nineteenth and early twentieth centuries. For example, Britain's position in the global network of labour migration was firmly established during the nineteenth century. Regional wage and employment differentials also emerged in the late nineteenth century and were accentuated in the interwar period when the north–south divide took on a form which is still partly recognisable today. Figure 2.1 indicates the timing of the mortality and fertility transitions which were clearly set in motion in earlier centuries and in this sense at least the period with which we have been concerned here has set a critically important legacy for today's British economy and society.

3 Human capital and skills

STEPHEN BROADBERRY

Contents

INTRODUCTION

Since the Second World War, many economic historians have come to see human capital as a weakness of the British economy since the late nineteenth century, particularly when compared with the United States and Germany. Although there is an element of truth in this, it is important not to exaggerate the British shortcomings in this area, particularly in the period before 1945. Britain can be seen as falling between an emphasis in the United States on formal education and a German emphasis on vocational training, but the extent of human capital gaps varied with the country of comparison, the time period and the sector of the economy.

There is strong evidence of a British shortfall in formal education compared with other rich countries including Germany as well as the United States in the mid-nineteenth century. However, Britain closed the gap in primary schooling during the late nineteenth century, and although the United States moved to a system of mass secondary education and rapidly expanded higher education in the first half of the twentieth century, Britain's increase in secondary schooling during this period was not unimpressive and remained on a par with Germany's. Although the modern German system of vocational training was already well established in industry and to a lesser extent in services by the early twentieth century, Britain still provided a supply of skilled workers for industry, through the system of apprenticeships, and for services, through professional qualifications, that far exceeded the supply of vocational training in the United States.

The main focus of this chapter is on the ramifications of education and training for productivity performance. The United States overtook Britain in terms of per capita income and labour productivity levels towards the end of the nineteenth century and pulled decisively ahead between the wars. This would be consistent with a positive role for mass secondary education and higher education in providing the social capabilities needed for modern high-volume methods (Goldin 2001; Broadberry and Ghosal 2002). Per capita income and labour productivity levels remained substantially lower in Germany than in Britain between 1870 and 1950, for although an impressive apprenticeship system had helped Germany to catch up in terms of industrial labour productivity, Britain remained a long way ahead in services and agriculture and had a more modern structure with a substantially smaller share of the labour force in the low value added agricultural sector.

FORMAL EDUCATION

All commentators agree that Britain lagged behind much of the rest of western Europe and North America in the provision of education during the nineteenth century, with universal primary education already a reality in the first half of the century in Prussia and the United States (Ringer 1979; Easterlin 1981; Sutherland 1990). In primary education, Britain largely closed the gap between 1870 and 1914 with a rapid expansion of primary enrolments that effectively established a system of universal primary education. However, despite an expansion of secondary and higher education in Britain between the wars, a significant gap opened up between Britain and the United States (but not continental Europe) in post-primary education.

The most significant development on the road to universal primary education (or elementary education as it was known until the 1920s) was Forster's Education Act of 1870, which provided for the creation of school boards in England and Wales, with the power to build and run schools in areas where there was a deficiency of voluntary (usually religious) schools (Armytage 1970: 143). Similar legislation for Scottish elementary schools followed in 1872 (Sutherland 1990: 146). The 1902 Education Act then allowed rate aid to voluntary schools, which were brought under the control of new local education authorities in England and Wales (Armytage 1970: 186). However, it was one thing to provide schools, another thing to ensure that everyone attended. Although the 1880 Education Act made full-time attendance compulsory between the ages of 5 and 10, by 1895 only 82 per cent of those on the register attended regularly (Sutherland

1990: 144–5). Furthermore, there have been suggestions that the quality of the education left something to be desired, with a system of payment by results leading to an excessive emphasis on drilling for examinations (Sutherland 1990: 145). Nevertheless, it seems clear that the introduction of universal primary education had a dramatic effect on illiteracy, with the proportion of grooms unable to sign at marriage falling from more than 30 per cent in the early 1840s to less than 1 per cent by 1914, and the proportion of brides unable to sign falling from nearly 50 per cent to less than 1 per cent over the same period (Schofield 1973; Mitch 1992). Furthermore, the quality of education surely improved as payment on established scales replaced payment by results after the 1918 Education Act and as more progressive ideas on child-centred learning associated with educationalists such as Dewey and Montessori replaced rote-learning (Sutherland 1990: 160).

During the nineteenth century, secondary schools were demarcated from elementary schools largely along lines of class rather than age. In practice, there was a two-grade system of 'public schools' for gentlemen and schools for those seeking respectability rather than gentility. Provision for those who were not members of the social elite was scant, with only a few receiving scholarships to a secondary school or becoming pupil teachers in elementary schools (Sutherland 1990: 148–50). The situation improved first in Scotland, where from 1885 education was a responsibility of the newly created Scottish Office, which pushed ahead with the provision of separate public secondary schooling (Sutherland 1990: 152–3). In England and Wales, the 1902 Education Act began a process that would lead to mass secondary education after the Second World War, charging local education authorities with responsibility for secondary as well as elementary education (Armytage 1970: 186–7). Fisher's 1918 Education Act raised the school leaving age to 14 and encouraged movement towards the systematic provision of secondary education in grammar schools (the most academic stream), modern schools (less academic) and 'senior classes' in elementary schools. The proportion of young people in the population fell between the wars, so that it was possible to increase the proportion of the school-age cohort attending school despite financial constraints (Sutherland 1990: 162). However, with many pupils continuing to receive their secondary education in elementary schools, the Spens Report of 1938 recommended moving towards an entirely separate secondary system based on grammar, modern and technical schools. This was implemented in Butler's 1944 Education Act, together with an increase in the school leaving age to 15 (Armytage 1970: 236). This act can therefore be seen as effectively establishing universal secondary education.

Although the dominance of the landed gentry and clergy was being challenged by the professional middle classes, higher education remained the preserve of a social elite. Despite the foundation of a number of new universities during the second half of the nineteenth century, the number of full-time students stood at little more than 20,000 in 1901. There was some increase in resources for higher education between the wars via grants to universities and scholarships, but the system remained small before the expansion following the Robbins Report of 1963 (Halsey 1988).

Data on formal schooling in Great Britain (combining England and Wales with Scotland), together with comparable data for the United States and Germany, are set out in Table 3.1, distinguishing primary, secondary and higher levels. The data are presented in the form of enrolment rates per 1,000 population under the age of 20, to facilitate international comparisons. The data suggest a trend increase of primary education in Britain before the First World War, followed by a rapid expansion of secondary education, particularly across the Second World War. There was also a trend increase of higher education during the first half of the twentieth century, but rapid expansion occurred only from the 1960s (Halsey 1988).

Although there are obvious difficulties in comparing enrolment data across countries, these issues have been worked over by a number of scholars, and it is now possible to draw fairly firm conclusions in several areas (Mitch 1992; Goldin 1998; Lindert 2001). First, it is clear that Britain lagged behind both Germany and the United States in the provision of mass primary education until about 1900, as was noted by Easterlin (1981). However, it is widely accepted that the official data on primary enrolments overstate the British shortfall due to underrecording. Lindert (2001) provides a corrected series using data on the number of child scholars from the 1871 Census of Occupations, which shows primary enrolments per 1,000 population

Table 3.1 Educational enrolment rates per 1,000 population under age 20, 1870–1951

	Primary	Secondary	Higher
A *Great Britain*			
1871	119.8		
1881	237.9		
1891	286.4		
1901	342.2		1.6
1911	373.1	11.0	
1921	366.4	30.8	3.8
1931	375.9	38.4	
1938	354.1	43.4	4.8
1951	325.1	162.1	8.7
B *United States*			
1870	390.6	4.2	
1880	404.5	4.6	
1890	492.5	10.3	
1900	478.9	18.7	
1910	475.6	26.8	
1920	472.9	56.1	15.8
1930	479.2	99.6	23.1
1938	472.2	147.1	29.8
1950	409.6	125.2	52.0
C *Germany*			
1871	364.7	9.5	0.8
1880	362.4	9.6	1.0
1890	365.5	10.1	1.3
1900	372.1	10.6	1.8
1911	372.4	10.9	2.3
1925	291.2	35.4	4.0
1933	383.2	38.3	6.4
1939	345.6	34.5	2.6
1950	410.6	52.3	6.9

Note: For Germany, primary and secondary enrolment data before 1911 refer to Prussia only.

Sources: Great Britain: primary and secondary school enrolments: Mitchell 1988: 798–810; higher enrolments: Halsey 1988: 270–2; population under age 20: Mitchell 1988: 15–16. United States: primary and secondary school enrolments: United States 1975: 368–9; higher enrolments: Tyack 1967: 478; population under age 20: United States 1975: 15. Germany: primary and secondary enrolments: 1871–1911: Königlichen Statistischen Bureau, *Statistisches Handbuch für den Preussischen Staat*; Statistisches Reichsamt, *Statistisches Jahrbuch für das Deutsche Reich*; 1911–39: Statistisches Reichsamt, *Statistisches Jahrbuch für das Deutsche Reich*; Länderrat des Amerikanischen Besatzungsgebietes *Statistisches Handbuch von Deutschland, 1928–1944*; 1950: Statistisches Bundesamt, *Statistisches Jahrbuch für die Bundesrepublik Deutschland*. Higher enrolments: 1871–1911: Ringer 1979: 272; 1925–39: Statistisches Reichsamt *Statistisches Jahrbuch für das Deutsche Reich*; Königlichen Statistischen Bureau, *Statistisches Handbuch von Deutschland, 1928–1944*; 1950: Statistisches Bundesamt, *Statistisches Jahrbuch für die Bundesrepublik Deutschland*. Population under age 20: Hoffmann 1965: 173–7; Königlichen Statistischen Bureau, *Statistisches Handbuch für den Preussischen Staat*.

under the age of 20 having already reached 300.9 by 1871. This suggests that the British lag in primary education may not have been as great as suggested by the official data in Table 3.1, but it does not eliminate the lag, particularly since there is an obvious upward bias in such data. Second, both Britain and Germany lagged behind the United States in the development of mass secondary education between the two world wars. This has been noted by historians of education such as Ringer (1979: 252–3), and has also been emphasised recently in the work of Goldin (1998). Third, both Britain and Germany lagged behind the United States in the provision of mass higher education after the First World War. By 1990, tertiary enrolment ratios in Britain and Germany were only at about the levels seen in the United States in the 1960s.

Two points should be borne in mind when interpreting these trends. First, the transfer from primary to secondary education has generally occurred at a later age in the United States and Germany than in Britain, affecting the breakdown between primary and secondary education. Second, however, it is not possible to give enrolment ratios for narrower age bands, as the difference between primary and secondary education was a matter of class as well as age before the Second World War.

Participation in education was not solely for economic purposes, and indeed Dent (1970: 108) writes of school as ‘a place where the aim is to help each boy and girl to develop his potentialities not for any ulterior purpose but for his own sake’. Nevertheless, it is widely accepted that education is an important way of investing in human capital, building up skills that raise productivity in the workplace. Formal education is usually seen as important for imparting general transferable rather than job-specific skills. This is certainly reflected in the curriculum of elementary schools in the nineteenth century with its focus on the three Rs of reading, writing and arithmetic, although further subjects including science and drawing as well as history and geography had been introduced by the late nineteenth century (Digby and Searby 1981: 33–6). It is also reflected in the focus on the classics in secondary schools, although science and modern languages had also been introduced by the late nineteenth century (Digby and Searby 1981: 36–40). Although the first half of the twentieth century saw a move away from rote-learning with the ending of payment by results, reform of the curriculum did not result in any radical change in academic content before the introduction of the tripartite system after the 1944 Education Act (Gordon *et al.* 1991: 278–93).

The content of the curriculum, with its academic emphasis, points to the role of formal education in preparing workers for white-collar occupations, which were more prevalent in the service sector than in industry, where blue-collar work predominated. Nevertheless, the observation by Digby and Searby (1981: 33) that the three Rs of reading, writing and arithmetic were often subordinated to the further two Rs of religion and respect for one’s betters points to a wider role of education in the development of social capabilities, preparing workers for the discipline of factory work, particularly with the development of modern high-volume techniques during the first half of the twentieth century. Goldin (2001) and Broadberry and Ghosal (2002) have recently emphasised the link between education and the advancement of the USA in the first half of the twentieth century.

Table 3.2 Average years of schooling of the male labour force in England and Wales, 1871–1951

	Years
1871	4.21
1881	4.69
1891	5.32
1901	6.02
1911	6.75
1921	7.41
1931	8.14
1951	9.21

Source: Matthews *et al.* 1982: 573.

The enrolment data refer to flows of investment in human capital. However, we are also interested in stocks of human capital, particularly when considering the implications for productivity performance. Indeed, the most widely used indicator of human capital in comparative growth studies is the average number of years of formal educational experience of the population aged 15–64. These data have been calculated by Matthews *et al.* (1982) for the male labour force in England and Wales, and are presented here in Table 3.2. These figures suggest a more than doubling of the educational experience of the average male worker between 1871 and 1951, or a growth rate of about 1 per cent per annum. It is likely that the growth rate of human capital was higher for female workers, since it started from a lower level.[1]

VOCATIONAL TRAINING: INTERMEDIATE-LEVEL SKILLS

Formal schooling, with its emphasis on general skills, is only one aspect of human capital formation. Vocational training is also important, particularly for the provision of job-specific skills. The modern literature proceeds on the basis of a distinction between higher-level and intermediate-level vocational training, and that distinction will be followed here. Higher-level training is taken to cover vocational qualifications at the standard of a university degree, including membership of professional institutions, while intermediate-level training is taken to cover craft and technician qualifications above secondary level but below degree level, including non-examined time-served apprenticeships (Prais 1995: 17). This section begins with intermediate-level skills, paying particular attention to the industrial sector, where there have been allegations

[1] Although Maddison (1987) provides a rough estimate of the average years of formal educational experience of the population aged 15–64 for six countries in 1913 and 1950, these estimates have been called into question by Goldin (1998). The problem is that Maddison's estimates show the British population in 1913 as having higher levels of educational attainment than the United States and Germany, despite the well-known lower levels of school enrolment.

of inadequate technical training in Britain, particularly in comparison with Germany (Wiener 1981; Wrigley 1986).

In fact, the standard view of poor technical training in British industry before the Second World War has been seriously questioned by a number of authors, and the recent literature offers a more balanced view. In many ways, the suggestion in the literature on economic growth that the British labour force was relatively unskilled has existed uneasily alongside a social history literature on the 'aristocracy of labour', particularly in the period before the First World War (Gray 1981). As More (1980) notes, the system of apprenticeship was adapted to the growing factory trades during the nineteenth century, and the five- to seven-year apprenticeship finishing at the age of 21 continued to provide the key framework for skill acquisition in modern factory industry in Britain as well as in Germany. This is in striking contrast to Britain's other major industrial competitor at the time, the United States, where the apprenticeship system all but collapsed (Elbaum 1989).

Nevertheless, the persistence of a flourishing apprenticeship system is not inconsistent with shortages of particular skills at particular points in time. Writers such as Landes (1969) and Wrigley (1986) stress shortages of the particular technical skills of the second industrial revolution, such as chemistry and electrical engineering. As Pollard (1989: 171) notes, however, it would be a mistake to think of technical training in Britain as a static system immune to change in the face of perceived skill shortages. Indeed, he argues that the changes in the provision of technical training should be seen as a vindication of the decentralised system that was so characteristic of late nineteenth-century Britain, and dismisses many of the criticisms of the education and science lobbies of the time as self-interested special pleading.

Technical training was first provided using public funds in the 1850s through the Charities Commission (Floud 1982: 157). More important in terms of the scale of funding, however, were the Department of Science and Art (DScA) and the City and Guilds of London Institute (CGLI). The DScA was established in the early 1850s following the Great Exhibition, and from 1859 it was able to provide grants for teachers' pay in certain science subjects (Pollard 1989: 171–2). The CGLI, founded in 1879, provided technical classes throughout the country and examined the students attending the classes. Neither the DScA nor the CGLI actually ran the technical schools, but they provided capital grants and payment by results to teachers in the schools and colleges that were increasingly run by local authorities and school boards (Floud 1982: 158). The Technical Instruction Act of 1889 allowed the local authorities to use rate money to finance technical instruction, while from 1890 use could also be made of the 'whisky money', originally intended to compensate the former licensees of redundant public houses (Pollard 1989: 171). The type of instruction was designed to supplement, but neither to precede nor to replace, instruction in the craft or industry carried out in the workplace. Such classes were normally held in the evening, in contrast to the day studies more common in Germany (Floud 1982: 160). The number of candidates examined by the DScA grew dramatically from 16,000 in 1870 to 151,000 by 1900 (Pollard 1989: 172). The number of students attending classes organised through the DScA and the CGLI grew even more dramatically from 10,000 in 1867 to 227,000 by 1896 (Floud 1982: 170).

Despite increased government involvement during the First World War through the Ministry of Munitions training schemes, developments in technical training between the wars were modest, focused initially on the retraining of disabled ex-servicemen and later on the needs of the unemployed (Sheldrake and Vickerstaff 1987: 8–9, 13–17). Concerns about shortages of skilled labour after the First World War were expressed in a Ministry of Labour enquiry into apprenticeship, but the government's response was to encourage the creation of an Interrupted Apprenticeship Scheme for the recommencement of training by those whose apprenticeship had been interrupted by military service (Ministry of Labour 1928; Sheldrake and Vickerstaff 1987: 12–13). Although the Education Act of 1918 stipulated a system of compulsory 'continuation schools' providing part-time technical education for school leavers between the ages of 14 and 16, it was never implemented due to financial stringencies (Argles 1964: 59–60). And although a National Certificate Scheme was introduced in technical subjects from 1921, the number of awards remained extremely modest before the Second World War (Argles 1964: 66). It was not until 1938 that the Spens Report recommended a tripartite system of secondary education that included separate provision of technical schools, and these plans were only implemented after the 1944 Education Act.

Table 3.3 provides apprentice-to-employment ratios in Britain, Germany and the United States. As well as economy-wide ratios, estimates are also provided on a sectoral basis where available. Data are taken from official sources including occupational censuses for all three countries and various enquiries into apprenticeship training. Traditionally, apprenticeships have been concentrated in the industrial sector, and this is reflected in Table 3.3. The most striking finding is the much lower proportion of apprentices in US industry compared with both Britain and Germany throughout the period. The most important factor here is the different approaches to industrial training on the two sides of the Atlantic.

To understand the transatlantic differences in training in industry, it is essential to take account of the distinction between 'mass-production' and 'flexible-production' technology (Piore and Sabel 1984; Broadberry 1994a). In mass-production, special-purpose machinery was substituted for skilled shopfloor labour to produce standardised products; flexible production, on the other hand, relied on skilled shopfloor labour to produce

Table 3.3 Apprentices as a percentage of persons engaged in Great Britain, Germany and the United States, 1880–1952

	Agriculture	Industry	Services	Whole economy
A *Great Britain*				
1906		4.19	0.65	2.48
1925		5.02	0.50	2.54
1951	0.17	3.22	0.59	1.87
B *Germany*				
1895		7.67	1.60	2.99
1907		6.38	1.60	2.87
1925		7.64	0.40	3.18
1933		6.48	0.48	2.28
1950	0.50	7.87	3.89	4.75
C *United States*				
1880		0.95	0.07	0.25
1900		0.87	0.06	0.28
1920		0.91	0.06	0.34
1930		0.56	0.03	0.19
1940		0.47	0.02	0.16
1952		0.74	0.03	0.26

Source: Broadberry 2003.

customised output. Although it would be an oversimplification to identify American manufacturing with mass-production and European manufacturing with flexible production, since in practice both systems coexisted on both sides of the Atlantic, mass-production was more prevalent in America and flexible production more prevalent in Britain and Germany, for reasons associated with both demand and supply conditions.[2] On the demand side, standardisation was facilitated in the United States by the existence of a large homogeneous home market, compared with the fragmentation of national markets and greater reliance on exports in Europe. On the supply side, mass-production machinery economised on skilled shopfloor labour (relatively abundant in Europe) but was wasteful of natural resources (relatively scarce in Europe). For a thorough discussion of these issues, including a detailed analysis of individual industries, the reader is referred to Broadberry (1997c).

These transatlantic differences in technology have important implications for the accumulation of human capital in the three countries under study here (Broadberry and Wagner 1996). In Britain and Germany, with an orientation towards flexible production, we see an emphasis upon the accumulation of intermediate level skills for shopfloor workers through apprenticeship. In the United States, however, with an orientation towards mass-production, we see much more emphasis on higher-level skills, with management hierarchies to supervise the relatively unskilled shopfloor workers, and research capabilities to produce the standardised designs and oversee the development process to volume production.[3]

Table 3.3 allows us to compare apprentice-to-employment ratios in Britain and Germany on the basis of the three broad sectors, agriculture, industry and services. In industry, there was a higher apprentice-to-employment ratio in Germany before the Second World War. This is

[2] See Scranton (1997) for a discussion of flexible production in an American context, and Herrigel (1996) for an analysis of German industrial performance stressing the coexistence of mass-production and flexible production.

[3] Although Goldin and Katz (1996) argue that US manufacturing increasingly employed workers with some high school education during the first half of the twentieth century, they did not have intermediate-level skills in the sense used here.

consistent with the fact that Germany had already overtaken Britain before the First World War in terms of labour productivity in industry (Broadberry, 1997a). Although apprentices also formed a larger proportion of the service sector workforce in Germany before the First World War, the absolute numbers involved were small, and we shall see in the next section that this was offset by a British lead in higher-level training. Only after the Second World War did the German lead in the provision of intermediate-level vocational training in services become substantial, as the apprenticeship scheme spread from industry to services in Germany but not in Britain.

Although it is sometimes suggested that the quality of training received by British apprentices left something to be desired, it should be noted that contemporary enquiries from the 1920s to the early 1960s generally concluded that Britain was not out of step with other European countries in this regard (Ministry of Labour 1928; Williams 1957, 1963; Liepmann 1960; OECD 1960). Similarly, Floud (1982) adopts a comparative framework to reject accusations of inadequate technical training of British apprentices before the First World War.

VOCATIONAL TRAINING: HIGHER-LEVEL SKILLS

An important aspect of human capital accumulation was the early development in Britain of professional bodies, a central function of which was to oversee professional training (Carr-Saunders and Wilson 1933; Reader 1966). The majority of these qualified professionals worked in the service sector, which was already highly developed in late nineteenth-century Britain. Table 3.4 presents data on the employment of professionals in the three countries since 1881. The British data allow a distinction between higher and lower professions, and data on the higher professions are shown in panel A. The definition is taken from Routh (1965), with higher professions defined as those requiring a qualification at the standard of a university degree. Although the key higher professions in the nineteenth century were in the church, medicine and law, the twentieth century has seen the growing importance of engineering, science and accounting.

To measure the growth of the professions on a comparative basis, it is necessary to include the lower professions as well as the higher professions, in panel B of Table 3.4. Although Britain started the period with a higher share of the occupied population in the professions, the United States had pulled ahead by the end of the nineteenth century. Although much of the existing literature on the professions concentrates on social aspects and eschews quantification, the idea of a leading role for Britain in the professionalisation of society during the nineteenth century and a leading role for the United States during the first half of the twentieth

Table 3.4 Professionals in Great Britain, the United States and Germany, 1880–1991

A Higher professionals in Great Britain, 1881–1951 (000)

	1881	1911	1931	1951
Church	38	44	48	49
Medicine	21	35	46	62
Law	20	26	23	27
Engineering	24	24	51	138
Writing	7	15	21	26
Armed forces	8	14	16	46
Accounting	13	11	16	37
Science	1	7	20	49
Total	132	176	240	434

B Higher and lower professions as a % of total employment in Great Britain, the United States and Germany, *c.* 1880–1950 (%)

	1880	1890	1900	1910	1920	1930	1950
Great Britain	3.6	3.7	4.0	4.1	4.3	4.4	6.1
United States	3.1	3.7	4.0	4.4	5.0	6.1	7.5
Germany			2.6	2.8	2.6	3.0	3.5

Notes: Church includes Anglican, Roman Catholic and Free Church clergy; Medicine includes doctors and dentists; Law includes barristers and solicitors; Engineering includes engineers, surveyors and architects; Writing includes editors and journalists; Armed forces includes commissioned officers; Accounting includes accountants and company secretaries; Science includes pure scientists. Lower professions include: Nurses; Others in medicine, including veterinary surgeons, pharmacists and opticians; Teachers; Draughtsmen, including industrial designers; Librarians; Social welfare workers; Navigating and engineering officers, aircrew; Arts, including painters, producers, actors and musicians. Dates for Great Britain are 1881, 1891, 1901. . .; Dates for Germany are 1895, 1907, 1925, 1933, 1950.

Source: Broadberry 2003.

century does seem to be widely accepted (Gilb 1966; Perkin 1996). In Germany, we see the effects of the large agricultural sector and low per capita incomes restricting the growth of the professions. Figures for the interwar period suggest a substantially smaller professional sector in Germany through to 1950 (McClelland 1991).

For some professional groups, it is possible to chart the growth of qualifications on a comparative basis. Data on the development of the accountancy profession in Britain, Germany and the United States are provided in Table 3.5. It seems clear that there has been a longstanding British reliance on professional accountants, although the difference between Britain and Germany is not as large as is sometimes suggested, if all accountants are considered rather than just chartered accountants. This British reliance on accountants is explained by Matthews *et al.* (1997) as deriving from the nature of the British capital market, which generated an early and growing need for independent auditors. Note that the growth of professionally qualified accountants in Britain mirrors the growth of the number of accountants enumerated in the higher professional occupational group in the census. The US data are derived from flows of Certified Public Accountant (CPA) certificates, which were established in 1896 following the British lead in professionalisation

Table 3.5 Qualified accountants in the United Kingdom, Germany and the United States, 1882–1961

A *United Kingdom*	ICAEW	Other UK bodies	Total UK membership	Professional accountants in census (000)
1882	1,193	290	1,486	
1891	1,737	1,092	2,829	9
1901	2,776	2,951	5,727	11
1911	4,391	6,950	11,341	11
1921	5,337	9,932	15,269	9
1931	9,213	16,340	25,553	16
1941	13,694	21,994	35,688	
1951	16,079	28,667	44,746	37
B *Germany*	**Chartered accountants**	**Tax advisers**	**Total**	
1932	540			
1943		22,588		
1945	3,043			
1955		22,000		
1961	2,741	23,761	26,505	
C *United States*	**Certified public accountants**			
1896	56			
1901	303			
1911	1,780			
1921	5,143			
1931	13,774			
1941	25,242			
1951	47,224			

Notes: UK: ICAEW = Institute of Chartered Accountants in England and Wales. Germany: Chartered accountants includes 'Wirtschaftsprüfer' and related occupations; Tax advisers includes 'Steuerberater' and related occupations. United States: stocks of Certified public accountants calculated from data on CPA certificates issued.

Source: Broadberry 2003.

(Edwards 1978: 69). The flow data have been converted to a stock basis using the perpetual inventory method, assuming an average working life of thirty-five years after qualifying. Allowing for the much greater population in the United States, it is clear that the density of qualified accountants was much greater in Britain.

Although data exist on the educational qualifications of American industrial managers in the late 1920s, comparable British and German data are available only from the early 1950s. These figures, which are presented in Table 3.6, suggest that the proportion of graduates among British and German management in the early 1950s was at about the level of American managers in the late 1920s, with Britain and Germany lagging equally behind America.

Table 3.6 Proportion of industrial managers who were graduates in industrial companies, Great Britain, the United States and Germany, 1928–54 (%)

	Great Britain	United States	Germany
1928		32	
1950–4	36	62	37

Source: Copeman 1955; Warner and Abegglen 1955; Hartmann 1959.

Table 3.7 Research and development expenditure in manufacturing in Great Britain, Germany and the United States, 1934–59 (% of net output)

	Britain	Germany	United States
1934	0.43		
1937			0.98
1938	0.43		
1950		0.46	
1959	3.49	1.12	5.82

Source: Derived from Broadberry and Wagner 1996.

Table 3.7 collects together the historical data on research and development in Britain, the United States and Germany, reaching back to the 1930s for Britain and the United States. For manufacturing, where the vast bulk of research and development (R&D) has been concentrated, the ratio of R&D expenditure to net output was higher in the United States than in Britain. However, as Edgerton and Horrocks (1994) have recently pointed out on the basis of firm level data for the interwar period, there is little evidence to support the idea of a greater German commitment to R&D. This is consistent with the findings of Sanderson (1972) that there were strong links between the British universities and industry during this period, and is a far cry from the allegations of an anti-technological bias in British society in much of the historical literature which alleges British relative economic decline (Wiener 1981; Barnett 1986). The transatlantic R&D gap confirms the concentration of American industry on higher-level skills compared with the greater emphasis on intermediate-level skills in European industry. It also illustrates the American commitment to science and technology that has been seen by Nelson and Wright (1992) as an important factor in US industrial supremacy in the twentieth century.

IMPLICATIONS FOR PRODUCTIVITY PERFORMANCE

Table 3.8 presents sectoral estimates of comparative labour productivity levels for the US/UK and Germany/UK cases over the period 1870–1950, derived from Broadberry (1997a, 1997b). The concept of labour productivity used here is output per person engaged. At the whole economy level, we see that in about 1870, aggregate labour productivity in the United States was about 90 per cent of the British level, and that the United States overtook Britain as the aggregate labour productivity leader during the 1890s and continued to forge ahead to 1950. Turning to the Germany/UK comparison, we see that at the whole economy level, German labour productivity in 1871 was about 60 per cent of the British level, and had still reached only about 75 per cent of the British level by the First World War. After a setback during and immediately after the war, Germany again reached about 75 per cent of the British level by the mid-1930s, rising to about 80 per cent by the late 1930s. After another setback during and immediately after the Second World War, Germany had again reached about 75 per cent of the British level by 1950.

Table 3.8 Comparative US/UK and Germany/UK labour productivity levels by sector, 1869/71 to 1950 (UK = 100)

	Agriculture	Industry	Services	Aggregate economy
A *US/UK*				
1870	86.9	153.6	85.8	89.8
1890	102.1	164.5	84.2	94.1
1910	103.2	193.5	107.3	117.7
1920	128.0	198.2	119.0	133.3
1929	109.7	222.9	121.2	139.4
1937	103.3	190.6	120.0	132.6
1950	126.0	243.9	140.8	166.9
B *Germany/UK*				
1871	55.7	86.2	66.1	59.5
1891	53.7	92.5	71.9	60.5
1911	67.3	122.0	81.3	75.5
1925	53.8	97.4	78.2	69.0
1929	56.9	101.7	84.3	74.1
1935	57.2	99.1	85.7	75.7
1950	41.2	95.8	83.1	74.4

Notes: For US/UK comparison 1870–1920, US dates are 1869, 1889, 1909, 1919; UK dates are 1871, 1891, 1911, 1920.

Sources: Derived from Broadberry 1997a; 1997b.

The sectoral patterns of comparative productivity performance are quite varied. The nine-sector analysis provided in Broadberry (1998) can be simplified into three sectors: agriculture, industry and services. Industry includes mineral extraction, manufacturing, construction and the utilities, while services includes transport and communications, distribution, finance, professional and personal services and government. Dealing first with the US/UK comparison, note that there has been a large US productivity lead in industry throughout the period. Industrial labour productivity was already in 1870 more than 50 per cent higher in the United States than in Britain, and by 1950 the average American industrial worker was producing nearly two-and-a-half times as much as the average British industrial worker. However, we can see in Table 3.9 that industry never accounted for more than a third of total employment in the United States and even in Britain never accounted for much more than 45 per cent of total employment. To understand the changing US/UK comparative productivity position for the economy as a whole, therefore, it is essential to consider developments in services and agriculture. Trends in comparative productivity in services mirror trends in comparative productivity in the economy as a whole. This is important because services became a more important employer of labour than industry before the First World War in the United States and during the 1920s in Britain. There was also an important shift of labour out of agriculture, where value added per person was lower than in industry and services. As the United States moved out of agriculture later than Britain, this acted as a force for US catching up and overtaking.

Turning to the Germany/UK comparison, it can be seen that Germany had already caught up with Britain in terms of industrial labour productivity before the First World War, despite Britain's productivity lead in the economy as a whole. The more disaggregated analysis in Broadberry (1997a) suggests that the German labour productivity lead in industry in 1911 extended to mining, construction and the utilities as well as to

Table 3.9 Sectoral shares of employment in the United States, the United Kingdom and Germany, 1870–1950 (%)

	Agriculture	Industry	Services
A *United States*			
1870	50.0	24.8	25.2
1910	32.0	31.8	36.2
1920	26.2	33.2	40.6
1930	20.9	30.2	48.9
1940	17.9	31.6	50.5
1950	11.0	32.9	56.1
B *United Kingdom*			
1871	22.2	42.4	35.4
1911	11.8	44.1	44.1
1924	8.6	46.5	44.9
1930	7.6	43.7	48.7
1937	6.2	44.5	49.3
1950	5.1	46.5	48.4
C *Germany*			
1871	49.5	29.1	21.4
1913	34.5	37.9	27.6
1925	31.5	40.1	28.4
1930	30.5	37.4	32.1
1935	29.9	38.2	31.9
1950	24.3	42.1	33.6

Source: Derived from Broadberry 1998.

manufacturing. Britain nevertheless retained an overall productivity lead due to Germany's low productivity in its small service sector and its very large agricultural sector. This suggests that the policy of free trade in Britain, allowing agriculture to shrink in the face of the grain invasion from North America, may have been better for overall productivity than the German policy of protecting agriculture and industry.

Our final task is to examine the linkages between this productivity performance and human capital. School enrolments is a very popular variable in explaining cross-sectional variation in growth rates amongst a large sample of countries in the post-Second World War period, so it may be expected to help in understanding the productivity differences between Britain, the United States and Germany outlined above (Barro and Sala-i-Martin, 1995). Comparing the educational enrolment data in Table 3.1 with the comparative productivity data in Table 3.8, the first point to note is that the differences in primary education in the nineteenth century do not seem to have been of much economic significance, since Britain had higher aggregate productivity than either the United States or Germany in 1870 despite lower levels of primary education, and began to lose that leadership as the educational gap narrowed. Second, however, the spread of mass secondary education in the United States is correlated with the United States pulling decisively ahead across the First World War. Note, third, however, that this is much easier to associate with developments in services than in industry, since the United States already had a large productivity lead in industry where mass-production methods required relatively unskilled labour. Indeed, it is much easier to see formal schooling as an appropriate preparation for the office work that characterises the service sector than for the factory work typical of the industrial sector at this time.

To assess the contribution of vocational training, we need to assemble the skills data on a stock basis for agriculture, industry and services as well as for the economy as a whole. This is done in Tables 3.10 and 3.11, taken from Broadberry (2003). Parts A to C of Table 3.10 provide estimates of the proportions of the labour force with higher- and intermediate-level qualifications c. 1910, 1930 and 1950.[4] For Germany and the United States, the same proportion of higher to lower professionals has been assumed as in Britain. Before 1950, there is no clear indication of a British shortfall of vocational skills. Although Germany was ahead in intermediate skills, particularly in industry, this was offset by a British advantage in higher-level skills, especially in services. And although Britain lagged behind the United States in higher-level skills, this was offset by a British advantage in intermediate-level skills.

Table 3.10 Stocks of vocationally qualified persons as a percentage of employees, by sector and skill level in the United Kingdom, the United States and Germany, 1910–50

	Higher level			Intermediate level		
	UK	US	Germany	UK	US	Germany
A 1910						
Agriculture	–	–	–	–	–	–
Industry	–	–	–	15.1	2.8	19.8
Services	2.0	3.0	2.4	2.0	0.2	1.6
Total	0.9	1.1	0.6	7.5	0.9	9.7
B 1930						
Agriculture	–	–	–	–	–	–
Industry	–	4.1	–	15.6	1.9	23.7
Services	2.6	3.5	2.1	1.5	0.1	1.2
Total	1.3	2.8	0.7	7.9	0.6	9.8
C 1950						
Agriculture	–	–	–	0.5	–	0.5
Industry	5.7	10.5	5.7	12.9	1.6	24.4
Services	3.8	4.0	3.1	1.8	0.1	3.9
Total	4.5	5.7	3.4	7.2	0.6	11.7

Source: Broadberry 2003.

The next step is to provide a measure of relative vocational skills, using the method of O'Mahony (1999). For each country, the proportions of the labour force in each category of higher, intermediate and lower (or no) skills are aggregated into a single unskilled labour equivalent. This is done by weighting each category according to its wage relative to the unskilled category:

$$H = \sum(w_s/w_u)(L_s/L)$$

where w_s is the wage of skill category s, w_u is the unskilled wage, L_s/L is the employment share of skill category s and H stands for human capital. The ratio of H for the two countries provides the estimate of relative skill levels, which is presented in Table 3.11 for the US/UK and Germany/UK cases. Relative wage rates for workers with intermediate skills declined from 1.6 times the unskilled wage in 1910 to 1.4 times in 1950, while relative wage rates for workers with higher skills fell from 4.2 times

[4] The intermediate-level qualifications are obtained by taking the apprenticeship flow data in Table 3.3 and converting them on to a stock basis using estimates of the ratio of journeymen to apprentices, obtained largely from the British sources. Although this may not be a particularly accurate method of estimation for the United States, where apprenticeship was much less widespread, it is equally clear that the US stock of skilled workers was so much smaller than in Britain or Germany that even a serious error would not significantly affect the comparative results. For the higher-level qualifications in industry, estimates of the proportion of industrial managers who were graduates have been taken from Table 3.6 and applied to data on the numbers of industrial managers from the occupational censuses. In services, higher-level qualifications have been obtained for Britain by using the number of higher professionals from Table 3.4. Note that the number of accountants in the census grows in line with the membership of professional accountancy bodies.

Table 3.11 Relative vocational skill levels, 1910–50 (UK = 100)

	US/UK	Germany/UK
A 1910		
Agriculture	100.0	100.0
Industry	93.2	102.6
Services	102.0	100.9
Total	96.9	99.8
B 1930		
Agriculture	100.0	100.0
Industry	105.5	103.8
Services	101.9	98.4
Total	100.9	99.2
C 1950		
Agriculture	99.8	100.0
Industry	106.3	103.9
Services	99.8	99.2
Total	100.4	99.2

Source: Broadberry 2003.

the unskilled wage in 1910 to 3.5 times in 1950, based on estimates in Routh (1965).

The first point to note in Table 3.11 is that, in 1910, Britain had higher aggregate vocational skills than either Germany or the United States, even though Germany had higher vocational skill levels than Britain in both industry and services. The British advantage overall arose in this case from the small size of the agricultural sector in Britain, since agriculture was more dependent on unskilled labour than industry or services. The second point to note is that relative vocational skills defined in this way did not change much over time, despite the large changes in comparative labour productivity levels. Furthermore, in industry, where we see the largest US labour productivity lead, Britain apparently had a vocational skills advantage in 1910 and only a small vocational skills disadvantage in 1930 and 1950.

The links between human capital and productivity performance are not therefore as simple as suggested by much of the literature on British relative decline. In particular, it is important to distinguish between the Anglo-American and the Anglo-German comparisons and also between the performance of industry and services. In industry, there was a large US productivity lead over Britain and Germany throughout the period despite the apparently better training of shopfloor workers in Britain and Germany. This US productivity lead was due largely to the adoption of mass-production methods, which did not require high levels of shopfloor skill. These methods were, however, dependent on educated managerial, supervisory and research workers, where the United States had a growing advantage during the first half of the twentieth century as a result of the move to mass secondary education and the expansion of higher education. In services, British productivity was higher than in Germany and not much lower than in the United States before the Second World War. Here, professional qualifications boosted human capital stocks in Britain's service sector.

CONCLUSION

As Floud (1982) notes, it is easy to point to differences between Britain and other countries that are perceived as having been more successful and to draw the conclusion that Britain should have been more like its competitors. There has been no shortage of commentators taking this position on human capital between the late nineteenth century and the mid-twentieth century, so that it is not difficult to paint a picture of Britain falling between the US emphasis on formal schooling and the German emphasis on vocational training. However, the extent of the differences should not be exaggerated, and it should be remembered that the situation changed over time. First, Britain closed the primary schooling gap during the last third of the nineteenth century. Second, although the United States moved to mass secondary education in the first half of the twentieth century, Britain's increase in secondary schooling during this period was not unimpressive and remained on a par with Germany's. Third, Britain continued to provide a supply of intermediate level skilled workers for industry through apprenticeships and higher-level qualified workers for services through professional qualifications. Fourth, Britain still achieved a higher level of gross domestic product (GDP) per employee than Germany throughout the period under consideration. Although Germany had caught up in terms of industrial productivity, Britain remained a long way ahead in services and agriculture and had a more modern structure with a substantially smaller share of the labour force in the low value-added agricultural sector.

4 Manufacturing and technological change

GARY B. MAGEE

Contents

THE SHAPE AND COURSE OF BRITISH MANUFACTURING

The global economic leadership that Britain enjoyed in the nineteenth century had its foundations in the nation's unprecedented industrial capability. To many Victorians and Edwardians this was a fact of life; it followed almost inexorably that should the uniqueness of that capability ever be lost, Britain's international pre-eminence would also be forfeited and decline ensue. The progress of manufacturing was seen as pivotal to Britain's economic fate.

To a large extent, this is also how Britain's decline has been cast in much of the economic history literature, where industrial decline and economic decline are taken as synonymous. As the manufacturing sector was a major employer that provided the vast majority of Britain's exports and was where the full brunt of the growing international competition was felt, it seems a reasonable focal point for the historical analysis of Britain's relative economic decline.

To some, the significance of manufacturing, because of its dynamic properties and integral place in the process of technological change, goes well beyond the size of its static contribution to national product. In this view, both economic growth and productivity are seen to be crucially determined by the expansion of the manufacturing sector (Kaldor 1966). Whether such a relationship applies in the late Victorian and Edwardian period is investigated later in the chapter, but it should be noted here that, despite the growing foreign challenge, manufacturing's place in the British economy was not in fact contracting. Rather, as Table 4.1 illustrates, its share of national output and the capital stock actually grew over the second half of the nineteenth century, while its share of employment remained constant. With around a quarter of the nation's output and a third of its employees in 1913, manufacturing's importance in the economy was stronger than ever. The sector also grew steadily over the period; by 1913 its output was more than two-and-a-half times greater than it had been in 1870. This progress was achieved, moreover, without substantial fluctuation. Between 1873 and 1913, growth rates rarely deviated markedly from the long-term trend of 2 per cent. This continuity of growth and general absence of instability in this period raises serious doubts about the existence of an industrial growth climacteric prior to the First World War. However, as Table 4.2 makes clear, the sector's annual average growth rate did decline dramatically in the transwar period between 1913 and 1920 when it fell to around 0.2 per cent. To a large extent this was a consequence of the war, a shock to the economy that saw the manufacturing sector contract at an average rate of 3.8 per cent each year between 1913 and 1918.

Table 4.1 Manufacturing's place in the economy, 1856–1913 (%)

	1856	1873	1913
Output (constant prices)	22.2	24.6	26.6
Employment	32.5	33.5	32.1
Capital stock	12.9	14.6	18.5

Source: Matthews *et al.* 1982: 222.

Table 4.2 Output and fixed capital growth in manufacturing, 1873–1924 (annual percentage growth rates)

Period	Output	Fixed capital stock
1873–82	2.3	2.3
1882–9	1.9	1.6
1889–99	2.3	2.8
1899–1907	1.6	2.7
1907–13	2.0	
1913–20	0.2	
1873–1913	2.0	2.6
1913–24	1.2	

Sources: Matthews *et al.* 1982: 228, 281, 381 and 378; Feinstein 1972: Table 51.

Inputs

The growth of manufacturing was paralleled by an expansion of employment in the sector. Between 1873 and 1913, employment grew on average at 0.8 per cent per annum (Matthews *et al.* 1982: 378), meaning that in 1913 around 30 per cent more workers were being employed in manufacturing than was the case in 1870. As Tables 4.2 and 4.3 show, capital accumulation in the sector also progressed strongly, especially after 1889, growing at an annual average rate of 2.6 per cent between 1873 and 1913. This had an impact on the capital intensity of work. Capital per unit of

Table 4.3 Gross reproducible capital, employment and capital per worker in manufacturing, 1869–1919 (1913 = 100)

	Gross reproducible capital stock	Employment	Capital per worker
1869	37.2	65.5	56.8
1875	44.4	70.7	62.7
1882	52.9	74.3	71.2
1889	56.7	80.6	70.4
1899	66.3	88.6	74.7
1909	90.1	90.4	99.6
1913	100.0	100.0	100.0
1919	125.3	97.4	128.8

Note: 1919 employment figure is an estimate calculated from the 1920 figure on the basis of the growth of output in that year.

Sources: Feinstein 1972: Tables 59 and 60; Feinstein 1988: Table XI.

output rose by 0.6 per cent per annum over the same period, while capital per worker more than doubled between 1869 and 1919.

Placed in a comparative perspective, however, this growth of capital intensity in British manufacturing was somewhat less than spectacular. In 1879 capital per unit of labour in British manufacturing was around 10 per cent higher than in the USA and almost 30 per cent higher than in Germany. By 1900, however, US manufacturing was nearly 90 per cent more capital intensive than British, while German capital intensity was almost on a par with Britain's (Broadberry 1997c: 106–7). Given the heavy focus in the literature on America's much greater capital intensity throughout the nineteenth century, a British lead in these regards up to as late as perhaps 1889 is somewhat surprising (Rostas 1948; Frankel 1957; Habakkuk 1962). Yet, as Broadberry (1997c: 108) points out, such a lead is not necessarily inconsistent with the view that the USA was indeed a much more machine-intensive manufacturer than Britain prior to 1889. Since machinery was in fact only one relatively minor component of each nation's capital stock at the time (Field 1985), it could well be that British manufacturers chose to invest more heavily in other forms of capital, such as structures, than their American counterparts.

There are alternative measures of capital. One such alternative is the quantity of energy consumed in manufacturing, a measure that in any case is potentially more revealing about machine usage, as capital equipment typically absorbed most of the sector's energy. Between 1870 and 1907 there was a massive growth of energy consumption in British manufacturing from approximately 1 million to 6 million horsepower, a rate of growth consistent with what is known about capital accumulation (Musson 1978: 166–70). The energy data, however, also lend support to the notion of the greater machine-intensity of American manufacturing throughout the latter half of the nineteenth century. In 1907/9, when the first reliable comparison can be made, horsepower per worker in American manufacturing was running at more than double the level of British manufacturing. Per capita energy use in German manufacturing by contrast was of the same order as British, whereas in France it was three-quarters of the British level (Broadberry 1997c: 108–9). These figures suggest that British, and indeed European, manufacturing before the First World War was significantly less mechanised than American. As will be seen later, this had important consequences for the relative levels of labour productivity found in each country.

Sectoral composition

The manufacturing sector was composed of a diverse collection of industries fabricating a wide range of products for the British and international marketplace. The first disaggregated data on the composition of the sector comes from the 1907 *Census of Production*, which supplied information on output and employment within the sector. This information, along with the comparable data compiled by the 1924 *Census of Production*, is given in Table 4.4. Despite the diversity of British manufacturing, it is immediately apparent from Table 4.4 that the textiles and clothing & footwear industries hold important places in the pattern of British manufacturing. Other prominent branches of the sector in 1907 and 1924 included food, drink & tobacco, mechanical engineering, metal manufacture and paper, printing & publishing. Overall, however, the majority of British manufacturing was located in the lighter industries, such as boot making, brewing and board making, which typically produced small or 'light' articles with relatively less capital-intensive production technologies. Thus, despite the emphasis placed in the literature on the heavy industries, such as chemicals production, engineering and the manufacture of metal goods, neither in 1907 nor in 1924 did these industries account for more than 40 per cent of the sector's workforce or net output.

What is more, across the transwar period, there is no significant shift in the sectoral composition of manufacturing. The dominant position of textiles and clothing remains, though it shows signs of erosion. These industries had in fact been declining as a proportion of the manufacturing sector's labour force since at least the 1870s. At the same time, other light industries, particularly food, drink & tobacco and paper, printing & publishing were becoming steadily more important; by 1924 they together were contributing almost as much to the sector's output as textiles and clothing. This development reflected the growing strength of the light industries in British manufacturing. By contrast, metals and engineering, which had been expanding prior to the First World War, contracted slightly over the transwar period, when the only growing branches of these industries were electrical engineering and vehicle manufacture.

Table 4.4 Sectoral composition of manufacturing in 1907 and 1924 (%)

	Employment		Net output	
	1907	1924	1907	1924
Chemicals	2.6	2.9	4.5	5.0
Coal and petroleum products	0.2	0.6	0.5	1.1
Metal manufacture	6.9	6.7	8.4	6.6
Mechanical engineering	8.4	7.8	9.6	7.0
Instrument engineering	0.4	0.4	0.4	0.4
Electrical engineering	1.3	2.9	1.4	2.9
Shipbuilding	4.3	4.4	4.4	3.4
Vehicles	6.6	8.4	5.6	7.7
Other metal goods	5.6	5.1	5.2	4.3
Textiles	25.0	22.5	19.8	18.1
Leather and fur	1.2	1.2	1.2	1.3
Clothing and footwear	12.4	10.9	8.3	7.9
Food, drink and tobacco	8.8	9.5	14.7	16.2
Brick, pottery, glass and cement	4.1	4.0	3.5	3.9
Timber and furniture	3.5	3.4	3.1	3.1
Paper, printing and publishing	6.3	6.5	6.8	8.2
Other manufacturing	2.4	2.8	2.6	2.9
Heavy industries	36.3	39.2	40.0	38.4
'New' industries	10.5	14.2	11.5	15.6

Source: Broadberry 1997c: 32–3.

A common criticism of British manufacturing since 1870 has been that the sector was slow to move into the new growth industries of the second industrial revolution, such as pharmaceuticals, automobiles and electrical equipment (Landes 1969; Kennedy 1987). A crude measure of the scale of these 'new' industries in 1907 and 1924 is given in Table 4.4, which is calculated by adding together the shares of the three industries most likely to encompass the new areas emerging: electrical engineering, chemicals and vehicle production. In 1907, these 'new' industries accounted for a small, though hardly negligible, 10 per cent of employment and output in manufacturing. Growth in these industries was in fact faster than in other branches of manufacturing, a fact that suggests that Britain's relative overcommitment to the old staples may have reduced the sector's overall rate of expansion. Between 1900 and 1913, the new industries grew at an annual rate of 3.8 per cent, whereas the sector as a whole grew at just 2 per cent. The contrast was even starker in the transwar period when between 1913 and 1924 the new industries grew at an average of 4 per cent every year, while manufacturing as a whole could only manage a relatively poor 0.7 per cent (Matthews *et al.* 1982: 257–8).

To what extent was the apparent failure to embrace the new industries due to underinvestment? It is often claimed that British investors had little interest or money for domestic industry, preferring instead to place their capital with projects initiated by overseas governments and enterprises (Kennedy 1987). This contention is taken up by Ross in chapter 15 below, but it is worth noting here that there is in fact little evidence to suggest that British investment projects were finding it difficult to raise capital at the time. Even new industries seemed able to secure the necessary funds when sought. If in fact insufficient resources were being devoted to new industries prior to the First World War, then, institutional impediments aside, this was chiefly due to demand-side rather than supply-side constraints.

Organisation

Another common criticism of British manufacturing is based on the perceived nexus between business organisation and economic performance. According to Chandler (1990), by the end of the nineteenth century competitiveness in manufacturing hinged crucially on the development of multi-unit, vertically integrated and professionally managed firms, a form of organisation uniquely adept at tapping into the economies of both scale and scope. Such firms, it is contended, were rare in Britain in the late Victorian and Edwardian period, at least relative to America and Germany. Indeed, in Britain, the small, family firm remained the norm well into the twentieth century. The dominant feature of British manufacturing, therefore, was its vertical specialisation and intense competition.

According to Elbaum and Lazonick (1986), it was the strictures imposed by this atomistic organisation of production that in fact represented the main constraint on the viability of British manufacturing going into the twentieth century.

There is no doubt that Elbaum and Lazonick are correct in claiming that the family-owned and family-run factory was the typical form of organisation in British manufacturing before the First World War. In the 1880s less than 10 per cent of the manufacturing sector was accounted for by the 100 largest concerns, a figure which had risen to just 16 per cent by 1909. This degree of concentration was slightly below the American figure of 22 per cent, though above the French figure of 12 per cent. Most industrial markets in Britain, therefore, were catered for by a large number of small price-taking firms. Competition in the manufacturing sector, consequently, was generally intense (Hannah 1983: 13, 23, 180).

Yet it would be wrong to assume from this that the British firm was necessarily inflexible, inefficient or amateurish. British marketing techniques, for example, often lambasted in the literature for their backwardness (Landes 1969: 337; Kirby 1981: 8), prove on closer analysis to be creative and adaptive (Nicholas 1984). In industrial districts, such as Lancashire or London, where competition was fierce, small and vertically specialised firms located in close proximity to downstream (or upstream) firms could prove as technically efficient as the vertically integrated firm (Godley 1996; Johnson 1996; Leunig 2001). The family firm Alfred Herbert Limited, for example, one of the most important companies in the machine tool industry, had an excellent record of profitability and innovation before 1914 and in the interwar period (Arnold 1999). Family firms in Germany at the time also proved remarkably adaptable and viable bases upon which to construct more efficient managerial forms (Schumann 1999).

Nor can it be said that British manufacturing firms were exceptionally small by international standards. The largest American firms certainly tended to be bigger than their British counterparts. In 1912, US Steel had a market capitalisation of issued equity stock more than double that of the largest British company, the textile firm, J & P Coats. J & P Coats, however, was more than twice the size of Krupps, the largest German firm at the time. Average capitalisation values similarly show the leading British firms lying between the Americans and Germans in terms of scale (Schmitz 1995: 23–7). Employment data add further weight to this picture. In 1906–13, the average manufacturing establishment in Britain employed sixty-four people compared to sixty-seven in the USA, fourteen in Germany and twenty-six in France. In certain industries, such as textiles, paper & printing, foods, ceramics and chemicals, the average scale of enterprises in Britain, at least as measured by employee numbers, was as large as, if not larger than, in both Germany and America. The largest British chemical firm in 1903, United Alkali, employed over a thousand more workers than BASF, Germany's biggest manufacturer of the time. It was only in the heavy industries, such as iron and steel, that British plant was comparatively small (Kinghorn and Nye 1996: 97–104). Indeed, the largest British firms were disproportionately located in traditional light industries, such as food, drink & tobacco and textiles, a reflection of the importance of these industries in British manufacturing (Schmitz 1995: 29).

The growing size of British firms over the latter half of the nineteenth century was accelerated by the increasing merger activity of the period. Driven by scale-intensive technologies, overproduction and a capital market which looked favourably upon larger concerns, the merger movement reached its peak between 1894 and 1903, when more than a thousand firms valued at £73.9 million disappeared. This, however, paled in comparison with the feverish activity taking place in the USA where in 1899 alone 979 firms with a value of over £400 million were merged. A second surge of merger activity in Britain, larger in terms of value, occurred across the transwar period as firms like Vickers and Nobel attempted to strengthen their peacetime positions by diversifying into non-military products (Hannah 1983: 17–29).

On the whole, then, the Chandlerian model does not fit terribly well with the British experience. British firms were small only relative to their American counterparts and even then the difference on average was not very large. Family firms were not incapable of efficiency. Industrial concentration levels were not exceptionally low. Most troubling of all for the model's explanatory power is that German industry, typically lauded for the relatively large size of its firms, in fact conforms even less to the ideal. Firm size is not a good predictor of industrial performance. British business organisation differed from the American, but this does not mean that it was necessarily inferior. Rather, the pattern of British business could just as easily be seen as a rational response to its unique environment. The relative abundance of skilled shopfloor workers and the legacy of craft control in Britain for one thing made it less profitable for British manufacturers to adopt the labour-replacing technology and managerial practices central to mass-production (Harley 1974).

British demand conditions also militated against the adoption of American practice. In 1860 America's population was already one-and-a-half times larger than Britain's; by the turn of the century it had grown to close on two-and-a-half times that of the British.

Protected by tariff walls and opened up by the railroads, the American market was thus far larger than the British home market and hence offered greater opportunities for mass-production. Yet, as we have seen, the average manufacturing establishment in Britain in terms of employee numbers was at least comparable to the American, a finding that suggests that the British market was clearly capable of supporting firms operating at levels of production obtained by the larger American manufacturers

(Rostas 1948). Where the difference between the countries lay was in the nature of the demand. In the nineteenth and early twentieth centuries standardised products were more marketable in the USA than in Britain, a fact that facilitated the adoption of mass-production techniques in that country (Hounsell 1984). There are number of reasons for this greater acceptance of standardisation in America. First, the greater income inequality and class distinctions of Britain created there a relatively small group of consumers, many of whom insisted upon high-quality, customised products (Rothbarth 1946; Williamson 1991). Secondly, the lower levels of income per capita in Britain also acted as a barrier to standardised production, especially in the more expensive consumer durables (Tolliday 1987; Bowden 1991). Finally, the growing orientation from the 1870s of the British exporter towards Empire markets that were spread over different continents and subject to varying cultures and income levels was hardly conducive to standardised production (Broadberry 1997c: 97). Whatever its sources, the very different demand patterns experienced by British producers made less standardised, flexible production technologies far more appealing than their American alternatives.

Table 4.5 National shares of world manufacturing output, 1860–1928

	1860	1880	1900	1913	1928
UK	19.9	22.9	18.5	13.6	9.9
France	7.9	7.8	6.8	6.1	6.0
Germany	4.9	8.5	13.2	14.8	11.6
Italy	2.5	2.5	2.5	2.4	2.7
Japan	2.6	2.4	2.4	2.7	3.3
USA	7.2	14.7	23.6	32.0	39.3

Source: Bairoch 1982: 296 and 304.

Table 4.6 Industrial growth in leading manufacturing countries, 1870–1913 (annual percentage growth rates)

	UK	USA	Germany	France
1870–80	2.3	5.7	5.9	2.6
1880–90	2.5	5.6	4.6	1.9
1890–1900	2.1	3.1	3.9	2.3
1900–13	2.1	5.4	4.4	3.3

Source: Lewis 1978: 148–50.

BRITISH MANUFACTURING IN INTERNATIONAL PERSPECTIVE

Relative scale and growth

As we have seen, British manufacturing exhibited strong and stable growth across the late Victorian and Edwardian era. This fact, however, did little to alleviate the concerns of many at the time and since who felt that the sector was in the process of losing its dominance. Comparative data, such at those given in Tables 4.5 and 4.6, have thus typically lain at the heart of the criticism of British performance after 1870. Yet such data are not entirely negative about British performance. Table 4.5, for example, confirms Britain's status as the world's largest manufacturer in the nineteenth century. In 1880 more than one fifth of all manufactured products in the world originated in Britain. From that point, however,

Britain's relative position did begin to slide; by 1913 it had fallen to third place behind the USA and Germany. This transition in industrial leadership is also reflected in the growth data presented in Table 4.6. The concern of observers of the time that Britain was losing its place in the world was thus not entirely without justification. Interpreting this loss, however, is no straightforward matter. Britain's relatively poor growth performance may indicate a failure, but also could just as well be the product of the evolution of the international economy as new industrial producers, often with large natural markets like those of America and Germany, emerged on the scene and as rising British wealth and living standards induced resources to be shifted out of manufacturing and into the service sector.

The slower growth of demand in Britain did, however, have consequences for the rate of technological change, by affecting the rate at which machinery was replaced. Investment theory shows that if an industry grows faster than another, it will, *ceteris paribus*, have on average a younger capital stock; and if, in turn, technological change is largely embodied in new capital equipment, this newer capital will be more efficient, granting the rapidly growing industry a lower cost structure (Solow 1960). Slower demand growth, therefore, accounts for the frequently reported reluctance of British manufacturers to discard their old machinery with the same relish as their American competitors. To the extent that protective tariffs also barred British exports from most of the rapidly expanding markets of Europe and North America, limitations of demand – both in terms of scale and nature – effectively reduced the capacity of British manufacturing to modernise at the same rate as the Americans and Germans. Such limitations were factors in the performance of the British steel and paper industries (Temin 1966; Tolliday 1991; Magee 1997b: 199–206).

Exports

As an island nation, Britain has always looked beyond its shores for markets and inspiration. In this regard, British manufacturing was no different. In 1913, 45 per cent of the sector's output was destined for foreign consumers. The corresponding percentages for Germany and the USA were 31 and 5 respectively (Maizel 1963: 223). The international trade in manufactured goods in the latter half of the nineteenth century was important both in terms of value and international pride. In 1913, it accounted for 36.7 per cent of all world trade and was larger in value than the trade in food (Alford 1996: 43). Furthermore, it was a rapidly expanding trade, whose volume tripled between 1880 and 1913 (Bairoch 1982: 296). Britain held a commanding position in this trade. In the early 1880s, British producers were responsible for 43 per cent of world trade in manufactured goods, a leading role that it was able to hold on to, despite growing competition from the USA, right up until 1929. For most of the nineteenth and early twentieth centuries, then, as Table 4.7 demonstrates, there is real substance to the claim that Britain was indeed the workshop of the world. It was, however, a workshop whose foundations were steadily being eroded. As Table 4.8 illustrates, British export growth was significantly slower than that of other leading industrial nations, especially in the 1880s. Furthermore, between 1913 and 1929, a period in which the volume of world trade in manufactures was expanding at an annual rate of 2.9 per cent, the exports of British manufactured goods actually contracted each year on average by 0.5 per cent (Matthews *et al.* 1982: 467). Not surprisingly, this period is characterised by a significant decline in Britain's share of world trade.

Table 4.7 National shares of world trade in manufacturing exports, 1881–1929

	UK	USA	Germany	Japan
1881/5	43.0	6.0	16.0	0.0
1899	34.5	12.1	16.6	1.6
1913	31.8	13.7	19.9	2.5
1929	23.8	21.7	15.5	4.1

Source: Matthews *et al.* 1982: 435.

Table 4.8 Growth of manufactured exports in selected countries, 1871–1913 (annual percentage growth rates)

	UK	USA	Germany	France
1871/5–1881/5	2.1	7.1		2.2
1881/5–1891/5	0.4	2.7	1.7	1.2
1891/5–1901/5	1.7	9.1	4.3	2.5
1901/5–1913	3.6	6.1	3.3	5.0
1871/5–1913	2.0	6.2		2.3
1881/5–1913			3.7	

Source: Hilgerdt 1945: 158–61.

Apart from the appearance of new foreign producers, Britain's relatively poor export performance had its origins to some extent in its waning price competitiveness from at least the early 1880s. This can be seen in the movements of the relative export price of UK and US manufactured products between 1879 and 1913, which show British prices slowly but fairly steadily drifting up by around 25 per cent vis-à-vis those of its main industrial competitor. In the early part of the 1890s, in particular, there is in a matter of a few years a sharp rise of some 15 per cent, which neatly corresponds with a surge in American exports (Greasley and Oxley 1996: 95).

A further factor affecting Britain's ability to export was the limits to free trade imposed by the commercial policies of different nations. Many industries appear to have been deleteriously affected by tariffs. The introduction of the McKinley Tariff by the American Congress in 1890, for example, is said to have had a major impact on the tinplate and iron and steel industries of Britain (Pollard 1989: 53). In 1890 the ratio of customs duties to imports, a measure of the degree of protection in place, stood at 29.6 per cent in the USA, 8.8 per cent in Germany and 4.8 per cent in the UK. Although all of these percentages subsequently fell in the years leading up to the First World War, they none the less illustrate the significant tariff barriers that British exporters faced in Europe and North America (Broadberry 1997c: 139–41). Despite these barriers, Britain remained a major exporter of manufactured goods throughout this period. Its main

Table 4.9 Main exports (excluding re-exports) of the United Kingdom (share of total), 1881–1913

	1881–90	1891–1910	1910–13
Coal	5.0	6.5	9.4
Iron and steel	11.3	9.8	11.3
Machinery	5.3	6.8	7.1
Electrical goods		0.7	0.8
Vehicles		0.08	0.6
Shipbuilding		0.8	1.9
Non-ferrous metals products	2.3	2.3	2.3
Cotton goods	31.4	27.8	25.7
Wool goods	10.1	8.8	6.7
Chemicals	4.6	4.9	4.3

Source: Alford 1996: 34.

comparative advantages lay in the unskilled labour-intensive commodities of the old staple industries. As Table 4.9 shows, textiles and iron & steel held the dominant place in the British export trade. Together these industries accounted for over a half of all British exports in the 1880s. In the following three decades, however, the share of the textile industry declined. In part this was due to the faster export growth of other industries; in part due to Britain's exclusion from the wealthy markets of Europe and America for all but the highest-quality cloth; and in part due to the resurgence of textile production in Asia (Crouzet 1982: 350). Britain's export data also reveal its lack of comparative advantage in most of the high-technology, human-capital-rich sectors of the period. The one exception was industrial equipment and machinery, though even this advantage had disappeared by 1929. By contrast, these emerging, technologically progressive sectors figured prominently among both American and German manufactured exports, a finding that suggests that Britain's human capital endowment may not have been sufficiently abundant for her to be competitive in these industries (Crafts and Thomas 1986; Crafts 1989b).

Productivity

To arrive at a rounded conclusion about the performance of British manufacturing, the sector must also be examined from the perspective of actual and potential development. One way to do this is to look at the comparative productivities of countries across time. Estimates of labour productivity in British manufacturing are given in Table 4.10. Apart from a plateau in the second half of the 1870s, output per worker in manufacturing increased steadily throughout, growing at an average rate of 1.3 per cent per annum between 1869 and 1913. During the war, however, labour productivity levels regressed and did not show growth again until after 1920. Over this entire period, British labour productivity in manufacturing remained approximately comparable to German, but consistently below American levels. As Table 4.10 demonstrates, the average American manufacturing worker tended to be twice as productive as his or her counterpart in Britain, with the lead, if anything, broadening over the Edwardian and transwar eras.

There was, of course, considerable variation in productivity levels within the sector. They were at their poorest in Britain in the heavy

Table 4.10 Labour productivity in manufacturing in the UK, USA and Germany, 1869–1925

	UK labour productivity (1913 = 100)	USA/UK labour productivity	Germany/UK labour productivity
1869	55.6	203.8	
1871	62.0		92.6
1875	65.0		100.0
1879	64.8	187.8	
1882	74.1		83.6
1889	77.5	195.4	94.7
1899	88.3	194.8	99.0
1909	91.0	208.5	117.8
1913	100.0	212.9	119.0
1919	94.8		
1920	93.9	222.8	
1925	119.6		95.2

Source: Broadberry 1997c: 42, 43, 48, 49, 127.

industries that were subject to significant economies of scale. In the automobile, copper, tinplate and iron & steel industries in particular, labour productivity in Britain in 1907/9 was between a quarter and a third of American levels. Poorer than average performance was also exhibited in the manufacture of soaps, detergents, hosiery, paper and board.

Yet it is important to realise that relatively low labour productivity need not necessarily imply failure. The case of the paper industry is instructive in that the roots of its lower productivity for most of the nineteenth century lay in its unique, yet rational, use of a raw material that required a more labour-intensive form of production. As the first nation to mechanise the process of making paper, Britain held a lead in the industry, both in terms of technology and market share, that was to be unchallenged at least until the 1860s when competition from German and American producers grew more marked. Despite the advent of these rivals, the industry remained innovative, with the average running speeds of British paper machines, an acknowledged industry gauge for technological progress, increasing at least as fast as the American until the 1890s. British paper makers also played a major role in the search for a solution to the industry's greatest problem of the late Victorian and Edwardian era: the urgent need for a new source of cellulose, the key ingredient of all paper and board. Traditionally paper had been made out of rags, but by the latter half of the nineteenth century, manufacturers were finding it difficult to obtain sufficient quantities of rag to meet the rapidly rising demand for paper. The ensuing search for a replacement for rag spanned the world and many of the leading British firms invested heavily in locating and testing the paper making properties of new materials such as bamboo and straw. In particular, British paper makers were instrumental in the development of a process to use esparto, a grass grown in North Africa and Spain, which proved itself capable of producing good-quality paper. As a result, esparto became the main substitute for rag in Britain until the turn of the century by which time the superiority of wood pulp, a material whose popularity had been growing in America since the Civil War, had become apparent. This British preference for esparto in the latter half of the nineteenth century had important implications for productivity. Because the conversion of esparto into cellulose required significantly more hands than was the case with wood pulp, its use reduced British labour productivity in the industry to levels significantly below American, even though British technology for most of this time was at least on a par with that on the other side of the Atlantic (Magee 1997b).

The labour productivity gap between the two countries, indicated in Table 4.10, also tended to be less extreme in the lighter industries, especially those associated with textiles, clothing and food processing where standardised mass-production either faced no demand-side constraints in Britain, afforded little competitive advantage or simply could not be easily applied. The tobacco industry provides a good illustration of a market that was sufficiently large for British producers to embrace standardised, capital-intensive methods of production. Between 1870 and 1914, the consumption of tobacco products, especially cigarettes, grew rapidly both in Britain and elsewhere. Major export markets opened up for British producers, most notably in the Empire. At the forefront of this expansion of the industry was the Bristol-based firm W.D. & H.O. Wills. Its exceptional success in this period was based on a twin-pronged strategy of using the latest technologies and pioneering the techniques of mass-marketing. In 1880 it acquired the exclusive rights to a mechanical packing machine; this was followed in 1886 by its adoption of Williamson's air-tight tin. The most important technological advance for the industry, however, came with the invention of the Bonsack cigarette machine in 1881. Wills, realising the potential, purchased the exclusive British rights to this technology in 1883, a move that, by placing the firm at the cutting edge of production technology, strengthened its position in the market significantly. As a result, by 1900 just over 10 per cent of the domestic market and nearly a half of all British cigarettes exported were manufactured by Wills. Around this time, however, serious competition from the American Tobacco Company began to be felt in the home market. To counter this, in 1901 Wills merged with other major British firms to form what was to become for a while Britain's largest company, the Imperial Tobacco Company. It proved a successful strategy and helped the British industry to remain internationally competitive well into the twentieth century (Alford 1973).

There were other successes as well. Indeed, in a handful of cases, such as in seed-crushing, the manufacture of lead and zinc and shipbuilding,

British labour productivity levels actually exceeded American in 1907/9. Of these, the success of the shipbuilding industry in this period is particularly noteworthy. More than 80 per cent of all new tonnage built in 1892 had its origins in British yards, a figure that, despite the growing protection afforded to many of its foreign competitors, still stood at more than 60 per cent in 1911. As the iron steamship was one of the technological wonders of the age, such a dominance of the world market by Britain represented a significant achievement. In this instance, the secret of British success, however, lay not in its adoption of mass-production, but rather in the flexibility and efficiency of its craft-based production system. In particular, British firms benefited from the fact that in shipbuilding the profitability of capital-intensive forms of production was severely limited by a demand that was highly cyclical and volatile by nature. A high proportion of fixed costs therefore exposed producers to exceptionally large losses during downturns. By substituting traditionally trained skilled labour, which was available in abundance, for machinery, British shipbuilders were to a large extent able to cushion themselves from such demand shocks while retaining their ability to produce efficiently. The concentration of shipyards on the Tyne, Wear, Tees and Clyde also encouraged the development of local economies that were tightly geared to servicing the specific needs of the shipbuilders. Thus, in the vicinity of yards, one could find some of the world's leading manufacturers of shipyard machinery, marine engineers and architects as well as a wide variety of multi-skilled craftsmen, the so-called 'amphibians' who could find work both in the shipyards and on land. The establishment of linkages between shipbuilders and shipping lines further helped by mitigating the impact of cyclical downturns in demand. Such external economies of scale greatly augmented the flexibility of British shipbuilding, helping it in turn to maintain its high productivity levels right up to the First World War (Pollard and Robertson 1979).

Labour productivity calculations, however, have their weaknesses, not the least being that they are only partial measures of productivity. They do not, for example, make allowances for changes in capital stock or energy use (Rostas 1948). An arguably better way of examining how efficiently an industry is using all the resources available to it is to calculate its total factor productivity growth (TFP). This technique measures the rate of growth of output not accounted for by the growth of all inputs (Brown 1966). Estimates of TFP are presented in Table 4.11. These estimates show TFP in manufacturing increasing on average by 0.6 per cent each year between 1873 and 1913. Such growth in the productivity of the sector accounted for 30 per cent of all manufacturing growth and 35.5 per cent of all TFP growth in the British economy in this entire period (Matthews *et al.* 1982: 228). Table 4.11 also lends further support to the notion of an Edwardian slowdown in productivity. Between 1899 and 1913, the rate of productivity growth fell to a third of what it had been in the last quarter

Table 4.11 Total factor productivity growth in manufacturing in the UK, USA and Germany, 1873–1925

	UK (%)		USA/UK (UK = 100)	Germany/UK (UK = 100)
1873–82	1.1	1869	204.9	
1882–9	0.4	1875		116.4
1889–99	1.1	1879	189.7	
1899–1907	0.1	1889	174.0	104.9
1907–13	0.3	1899	166.8	99.8
		1909	179.7	118.5
1873–99	0.9	1913		117.2
1899–1913	0.3	1919	179.5	
1873–1913	0.6	1925		110.5

Sources: Feinstein *et al.* 1982: 178; Broadberry 1993.

of the nineteenth century. Up to 1907 TFP showed virtually no improvement at all. It picked up slightly in the years leading to the war, but still grew at what was a comparatively low rate of 0.3 per cent per annum.

Relative to the USA and Germany, Britain's TFP performance in manufacturing was once again not impressive. TFP in America in 1869 stood at twice the British level, but unlike the labour productivity gap at least the TFP levels converged somewhat up until 1899. German TFP by contrast tended to operate at a level on average about 10 per cent above the British throughout the period in question. It is worth noting that against both countries, British TFP lost ground in the first decade of the twentieth century. In the following section, technology and other factors influencing this relatively poor productivity performance are discussed.

TECHNOLOGICAL CHANGE

The ability to create, develop and implement new technologies is generally held to be central to the attainment of long-term industrial competitiveness (Pavitt and Soete 1981: 106). Not surprisingly, then, most theories of Britain's industrial decline in some way touch, if not actually focus, on the process of technological change. As Mokyr (1990: 266) succinctly puts it, for many the failure of late Victorian Britain 'was not an economic failure, but a technological and scientific one'.

This failure, of course, related to not just the generation of ideas, but also technical choice: the seeming inability or unwillingness of British manufacturers to adopt cutting-edge equipment when it became available. The cotton industry's failure to adopt ring spinning and automatic looms, the dyestuff manufacturers' reluctance to capitalise on Perkin's synthesising aniline, and the alkali manufacturers' clinging on to the

Leblanc process, are just the better-known instances of this phenomenon. Proponents of the entrepreneurial failure thesis claim that this has steadily eroded British industrial competitiveness since the latter half of the nineteenth century. While the specific question of the quality of British entrepreneurship is considered in chapter 9 below, it is worth noting here that most of these alleged irrational choices in fact tend to make perfect sense once allowance has been made for factor costs, demand conditions and the state of knowledge (McCloskey and Sandberg 1971). Thus, it was the cotton industry's emphasis on the finer grades of cloth combined with the relative abundance of skilled labour and dense co-location of spinning and weaving firms in Lancashire towns – and not irrationality – that explained the cotton manufacturers much-debated predilection for mule spindles (Sandberg 1974; Leunig 1997). Similarly, the paper makers' apparently peculiar preference for esparto grass over wood pulp as a source of cellulose at the turn of the century becomes more understandable when due consideration is given to the sources, timing and flow of new information about the competing raw materials available at the time (Magee 1997b). Indeed, the only failure that is widely accepted in the literature was the soda manufacturers' retention of the Leblanc process long after the superior profitability of the alternative Solvay process had been established; this is a somewhat atypical example in that it occurred in a heavily cartelised industry largely sheltered from foreign competition (Lindert and Trace 1971). Where competition was stronger, the application of sufficient entrepreneurial vigour (Magee 1997a) to technical choice does not appear to have been a major problem.

The soundness of British invention and innovation, however, is less easy to establish. The late nineteenth and early twentieth centuries were a period of major technological transformation, an era in which *inter alia* the internal combustion engine, electricity, synthetic dyes, aspirin, telephony, the automobile and the wireless radio came of age. To what extent was Britain in the van of these technological revolutions? One problem in addressing this question is that there is no unambiguous index of a nation's technological performance. There are, however, a number of measures, which might serve as a proxy. Streit (1949), for example, provides a list of 1,012 major inventions made between 1750 and 1950 and their countries of origin. To the extent that these inventions constitute a meaningful sample of inventive activity, the list, summarised in Table 4.12, sheds some light on the changing location of technological leadership over this period. It shows that the relative contributions of Britain and America to the first industrial revolution (1776–1825) are almost exactly reversed in the second

Table 4.12 Major inventions by country of origin, 1776–1926 (percentage of total)

	Total	Britain	USA	Germany	France
1776–1825	163	43.6	11.7	9.8	26.4
1826–75	292	22.6	24.0	21.2	21.6
1876–1926	343	14.0	43.7	17.5	14.0

Source: Streit 1949.

Table 4.13 Foreign patents granted in the USA by country of origin, 1883–1929 (%)

	1883	1890	1900	1913	1929
Austria	2.6	3.4	3.4	4.0	2.5
Belgium	1.6	0.9	1.4	1.3	1.3
France	14.2	8.5	9.8	8.1	9.8
Germany	18.7	21.5	30.7	34.0	32.4
Sweden	1.0	1.5	1.3	2.1	3.2
Switzerland	1.8	2.7	2.3	3.1	4.5
UK	34.6	36.2	30.5	23.3	22.2

Source: Pavitt and Soete 1981: 109.

(1875–1926). Britain's inventive dominance is steadily lost over the course of the nineteenth century, so that by 1875 it is just one of the sources, albeit still an important one, of new technological ideas. This impression is supported by the patent data from the USA presented in Table 4.13. It confirms both the massive scale and the relative decline of British inventive and innovative activities at the turn of the century. Table 4.13 also shows the growing capacity of Germany, which by 1900 was rivalling Britain. The relative rise of German capability is more starkly seen in per capita terms: whereas the average Briton was patenting more than twice as frequently in America as the average German in 1886–90, by 1910–15, the gap had narrowed to just 17 per cent (Edgerton 1996: 64).

Moreover, the composition of British patenting in the USA between 1890 and 1912 provides further ground for concern. British inventors and firms tended to patent disproportionately in technologies associated with traditional industries, which offered fewer opportunities for rapid change. In the twenty-five years leading up to the First World War, Britain's greatest technological strengths still lay predominantly in industrial engines and turbines; rubber, coal and petroleum products; shipbuilding; soaps, detergents and fertilisers; textiles; and radio and telegraphic equipment. By contrast, German patenting was characterised by a much stronger commitment to the new industries of the second industrial revolution: chemicals, especially dyestuff and paints; pharmaceuticals; lighting and wiring; radio receivers; and electrical operating systems (Cantwell 1991: 46–7). It is clear that Britain was not at the forefront of the new wave of technologies breaking at the end of the nineteenth century.

What accounts for Britain's relative technological decline after 1870? One feature of British manufacturing that has constantly cropped up throughout this chapter is the sector's somewhat limited engagement with the new industries and technologies of the period. That these industries tended on the whole to be more scientifically orientated has prompted claims that the British worker and manager was simply inadequately trained to meet the challenges of the new technologies (Crafts 1989b: 135). Yet, as the discussion of human capital in chapter 3 above demonstrates, such claims have tended to be overstated. Technical education in Britain was not non-existent, as often asserted, but simply different with a greater emphasis on intermediate level skills than was the case in the USA.

In evaluating the strengths of Britain's technological system, it is also important to bear in mind that, in the late Victorian and Edwardian period, innovative activity was still largely the preserve of the independent inventor. Research and development (R&D) was typically carried out on the shop floor in a rather *ad hoc* manner with little direct application of scientific expertise. Admittedly, consulting chemists and engineers did exist, but when engaged they tended to undertake specific tasks rather than initiate systematic R&D programmes (Saul 1968: 117–18; Magee, 1997b: 38–9). To an extent, the existence of a relatively sophisticated international market for technological ideas obviated the need for more in-house research. By acquiring machinery from specialised capital good producers or through the patent system, the immediate technological needs of most firms could be easily met without incurring the significant costs of doing in-house R&D (Magee 1999, 2000). Indeed, costs were a real consideration for firms since in most instances such activity would have had to have been funded out of retained profits and, hence, be paid up front. Nor did the state offer much by way of relief. Other than providing indirect support through the funding of universities, museums and other institutions such as the National Physical Laboratory established in 1900, the state's engagement in Britain's R&D effort in this period was almost entirely restricted to purely defence-related matters (Edgerton 1996: 42).

The contribution of Britain's higher education sector was also limited. Unlike the situation that was emerging in the USA, where by the first decade of the twentieth century tertiary institutions such as Massachusetts Institute of Technology (MIT) were already involved in commercially funded research in electrical and chemical engineering, the research links between British industry and universities were comparatively weak and rare (Mowery and Rosenberg 1998: 23–5, 82). British tertiary education was also seemingly less focused on technical and scientific subjects than American. In 1870, only nineteen students graduated with degrees in science, mathematics or technology in England. In that year neither Oxford nor Cambridge offered courses in these fields. While thirty years later the situation had improved somewhat, England still only managed to produce just 677 science, mathematics and technology graduates in 1900, a small minority of the students who graduated in that year (Edgerton 1996: 20). The contrasts with Germany are striking. In 1872, there were fewer students reading for degrees or engaged in research in chemistry in England than there were at the University of Munich alone. This situation had not changed dramatically by 1908 when there were still fewer than 300 students enrolled in applied science courses in the entire country; at this time German universities were churning out over 400 graduate degrees in chemistry alone each year. The story is much the same in engineering. Between 1900 and 1910, German *Technische Hochschulen* were producing on average around 1,000 graduate engineers each academic year; the corresponding figure for Britain was about 400 (Sanderson, 1972: 271; Aldcroft 1975: 293; Fox and Guagnini

1993: 80). The implication of these figures is that, relative to its competitors, British industry may have been starved of scientifically trained personnel capable of working with the cutting-edge technology of the time.

To what extent was this true? While most comparative studies do tend to identify a British shortfall in scientifically trained workers, especially relative to the USA, the scale of the disparity was probably not as stark as has often been supposed. Owens College in Manchester alone, for example, saw seventy-one of its honours graduates in chemistry between 1884 and 1901 find employment in industry. Similarly, between 1870 and 1914, the membership of British engineering institutions rose tenfold from 4,000 to 40,000. These figures suggest that scientific skill was far from absent from British industry. Such skill was also making progress in entering the ranks of management. Between 1875 and 1895, 14 per cent of active partners or executive directors of British steel firms had had formal technical training, a share that rose to 16 per cent between 1905 and 1925. It is noteworthy that in the latter period, around a third of those technically trained managers had acquired their training at Oxbridge (Edgerton 1996: 25–7). How did this situation compare with other countries? Comparable data are sparse, but a number of scholars have argued that a larger proportion of American managers in this period had university qualifications than was the case in Britain (Chandler 1977). Similarly, a study of leading businessmen in Germany and Britain between 1870 and 1914 has found that only 13 per cent of British businessmen had any form of higher education, whereas nearly double the proportion of the Germans, some 24 per cent, had experienced it. Revealingly, though, there was virtually no difference between the countries among those businessmen born after 1860, a finding that indicates that the higher education gap must have progressively narrowed over the period (Berghoff and Moeller 1994).

At the turn of the century, the *ad hoc*, uncoordinated nature of nineteenth-century invention started to change, as an increasing number of firms, cognisant of the strategic need to keep abreast of technological knowledge, took it upon themselves to establish their own independent R&D capability. Although German and American corporations led the way in this process, British firms were also involved. By the first decade of the twentieth century, it has been estimated that around £0.5 million was being expended by British firms on R&D each year; by the 1920s this figure had risen to more than £2 million. The vast majority of this British R&D effort was concentrated in a few large firms manufacturing chemicals and naval shipping (Edgerton 1994; Edgerton and Horrocks 1994). Such levels of spending, however, were almost definitely lower than the amounts being invested in both Germany and the USA. Certainly, in Britain there was nothing to compare to the massive research laboratories that by this time were being operated by the likes of General Electric, Eastman

Kodak and Bell Telephones in America or Bayer in Germany (Mowery and Rosenberg 1989: 101, 107). In relation to its competitors, then, there is certainly some evidence to suggest that late Victorian and Edwardian Britain may have underinvested in R&D and higher-level scientific and technical training, even if the magnitude of the gap between it and its main competitors prior to 1914 was probably not as large as many critics have maintained.

Another distinctive feature of British manufacturing, which may have affected its productivity and technological performance, was its high and increasing rate of unionisation. In 1892, 13 per cent of the manufacturing workforce were paid-up members of a union; by 1911 that percentage had risen to 18.6 per cent. During the war, unionisation, tacitly encouraged by government in order to advance the war effort, increased dramatically, so that by 1925 slightly under a half of the entire manufacturing workforce had been unionised. By contrast, while there were some exceptions (Magee 1997b: 169–73), American manufacturing on the whole appears to have been conspicuously less unionised. Only 4.3 per cent of American manufacturing workers were in unions in 1897, a figure that had risen to just 18.1 per cent by 1920 (Broadberry 1997c: 145–6).

Such a difference in unionisation may have had significance for the very different rates of technological development achieved by each nation, especially after 1890. In fact, a major theme in the literature of the period is the hostility of British unions and workers in general to changes that altered the existing customs and arrangements regarding employment in their industry. Because of regional concentration, vertical specialisation and a traditional emphasis on skill-intensive flexible production methods, British industry in the nineteenth century tended to depend heavily on its craftsmen to co-ordinate production. Manufacturers, thus, typically left the management of the shop floor, from hiring and training of employees right through to setting of work rates and manning ratios, to the most experienced and skilled workers, an arrangement which gave these workers and their organisations considerable industrial power and prestige (Lazonick 1979, 1994).

While such craft control undoubtedly could work and even adapt efficiently within the confines set by nineteenth-century technologies, in the longer term it proved less malleable and tended to impede shopfloor flexibility. Increasingly menaced by the advent of skill-displacing technologies, which threatened to challenge their dominance of the workplace, craft unions used their power on the shop floor to enforce traditional practices in the workplace in terms of the numbers employed, training, routines and piece-rates. Such attempts were more successful in industries, such as shipbuilding and cotton, where skilled craft labour could not be easily replaced and was relatively better organised than its employers. Irrespective of outcome, however, the increasing frequency and pervasiveness of such disputes over shopfloor control as the end of the century drew nearer only served further to sour relations with management and make the labour force even more defensive about technological change in general: hardly developments likely to spur on innovative effort at the grassroots level. Lewchuck (1987: 221–5) contends that such mistrust between management and labour in the automobile industry produced a sub-optimal outcome in which British manufacturers, fearful of union objections, opted not to pursue the adoption of American mass-production technologies, while workers, suspicious of employers' intentions, chose not to co-operate in shopfloor reorganisation.

But poor technological choice was not the only drawback of such a restive workplace. Given that a significant proportion of technological change in manufacturing originates in the ideas and innovations of those who work in it, matters of industrial relations also clearly play an important part in determining the degree of technological change that is realised. Working in an atmosphere of industrial conflict, characterised by friction between labour and capital and resentment of the owner, a worker may simply have no desire to help the boss out by improving his machinery; at least, not unless something is given in return. Where, however, the benefits of such learning acquired through production were considered important enough, employers could opt for remuneration plans favourable to its employees and the generation of further home-grown innovation. Apart from piece-rates, other incentive-driven remuneration policies that can be employed include profit-sharing plans, bonuses, promotions or even partnerships for those who introduce or suggest innovative ideas.

While there is evidence to suggest that some Victorian and Edwardian manufacturers clearly did explore ways of rewarding and encouraging shopfloor invention, the practice was probably not widespread, at least relative to the USA (Magee 1997b; MacLeod 1999). In fact, it would seem that American manufacturers on the whole appeared to have appreciated, better than British, the necessity of providing a suitable work environment and conditions for their workers, and of instilling them with positive and desirable attitudes to technological change. American firms were certainly more active in experimenting with various fringe benefits for their workers such as free technical education and the establishment of mutual relief and insurance associations. More importantly, a system of giving premiums, bonuses and promotions for improvements and suggestions made by an employee was commonly used in the USA and, apparently, frequently brought beneficial results all round (Hatton 1988a; Magee 1997b: 221–30).

Yet, while perhaps inimical to long-run technological performance, this relative absence of higher-level scientific and technical education, R&D and shopfloor incentives for innovation in British manufacturing may have had a rational explanation. The point is best, and most often, made through a comparison of British and American production technologies. Broadberry (1997c) contends that two factors succinctly explain the divergent paths of British and American manufacturing since 1870: the standardisation of demand and the relative abundance of skilled shopfloor labour. As was seen earlier, in the USA the demand for standardised products was high. Skilled craftsman, however, were in relatively short supply especially in the manufacturing heartlands of the mid-west and eastern seaboard. Almost as compensation for this, though, America was blessed with a richness of resources. This specific combination of shortages and abundances acted as a stimulus to the development and utilisation of labour-saving technology in those branches of manufacturing where skilled labour was particularly important (Ames and Rosenberg 1968; James and Skinner 1985). Such machine-intensive production, coupled with a rich potential for standardised products, provided American manufacturers with fertile ground in which to lay the seeds of mass-production.

The situation in Britain was very different. Demand there tended to be much more fragmented and customised and natural resources less plentiful than was the case in America. Moreover, unlike in America, skilled shopfloor labour was readily available and, hence, comparatively inexpensive in Britain, especially in the industrial regions of the country. Faced, therefore, by a less urgent need to find substitutes for expensive labour and a pattern of demand that did not lend itself to standardisation, most branches of British manufacturing offered little scope for the introduction of mass-production technologies. Instead, they opted for a more flexible form of production, based on general purpose machinery, skilled labour and customised demand; a form much more suited to British conditions.

To the extent that this depiction of British manufacturing is true, it has a number of implications for the interpretation of the sector's pattern of development. First, given that flexible production and craft control of the shop floor was rational in British circumstances, there was less perceived need on the part of manufacturers to provide formal higher-level scientific and technical education for their workers. Traditional workplace training through apprenticeships would suffice. Secondly, because of British manufacturing's abundance of skilled craft labour, it was only natural that the sector's comparative advantage should lie in the old staple industries, such as textiles and iron and steel, where such labour was used most intensively. Since these industries also required less scientific knowledge and understanding, it follows that they had less need for organised R&D capabilities. Thirdly, as most major technological improvements in this era were tied to mass-production, Britain's adherence to more traditional flexible production methods, as well as its slower rate of expansion, meant that it was less capable of achieving as rapid a rate of technological change as was America. Finally, the analysis provides an explanation for why the American manufacturing workforce was twice as productive as the British throughout the late Victorian and Edwardian era and beyond. Because British demand conditions and factor endowments dictated smaller production runs and greater labour input than in the USA, British manufacturing was significantly less capital intensive by a margin of about two to one in 1900. With less machinery at his or her disposal, the average British worker was not surprisingly less productive.

MANUFACTURING AND THE BRITISH ECONOMY

Between 1870 and 1913, manufacturing was a large and expanding part of the British economy. But was manufacturing's place in the economy more important than the weight of its contribution to national output? At the beginning of the chapter reference was made to the Kaldor (1966) thesis, the view that manufacturing had dynamic properties that made it of special importance to the economy. Central to this hypothesis is an alleged correlation between the sector's rate of expansion and productivity growth. Attempts to test for this supposed relationship in the British economy over the long term provide no clear evidence of its existence (Matthews *et al.* 1982: 277–8; Crafts 1988: xii). Interestingly, though, the alleged correlation is most evident in the period between 1873–99 and 1899–1913, when a fall in the average rate of manufacturing growth from 2.2 to 1.8 per cent coincided with a steep decline in productivity from 0.9 to 0.3 per cent per annum. Yet, while such a finding is certainly consistent with the hypothesis, it is hardly proof of it. After all, factors other than manufacturing's dynamic economies of scale can clearly affect productivity and it may well be these that are of greater importance in the period under investigation. Furthermore, comparisons of growth and TFP rates reveal nothing about the direction of causation. Indeed, it could just as plausibly be that it is faster (slower) productivity growth that leads to an acceleration (deceleration) of output growth, and not vice versa. In an environment like late nineteenth-century Britain, where new productivity-enhancing technologies were being regularly developed and applied, such an explanation would have currency.

The hypothesis that manufacturing held an indispensable position in the economy is also undermined by other factors. A common corollary of this view is that a growing service sector is deleterious to an economy's well-being if its expansion is fuelled by drawing resources away from manufacturing (Baumol 1967). As employment in the service sector grew faster than in manufacturing between 1870 and 1913, this charge could be made for the late Victorian and Edwardian period. It would, however, be an ill-founded one. Manufacturing and services are interdependent, rather than in competition with each other. Banking, insurance, shipping and education, for example, all provide vital services that facilitate the smooth running of the manufacturing sector. Without a reliable means of bringing cotton from the USA or financial institutions capable of funding such international transactions, Lancashire's cotton industry simply could not have functioned. Moreover, it would seem that as economies become more complex, the need for such services increases. Thus, as Britain moved into science-based industries, it created a demand for greater numbers of scientifically trained workers, a demand that in the long run could only be met by expanding the number of science faculties in the country. The rise of the service sector is not symptomatic of the failure of manufacturing.

A final consideration is the performance of British industry: did late Victorian and Edwardian manufacturing really fail as is often claimed? As this chapter has demonstrated there is certainly reason for concern. After all, relatively slow growth rates and declining market share are usually not taken as signs of economic vitality. Yet such an assessment would ignore the historical context in which these phenomena occurred. By the latter half of the nineteenth century industrialisation, pioneered in Britain, had begun to take root in a growing band of nations in Europe and North America. At the beginning of their industrial revolutions, with large shares of their workforce engaged in agriculture, an abundance of industrial potential to tap into and often imposing tariff walls to protect themselves, these nations had the ingredients necessary for rapid industrial expansion. By contrast, Britain in 1870 was already a mature industrial economy, whose potential for industrial growth was far more limited. Moreover, as the products of these new industrial centres appeared in the marketplace, it was only natural that Britain's share of world manufacturing activity should diminish accordingly. And it did. But this was not a zero-sum-game, as the volume of British manufactured exports continued to grow throughout this period, despite its declining proportion of the world trade. This is, of course, what one would expect in an international economy that was both expanding and integrating at an unprecedented rate.

Assessment of British manufacturing is also clouded by a tendency in the declinist literature to equate the sector's performance with that of a handful of high-profile industries, whose record appears far from impressive in this period. Typically, these were the industries, such as steel, automobile and electrical engineering, where Britain's competitiveness is said to have been undermined by its slowness to adopt the techniques of mass-production. But, as discussed earlier, even these 'failures' can be accounted for by Britain's unique factor endowment and demand conditions, which made mass-production less, and flexible craft-based production more, profitable in Britain than elsewhere, particularly the USA.

The declinist perspective is further weakened when consideration is extended beyond the heavy industries where mass-production came to dominate. In some industries, such as food, drink and tobacco, soaps, shipbuilding and textile machinery, British performance was distinctly respectable, with high productivity levels, significant technological progress and healthy shares of world exports. When the full diversity of British manufacturing experience is considered it is hard to be adamant about the sector's failure. Indeed, it could be said that on the whole British manufacturers did reasonably well in adapting their industries to the changed and much more competitive international environment after 1870. There is no evidence of widespread entrepreneurial ineptitude. Failure, in the sense of a rapid loss of markets, was an issue in only those industries for which upon reflection it can be seen that the nation was not well suited. Elsewhere British manufacturers appear to have held their own.

5 The service sector

MARK THOMAS

Contents

The importance of services to the achievements of the industrial revolution is gradually becoming realised. Britain may have been by 1851 the 'workshop of the world', but it was also the pioneer service economy, with over 30 per cent of its labour force already devoted to the provision of services to domestic and overseas markets, contributing almost half of national income. Services further increased in statistical significance after 1850: by 1939, half the labour force was employed in the tertiary sector. It seems right to argue that services played an important role in the maturing of modern Britain. Yet it may also be right to argue that they played a role in slowing down British economic growth and contributing to the catch-up by other economies.

Table 5.1 A taxonomy of services (including numbers employed, England and Wales), 1851–1931 (thousands)

	1851	1871	1891	1911	1931
A *Social overhead capital*					
(i) Transport and communication	356	556	981	1,550	2,045
(ii) Public utilities					
(a) Education	90	127	201	264	261
(b) Police, defence, justice and administration	107	172	186	339	
(c) Social and environmental services	14	32	49	114	300
B *Business services*					
(i) Retail and wholesale trade (inc. catering)	616	908	1,158	1,876	1,865
(ii) Finance (banking, insurance, brokerage, etc.)	4	18	53	144	112
(iii) Professional business services (accountancy, surveying, architecture, engineering, etc.)	19	32	46	56	105
(iv) Commercial clerks	38	91	247	478	1,279
C *Personal services*					
(i) Domestic service	853	1,341	1,535	1,564	1,421
(ii) Artisan personal services (hairdressing, laundries, clubs, etc.)	279	351	494	573	689
(iii) Professional personal services (medicine, law, domestic architecture, etc.)	70	83	126	174	189
D *Community and co-operative services*					
(i) Religion	31	43	59	67	59
(ii) Professional associations, trade unions, co-operatives, etc.	–	–	2	4	5
E *Recreation and culture*					
(i) Entertainment and sport	16	24	58	115	137
(ii) Cultural services (fine arts, literature, museums, etc.)	14	23	35	65	66

Notes: 'Commercial clerks' in 1931 incorporate all clerical staff other than law clerks; in previous years, non-commercial clerks are allocated to their respective sectors. Blanks indicate insufficient detail to allocate workers.

Sources: Taxonomy adapted from Hartwell 1973; numbers employed calculated from Census of England and Wales, 1851, 1871, 1911, 1931.

THE TERTIARY SECTOR

The boundaries of the service sector are famously imprecise, its content notoriously heterogeneous. Fisher (1952), who coined the term, 'tertiary sector', to distinguish services from primary (agriculture, mining) and secondary (manufacturing, construction) activities, noted that it was defined not from any positive attributes, but rather as a residual claimant, 'a miscellaneous rag-bag into which everything has to be thrown that cannot conveniently be fitted anywhere else'. The heterogeneity is reflected in Adam Smith's famous compilation, 'some both of the gravest and most important, and some of the most frivolous professions: churchmen, lawyers, physicians, men of letters of all kinds; players, buffoons, musicians, opera singers, opera dancers, etc.' (Smith 1976 [1776]: 331).

Table 5.1 reproduces (with some minor modifications) the classification suggested by Hartwell (1973) in his pioneering treatment of services

Table 5.2 Industrial classification of service workers, UK, 1861–1938 (thousands)

	1861	1871	1881	1891	1901	1911	1921	1929	1938
Social overhead capital									
(i) Transport and communication	590	760	860	1,110	1,450	1,580	1,540	1,600	1,690
(ii) Public utilities									
(a) Education	140	160	210	240	280	310	260	280	290
(b) Central government	40	40	50	70	80	120	250	170	250
(c) Local authorities	100	130	170	200	270	320	390	460	560
(d) Defence	310	250	240	280	530	400	490	330	430
Business services									
(i) Retail and wholesale trade	850	1,050	1,300	1,640	1,990	2,460	2,190	2,670	3,090
(ii) Finance	20	40	70	110	150	230	330	410	480
Professional services									
(i) Medical and dental	65	70	80	100	120	150	130	150	190
(ii) Other (including law)	130	160	240	260	320	370	220	230	290
Personal services									
(i) Domestic service	1,510	1,790	1,850	1,940	1,980	2,000	1,270	1,510	1,680
(ii) Catering, hotels, etc.	200	240	350	430	460	610	370	390	490
(iii) Other	250	280	320	390	430	450	320	360	580

Notes: All numbers rounded to nearest 10,000. Numbers occupied, 1861–1911; numbers employed, 1921–38. Eire excluded after 1920. Data may also not be strictly comparable between 1861–1911 and 1921–39 because of changes in classification.

Sources: 1861–1911: adapted from Feinstein 1972; 1921–38: Chapman and Knight 1953.

in historical perspective. Hartwell's taxonomy classifies services by end-use, distinguishing infrastructure (social overhead capital; community services) from market services, and intermediate (business) from consumer (personal) services. Within these broad categories, other characteristics deserve mention – the public provision of communications distinguishes it from the private provision of transportation, for example; while public utilities, as non-marketed services, could be distinguished from the rest of the sector, where market forces rule. Moreover, as Hartwell noted, all taxonomies are static by conception, whereas a historical study of services should focus on how, and how much, things have varied over time and place.

Table 5.1 begins this process by matching census respondents in England and Wales in at twenty-year intervals between 1851 and 1931 to Hartwell's taxonomy. The table is drawn from the occupational classification of the census, and therefore tends to understate the true number of workers in each sector, since it excludes all those recorded as 'general labourer', even though they may have been employed in a service. An industrial classification is provided for the UK in Table 5.2, which allocates general workers (and clerks) to specific trades. The classification is less fine and some of the allocation of occupations to industries is quite rough. But between them, these tables give a strong sense of the structure of the service sector and how it changed over time.

It is impossible in a short essay to do justice to the complexity and diversity of experience of the service sector. This essay instead focuses on the central players in a historical narrative that tries to locate the service sector in the primary developments of the period from 1850 to 1939. The narrative emphasises interdependence, both among the service sectors and between services and the rest of the economy. It is a story about change, but also about the limits to change.

We begin with internal transportation and its place in the transformation of the marketplace in Victorian Britain – the decline of local and regional loyalties in favour of a more national economy, which allowed the producers of standardised products to develop sales strategies and organisations to reach a gradually more prosperous populace. The falling costs of moving goods around the economy in turn stimulated changes in the distributive network, most notably with the creation of new types of retail outlet. The spatial lengthening of market transactions increased the need for networked systems of information and finance; at the same time, the temporal shortening of market transactions reduced the power of credit and encouraged the monetisation of exchange. Finally, transportation and communication improvements on the open seas promoted an increasingly integrated global market, for which Britain served as entrepôt and finance house. That, in précis, is the story. What follows puts flesh on these bare bones.

Inland transportation

The railway age was firmly in place by 1851: over 6,000 miles of track had been laid and over 65 million passengers were carried each year (an average of 3.2 train journeys for every Briton). Locomotives roared through the countryside at speeds of up to 40 miles an hour, slow by today's standards, but lightning compared to the other means of movement of the time, canal barges, horse-wagons and stagecoaches, which were limited literally by horsepower. By 1913, when the railway system was at its zenith, there were 20,000 miles of track; almost 1.5 billion passengers were carried each year (an average of thirty-five journeys per person); and railway wagons carted almost three-quarters of the goods that circulated around the economy (Armstrong 1987).

Table 5.3 charts the progress of railway services between 1850 and 1938, in terms of miles of track open, the volume of freight (ton-miles) and passenger traffic (passenger-miles). The table shows three basic stages in the growth of railways: a mid-Victorian boom (1850–70), followed by gradual deceleration to 1913, and stagnation, if not decline, between the world wars.

The spectacular growth of freight in 1850–70 was due largely to the expansion of mineral traffic as the railway supplanted canal and coastal shipping of iron ore and, especially, coal. Traffic was stimulated both by falling prices over time and, more significantly, by lower prices relative

Table 5.3 Growth of railway services, 1850–1938

	Change in road miles open (% p.a.)	Change in passenger-miles (% p.a.)	Change in freight (ton-)miles (% p.a.)
1850–70	3.8	6.1	9.8
1870–90	1.3	4.5	3.3
1890–1913	0.7	4.5	2.8
1913–38	0.0	1.2	−0.0

Sources: Col. 1: Mitchell and Deane 1962, 225–8. Col. 2: number of passengers x average length of journey; adapted from Hawke 1970: 48. Col. 3: tons of freight x average length of haulage; adapted from Hawke 1970: 88 and Cain 1988: 123.

to other means of transport. Canals, the mainstay of transportation improvements before 1830, rapidly fell into disuse and disrepair. A government official declared as early as 1846, 'the railway can always carry cheaper' (Clapham 1932: 199). There were exceptions: well-constructed and well-maintained canals did have a competitive advantage in carrying goods with a low ratio of value to weight, as the Weaver (salt) and Aire and Calder (coal) Canals demonstrated. But most canals could not compete; they were unable to raise the revenue necessary for routine maintenance, let alone capital improvements. And where canals did promise competition, railways were not averse to buying them up. By 1913, less than 2 per cent of freight was carried on inland waterways.

Initially, railways out-competed coastal shipping as well. In 1851, 98.5 per cent of London's coal supplies were sea-borne; by 1873, less than 35 per cent. However, the competitive advantage of rail over ship slipped in the last quarter of the century. By 1900, coastal shipping once again accounted for more than half the coal imported into London. The turnaround has been explained (Bagwell and Armstrong 1988) by technological innovation in shipping (the shift from sail to steam colliers) and technical conservatism in rail (the failure to move to bigger coal wagons). Others have disputed the culpability of rail companies (van Vleck 1997); it is none the less clear that there was a drop in the relative competitiveness of rail freight after 1880 or so. Indeed, by the interwar period, railway traffic was beginning to be bid away by new, more flexible means of moving goods around the economy inland. The number of motor trucks on British roads increased from 101,000 in 1920 to 495,000 in 1938.

That passenger traffic on railways continued to thrive up to 1913 indicates the absence of alternative ways for people to travel quickly and cheaply. Predictably, the fastest rate of growth was in the early years of expansion. Railway carriages transported almost five times as many passengers in 1870 as twenty years earlier; but since most of the new customers were shorter-distance travellers, the impact on passenger-miles (the preferred measure) was less. The average length of journey fell from 16 miles in 1850 to 9 miles in 1890. The increasing use of trains to travel to work accounts for much of this decline (with an added fillip from customers travelling to markets). So it does also for the rise in average travel distance to 17 miles by 1913 and 22.5 miles in 1938, as a rising rent gradient forced workers to live further out from city centres. As late as 1938, travel to work still accounted for over two-thirds of all passenger journeys.

Railways contributed little to transportation within urban boundaries, tending instead to deposit suburban passengers on the fringes of the city. Horse-omnibuses, supplemented by horse-tramways, dominated urban transport in the Victorian era. By 1900, electrification was transforming transport above and below ground through the electric tram, which became part of every major city's urban plan, and the tube, limited to London. Taxis, like hansoms before them, remained a luxury of the well-to-do (and declined in importance over the interwar period), while the motor bus became an increasingly common sight on town streets. The flexibility of bus routes over tramlines benefited shoppers and commuters; between 1920 and 1938, the carrying capacity of buses and coaches increased by 20 per cent a year; by 1938, they accounted for as many passenger-miles as the entire railway network, above and below ground (Stone and Rowe 1966: 71).

For long-distance passenger travel, in contrast, the railway remained supreme into the 1940s. Coach networks developed in the interwar period to link small villages and towns that could not be reached by rail. The motor car also blossomed (there were almost 2 million private cars on the roads by 1938 and half a million motor cycles), but the relatively poor quality of trunk roads (plus concerns about vehicular unreliability over long distances) restricted their use. Aeroplane travel was even more remote for most Britons.

The economics of railway management

Railways are the classic decreasing-cost industry. Fixed costs – the expenses associated with the track, locomotives, rolling stock, stations, freight depots, signal-boxes and other fixed assets – are much higher than operating or variable costs (such as labour and fuel). Average total costs therefore decline continuously as output increases, at all conceivable levels of output. In such a situation, even with competitive beginnings, the tendency will be towards concentrated ownership over time, as larger (and hence more efficient) firms buy up or take over smaller ones. Economic Darwinism will eventually generate market control by a single producer – the most efficient. This constitutes a natural monopoly.

Whether railways would, if left alone, eventually have fallen under the control of a single firm is not known. But the tendency towards bigness was already evident in the amalgamations of the 1840s (the age of Hudson and Huish) and the 1860s. By 1874, the top four companies owned 39 per cent of track mileage and earned 47 per cent of total receipts (Cain 1988: 103). A Select Committee in 1872 declared 'amalgamation inevitable; and perhaps desirable', but its recommendations were thrown out by a more wary parliament, fearful of the potential for monopoly. For the next thirty years there were no new amalgamations as the government, increasingly sensitive to complaints equally directed at anti-competitive ownership and uncompetitive management, resisted. The result was not monopoly, but oligopoly.

The problem with oligopolies is not, as contemporary critics feared, too little competition, but rather too much. The problem for the oligopolist is excess capacity, the challenge how best to eradicate it. Oligopolistic industries are characterised by intense rivalry; each firm tries to reduce its excess capacity by charging lower prices or offering a better product than its competitors in order to capture a larger share of the market. Rivalrous competition is likely to be at its most intense when demand is depressed, spilling over into price wars or dramatic product innovations. In calmer times there are incentives for co-operative behaviour among firms, since rivalry tends to lower profits for everyone. Co-operation may take the form of collusion (price-setting by agreement) or price leadership by a single firm (price-setting by example). The incentives to cheat by charging a lower price are strong, although other firms will be quick to catch up rather than sacrifice market share. If the firm can cheat in secret, through negotiation with favoured customers, so much the better.

The scramble for profits and market share also leads firms to practice price discrimination, by charging different prices to different customers for the same product. At the extreme, firms will try to charge a different price for every customer (first-degree price discrimination). The excessive monitoring costs of identifying the right price for every customer renders this unfeasible. But third-degree discrimination (charging different prices to different *types* of customer) can significantly improve a firm's profit position with relatively limited bureaucratic expense.

The railway industry after 1870 was intensely competitive, all the more so given the density of track, which ensured that there were often many different routes between any two locations. Competition rarely deteriorated into bruising battles between firms; instead informal sharing arrangements and more formal working agreements became increasingly common. Pricing norms were established by which railway companies charged the same rate to take freight from point A to point B by any route (part of the motivation for this arrangement was that freight movements between A and B often required carriage on track owned by different companies). Firms participated in pooling arrangements, sharing locomotives and rolling stock to permit each firm to reduce its fixed costs and lower the burden of excess capacity for the industry as a whole.

'There were said to be 3–4 million local rates on the North Eastern Railway, 2 million freight and 1 million passenger rates on the Lancashire & Yorkshire Railway, and a million rates with 20,000 alterations each year on the North Staffs. Railway' (Hawke 1970: 333). The bureaucratic implications of such numbers are staggering, if they are to be believed (they are not). But price discrimination did not have to go this far to become effective. In the late Victorian period, the development of increasingly complex price tiers were clearly designed to capture a greater share of consumer surplus – third-class, workmen's, excursion, season-ticket passengers. Spatial and product discrimination were standard practice in the freight business. A uniform price for all railway services would certainly have reduced the profitability of any given company, and of the industry as a whole.

Competition focused less on pricing than on the provision of services. Indeed, one of the criticisms of railway companies was that rates were not falling as fast as prices in general. Instead, they participated in an increasingly expensive game of improving services – by building better railway stations, by adding dining cars and lavatories to carriages, by providing refrigerated wagons – a form of competition less apparent to critics but no less expensive to the companies. The burden of the continuous pressure to improve services was recorded in a rise in operating expenses, falling profits and, perhaps, a slower rate of productivity growth (if only because improvements in the quality of service are not measured as an increase in output).

The difficulties of running a railway were intensified by the strong network effects that came from single ownership of both the means and mechanisms of transportation (in contrast to canals, where there was a legally enforced separation of ownership of barge and waterway before 1845, and shipping, operating on the open seas). Many commentators considered the solution to the problems of the railway to be increased state oversight, if not overt control. Bagehot, the influential editor of the *Economist*, certainly believed this was necessary as an antidote to 'the present mode of railway management . . . trading management at its worst'. A Royal Commission rejected the possibility in 1865–7; a second, established in 1914, was interrupted by war before it could make any recommendation. The railway companies were put under state control during the First World War in an experiment that ended with the rush to decontrol once peace was signed. But the Railways Act of 1921 essentially legitimated oligopolisation with state oversight, by dividing up the railway map of Great Britain into four regions, each under the control of a single company, operating under government regulation. From there, it was not a big step to full nationalisation, as the rail companies discovered in 1947.

Overseas transportation

At the start of our period, two-thirds of all freight clearings (by tonnage) from British ports were due to coastal trade. But over the rest of the nineteenth century, foreign clearances outpaced coastal (increasing at 3.1 and

1.4 per cent p.a. respectively between 1870 and 1910). By 1913, two-thirds of all freight clearings were bound for foreign or colonial destinations.

The growth of overseas traffic reflected the expansive nature of Britain's export and import trades in the Victorian period. Britain was among the most open of all economies, with the combined value of exports and imports equalling 60 per cent of national income in 1913. The volume of commodity trade grew substantially: at over 4 per cent a year, 1850–70, and at over 3.2 per cent p.a. from 1870 to 1913. All of these goods had to be carried into and out of British ports and harbours. For most of the period, British ships dominated overseas carriage. The rising share of foreign (especially German) ships in overseas clearings in the late nineteenth century (from 28 per cent in the 1870s and 1880s to 45 per cent in 1913) caused consternation among British shippers and commentators, fearful of its meaning for British mercantile (and by extension, naval) supremacy. None the less, British shipping still dominated world markets – in 1913 fully a third of world shipping capacity sailed (or steamed) under the British flag.

The period between 1870 and 1914 saw a revolution in ocean shipping, with the shift from sail to steam (steam had already conquered the coastal trade by 1870). In 1870–4, only 14 per cent of sea-going vessels were steam, and only 26 per cent of the merchant tonnage; by 1910–14, 59 per cent of the ships and fully 92 per cent of the tonnage was steam. Steam vessels were not subject to the shifting fortunes of wind and weather; their average speeds increased over 1880–1914 as engine capacity and design improved; and, perhaps most important, their carrying capacity rose relative to wooden sailing vessels as the technology of construction improved. In 1870, steamships already had an average tonnage twice that of sailing ships; by 1910, it was eight times as large. Many of the largest vessels (the great liners culminating in the 47,000 ton *Aquitania* in 1914) carried passengers (migrants and tourists) across the North Atlantic; but cargo ships also became bigger. Sharply declining costs were the result.

The interwar period tells a very different story. Freight rates continued to fall, but due to falling demand, not rising efficiency. Much merchant tonnage was destroyed during the First World War, yet the 1920s and 1930s were characterised by excess capacity (partly because of the rapid shipbuilding boom of the early 1920s). The passenger traffic of the North Atlantic, on which the fortunes of many shipping companies depended, collapsed after 1914, as migration to the 'New World' was halted, first by war, then by the passage of US immigration quotas. Over 700,000 passengers left British ports for non-European countries in 1913; only half as many in 1925. Cargo traffic held up better in the 1920s, but hit a deep reef in 1929–31, with the onset of the great depression. The British merchant marine maintained its competitive position during the troubled 1930s, accounting for more than a quarter of the world's carrying trade in 1931 and 1936 – but it was a much-diminished level of trade. Much of the 1930s was spent trimming supply to meet falling demand: between 1931 and 1937, British ship owners scrapped over 40 per cent of the fleet's carrying capacity. The fortunes of the industry slowly improved as world trade picked up (despite a continued weakness in coal exports). But any reprieve was temporary.

Communication

The development of an integrated, increasingly flexible national market depended in no small part on the speed, reliability and frequency of transmitting information. The gains from expanding communication services were concentrated in the business sector, which accounted for three-quarters of all telegrams sent and two-thirds of all letters mailed; business calls accounted for 90 per cent of telephone usage before 1913, 80 per cent in 1924 and 66 per cent in 1938.

The Penny Post came to Britain in 1840. The benefits of post-haste may have originated with the stagecoach, but it was the railway that sustained its expansion. By 1851, 334 million pieces of mail were placed in British post-boxes, a rate per capita well over twice as high as in the leading economies of the rest of Europe. The mail system grew by over 4 per cent p.a. between 1851 and 1871 and by almost 3 per cent p.a. between 1871 and 1913. Only with the diffusion of the telephone did the postal service slow (1.7 per cent p.a., 1913–38). Even as late as 1938, however, per capita mailings were significantly higher than in France or Germany.

The place of the telegraph in promoting improved market communication is much harder to evaluate. On the face of it, it looks quite unimpressive. As late as 1913, the number of inland telegrams sent was only one sixtieth the number of mail pieces posted. The capital stock invested in the telegraph system was trivial. Yet Marshall (1919: 363) argued that the 'centralised administration of railways has always owed much to the telegraphic communication which the exigencies of the traffic require', although he considered the telephone superior for business administration, especially within large manufacturing enterprises requiring flexible management rather than routine administration. The expansion of telegraphic messages slowed over time (5 per cent a year, 1873–90; 1.4 per cent a year, 1890–1913), indicating the limits of use. There were fewer telegrams delivered in 1938 than in 1920. A government inquiry in the 1920s characterised the telegraph service as 'lying between the upper and lower millstones of an expanding Telephone Service and of a Postal organisation which . . . ensures the delivery of a letter anywhere within the boundaries of the British Isles within 24 hours of posting' (Stone and Rowe 1966: 73). In the compact geography of Great Britain, the speed of the telegraph added little. The one area in which it was a clear aid to business efficiency was in overseas communication. The transatlantic submarine cable, laid successfully for the first time in 1866, was followed by other sub-oceanic initiatives (and later by wireless telegraphy). Here distance was a deterrent to commerce, and here the telegraph mattered. The world was a smaller place in 1913 than in 1851.

The telephone arrived in Britain in 1877; it was slow to develop, but by 1895, there were over 2,500 miles of trunk lines. The number of trunk (long-distance) calls grew steadily at 12 per cent a year between 1896 and 1913 and at almost 10 per cent p.a. during the interwar period; there are no data on local calls before 1913, but these increased at about 7.5 per cent a year between 1921 and 1938. The industry was heavily criticised. An American visitor to London in 1913 was scathing: 'nowhere under the canopy is there a telephone service so dreadful and so exasperating' (van Antwerp 1913: 341). Telephone use in Britain was lower, and the average cost of a call higher, than in many other countries (especially Germany and the USA), largely because of the prior existence of an inexpensive and efficient alternative (the post), which reduced demand, and the inability to take advantage of scale economies in production, which kept costs high.

In contrast to the transportation networks which were privately owned though publicly monitored, the communication services were perceived as public goods and were operated as national monopolies (the BBC joined the list in 1926). Some critics have suggested that the absence of a profit motive, as well as political pressures on the highly visible Post Office, created inefficiencies. Perhaps, but the evidence from the telegraph industry before it was nationalised in 1870 and the telephone system when in private hands before 1912 does not suggest that private ownership was inevitably superior.

Improved transportation and communication benefited the British economy by lowering the costs of trade and commerce, thereby increasing the extent of the market. The cost of moving goods by rail fell by over 35 per cent between 1850 and 1913; overseas shipping rates fell by 34 per cent, 1870–1913; coastal rates by perhaps 40 per cent, 1865–1910. What contribution did such changes make to the size and prosperity of the overall economy?

Social savings

In 1866, Dudley Baxter measured 'the saving to the country' of the railway system, estimating that, 'had the railway traffic of 1865 been conveyed by canal and road at the pre-railway rates, it would have cost three times as much'. Baxter anticipated by almost a century the social savings technique for measuring the contribution of railways to the economy. The social savings methodology asks the question, 'how much smaller would the economy have been in a given year in the absence of the railway'. The answer is given by calculating how much more it would have cost to move railway traffic by canal and road, at current prices, had the rail system been closed down for the year. It is implicitly assumed that prices capture the market value of all the resources embodied in the transportation service – in the case of road or canal traffic, the coachmen or barge-men, the rental costs of the wagons or barges, road or canal tolls, and the horses used for haulage; in the case of railways, the locomotive engineer, fireman, guard, the rental cost of the locomotive, rolling stock, railway track and other facilities, as well as the cost of fuel, etc. Prices are higher on canals, on roads and at sea than on the railway because they require more resources; the added cost of the more expensive alternatives thus represents the resource, or social, savings of the railway system. These savings may be compared to the size of the national income, which measures the market value of resource consumption for the economy as a whole.

The basis of the calculation of social savings is shown in Figure 5.1a. The shaded area represents the additional resources consumed by using roads and canals in place of rail. The diagram maintains certain working assumptions that simplify the arithmetic: that transportation demand is inelastic (this assumption tends to overstate the extent of social savings); and that the marginal resource cost on the alternative systems does not increase as more traffic is transferred to it (this assumption tends to understate the extent of social savings). In Figure 5.1b, the two assumptions are relaxed simultaneously. It can be seen that the direction and scale of bias stemming from such assumptions cannot be determined a priori: it depends on the relative size of the triangular areas, A and B.

Baxter's crude estimate of social savings amounts to some 9 per cent of UK national income in 1865. Hawke (1970, 1981), applying a more sophisticated treatment of statistics and method, arrived at an estimate for English railways on the same basis as Baxter of 4 per cent (part of the reason for the difference in these two estimates is that Hawke believed that the lower prices charged by canal and coach companies after the coming of the railways reflected the eradication of monopoly profits, rather than true resource savings). Savings on freight were marginally higher than savings on passenger travel. Hawke also added allowances for more efficient movement of livestock and the reduced use of wagon haulage to carry goods to railway stations than canal and dock wharves, which increased the freight component of social savings to 4 per cent, and the overall figure to 6 per cent of national income. Finally, and most controversially, Hawke added an allowance for the increased comfort of travelling by rail carriage than by stagecoach; this alone raised his social savings estimate to 11 per cent overall.

Each of these calculations applies the procedure shown in Figure 5.1a, making no correction for elasticity of demand or supply. There is no reason to anticipate congestion problems leading to higher marginal costs on coach travel, so triangle B should be small for passenger transportation;

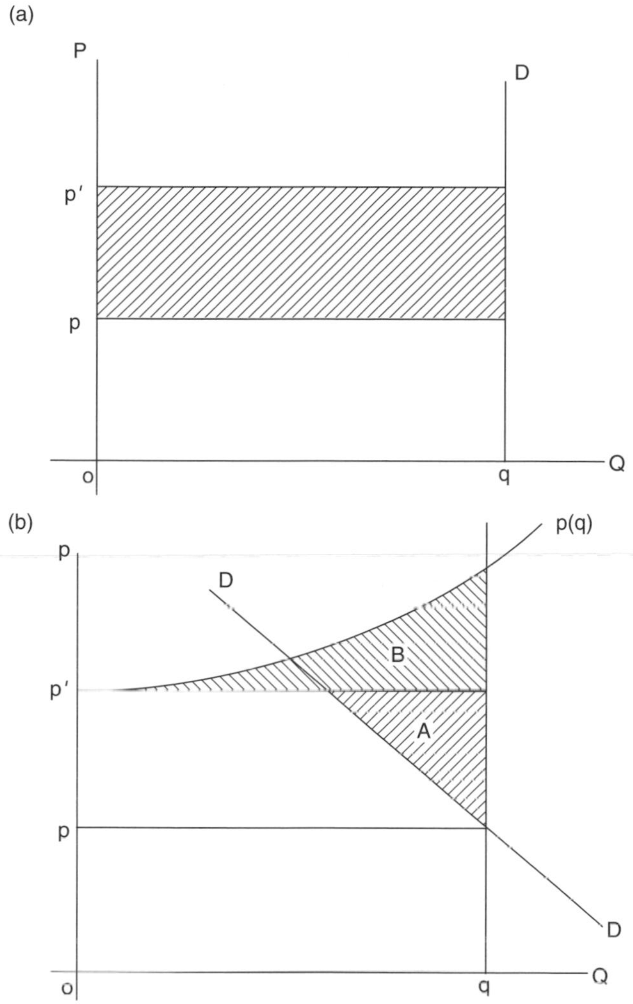

Figure 5.1 Social savings

the same logic applies to coastal shipping and land haulage of goods, while Hawke has figures that imply constant costs on canals. There is the possibility that the redistribution of freight from the railways would have overwhelmed the carrying capacity of canals in 1865, shifting the burden to more expensive road haulage and raising social savings accordingly; but Hawke has implicitly assumed that in the absence of the railways, more canals would have been built to accommodate increased goods traffic. Demand is likely to be inelastic for freight carriage, making triangle A unimportant; but Foreman-Peck (1991) is surely right to observe that demand for passenger transportation was highly price-elastic, and triangle A therefore large. His correction reduces the social savings from passenger travel by 3.5 to 4 per cent; the revised total for 1865 is 7 to 7.5 per cent of national income.

Since the growth of railway traffic was faster than national income after 1865 (at least until 1913), social savings should have been larger in later years: two or three times higher by 1890, according to Gourvish (1980). Foreman-Peck's approach (1991) implies a social savings of 15 per cent in 1890 and 17 per cent in 1910.[1] All such calculations should, of course, be treated as upper bounds, limited as they are by the implicit assumption that transportation technology in the absence of the railway would have been stuck in the age of the *Rocket*. If the railway had never existed, it seems likely that some alternative and more efficient transportation system would have developed, whether through modifications to prevailing technology or through developments of new initiatives.

If we wish to evaluate, not the gains from a specific innovation, but the benefits that accrued to the economy from the overall improvement in transport and communications, we could adapt the social savings approach to ask, 'how much smaller would the UK economy have been if transport technology had not advanced beyond 1850'. The resulting counterfactual takes us back to Baxter's original contribution, by focusing on the price differential between the base-year and end-year as the measure of per unit resource saving. But, as Foreman-Peck (1991) observes, a static calculation of this sort is bound to understate the true figure, because it ignores the dynamic consequences of technological improvement. His model emphasises the higher level of savings made possible by the railway; a more mundane (and inherently less quantifiable) approach would emphasise the gains from additional trade on institutions and individuals.

[1] The standard formula for the social savings is $(p' - p) \times q$ where q refers to the volume of traffic carried by railways, and p and p' represent the cost (market price) of rail and non-rail transportation respectively. The social savings (SS) may be expressed relative to total revenue ($R = p \times q$) and simplified as follows:

$$\frac{SS}{R} = \frac{(p' - p)q}{pq} = \frac{p' - pq}{pq} = \left(\frac{p'}{p} - 1\right)$$

This expression may be multiplied by the share of railway revenue in gross domestic product (GDP) to generate the ratio of social savings to national income.

The total factor productivity (TFP) index can be represented as either the difference between the change in output and the weighted average change in inputs, or as the difference between the change in output price and the weighted average change in input prices (the so-called 'price dual' formulation). The TFP index thus measures the resource savings created by improvements in technical efficiency in the production of output.

The TFP index may be used to extrapolate (SS/R) for years in which price data are not secure. The ratio of p'/p in 1865 may be calculated from known parameters ($R/GDP = 0.044$; and the benchmark calculation of $SS/GDP = 0.075$) at 2.7045. In 1890, $R/GDP = 0.061$; the value of the TFP index (with 1865 = 1) was 1.28 (calculated from the annual rate of 1 per cent p.a. reported by Hawke 1970; and Foreman-Peck 1991). The ratio of social savings to national income is thus:

$$SS_{90}/GDP_{90} = (R_{90}/GDP_{90})[(TFP)(p'/p) - 1] = 0.061 \times [(2.7045 \times 1.28) - 1] = 0.15$$

or 15 per cent, as noted in the text.

Economies of speed

The social savings methodology focuses on resource savings due to lower prices. But many contemporaries argued that the largest savings came from the increased speed that rail travel and telegraphic communication afforded. 'Railways save time', observed Wyndham Harding in 1848, arguing that the more rapid flow of goods through the economy released capital otherwise 'unproductively locked up in the shape of goods in transit . . . to be invested reproductively in the transactions of commerce' (Harding 1848: 341). Newmarch (1857) suggested that the increased speed of moving goods from factory to shop enabled retailers to reduce their stocks of manufactured goods from ten days consumption to three days (quoted in Hawke 1970: 190). Stock turnover certainly sped up for retailers between the 1830s and the end of the century (Jefferys 1954; Alexander 1970). By 1919, Marshall could write that, 'the post, the telegraph, the telephone, and the almost omnipresent quick railway service of a compact western country, supplemented by motor traffic' ensured low inventory holdings by dealers (Marshall 1919: 278).

But we should not exaggerate the gains from lower inventories. In part, this is because the diffusion of faster rail transport merely redistributed the storage problem from retailer and wholesaler to producer. If a producer wished to respond quickly to an increase in orders in order to remain competitive, maintaining stocks of materials was essential. This was, in certain industries, offset by the increasing speed of production, which reduced the time between receipt and fulfilment of orders. But for those industries which were not characterised by faster throughput, which produced for relatively narrow markets, or which made a wide array of products (or were otherwise risk-averse about the extent to which 'made to order' production was possible), stocks remained essential.

More important were reductions in the stocks of overseas goods, especially raw materials. In the *Statist* of 8 August 1903, it was noted that 'In the old times it was so uncertain when goods would be received that it was absolutely essential to keep large stocks always on hand'; all that had changed as 'one of the consequence[s] of the beneficent invention' of the international telegraph. But it was not simply improvements in communication. Faster and more reliable steamboats also permitted lower equilibrium stock-holdings.

Distribution

The extent to which improvements in transportation and communication contributed to the maturing of the British economy depended in no small part on the responsiveness of the distributive sector, which provided the infrastructure for trade. Certainly, the state of retail and wholesale trade in 1850 was not compatible with a modern economy. How did it adapt?

The distributive trades in mid-century reflected the persistence of pre-industrial modes of commerce. Consumers could buy from a variety of sources: fixed retailers in towns and villages (grocers, haberdashers, etc.), who in turn bought their goods either directly from producers or from intermediaries (wholesalers); the retailer/producer, skilled tradesmen who made and sold their own wares (e.g., tailors, shoe makers, tinkers); weekly or daily markets, where farm produce could be bought; fairs, offering a wider variety of goods; and peddlers, chapmen and other itinerant traders. Higgling over price was standard practice. The wholesale trade, which linked producer to producer as well as producer to consumer, was a complex network of traders and hierarchies, with a confusing mêlée of names (jobbers and braggers, factors, brokers and bummarees); imported and manufactured goods usually passed through at least two stages of intermediation. The crux of the network was information and credit: information about producers and their supplies, consumers and their demands; credit to permit purchases in an economy still geared to a significant degree to the seasonal rhythms of agricultural production.

Urbanisation and rising real incomes effected changes in the demand side of the market; the rise of larger-scale production of manufactures, alongside the improvement of transport and communications, stimulated rationalisation on the supply side. Changes in retailing between 1850 and 1914 were largely a matter of sloughing off archaic forms of trade: the retailer-producer, forced out by competition from factory-made consumer goods and the substitution of imported for home-grown foodstuffs; and the replacement of the pedlar by the shop, so that consumers travelled to the retailers, rather than the other way around. The process of change was inexorable, but slow; connections and arrangements that had formed over generations did not melt away overnight.

Wholesale trade became more streamlined, as improvements in both transport and communication reduced the need for so many layers of intermediation. At the same time, the decline in retailer-producers (and the rise of imported goods) opened up new opportunities for middlemen, as the gap of time and space between producer and final customer widened. The increased volume and range of goods available in the market made it increasingly difficult for wholesalers to sell everything; moreover, retailers demanded of them more information on products and suppliers. The inevitable result was greater specialisation among middlemen; the general wholesaler was an endangered species by 1870.

The manufacturers also created change. Brand-name products bearing the producer's imprint began to replace generic goods for a wide array of manufactured consumer items. Branding (with the attendant advertising) was made possible by the development of standardised production; it was made attractive by the geographical widening of the market and the opportunity to establish a national reputation for firms that had been previously limited to local custom (Alford 1977). It also enabled producers to lower their selling costs, by cutting out the middleman – how much specialised knowledge could a wholesaler have about a standardised, packaged product that was known intimately by every consumer? The establishment of specialised sales departments within manufacturing firms also overcame the 'principal-agent' problem inherent in wholesale trade – how to monitor and improve sales effort and presentation – by internalising a function that had been previously met outside the firm. By 1938, only 40 per cent of retail goods were handled by wholesalers.

In the long term, the most dramatic transformation in the distributive system was the replacement of the small-scale independent retailer by large-scale, high-volume emporiums of trade – the multiple shop, the department store and the Co-operative store. The process of retail reorganisation began in Victorian Britain. W. H. Smith in stationery and bookselling, Jesse Boot in pharmaceuticals, Thomas Lipton in groceries, Freeman, Hardy and Willis in footwear and Singer in sewing machines are among the best-known examples of the multiple shop, or chain-store. The advantage that the multiples had over unit retailers was their ability to buy in bulk, at a discount. They too were able to internalise the services of the wholesaler, by establishing purchasing departments that could negotiate directly with manufacturers. By 1930, multiples bought only 5 per cent of their goods from wholesalers, compared to over 30 per cent for unit retailers.

The department store is associated pre-eminently with Bon Marché in Paris, although A. T. Stewart and Macy's in New York also have claims to first-mover status. The pioneers in Britain were Whiteley's and Harrods of London. The idea of the department store was to combine an array of different products (groceries, shoes, clothing, draperies) under one roof and one management, to attract customers by making shopping less arduous. Inevitably, it was aimed at a more exclusive clientele; the emphasis was less on cheap prices for standardised goods than on quality service at a reasonable price. It would, of course, do no good to be out-competed by specialist shops; and the administrative expenses of running a large department store were significantly larger than for the unit retailer. So steps were taken to increase stock turnover to keep transactions costs down, and to ease administrative burdens. Department stores were among the pioneers of store advertising, the window display, loss-leader promotions, and other mechanisms to bring customers into the store and send goods out. Within the store, costs were carefully monitored by the careful use of records, department by department.

The Co-operative store began in the 1840s as a regional initiative, a statement of political solidarity in the marketplace. The 'Co-op' spread rapidly in the north, before gaining strong representation in London and the south-west. The Co-operative societies developed a market strategy quite different from anything that existed previously or elsewhere in retailing. First, they practised profit sharing, by providing dividends to regular customers. This was partly motivated to ensure loyalty to the firm, but was also a reflection of underlying distributive principles. Second, they practised backward vertical integration, first establishing Co-operative Wholesale Societies, and later Co-operative Productive Societies. By 1938, fully 40 per cent of the goods sold in Co-ops were produced by Co-operative societies; the proportion of all other goods that were sold under retailer imprints was only 6 per cent.

All of these elements, taken in tandem, have suggested to some historians that there was a retailing revolution between 1850 and 1940. But this is to exaggerate the pace of change. The corner store was still very much alive in urban (working-class) districts in 1940, as was the village shop in the countryside. The revolution in goods transportation had not yet been combined with a revolution in personal transportation that would permit every customer easy access to the new stores. Of the 607,000 retailers recorded at the 1911 Census of England and Wales (a retailer for every fifty-nine people), over 95 per cent were single shops; unit retailers in 1938 accounted for 88 per cent of the 750,000 retail outlets recorded in the UK (one for every sixty-three people) (Jefferys 1954; Winstanley 1983: 40–1). The distribution of goods was somewhat more concentrated, as we would expect. But here, too, a cautious appraisal seems best. In 1938, co-operative stores accounted for 11 per cent of consumer sales in the UK; department stores for 5 per cent; multiples for 19 per cent; and unit retailers for 65 per cent (mail-order accounted for less than 0.5 per cent). The share of unit retailers had shrunk from 88 per cent in 1900, and 80 per cent in 1920, but the transformation was far from complete. Retail distribution was one of the last habitats of the small entrepreneur.

Unit retailers survived partly because of the thinness of transportation networks, and partly because of the limited opportunities for change in the distribution of many consumer goods. Fruits and vegetables, fish, tobacco, newspapers and other perishable (or time-sensitive) goods were invariably sold by small shops; so too were petrol (and motor cars), jewellery, books, radios, etc. Trade in many of the sectors that had pioneered multiple shops in the 1870s was still dominated by unit retailers sixty years later (magazine and periodical sales, despite Smith's and Menzies; tobacco, despite Salmon and Gluckstein). Jefferys (1949) noted a strong correlation between the resilience of unit retailers and changes in wholesale distribution networks. Where direct links between producer and retailer were economically viable, small shopkeepers were squeezed out of the marketplace. The survival of the rest (and the 25,000–30,000 wholesale merchants who supplied them) reveals the incompleteness of the revolution in distribution.

Change was probably also slowed by the blunting of the competitive edge of the new retailers after the adoption of resale price maintenance (RPM), by which producers established a fixed price for their goods, and refused to supply any retailer who did not agree to sell at that price. RPM was a coalition between manufacturers, anxious to weaken the bargaining power of the multiples, and retailing associations, anxious to curtail the discount system by which suppliers negotiated special arrangements with preferred customers. By 1900, perhaps 3 per cent of consumer goods (concentrated in grocery, pharmacy, and tobacco products) were covered by fixed prices; by 1938, the proportion had risen to 30 per cent, and products covered included books (through the Net Book Agreement), clothing, milk and motor vehicles (Winstanley 1994). RPM forced retailers to place more emphasis on improved service to attract customers. The days of haggling over price at the local store had long since passed.

Finance

The financial sector provides services to both individuals and businesses. The provision of financial services to private customers is primarily involved with management of funds over time: in the short run, by providing current accounts (and overdraft facilities) to smooth expenses against current income; in the longer term, by facilitating the purchase of big-ticket items, by accumulating deposits or by lending against future income (via mortgages, or hire purchase scrip). The sector also provides instruments to reduce the burdens of risk, including life and property insurance. (See also chapter 10, which considers the impact of financial services on the economy.)

Financial services to businesses involve fund management over time and space. Businesses have many of the same needs as individuals - the need to smooth payments against revenues; the need to finance large-ticket expenditures out of expected future income; the need to minimise the consequences of risk. The spatial component arises (and becomes increasingly important as the marketplace expands) because businesses undertake transactions at a distance. Manufacturers operate in the local community; banks and finance houses provide the network (either informally through arrangements with peers, or formally by having branches or offices) that links producers and customers, or producers and suppliers. Financiers also assist businesses by turning credit notes (the inland bill of exchange at the beginning of our period, the cheque at the end) into cash, which can then be used to pay wages or meet other liquid obligations.

The history of the financial sector between 1850 and 1939 is in large part the rationalising of these services through market segmentation. Bill brokers dealt with discounting; banks with advances (overdrafts and short-term loans) to tide businesses over; the stock market with the provision of long-term capital for business expansion; savings banks with small private depositors; building societies with house purchases; insurance companies specialised by type of risk (fire, life, marine, etc.). The boundaries, while not absolutely rigid (banks continued to discount notes, for example), may be viewed as a defensive reaction to the added complexity of finance arising from the increased scale, geographic spread and speed of market transactions. The best way to maintain efficiency in such a system was by limiting the range of activities on offer and by developing knowledge and establishing routines to carry out those tasks effectively and at low cost to the customer.

The volume of deposits held at banks increased more than sixfold between 1850 and 1913. Bank remittances also increased at a rapid pace before 1913, reflecting the rising monetisation of transactions and the shift towards an increasingly national system of payments (Collins 1994). The number of bank offices increased by 3 per cent a year between 1855 and 1913 (Nishimura 1971: 80–1). The majority of these were branches of joint-stock banks; the private country banking system, so important during early industrialisation, fell away rapidly after 1850. The informal arrangements that characterised dealings among private banks (especially between the provinces and London) were abandoned in favour of a formal network of interlinked facilities. The routinisation of bank business permitted delegation of operations to branches, co-ordinated but not controlled by head office.

The efficiency advantages of joint-stock over private banks resulted in the consolidation of the system. The period from 1896 to 1913 is known as the era of bank amalgamation; more truthfully, it saw the acceleration of a well-established trend towards concentration. In 1855 there were over 400 banks in England and Wales; by 1896, fewer than 200; and by 1913, only 70. The data on bank branches emphasise the extent of consolidation – by 1913, 94 per cent of all offices were in the hands of twenty-one banks, with the top three accounting for a third of the total (Midland having 846 branches; Lloyds, 673; and Barclays, 599).

A second wave of concentration between 1915 and 1920 had a different character, involving the merging of joint-stock banks with established branch networks, rather than the takeover of private banks with limited branch facilities. Barclays, for example, merged its 839 branches with the 601 branches of the London, Provincial and South Western in 1918, gaining 277 additional branches in two other mergers in 1919 (Ackrill and Hannah, 2001). The move towards bigness appeared inexorable. As with the railways, whether amalgamation would have proceeded to its logical conclusion, we shall never know. Governmental unease with the entire process led to informal control of any future mergers in 1920; consolidation was effectively stopped in its tracks (Balogh 1947).

Banking had become an oligopoly. The 'Big Five' (the three above, plus the Westminster and National Provincial) controlled 80 per cent of deposits. The 'growing tendency to . . . restrictive cartel agreements' before 1913 (Goodhart 1986: 188) was intensified. By 1921, the banks had agreed on a ceiling on interest on deposit payments, set 2 per cent below bank rate (with a minimum of 0.5 per cent), and minimum overdraft rates of 5 per cent. During the depressed 1930s, overdraft rates could fall to 4 or even 3 per cent, but the incentives to cheat on the 'gentleman's agreement' were limited by the interest inelasticity of borrowing. The exceptions to the 5 per cent rule are perhaps better viewed as a means of first-degree price discrimination, offered to local (usually large) businesses to ensure their continued loyalty to the bank. The personal touch had not disappeared completely, even in the routinised world of the 1930s, and it contributed to client bargaining at the margin.

Banks, like railways, tended to compete not on price but on service, primarily by building more branches to facilitate access to the system of payments and advances. The number of bank offices in England and Wales increased by over 40 per cent between 1921 and 1931 (increasing the density from 1 bank office per 5,000 in 1921 to 1 per 4,000 in 1931 – a far cry from the 1855 ratio of 1 per 23,500). The beneficiaries were producers and merchants rather than individuals (as late as 1936, two-thirds of loans from Barclays banks were to businesses, much of the rest to professional clients who maintained joint business/private accounts). The expansion of branches no doubt increased the speed of transactions, but given the 'wasteful duplication of facilities' (Clapham 1938: 283), it is by no means clear that the social benefits outweighed their costs. That the banks themselves benefited seems evident from the average profit rate of the 'Big Five' of 8 per cent in 1938.

The rise of branch banking, as well as the consolidation of banking firms, placed a premium on efficient organisation and cost control. Centralisation of authority was essential to effective management of the branch system; it also enabled consolidation of certain tasks at head office, and promoted functional specialisation in general. Cost control, as practised by the Big Five banks during the interwar period, included the introduction of accounting machines, standardised book-keeping and hierarchical systems of management (Wardley 2000). Mechanisation only slowly diffused to the branches, beginning with the largest, where the greatest efficiency gains could be realised. Even by 1938, fewer than 12 per cent of Lloyds' branches used office machines.

The logic of market segmentation dictated that joint-stock banks dealt almost exclusively with 'people of private means', leaving the market for lower-middle-class and working-class funds to the savings banks and the building societies. Savings banks were considerably more generous with deposit rates (2.5 per cent on ordinary accounts) and building societies even more so (4.5 per cent after tax). By 1939, there were 2.5 million depositors in the Post Office Savings Bank, with accumulated funds of £550 million; trustee savings banks accounted for a further £250 million. The real value of deposits in all savings banks rose by almost 4 per cent a year, 1870–1913, and at over 7 per cent p.a., 1920–38. These growth rates reflected not only rising incomes, but also a move towards thrift, or at least a shift towards more liquid savings vehicles, away from consumer durables (furniture, clothing, etc.) that had been the dominant means for working-class households to meet precautionary needs before the First World War (Johnson 1985).

The fastest-growing component of consumer banking between the wars was the building society, the assets (shares and deposits) of which, in 1938 prices, stood at £51 million in 1920 and £717 million in 1938. The societies had a narrow economic role, being designed to pool funds for house building and purchase – another example of market segmentation. Glimmerings of another revolution in consumer finance may be seen in the 1930s, with the innovation of hire purchase agreements to buy durables, such as cars and radios, at 8 per cent interest. But the movement was very much in its infancy.

Businesses interested in long-term funds did not look to the banks, but relied instead on reinvested profits or on capital raised on the stock market. We have no data on the number of trades on the London (or provincial) stock exchanges before 1939; the available data on new capital issues (which grew at 2 per cent a year in real terms between 1870 and 1913, but largely stagnated during the interwar period) exclude the trading of established stock. The nominal value of all stocks quoted on the London exchange rose at almost 4 per cent a year between 1853 and 1913, but we have no way of knowing the average rate of stock turnover. The membership of the London exchange increased sixfold between 1850 and 1905 (when restrictions on entry were imposed), but this probably understates the scale of increase, since it excludes any productivity increase. Certainly, in the interwar period, the volume of business continued to increase, albeit slowly, even as the number of brokers and jobbers registered on the exchange fell.

Clapham (1938) opined that 'of stock-exchange companies there was probably no group so important as the Insurance Companies', who were conservative investors with a great deal of money to invest. The reported capital assets of life assurance companies alone in 1910 were over £450 million, or more than 20 per cent of national income. Burial insurance had become part of the fabric of Edwardian working-class life, with 31 million policies in force in 1910, each valued at about £10. Ordinary life assurance was designed for wealthier customers; there were some 2.8 million policies in 1910, each valued at £285. The real value of life insurance premiums rose by 3.3 per cent a year between 1913 and 1938; only one other part of the insurance industry grew faster – premiums on motor vehicles.

Much of the demand for British financial services before 1914 came from overseas. From Lloyd's of London in marine insurance, to Barings, Hambros and Rothschilds in (international) merchant banking, British companies were at the core of the international system of financing and underwriting international trade. British dominance was established by the 1860s. In the absence of any serious rival, it intensified over the next half-century, as the international economy expanded in a burst of globalisation. In 1903, Felix Schuster could confidently state, 'we are . . . the financial centre of the world'. By 1938, however, that would have seemed a hollow claim, after a quarter-century in which the city was battered first by war, then by slump and financial crisis; between 1920 and 1935, receipts from the export of financial services fell by half.

Personal services

Our knowledge of personal service expenditures in the Victorian period is fragmentary at best, but it probably doubled in real terms per head between 1871 and 1900, rising faster than consumer expenditures overall. The share of services in the average consumption bundle roughly increased from 25 per cent in 1871 to 30 per cent in 1891 (Jefferys and Walters 1955).

The data for the twentieth century are more detailed and sound. The top line in Figure 5.2 displays the level of personal service spending per capita for 1900–38, measured in constant (1938) prices. The line is drawn on a semi-logarithmic scale to ease interpretation of growth (a steady line indicates a steady rate of growth). An Edwardian plateau is evident; service spending then fell slightly during the war, as disposable incomes were reduced, before rising steadily (at about 1.7 per cent a year) over the interwar period. The lower lines in the graph indicate the share of services in total consumer expenditure, in real terms (the solid line) and at current prices (the dotted line). The proportion in real terms held steady at 30–2 per cent over the entire period, indicating that service spending grew in line with consumption overall. The divergence between the real and nominal shares arises from movements in the price of services relative to goods. The stable difference between 1900 and 1913 indicates a steady price differential, while the collapse in the nominal service share across the First World War was due to price stickiness in rents, domestic service and other services, relative to the goods sector of the economy. Price stickiness also accounts for the convergence in the interwar years, as the average price of services grew more slowly than goods prices between 1920 and 1931 and fell less drastically during the depression.

Table 5.4 allocates consumer spending by product. The dominant category is housing, covering not only rents, but also payments to local authorities in the form of rates (see section on public utilities, below). This figure is not restricted to actual payments to landlords but includes the imputed value of owner-occupied housing. The other large personal service sectors are catering (hotels and restaurants), public transportation and domestic service. No other service category accounted for as much as 2 per cent of total consumer spending in 1938. Rising incomes enabled consumers to experience both a greater volume and a greater diversity

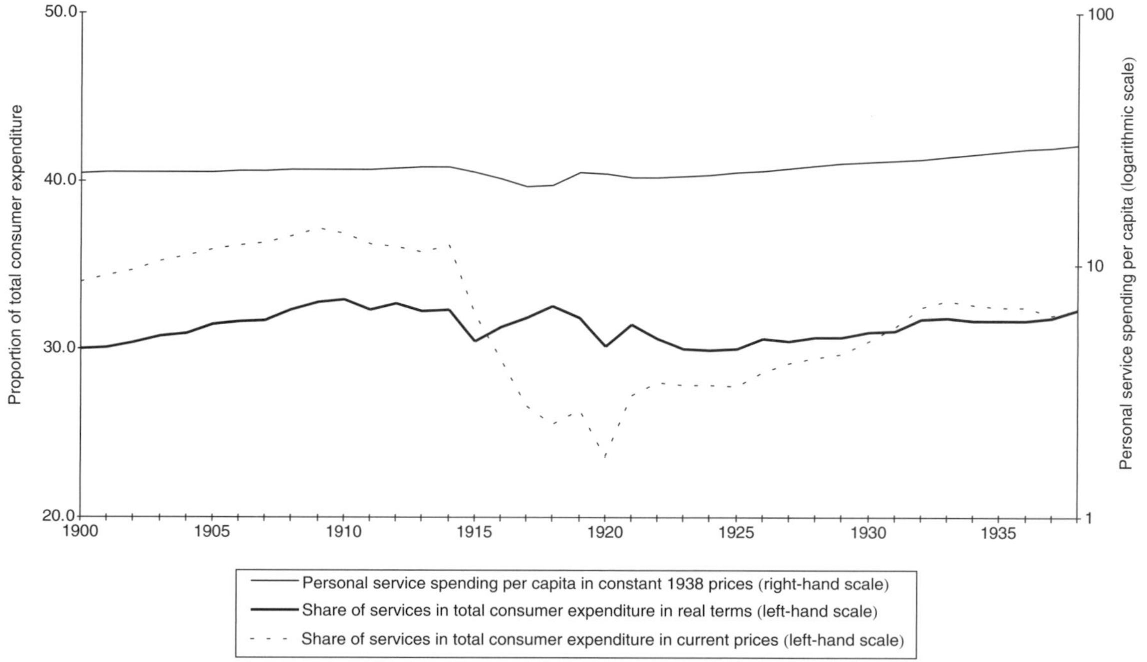

Figure 5.2 Consumer expenditure on personal services, 1900–38

Source: Calculated from Feinstein 1972.

Table 5.4 The distribution of consumption expenditures on market services, 1900–13 and 1920–38 (% by category)

	1900–13	1920–38
Housing (rents and rates)	29.6	30.1
Catering[a]	21.5	16.7
Public transport	10.7	14.7
Domestic service[b]	10.4	8.1
Private medical care	5.6	3.4
Laundry and other household services	5.3	6.9
Entertainment	4.1	5.9
Insurance	2.5	4.2
Religious and charitable organisations	2.5	1.9
Private education	1.9	1.7
Fees paid to local authorities[c]	1.2	1.7
Communications	1.1	1.8
Personal care	0.9	1.5
Other miscellaneous services	2.7	1.3

[a] Includes cost of food served, but excludes alcoholic drink.
[b] Includes imputed costs of room and board for live-in servants.
[c] Local authority fees include charges for museums, libraries, educational charges, etc., but exclude rates.

Sources: Calculated from Prest 1954; Stone and Rowe 1966; Feinstein 1972.

of services, as the expansion of public entertainment (cinema, theatre, spectator sports) and personal care (chiropodist, hairdresser, manicurist) attests. But we should not exaggerate the changes: for example, although private telephone usage boomed between 1920 and 1938 (local calls grew at 10 per cent a year), fewer than 10 per cent of households rented a handset in 1938.

Domestic service

Domestic service was the largest personal service sector in 1851 and grew rapidly over the next twenty years (see Table 5.5). By 1871, fully a third of working-women were in service. The continued expansion was due in large part to the growth of the middle class, which according to some sources doubled in size between 1851 and 1871. The typical domestic servant in this period was the 'maid of all work', working alone: about two-thirds of servant-keeping households in 1871 had only one servant (Ebery and Preston 1972). The large retinues beloved of popular fiction were rare even in the high Victorian age.

The sharp deceleration in employment growth after 1871 was due primarily to changes on the supply side, as employment opportunities elsewhere beckoned. The supply pressure intensified during the First World War, as male servants left for combat, and many women abandoned service in favour of higher wages and greater freedom in munitions factories,

Table 5.5 Domestic service in England and Wales, 1851–1931 (thousands)

	Indoor service		Outdoor service	
	Male	Female	Male	Charwomen
1851	74.3	751.6	–	55.4
1861	62.1	962.8	–	65.3
1871	68.4	1,204.4	–	77.7
1881	56.3	1,230.4	160.4	92.5
1891	58.5	1,386.2	–	104.8
1901	64.2	1,330.8	180.3	111.8
1911	54.3	1,359.4	226.3	126.1
1921	61.0	1,148.7	–	118.5
1931	78.5	1,332.2	–	140.1

Notes: The number of indoor servants is inflated in 1891 by the inclusion of 'women engaged in domestic service about the[ir] home'. The extent of overe-numeration was probably about 100 thousand.

Outdoor service (domestic gardeners, domestic coachmen and grooms, gamekeepers, domestic chauffeurs) can only be measured with accuracy in 1881, 1901 and 1911. In other years it is aggregated with commercial activities.

Source: Census of Population.

on public transport and elsewhere on the home front. The government appointed the Domestic Service Committee in 1918 to investigate the problem of the 'servant shortage'. As it happened, there was a resurgence in service employment after the war, especially for women, who were faced with the evaporation of wartime jobs and limited employment opportunities (and rising unemployment) in shops and offices.

The character of domestic service changed slowly, most notably with the replacement of the live-in maid by the 'daily'. The rise of charwomen and other day servants (the fastest-growing category of servant after 1871) reflected the transformation of domestic service from indivisible to divisible consumption. Domestic servants were becoming increasingly expensive, especially given the imputed costs of living-in. The sub-division of service (effectively sharing servants among households) was a means to overcome the problem of rising expense (it also passed the burden of living costs to the servant). Technological change in the home helped make this a feasible solution. The diffusion of electrical appliances such as the vacuum cleaner increased the productivity of servants, while the replacement of coal hearths by electric and gas heaters significantly reduced the need for hours of cleaning. By 1931, perhaps a third of female 'indoor domestic servants' were 'dailies' (calculated from Chapman and Knight 1953: 219).

The trend towards daily cleaners and charwomen began among the lower middle classes – the Mr Pooters who had been able to afford (if barely) a maid-of-all-work in 1900, but could no longer in 1930. The average lower-middle-class household consumed about 1.5 days of paid help a week in 1937/8 (calculated from Prais and Houthakker 1955). After 1939, the pattern spread to better-off households, such that by 1951 there were twice as many non-resident as resident female domestic servants (and only 260,000 of both combined). The shift from servant to domestic was all but complete.

Public utilities

Not all services were provided by the private sector; nor were all services purchased in the marketplace. We have already noted the transfer of certain 'public services' from private to government control (telegraphs, telephones). Other services have always been the province of local or central government, many of them related to the creation and maintenance of the market infrastructure. Defence protects property against foreign aggression, and lowers the risks of overseas trade and finance; the police system defends property as well as life against criminal acts; the justice system prosecutes criminals, and also enforces the law of contract. None of these services is controlled directly by the price mechanism; they fall instead into the category of non-market services, in which decisions about resource allocation are made administratively.

The scale of non-market services clearly grew in this period. In 1870, current expenditures on goods and services by central and local government was 5 per cent of national income; by 1913, it had risen to 8 per cent; by 1937, to 12.5 per cent. The rising share reflects a broadening sense of what constituted the public interest and, therefore, the purview of government. In the words of the *Economist*, 'little by little, and year by year, the fabric of State expenditure and State responsibility is built up like a coral island, cell by cell' (Clapham 1938: 398).

The accretion of direct government service expenditures was located primarily in education and (after 1911) health. Health spending grew rapidly during the interwar period (at about 5 per cent a year), although its share of total expenditure was only about half that of education in 1938. Educational expenses accounted for 22 per cent of non-military expenditures in 1890, and 28.5 per cent in 1938. The number of children attending elementary schools rose from 387,000 in 1851 to over 6 million in 1913 (plus 208,000 in secondary schools). In 1911, over three-quarters of children aged between 5 and 14 attended school; fifty years earlier the proportion had been only 18.5 per cent; by 1931, it had increased to 83.6 per cent. This was an expansion in government services that clearly brought benefits for workers and the economy as a whole. But for many critics, the commitment to formal human capital investment had come late and remained incomplete, especially at the secondary and technical levels. The new reforms introduced during the Second World War (the 1944 Education Act) were designed to redress some of these imbalances.

Almost the entirety of educational spending was undertaken by local authorities, which took ultimate responsibility for shaping classroom policy in the years between the Education Acts of 1870 and 1944, albeit within parameters set by central government. But local authorities were not responsible for the entire bill; their expenditures were partly financed by grants-in-aid from the central government, transferred from income tax revenues. The same structures of financing applied to health expenditures. Local rates (property taxes) were to be used for more clearly local obligations, such as (local) roads and public lighting, fire service, water, sewage and garbage disposal, park maintenance and other 'environmental services'. These also grew in significance over time, in part because of the increased demands placed on urban communities by population growth, as well as the diffusion of ideals of civic virtue.

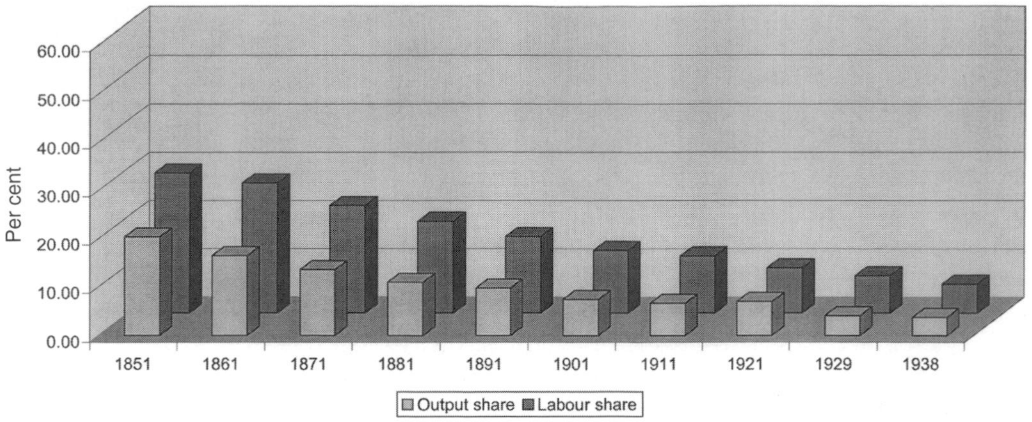

(a) Primary sector

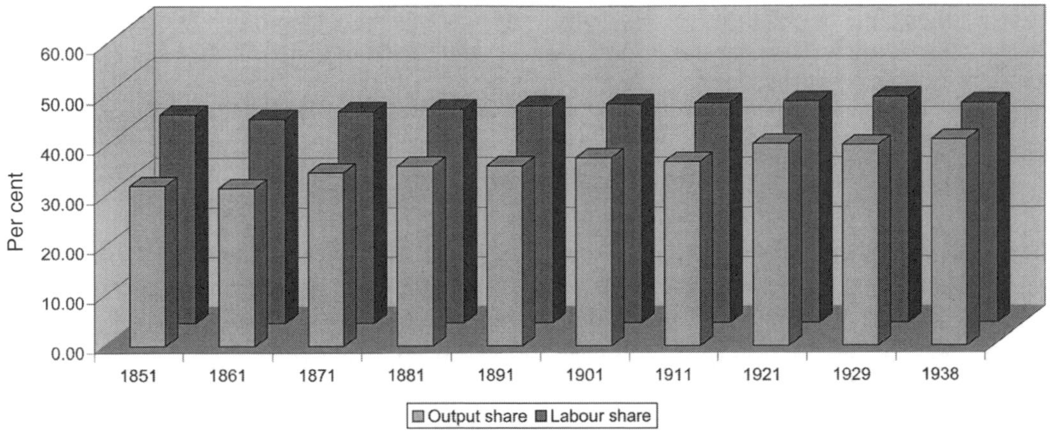

(b) Secondary sector

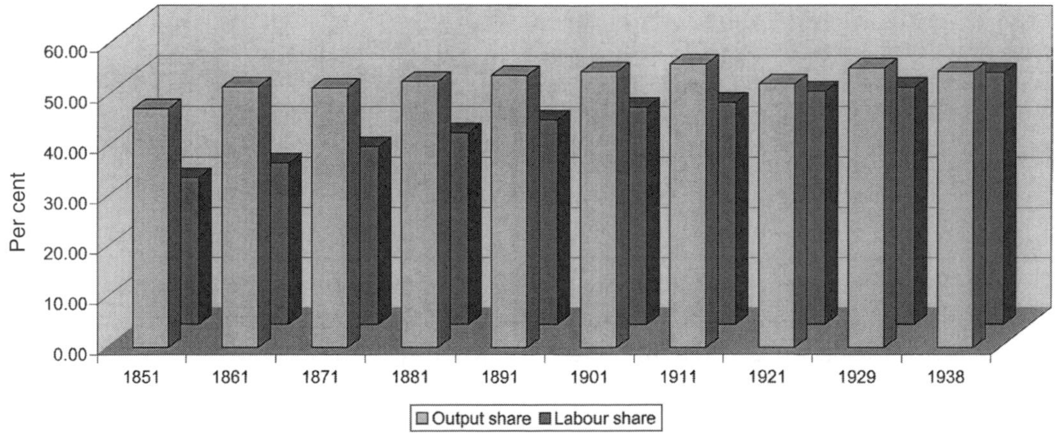

(c) Tertiary sector

Figure 5.3 The share of primary, secondary and tertiary sectors in output and employment, 1851–1938

Source: Calculated from Feinstein 1972.

THE GROWTH OF THE SERVICE SECTOR

Colin Clark (1940) argued that the relative size of the tertiary sector is bound to increase in mature economies. Because the income elasticity of demand for services is generally greater than one, its share of total consumption grows as incomes rise; and since productivity growth in services is slower than in the rest of the economy, it needs to hoard an ever-larger share of total resources to keep up with demand. A corollary (attributed to Baumol) is that the growth rate in the economy as a whole will inevitably decline, as more resources are locked into the slow-growing tertiary sector.

The historical evidence for the Clark hypotheses is displayed in Figure 5.3, which charts the share of the primary, secondary and tertiary sectors in aggregate output and employment between 1851 and 1938. It is clear that employment grew faster than output in services, and that the share of services in national income increased in both (albeit very slowly in output terms). Resources were being continuously transferred to a slow-growing sector. How should we explain this paradox?

Table 5.6 reconfigures the evidence from Figure 5.3to measure the relative productivity performance of the three sectors for 1851–1938. Relative productivity is calculated by dividing the output share of each sector by its labour force share; the average for all sectors combined is 100 in each year. Services are revealed as the high-productivity sector in the UK economy throughout the period; in 1851, labour in services is more than twice as productive as in either agriculture or services. By the late 1930s, services were 15 per cent more productive than industry. Resources flowed into services to earn larger returns through higher productivity. Once we distinguish levels from changes in levels, the paradox disappears.

Over time, resource transfers narrowed the productivity advantage of services. The primary sector played almost no part in this process (the apparent jump in the relative productivity of agriculture and industry between 1911 and 1921 is largely due to the separation of Eire); convergence was due almost entirely to the relative productivity performance of industry and

Table 5.6 Relative productivity growth by sector, 1851–1938

	Primary	Secondary	Tertiary
1851	70.3	76.9	162.7
1861	61.3	77.5	161.1
1871	61.1	82.3	145.6
1881	57.8	84.3	138.7
1891	61.8	83.1	133.0
1901	57.2	86.1	127.0
1911	56.5	84.0	127.6
1921	74.8	91.6	113.1
1929	53.2	89.3	117.9
1938	62.9	94.1	109.6

Notes: Calculated as the ratio of the sectoral share of national income to the sectoral share of employment.

Source: as for Figure 5.3.

Table 5.7 Labour and total factor productivity growth by sector, 1856–1938 (% p.a.)

	Output	Factor inputs		Total factor inputs	Labour productivity	Total factor productivity
		Labour	Capital			
Primary sector						
1856–1873	1.03	−0.63	1.43	−0.11	1.66	1.14
1873–1913	0.72	0.03	1.18	0.32	0.75	0.40
1913–1924	−0.55	−0.23	−0.20	−0.22	−0.32	−0.33
1924–1937	0.46	−2.00	0.06	−1.48	2.45	1.94
Secondary sector						
1856–1873	2.67	0.47	3.09	1.13	2.20	1.54
1873–1913	2.01	1.11	2.45	1.45	0.90	0.57
1913–1924	1.32	−0.34	2.48	0.37	1.66	0.95
1924–1937	3.63	1.35	1.50	1.39	2.28	2.24
Tertiary sector						
1856–1873	2.29	0.96	2.32	1.30	1.33	0.99
1873–1913	2.02	1.46	2.21	1.76	0.56	0.26
1913–1924	−0.24	−0.39	0.80	−0.09	0.15	−0.15
1924–1937	1.89	1.89	1.96	1.91	0.00	−0.02

Sources: Output and labour calculated from Feinstein 1972; capital from Feinstein (1988) for 1856–1920; Feinstein 1965, for 1920–1938. In all cases, the data were corrected for the separation of Eire after 1922.

services. The table confirms the slower relative growth of productivity in services, but also shows that the service sector remained the most productive part of the economy on average, at least in terms of output per worker.

TOTAL PRODUCTIVITY PERFORMANCE IN SERVICES, 1856–1937

Table 5.7 provides estimates of total factor productivity (TFP) growth, by sector, for subperiods within 1850 and 1939. The table uses data on the growth rate of output, labour and capital across cycle peaks to measure the growth rate of total factor inputs (a weighted average of labour and capital); growth in labour productivity (the difference between the growth rates of output and labour); and growth in TFP (the difference between the growth rate of output and total factor inputs).

The table reiterates the finding that employment growth was faster in the tertiary sector than in the rest of the economy (and that the primary sector shed labour); note also that capital growth in services was relatively rapid in all periods except 1913–24. The output data are consistent with Clark's hypothesis regarding the income elasticity of demand for the products of the three sectors, although we should be

Table 5.8 Labour and total factor productivity growth within the service sector, 1924–37 (% p.a.)

	Output	Factor inputs		Total factor inputs	Labour productivity	Total factor productivity
		Labour	Capital			
Distribution	1.88	2.60	1.32	1.88	−0.72	0.00
Transport and Communication	1.54	0.58	0.06	0.41	0.96	1.13
Finance, etc.	1.63	1.88	–	–	−0.25	–
Professional services	1.34	1.69	4.85	2.95	−0.35	−1.61
Public administration	1.30	1.52	2.08	1.80	−0.22	−0.50
Dwellings	1.92	–	3.19	–	–	−1.27
Miscellaneous services	1.82	2.20	1.04	1.74	−0.38	0.08

Sources: Output and labour calculated from Feinstein 1972; capital from Feinstein 1965.

careful not to ascribe all of the output change in the primary sector to demand-side factors – there was a shift towards imported foodstuffs and raw materials and away from domestic production during much of this period.

The table not only confirms that labour productivity growth was clearly lower in services than in the rest of the economy, it also shows that the productivity gap grew larger over time. During the interwar period, labour productivity in services was zero, but above 2 per cent a year in the other sectors. The difference is even more pronounced in TFP terms: during 1913–24 and 1924–37, correcting for capital growth creates negative productivity growth in services.

Statistical exercises of this sort are always hazardous, and the hazards of easy inference are even greater with historical than with contemporary numbers. We should treat these calculations as suggestive rather than definitive, and should place wide margins of error around the results. But even if we recognise their limitations, the results none the less provide strong support for a pessimistic interpretation of the role of services in Britain, especially after 1913. It is worth emphasising that the role of services is at its most negative in the period (1924–37) when the data are at their most reliable, and conform most closely to modern measurement conventions.

Is it possible that the result is due to a rogue sector within services, pulling the average down? Table 5.8 suggests not, at least during 1924–37: productivity growth, though variable, appears weak across the board. Transportation and communication is the only sub-sector to show relatively strong labour and TFP growth, but it is shrinking in relative importance during this period.

There is one final, and perhaps counter-intuitive, matter to consider. Even though productivity in services was slower than in the rest of the economy, and even though the sector was increasing its consumption of available resources, it does not necessarily follow that tertiary production was acting as a drag on the economy as a whole. The crucial issue is the productivity growth rate in those services that provide intermediate inputs to the rest of the economy.

Improvements in the efficiency of producing an intermediate good will permit expansion of final output, even if the rate of productivity growth is slower than in the rest of the economy.[2] Higher productivity either releases resources to work in other sectors, or it increases the volume of materials to be made into finished goods, or it lowers input prices. In each case, the effect is equivalent to a rightward shift in the supply curve of finished goods. Conversely, an intermediate sector that experiences negative productivity growth is clearly counterbalancing any gains in the rest of the economy.

A significant proportion of the service sector (perhaps half) was concerned with the production of intermediate rather than final products during our period: business services, including both distribution and finance, much of transportation and communication and some part of government. What is the historical productivity record for intermediate services?

Before 1913, productivity in intermediate services rose slowly. TFP growth was about 1 per cent a year in railways, 1870–1910 (Foreman-Peck

[2] Consider a world in which there are only two activities: the production of coke and the production of coal. Coal is a raw material for the production of coke; it is not used for any other purpose. Coal is mined by labour from the ground without any additional factors; coke is produced by labour and coal in combination (some of the coal heats the coke oven, the rest of the coal is the raw material for making the coke). Let us imagine that there is a fixed amount of labour (100 workers), which can be used to dig coal, or to shovel coal into the coke oven (we hold capital fixed in this case on the assumption that the same coke oven can produce larger volumes of coke). Let us assume that the equilibrium in the first period assigns twenty workers to the production of coke and eighty to coal mining. Each coke maker produces 10 tons of coke; each ton of coke requires 2 tons of coal. The labour productivity of coal miners is clearly 5 tons per period. The total make of coke is 200 tons; of coal, 400 tons.

We begin by assuming that labour productivity in coke making rises by 25 per cent. The coke industry can shed labour; indeed, it will have to in order to raise the additional coal to feed the oven. The amount of labour that will be redistributed from coke to coal will depend on the productivity performance of coal mining. If productivity down the pit remains constant, 3.33 workers will be reassigned; coke output will rise to 416.5. If coal productivity rises by 10 per cent (a rich seam is discovered), only two workers will be reassigned, and coke output will rise to 450. As long as productivity below ground is non-negative, overall output will increase, even if mine productivity is slower than in the rest of the economy.

What if productivity falls below ground (via diminishing returns to already overworked seams)? More labour will have to be reassigned, and some of the benefits of higher productivity in coke will be lost. There is an indeterminate range in our example within which combined productivity still increases; but if productivity below ground falls too much (by more than 5 per cent in this case), it will reverse the gains in coke productivity and the output of both products will fall.

Finally, if coal productivity declined and there was no productivity improvement in coke production, overall output would be bound to fall, as workers would have to be reassigned from coke production to work underground to produce enough coal to keep the coke ovens at full capacity.

1991) and about 0.45 per cent a year in shipping, 1873–1913; labour productivity grew at about 0.3 per cent a year in banks and 0.25 per cent a year in communications, 1873–1913 (author's calculations). These sectors, by providing business services more efficiently, released resources to be employed in expanding output elsewhere. No such optimism, however, applies to the interwar period, as reference to Table 5.8 makes clear. For this period, the tertiary sector remains, on balance, a drag on overall economic performance.

It remains to ask, why was productivity growth slower in services than in the rest of the economy? Baumol has noted that productivity growth in certain services must, by definition, be zero – a Mozart Symphony takes the same amount of time (and labour) to play today as it did in 1780 (since it is now played with better (i.e., more expensive) instruments, it may be argued that its TFP growth is by definition negative). But this observation surely only affects a very small part of service output (broadly, cultural services). Other explanations work less well. The argument that services tend to be dominated by small-scale producers (so that the gains from large-scale production are absent) is refuted by evidence that banks, insurance and railway companies were among the largest firms in the UK in this period (Wardley 1991). Similarly, the suggestion that services are characterised by relatively low capital-output ratios (so that the gains from capital accumulation and new technology are missing) hardly applies to finance, transportation, communications or distribution, where the average capital-output ratio is higher than in many manufacturing activities (Gemmel and Wardley 1990). The share of non-marketed services is too small to make this the source of the problem (besides, productivity performance was poor in marketed services too). The puzzle becomes even more acute when it is recognised that certain service activities (sales, accounting, other clerical work) were transferred to the manufacturing sector, with the internalisation of outside services that accompanied the rise of large-scale production.

One possible explanation, which has not been much discussed in the literature, is that the output measures that underlie the calculations of productivity growth fail to capture improvements in the quality of product provided by service providers – the better service offered by retailers, railways and banks, noted above; the rising productivity of domestic servants due to new cleaning regimens; improvements in the quality of medical care, of housing and perhaps in the level of entertainment (talkies vs. silent movies, for example). Accounting for higher quality would raise productivity growth in services; it would, of course, only change the relative position of the sector if quality improvements were less important for manufactured and agricultural goods. Whether it could alter the negative perception of services in interwar Britain is an empirical question that we are not yet ready to answer.

CONCLUSIONS

We have taken a generally optimistic perspective on the role of services in contributing to the growth and maturity of the Victorian economy, but the tone has been more critical when assessing the service sector in the interwar period. The argument for the nineteenth century is that innovations in the service sector, from transportation and communications to finance and distribution, assisted in the development of a national marketplace and contributed to the broadening and deepening of economic change. This is a highly stylised depiction of change, which clearly compresses a great deal of detail (we have, for example, ignored professional services entirely) and may give a superficially optimistic gloss. For example, recent work on Britain's productivity performance in international perspective identifies 'the loss of labour-productivity leadership in services' as the major source of 'Britain's relative economic decline' relative to the US and Germany between 1870 and 1913 (Broadberry 1998: 392). TFP growth in railways was perhaps twice as rapid in the USA as in the UK between 1870 and 1910 (Foreman-Peck 1991). Comparisons of this sort beg certain questions, such as the impact of geography on journey lengths in the two countries and on consequent productivity performance, and whether UK companies would have been able to emulate the standards of transcontinental rail transport. But they certainly raise legitimate questions worthy of further thought.

Similarly, the negative evaluation of productivity performance in the interwar years may be viewed as too harsh, too monochromatic, too dismissive of service activities in which innovation and efficiency were strong. After all, there was considerable continuity between the two periods and perhaps some improvement in the latter – the pace of innovation in distribution, for example, clearly accelerated after 1920. One possible explanation for poor productivity growth in this period may have been the increasing oligopolisation of British service provision, which resulted either in directing energies towards unmeasurable service improvements, or in compromising efficiency. But here an American comparison once again leads in a different direction. Banking was an oligopolised industry, whose negative labour productivity growth between the wars may have been caused by excessive investment in new branches. But it was the absence of branch banking in the US, outlawed by government, that has been identified as a primary cause of the bank collapses of 1930–1 that did so much to intensify the great depression. Not a single commercial bank failed in Britain.

6 Agriculture, 1860–1914

MICHAEL TURNER

Contents

INTRODUCTION

The one great sector of the economy that seems to have been in more or less unremitting decline from 1860 down to the Great War was agriculture. Agriculture's share of national income fell from about 20 per cent in 1851 to 10 per cent by 1881 and 6 per cent in the first decade of the twentieth century (Collins 2000b: 9–10, 13). Agriculture's share of capital fell from three-fifths in 1832 to less than a quarter in 1885 and under 10 per cent by 1912 (Collins 2000b: 14). Agricultural rents as a proportion of total domestic income fell from about 7 per cent in the early 1850s to 2 per cent by the Great War (Collins 2000b: 7, citing Feinstein 1972: T4–5, column 7). The greatest declines were in England and Wales where the numbers employed in the farm sector, including farmers and their relatives living on the farms, fell from 1.7 to 1.2 million from 1851 to 1911 (Collins 2000b: 7). By 1901 no counties of England or Wales had more than 45 per cent of their working populations employed in agriculture. In 1851 twenty English and five Welsh counties had over 20 per cent of their total populations employed in agrarian occupations, but by 1911 only eight

English counties had more than 10 per cent and sixteen counties had 3 per cent or under. However, those that remained were involved in a more complex 'industry': in 1841 100 farm workers generated subsidiary work for 27 others off the farm; in 1881 they were supported by 47 others; and in 1911 by 67. In consequence the external inputs from 'off-farms' generated employment and income and reduced the real impact of the decline in direct employment (Thompson 1989: 197; Collins 2000b: 8). With the decline in the agrarian population there was also a decline in seasonal employment, and work was performed more often by the hard core of full-time labour, increasingly using labour-saving mechanical techniques (Walton, 1979; Collins 2000b: 9–10).

Surrounding the small islands of success such as the rise of market gardening and the supply of fresh milk to the urban areas, there was a sea of unparalleled decline. The demands of urban society became paramount. While it was a good thing that the development of railways provided fresh fruit, milk and vegetables to urban areas this benefit came at a price, because the same railways also brought non-British goods to areas where British agriculture formerly had a monopoly. The benefits of bulk carriage and the attendant economies of scale meant that even after incurring substantial freight charges many overseas suppliers from the 1880s could compete more successfully in home markets than home producers (Collins 2000b: 2–3).

THE LEGACY IN 1860 – AND LOOKING FORWARD

Any starting point is endowed with the legacy of an important past. In the case of agriculture the preceding great landmark was probably the repeal of the corn laws in 1846, and more generally the beginning of the period of free trade. By 1860 it was clear that the worst fears of protectionists – that the removal of the corn laws would result in a great influx of cheap overseas food – were ill founded. Fears that the approaches to British estuaries and ports were heaving with merchant vessels creaking with surplus foreign produce were not realised. The feared countries were themselves going through a demographic transition, industrialising and consuming their own increased output. An influx of grain did eventually swamp an unprotected market but not for a decade or more. In the 1850s over three-quarters of the wheat available to home consumers was still produced at home, despite the fact that the population had doubled in the previous half-century, and in the 1860s approximately 65 per cent of wheat consumption was still home produced (see Table 6.1).

From the 1860s the flow of imports increased and eventually flooded the home market. From 1900 to 1914 perhaps only one quarter of the wheat available to home consumers was produced at home. Large, bulk-carrying, iron ships and steam railways allowed North American wheat

Table 6.1 Wheat imports into the UK – five-year averages

Annual averages	1841–5	1851–5	1861–5	1871–5	1881–5	1891–5	1901–5	1911–15
				(in 000s cwt)				
Russia	485	3,262	5,602	11,773	8,870	13,754	15,070	8,031
Germany	2,819	3,035	6,467	3,554	2,076	630	595	
Canada	172	150	1,948	3,242	2,173	2,976	7,967	21,779
USA	57	1,790	8,957	17,703	28,853	28,417	23,714	28,570
Argentina						7,746	14,243	13,389
India				827	9,439	9,170	15,509	17,795
Australia				1,092	3,700	2,811	8,047	9,864
Other	3,445	7,917	4,928	5,950	3,756	4,205	3,791	1,796
Total imports	6,978	16,154	27,902	44,141	58,867	69,709	88,936	101,224
Home production		60,353	66,983	51,507	43,502	31,531	28,644	34,902
Total available		76,507	94,885	95,648	102,369	101,240	117,580	136,126
Home as a % of total		78.9	70.6	53.9	42.5	31.1	24.4	25.6
				(percentages)				
Russia	7.0	20.2	20.1	26.7	15.1	19.7	16.9	7.9
Germany	40.4	18.8	23.2	8.1	3.5	0.9	0.7	
Canada	2.5	0.9	7.0	7.3	3.7	4.3	9.0	21.5
USA	0.8	11.1	32.1	40.1	49.0	40.8	26.7	28.2
Argentina						11.1	16.0	13.2
India				1.9	16.0	13.2	17.4	17.6
Australia				2.5	6.3	4.0	9.0	9.7
Other	49.4	49.0	17.7	13.5	6.4	6.0	4.3	1.8
Total	100	100	100	100	100	100	100	100

Note: Germany in fact Prussia to 1856, and Germany thereafter.

Sources: Imports from Mitchell 1988: 229–32; home production prior to 1885 from Lawes and Gilbert 1893: 132, assuming bushels of 62 lb; home production post-1884 for GB from MAFF 1966: 108, Table 56; Ireland from Mitchell and Deane 1962: 88–9.

to cross half a continent and then an ocean and still compete favourably against home-grown produce in home markets in the 1890s. Historically, whenever the home supply required topping up there had been a ready local source from Europe, especially northern Europe and Russia. Russia continued to be a major supplier in the late nineteenth century but it was overshadowed by grain imports from North America. In many years in the 1870s, 80s and 90s as much as one half of the wheat imports came from the USA. In some years that country alone accounted for 30 per cent of the total wheat available to British consumers.

Yet as Table 6.1 shows, the worst fears of those who opposed the open-door, free-trade policy were eventually realised. The influx of foreign wheat was a kind of double jeopardy: home-produced wheat was displaced as the major cash crop; and it awakened psychological fears of vulnerability with the loss of self-sufficiency. The period under review in this chapter therefore is a vital turning point in the history of British agriculture.

The importance of wheat cannot be overstressed. Traditionally it was the cash crop *par excellence*, and from sometime in the eighteenth century and increasingly in the nineteenth wheaten white bread became psychologically a thermometer of success in production and consumption. As for potato consumption, Ireland was not dependent on wheat except as a means of earning income and paying rents, but in the other countries of the United Kingdom wheaten bread consumption increased rapidly. As early as 1800 perhaps 58 per cent of the population consumed wheaten bread, and by 1850 it was probably closer to 80 per cent. By 1900 something like 95 per cent of a yet further expanded population ate wheat. Even in Scotland the consumption of oaten bread had been overtaken (Collins 1975: 97–115, Petersen 1995: 205–6).

The moated settlement that is the British Isles allowed parts of the agricultural economy to enjoy some natural protection. It was another twenty years or more before the perishable food market was seriously threatened by the development of the tin can and refrigeration, both of which erased the benefits of relative isolation and distance. Legislation also afforded some respite in the guise of the contagious diseases acts of the mid-1860s. Initially these restricted the landing of live animals at selected ports but in time further restrictions were introduced on both the landing of those animals and their internal movements within Britain. Different restrictions applied according to the country of origin. These acts, as far as they applied to animals, were implemented less for the protection of trade and more to preserve the reputation of a disease-free national herd in the wake of the cattle plague (rinderpest) which entered the country from the Baltic in 1865 (Perren 1978: 106–14). Nevertheless, a residual degree of economic protection to the fresh meat industry ensued.

Table 6.2 captures the trend of UK meat supply that took place under free trade. The table compares the rising trend of meat imports, with an estimate of the domestic meat supply (Perren 1978: 3). Essentially this is the sum of cattle, sheep and pigs entering the country but reduced to a simple measure of total weight (for example, see Mitchell 1988: 233), applied to an estimate of the annual enumeration of animals that were slaughtered for the meat market.[1] On this evidence the estimates in

[1] In this last context it is assumed that 25 per cent of the cattle were slaughtered each year, 40 per cent of the sheep and 116 per cent of the pigs. The high slaughter rate for pigs arises because they produced litters more than once a year, a feature that the annual agricultural census does not pick up. To these slaughter estimates are applied the average weight of meat each animal yielded. In reality slaughter weights and their trend over time are notoriously difficult to measure. A report of 1904 was that it was 'probably true to say that animals, being sold at an earlier age, are not now fattened to so great a size as formerly'. This is a clear enough warning against using slaughter weights as indicators of productivity. But the report continued that 'the progressive improvement of farm stock has tended to the more general production of animals which, in butchers' phraseology, 'die well', and has possibly increased to some extent the proportion of the 'carcase' to the live weight' (Rew 1904: 416–17). The latest researches on slaughter weights suggest plausible

Table 6.2 Meat imports and domestic meat supply in the UK, 1851–1914

Period	Domestic supply (000s tons)	Imports (000s tons)	Total supply (000s tons)	Imports as a % of total	Per capita consumption (lb)
1850s	1,047.0	44.0	1,091.0	4.0	87.3
1860s	1,078.0	131.0	1,209.0	10.8	90.0
1870s	1,326.4	276.0	1,602.4	17.2	109.7
1880s	1,306.0	469.0	1,775.0	26.4	110.8
1890s	1,405.6	803.3	2,208.9	36.4	126.6
1900s	1,456.3	1,033.2	2,489.5	41.5	130.3
1910–14	1,484.4	1,091.0	2,575.4	42.4	126.9

Source: Perren 1978: 3.

Table 6.2 are something of a lottery, but they may faithfully pick up the overall trend. Meat imports as a percentage of total supply were trivial just after the introduction of free trade, but by the 1880s they had reached worrying levels, and by 1900 Britain was dependent on foreign suppliers. By 1914 two-fifths of UK consumed meat almost certainly came from overseas.

Once a policy of free trade was in place the major obstacle that restricted meat imports was the problem of putrefaction, and this had implications for the geographical range of supply. As preservation techniques were developed and perfected this geography was extended. Early methods relied on salt and brine. For example, this allowed supplies of surplus hog products from Chicago to appear on the Liverpool market almost as soon as free trade was declared. The development of the chilled meat trade meant that by the 1880s the potential meat supply stretched round the globe to Australasia and South America. Indeed, these supply sources became so important that by the turn of the century they had eclipsed the chilled meat trade from North America and Europe (Perren 1978: *passim*). In contrast, the popularity of canned and other methods of preserving food has probably been exaggerated (Perren 2000: 1093–7). By 1907 perhaps 34 per cent of total meat supply came from overseas and a further 10 per cent from British possessions (Turner 2000: 224).

There was also an internal trade in meat supply, especially from Ireland to Britain. A combination of the annual agricultural census and the records of shipping suggest that from 1875 to 1891 between 14 and 20 per cent of Irish enumerated cattle were exported to Britain. This was in the ratio of 40 per cent fat cattle, 53 per cent stores cattle and 7 per cent

upper and lower bound carcass weights of 600–700 lb per head of cattle, 50–70 lb per head of sheep and 120–200 lb per pig (Holderness 1989: 152–6, though heavily reliant on Herbert 1859: 475–6; Turner *et al.* 2001: 186–7). The estimates in Table 6.2 take the lower cattle figures of 600 lb, the upper sheep figure of 70 lb, and a pig weight that was closer to the lower end of the scale at 134 lb. An 1873 estimate of average slaughter weights quotes cattle at 514 lb per head, sheep at 67 lb and pigs at 134 lb, which by the late 1870s had risen to 637, 69 and 149 lb respectively (Craigie 1883: 26).

calves. Over the same period 17 or 18 per cent of all Irish-born sheep were exported to Britain in the ratio of two sheep to one lamb, and a fairly constant 36 per cent of Irish pigs came to Britain (and an untold quantity in terms of bacon (Turner 1996: 58–9, 2000: 279–80).

In 1867 the total of grain and meat imports constituted about 20 per cent of food supply. By 1878 this had risen to 25 per cent, by which time nearly 40 per cent of basic grain was foreign supplied. By 1907 Britain produced less than one fifth of its own grain. A further one third came from British possessions, but as much as 50 per cent was supplied from countries outside British Empire influence or control (Turner 2000: 224–5). The vulnerability of British food supplies was plain to see yet a policy of free trade persisted. If safeguarding the nation's food supply was a key part of British economic strategy then it was to be achieved through a combination of accumulated colonial sources of supply and an extension of the so-called 'blue water' policy. Food supply was safeguarded by a combination of a strong navy and the formation of Atlantic alliances, policies that were truly tested by the German submarine campaign of the Great War with one of its solutions, the development of the convoy system (Offer 1989; Collins 2000a: 2000b: 28, 34). It was not achieved by supporting home supplies.

THE 'GOLDEN AGE' OF HIGH FARMING

An important component of agricultural change, especially of productivity change, is the trend of crop yields, and especially the trend in wheat yields. In the depression that followed the French wars of 1793–1815 wheat yields reached unprecedented heights (see Table 6.3). At a time when farms were being repossessed by landlords because tenants were having trouble paying their rents, yields began an unmistakable rise towards a mid-century plateau. In the crisis of supply during the French wars farmers responded by extending the arable acreage, especially for wheat cultivation, and investing heavily. By so doing they raised output. From 1815 onwards for several decades Britain was more or less self-sufficient in basic grain supply. The corn laws that were in place merely served to frustrate the farming and commercial communities alike. The farmers were frustrated because peace prices were not nearly as high as they had been in war, but at the same time they responded successfully to population change and made sure that prices remained low (on the likelihood of much lower grain prices in the hypothetical absence of protection see Fairlie 1965; Wordie 2000: 44–9). The per capita grain availability index either rose or remained stable, thus indicating a matching supply response to a growing demand (Wilkes 1980: 92, based on Fairlie 1969). The commercial interests were frustrated because they thought prices could be lower still with a free market, and this would help them in their desire to hold wages in check.

By the end of the 1830s the agricultural depression had subsided, and the removal of agricultural protection followed in the mid-1840s. Thus began the period known popularly as high farming. It lasted until the 1870s. Under the economic circumstances that agriculture faced, especially a growing international market in which increasingly British producers became price takers, the prevailing prices that farmers found at their markets were relatively stable. In addition, the productivity changes that had characterised British agriculture and which enabled British producers to feed the headlong British population growth had probably reached their limits. This occurred without a substantial recourse to imports or a severe, if indeed any, deterioration in living standards (Turner *et al.* 2001: ch. 7). High farming therefore referred to alternative means by which to raise output and productivity, essentially by increasing the capital component of the inputs, perhaps as a substitute for other inputs, and thereby achieving improvements in productivity. An important additional component is thought to have been improved drainage. From 1845 to 1899, but mostly before 1870, about 4.5 million acres of England were drained. Out of a total cultivated acreage of 22–3 million acres this was a considerable investment (Phillips 1989: 242). With the weight of all this capital investment farming was once said to have entered a 'golden age', a clear reference to healthy crops of sun-ripened grain (Perren 1995: 1–6).

Table 6.3 Mean wheat yields in England, 1790s to 1900s

Period	Mean wheat yield per acre (bushels per acre)
1790s	19.0
1800s	21.0
1810s	21.2
1820s	23.6
1830s	26.7
1840s	30.6
1850s	27.5
1860s	28.6
1870s	28.9
1880s	26.5
1890s	27.1
1900s	28.1

Source: Turner *et al.* 2001: 129.

Many modern researchers now doubt the appropriateness of the appellation 'high farming', since it is unlikely that the investments made strict economic sense, even before 1870, when compared with alternative forms of investment (Perren 1995: 4). Such doubts apply particularly to clayland areas where underdrainage was supposedly most important (doubts expressed by Collins and Jones 1967, responding to an opposing optimistic view by Sturgess 1966). One component of high farming was high feeding, that is the application of alternative sources of both animal and crop sustenance. It is usually argued that non-farm manure, such as imported natural substances and industrial and artificial fertilisers, were heaped on the land in prodigious quantities. Yet what effect did this application of fertiliser have? The data suggest that there was no obvious response in wheat yields. Instead, average yields seemed to reach something of a plateau. They fluctuated between a low of 26 bushels per acre in the 1830s and 1880s, and a high of 30 bushels per acre in the 1840s, but around a mean which remained more or less constant at 27–8 bushels per acre (Craigie 1883; Lawes and Gilbert 1893; Turner *et al.* 2001: 129). Historians may have exaggerated the impact of home-produced and imported non-natural manure-based additives. Thompson dubbed the period from 1815 to 1880 as a 'Second Agricultural Revolution', pointing out that between 1810/14 and 1887/91 externally purchased feed applied to British farms increased from 27,000 tons to 2.4 million tons, and net retained fertilisers increased from 26,000 to 654,000 tons (1968: 76–7). In the early 1850s about £10 million per annum of purchased inputs was applied to British farmland, rising to £17 million per annum by the early 1870s (Perren 1995: 2). Yet when we measure the application of these external inputs in different ways we struggle to find a revolutionary response. The rate of growth of imported and artificial fertiliser application was exponential, but at only 96 pounds per arable acre as late as 1872 it was spread very thinly (Turner *et al.* 2001: 140). There is surely room to doubt the overall impact. The application of traditional home-produced farmyard manure tells a similar tale: in the 1860s it amounted to 1.75 tons per acre, but it rose only to 1.85 tons per acre by 1914 (Brassley 2000: 539). From 1850 to 1914 there was a fivefold increase in non-farm and non-lime-based fertilisers but still no comparable increase in wheat yields beyond a seemingly irreducible minimum of 30 bushels per acre (Brassley 2000: 541n).

So what precisely was the value of external inputs if all they did was to allow farmers to maintain a stable wheat yield? Possibly they were cost saving since artificial fertilisers or external additives were more concentrated relative to traditional muck and lime. Whether this made them relatively labour saving remains an open question. What is not in doubt is the failure of agriculture to break through the apparent upper limit of 30 bushels of wheat per acre. A not dissimilar tale can be told for animal feeds, casting doubts on the high feeding aspect in the story of high farming (Brassley 2000: 581). Perhaps contemporary farmers were content with yields at an upper limit of close to 30 bushels per acre, because they were achieving other forms of productivity improvements, such as improving seeding rates by more efficient methods of preparing and seeding the ground. Of more importance was the fact that increasingly artificial fertilisers were applied to root crops, which were particularly responsive to phosphates, and these were a main source of food supply for animals, especially after 1880. This was a response to the shift in the terms of trade towards animal products (Brassley 2000: 542). Even within grain production, and depending on the varieties of wheat or barley employed, the fertilisers might have had the effect of increasing the length of straw stalk, rather than of grain yields, as another response to the demand for fodder (Walton 1999: 39–41).

In later years the period of high farming was seen as a golden age but some trends belie this description. Over the period *c.* 1840–90 the acreage

Table 6.4 Indexes of grain, live meat and dairy product prices, and rents per acre 1870/4–1910/14 (1870/4 = 100)

Annual averages	Wheat	Barley	Oats	Bread	Rent	Live cattle	Live sheep	Milk	Butter	Cheese
1870/4	100.0	100.0	100.0	100.0	100.0	100.0	100.0	100.0	100.0	100.0
1875/9	86.7	96.9	101.2	87.5	101.4	99.4	109.5	112.5	100.0	100.0
1880/4	77.1	82.2	86.4	83.8	93.0	97.8	108.5	112.5	100.0	92.3
1885/9	57.4	70.1	72.0	71.0	82.7	82.0	92.3	87.5	83.3	92.3
1890/4	53.9	68.8	75.1	70.6	78.5	80.1	91.8	84.4	83.3	84.6
1895/9	50.7	62.6	65.1	63.8	74.2	75.0	89.4	81.3	66.7	76.9
1900/4	49.8	62.4	71.5	63.3	80.4	79.5	92.1	87.5	75.0	100.0
1905/9	57.2	65.3	72.7	67.4	75.2	79.3	92.9	100.0	81.7	113.8
1910/14	59.9	70.0	77.9	68.6	76.8	88.8	98.5	112.5	90.0	164.6

Notes: Base prices: wheat 55.0 sh. per qtr; barley 38.7 sh. per qtr; oats 25.1 sh. per qtr; bread 8.4 pence per 4 lb; rent 27.1 sh. per acre; cattle 9.1 pence per lb; sheep 9.9 pence per lb; milk 8.0 pence per imp. gall.; butter 6.0 pence per imp. gall.; cheese 6.5 pence per imp. gall. Years: milk, butter, cheese 1871–5, 1876–80 . . . etc. . . . to 1911–14.

Sources: Grain prices from Afton and Turner 2000: 2044–5; bread prices from Mitchell and Deane 1962: 498; rent from Turner *et al.* 1997: 312–13; cattle and sheep prices based on maximum annual quotation at the Metropolitan cattle market and listed in Afton and Turner 2000: 2057–8, 2069–70; dairy product prices from Taylor 1976: 590.

under wheat in Britain declined from *c.* 4 million to 2.4 million acres. Ordinarily, if the worst wheat lands were deserted first, there might be a resulting improvement in the overall unit land productivity. But the stable, or at best modest, improvement in wheat yields was accompanied by a large downturn in labour usage, and, as we have demonstrated, only modest increases in fertilisers and other land improvement inputs. Only in Ireland did average wheat yields markedly improve, but then the decline in the wheat acreage was more dramatic here than in the rest of the UK (Turner 1996: 227–8).

THE GREAT DEPRESSION

There was a slump in wheat yields in the 1880s, in line with what became the darkest decade of the agricultural depression. Several years of bad weather injured arable crops, and at times livestock farmers suffered equally when liver fluke and foot rot in sheep was particularly severe (Jones 1964; Perren 1995: 7). Under normal domestic market conditions these circumstances would have led to a rise in prices, but quite the opposite occurred. British prices were determined now more by external considerations.

The first three columns of Table 6.4 gives the average annual price of the three main corn crops – wheat, barley and oats – the cash crops which were the main source of income to the arable farmer. The slump in wheat prices was particularly severe and was the main result of Britain's open-door policy. The slump in barley and oats was less severe and the recovery from the 1890s more pronounced because there were alternative markets

Table 6.5 Trend of agricultural rents, 1850–1914

	Arable rents (sh./acre)	Pasture rents (sh./acre)	Pasture rents as a % of arable rents
1850/4	21.9	17.9	81.8
1855/9	24.1	20.3	84.5
1860/4	25.6	22.6	88.6
1865/9	26.6	23.2	87.1
1870/4	26.5	27.6	104.2
1875/9	27.1	28.1	103.6
1880/4	24.8	27.2	109.7
1885/9	22.1	25.8	116.4
1890/4	20.9	24.5	117.0
1895/9	19.3	23.7	123.3
1900/4	18.2	21.8	119.9
1905/9	18.6	21.4	115.1
1910/14	19.9	22.2	111.8

Source: Derivation explained in Turner *et al.* 1997: 193–5.

for these two crops, in malting for barley, and as animal feeds for both crops (on farmer responses to relative price movements, even in Essex the supposedly hardest hit depression county, see Hunt and Pam 1997, 2002). The lighter side of the depression was the relatively better fortunes enjoyed by the pasture farmers. The prices for animal and dairy products also fell, though less severely (Table 6.5). The price of milk declined, but then recovered. This reflected less the impact of the agricultural depression and more the impact of urban demand, changing diets and the ease of supplying that market once the railway network was completed. In responding to these factors the milk sector had an influence on regional agricultural activity, perhaps to a greater degree than any other area of agricultural activity in the second half of the nineteenth century. Butter and cheese, however, both suffered from foreign competition and did not respond by way of technical improvements (Taylor 1976: 591). Nevertheless, cheese prices recovered, but as much as anything because cheese became a much scarcer product with a dramatic decline in regional varieties. English cheese production fell by two-thirds from 1860 to 1910 and while cheese making consumed 40 per cent of milk output in the 1860s, by the first decade of the twentieth century it probably consumed not much more than 5 per cent (Taylor 1976: 590).

The prices of all these products translate eventually into farmers' incomes. One of their main costs was rent, the main income to the landowners. The slump in rents through the course of the depression was severe, but on arable farms it was very severe. This afforded some respite to the arable farmer, but constituted a major loss of income to arable landlords. Even for the arable farmers the decline in rents was not sufficient to overcome the decline in product prices that they endured (compare rents with grain and bread prices in Table 6.4). In contrast, the decline in pasture rents was far less dramatic and reflected the more buoyant conditions that animal and animal product farmers faced (Table 6.5, but see also product price differentials in Table 6.4). Another important feature of the differing trends in arable and pasture rents was the way that the latter caught up with the level of the former (a process complete in the 1870s) and indeed proceeded to open up a sizeable gap. This was especially the case by the mid-1890s, the lowest point in the depression.

From the mid-1890s onwards there was a modest general recovery in agriculture that lasted until the First World War, but no corresponding recovery in the acreage of land devoted to wheat. It tumbled throughout the period from 3.4 million acres in England in 1870 to 2.2 million acres by 1890, and fell further to 1.7 million acres by 1900. At its lowest point in 1904 there were just 1.3 million acres in wheat production. In the decade prior to the war acreage averaged close to 1.7 million (the addition of Wales and Scotland to these totals is trifling) (Afton and Turner 2000: 1770–1). Wheat yields remained fairly flat at something close to 28 bushels per acre. English wheat output therefore declined from close to 2 million tons in the late 1880s to a low point of less than 1 million tons in 1904, and on average a little under 1.5 million tons in the decade prior to 1914 (MAFF 1966: 108).

It is surprising, perhaps, that wheat yields did not fluctuate given the changing acreage involved. We might have expected the relatively inferior wheat-growing lands to be converted into other uses, with a resulting rise in average yields. But these were difficult times for arable farmers. Their costs of production remained high relative to agricultural incomes. Therefore, conjecturally, they may have maintained unit acre yields by reducing inputs. Alternatively, the best wheat land may not have remained in wheat production, but instead was converted to higher-value products like milk or market gardening.

OUTPUT

Whether a sector of the economy is performing well is demonstrated by its contribution to the national economy. The share of agriculture within gross domestic product declined dramatically. Yet this may be partly or wholly a reflection of activities outside the control of agriculture itself. There is a case for suggesting that agriculture was not performing as badly as has sometimes been thought.

The internal performance of agriculture has been assessed and reassessed many times (Ojala 1952; Bellerby 1953, revised 1968; Ó Gráda 1981, 1994; Turner 2000). The latest estimates are summarised in Table 6.6 showing five-year averages at selected ten-year intervals (annual values in Afton and Turner 2000: 1895–900). These show the values of output for the most important agricultural products. The item labelled 'Other' includes estimates for animals like rabbits and game, and for crops like flowers and nursery stock. In facing unprotected competition from overseas in a market where price was increasingly determined externally, agriculture went through important decades of change. A benchmark figure for the total agricultural output of the UK is available for 1851 of about £180 million.[2] This value had risen during 'high farming' to £215 million in

[2] Based on Bellerby 1959: 103, which is a net estimate here grossed up on the basis of Bellerby 1968 where the value of net agricultural income was always about 65 per cent of the gross.

Table 6.6 Agricultural output in the United Kingdom, by product, 1871–1914 (five-year averages – all in £s million)

(i) Crops Year	Wheat	Barley	Oats	Potatoes	Hay	Straw	Veg.	Fruit	Hops	Flax	Rye
1871/5	24.0	16.4	6.6	15.7	11.9	7.1	6.1	1.7	3.5	1.0	0.02
1881/5	11.9	11.6	7.0	11.0	18.2	5.5	4.4	2.0	2.7	0.7	0.02
1891/5	7.0	8.4	6.9	10.4	16.0	5.0	4.7	2.5	2.3	0.5	0.02
1901/5	6.2	7.5	7.7	8.5	17.9	4.0	6.0	3.9	2.1	0.4	0.01
1911/14	9.1	7.5	7.1	10.6	12.3	3.0	8.5	4.9	2.5	0.5	0.04
(ii) Livestock and livestock products	Cattle	Sheep	Pigs	Milk	Eggs	Poultry	Horses	Wool			
1871/5	24.7	13.1	18.7	36.9	5.6	1.9	3.9	11.2			
1881/5	24.2	12.5	19.2	33.6	5.5	1.9	3.6	4.6			
1891/5	25.0	11.7	18.3	33.1	5.9	2.1	3.4	4.8			
1901/5	26.2	12.0	22.2	36.6	7.0	2.5	3.4	3.8			
1911/14	31.3	13.2	16.6	50.4	10.0	3.9	3.2	5.0			
(iii) Totals	Crops	Livestock	Other	Total							
1871/5	93.9	116.0	5.2	215.1							
1881/5	75.0	105.1	4.5	184.6							
1891/5	63.7	104.1	4.9	172.7							
1901/5	64.3	113.8	5.7	183.7							
1911/14	65.9	133.5	7.1	206.5							

Source: Turner 2000: 263. Annual figures given in Afton and Turner 2000: 1895–1900.

1871–5, but fell thereafter to £172.7 million in 1891–5. This fall of 19.7 per cent represents the full extent of the impact of the great depression. It was particularly evident in arable farming (a fall of 32.2 per cent) relative to livestock and livestock product farming (10.3 per cent).

The five-year average value for output in 1871–5 was abnormally high as a result of a particularly good year in 1874, one of the best years ever and second only to the most productive year, 1868. This may exaggerate the successes of 'high farming'. Yet there was a clear shift in emphasis towards livestock farming and its allied products. These represented 54 per cent of output in the early 1870s, but 65 per cent by 1914. The greatest problem facing the agricultural sector as a whole was the collapse of grain output, and in particular the farmer's traditional cash crop, wheat. It declined from about 11 per cent of gross output in the early 1870s to about 3 per cent by the end of the century, recovering only marginally by 1914. The grains together (wheat, barley and oats) declined from 22 per cent to 11 per cent over the period. The main change in the animal economy was the rise in the value of cattle output, and more particularly the rise in the value of milk products. In the early 1870s cattle and milk represented 11.5 and 17 per cent respectively of gross output, but 15 and 24.5 per cent by 1914. Estimates of milk yields varied enormously across the country, but a

Table 6.7 Labour productivity in UK agriculture, 1871–1911

Date	Output 1 (£m)	Labour force 2 (000s)	Average weekly wage 3 (sh.)	Wages cost 4 (£m)	Productivity estimates 5 (£/head)	6 (£output/£input)
1871	206.6	2,809	12.42	90.7	73.55 (100.7)	2.26 (108.1)
1881	184.8	2,561	13.75	91.6	72.16 (98.8)	2.02 (95.8)
1891	175.7	2,405	13.33	83.4	73.06 (100.0)	2.11 (100.0)
1901	185.1	2,181	14.67	83.2	84.87 (116.2)	2.23 (105.6)
1911	196.2	2,183	16.75	95.1	89.88 (123.0)	2.06 (97.9)

Notes and sources: Revised version of Turner 2000: 315.
Column 1 Annual averages centred on the years shown, from Turner 2000: 1899–1900.
Column 2 Labour force from Ojala 1952: 85.
Column 3 National average weekly wages for agricultural labourers for 1867–71, 1879–81, 1892–3, 1902, 1914 from Orwin and Felton 1931: 233, 247, 255.
Column 4 National average agricultural wage cost: column 2 × column 3 × 52 weeks, and converted into £m.
Column 5 Column 1/column 2 (and indexed on 1891).
Column 6 Column 1/column 4 (and indexed on 1891).

trend is discernible demonstrating a productivity improvement over time (Rew 1892a, 1892b; Fletcher 1961b; Taylor 1976). At a lower level of output, but a significant level of new production, fruit farming also represented something of a success story (Robinson 1981, 1983).

The national farm looked like a mixed farm at the beginning of the period, but ended up in a much more specialised state with cattle and milk together contributing two-fifths of the value of all agricultural output. This was a triumph for adaptation: adapt or perish, specialise and survive became important radical ideas for an otherwise conservative agricultural sector.

This trend was already under way. The particularly bad year in 1879 stands out when all the environmental elements conspired against farming; the weather was bad for crops and animals alike (Perren 1995: 7), and then the drift into deep depression in the 1880s locates the onset of depression. But the distribution of output in the late 1860s and 1870s indicates that the realignment from the grain to the livestock economy was already well in motion. Leaving that aside, the resultant shortfall in output in 1879 might ordinarily have signalled an increase in unit agricultural prices, and thereby bolstered agricultural incomes. In the event, the real impact of the open market was felt, especially in grain production with the great surge in grain imports.

The annual figures and trends that underlie Table 6.7 are shown in Figure 6.1, highlighting the difference between the crop and livestock economies. The crash in 1879 is plain to see, but the long-term broad 'U' shape of total output is more important. Leaving aside short-term fluctuations there was a shallow downturn in livestock output from the mid-1870s to about 1890, followed by a continuous upturn. For crops there was a sharper downturn reaching a low point in 1895, followed by a slight, almost imperceptible, upturn. These differentiated trends are sharply

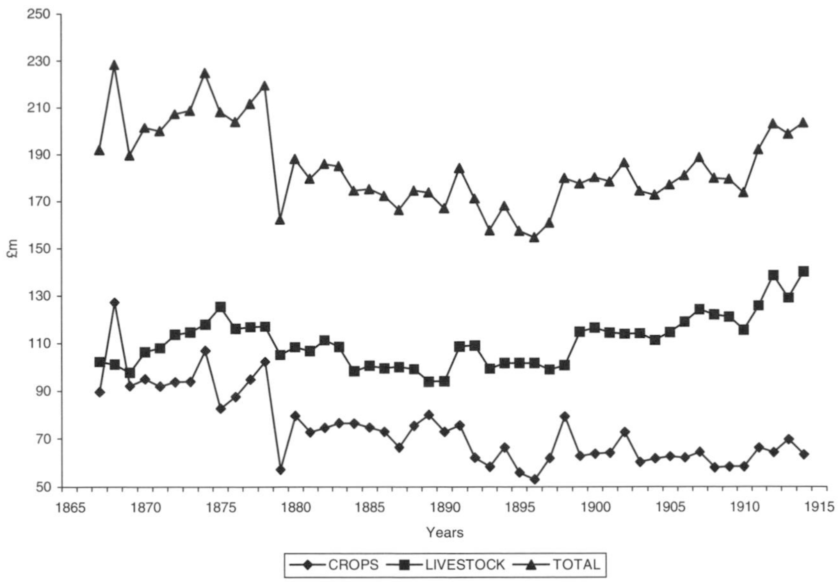

Figure 6.1 Crop and livestock output in the UK, 1867–1914

Source: Turner 2000: 266.

focused in Figure 6.2, showing starkly the variable fortunes between grain output, and cattle and milk output.

The familiar landmarks in late nineteenth-century general price history are evident, typically the price peak of the early 1870s and the trough in the early 1890s. But the value of output is not determined by price alone. The observable decline in the value of output could have been caused by this price fall, but also by an actual decline in the quantity produced, or indeed a combination of the two. On closer inspection, it arose from the decline in prices, but in the face of an actual improvement in physical output.

The nominal output series has been deflated by an agricultural price index (Turner 2000: 295–300) to produce a real volume output series, thereby adjusting for price changes taking place wholly within agriculture. The outcome is shown in two versions in Figure 6.3. The first version uses a deflator determined by a price index based on product distribution weights pertaining in 1870, and the second on the weights pertaining in 1910. The difference between the two therefore picks up the demonstrable change in product distribution we have described. For comparative purposes the trend of nominal output is also displayed in Figure 6.3. Nominal output fell by 22 per cent from 1867–9 to 1895–7, but the volume of output actually rose by 8 per cent (using 1870 weights in the deflator). This puts the idea of a national depression into a different perspective. The substantial downturn in nominal output from the early 1870s to 1895/6 is the most compelling evidence for a great depression, but in real volume terms agricultural output actually increased. It was not a smooth increase, and in particular there was a reversal from 1888

Figure 6.2 Grain and cattle and milk output in the UK, 1867–1914

Source: Turner 2000: 266.

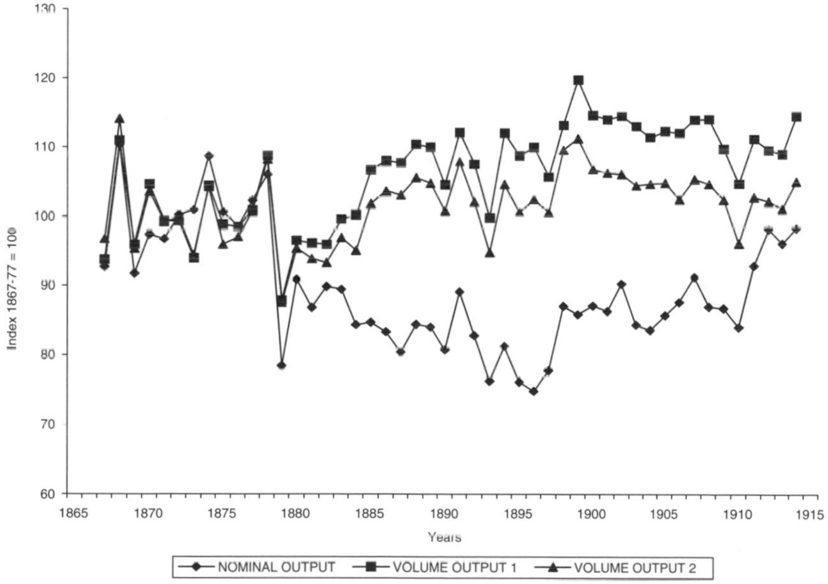

Figure 6.3 Nominal and volume indicators of UK agricultural output, 1867–1914

Source: Turner 2000: 301.

to 1893, but all the same it was an increase. In the period of recovery traditionally dated from *c.* 1896 the nominal output rose by 28 per cent down to 1912–14. This rise was a price effect, and not really the result of a genuine increase in output. The real volume of output continued to rise to 1899 but declined thereafter.

There is some confirmation of these trends in Drescher's physical volume index. He converted output into starch equivalents and demonstrated a nearly continuous rise in livestock production from the late 1860s to 1914, but an arable index that trended downwards (Drescher 1955). A more or less equivalent estimate of output for England and Wales alone, based on conversion to calorific values, shows a similar rise in gross livestock production from 1885 to 1914, but a decline in crops from 1885 to 1904, a small recovery in 1905 to 1909, and then the resumption of decline (Beilby 1939).

The construction of separate price indexes for composite grain and composite animal production clarifies the position a little further (Turner 2000: 295–305). The terms of trade moved almost continuously in favour of animal products in which the major trend reversals were caused by the more volatile nature of grain prices. There are no surprises here given the open, free-trade nature of the economy, with the opening up of grain production in otherwise virgin international territory, but still the safety of distance for many perishable animal products.

The commodity price depression was an international phenomenon and is reflected in the price indexes, especially for grain. The price recovery down to the 1914–18 war is equally evident for animal products. But grain prices at best levelled off in the period of so-called recovery. To this extent the depression for grain lasted not twenty years but at least forty years, and but for a brief respite during the war it lasted for sixty years or more. Significantly Perren chooses the boundary dates of 1870–1940 in his analysis of the agricultural depression. Although price was an important signal to contemporaries, who, like all of us, suffer from money illusion (Thompson 1991), in real volume terms the traditional turning points in late nineteenth-century price history – 1873 and 1896 – more or less disappear. In addition, the divergence between the arable and the animal economies was a long-run, more or less continuous, phenomenon. Even the massive and infamous decline in the fortunes of grain production in 1879 can only be recognised as a single aberrant year, not as a catalyst for a change, since that change was already in motion.[3]

The delicate equation facing grain farmers especially involved the decline in the value of their output relative to movements in their costs,

[3] See also the discussion of long-term change in Thompson 1959: 98–9; Offer 1989: 116; Ó Gráda 1994: 147. See also Hunt and Pam 1997 and 2002, who suggest that the contrasting fortunes of arable and livestock farmers in Essex have been misunderstood by historians at least partly because they have underestimated the adaptability of contemporary farmers.

especially wages and rents. Wages more or less rose throughout the period. Both rent and output fell down to the mid-1890s, but the fall in rent lagged behind the fall in output. From the mid-1890s, however, output rose but rents only modestly recovered. The lags in revenue and cost adjustments of those who had a call on the land – the landlords, tenants and labourers – helped to define the changing fortunes of those people. Initially the depression was felt more by the farmers than by the other two groups: they experienced an absolute decline in gross output, and the initial stickiness in rents meant there was a squeeze on their net income (Offer 1989: 116; Turner *et al.* 1997: 210–14; Turner 2000: 271, 305–7). But after a decade of rent arrears and rent abatements there was a shift in the impact of the depression away from the farmers and on to the landlords as output rose faster than rents. There was certainly a contemporary perception that the main burden of the late nineteenth-century depression eventually fell mainly on the landlords, though this may be more the result of government inquiries seeking the views of the landlords rather than the farmers.

Yet this does question the accounting senses of the landlords who apparently allowed their tenants to enjoy some recovery in income without a very obvious or positive attempt to share in that recovery. The share of income accruing to landlords in the early 1860s was 22 per cent, rising to 27 per cent by *c.* 1880, and calamitously falling to 18 per cent in *c.* 1910. In almost a mirror image the farmers' share over the same period fell from 35 per cent to 22 per cent, but then rose back to 35 per cent. In between, the farm labour share rose from 43 per cent to 51 per cent before falling back to 47 per cent (Ó Gráda 1981: 177; and for slightly different numbers for slightly different years see Ó Gráda 1994: 146). Most commentators agree on these trends and relative shares (Feinstein 1972: table 23, p. T60, suggests a higher proportion accruing to rent, but similar trends, and the same story is portrayed by Offer 1989: 114–15).

PRODUCTIVITY

Traditional methods of measuring productivity change, through unit acre yields and animal carcass weights, have already been discussed. But productivity change was actually more complex. In response to changing circumstances which were a function of the prices they received and the incomes they achieved, farmers adjusted their costs through the mix of inputs. The move out of grain and into animal production automatically necessitated an adjustment of inputs, especially the mix of labour and capital. It usually meant less labour and some capital expenditure on new equipment and specialist buildings. Under the right combinations of those factor inputs farmers could adjust to lower income per acre as long as there was a compensating higher output per man and per unit of capital employed. In short a lower income was balanced by lower unit costs (Thompson 1959).

The margin for adjustment was tight. The total area of land did not change a great deal; rent per acre shows an increase in the unit value, and therefore in the productivity of land down to about 1880, but a decrease thereafter. It also shows a clear divergence after about 1895 in the distribution of agricultural income away from the landlords and towards the farmers. The available wage series simply shows a rise in average earnings (in fact weekly wages), but at the same time there were fewer agricultural wage earners from 1881 to 1911. The resulting mix of the value of output relative to the cost of labour input produces the labour productivity estimates summarised in Table 6.7 (revised version of Turner 2000: 314–15). A simple trend of the value of output per head of labour input shows stability before 1891 and then a significant rise from 1891 to 1911 of 23 per cent (see also Ó Gráda 1994: 148), but if the labour input is costed then the value of output per £ of labour cost input produces a measurable fall in productivity from 1871 down to 1891 of 7 or 8 per cent, a modest rise thereafter and then a further fall. Therefore, while each worker increased his or her output he or she did so at a relatively long-run stable unit cost to the farmer, though there were quite divergent regional productivity trends (Hunt 1967, 1986).

But labour is only one of the inputs in the productivity equation, if still the most important during this period. A total factor productivity (TFP) approach considers the combined contribution to output of all factor inputs and analyses the ratio of output to the weighted sum of all the inputs (land, labour, capital). The inputs are weighted according to their respective shares of the returns, as measured by rent, wages and interest. Over the period 1870/2–1910/12 Ó Gráda suggested a TFP growth rate of 0.3 per cent per annum for British agriculture (later revised with different boundary dates to 0.4 per cent per annum). This is positive, but less significant by comparison with some other contemporary world examples which show growth rates of 1 per cent per annum in both Japan and the USA (Ó Gráda 1981: 178–9, 1994: 148–9; relatively modern productivity growth in UK agriculture was of the order of 1.9 per cent per annum from 1967 to 1990, including growth of over 3 per cent in 1975–84, Thirtle and Bottomley 1992: 381, 391). New estimates for the UK in the late nineteenth and early twentieth centuries are compared with Ó Gráda's British estimates in Table 6.8, though they turn on different years (full explanation of sources in Turner 2000: 317–19).

At all times productivity growth in the UK was positive, and in sympathy with the findings reported earlier. The greatest gains were made during the decades of the agricultural depression. The so-called recovery in Edwardian times was in fact a slowdown. All of these estimates add to the reappraisal of the doctrine of depression. There was clearly an Irish influence in the wider UK estimate. The relatively strong growth in the

Table 6.8 Total factor productivity in UK agriculture, *c.* 1871–*c.* 1911

	Total factor productivity (Real output/weighted factor input) × 100			Annual rates of growth		Ó Gráda's estimates			
	1870 base	1910 base		1870 base	1910 base		TFP indexes		Annual rates of growth
1871	100.0	100.0	1871–91	0.79	0.56	1862	100.0	1862–96	0.52
1891	117.0	111.9	1891–1911	0.52	0.37	1878	110.3	1878–96	0.43
1911	129.8	120.6	1871–1911	0.65	0.47	1896	119.2	1896–1913	0.25
						1905	119.5		
						1913	124.0	1862–1913	0.42
								1878–1913	0.35

Notes and sources: Output is based on five-year annual averages centred on 1871, 1891 and 1911, and deflated into a real volume index first by a price index based on weights pertaining to 1870 and then to weights pertaining to 1910. Labour is defined as the occupied labour force. The land factor is the extent of land on which rent was paid. The capital input represents the current values of animal feed, the stock of animals and crops, seeds, fertiliser, machinery, maintenance and some miscellaneous items, as well as the fixed capital or occupiers fixtures. The shares of factor returns are more or less the same as those employed by Ó Gráda. A full digest of the statistics and the method of construction is given in Turner 2000: 318–19; Ó Gráda 1994: 149, but see also Ó Gráda's first estimates in 1981: 179.

UK from 1871 to 1891 should be compared with weaker growth in Ireland for the same period, though conversely the downturn in growth in the UK in 1891–1911 masks much stronger growth over the same period in Ireland (Turner 1996: 138). Growth in GB alone in the decade of so-called recovery (1896–1905) was probably close to zero (Ó Gráda 1994: 149). Real output was maintained not by significant additions of land, but instead by a large fall in the labour force and modest additions to real capital of less than 1 per cent per annum. The agricultural sector traded off one factor against another and modestly bought its way out of depression. These estimates confirm the view that the real volume of agriculture was maintained or even rose throughout most of the period, providing further reasons for laying the ghost of the great agricultural depression to rest.

REGIONAL IMPLICATIONS

Yet can it really be true that the depression was a figment of contemporary imagination? Fletcher first suggested a moderation in the full impact of the late nineteenth-century depression, and he was also instrumental in pointing to regional nuances, especially through his intensive study of Lancashire (Fletcher 1961a, 1961b). In his turn Perry thought that the depression lasted from 1875 to 1939, with just a brief respite during the Great War and immediately after (Perry 1972, 1973: 'Introduction'). His main evidence was the incidence of bankruptcy, which also identified the geography of depression as well as its temporal nature. The worst period of bankruptcy was in 1881–3, and regionally it appears that agricultural failure was greatest in eastern and Midland counties, and least in the west. This is crudely the arable east and south versus the pastoral west and north. But the bankruptcy evidence alone cannot support Perry's pessimistic conclusion regarding almost unremitting depression, because bankruptcy treated regionally in this way simply shows that there were more failures in region A than in region B, not that region A was absolutely depressed.

Thompson actually measured regional output and therefore captured both the regional differences and the absolute expression of failure. The real gross value of output (or volume of production), fell by 4 per cent from 1873 to 1894 in England, but ranged from an increase of over 10 per cent in Cheshire (11 per cent), Lancashire (12 per cent) and Sussex (16 per cent), to a 20 per cent decrease in Oxfordshire and Berkshire. In the recovery period 1894–1911 the volume of English output rose by 4 per cent, ranging from increases of over 10 per cent in Cornwall, Cheshire, Shropshire and Devon to decreases of over 20 per cent in Herefordshire, Surrey, Sussex and Kent (Thompson 1991: 232–3). Some counties have been disadvantaged in this analysis because of the failure to measure the rising horticultural sector with its flourishing market gardens in Kent, Essex, Bedfordshire, Cambridgeshire and Worcestershire (Collins 2000a: 160–2). Nevertheless, the overall message is clear: from 1873 to 1911, through depression and recovery, the volume of production remained more or less stable. Farmers in the north and west of England experienced a rise in production and those in the south, east and central counties suffered a decline. Farmers in half a dozen counties flourished or even prospered, those in a further dozen faced serious difficulties and many were severely depressed, but those elsewhere, covering perhaps three-quarters of the land area were neither dynamic or expansive, neither contracting nor in decline (paraphrasing Thompson 1991: 234–5).

This combination of analyses based on the national farm and on crude regions suggests that the idea of a depression and subsequent recovery is not entirely discredited, but surely requires more sophisticated language than we have inherited, largely unchanged until recently, from the Royal Commissions of the 1890s.

FARMERS AND LANDLORDS

The returns to land, labour and capital were returns to real people, not just impersonal returns to the economists' factors of production. The return to land included rent, but was affected by other calls on income such as land taxes and local rates. So far as labour is concerned there needs to be an estimate of the return to the farmers and their families for their own labour deployed on the farm, as well as of the wage component to their labourers (Bellerby 1953). The return to capital is far less straightforward to estimate, let alone to measure in any direct sense (Feinstein 1988a).

Rent and wages were costs to the farmer. In turn they formed a return to the owners of the land and the owners of the labour – the landlords and the workers. They are also neatly encapsulated in rigid time horizons. The agricultural cycle was mainly an annual affair. The rent was paid half-yearly; the workers were hired by the year though casual labour was hired by the day. This is all rather neat, but the expenditure on, and the return from, capital stretched over longer periods. Not all the return to some capital expenditure was realised within the same agricultural cycle. An application of fertiliser or manure in one year may have had the most important income-bearing benefit in the same harvest year, but there might have been some return in subsequent years. This was certainly the case with fixed capital such as the erection of buildings, but was also the case with other items of expenditure such as the purchase of machinery, and land improvements such as drainage. This can be catered for with allowances for depreciation. But most farmers thought in terms of money in and money out, very rarely making any allowances for foregone income in the form of opportunity cost, or of depreciation in the value of capital stock.

The stock of land was more or less fixed; the stock of labour declined by 27 per cent from the 1860s to 1911; and current estimates suggest that the capital stock increased by 5 per cent early on but eventually declined to a level of 96 per cent of its original size by 1913 (Ó Gráda 1994: 5). But the factor returns did not necessarily move in line with the fluctuations in these absolute factor inputs. There was a decline in the land share of agricultural income (and thus its factor return) from 23 to 18 per cent, a capital share that stabilised at 12 to 13 per cent, but a labour share that increased from 64 to 70 per cent of agricultural income. The agricultural labour force declined but unit wage costs increased in real terms during the last quarter of the nineteenth century, at a time when rents declined and there was a deterioration or depreciation in capital stock. If land was the landowner's capital, and capital expenditure was the farmer's capital, there occurred a late nineteenth-century shift in the returns to farm capital, and thus a redistribution of income away from the landowners towards the farmers. At the same time there was a relatively steady share for a declining pool of farm labour whose individual stakes increased.

But farming was a matter of co-operation, joint management and partnership between the landlords and their tenants. It was reinforced by the nature of their tenancy agreement. By the middle of the nineteenth century these arrangements were formalised to a very high degree. And so they should have been, given that any transformations in farming across the full spectrum of choices from predominantly arable, through mixed, to predominantly livestock production was a costly exercise. So much is clear, for example, from the involvement of the duke of Sutherland in the farming of his Shropshire and Staffordshire estates both during the classic period of agricultural investment and high farming and also during the agricultural depression. Nature had been kind to the duke because his lands were better suited to mixed or livestock production.

Therefore when change was signalled in the second half of the nineteenth century it became a case of adding to the comparative advantages already enjoyed by the farmers on his estate, rather than financing a complete transformation. Yet to a degree the estate did anticipate the slump in grain price which was so much the hallmark of the depression. The result was that rents and estate net incomes held up remarkably well in the late nineteenth century. In contrast, nature was not nearly so kind to the duke of Bedford at Woburn in Bedfordshire and Buckinghamshire. Once it became evident that the agricultural depression was more permanent than a passing phase, changes took place in something of a rush (Perren 1970).

The onset of the agricultural depression was not a signal for landlords to spend lavishly to overcome the problem, nor was it a signal for them to retrench. Twenty-nine great estates gave detailed factual evidence to the Royal Commission of the 1890s. Together they accounted for nearly half a million acres in 1892, let out in over 5,000 holdings of which nearly half were over 20 acres in extent. The proportion of the landlords' rent that was spent on repairs, fences, insurance, new buildings and permanent improvements increased from one quarter to nearly one third between 1872 and 1892 (Perren 1970: 39–40; Turner *et al.* 1997: 22–4). Some of these estates did one thing – retrenchment at Holkham in north Norfolk for example, and also at Woburn – and others did the opposite – an expansion on an anonymous Suffolk estate for example – and yet others were 'steady as she goes', as on Lord Fitzhardinge's estate in Gloucestershire (Royal Commission on Agriculture 1896). In general most retrenchment took place in the arable east of England. But the decline in rents was dramatic, and therefore in some cases landlords' expenditure relative to their rents grew enormously, so that their net incomes were squeezed considerably.

There was obvious concern and involvement of landlords in the process of agricultural transformation in the face of external pressures that were beyond their control. But what of the farmers? The Royal Commission of the 1890s essentially told the landlords' story. The influential witnesses represented the great estates, including agents for the ecclesiastical commissioners, the duchies of Lancaster and Cornwall, the commissioner of Her Majesty's woods and forests, the treasurer of Guy's Hospital, and the bursar of Oriel College. Not once were any of their tenants called to London, but instead their evidence was told second hand and refracted through the lenses of these agents.

The landlords offered respite to their hard-pressed tenants by remitting a proportion of the rents, but this was a short-term solution. In the long term the only solution was a reduction of rent, but from the farmers' point of view this was often inadequate to meet the continuous fall in prices. Many tenants therefore ended up paying for a proportion of their rents out of their own capital. The situation was just as bad for many occupying owners. They were not encumbered by rents, but many of them were burdened by inherited mortgages or new mortgages on purchase. Many had become independent men during the period of high farming, taking out mortgages at fixed interest rates when prices and incomes were bouyant if not rising. In the 1890s these men were in a worse plight than mere tenant farmers. There was no question of mortgagees offering remissions of interest, and the fall in interest rates in the 1890s was no help. With the declining value of the land, but without remission on interest, as a charge on the land the interest repayments became a heavier burden, larger than the land might have been worth in rental payments to a landlord. These occupying farmers had 'to bear both the losses of the landlord and the losses of the tenant'. A farmer from Market Deeping in Lincolnshire owned 9 acres and rented 11 more of similar quality. On the owned land he paid between 90–100s. per acre in interest, but on the rest he paid only 45–60s. per acre in rent, thus demonstrating 'the difference in the profits of the land lender and the money lender' (Royal Commission 1897: paras. 106–8, 113, 116–18). Tenants faced nothing worse than unemployment, which was bad enough, but the occupying owners also faced bankruptcy, and then only if they were lucky enough to find purchasers for their land and were therefore able to clear at least a proportion of their debts.

FARM COSTS AND FARMING RETURNS DURING THE GREAT DEPRESSION

Even though the Royal Commission was essentially a landlord's response, it was reported that the average farmer's profit from 1875 to 1894 was just over a quarter of his rent. It was admitted that this compared unfavourably with a return of over two-fifths, which was the old basis on which income tax was determined. The farmers received an average of only 60 per cent of what was once regarded as the ordinary and average profit (Royal Commission 1897: paras. 110–11). This rather terse conclusion of the Royal Commission is purportedly based on a summary of over ninety farm accounts that they collected and collated. Our independent analysis of the same data is rather more pessimistic, and more in line with the minority report made by one critical commissioner, F. A. Channing. In his view, at best, 'some [occupiers] are making a little more than nothing, some also are making less than nothing' (Royal Commission 1897: 274–5).

Details of profit and loss are available for sixty-four of the farms, and so also is the size of tenants' capital employed. This is not the same as the expenditure on feed, manure, machinery and other items of circulating capital. Neither is it the annual expenditure on replenishing stock, but rather it represents the valuation of the farm stock (animals, seed, equipment, etc.) at one year end, and therefore the value of stock available for

Table 6.9 Distribution of factor costs on sixty-two English farms, *c.* 1892

County	No. of farms	Average acreage	Total expenditure (£s)	Distribution of expenditure (%)			Unit expenditure (sh. per acre)		
				Rent	Labour	Other	Rent	Labour	Other
Cambs	2	759	6,304	21.7	33.5	44.8	18.1	27.8	37.2
Essex	12	895	59,084	15.1	32.4	52.5	16.6	35.6	57.8
Hunts	1	462	1,082	24.3	28.9	46.8	11.4	13.5	21.9
Lincs	10	734	27,437	28.0	29.1	42.9	20.9	21.8	32.1
Norf	4	576	8,589	22.4	31.3	46.3	16.7	23.4	34.5
Suff	6	662	20,221	15.3	27.5	57.2	15.6	28.0	58.2
Sub total	35	752	122,717	19.0	30.8	50.2	17.7	28.7	46.8
Beds	9	528	16,389	26.9	34.9	38.2	18.6	24.1	26.3
N'ton	4	322	4,531	32.3	24.4	43.3	22.7	17.2	30.5
Sub total	13	465	20,920	28.1	32.6	39.3	19.5	22.6	27.2
Devon	1	245	1,490	26.0	24.0	50.0	31.6	29.2	60.8
Dors	7	628	12,886	27.2	30.7	42.1	15.9	18.0	24.7
Wilts	2	794	6,273	17.5	24.7	57.7	13.9	19.6	45.6
Sub total	10	623	20,649	24.2	28.4	47.4	16.0	18.8	31.5
N'land	1	494	1,334	30.9	35.1	34.0	16.7	18.9	18.4
Yorks	3	629	6,248	26.4	29.1	44.4	17.5	19.3	29.4
Sub total	4	595	7,582	27.2	30.2	42.6	17.3	19.2	27.1
TOTAL	62	661	171,868	21.1	30.7	48.2	17.7	25.8	40.5

Source: Collated from Royal Commission on Agriculture 1897 (subject to rounding errors).

the start of the following year. There is of course an element of circulating capital in this valuation in so far as some of the stock purchased afresh in one year remained on the farm in the following year.

The farm accounts allow an analysis of the distribution of factor costs and the returns on farmers' capital. While they give a record of farmers' expenditure, we can only guess at the investment strategies that the farmers employed to meet the agricultural crisis. The farms were located in fifteen counties, but fifty-six of the ninety-one farms were located in Essex, Norfolk, Suffolk, Lincolnshire and Cambridgeshire, and only eleven in south-west England (Dorset, Devon and Wiltshire). So undoubtedly the evidence came from the arable east where the depression was felt the most severely. Detailed expenditure on rent, labour and a miscellany of capital expenditure was included in the accounts of sixty-two of the farms. Table 6.9 is a summary of the main features. These were large farms, with an average size of 661 acres, ranging from 150 acres in Lincolnshire to 3,470 acres in Essex. In consequence the total annual expenditure also ranged widely. The data mostly summarise the situation at the bottom of the depression in the early 1890s but many of them stretch back to the early 1880s. However, short run or long run, the farm accounts reflect the influence of the depression.

The evidence shows perhaps what we would expect at the bottom of a depression: a relatively small proportion of expenditure on rents in eastern England, especially in Essex and Suffolk, the two worst-hit counties in terms of the decline in rent from 1872/3 to 1892/3 (Thompson 1991: 226). Yet there was a countervailing large expenditure on feed and manure and other items of tenants' capital expenditure (in line with the recent researches on Essex by Hunt and Pam 2002). There was a switch in the relative importance of landlords' capital vis-à-vis tenants' capital. Expenditure on labour remained more or less buoyant at around 30 per cent of all expenditure. Given the decline in the labour force from the 1860s the distribution of factor costs suggests a redistribution of income down the agricultural ladder towards the labourers. There was a general shedding of labour from agriculture from about 1860, but those that remained in work did relatively well. This is the story from eastern England, but elsewhere rents remained more buoyant, capital expenditure was at a lower relative level and the implied redistribution of income towards the agricultural labour force was less pronounced or not present at all.

This is a regional approach to the distribution of factor costs in the face of an agricultural crisis, but we can cut the database in different ways. A subset of forty-seven farms allows insights into the degree to which the more or less arable farms had different factor cost patterns. A simple correlation emerges: the greater the proportion of arable on the farm the less was the proportion of expenditure on rent (correlation coefficient of −0.45), but the greater was the proportion of expenditure on other items, especially labour (correlation coefficient between the degree of arable and the expenditure on labour, 0.46). This accords with what we have come to expect: the remission or lowering of rents, or indeed tenants going into arrears, were offset by a relative increase in other expenditure, especially the maintenance of a labour force in what was always a highly labour-intensive arable sector. The expenditure on what we take to be capital items was not sensitive to the relative mix between arable and non-arable production. Instead it was high everywhere. There is no statistical relationship at all between farm size and the relative distribution of factor costs; it was the *degree* of arable rather than purely farm size which was a determining factor.

While the distribution of factor costs tells a particular tale, there was also a particular pattern in the unit acre costs. The single Huntingdonshire farmer in the sample was a parsimonious fellow of the most extreme kind compared with his contemporaries, but elsewhere in eastern England this was not the case. The labour cost was highest in the east, and so was the unit expenditure on capital, but conversely the rents were by no means the lowest. In contrast, the single farmer from Devon was extravagant beyond his peers – he paid good wages, spent a lot on his land and endured the highest rent. In fact he paid the highest unit rent of all the sixty-two farms (but he had one of the smallest farms), and was

Table 6.10 Rate of return on farmers' capital on sixty-four English farms, *c.* 1892

County	No. of farms	Acreage	Profit or loss (£s)	Tenants' capital (£s)	Tenants' capital (£s per acre)	Rate of return on capital
Camb	4	2,318	−15	15,828	6.83	−0.1
Essex	16	11,944	−97	93,684	7.84	−0.1
Herts	2	750	−104	5,765	7.69	−1.8
Hunts	2	862	−39	7,500	8.70	−0.5
Lincs	13	10,271	−2,954	67,327	6.56	−4.4
Norf	4	1,763	−401	12,399	7.03	−3.2
Suff	6	3,970	−156	27,781	7.00	−0.6
Sub total	47	31,878	−3,766	230,284	7.22	−1.6
Beds	4	1,591	−2,023	11,793	7.41	−17.2
N'ton	5	1,585	−515	14,613	9.22	−3.5
Sub total	9	3,176	−2,538	26,406	8.31	−9.6
Dors	4	1,545	−1,336	11,217	7.26	−11.9
Wilts	1	827	−304	7,000	8.46	−4.3
Sub total	5	2,372	−1,640	18,217	7.68	−9.0
N'land	1	494	130	3,052	6.18	4.2
Yorks	2	1,387	650	15,944	11.50	4.1
Sub total	3	1,881	780	18,996	10.10	4.1
TOTAL	64	39,307	−7,164	293,903	7.48	−2.4

Source: Collated from Royal Commission on Agriculture 1897 (subject to rounding errors).

in the top ten of unit capital expenditure, and twenty-first in terms of unit acre labour costs. Apart from these individual outliers, the unit cost distributions in Table 6.9 show that the highest unit costs in labour and capital were experienced where the depression was most felt.

We have already identified that annual expenditure on capital was very high, especially in the east of England where the depression hit the hardest. Was this capital wisely spent? The combination of profit and loss and the size of tenants' capital employed allow a measure of the crude rate of return on that capital (but ignoring the opportunity cost of investing the capital in alternative ways). The aggregate for the sixty-four farms reveals a negative rate of return on capital employed of 2.4 per cent. But this varied dramatically from a positive return of 46 per cent on a farm of 120 acres in Essex to a negative return of 74 per cent on a 400 acre farm in Cambridgeshire. Table 6.10 summarises these returns on tenants' capital on the same regional basis as the analysis of the distribution of factor costs. The unevenness of this regional distribution cautions against hard and fast conclusions. Nevertheless, despite the severity of the depression the farmers in the east of England were by no means the most severely hit in terms of the return on their capital. They may all have made annual running losses, but the extreme of their plight was held in check by their landlords who shared the problem by reducing rents, and thus encouraged their tenants to invest their way out of trouble. In contrast, farmers in those counties in the middle and west of England fared much worse in terms of their capital returns. Those few farmers in the sample from the north of England fared much better, but at a contemporary rate of interest of about 4 per cent even they were only just matching the opportunity costs of other investments.

CONCLUSION

We have shown that the history of British agriculture from the mid-nineteenth century to 1914 cannot be depicted in terms of a neat cyclical pattern of first relative prosperity and then tragic depression, followed finally by modest recovery. The course of events was much more complicated, not least because there were external considerations involved. The repeal of the corn laws may not have sacrificed agriculture on the altar of free trade as is so often suggested, but the presence of free trade allied with technical developments in transportation and food preservation was important in shaping the course of events in British agriculture. More considered measurements of the performance of the agricultural sector also suggest that an otherwise straightforward story enshrined in textbook literature is rather more complex. Certainly the language of 'high farming' and 'agricultural depression' sometimes hides more than it reveals.

Yet there is no denying that British agriculture as a vital force in the national economy was in its death throes by 1914, though not yet completely expired. Agriculture's share of national income, share of national capital stock, share of rents as a proportion of total income, proportion of total employment, had all fallen below 10 per cent by 1914, and mostly well below 10 per cent. But it still supplied one fifth of home grain consumption and three-fifths of the meat, which argues for a relatively productive sector.

The First World War came and went, but not without apprehension, especially in Whitehall about the protection of food supply (Wilt 2001: 14–20). For the first two years of the war the government continued its more or less *laissez-faire* stance (Dewey 1989: 23–87). The indiscriminate enlistment into the armed services from the agricultural sector mirrored the general enlistment process of the war (Dewey 1975, 1991: 242–3). According to one theory Britain and her allies were triumphant because of agriculture, but not necessarily because of home agriculture (Offer 1989). Rather, it was the inadequacy of agricultural supply on the part of the enemy which, unlike Britain, had not secured massive supplementary sources through a successful history of empire building, sources that for Britain enjoyed the protection of distance and were not vulnerable to invasion and dispossession. They were, however, vulnerable to destruction when the ships bearing produce entered home waters at the end of their passage from Canada, South Africa or New Zealand.

The German submarine campaign was a real threat. However, once the German surface fleet had retreated to home ports in 1916 after Jutland, and once the vulnerability of lone merchant ships was solved by developing the merchant convoy system, considerations about the inadequacy of self-sufficiency abated, though they did not disappear. Every merchant ship that carried food to the British Isles could not carry armaments, troops or the other essentials of war. Self-sufficiency was in these terms a virtue. In general Lloyd George's national coalition government became more interventionist in agricultural as well as in other affairs. In late 1916 a decision was made to consider minimum price guarantees for the 1917 harvest (Dewey 1989: 91–105), and the Corn Production Act of 1917 actually guaranteed prices. This was too late to influence the 1917 harvest but the encouragement it gave to farmers was evident in the plough up of 1918. The arable acreage of Great Britain increased from 14.3 to 15.9 million acres 1914–18, of which wheat acreage alone increased from 1.9 to 2.6 million acres (MAFF 1966: 94–9).

The end of the war resulted in European dislocation, coincided with poor harvests and saw Australia, for example, impose a ban on grain exports. Food supply was put at risk. When the 1917 provisions were replaced by the 1920 Agriculture Act, offering price support for wheat and oats for four years, it looked like a sensible idea. But almost as soon as the act was passed the economic justification for it vanished as countries began to trade again and there was a ready supply of international grain. Grain prices halved in 1921 and it was no surprise that the Agriculture Act was repealed and price support removed. Whether this was the 'Great Betrayal' that many contemporaries thought is open to debate (Perren 1995: 38–44; Martin 2000: 4–6). The creation of marketing boards in the 1930s and the generally more attentive attitude of governments after the ending of free trade in 1932 may have lifted some of the gloom that had otherwise descended on the agriculture sector (Martin 2000: 23–8; Wilt 2001: 30–51). However, but for that brief respite at the end of the war agriculture seemed to labour under a state of benign neglect from the late 1870s until the Second World War.

7 Trade, 1870–1939: from globalisation to fragmentation

C. KNICK HARLEY

Contents

INTRODUCTION

In 1870 Britain appeared to dominate the international economy; by 1939 things looked very different as export industries struggled in a moribund international economy. In the eighteenth century Britain had become Europe's leading trading nation, and, during the industrial revolution, industrialisation and export growth went hand in hand to make Britain the 'workshop of the world'. In the late nineteenth century the international economy grew rapidly – during an era of globalisation that was not rivalled until the late twentieth century. Although the dominance of British firms diminished as foreign (particularly American) firms increased their share of world export markets, British export industries continued to prosper. Furthermore, British shipping, banking and mercantile services remained at the centre of the world economy.

By 1939, Britain's relationship with the rest of the world was altogether gloomier. The First World War had ended the era of a liberal expanding global economy. In Britain, as in other combatant nations, firms had turned their resources towards the war effort. Foreign customers found themselves ignored by their usual suppliers and looked elsewhere

Table 7.1 Britain and world trade in manufactures, 1899–1937 ($ million)

	British exports to		World exports to		
	Industrial countries	All markets	Industrial countries	All markets	British imports
At 1913 prices					
1899	479	1,327	1,923	3,677	545
1913	624	1,960	3,248	6,497	763
1929	537	1,821	4,212	8,936	810
At 1955 prices					
1929	1,547	5,176	11,272	23,841	2,115
1937	1,056	4,034	8,031	19,895	1,692
Annual rates of change:					
1899–1913	1.9	2.8	3.8	4.1	2.4
1913–29	−0.9	−0.5	1.6	2.0	0.4
1929–37	−4.7	−3.1	−4.1	−2.2	−2.8

Source: Maizels 1963: Table A4.

for alternatives. During the 1920s Britain returned to the pre-war gold-based monetary standard at an exchange rate that made British exports expensive. At the end of the 1920s, strains from the war and the imperfect return to gold contributed to the great depression in the 1930s. As depression and monetary instability spread, governments responded by circumscribing international trade to protect domestic firms and jobs and to insulate the monetary system from international pressure. In response to depression and the changed world, Britain abandoned the gold standard in 1931 and moved from a policy of free trade to one of tariff protection. Between 1929 and 1937 total world trade declined by about 5 per cent and exports of manufactured goods declined by nearly 20 per cent. Britain's situation was worsened by the loss of competitive position particularly in industries that had dominated the economy since the industrial revolution and that exported disproportionate shares of their production. These industries were geographically concentrated and their decline was a principal source of intractable long-term regional unemployment in the interwar economy.

Table 7.1 outlines Britain's relative position in the world trade in manufactured goods between 1899 and 1937. At first, British firms still held a disproportionate share, but that share was declining. In the interwar years trade contracted and Britain's share continued to contract. None the less, Britain was a major industrial exporter. Throughout the period trade continued to be important to the British economy, as Figure 7.1 illustrates. At the outbreak of the war about 30 per cent of the economy's goods and services were sold abroad. In the fragmentation of the interwar years that proportion was more than cut in half.

World trade in the nineteenth and twentieth centuries can be visualised, at the cost of some oversimplification, as falling into four eras.

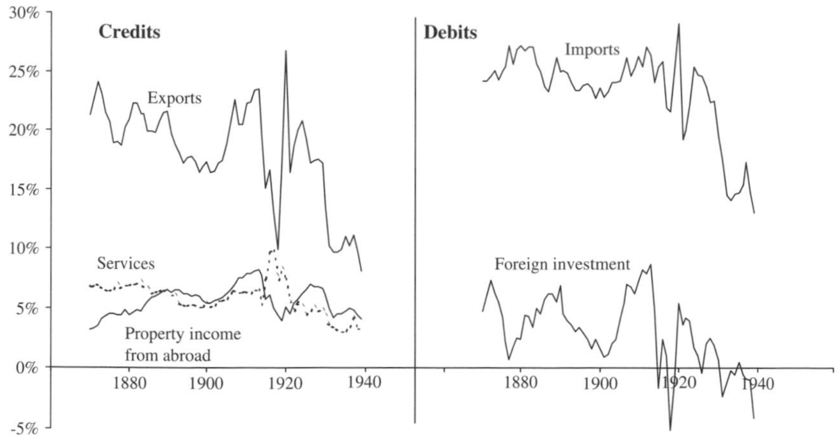

Figure 7.1 Balance of payments as percentage of GNP, 1870–1939

Source: Feinstein 1972: tables 3 and 15.

The first era was that of the industrial revolution and reflected British technological leadership. British firms invented new technologies in cotton and then in other textiles, in iron production and in the development of machinery of many types. Costs fell dramatically while the Revolutionary and Napoleonic Wars hindered foreign emulation and lower British prices attracted foreign buyers. British firms maintained their technological advantage for much of the century, most strikingly in cotton textiles where British firms continued to dominate international trade in 1913. The technology of the industrial revolution dominated Britain's early nineteenth-century trade, but population pressure on domestic agricultural resources also played an important role (Harley and Crafts 2000).

In the second era, covering the second half of the nineteenth century, transportation technology and population pressure drove change. Iron and steam technology had its greatest impact on railroads and steamships and caused dramatic reductions in transportation costs. Population pressed on limited European resources at the same time as the abundant agricultural resources of continental interiors became accessible. Together these forces generated an unprecedented growth in intercontinental trade in food and raw materials. With lower transportation costs, trade could exploit differences in factor endowments. In response, transportation networks and settlement expanded into hitherto inaccessible regions. Growing trade required investment which was provided by British investors. The growth of trade required the expansion of the international transactions services – such as finance and insurance – that British firms also provided.

The great period of globalisation driven by falling transportation costs and expanding settlement drew to a close by the early years of the twentieth century. We can see with hindsight the beginnings of the trade pattern of the late twentieth century. Today, although trade of manufactured goods for raw materials remains important, the bulk of trade consists of the exchange of differentiated manufactured goods among developed nations. That sort of trade was beginning to develop in the late nineteenth century and by 1913 Britain was deeply involved. Although we now see that advanced nations principally trade manufactured goods with one another, many commentators at the time, and some historians since, were concerned that Britain – the mid-century 'workshop of the world' – had become the most important import market for the manufactured goods of the other advanced economies. However, trade did not develop smoothly towards its late twentieth-century pattern. The First World War savagely disrupted the international economy.

During the war, neutral firms (particularly American and Japanese) supplied the goods which Europeans could no longer provide and import-competing industries developed within Britain's customers. In the years after the First World War, the third era, tariffs and quotas protected threatened industries in many countries. Attempts to restore the pre-war *status quo* foundered as a result of falling aggregate demand and the monetary disruptions of the great depression. In 1938, the total exports of industrial Europe in real terms (that is adjusted for inflation and deflation) were only just over three-quarters what they had been in 1913. Globalisation had been reversed and Britain's traditional exports suffered more than most other commodities. Globalisation was to return only in the late twentieth century during a fourth era of expanding world trade.

LATE NINETEENTH-CENTURY TRADE AND BRITISH PERFORMANCE

Early in the nineteenth century, Britain's trade had expanded rapidly because British firms had lowered the prices of textiles, iron and machinery. After mid-century, British firms retained technological leadership in these industries for many more years, but innovation activity shifted to industries where British firms now shared technological leadership with American and continental European rivals. Globalisation replaced technological leadership as the primary engine driving an unprecedentedly fast expansion of trade. Much of the growing trade involved exports of food and raw materials from newly settled regions, particularly, but not exclusively, in the western hemisphere. Falling transport costs, growing European population, an international policy regime of relatively free trade and the monetary stability that the gold standard provided also supported the expansion of trade (Irwin 1996; O'Rourke and Williamson 1999; Estevadeordal *et al.* 2002).

A densely populated industrialised core – western Europe and the eastern United States – traded manufactured goods for the raw materials of a primary-producing periphery. Much of the periphery was frontier brought into use by immigrants responding to export opportunities. In the 1850s the frontier stood in the American mid-west; in the following decades, it moved into the high plains of North America, the steppes of southern Russia and eventually into the southern hemisphere. Two forces unified the world into a single market. First, steam power and improved metallurgy revolutionised long-distance transportation; new railroads and steamships dramatically cheapened shipment. Second, population grew rapidly in Europe and older settled areas of the United States. Population growth put upward pressure on European food prices and falling transportation costs meant that a given Liverpool price produced a higher local price in remote areas of the world. As local prices rose, production of staple foodstuffs and raw materials became profitable where it had previously been unattractive (Harley 1980, 1986, 1992; but see Olson 1974; Latham and Neal 1983; Sugihara 1986; O'Rourke 1997; O'Rourke and Williamson 1999). A global economy for tropical goods had existed since the eighteenth century, but until the late nineteenth century high transportation costs largely separated two trading networks of temperate goods. One centred on the industrial areas of north-western Europe extended into a Baltic hinterland for agricultural supply; the second, centred on the north-eastern United States, extended into the American mid-west. As transportation costs fell, these trading blocks integrated and extended their influence beyond the Black Sea in one direction and beyond the Mississippi in the other, finally to encompass the entire globe.

During approximately a generation, between 1860 and 1890, the cost of shipment by rail and ship fell rapidly and the interior of North America, the Ukraine and central Asia, South America and Australasia and significant portions of South Asia entered a Europe-centred food economy. The general outlines of the developments of railroads and steamships are well known, but the extent of the change is often underestimated. The new transportation revolutionised spatial relationships; primary product prices rose in the frontier regions while they fell in Europe, despite an approximate doubling of Europe's population. The contrasting trends are illustrated by grain and meat prices in the American mid-west and Britain in Figure 7.2. British prices fell dramatically but the cost of shipment from Chicago to Liverpool fell (from equalling the Chicago price to insignificance in a half-century) so much that prices rose gently in Chicago and more rapidly in newly settled exporting regions farther west.

European agriculture came under tremendous pressure (see chapter 6 above). Seldom before had trade forced a fall in the prices of well-established activities on such a scale (although the impact of British textiles on foreign competitors earlier in the century provided some parallel). Globalisation in the previous centuries had seen dramatic increase in trade as new products – sugar, tobacco, tea and cotton – not produced in the importing region became international staples. From the late eighteenth century, Britain's timber imports had grown very rapidly, but in response to domestic depletion and rising prices. The great late

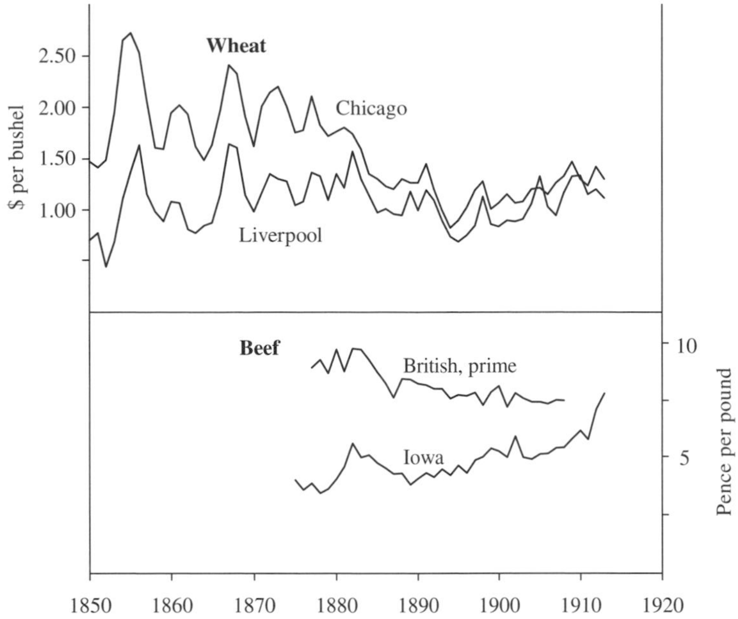

Figure 7.2 Wheat and beef prices, US and UK, 1850–1914

Source: Harley 1999.

nineteenth-century expansion of trade in agricultural commodities, in contrast, generated dramatic declines in the price of food in the consuming regions.

Lower transportation costs and the elimination of tariff barriers stimulated trade and caused the prices of traded goods to rise in exporting and fall in importing countries. In the process, factor prices also converged. Countries tend to export goods that use their abundant, and thus cheap, factors intensively, while imported goods use scarce, and thus expensive, factors intensively. The growth of exports increased the demand and price of abundant factors while imports lowered the price of expensive factors used in import-competing industries. Rents on scarce British agricultural land had long been high. This was perpetuated after the Napoleonic War by the corn laws and maintained after their repeal by growing population. In the 1880s, by contrast, rents declined dramatically in the face of growing food imports from distant frontiers. At the same time, exports increased British wages – over and above the benefits from cheaper food – although this effect was more restrained because only a minority of workers worked in exporting industries while all land competed with food imports (O'Rourke and Williamson 1999).

In continental Europe, governments responded to pleas from agricultural interests (Kindleberger 1975; Irwin 1996; O'Rourke 1997) and imposed tariffs on imported food from the 1880s. Britain's commitment to free trade, however, remained unshaken. British agriculture was already a small sector with modest electoral impact and more importantly, with the repeal of the corn laws the aristocratic landowning classes had abandoned protection for continued political dominance. The effect was quick and decisive; British food prices fell from the 1880s until the end of the century.

The era of transportation improvement ended around the turn of the century and food prices began to rise slowly. Primary product prices soared during the First World War and stimulated the final geographical expansion of agriculture in distant Canadian prairies and Argentine pampas. Thereafter the primary product producers in the periphery suffered from declining prices that persisted until the Second World War. In the twentieth century, agricultural output continued to grow but now as a result of advances in biotechnology rather than through geographic expansion, although protective policies discouraged international trade in foodstuffs. By the First World War, the era of expanding trade based on the exchange of agricultural commodities for manufactured goods was ending. Already, particularly in Europe, the more modern pattern of trade dominated by the exchange of manufactured goods among advanced economies was emerging.

Globalisation extended beyond international commodity flows. Settlement of continental interiors required people and capital and the construction of transportation and distribution networks. Railroads and cities to serve frontiers in the plains of North and South America needed far more resources than were available locally and capital was drawn from older areas. British investors found the securities issued by overseas railroads and governments attractive investments and bought them in large amounts. Nearly 70 per cent of the foreign securities issued in London in the late nineteenth century were to finance railroads and other forms of overhead capital (see chapter 8 below).

Long-distance trade required extensive modification of age-old methods of distribution. Traditionally, for example, local butchers had slaughtered local livestock to provide meat. By late Victorian and Edwardian times, however, much of the British consumer's beef came in a much less direct manner. The calf may have been born in Texas: driven as a yearling to grass lands in Montana; shipped by rail to a feedlot in Iowa to fatten on mid-western American corn; and finally shipped to Chicago and slaughtered in Swift's or Armour's mammoth packing houses. From there, meat made its way thousands of miles to British tables. Meat, because it is a valuable and highly perishable commodity, must be shipped quickly and reliably under refrigerated conditions. Refrigerated railroad wagons moved the meat to east coast ports where it was kept temporarily in specialised cold stores. Then it was packed in refrigerated storage compartments on Atlantic liners, shipped to Liverpool or London and transferred again to specialised cold storage. Only after all this did it appear on the butcher's counter for housewives to buy. The story was similar for many other commodities. Frozen lamb and mutton from New Zealand, Australia and Argentina followed nearly identical distribution paths. Even less perishable goods like wheat and wool now travelled long distances and were graded, stored and traded at various points along the way. All this distribution needed transportation, co-ordination and finance.

British firms had acquired experience in marketing, financing, insuring and transporting goods on an intercontinental scale since the eighteenth century and their activities expanded along with the world economy. British capital in the exporting regions further directed business toward them. As a result the world's commercial co-ordination and finance centred on London. In addition, British-owned ships made up about half the world's merchant marine so the increase in demand for shipping also generated business for British firms.

LAGGING EXPORTS AS AN ENGINE OF DECLINE?

In the late nineteenth century the volume of Britain's exports continued to grow more rapidly than national income (a considerable fall in the price of manufactured export goods relative to non-traded services resulted in the share of exports in income remaining roughly constant as Figure 7.1 illustrates). However, Britain's position in the trading world appeared different from that which it had enjoyed a half-century earlier when British technological leadership drove trade expansion. Export growth slowed, imports grew more rapidly than exports and other industrial countries, particularly the United States and Germany, appeared to dominate trade in the latest technology, even capturing large markets in Britain (see Table 7.1). Britain lost its dominance as 'workshop of the world' and its economy grew distinctly more slowly than those of its foreign rivals. By the 1890s editorial pages and parliamentary debate spoke of 'defeat' in a German commercial 'invasion', or of the 'conquest' by Americans of another 'outpost' of British exports (Hoffman 1933). Just as many scholars see Britain's growth to international prominence in the industrial revolution as dependent on foreign trade, so many also blame developments in the international economy for Britain's relative decline after 1870. Both judgements are probably unfounded but examining the case helps us to understand the nature of the late nineteenth-century international economy.

The seemingly common sense notion that demand causes growth underlies the belief that trade growth crucially influenced British growth, first for good and then for evil. Simple Keynesian income analysis, in which the level of demand determines the level of national income, reinforces this view. If the economy is not fully employed then an increase in export demand will increase the nation's income. Higher income will come directly by setting men and machines to work in producing ships and coal and machinery for export; it will also come indirectly by setting men and machines to work making steel for the shipyards, pit-props for the collieries and machine tools for the machine shops, as well as producing food, housing, transport and so forth for the men now earning and spending incomes. In this situation, buoyant export demand gives the economy a 'free lunch' by productively using involuntarily idle resources; sagging export demand took it away.

The assumption of less than full employment is suited for the understanding of an economy coming out of bust and moving into boom, for it is plain in such a case that workers are indeed being drawn out of involuntary idleness as the economy expands. It is doubtful, however, that the assumption helps understanding growth between peaks of the cycle of boom and bust; this is crucial, since a Keynesian interpretation depends on the British economy not being fully employed at the successive peaks of boom and bust in the late nineteenth century (Matthews 1959: 74). Doubts on this score have not deterred students of the late Victorian economy in the heyday of Keynesian analysis from using a demand-led model to explain growth (Rostow 1948; Meyer 1955; Coppock 1961). The evidence, however, suggests that there were simply no large reserves of unemployed resources that could have been set to work if exports had been larger. The limits on the late Victorian economy, in other words, were limits of supply (McCloskey 1970).

In a fully employed economy an increase in demand for, say, exported cloth increases the output of cloth, but only by reducing the output of another domestic commodity. In the language of economics, in such an economy there are opportunity costs or, colloquially, no 'free lunch'. An increase in demand for exports does not increase total output, but merely reallocates resources and restructures output. In the absence of unemployed resources events in the international sector may have a large impact on economic structures but only modest influence on the size of national income. This was true when exports boomed after the industrial revolution and also in the late nineteenth century when export growth slowed.

The argument linking export deceleration with late Victorian decline has not, however, depended exclusively on the existence of unemployed resources. More promising arguments explore ways in which Britain's international transactions may have limited the growth of capacity of the economy. Some have argued that sluggish markets for exports reduced the scope for investment in export industries at home and drove British savings (already low by international standards) overseas, to Indian railways or Brazilian plantations. The private returns from such reallocation of resources, it is said, were satisfactory, but the social return was not (Coppock 1956: 2; Kennedy 1974, 1987; Crafts 1979, 1985: ch. 8). Even if this last is true, however, it does not follow that the effects of misallocating savings were large (McCloskey 1970, 1981; Harley 1989). In an important study of British long-term growth, R. C. O. Matthews, C. H.

Feinstein and J. C. Odling-Smee presented a demand-influenced view of growth that included an opinion that slower export growth seriously hurt late nineteenth-century growth (1982: 445–65). They concluded that, although unemployment did not increase, the slower growth of exports depressed British activity by encouraging disguised unemployment and, most importantly, by slowing growth of total factor productivity. They presented no direct evidence for this conclusion but appealed to a supposition (the 'Verdoorn Law') that total factor productivity growth is caused by output growth in manufacturing. The conclusion, however, can hardly be regarded as established. The Verdoorn proposition is by no means generally accepted; the slowdown in exports and manufacturing growth that Matthews *et al.* document occurred almost exclusively in textiles, where they point out there was little scope for total factor productivity growth.

It is hard to see how British manufacturing exports could have continued their earlier growth. Britain's share of world manufacturing at the middle of the nineteenth century was uniquely high and could only have been expected to decline. The manufacturing sector already employed modern proportions of the economy's resources and failure to continue to increase its share is hardly surprising. In 1913, after all, Britain still accounted for nearly 32 per cent of internationally traded manufactured goods, although it produced only around one fifth of total world manufactured goods. Britain's share of world manufacturing had been declining from its peak early in Queen Victoria's reign as industrialisation occurred elsewhere. Modern economic growth inevitably involves the economy in readjusting its use of resources and the mix of goods it produces as technology and demand change; the late nineteenth century seems little different from other periods. While it is conceivable that particular adjustments, towards the growing international service sectors together with continued exports of products from the now old industries of the industrial revolution in particular, combined to hamper growth, a simple connection of exports to income is hard to support.

Critics have certainly pointed to the pattern of British trade as evidence of failure. In every year after 1822 the value of Britain's commodity imports exceeded the value of commodity exports and the disparity increased as time went on. Mathias (1983: 289) summarised a prevailing view:

> The conclusion to be drawn from Britain's accounts with the rest of the world in 1913 is to see to what a great extent the economy was being protected, or cushioned from the failure of exports to pay for imports, by the £4,000 million of capital invested abroad . . . Even quite a marked degree of failure in the competitive standards of some British export industries might be tolerated without much strain, as long as the £200 million came in interest each year.

The fixation on commodity trade and its deficit is usual but it is inappropriate to ignore the spectacular successes in the export of services and the receipt of interest and dividends that past lending provided. The growing deficit on commodity trade was more than covered by receipts from the international sale of shipping, commercial and financial services, and by the interest and dividends from foreign assets (see Figure 7.1). In 1913, for example, the deficit of £82 million in commodity trade was more than balanced by a £121 million surplus on services. This surplus, together with net property income from abroad of £200 million, financed enormous new overseas investment equal to more than 8.5 per cent of gross national product (GNP) (see chapter 8).

The market and commodity structure of British exports, however, enhances the impression of weakness in exports and industrial performance. Exports throughout the nineteenth century came mainly from the few industries that had been in the forefront of the industrial revolution. Even on the eve of the First World War, textiles, iron and steel and coal contributed two-thirds of commodity export earnings and these exporting industries were heavily oriented toward export markets. The dependence of export earnings on a few industries whose technology had been set during the industrial revolution and whose prosperity was dependent on export markets has been seen as a weakness in the British economy of the early twentieth century. 'Overcommitment', it is said, produced vulnerability to change in international conditions, for newly industrialising countries were stimulating these very industries with tariff protecting. Their predominance in Britain made adjustment of the economy toward the newer light engineering industries, emerging around 1900 as technological leaders, more difficult. The experience of these industries between the wars reinforces this position (Richardson 1965; Aldcroft and Richardson 1969; Crafts 1985: ch. 8; see also chapter 4 above).

The British economy apparently clung to its traditional industries and failed to take advantage of the new technologies. When tariffs and industrialisation severely curtailed sales to traditional markets in Europe and the United States, British firms found less challenging export markets. In the 1850s customers in western and central Europe and the United States purchased more than 40 per cent of Britain's exports; in 1870 these customers still took nearly 40 percent; by 1910 the proportion had declined to well under 30 per cent. In their place British exporters found customers in Empire markets and in Latin America and Asia where less formal but still important ties bound primary-producing areas to Britain. Specialisation in such less sophisticated markets worried observers. Nor were foreign markets the only problem. By the early twentieth century, foreign manufactured goods were becoming increasingly evident in Britain. Shipbuilders and other steel users purchased German steel and British engineering firms bought American machine tools. Surely something had gone wrong. Many began to believe that the British entrepreneur had failed, or that the policy of free trade was a mistake.

The conclusion that there was a failure in performance does not, however, necessarily follow from the observed patterns of trade. It seems more likely, in fact, that Britain's trade pattern emerged as a consequence of globalisation. Exports from Asia and the Americas revolutionised the supply of primary products to Europe, and European trade patterns adjusted. The growing staple-producing areas drew large amounts of British capital, which in turn generated large return flows of interest and dividends; and the export of staple products required services which British shipping, financial and commercial firms provided.

Conclusions about economic performance cannot easily be drawn from patterns of trade, because comparative, not absolute, advantage determines trade. Britain exported the things it could produce cheaply relative to the other things it could produce – cheap coal, cotton goods, insurance, shipping relative to food, timber and in the end steel – not necessarily the things that it could produce with less labour or capital than could other nations. For example, British agriculture was so efficient that it could produce food using fewer resources than were used in Argentina or Illinois. But it would have been foolish to do so in 1900, as Britain's continued adherence to free trade recognised. British resources were better used making machinery and insurance policies. The 'failure' of Britain to export food, the 'decline' in the size of agriculture and the 'invasion' of British markets by imports was no sign of technological inferiority in agriculture. So too elsewhere in the economy.

As world markets became integrated, Britain became the centre of the international economy. Other industrial economies were initially preoccupied by domestic industrialisation and, after 1880, unlike Britain, insulated themselves from international forces with tariffs on both manufactured goods and agricultural imports to protect domestic interests (Kindleberger 1975; Bairoch 1989; Irwin 1996, 2002). British trade in the late nineteenth century reflected more the world that Britain dealt with than any peculiar developments in British economic character. Food and raw materials came from distant, often frontier, areas. Britons migrated to these areas, and British firms and investors helped to construct the transport and urban infrastructure needed to support new production. Not surprisingly British firms traded actively with these regions, providing the consumer and investment goods that the pioneers demanded – textiles, railroad iron and other heavy investment goods that Britain had long produced with such skill. Trade needed commercial services that Liverpool shipowners and London bankers provided. The commodity composition and the markets of British exports and the bilateral payments patterns at the end of the nineteenth century were imbedded in the multilateral globalisation driven by staple supply. Figure 7.3 illustrates multilateral trade balances around 1910. Britain imported much more, including manufactured goods, from Europe and America than it sold to these countries – features that have been ascribed to British weakness.

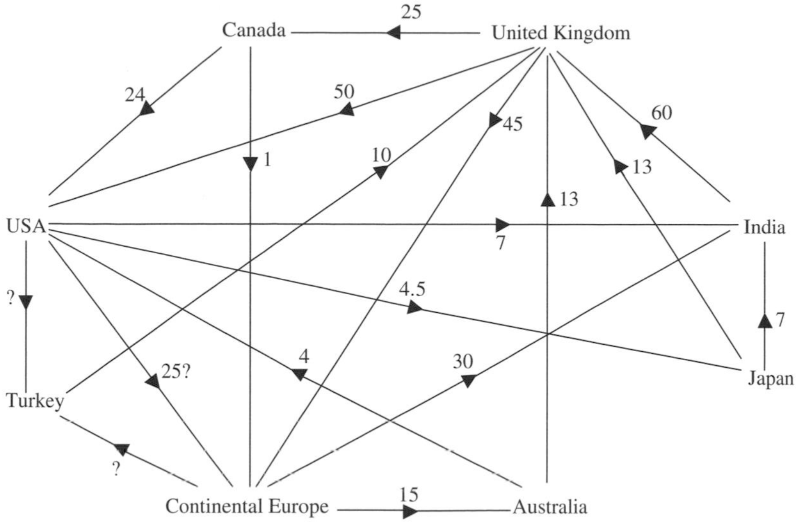

Figure 7.3 Patterns of world trade settlements, 1910

Source: Saul 1960: 58.

British exporters sold large amounts of manufactured goods to the staple-exporting areas – including, importantly, India – and generated surpluses there. These had their counterpart in the import surpluses which Europe incurred with all the primary exporters and the United States incurred with the tropics. Britain's large overall commodity deficit, equalling more than a third of imports, was more than paid for by interest and dividends and by foreign purchases of British service (Hilgerdt 1942; Saul 1960: chs. III, IV; Harley 1995).

Britain's deficits with the industrial economies and surpluses with the primary-producing economies therefore need to be seen within a world network. Other industrial economies balanced deficits with the primary-producing areas by running surpluses with Britain. The pattern could have emerged and been maintained in more than one way. Those who see weakness in the British economy believe that British firms lost the ability to compete in the markets of developed countries. Ties of formal and informal empire, it is said, allowed increasingly non-competitive British firms to sell in primary-producing countries. Imperialism supported the sale of non-competitive exports. Those who have studied world trade in detail see the pattern differently: '[the] world-wide interconnecting network of trade [emerged] in the last three decades of the nineteenth century mainly from the rapid growth of primary producing countries and the demand for their products arising in Europe and America' (Saul 1960: 62). As continental Europe imported more primary products it had to finance them. Since the means for multilateral settlement existed, these countries exploited comparative advantage multilaterally rather than bilaterally. The competitive advantage of Germany and America did not lie in the products demanded by the primary producers, but in the products of new industries demanded by richer consumers and more sophisticated firms in developed economies. Exports to the British market, where consumers and investors demanded new products and access was unhindered by tariffs, proved the best way for Germany and America to finance primary imports. In 1913, British importers spent nearly 50 per cent more on manufactured goods from continental Europe than British firms earned on sales to this region.

Earnings from foreign investment and transactions service that the international economy required were not an artificial cushion; rather they were payments to British firms and investors for important contributions to the international economy. These receipts had repercussions on Britain's commodity trade. To the extent that the British were unwilling to invest abroad amounts equal to these earnings, the surpluses on the investment income and service accounts had to be balanced by deficits in commodity trade. International prices adjusted to support this equilibrium so service earnings resulted in a higher price level in Britain relative to her competitors (a higher 'real exchange rate') than would have been the case in their absence. Earnings from service and investment retarded British export growth just as earnings from Dutch natural gas exports in the 1960s hurt Holland's other export industries – late nineteenth-century Britain had a variety of what economists later came to call 'the Dutch disease' (Matthews *et al.* 1982: 455–6, 526; Crafts 1985: 163).

British firms continued to export the products of the old industries and sold outside the industrial nations while Germany and America gained markets in richer industrialised countries with their new industrial products. This pattern emerged from three characteristics of the late nineteenth century. First, tariffs on industrial products inhibited the sale of British manufactured goods in industrial countries. Second, many areas of primary production had expanded with the aid of British capital and commercial expertise and the trade of these areas was naturally oriented towards Britain. Third, when British industries were compared with their German and American counterparts it was clear that Britain's competitive position was strongest in certain old industries – textiles, shipbuilding, heavy engineering and some branches of metal production. This advantage was based on Britain's early lead and the practical skills that the labour force had developed over a century of industrial experience (see chapter 3 above). Although British firms appeared old-fashioned in their use of skilled labour and their relatively late adoption of new machine processes, they produced more cheaply than they could have done with more mechanised methods and also more cheaply than could foreign competitors. In newer branches of industry, however, Britain did not enjoy these advantages of an early start. Here mechanised production was the rule in Britain, as elsewhere, and Britain was comparatively disadvantaged (Harley 1974; Broadberry 1997c). In short, because it industrialised first, Britain's comparative advantage lay in the old industries while her rivals' comparative advantage lay in newer industries. This finding about comparative advantage provides no insight into the relative technological or economic efficiency of production in the various countries. Investigation of that issue requires detailed study of the technological choices that industries faced (see chapter 4 above).

The concentration of British exports in a few industries was therefore the legacy of the lead that Britain achieved in the industrial revolution. Technological precocity led British industries to supply a substantial portion of world industrial demand in historical circumstances where demand was highly concentrated in a few commodities. The legacy of early leadership shaped British trade into the twentieth century and may have imposed costs of 'overcommitment' and late adoption of new technology. Learning by doing appears to generate a large part of technological change, both in Britain early in the century and in America and Germany late in the century. Britain's productivity growth may have suffered because trading opportunities concentrated resources in old industries where technological opportunities were meagre at the expense of new industries with potential for technological advance. Certainly productivity growth appears to have slowed in the years before the war (Matthews *et al.* 1982: 229; Crafts and Thomas 1986; Crafts 1985: ch. 8). Crafts and Thomas show that Britain's export industries did not require skills imparted by formal education. In contrast the comparative advantage of German and American firms lay in new industries that used human capital. British commitment to education and human capital formation may have lagged in consequence. The British economy provided less basic education to its general labour force and directed educational reform toward clerical skills, demanded by Britain's internationally dominant service sectors, rather than towards scientific skills (see also chapter 3 above). This left Britain relatively poorly placed to take advantage of new technology of the so-called 'second industrial revolution' in fine chemicals, industrial equipment, electrical goods and cars and aircraft. This was a legacy that was to cause twentieth-century difficulties; it was an efficient response to Britain's position as the first industrialised country, perhaps, but a restraint on future growth.

With the benefit of hindsight we can also see that twentieth-century Britain paid a price for the industrial concentration caused by large exports of a few commodities to a few markets. Interwar unemployment was concentrated in the old industries. Labour drawn to these industries in the pre-war period did not move easily to other employment. The loss to the economy was enormous. Still this does not imply that the industrial structure prior to the war was necessarily wrong. Even if we leave aside the issue of the management of the international value of the British pound in the interwar period – perhaps no small leaving aside – it is not clear that hindsight is appropriate for historical judgement. To be sure, adjustment would have had to occur even without the trauma of the war and the associated disruption of the international system in which Britain was so involved but it would have been slower. The British economy began to adjust long before the war. Traditional industries were declining as a proportion of national income and of foreign earnings. As the twentieth century unfolded, it was unfortunate that much of the shift went into international services that depended on the stable international economic environment that was so shaken by the war and its aftermath. And it is an irony of history that the interests of these service industries heavily influenced the exchange rate policy of the interwar years.

Perhaps an appropriate question to ask is: would an omniscient, but not prescient, planner have made a different choice than that which the British economy actually made through the workings of atomistic markets? That question is hard but does not obviously demand an affirmative answer. Britain's international specialisation conformed to her comparative advantage: there were gains from trade that would have been lost by some other structure. The newer industries that expanded slowly in Britain were the wave of the future where technological change was developing most rapidly. Perhaps dynamic gains, in learning-by-doing and human capital formation, were overlooked but those are hard to identify even now. Future advantage does not imply that the economy should have shifted immediately to its future structure more rapidly. The concentration of export markets and the concentration in industries certainly increased the risk to the economy – as the interwar period dramatically revealed – and a cautious planner might have chosen to forego present gains from trade to reduce this risk. But it turns most of the historical literature on its head to suggest that the structure of the British economy before the First World War was inappropriate, not because of excess caution being exhibited through the market decisions, but instead because of paucity of caution.

THE FIRST WORLD WAR: DRAMATICALLY CHANGED CIRCUMSTANCES

The First World War irrevocably changed Britain's trading world although the full impact was not apparent until the 1930s. The war itself, of course, horrendously disrupted trade. Trade ceased between the belligerents but it was of longer-term significance that it diverted European industrial capacity to military needs; customers used to purchasing European manufactured goods looked elsewhere for supplies. Alternatives became available from non-European exporters and from import-substituting domestic production. American and Japanese firms permanently increased their exports. Between 1913 and 1929, the United States' share in world exports of manufactured goods increased from 13 per cent to 21 per cent, while Japan's share rose from 2.3 per cent to 4 per cent. European exporters all lost market share, none more so than Britain whose share of trade in manufactured goods fell from 30 per cent to 23 per cent (Maizels 1963; Hartach 1977: ch. 9).

The war also fundamentally altered international asset positions. Britain entered the war with international assets worth approximately half of the value of the domestic capital stock. Income from these assets, as we have seen, financed imports and new foreign investment. During the war, the government acquired and sold assets located in the United States to purchase war materials and other goods to aid the war effort. In addition, the government borrowed large amounts in New York. At the same time, the British government followed its traditional policy of providing financial aid to its continental allies – in this case principally France and Russia.

The most important long-run economic effect of the war, however, was the destruction of the international monetary equilibrium under the gold standard that had supported the previous half-century of globalisation. At the outbreak of war prudent investors sold assets in belligerent countries and demanded foreign exchange or gold in order to move their funds from the war zones. Governments responded to the threatened loss of gold by *de facto* (although usually not *de jure*) abandonment of the gold convertibility of national currencies. Of greater long-run significance was that the cost of the war led governments to manipulate the monetary system to aid wartime finance. Tax increases were insufficient to pay much of the cost of the war and government borrowing, although quite successful in Britain, provided insufficient funds for the war's requirements, at least at interest rates that the state was prepared to pay. Governments paid many of their costs with newly issued government currency or, more usually, by selling short-term debt to the central bank and the banking system, thus increasing the supply of bank money. This increased money supply caused inflation inconsistent with the gold standard. Prices rose much faster in the combatant countries, including Britain, than in noncombatants – most importantly in the United States until it joined the war on the Allied side in 1917. The result was that, if the gold value of the pound was to be restored after the war, British firms would find their prices above those of American goods in domestic and international markets. Exports sales would fall and imports increase. Maintaining the exchange rate would threaten British gold reserves (Hardach 1977; Temin 1989; Eichengreen 1992).

POST-WAR ADJUSTMENT: INFLATION, EXCHANGE RATES AND THE RETURN TO GOLD

Armistice in November 1918 ended the immediate stress of war but brought many other problems. Trade was no small issue since in 1913

Britain had sold goods and services worth 30 per cent of national income to foreign customers and received an additional 8 per cent of national income from overseas assets. The war jeopardised this income. Markets had been lost and the war reinforced nationalism globally. A socialist state in Russia repudiated Czarist debts and largely withdrew from trading networks. New states created from the defeated Central Powers (Germany and Austria-Hungary) asserted sovereign rights to tariff protection. Elsewhere, firms created by wartime demand clamoured for protection from European imports. International assets had been liquidated and debts taken on to support the war. There were offsetting claims on allies and reparations to be claimed from Germany but the balance was uncertain.

Exports boomed immediately the war ended as firms and consumers world-wide placed orders to offset wartime privation. This sharp boom was accompanied by continued inflation. Private individuals and firms spent money accumulated, but not spent, during the war. At the same time governments faced continued fiscal difficulties and refinanced short-term wartime debt by direct or indirect money creation.

The boom, although it stimulated new investment, proved ephemeral for many British export industries. Initially problems arose from monetary adjustment. The boom had been supported by American lending and monetary expansion that came to an abrupt end in 1921 when the newly created Federal Reserve took steps to bring prices down towards pre-war levels. Tighter money in New York curtailed American lending and caused contraction elsewhere. In Britain, the Bank of England and the Treasury initiated a regime of tight money to begin the process of returning sterling to the gold standard at its longstanding value. Return to gold posed a challenge. The stability of domestic and international monetary arrangements that the gold standard had provided was widely seen as an indispensable foundation for a prosperous pre-war international economy. Britain's international financial service industries – 'the City' – in particular felt that success in finance and commerce required stable money both domestically and internationally. Consequently, there were strong pressures to restore the gold standard after the war, just as it had been restored in similar circumstances a century earlier after the Napoleonic Wars.

Return to gold involved both constraints on domestic money supply and a fixed exchange rate with other countries with a gold-based currency; in this case, particularly with the United States. The gold standard and the fixed exchange rates had been abandoned under the pressure, initially, of capital flight and, subsequently, of inflationary wartime finance. Market-determined (or flexible) exchange rates prevailed immediately after the war and the value of sterling had fallen by 1920 to less than 80 per cent of its pre-war dollar value. Fixed exchange rates lower the costs of international transactions but equilibrium at a specific fixed exchange rate between two currencies also requires a specific relationship between price levels. If a country's price level is too high, imports will exceed exports and gold will leave the country to cover the deficit (and perhaps also in anticipation of the currency being forced from its gold basis). If the process is gradual, the loss of gold will reduce the money supply, lead to lower prices and bring about international equilibrium. In the years before the war, central banks acted to maintain the convertibility of paper money to gold and the balance of payments equilibrium at fixed exchange rates that implied. As the world economy evolved long-term trends required modest changes in the price levels between countries but, at least from the perspective of Britain and other core industrial countries, these had generally occurred at a modest pace. In addition, international confidence in the gold standard supported international lending to ease transitions (Eichengreen 1992; and see chapter 12 below).

The situation after the war was more complex. Countries had different inflationary experiences. War debts and large reparations imposed on the Central Powers added additional disequilibrium and uncertainty to the international financial picture. A restored gold standard either had to adjust the gold value of domestic money and the exchange to reflect inflation and new financial obligations or there had to be large changes in domestic price levels among countries to achieve consistency with the old gold value of currencies. Inflation in the United States had been the lowest among the major economies. Britain's inflation had been considerably above the American level, but moderate by the standards of the other combatants. On the European continent, the currencies of most of the Central Powers collapsed in hyperinflation in the early 1920s. The victorious Allies were in a happier situation and could expect to receive reparations, but inflation had been high and the fiscal situation was more difficult than in Britain. The continental economies found themselves unable to control inflation, permitted the exchange rate to float and eventually resumed gold-based currencies at substantially lower gold values than had prevailed before the war. Even in this environment of the early 1920s, it became clear that Britain would return to gold at the pre-war parity of $4.86 to the pound. However, British inflation had exceeded American by some 10 per cent, and the loss of overseas assets and the wartime erosion of British export markets suggested that the British price level needed to be lower relative to that of the United States than before the war.

The return to gold with the domestic price level too high to correspond to the exchange rate placed enormous pressure on the British economy. The success of restoration to the pre-war parity required macroeconomic adjustments to lower the domestic price level. The export industries were particularly hard hit. Although most economists believe that the absolute level of prices has little or no effect on the real economy, they also agree that lowering the price level, as Britain's return to gold required, entails a period of depression and unemployment. John Maynard Keynes opposed the return to gold and outlined its costs in a brilliant 1925 polemic – *The Economic Consequences of Mr. Churchill.* He pointed out that the initial impact of the overvalued exchange rate would fall on export industries forced to sell at international (or dollar-determined) prices that were now some 10 per cent lower in sterling while their costs of production were still determined by British domestic prices. This situation, of course, would force losses on the export industries and some firms would curtail operations. Unemployment in the export industries would tend to put downward pressure on wages but would initially have little effect on wages and prices (all of which needed to fall) elsewhere in the economy. In Keynes' view the coal industry was particularly vulnerable and the miners 'victims of the economic juggernaut'. Eventually, he pointed out, falling prices in the export industries, cheaper imports and unemployment would result in lower prices and wages in the economy overall. The cost in terms of lost markets and unemployment in the export industries, however, would be irresponsibly high. His foresight was good: high levels of unemployment, particularly in the export industries, accompanied the return to gold. However, the problems of the export industries and high levels of unemployment in the regions where they were concentrated persisted beyond a reasonable period of macroeconomic adjustment. There were longer-run problems.

'OVERCOMMITMENT': COAL, TEXTILES AND STEEL

The interwar years saw the collapse of the comparative advantage of Britain's old export industries. By the early twentieth century, the technology in these industries had stabilised and had been transferred around the world by British machine-making firms which sold complete factories to foreign competitors and provided advice to get them operating. Foreign firms, with much cheaper labour, could compete very effectively. This process had been evident for some time and British cotton textile firms, for example, had gradually concentrated on the finer yarns and fabrics in which the advantage of their experience had greatest impact (Kowakatsu 1998). The war and protectionism in the uncertain post-war environment greatly accelerated the trend and British textile firms rapidly lost market share to low-wage producers in a market that was growing only slowly. Japanese cotton mills, in particular, responded to wartime opportunities by expanding output and exports and in 1929, Japan produced nearly twice the amount of cotton goods it had produced before the war and exports of 2.2 times as much. Textile firms expanded in many other countries and trade in textiles declined despite continued growth of world output of textiles. The most important expansion of import substitution occurred in India where, by 1929, imports had fallen to just over two-thirds of their level in 1913. Similar trends existed in steel, chemicals and capital goods. Britain's share of world exports shrank, but here the loss of markets was primarily to American exporters. British share of world exports of steel fell from 23 per cent before the war to 14 per cent in the late 1930s, of chemicals from 20 per cent to 16 per cent and of capital goods from 31 per cent to 19 per cent. Before the war Britain had also been the world's main exporter of coal – the principal industrial fuel. This market also contracted as low-cost American mines expanded, wartime-induced expansion in Europe continued to develop and petroleum became an increasingly important source of fuel (Maizel 1963; Supple 1987).

It would be a mistake, however, to see British industry entirely as failing in international markets for manufactured goods in the interwar years. British firms remained major exporters of capital goods and developed important positions in new consumer durable industries. None the less, the old exporting industries of the industrial revolution went into decline from which they never recovered. The problems of these industries affected the economy disproportionately primarily because many of them were highly concentrated geographically. Concentration had provided advantages of information, labour supply and complementarity during the industries' prosperity but in the interwar years it created serious regional problems of unemployment and decline. New industries provided little compensation because they located in the Midlands and the south-east in order to be close to the main consumer markets centred on London and away from the old industrial regions.

The distress that accompanied the loss of export markets was very real and regional unemployment was a major political and social issue. The problem began with the return to gold and intensified during the depression. Many firms failed and workers lost jobs in Lancashire, with its declining cotton industry, the north-east, South Wales and parts of Scotland, where the coal mines and the steel works lost export markets. The regional economies adjusted very slowly to the changed opportunities because local skills and resources had long been directed to the export staples and the new industries were locating elsewhere. Government policy attempted to preserve jobs. Some initiatives ameliorated immediate distress, but they tended to support existing firms with little long-run prospects and delayed adjustment to new sustainable economic structures. Overall, attempts to save jobs probably distorted incentives and slowed long-term growth (Heim 1986; Broadberry and Crafts 1992a; Bowden and Higgins 1998).

INTERNATIONAL FINANCE AND WORLD DEPRESSION

After 1928 the world economy slipped into depression with international trading and financial relations playing an important role. Among the industrial countries, the large reparations obligations imposed on Germany by the peace, the war debts which Britain had incurred with America and the debts which the other Allied powers had contracted with Britain and the United States all complicated international economic relations. Although there was some pressure to negotiate reduction or eliminate these obligations, America insisted on repayment of war debts and France on reparations. Through most of the 1920s these financial flows were financed primarily by German public authorities' and private firms' borrowing in New York.

Additional international financial complications arose in the periphery. High food prices during the war and its immediate aftermath stimulated agricultural expansion and agricultural suppliers, like Canada, Argentina and Australia, had financed expansion with foreign borrowing. In the 1920s, agricultural exporters faced sharply falling prices that reduced foreign exchange earnings, just as their new production came to compete with traditional sources that had faced wartime disruption. Lower earnings from staple exports accompanied unchanging debt obligations from foreign borrowing and many primary product exporters confronted balance of payments deficits. During the 1920s additional borrowing in New York financed the shortfall (Kindleberger 1973; Eichengreen 1992).

International economic relationships thus rested heavily on borrowing from New York but in the late 1920s, an American boom and rapidly rising stock prices led the Federal Reserve systems to impose a restrictive monetary policy. American financial markets reacted by curtailing foreign lending, with immediate repercussions on foreign borrowers. Primary exporters in Latin America and the British Dominions, whose economies had relied on American lending to cover the shortfall of international receipts relative to obligations and to finance government expenditures that exceeded tax receipts, now found themselves in very difficult positions. Without new loans from New York demand for foreign exchange exceeded its supply at gold standard exchange rates. Maintenance of the gold standard required central banks to meet the excess demand with reserves of gold or foreign currency. These reserves, however, were severely limited so long-term equilibrium required that the price level in these countries should fall relative to the rest of the world.

Deflation is always difficult, as the British had found in the immediate post-war years. It requires monetary restriction and entails a period of adjustment characterised by bankruptcies and unemployment. The Latin American borrowing countries, which depended on American finance to cover their public budget deficits as well as their balance of payments shortfalls, were particularly hard hit. With American loans curtailed, these governments continued to finance budget deficits by money creation. The combination of reduced American lending and budget deficit was inconsistent with the gold standard and the prevailing value of the currency. The situation quickly deteriorated as domestic wealth holders and international speculators rushed to sell the currency to avoid losses (or achieve gains) when the logic of the situation predicted devaluation. Reduced American lending and capital flight drove many primary exporters off gold in 1929 (Eichengreen 1992).

Abandonment of gold by primary product exporters in the 'periphery' was inconvenient but not devastating to the system. Britain as a major creditor and exporter to these economies felt pressure on its own exchange reserves that reinforced existing deflationary pressure. In the heyday of the gold standard before the war, primary producers had experienced this sort of difficulty and been forced to abandon gold and devalue their exchange rates without systemic damage. In the late 1920s, however, the situation was much more precarious because weakness was also present in industrial nations at the core of the world economy. Germany, Austria and other successor states of the Austro-Hungarian Empire also depended on borrowing from New York. This was partly a consequence of reparations obligations imposed by Versailles, but it also stemmed from a governmental policy choice (conditioned to be sure by reparations) (Kindleberger 1973; Temin 1989; Eichengreen 1992; Ritschl 1998).

International financial crisis occurred in 1931, triggered by central European banking systems which were weakened by depression and by large short-term borrowing by governments and banks in those countries. The crisis began in the spring in Austria when it became apparent that the largest private bank, the Credit-Anstalt, was in serious difficulty from loans that the recession had made uncollectable. Domestic and foreign depositors in the bank prudently attempted to remove their deposits from the weakened bank. The bank turned to the Austrian central bank for assistance. The central bank followed normal central banking procedures of increased liquidity to aid the banking system by purchasing assets and extending loans to the banking system. In the process the central bank's own reserves fell. After more than two years of recession, investors' confidence had declined and the reduction in a central bank's reserves brought its ability to maintain a fixed exchange rate into question. Austrian and foreign investors lost confidence and converted Austrian assets into foreign exchange, greatly intensifying the pressure on the central bank. Some international loans assisted Austria and President Hoover of the United States initiated a moratorium on intergovernmental debts. By the end of the summer, however, it was clear that the international assistance was inadequate. Austrian authorities imposed strict exchange controls and other restrictions on international transactions to limit the damage to the banking system, effectively leaving the gold standard.

The events in Austria presaged a similar loss of confidence in neighbouring countries. In Hungary, with close connections with Austria, depositors lost confidence in the banks and the currency only days after the crisis began in Vienna. By July the banks and the stock exchange were closed to prevent the loss of reserves. They only reopened when the government effectively left the gold standard by freezing foreign deposits and imposed exchange controls.

More serious problems for the international economy arose as the crisis spread to Germany. Investors withdrew assets from German banks and converted them into foreign currency. A banking panic erupted in July. The Reichsbank sought international support for the mark at its gold standard value. American distrust of European finance and French distrust of Germany's political situation and its attempts to end reparations inhibited international co-operation. During the summer, the German authorities, too, instituted exchange controls that limited international transaction.

The continental crisis spread to London. British earnings had been reduced by events in the primary producers; exchange controls in central Europe further restricted their overseas earnings. The minority Labour government faced a serious budget deficit as a result of growing unemployment insurance payments. In this situation, holders of sterling deposits questioned the ability of Britain to stay on gold. During the summer, the Bank of England found that it had to use its reserves to maintain the gold standard. The Bank received some American assistance, but it was too little and too late. On 23 August, the Labour government split on issues of reducing the budget deficit and fell. A National Government under Ramsey MacDonald (the prime minister of the previous Labour government), composed of a coalition of part of the Labour party, Conservatives and Liberals, took office and took difficult steps to reduce the government deficit; however, pressure on sterling continued. On 19 September 1931, Britain left the gold standard and allowed the value of sterling to fall. New exchange rates were thus determined by the market (Cairncross and Eichengreen 1983).

Britain's abandonment of the gold standard did not end confusion in the international economy but moved it into a new phase. Many of Britain's trading partners, particularly in the Empire and in Scandinavia, allowed their currencies to follow sterling. The United States and most of western Europe, however, maintained the gold value of their currencies. Abandoning gold and devaluation removed the pressure from the British financial system. Unlike in the United States and much of continental Europe, there was no banking crisis to intensify the depression; in addition, devaluation, by lowering the foreign price of British exports and increasing the domestic price of imports, provided some assistance to British firms, both exporters and those who competed with imports. A gradual recovery from the depression can be dated from the abandonment of gold.

The early thirties, however, were an inauspicious time for international economic transactions. The countries that remained on gold (most notably the United States and France) continued to face deflationary

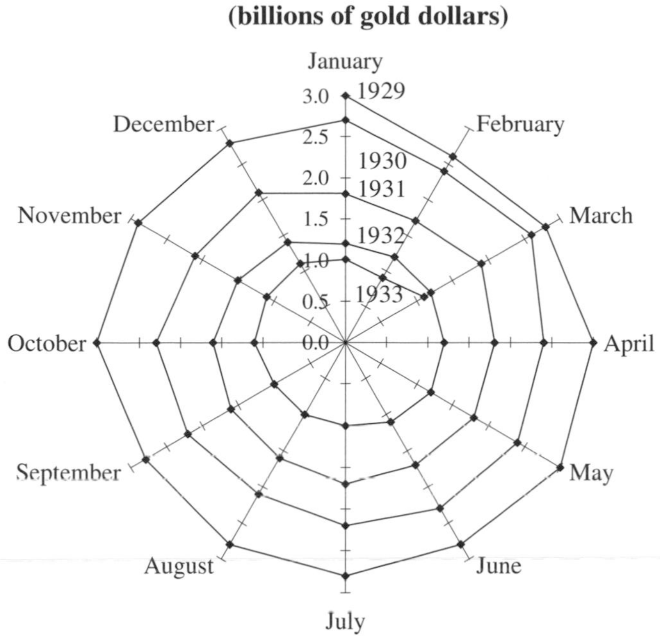

Figure 7.4
Contraction of world trade, 1929–33
Source: Kindleberger 1973: 172.

pressure from the need to defend their gold parity. The onset of the depression had strengthened the political argument for protecting domestic markets for domestic producers and balance of payments pressure added further arguments for restricting imports and financial flows. Protectionist interests were successful in passing tariffs. The financial crises of 1931 led to further tariffs and exchange controls. Britain's departure from gold and the depreciation of sterling put further pressure on those countries that remained on gold and they responded with increased protection. The result was the downward spiral in world trade after 1929 illustrated in Figure 7.4.

Over the course of 1929 the value of world trade contracted by about around 10 per cent, in 1930 by 30 per cent, in 1931 again by around 30 per cent and in 1932 by 17 per cent. In January 1933 the value of international trade was just one third of its January 1929 level. Since Britain was still the largest exporter of manufactured goods, this decline in international trade hit the domestic economy hard. For example, in 1924 Britain produced over 6,000 million square yards of cotton piece goods, of which 73 per cent was exported. By 1930 production had fallen to just 3,500 million square yards, and although it rose to 4,288 million square yards by 1937, exports now accounted for only 45 per cent of output (Allen 1951). Total exports of the British economy, which formed 23.2 per cent of net national income in 1913, had declined in scale to 17.6 per cent of net national income by 1929, and to just 9.8 per cent by 1938 (Aldcroft 1970: 245).

THE RISE OF PROTECTION

The Abnormal Imports Act of November 1931 marked Britain's definitive abandonment of free trade – another strong commitment of Britain's pre-war international economic stance – and quickly followed departure from the gold standard. Three months later, the Import Duties Act imposed duties (initially of 10 per cent, soon increased to 20 per cent) on manufactured imports and stipulated preferential treatment for imports from the British Empire.

While the depression played a role in the enactment of the tariff, political pressure had been developing since before the war. Although there are circumstances in which economic theory indicates that a country as a whole can benefit from a tariff, because restricting exports increases the price received from foreigners or because expansion of an industry generates technological advance, economists usually argue that tariffs hurt the economy imposing them. This is true because with a tariff higher-cost domestic sources replace low-cost imports. The overall costs may be quite small and a tariff's greater effect is to alter the distribution of domestic income in favour of those receiving protection. The political economy of the passage of tariffs rests on these distributional effects. In an election voters must weigh a range of issues and while ideology certainly plays an important role, they are best informed and most active in lobbying and voting for those issues that have the greatest impact on their personal situation. In contrast they pay little attention to issues that they personally find peripheral. Since production is concentrated and consumption is diffuse, policies that distribute income to well-defined groups of producers have political advantage over those that benefit heterogeneous groups of consumers (Smith 1776; Olson 1965, 1982).

As frontier expansion and transportation costs lowered food prices in Europe, agricultural interests – both landlords and peasants – suffered. On the continent, landlords were the ruling elite and peasants an important source of conservative support for the established order. It is hardly surprising that soon after food prices started to fall in the 1870s these groups succeeded in getting tariffs passed to maintain agricultural prices at home at the expense of urban workers. Britain differed in several ways. First, by 1870 only about a fifth of the male labour force was in agriculture compared to about a half in most continental economies. Furthermore, unlike continental peasants most British agricultural workers had little property stake in agriculture. Aristocratic landlords, of course, were the main losers from cheap American grain and meat and, as on the continent, they still dominated political life. However, with the 1846 repeal of the corn laws (see Volume I) the aristocracy traded protection of their agricultural interest for continuing political power. The repeal of the corn laws and then the fall in food prices had instilled in the industrial classes – middle-class factory owners and urban workers alike – an awareness which forcefully entered political debate that free trade meant cheap food.

In the twentieth century some of these conditions changed. Even before the war, increasing imports of manufactured goods – most noticeably steel – had started to alter the interests of some of the manufacturing classes. Nationalism also entered the debate. Joseph Chamberlain's early twentieth-century campaign for 'Fair Trade' and for a self-sufficient British Empire emphasised that Britain's economic and potential military rivals had promoted their industries with tariffs on British manufactured goods; it urged that the Empire should do the same. However, Chamberlain's arguments lost decisively when put to the voters during the 1906 election.

The war, however, gave protectionist politics a significant boost. After four years of total war, no one could deny the strategic importance of the iron and steel and machinery industries – 'heavy industry'. The steel industry quickly warned of the perils of Germany regaining a significant share of the British market and reducing the size of their strategic industry. Post-war unemployment provided another protectionist argument: imports had cost British workers jobs. Even Empire solidarity was strengthened by the war. The White Dominions had made disproportionate contributions to the war effort. To be sure, they had instituted protective tariffs in the late nineteenth century to promote their own industrialisation, but they had allowed British goods in at preferential rates. Should Britain not reciprocate?

The free-trade tradition was breached during the war. Government control of the economy had been pervasive and shipping space was tightly rationed. In 1915, the so-called McKenna (after the chancellor of the Exchequer) duties of 33 per cent *ad valorem* were imposed on a limited range of manufactured goods as a temporary wartime measure. They were, however, renewed (with a brief lapse in 1924) through the interwar years and remained as rates above the general tariff rates in 1932. The coverage of these duties was limited but included the important automobile industry (Foreman-Peck 1979). In the chaotic years after the war industrial groups, most notably steel producers, argued for protection in the face of alleged German dumping (selling in Britain below the price in the home market) and argued that the depreciated German exchange rate gave their rivals unfair advantage. The Liberal and the Labour parties, however, successfully resisted, primarily by appealing to the need for cheap food.

The depression, however, gave protectionist arguments additional force. By the 1930s unemployment and excess capacity in established industries had become the major issue. It seemed only reasonable to guarantee the home market to domestic producers, particularly when foreign markets were contracting, in part, at least, because of foreign protection. The deteriorating international political scene in Europe and pressure from the Dominions for preferential treatment also strengthened the case for protection. In any event, Britain joined the world-wide protectionist trend in the early 1930s. It is unlikely that the tariff made a major impact on employment but it certainly helped to fuel the global climate of contracting world trade. The 'deglobalization' of the interwar years was only reversed with American leadership in the post-war years (Drummond 1974; Capie 1983).

CONCLUSION

In the years covered by this chapter, the international economy underwent two major transformations. In the late nineteenth century, revolutions in transportation technology and liberal trade policies in Europe combined with largely unfettered movements of people and capital to produce a great era of globalisation. This era ended with the First World War. The war disrupted trade. Equally important, war finance resulted in monetary expansion that severely disrupted domestic and international financial arrangements that had been based on the gold standard. Protectionist policies and financial disruption fragmented the international economy in the aftermath of the war. Attempts to restore the liberal pre-war regime failed to overcome the obstacles that the war had created. After 1929, depression and financial crisis led to the decade-long great depression. Seen as a whole the half-century after 1913 was one of deglobalisation that contrasted sharply with the preceding half century of globalisation.

By 1850 geography and history had enmeshed the British economy uniquely in the international economy. British firms had played important roles in the eighteenth-century expansion of Europe's world trade. Then British firms responded to the industrial revolution by developing extensive export trade in a few industries. After 1850, British manufacturing industry no longer enjoyed undisputed technological leadership, but trade continued to loom large in the economy. Firms in the industries of the industrial revolution – textiles, iron and steel and engineering – continued to serve world markets, which often took more of their production than domestic consumers. In the expanding world economy, British firms provided needed distribution services. Throughout the half-century before the First World War, between 25 and 30 per cent of the goods and services produced in Britain were sold to foreign customers. Export industries – both goods and services – were dynamic sectors of the economy. It is probably incorrect, however, to credit export expansion with much of the underlying growth or its variation. Certainly exports influenced the structure of production but the sources of growth were located in more fundamental characteristics of the economy.

Britain's heavy involvement in the international economy created difficulties in the troubled interwar years. World trade faltered badly and technological transfer, low foreign wages and protection hurt British firms in textiles, metallurgy and engineering. In addition, Britain's specialisation in old industries and services implied that fewer firms had experience in newer technologies such as electrical engineering and chemicals. The large service sector was hurt by the overall contraction of the international economy. International monetary problems added to the difficulties emanating from the international economy. The decision to return to gold at its traditional value in 1925 placed exporters at a disadvantage and necessitated tight money and deflationary pressure in the early 1920s. The collapse of trade that accompanied the great depression after 1929 appeared to sound the death knell of the liberal international economy. Britain left gold and abandoned free trade in 1931 under pressure from international forces and turned inward for a generation.

8 Foreign investment, accumulation and Empire, 1860–1914

MICHAEL EDELSTEIN

Contents

INTRODUCTION

Great Britain's immense capital export is among the most important historical phenomena of the period between 1860 and 1914. Rising in the 1850s and 1860s, the flow of net foreign investment averaged about a third of the nation's annual accumulations from 1870 to 1914. As a result of these annual flows, net overseas assets grew from around 7 per cent of the stock of net national wealth in 1850 to around 14 per cent in 1870 and then to around 32 per cent in 1913. Paish (1914), estimating the value of the stock of British overseas assets just before the First World War, net of repatriations and foreign sales, suggested that the total stock at the end of 1913 was not less than £4,000 million (see also Platt 1986; Kennedy 1987b; Feinstein 1990b). Never before or since has one nation committed so much of its national income and savings to capital formation abroad.

To some observers the immense capital export went abroad because of the high profitability of railroad and other social overhead investments in the emerging primary product economies of North America, South America and Australasia. Others have argued that the capital export was a result of weaknesses in the domestic British economy. In one argument domestic investment demand weakened due to a pause or slowdown in British productivity growth – a productivity climacteric – and, because Britons continued to save despite slowing domestic investment demand, funds moved abroad by default. Another argument is that the British distribution of income and wealth led to tendencies to oversave, with the excess carried off abroad. Institutional factors are also said to have influenced the capital export.

If there is controversy about the reasons for the immense capital export, there is also controversy concerning its effects. On the positive side, it is often argued that the capital exports received a higher private rate of return than domestic investment and, given a generally low unemployment rate, thus augmented British incomes more strongly than alternative domestic investments. Furthermore, by helping to lower the costs of overseas transport and extending the margin of cultivation and mineral extraction into hitherto inaccessible but highly productive soils and deposits, British capital exports helped to lower the cost of British imports of food and raw materials.

Sceptics, however, have argued that the capital export may have had a number of pernicious effects. First, some have argued that, in fact, the realised return from investment abroad was lower than at home due to widespread defaults by spendthrift overseas governments and railway executives. Second, it is sometimes argued that the distribution of British incomes was more sharply skewed by directing British savings abroad. Had these funds remained at home they would have helped to augment the stock of domestic housing and other urban social overhead projects which would have benefited the British populace more widely than the uses to which the overseas profits were employed. Finally, modern studies of technical progress have found that an important source of productivity growth stems from the accumulated experience of production, often termed 'learning-by-doing'. If, as seems to be the case, British capital exports tended to increase the demand for the products of the older export industries, it might be argued that the newer segments of the British capital goods industry were inadvertently starved of demand during their infant and later learning years, with consequent effects on the growth rate of British per capita incomes.

The period from 1860 to 1914 is also notable for the continued expansion of the British Empire and British political influence in the independent nations of the underdeveloped world. Expansion of the British Empire in the seventeenth and eighteenth centuries had often involved competition with Holland, France, Portugal and Spain. During the first three-quarters of the nineteenth century, British expansion was largely a quiet, uncompetitive affair. In the last quarter of the nineteenth century expansion again took place within what can only be termed an international scramble. The maintenance and expansion of the Empire presents a number of important issues. The difficulty, in fact, is that there are too many important questions to give each of them their due. In the section on the economics of Empire which closes this chapter, the problem which receives most attention is whether the British Empire represented a net gain or loss to the domestic economy.

THE PATTERN OF FOREIGN INVESTMENT

Rates

In the seventeenth and eighteenth centuries joint-stock trading and colonising companies, interloping merchants and the individual owners of West and East Indian plantations gathered a certain amount of long-term funds for ships, warehouses, plantations and slaves. Wealthy Britons also held a certain amount of interest-bearing debt of various European governments. For most of the eighteenth century it is likely that these outflows of long-term capital were roughly balanced by inflows of Dutch and other foreign funds, Britain becoming a small net creditor on international account in the late eighteenth century (Feinstein 1988b: 164). This low level of international lending continued after the Napoleonic Wars, net foreign investment averaging 1–1.5 per cent of gross national product (GNP) from 1811 to 1850 (Table 8.1). In the 1850s, however, the rate rose to 2.1 per cent and in the 1860s rose again to 2.8 per cent. From 1870 to 1914, the average rate was 4.3 per cent. There was therefore a

Table 8.1 UK rates of savings and investment (%), 1830–1914

Period	GNA/GNP	GDFI/GNP	II/GNP	NFI/GNP	GPS/GNP	GS/GNP	E/GNP	PH/GNP	PO/GNP	Yr	OA/GNW	OA/NNW
1830–9	7.83	6.56	0.36	0.91								
1835–44	8.57	7.37	0.29	0.91								
1840–9	9.84	8.38	0.70	0.76								
1845–54	10.96	9.15	0.90	0.92						1850	6.02	7.04
1850–9	10.08	7.42	0.60	2.05								
1855–64	10.68	7.22	0.92	2.55			48.94	48.49	2.57	1860	8.91	10.57
1860–9	11.44	7.55	1.08	2.81			47.69	49.27	3.05			
1865–74	13.90	8.04	1.18	4.67			47.02	49.23	3.76	1870	11.90	14.16
1870–9	13.31	9.12	0.20	4.00	12.31	1.00	47.69	47.65	4.66			
1875–84	12.16	8.66	0.51	2.99	11.16	1.00	49.07	45.63	5.29	1880	14.83	17.74
1880–9	13.17	7.03	1.42	4.72	12.17	1.00	49.17	44.84	5.99			
1885–94	12.42	6.61	0.87	4.94	11.42	1.00	50.34	42.95	6.70	1890	21.05	25.46
1890–9	12.02	7.61	1.04	3.37	11.02	1.00	51.05	42.38	6.57			
1895–1904	11.76	9.12	0.67	1.97	11.76	0.00	50.93	42.85	6.22	1900	22.65	27.84
1900–9	12.61	8.75	0.19	3.66	12.61	0.00	50.70	42.54	6.76			
1905–14	14.13	7.20	0.42	6.51	13.13	1.00	50.15	42.05	7.80	1910	26.23	32.12

Abbreviations: GNP = gross domestic product at market prices plus net property income from abroad; GNA = gross national savings = gross national investment; GDFI = gross domestic fixed investment; II = change in inventories; NFI = net foreign investment; GPS = gross private savings (= GNA − GS); GS = government savings; E = income from employment; PH = income from home property (= GNP − E = PO); PO = net property income from abroad; OA = stock of overseas assets; GNW = gross national wealth, including domestic reproducible assets, land and overseas assets; NNW = net national wealth (GNW less depreciation on domestic reproducible assets).

Sources: The sources for domestic investment, foreign investment, public and private saving and gross national product are Imlah 1958: 70–5; Edelstein 1982: 315–23; Feinstein 1988: 462–3 and Mitchell 1988: 831–3. The factor income ratios derive from Mitchell 1988: 828–9 and the wealth stocks from Feinstein 1988: 464–5. Platt 1986 argues that the overseas wealth stock estimates presented here are too high but his methodology involves some serious flaws (see Kennedy 1987a; Feinstein 1990b).

major shift in the nature of British capital accumulation in the third quarter of the nineteenth century.

Another feature of British overseas investment in the late nineteenth and early twentieth centuries was its volatility. As Figure 8.1 illustrates, this volatility was set in a repeating pattern of long cycles lasting between sixteen and twenty-four years. Up to the early 1870s, the broad fluctuations in the overseas investment rate roughly paralleled the fluctuations in the domestic investment rate, but thereafter the long movements in overseas and home investment moved inversely.

Direction

In the early 1850s about half the stock of UK overseas wealth was in European securities and other assets, a quarter in the United States, a sixth in Latin America and the rest in the Empire. Over the next ten years or so, India and the Dominions replaced Europe as the dominant hosts of the British capital export (Jenks 1927: 64, 413, 425–6).

From 1865 to 1914 the cumulative sum of annual money calls for new overseas issues totalled £4,079 million (Stone 1999: 381; see also Simons 1967). In its continental directions, 34.3 per cent were placed in North America, 16.8 per cent in South America, 14.0 per cent in Asia, 12.6 per cent in Europe, 10.8 per cent in Australasia and 10.6 per cent in Africa (Stone 1999: 381, 409).[1] In terms of Stone's climatic-ethnic breakdown, most, 59 per cent, of the 1865–1914 new issues went to the regions of recent European settlement, followed by 23.4 per cent to the tropics and only 12 per cent to Europe. Stone also found that 71.4 per cent of all overseas railway money calls between 1865 and 1914 went to the regions of recent settlement, regions likely to have had a disproportionate need for an initial stock of social overhead capital (Stone 1999: 414). The British Empire received 39.6 per cent of all money calls for new overseas issues, 1865–1914.

Direct versus portfolio investment

Before the nineteenth century and after 1945, most British overseas assets took the form of direct investments in overseas structures, land, plant, equipment and inventories by British businesses. Between those dates the bulk of British overseas placements took the form of British purchases of portfolio investment (Cottrell 1975; Edelstein 1982; Dunning 1983; Wilkins 1988).[2]

[1] The top ten national or colonial hosts, 1865–1914, were the United States (20.5 per cent), Canada and Newfoundland (10.1 per cent), Argentina (8.6 per cent), Australia (8.3 per cent), India and Ceylon (7.8 per cent), South Africa (6.4 per cent), Brazil (4.2 per cent), Russia (3.4 per cent), New Zealand (2.1) and Mexico (2.0 per cent) (Stone 1999: 411).

[2] Overseas investment is called portfolio investment when the assets purchased are either the debentures of governments or the equity and debentures of private enterprises in which Britons own less than 30 per cent of the equity interest. When Britons own more than

In the years between 1850 and 1914, the proportion of portfolio investment was probably in the range of 70–80 per cent (Cottrell 1975: 11; Stone 1977: 696; Svedberg 1978: 769; Edelstein 1982: 33–7; Dunning 1983: 85). The explanation probably lies in the nature and size of the real capital which was purchased with British funds. Between 1865 and 1914 almost 70 per cent of British new security issues went into social overhead capital (railways, docks, tramways, telegraphs and telephones, gas and electric works, etc.) and 12 per cent went into extractive industries (agriculture and mining) (Simon 1967). Very little, 4 per cent, went into manufacturing.

Social overhead capital is lumpy; that is, the initial size necessary to give service, let alone to make a profit, is very large relative to the resources of wealthy individuals or businesses. Consequently, social overhead capital has rarely been financed from the personal resources of a few individuals or businesses. The typical borrower for social overhead capital projects in modern times has been a government or a large joint-stock company. Indeed, the institutions of joint-stock organisation and public issue of securities were created in the early seventeenth century, at least in part as a private solution to the problem of the size and risk of social overhead projects and the resources of individual wealth holders (see Volume I, ch. 11.) In the mid-nineteenth century, the principal overseas borrowers for social overhead capital projects were either governments or mixed government–private enterprises (Simon 1967). During the second half of the nineteenth century, however, the trend was toward placements in wholly private, limited liability companies, probably reaching over 50 per cent of social overhead borrowings by 1914.

Short bursts

Except for the United States, British investment in particular countries or colonies between 1865 and 1914 tended to be concentrated in short periods of time. Thus, the greater part of British investment in Australia occurred in the 1880s and early 1890s, in Canada after 1900, in South Africa in the early 1900s and in Europe in the early 1870s and just before the First World War. Hall (1963) attributed this spurt-like involvement of British capital to the flexibility of British investors who shifted their horizons in the wake of the appearance of new opportunities. Unquestionably, British investors were quite flexible in this respect, but the nature of the opportunities was also important. To some extent the 'one-shot' pattern of British overseas investment reflected the lumpiness of the social overhead needs of the regions of recent settlement, their initially limited savings resources and their immature capital markets.

30 per cent of the equity interest in an overseas private enterprise, their holdings of the latter's equity and debentures are termed direct investment and it is believed that British owners were thereby able to control the use and management of their savings. Control is assumed to rest elsewhere with portfolio investments.

In a small country recently settled, a large backlog of lumpy social overhead capital projects might have to accumulate before the return was sufficiently great to draw attention to the need for the special funding arrangements just mentioned. Going overseas for some of the entrepreneurship and capital might then be thought of as the cheapest means of arranging for these lumpy projects, and this would lead to a spurt of foreign investment. Later economic development either did not generate as many lumpy social overhead projects or local savings and capital markets were now able to handle the lumps that did appear (Davis and Gallman 2001).

American borrowing from Britain was also variable, but it was always important. Given the size and pace of the aggregate movements in the US economy and its expansion into unsettled territory until the end of the nineteenth century, the continuous flow of British capital is not surprising. The major use of British funds was for lumpy social overhead capital projects. Of the £836.4 million in money calls for new US securities raised in Britain, 1865–1914, 61.6 per cent went to new railway issues and another 9.5 per cent to urban public utilities (Stone 1999: 51).

THE CAUSES OF FOREIGN INVESTMENT

Hypotheses

In the late nineteenth and early twentieth centuries there were two streams of thought concerning why overseas investment had surged to such heights. One stream relied upon classical economic thought and saw the money flowing abroad because the rate of return on European capital had reached some sort of diminishing returns. By the late nineteenth century, many observers were aware that technical progress in transportation, manufacturing and agriculture might limit or prevent a fall in rates of return, but either the rate of invention or the diffusion of new technologies did not provide enough profitable domestic opportunities or there were even more natural resource, transportation and industrial investment projects with high returns abroad. The dispute is whether the funds were pushed out by fading domestic returns or pulled out by eruptively high overseas returns.

The second stream of thought is best represented by J. A. Hobson's work (1902). Hobson held that because too little of Britain's national income was allocated to wage earners, who did most of the nation's consumption, and too much income was allocated to property owners, who did most of the nation's savings, there was a strong tendency for a prosperous Britain to generate too little consumption and too much savings. Property owners were assumed to save irrespective of the rates of return they received. Given this insensitivity to rates of return and the tendency to generate too much savings, British funds were inevitably pushed abroad searching for any use.

In sum, the literature suggests that there were two possible reasons for funds being pushed out of Britain, fading domestic returns and surplus savings, and a single reason for funds being pulled from abroad, that is, newly high overseas returns.

The 1850s and 1860s

As already noted, the rate of net foreign investment first jumped to significant levels in the 1850s and 1860s. It would appear that during this first period overseas flows were pulled abroad by newly high overseas returns rather than pushed by fading domestic returns or an excess of British savings, invariant to rates of return. Many overseas regions were growing quickly and needed social overhead capital – but had small local savings and immature capital markets. In Australia the gold discoveries and subsequent broader economic developments provided a strong field for British capital exports. After the Mutiny of 1857, the British wished to extend the Indian railway system, the better to move troops and emergency foodstuffs. Europe also offered an excellent field for railway investments. But the widest field was the United States. With nearly half the world's track mileage during this period, the US system tripled in size in the 1850s and then doubled in the 1860s.

Great Britain's railway system was also expanding in the 1850s and 1860s, doubling its trackage. Industry-wide averages of the return on real and financial railway capital showed no sign of any downward movement (Broadbridge 1970; Hawke 1970). Thus it seems likely that if the surge of foreign investment in the 1850s and 1860s was motivated by a disequilibrating gap between overseas and home returns, the gap was created by newly high returns abroad rather than fading returns at home. Notably, a strikingly similar pattern characterises French domestic and foreign investment in these decades.

1870–1914: the role of return and risk

Having risen in the 1850s and 1860s, the ratio of British net foreign investment to GNP rose still higher after 1870, to average around 4.3 per cent, 1870–1914. As Table 8.1 and Figure 8.1 make obvious, British foreign investment was highly variable during these years. There were two surges in British overseas lending, one which began in the early 1880s and peaked in 1891, and another which began in the early 1900s and peaked in 1913. The principal use of these funds was railway and other social overhead capital and the chief borrowers were the regions of recent European settlement. As in earlier years, the proportion going to the Empire was steady at about 40 per cent. What balance of

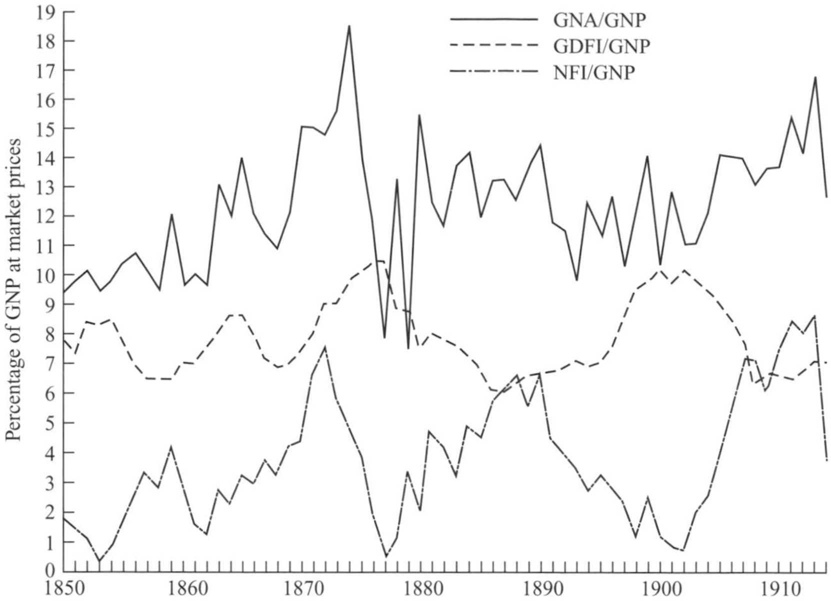

Figure 8.1 British savings and investment rates, 1850–1914

Source: Floud and McCloskey 1994: 176.

push and pull forces was responsible for the massive capital outflow of these years?

First, it must be asked whether overseas portfolio returns were greater than those available at home and, if so, when. If the capital market is reasonably competitive, differences among expected rates of return from one investment to another should not appear unless there are differences in the market's evaluation of their relative riskiness. Thus the only way one can examine whether there were differences in portfolio rates of return is to tabulate the historical record of capital gains and losses, dividends and interest payments, and compute indices of realised returns. One study examined a sample of 566 home and overseas, first and second class, equity, preference and debenture securities (Edelstein 1982: chs. 5 and 6). The sample included issues from every sector of the capital market except overseas mining and foreign governments.

Table 8.2 Realised rates of return to home and overseas railway securities, 1870–1913 (%)

Region	Equity	Debentures
United Kingdom	4.33	3.74
Eastern Europe	2.58	5.33
Western Europe	6.31	5.28
India	4.97	3.65
United States	8.41	6.03
Latin America	8.43	5.33

Source: Edelstein 1982.

Where direct comparisons are possible in railroads, governments, municipals, other social overhead investments and banking, Table 8.2 shows that overseas portfolio investments yielded a higher realised return than domestic portfolio investments, 1870–1913. When the entire sample of 566 securities including assets issued by domestic manufacturing and commercial enterprises is aggregated into weighted home and

Table 8.3 Realised rates of return, aggregate indices, selected sub-periods 1870–1913 (%)

	1870–1913	1870–6	1877–86	1887–96	1897–1909	1910–13
(A) *Domestic*						
(1) Equity	6.37	11.94	7.19	8.93	0.92	6.64
(2) Preference	4.84	9.08	5.70	6.10	1.85	3.25
(3) Debentures	3.21	4.36	4.12	4.92	1.40	1.84
(4) Total	4.60	7.62	5.37	6.42	1.35	3.60
(B) *Non-domestic*						
(1) Equity	8.28	7.34	13.77	5.34	9.54	1.37
(2) Debentures	4.92	6.29	6.40	5.16	3.82	1.90
(3) Total	5.72	6.60	8.06	5.23	5.20	1.79
(C) *Non-domestic minus domestic*						
(1) Equity	1.91	−4.60	6.08	−3.59	8.62	−5.27
(2) Debentures	1.71	1.93	2.28	0.24	2.42	0.06
(3) Total	1.12	−1.02	2.69	−1.19	3.85	−1.81
(D) *Market*	4.90	7.72	6.51	5.92	2.97	2.84

Source: Edelstein 1982.

overseas return indices, overseas placements still offered a superior return to home issues (Table 8.3, column 1). On average, 1870–1913, overseas first and second class investments yielded a return of 5.72 per cent per annum while home first and second class investments offered a return of 4.60 per cent. When evidence on returns to overseas mining (Frankel 1967) and foreign government debentures (Cairncross 1953) is taken into consideration, the average gap was probably somewhat larger.

Was the higher return abroad a reward for undertaking more risky investment? One can measure risk first by examining the amount of variation around the mean return on home or foreign assets, to see if returns varied more abroad. They did not; the variation was roughly equal for both types of assets. In addition, the return on foreign assets was less closely correlated with the rate of return on all assets than was the return on home assets (Edelstein 1982: 139). Overseas returns, in other words, were slightly less affected than home returns by the unavoidable risks of major economic disruptions and political events. In short, it does not appear that foreign assets were significantly more risky than home assets.

What accounts for the gap in risk-adjusted returns? The most plausible hypothesis is that overseas regions tended to generate greater amounts of profitable natural resource, transportation, industrial and marketing opportunities which periodically led to higher returns abroad than at home. That is, the places were newer, like the American west (Clemens and Williamson 2001).

Contemporary observers of the British economy were concerned to know whether the absolute level of British rates of return was declining.

If one wants to know why capital flowed overseas, the more appropriate question is whether the gap between home and overseas returns was steady, increasing or had some other pattern. The evidence of the first and second class securities is that the trend of both home and overseas realised returns was downward from 1870 to 1913. Yet, a far more prominent feature was an inverse long swing in which one or the other dominated. Table 8.3 gives the aggregate indices of home and overseas returns during the alternating periods of home and overseas dominance. Importantly, Table 8.3 shows that overseas returns tended to dominate their periods of ascendance more strongly than domestic returns dominated theirs, thereby yielding the overall edge of overseas returns noted earlier.

1870–1914: the role of domestic savings pressures

The mere fact that overseas returns exceeded home returns at various points in the period from 1870 to 1913 does not mean that Hobson's push forces were not also present. It could be that there were gluts of private savings from British households and corporations but the gluts were not large enough to satisfy all foreign investment demand and thus reduce overseas returns to the level of home returns. What evidence is there that the forces of return, income and wealth tended to deliver too much savings?

One method of examining this question is to ask whether econometric estimates of the likely amount of British savings for the years 1870–1913 predict more British savings at foreign investment upturns than actually took place. A recent study of British savings behaviour, 1870–1914, shows that estimates of the likely (ex ante) amount of savings (based on relationships of savings to its income, interest rates, etc. determinants) were much higher than the actual amount of total investment in two periods, 1877–79 and 1902–4 (Edelstein 1982: 185). An examination of Figure 8.1 reveals that both periods were the last years of a home investment boom and the first years of a strong foreign investment boom. The implication is that, at least in its initial stages, a boom in foreign investment was the result of a tendency for Great Britain to generate too much savings during the peaks of home booms. This is Hobson's observation, though not explained in the way he proposed.

Another secular phenomenon which may have affected UK saving rates towards the end of this period was the shifting age structure of the UK population. With lengthening life expectation and declining birth rates from the 1870s, the age structure of the UK population shifted strongly (Mitchell 1988: 5–7 and see chapter 2 above). The proportion of the population 14 or younger was 35–6 per cent from 1851 to 1891 but then dropped across the 1890s and 1900s to 30.8 per cent in 1911.

The proportion 65 or older rose slightly. Thus the total share of these dependent age cohorts fell from 39.9 per cent in 1891 to 36.1 per cent in 1911. Equally significantly, the share of the population in the prime savings years, 45–64 years old, averaged around 14.4 per cent, 1851–91, but then rose to 14.9 per cent in 1901 and 16.1 per cent in 1911.

Modern demographic and savings research suggests that life-cycle needs would cause saving rates to rise when the share of dependants fell and when the share of adults in the years of maximal saving rose. Whether the increased savings resulting from a reduced proportion of children was for the children's future education expenses, *in vivos* gifts to the children to start businesses or parental semi- or full retirement in old age is not known but all of these saving goals were of increasing importance from the 1890s onward. And, as with Hobson's hypothesis, pressure to save occurs independent of return.

1870–1914: institutional and legal factors

There may also have been institutional and legal factors which tended to push capital abroad. Many observers have felt that London, as the central capital market of the nation, tended to ignore domestic industry, especially small- and medium-sized firms, and favour overseas governments and enterprise (Kindleberger 1964; Landes 1969; Cottrell 1980; Kennedy 1987a). It seems curious that a central capital market which was so flexible with respect to overseas regions could fail to see new industries and opportunities for profitable intermediation close to home. It is therefore sensible to ask whether in fact domestic industry had a significant unsatisfied demand for funds from London.

Probably it did not. First, in the mid-nineteenth century, the older industries of Britain had strong internal sources of funding and easy access to local, provincial financing. In the late nineteenth century firms in some older sectors began to enlarge due to the scale requirements of new technologies or in pursuit of monopoly (Davis 1966; Hannah 1976; Cottrell 1980: ch. 6). These expanding firms found it fairly easy to raise external funding, from the 1880s onwards issuing stocks, preference shares and bonds. The new issues were offered locally, though often in London as well (the larger the new issue the more likely the reliance on London: Cottrell 1980: ch. 6; Michie 1987: chs. 1 and 4; and see chapter 10 below).

Second, virtually all of the newer industries, such as automobiles, artificial fibres, bicycles, telegraphs and telephones, found elastic supplies of venture capital either from local or London sources (Aldcroft 1968). Two new sectors which may have had some difficulty raising funds in the domestic securities market were electrical supply and electrical equipment manufacturers. New firms involved in electrical supply found funding quickly in the early 1880s, but provincial and London capital markets were less welcoming thereafter. The evidence suggests, none the less, that the problem was not the structure of financial intermediation but rather that electrical supply firms faced obstruction from local and central government politics and regulation, and these obstructions dampened capital market enthusiasm (Hughes 1988: ch. 9). Electrical equipment manufacturers had little trouble in finding initial finance. Their trouble was the limited market set by the stunted growth of the electrical supply system.

Automobile investment in the UK appears to have lagged behind the United States, France and some other European countries. The problem, however, was legislative restraint, not British capital markets. Legislation passed in the 1860s required a person to walk in front of an automobile with a red flag, warning pedestrians and horse-powered transport, and imposed a maximum speed of 2 miles per hour. When the law was modified in 1896, automobile manufacturers received immediate attention from provincial and London financial intermediaries and wealth (Lewchuk 1987: 138, 157; Michie 1988: 518–26). Again, initial British research on artificial silk, viscose, was backed by two private limited liability companies whose shares were held by British and German manufacturers. Courtaulds used £100,000 from its conversion to a public company to purchase the relevant patents, an investment which paid extremely handsomely (Cottrell 1980: 188).

Direct testing for investor bias in the pricing of capital market assets suggests that if there was a bias it was small and did not always operate in favour of overseas assets (McCloskey 1970; Edelstein 1982: 65–71). Indeed, recent research has suggested that the global integration of international capital markets may have been greater in the late nineteenth century and the early twentieth than at any other point in modern economic history, except possibly the very late twentieth century (O'Rourke and Williamson 1999; Taylor 2002).

Nevertheless, Britain did not have an institution which was widely considered quite important to the rapid advance of the German and US economies in this period. This was the large investment bank, capable of nursing large industrial firms from cradle to adulthood, complete with short- and long-term financing, engineering and accounting advice, and entrepreneurship. According to Kennedy (1987a) the fundamental problem was that information about British industrial firms, particularly new ventures, was largely held within the firm by the principal owners. The wider public was therefore ill-prepared to support industry's external financing needs. Some sort of financial intermediary, Kennedy posits, was necessary to collect and analyse such information, and then fashion a financing package which would diversify the high risks of these new ventures for the often quite conservative investing public. In Germany the financial intermediary that performed this function was the large investment bank. Similar financial intermediaries became involved in US industrial financial affairs in the late 1890s.

From the early nineteenth century British banks developed good information concerning their industrial clients and used it to provide a mix of short- and some longer-term financing. But as British firm sizes rose after the mid-century, the banks lending for long periods to the larger industrial firms put themselves and their depositors at some risk. After the banking crises of the 1870s the banks apparently left the field of long-term industrial lending (Cottrell 1980: ch. 7; Collins 1989, 1990). The subsequent banking amalgamation movement created institutions big enough to handle large enterprises comfortably but they too remained cautious in their long-term financing assistance before the First World War (Cottrell 1980: ch.7; and see chapter 10 below).

With the banks less involved, new British ventures had to rely more heavily upon the hodge-podge of provincial and London new issue firms and specialists which first appeared in the limited liability booms of the 1860s and 1870s. In the provinces, new issues were mostly handled by lawyers but sometimes by accountants or specialised company promoters. The latter specialists were usually based in the larger capital markets of Glasgow, Manchester and London, appearing when the new issues were large, warranting non-local participation. Kennedy argues that there were only a few honest company promoters (e.g., Chadwicks, Ellerman, O'Hagan) and, in any case, they offered little or no aftercare for the firms and sectors which they had assisted at birth. The honest company promoters certainly made money so the question becomes why were they so few and why was aftercare so limited.

One important reason is that the problems of British industry were different from those of German or American industry. Davis (1966) found that British industry showed little tendency to change its location or sectoral distribution, and only a few sectors displayed significant economies of scale. This meant that industrial investment spending put less stress (demands for new facilities or lumpy firm and sectoral funding needs) on the existing British financial system than was the case in Germany or the USA.

It is also notable that the new vertically integrated firms appearing in the USA in the 1870s and 1880s, for example, Swift and Armour in meat packing, Rockefeller in kerosene refining and supply, McCormick in reaping, all relied upon local (i.e., provincial) capital markets and internal profits to get to their immense scales, not on the New York capital market. Until the merger movement in the late 1890s, American new ventures faced virtually the same hodge-podge of personal and local capital market structures and services as did the British. Certainly Cleveland, Cincinnati, Chicago, etc., were wealthy towns but so too were Manchester, Liverpool, Birmingham, etc. Furthermore, good information about industrial enterprise was no more widely distributed locally or nationally in the USA in these decades than in the UK.

The involvement of investment banking with American industry began in the late 1890s with the merger movement, a movement whose major advertisement and outcome was probably a significant increase in the degree of monopoly power, importantly buttressed by protective tariffs (Chandler 1977; A. P. O'Brien 1988). With free trade and a very high degree of competition, Britain was infertile territory for investment banking interested in financing monopolies.

The constellation of long-term British financing facilities for industry was not static. The 1880s saw increasing use of preference and debenture new issues by industrial firms, clearly tailored to attract conservative investors. Furthermore, the diffusion of telegraph and telephone facilities improved the communication between provincial and central capital markets, giving greater depth to the nation's markets for outstanding securities, thereby offering safer prospects for new issues and venture capitalists (Michie 1987: chs. 1 and 4).

Investment banking was a well-known European institutional innovation by the mid-nineteenth century. Continental investment banks were quite willing to set up branches or new banks in other countries (Cameron 1961; Crisp 1967). Kennedy found several unsuccessful British attempts to start investment banks in the 1860s and 1870s. In describing the boom conditions in the domestic new issues of the 1890s, Michie notes that several experienced émigré firms promoted new issues of both provincial and London enterprises. Given the availability of the continental model and the inability of the model to take root in Britain, together with the vigorous new issue markets in the provinces and London, it seems fair to conclude that there was simply no demand for domestic investment banking of the continental variety. If British financial institutions and wealth paid attention to overseas opportunities, it was the demand for financing which called the tune, not biased capital markets.

Another aspect of the institutional framework for investment was the set of regulations on the purchase of assets by trustees (Keynes 1924). Up to 1889 the list consisted of Consols, Bank of England and East India stock and mortgages of freehold and copyhold estates in England and Wales. The list was enlarged by the Trustee Acts of 1889 and 1893 to include the stocks of English corporations and guaranteed Indian railways, the debentures of British and guaranteed Indian railways and a number of other securities. The Colonial Stock Act of 1900 extended the list to registered and inscribed stocks of colonial governments. Davis and Huttenback (1986: 171–4) examined the yields on 944 domestic, colonial and foreign government securities issued in Britain from 1882 to 1912 and found that the regulations reduced the yield by 0.16 percentage points, suggesting a very small bias.

THE CONSEQUENCES OF FOREIGN INVESTMENT

The role of defaults

What were the consequences of the massive capital outflow? Economic theory does not suggest that overseas investment by private investors will necessarily lead to increases in the welfare of the investing nation (Pearce and Rowan 1966). Even if the private realised rate of return is greater abroad taking into account defaults and bankruptcies, there are several factors which may make the social rate of return differ from the private rate of return.

At one time it was argued that one advantage of home over overseas portfolio investment was that, if there was default or bankruptcy, then the domestically located machinery and plant would remain in the UK (Keynes 1924). The argument, however, has a number of ambiguities. The ultimate receivers of a bankrupt overseas firm might be British citizens. Alternatively, consider a domestic firm which entered a new home market, found the profit too small and ended in bankruptcy. Is this firm's specialised capital equipment convertible to other uses? Rather than undertake an examination of each case of default and bankruptcy, it seems sensible simply to ask whether the loss from overseas default and bankruptcy was so much higher than the loss at home that it outweighed the differential in rates of return.

Something like a billion pounds were lost through domestic company bankruptcy, 1870–1913 (Edelstein 1982: 129–30). Domestic portfolio capital fell from around 67 per cent of UK-held long-term negotiable capital in 1870 to 55 per cent in 1913. Assuming the average was 61 per cent, net losses from overseas investment would have to be £640 million for overseas and domestic portfolio holdings to have been equally risky.

The gross nominal value of defaulted overseas government issues in the 1870s was around £60 million (Cairncross 1953), but at least 50 per cent of this was recovered. From 1880 to 1913 the worst overseas government defaults occurred during the early 1890s when various Argentine government bodies defaulted on £40 million of debentures, but most of this amount was recovered by the mid-1900s. Thus, £50 million appears to be a plausible upper-bound estimate of the net losses from overseas government defaults, 1870–1913.

If it were assumed that the overseas rate of net insolvency was the same as that at home, some £450 million would have been lost on overseas companies. However, because the overseas portfolio contained a higher proportion of social overhead firms (railways, gas works, etc.), which usually had some degree of monopoly power or government backing and thus were less risky, it is likely that something less than £450 million were so lost.

Combined with the £50 million of overseas government defaults, the total lost overseas was probably less than £500 million, short of the £640 million amount which would have made the default losses on Britain's overseas and domestic portfolio capital equivalent. In short, the differential between overseas and domestic private rates of return seems to have been substantially unaffected by home and overseas financial failure.

Terms of trade

Consider the various factors involved in the balance of the social rate of return. One is the terms of trade. From 1870 to 1913 the terms of trade – the ratio of British export to net retained import prices – rose gently, by about 0.1 per cent per annum (Imlah 1958). The sources of this change are several, but few would question the importance of social overhead and extractive capital formation abroad. In places like Australia, Argentina, Brazil, Canada and Mexico where the alternatives of water and road transport were missing the railway made a significant contribution to reducing the cost of transport from the interior regions to the coast. In the United States the gains were relatively smaller due to the excellent alternative of river and canal transport but were still substantial. A substantial amount of hitherto inaccessible but productive soils and mineral resources became the cheapest sources of the world's agricultural and mineral goods. So, the price of imports to Britain fell, bettering the terms of trade.

It is difficult to judge how much of the change in the British terms of trade was due to the capital exports for such projects. Technical change in agriculture and mining was partly responsible. Furthermore, in the absence of capital inflows from Britain the social overhead and extractive industry capital stock of the US, Australia, Canada, etc., would not have been smaller by the size of the actual British capital export. The capital import into these countries occurred because local savings supplies were relatively small and local capital markets were relatively immature (Davis and Gallman 2001: chs. 3–6). Borrowing from Britain represented a cheaper solution than relying on domestic resources, but not the only solution. While British funds to the smaller economies were often a high percentage of total local saving for a short period, they were never the only source of local savings. In the absence of British funds the local rates of return – for example, on the profitable United States railways – would have been somewhat higher, encouraging more local savings and financial intermediation services. Nevertheless, in some of the smaller economies overseas, such as Canada and Argentina, British funds mattered a great deal; if British capital had remained at home, Canadian and Argentine development would have been slower and later, which would have affected the speed at which the British terms of trade fell. It is difficult to calculate how much of the movement in the terms of trade was due to this irreducible contribution of British capital export, However, a broad swathe of British society benefited from this relationship in the form of cheap grains, meat, and industrial products dependent on overseas raw materials (compare chapter 6 above).

Another potential effect of a pattern of capital export which is focused on a particular region is that it may depress returns on British wealth which has previously been accumulated in that region, assuming all else held constant. The spurt-like character of British investment in most regions of the globes tended to minimise this problem, even if the evidence of declining returns in Table 8.3 suggests that it could not be totally avoided. Of course, a similar pattern of incremental investment pursued at home might, all else held constant, lower rates of return on the existing stock of domestic capital. To complicate matters further, suppose that in the absence of incremental British capital exports, other foreigners replaced British investors or overseas locals saved more, thereby driving down the overseas rate of return. In this case, existing British investments abroad would still decline in value. If returns on the incremental investment were greater abroad than at home, Britain as a nation might lose more by not adding to their overseas holdings than by adding to them.

We have seen that there was a persistent, risk-adjusted gap between overseas and home returns in favour of foreign investments. Except in Canada, Argentina and a few of the smaller colonies, British contributions were small relative to local savings (Green and Urquhart 1976). It seems likely therefore that the good effects on the terms of trade outweighed the effect of diminishing returns. If this is so, the social rate of return to overseas investment would still be larger than the private return.

Home investment and growth effects

The allocation of British savings between home and overseas outlets was largely a private affair in the nineteenth and early twentieth centuries, each investor balancing ambitions of return and risk. The capital market did not evaluate the social benefits of a project; indeed, due to information costs and other phenomena, the capital market does not perfectly evaluate private returns. For example, housing typically pays a low return spread over a long period. If investors tended to be risk averse and myopic, the private rate of return on housing would have been lower than the social return and in consequence private markets would not have built enough housing. If foreign investment had been restricted, and if, as suggested earlier, British property owners had continued to save, the fall in the rate of return would have lowered the rate of British total investment but there still would have been more domestic investment than actually obtained. It is, however, difficult to know what form that increased domestic investment would have taken; given the *rentier* character of much foreign investment, funds seeking steady income and security of principal might have moved to mortgages on urban property. It is an open question, however, whether the social gains from more housing would have counterbalanced the effects which overseas investment had on the purchasing power of labour over food and other imported necessities.

Perhaps more controversial is the question of whether any significant part of a counterfactually restricted flow of British foreign investment would have gone to domestic industry, especially the new industries of the late nineteenth century, or to domestic human capital formation, especially technical education. First, since few new industries in Britain complained about capital shortage, one wonders where and how much the counterfactual funding would have taken hold. Furthermore, the cost of financial capital was not a serious consideration for the expansion of British educational plant and equipment at the secondary or university levels.

The closest industrial competitors with Great Britain were in western Europe and the US. Their social structures for encouraging technical change were quite different from the UK. Infant industries were protected by general tariffs; industry in general was often thought to be infant relative to the UK. Scientific and technical education on the secondary level in Europe and in the universities in the US and Europe was widely supported by regional and national businesses and governments, in some places explicitly to challenge British technical competence. These same nations had developed strong traditions of universal primary education, fundamental to the production of a large corps of secondary and tertiary educated technologists and scientists. Britain probably fell behind its closest industrial competitors in secondary school science education in the late nineteenth century, and university technical education and research clearly lagged in the 1870s and 1880s (Pollard 1989: ch. 3). These developments were significant because in the latter half of the nineteenth century the applicable scientific knowledge involved in electricity, chemistry, load-bearing, etc., became substantially greater and more complex. Formal education in basic science and technical applications from professors engaged in mixtures of university and private research were becoming the standard method for generating technical personnel and ideas for industry (but see chapter 3 above).

In sum, restrictions on overseas capital embargoes were not the prevailing method for encouraging domestic, scientifically based, industry; tariffs and publicly supported general and technical education were. British private and social rates of return to industry might have diverged but it is unlikely that substantial sums were needed or would have found their way into the new, science-based, industries of the late nineteenth and early twentieth centuries with an overseas capital embargo. Such a policy would not have been sufficiently focused to obtain the desired result. Had Britain wanted to alter its industrial direction, infant-industry tariffs and publicly supported secondary and tertiary technical education and research would have more certainly altered the private rates of return towards their social rates; these were the policies used successfully in the US and Europe and the ones closest to consideration in Britain.

THE GROWTH OF THE BRITISH EMPIRE

The expansion of British investment abroad from 1860 to 1914 was paralleled by expansions of trade, migration, culture and political sovereignty. Of the earth's land area, 10 per cent was added to the British Empire. By 1914, with nearly a quarter of the earth's population and land mass, the British Empire was the largest the world had known. The amounts of new territory taken in each half of the hundred years between 1815 and 1914 were roughly equal; many historians have given the last quarter of the nineteenth century the title 'the age of high imperialism', but this overemphasises the extent of the territory acquired in that period. If there is a case to be made for singling out the period from the early 1880s to the early 1900s, that case must be that the acquisitions of these years were motivated by factors which were substantially different from those operating in the earlier part of the century (Wehler 1970; Fieldhouse 1973; Hopkins 1973).

The following factors are thought by some historians to have changed the nature of imperialism in the fourth quarter of the nineteenth century: the altered balance of European power following the Franco-Prussian War of 1870; the higher tariff levels emerging in the rapidly industrialising nations such as France, Germany and the USA after the mid-1870s; the possible slowing of investment opportunities at home and the fear of reductions in opportunities in other industrial and independent nations; the problems of integrating a newly emergent and vocal urban working class into national political life; and finally the faltering political economies of the independent African regions which were involved in important trading relations with coastal European trading settlements. Similarly at various times in the nineteenth century, Britain brought its political power to bear on a number of independent nations. This is often termed 'informal' imperialism, although a good deal of controversy surrounds just where such power was employed, how often and to what end (Gallagher and Robinson 1953; Fieldhouse 1973; Platt 1973; Louis 1976; Cain and Hopkins 2001: chs. 9, 12, 13).

There are two aspects of these extensions of British political power which are of interest to British economic historians. First, there is the question of what role economic forces at home and abroad played in the extension of formal and informal empire. Second, there is the question of the economic benefits and costs of formal and informal empire. To some degree these two questions are separable; what caused extension of the Empire might have nothing to do with the consequences. For example, one motive of Britain's informal imperialism in China was the high profit expectations of Lancashire and overseas British merchants who saw the potential of the immense Chinese market; it is doubtful, however, whether the excess of benefits over costs ever approached these expectations. Conversely there were several territories which were acquired for substantially non-economic reasons but which yielded a large economic reward. Since these questions are to some degree separable the remainder of this chapter is concerned with the realised return to formal and informal empire; the motives for imperialism have been widely discussed (Cain and Hopkins 2001).

THE GAINS FROM THE EMPIRE: MEASURING STANDARDS

By what standard should the gains from formal and informal empire be measured? One might, for example, add the net amounts of profits, rents and wages shipped home to Britain to the net transfer of government monies to Britain, and divide this sum by the total of public and private capital placed abroad. The result would be the 'social' return from possessing, for example, India at a particular moment in time or over a specified period. The same sum of net private and public transfers home might be divided by British GNP, thereby making it possible to compare the possession of India with that of other types of British incomes. Either method, however, implicitly assumes that, in the absence of British imperialism, there would have been no economic entity called India from which Britons might have derived an economic return. Britain did very well in its economic relations with the United States without much, if any, employment of formal or 'informal' imperialism after the Treaty of Ghent ending the Anglo-American War of 1812–14. The Treaty restored the equal *status quo ante bellum* with regard to the trade and impressment issues but, more significantly for the future, it provided for joint Anglo-American commissions with equal weight for each nation to determine disputed boundary issues. To some undefined degree, a similar pattern of settlement and economic opportunities would have occurred in Australia, Canada and some other parts of the British Empire, even if Britain had not ruled them.

To determine what are the gains from Empire or imperialism, one must first define the 'non-Empire' or 'non-imperialist' economy with which the 'Empire' or 'imperialist' economy is to be compared. Lenin (1915) avoided this issue by arguing that imperialism was a stage of capitalism, thus making possible the interpretation that the world of the late nineteenth century could not present examples of 'non-imperialist' economic and political relations. It seems likely, however, that Lenin would not have characterised Britain's actual relations with Germany, for example, as imperialist. There was a sufficient balance of power between Britain and Germany to prevent any abuse of political sovereignty or interregional economic exploitation whether through a negotiated treaty or any other economic relationship. This reasoning suggests an alternative methodology for measuring the gains from imperialism.

If the state of political and economic relations between Britain and Germany (or France or the US) provides an example of 'non-imperialist' economic and political relations, then the gains to Britain from ruling India (for example) can be measured as the amount by which Britain benefited from its economic relationship with India minus the benefits Britain would have gained if Britain had not ruled India but merely traded with India as she did with Germany, France or the US. To be specific, as a direct consequence of British rule in India all Indian railway equipment in the nineteenth century had to be purchased from Britain. The gain from this exertion of political power was not the profit from all British railway equipment sales, only that portion specifically due to the Raj purchase requirement or any other colonial policy affecting trade. Some railway equipment probably would have come from British factories even without the regulation. This standard of 'non-imperialism,' however, has a hidden and somewhat artificial assumption, that roughly the same economic opportunities would have been available in the colonised regions without British formal and informal imperialism. This counterfactual is artificial because if Britain had not meandered and fought its way into its nineteenth-century Empire, it is likely that there would have been fewer regions of the globe involved in the world economy. Furthermore, other European powers might have filled the vacuum, and then imposed extra costs on Britain.

In the following discussion of the gains from Empire, therefore, two standards of 'non-imperialism' will be employed. They will be termed, respectively, the 'marginal non-imperialist' standard and the 'strong non-imperialist' standard. The 'marginal non-imperialist' standard assumes that the Empire had the actual economic development that it underwent in the nineteenth and early twentieth centuries, but that at the moment of measurement of the gains it acquired the political independence and power of the USA, Germany or France in its economic and political relations with Britain. This 'marginal non-imperialist' standard underestimates the British gains from Empire because it overestimates the degree of economic development which would have taken place if there had never been a British Empire; it does, however, measure the benefit of not relinquishing control of the territories at that particular moment. The 'strong non-imperialist' standard assumes that the countries of the British Empire were independent from British rule throughout modern economic history with consequent effects on their involvement in the world economy and their political power vis-à-vis Britain.

There is a further issue, not considered here, that of the benefit to the countries of the British Empire. Britain's net gain from its Empire does not imply that India, Nigeria, Canada, etc., had a net loss from membership in the Empire. For example, Britain may have been able through manipulation of trade, investment or other government policies to extract a net gain from India. Yet, it is possible that the civic order imposed on India by British rule gave India economic advantages which would not have occurred in the absence of Empire. Alternatively, the policies of the British Raj may have delayed an Indian industrialisation even as Britain may have lost due to the burdens of defence or other expenses. A separate calculation is required for each colony to assess whether it gained or lost from membership in the Empire, independent of whether Britain gained or lost.

THE GAINS FROM TRADE WITH THE EMPIRE

Some theory

In matters of international trade, political sovereignty over the Empire gave Great Britain two powerful policy levers; colonial tariffs, and the regulations guiding the purchase of supplies for colonial government and mixed government–private enterprise projects. Both presented opportunities to favour domestic producers. Were they employed and with what gain or loss to Great Britain?

If we use the 'marginal non-imperialist' standard it is immediately evident that Britain gained from its Empire. Tariff levels imposed by France, Germany or the United States were substantially higher than those of the colonies, even the white-settler colonies which were increasing the degree of their political autonomy across this period and imposing protective tariffs against heated opposition in the British parliament.

However, if one wishes to demonstrate the full power of domestic British interests the Indian case is revealing (Harnetty 1972). The British Indian government was short of funds due to expenditures connected with the Indian Mutiny of 1857 and wished to enlarge its tax base. The proposed method was to increase tariffs by a small amount. The duty would cover all imports, including cotton yarn and cloth. Lancashire cotton interests mobilised to put pressure on London to defeat the Indian government's proposal. The threat to their interests was clear; an infant Indian cotton textile industry of perhaps a half-dozen firms had recently appeared. Although Manchester interests were quite prepared to allow the proposed tariff to remain on other imports, they felt an exception should be made for British yarn and cloth. In the event, despite pleas from the Indian government, Manchester interests were successful and the British Raj financed the deficit by issuing debentures.

The trade flows in railway equipment are another example of the supposed gains from imperialism. Nearly all the Indian railway equipment was ordered from Great Britain in the nineteenth century. Legally, there was no choice because the British Indian government stipulated this pattern of purchase. But, given that many of the entrepreneurs guiding the construction and maintenance of the Indian railway system were Scots who wanted Scottish and English materials, the near-zero tariffs were probably more important than the stipulation. The pattern of Canadian railway purchases was also overwhelmingly British until the appearance of their first tariffs (Saul 1960). At this point, as in a number of other Canadian industrial branches, a substantial resident Canadian industry appeared. The Indian railway system was larger than the Canadian until just before the First World War. Furthermore, as evidenced by the Indian cotton textile, jute and iron industries Indian and British entrepreneurship, engineering and capital were not lacking in late nineteenth- and early twentieth-century India. It must, therefore, be concluded that here also free trade rather than direct regulation was the source of Britain's advantage.

The marginal standard

In exploring the size of this advantage in general, let us make the assumption that the relatively low tariff of the white-settler colonies was due to British rule. There is good reason to doubt the full force of this assumption; colonial parliamentary debate suggests that British politics and policies were not often involved directly in their tariff decisions. Still, the tariff levels of these white-settler colonies certainly gave political expression to the closer economic links between the manufacturing metropolitan country and the primary product economies overseas than was the case for countries outside the Empire. Further, it will be initially assumed that the supply of British output is quite elastic, so that the actual level of British output was determined by demand forces and any shift in demand would have low costs. Obviously, these assumptions are questionable. For that reason the numbers which follow are to be taken as conjectures of direction and order, not precise magnitudes.

Assume that the colonial tariff rate was zero, while the 'non-imperial' rate was 20 per cent in 1870 and 40 per cent in 1913. These latter rates are close to the average tariff imposed by the United States at these two dates (Davis *et al.* 1969). British commodity and services exports were 30.3 per cent and 33.0 per cent of GNP at these two dates. The shares of commodity exports to the colonies in total British exports were 26 per cent. *c.* 1870 and 36 per cent *c.* 1913. Assuming that the colonies bought the same shares of invisible service exports (an underestimate in all likelihood), colonial purchases of commodity and service exports represented 7.9 per cent (i.e., 26 per cent of 30.3 per cent) of GNP in 1870 and 11.9 per cent of GNP in 1913.

What percentage of GNP would have been lost if Britain had faced 'non-imperialist' tariff levels in its colonies. Assuming that Canada, India, etc., had exactly the same level of economic development as actually prevailed at these dates, the only hypothesised difference is the tariff-raising power they would have had if they became as independent as, for example, the US.

Wright's studies (1971, 1974) of nineteenth-century cotton markets suggest that the price elasticity of British demand for colonial products was probably below unity, say 0.75, and that the price elasticity of colonial demand for British goods was somewhat above unity, say 1.5 (see also Hatton 1990). If we assume first that the home and colonial marginal propensities to import were equal to 0.2, secondly that (as noted above) Britain's supply curves were highly elastic and thirdly that the imposed tariff levels would have been 20 percentage points and 40 percentage points higher than the existing tariff levels of 1870 and 1913 respectively, then we can calculate the gain to Great Britain from the actual state of near-free trade with the colonies. On the basis of these assumptions, it was 1.6 per cent of GNP in 1870 and 4.9 per cent of GNP in 1913.[3]

Enhanced political autonomy for the white-settler colonies (Canada, Australia, New Zealand and South Africa) meant that the gap between their tariffs and the 'non-imperial' tariff was smaller than 40 per cent in 1913. About 45 per cent of Britain's colonial exports in 1913 went to the Dominions; if it is assumed that their average tariff was 20 per cent (an overestimate) then the gain to Great Britain from 'freer' trade with the Dominions and other possessions becomes 3.8 per cent of GNP in 1913.

The strong standard

If we now use the 'strong non-imperialist standard' it must be argued that had the Empire territories remained independent of Empire rule, they would not have participated in the international economy to the same extent. One example is India where it is likely that the British Raj brought a more peaceful, unified and commercially oriented political economy than would have been the case in its absence (Morris 1963; Mukerjee 1972). As a guess, let us assume that Britain's trade with India and the other non-Dominion regions would have been 25 per cent of its existing level in 1870 and 1913 if there had never been British rule.[4]

To what degree would the economic development of the white-settler areas have been similarly inhibited by the absence of British rule? The US experience might be thought instructive because the US was also founded by British migrants who had a common core of political, cultural and economic institutions. Still, the US industrialised much earlier

[3] Let Ecc and Ebb = the price elasticities of colonial demand for British products and of British demand for colonial products; Cc and Cb = the marginal propensities to import of the colonies and Britain; qX = the share of British exports to the colonies in British GNP; dt = the change in tariffs; and dW = the percentage change in British GNP due to the tariff change. Then, from Pearce (1970), dW = qX(Ecc+Cc)/(Ecc+Cc+Ebb))dt.

[4] West African purchases of British goods quadrupled between 1870 and 1913 at the same time that British rule spread from a few enclaves to significant territorial sovereignty.

Table 8.4 Some conjectures on the gains from imperialism in 1870 and 1913 (% of GNP)

	Standard of 'non-imperialism'			
	'Marginal': same level of economic development: US, German, French standard of international economic policy		'Strong': independent nineteenth-century political and economic development	
	1870	1913	1870	1913
Exports of commodities and services	+1.10	+2.60	+4.30	+6.50
Overseas investment	−0.20	−0.94	+0.31	+0.45
Net government transfers				
a direct assist.	−0.06	+0.11	−0.06	+0.11
b defence	−0.04 to −1.01	−0.23 to −1.40	−0.04 to −1.01	−0.23 to −1.40
Total	−0.17 to +0.70	+0.37 to +1.54	+3.54 to +4.51	+5.66 to +6.83

Source: see text.

than the white-settler colonies of the nineteenth century, and had earlier and much stronger income and population growth. One alternative standard might be the pattern of growth and development in Argentina. Although the political and cultural traditions of Argentina were different from those of the British white-settler colonies, Argentina entered the international economy at about the same time as the future Dominions and had a very similar pattern of economic development. Argentina grew through extensive development of land and mineral resources, using largely British funds to build its railway and other social overhead capital. Argentina's consumption of British exports per capita was about 70 per cent of the average for the white-settler colonies, so let it be assumed that British exports to the white-settler colonies would have been 70 per cent of their actual level if these colonies had been independent.

Summing the 75 per cent reduction to British exports to the non-Dominion colonies and the 30 per cent reduction to British exports in the Dominion regions (weighted by their respective shares in British colonial exports), British colonial exports in 1870 and 1913 would have been 45 per cent of their actual levels under this 'strong non-imperialist' standard of the gains from Empire.[5]

The 'strong' gain is the difference between the actual British Empire exports and this hypothetical 45 per cent level in the absence of Empire. British exports of goods and services to the Empire were approximately 7.9 per cent and 11.9 per cent of GNP in 1870 and 1913; therefore, the 'strong' gain from Empire was 4.3 per cent (i.e., 55 per cent of 7.9 per cent) of GNP in 1870 and 6.5 per cent of GNP in 1913 (Table 8.4).

[5] The shares of white-settler and non-white-settler colonies in British exports to the colonies were approximately 45 per cent and 55 per cent, respectively. With their 'strong' non-Empire levels hypothetically reduced to 0.7 and 0.25, respectively, of their actual levels, British exports to both types of colonies would have been = 45 per cent (0.7) + 55 per cent(0.25) = 45.25 per cent of actual levels.

THE GAINS FROM INVESTMENT IN THE EMPIRE

The marginal standard: analysis

Would the amount of Britain's investment in its colonies or its returns have differed from the actual amounts in 1870 and 1913 if we assume that the colonies were as integrated into the world economy as they in fact were, and as independent as the US, France and Germany, that is, the 'marginal non-imperialist' standard. First, it seems fairly certain that both Dominion and non-Dominion regions would have had many social overhead and primary product capital projects worthy of local and international financial interest. Furthermore, it is likely their governments (assumed independent) would have participated in the financing of the social overhead capital projects. From 1850 to 1871 the government of the United States regularly gave land grants to help attract domestic and overseas investors to the equity and debenture issues of US private railway companies; the same policy was pursued in Canada and Argentina. In nineteenth-century France, Germany, Russia and, indeed, throughout Europe, railway networks were constructed partly at state expense (financed with government debentures) and partly privately (the interest on railway company debentures guaranteed by the state). Government subsidies and government guarantees of internationally marketed, private railway debt instruments were standard financing modes for the independent nations of Latin America and Asia. It is therefore likely that under the 'marginal non-imperialist' standard similar types of debt instruments would have been issued to finance social overhead investment projects and, given the lumpiness of this sort of investment, these securities would have been internationally marketed like those of the USA, Argentina, etc.

The question of the gains from imperialism ('marginal non-imperialist' standard) now becomes how much of this debt would have been funded in Britain and at what cost to the (hypothetically independent) borrowers. There can be little question that the British capital market treated Empire borrowers differently from foreign borrowers. Davis and Huttenback (1986: 171–4) examined the yields on 944 domestic, colonial and foreign government securities issued in Britain from 1882 to 1912. Indian government interest rates were 0.64 percentage points above the UK municipal government rate, dependent colonial governments were 0.84 percentage points above, responsible colonial government issues were 1.14 above, independent developed countries were 2.04 above and underdeveloped independent countries 4.26 percentage points above.

Recasting Edelstein's sample of first and second class securities into domestic, colonial and foreign groupings, Davis and Huttenback found that the average realised return per annum, 1870–1913, on UK railway debentures was 3.77 per cent, colonial railways, 4.48 per cent and foreign railways, 5.72 per cent (Davis and Huttenback, 1986: 81). A similar rank order characterised domestic, colonial and foreign railway equities and non-railway social overhead equity. In sum, government and railway securities issued by Dominion and non-Dominion colonies were typically financed at lower interest rates than in independent foreign nations at similar levels of economic development.

Some portion of the explanation for the lower colonial rates derives from parliamentary loan guarantees. Indian government bonds carried the full backing of the British government and were listed in the official rosters of the London Stock Exchange with 'British funds'. Parliamentary loan guarantees were used for the debt issues of the white-settler colonies with responsible government through the 1870s but little thereafter. Before 1900 debt issued by the governments of the dependent Empire nearly always came with some sort of London guarantee. With the passage of the Crown Colonies Loan Act of 1899 and the Colonial Stock Act of 1900, unguaranteed issues from the governments of the dependent Empire began to appear.

But, even when London backing and oversight were absent from colonial government issues (e.g. colonial municipal debt), the British capital market charged lower interest rates than on comparable securities from independent nations at similar levels of economic development. Private colonial railway issues usually involved colonial government support but no more than Argentine or US private railway issues and these colonial securities also showed lower issue yields and realised returns. The strong inference is that colonial status, apart from the direct guarantees, lowered whatever risk there was in an overseas investment and that investors were therefore willing to accept a lower return. In some colonies, particularly the newer ones, British rule and law directly reduced the potential losses from default and bankruptcy. In others, risk and uncertainty were reduced by the justice which was expected from colonists of British extraction.

The marginal standard: measurement

It is thus clear that membership of the British Empire involved a more favourable interest rate on the financing supplied by Britain to both the responsible and the dependent Empire. Attempting to measure the extent of the subsidy, Davis and Huttenback use their regression equation for government yields to estimate how much the colonies would have paid if they were forced to pay interest at rates similar to foreign governments. In this exercise, the colonies with responsible government (synonymous with Dominion status by 1914) are treated as if they were foreign governments with developed economies and the colonies with dependent governments (non-white-settler, non-Dominion) are treated as foreign governments with underdeveloped economies. It is further assumed that these governments borrowed as much as they did as colonies. Davis and Huttenback thus provide us with a highly useful estimate of the value of the implicit interest subsidy paid by Britain to the members of the British Empire.

This subsidy constitutes a cost of imperialism to the British under the 'marginal' standard of non-imperialist behaviour. If the colonies are assumed to attain the independent power status of the US, France, etc., in 1870 or 1913, this cost would disappear because the ex-colonial regions would pay interest rates something like Davis and Huttenback's hypothesised market rates. The subsidy to colonial government borrowers, *c.* 1870, was about £0.5 million or 0.05 per cent of 1870 GNP and *c.* 1914, £9.2 millions or 0.36 per cent of 1914 GNP (Davis and Huttenback 1986: 176).

As Davis and Huttenback note, these estimates do not entirely capture this cost of Empire. It would be highly useful to have a regression analysis of private railway yields similar to Davis and Huttenback's for government securities. Colonial railway borrowing was three times that of colonial government borrowing *c.* 1870 and about 1.6 times, *c.* 1914 (Edelstein 1982: 48). If it is assumed that the colonial railways received similar subsidies at the margin and a similar ratio of private railway borrowing between colonies of responsible and dependent government, the total subsidy (government and railway securities) *c.* 1870 becomes 0.20 per cent of 1870 GNP and *c.* 1914, 0.94 per cent of 1914 GNP, entered in Table 8.4 with a negative sign to denote they were a cost of Empire, not a gain.

These estimates of the total government and railway subsidies are, however, quite crude. First, the yield differentials between colonial and foreign railway borrowers of similar levels of development were probably smaller than for government borrowers; it would appear that British lenders thought Empire reduced the risks of government securities more than railway issues (Edelstein 1982: 123,125). Second, according to Davis and Huttenback, responsible governments borrowed three times as much as dependent governments while their private railway borrowed twice as much. The first factor would tend to lower the total subsidy and the second raise it.

There are other difficulties. The subsidy to Empire borrowers may have had wider effects. With the colonial imprimatur, colonial government and railway borrowers were placed in lower-risk categories by the British lenders, but it is possible that some domestic and foreign 'safe' borrowers were thereby displaced or perhaps higher interest rates prevailed in the 'safe' sector of the capital market. Furthermore, the reduced presence of colonial government and railway borrowers from the riskier sectors of the capital market may have meant that more funds were available for riskier domestic and foreign borrowers and perhaps at lower interest rates. If we make the bold but plausible assumption that for given use (e.g., tramways), domestic borrowers were always treated as less risky than foreigners, it was likely foreigners were the most affected by the colonial subsidy. Foreign borrowers were the most displaced in the 'safe' market due to the subsidy, perhaps paying a higher interest rate as well, and they were likely to be the ones who most benefited in the market for risky securities. What direction these wider effects would have had and how much is difficult to evaluate. It is plausible that these two, general equilibrium, readjustments just cited more or less cancelled each other, hence the wider effects were small, but clearly more research is warranted.

Finally, the Davis and Huttenback estimates only contend with the 'price' effects of the subsidy, not the quantity effects. In their calculation of the subsidy the colonies pay a higher interest rate but borrow the same amount. Hypothetically freed from colonial rule in 1870 or 1913, it is doubtful that an independent Nigeria, India, Malaya, etc., would have been able to attract the same attention from the London or any other capital market. If they counterfactually borrowed less because of higher interest rates or other effects, the implicit subsidy is less than the Davis and Huttenback calculation. How much less is difficult to hazard; again more research is warranted.

The strong standard

Turning to the 'strong non-imperialist' standard, the issue becomes how much British investment would have taken place without Empire rule in the nineteenth and twentieth centuries. With regard to the white-settler colonies, it seems plausible to assume that British investment per head in Canada, Australia, New Zealand and South Africa would have been closer to the Argentine per capita investment. The required rate of return, however, would probably have been higher to compensate for the greater risk of foreign political pressures and court systems. British investment per head in Argentina was approximately 70 per cent of what it was in Canada, Australia, New Zealand, and South Africa but the realised rate of return on Argentine (and US) securities was about a third higher than on the Dominion securities. Thus, it seems likely that whatever income for Britons would have been lost from a drop in the quantity of investment in the white-settler colonies, under these rough assumptions it would have been made up through a higher rate of return.

It seems safe to suggest that under the 'strong non-imperialist' standard there would have been less investment income from India and the remainder of the non-Dominion Empire. Plausible political and economic analogies to India without Empire rule in the nineteenth century might be the experience of China and Turkey. Clearly, there was some amount of 'informal' imperialism in these regions affecting their openness to foreigners (McLean 1976; Cain and Hopkins 2001). It is therefore quite generous to assume that the non-white-settler colonies would have had

British investments one fifth their actual £140 and £480 million levels in 1870 and 1913. The realised rate of return was approximately 4 per cent on colonial investments, 1870–1913, but in order to draw funds into these hypothesised independent regions, the required rate of return would probably have had at least to double to compensate for the perceived increased risk. If we reduce the non-Dominion colonial investments by 80 per cent and assume an 8 per cent return, the gain to Great Britain from Empire investments based on a 'strong non-imperialist' standard was 0.3 per cent of GNP in 1870 and 0.5 per cent of GNP in 1913 (Table 8.4).[6]

NET GOVERNMENT TRANSFERS TO AND FROM THE EMPIRE

Monetary transfers

Throughout the late nineteenth and early twentieth centuries a fundamental tenet of Colonial Office oversight was that colonial governments were to find sufficient local revenue sources to finance current (non-capital) expenditures. Most colonies came close to this in normal times, relying upon direct assistance from London principally when a major military campaign or natural disaster caused fiscal stress. India, however, was a different matter. Not only was India self-supporting but Indian troops and funds were regularly used for Empire military actions in Africa and Asia. According to Mukerjee (1972), some £0.4 million *c.* 1870 and, employing his methods, £4 million *c.* 1913 were transferred to Britain for (a) unjustified debt service for wars which an independent India would not have undertaken, (b) military expenditures for campaigns in Africa and Asia and (c) civil charges for Empire operations outside India. These Indian transfers, however, must be matched against the direct assistance to other colonial governments from London government under unusual fiscal stresses. Such direct assistance averaged perhaps £1 million *c.* 1870 (Feinstein 1972) and £1.3 million *c.* 1913 (Kesner 1981: 34–43). Both the British outflows and inflows from India would disappear under either a 'marginal' or 'strong non-imperialist' standard.

A second form of colonial expense was the shipping and cable subsidies to maintain mail and telegraphic communication within the empire (Davis and Huttenback 1986: 181). Since other advanced nations subsidised their shipping and cable companies for mail and telegraphic benefits, or would have, in the absence of British services, we have to

[6] The stock of British portfolio capital in non-Dominion colonies was £140 million in 1870 (Hall 1963) and £480 million in 1913 (Saul 1960). British GNP was £1081 million in 1870 and £2542 in 1913 (Feinstein 1972: T8–T9). The change in British GNP from the assumed lowered rate of investment in non-Dominion colonial areas in 1870 would thus be [(0.04)(140) − (0.08)(0.2)(140)]/1081 = 0.0031 and in 1913, 100[(0.04)(480) − (0.08)(0.2)(480)]/2542 = 0.0045.

Table 8.5 Average annual defence expenditures, 1860–1912 (£s per capita)

	Davis and Huttenback (1860–1912)	Offer (1870–1914)	Offer (c. 1908)	Offer (1907–10)
United Kingdom	1.14	1.07	1.41	1.26
UK colonies				
Responsible governments	0.12		0.26	
India	0.10		0.07	
Dependent governments	0.04		} 0.03	
Princely states	0.03			
Special princely states	0.03			
Foreign developed nations	0.46			
France and Germany	0.62			
France		1.05		1.18
Germany		0.69		0.90
Foreign underdeveloped nations	0.18			

Sources: Davis and Huttenback 1986: 161; Offer 1993: 224, 226–7.

assume that these expenses would remain under either standard of imperialism.

Transfers in kind: defence

A third form of budgetary assistance provided by the British Empire was an 'in kind' transfer, national defence. One of the central arguments of Davis and Huttenback on the political economy of imperialism is that none of the colonies, with or without responsible government, paid for anything like a reasonable defence establishment. The data shown in Table 8.5 illustrate their hypothesis (Davis and Huttenback 1986: 161):

> The colonies with responsible government [the white-settler colonies] appear to have paid around a quarter of what foreign developed nations spent on defence, and the dependent colonial governments and the princely states paid about a fifth of what foreign underdeveloped nations expended. India, as we have already noted, paid more, but it too expended about half of what foreign underdeveloped nations spent. Davis and Huttenback's estimates also show Britain's defence spending per capita was double the rate of France and Germany, suggesting that Britain was buying two defence establishments, one for home defence and one for its empire.

Two problems are evident in the Davis and Huttenback defence expenditure comparisons. First, a substantial part of the difference between the defence expenditures of foreign underdeveloped countries and the Empire's dependent colonies appears to be due to the fact that the Empire had separate police forces whereas in many foreign underdeveloped countries the military served this function (Davis and Huttenback 1986: 164).

Second, a subsequent critique by Offer (1993) presents evidence (see Table 8.2) that Davis and Huttenback missed certain secret French and Germany military and naval expenditures (see also P. K. O'Brien 1988, 1989; Kennedy 1989). Given Offer's substantially higher estimates of French and German per capita defence costs it seems plausible to surmise that more of Britain's expenditures were meant for home island security and less were devoted to Empire defence. As Offer argues elsewhere (1989: 215–318), Britain's strategic planners viewed the nation's food and raw material imports as an important part of home island security and felt these resources required extensive naval and military protection. British naval and military forces stationed overseas thus served both home and colonial security purposes.

On the 'marginal non-imperialist' standard, the portion of the British defence establishment and its expense devoted to colonial security would hypothetically disappear. According to Davis and Huttenback's data this overseas military establishment cost £10.9 million, *c.* 1870, and £30.3 million, *c.* 1909, or 1.0 per cent and 1.4 per cent of UK GNP.[7]

However, because this assumes that all of the forces committed abroad are for Empire defence it must be considered an upper-bound estimate of the defence subsidy to the Empire. A lower Empire defence subsidy would result if part of the overseas military and naval expenses is credited to keeping shipping lanes open for essential food and raw material imports for Britain's home defence.

Assume that all of the difference between the defence expenditures of the independent underdeveloped countries and India and the dependent colonies was due to differences in accounting for police functions. Second, assume that the Dominions would have spent per capita the amount that the US spent if they, hypothetically, were to become independent in 1870 or 1913 and the difference represents the British subsidy for their defence. The US appears to have spent approximately double the per capita Dominion rate.[8] The resulting hypothetical increment for the Dominions would be approximately £0.5 million in 1870 and £5.0 millions in 1913, or 0.04 per cent of 1870 GNP and 0.23 per cent of 1913 GNP (Feinstein 1972: T8–T9; Davis and Huttenback 1986: 28, 161). Table 8.4 displays

[7] Averaging Davis and Huttenback's data (1986: 164) for 1860–9 and 1870–9, total British defence costs were approximately £0.70 per capita, *c.* 1870, of which £0.35 per capita was for imperial defence, that is, 50 per cent of total British defence costs. Average annual total defence costs, 1905–12, were £1.58 per capita, of which 0.68 per capita were for imperial defence, 43 per cent of total British defence costs. These figures include the Mediterranean fleet in home defence costs. Given that other major European powers maintained Mediterranean fleets, assuming Britain would maintain one in the absence of an overseas Empire appears plausible. The total defence budget in 1870 was £21.1 million and £73.5 million in 1913 (Mitchell 1988: 588). Thus, the empire expense was 0.50 £21.1 millions in 1870 and 0.43 £73.5 million in 1913. British GNP was £1,081 million and £2,150 million in 1870 and 1913, respectively (Feinstein 1972: T8–T9).)

[8] United States: United States (1975: Series A7, Y458–9). Australia: Maddock and McLean (1987: 353, 359). Canada: Urquhart and Buckley (1965: Series A1, G26).

these upper- and lower-bound estimates of these subsidies as costs of Empire.

On the strong non-imperialist standard, a similar assumption seems equally plausible. Part of Britain's military expenditures involved a naval presence which guarded British shipping lanes from predatory states and privateers. Given their level of commercial development in the late nineteenth and early twentieth centuries, the hypothetically freed regions of the British Empire ('marginal non-imperialist' standard) might be expected to continue to maintain order in their adjacent trade-routes. The 'strong non-imperialist' standard counterfactually assumes that the Empire never came into being, hence a trading (Empire-less) Britain would have had to spend something to make the waters off Asia, Africa and the Americas safe for commercial activity in the eighteenth and nineteenth centuries. How much naval expense would have been necessary? France and the United States, with lower naval expenditures than the UK, made their presence felt when privateers were a problem in the nineteenth-century Mediterranean and elsewhere. Since France and Germany, two substantial European commercial and naval powers, had considerably larger defence expenses than the typical developed countries, and British *home* defence was similarly expensive, it seems likely the cost of imperialism was similar for under both standards of 'non-imperialism' (see also P. K. O'Brien 1988, 1989; Kennedy 1989; Offer 1993; Cain 1998).

SUMMARY OF THE ECONOMICS OF EMPIRE

The net gain, 1870–1914

These rough calculations, summarised in Table 8.4, suggest three important features of the economics of Empire. First, the Empire meant more for the economic well-being of Great Britain in 1913 than it did in 1870. This trend was largely due to the increased proportion of British commodity and service exports which were marketed in the Empire.

Second, if we employ the 'marginal non-imperialism' standard, the gains to Britain from her Empire do not appear to have been very large. The ability to manipulate the international trade, investment and fiscal policies of the developed colonial economies appears to have yielded very little *c.* 1870 and perhaps 1 per cent in 1913. Whatever the trade and investment advantages, they were negated by the direct and indirect subsidies to Empire. In addition, the trade calculation assumed that the relatively low tariffs of the white-settler colonies were due to British rule. Colonial parliamentary debates suggest that this assumption must be modified. If, for example, it is totally dropped, the trade gains from the 'marginal' standards are halved. Needless to say, the fact that the nation as a whole did not gain much according to this standard does not mean that certain sectors of the British economy did not benefit from freer trade with the Empire. The cotton trades, shipping, overseas insurance and banking and railway equipment manufacturers are good examples but they are not alone. In other words, private rates of return may have been higher than the social rate of return.

Third, Britain probably received a more significant return if we use the 'strong non-imperialism' standard. This is best viewed as an estimate of the return on the role which Empire played in enlarging the extent of the nineteenth-century world economy. Furthermore, because the gains from 'informal' Empire have been largely ignored, the gains from imperialism in Table 8.4 may be understated. Argentina, which was used here as an example of a 'non-imperialist' economy was subject to the pressures of Britain and other imperial powers at various points in the nineteenth and early twentieth centuries, although it should be noted that Argentina, like the USA, successfully fought off a British military invasion during the Napoleonic Wars.

The size of the gains reported in Table 8.4 must be examined in the light of our earlier assumption that supply curves were elastic and hence British output was set by the level of demand. To assume elastic supply curves means that if there had been no Empire the domestic labour and capital resources employed in Empire-induced activities would have either never participated in the economy or, through lower population growth rates, never come into existence. Alternatively, it might be assumed that some portion of the labour and capital involved in Empire-induced activities would have been employed in other economic activities, albeit less productively. Unfortunately, it is quite difficult to measure accurately how much of the labour and capital resources involved in Empire-induced activities would have been employed elsewhere in the economy. It is possible, however, to specify a range of possibilities. If, on the one hand, all factors of production were employed elsewhere and the only change was a drop in their rate of return by one percentage point, after forty-four years without the Empire-induced growth British GNP would have been lower by around 1 per cent. If, on the other hand, it is assumed that the resources involved in the Empire-induced economic activity had remained unused (or never come into existence) and the pace of technical change is proportionately lowered as well, British GNP would have been lower by somewhat more than 5 per cent after forty-four years.

How can we tell whether this range of proportions is large or small? One way is to compare the gains from Empire with the gains from various forms of technical progress. Hawke's study of the diffusion of the railway in Great Britain indicates that in 1860, after thirty-five years of the railway, GNP was at most 10 per cent higher than it would have been without the railway (Hawke 1970). Since it is likely that the railway was the most important single technological innovation of the nineteenth century, the Empire does not appear to have been as important as is sometimes thought. Still, the Empire made a significant contribution to the growth in the income and output of Great Britain in the nineteenth and early twentieth centuries. Chapter 1 above suggested that between 1870 and 1914 the forces of innovation and economies of scale were exerting a diminishing effect on growth. By contrast, the contribution of the Empire was increasing.

The First World War

Finally, in September of 1914 Britain entered into a European war of immense carnage and cost. The Empire came quickly to the defence of Britain and in key battles towards the end carried an especially heavy combat role (Offer 1993: 235). How does the Empire's contribution to the First World War fit in a cost-benefit calculus of the late Pax Britannica. First, it is best to think of the contribution of Empire to the First World War as quite separate from its contribution during the relatively peaceful years of the nineteenth and early twentieth centuries. During the latter period, economic goals were important motivators for individual and social life. But for the survival of an autonomous national life, 1914–18, governments and peoples were willing to throw immense human and other resources into battle with little reference to economic considerations. This distinctive motivational structure means that any calculation of wartime costs answers different questions.

The Empire was not settled to provide a reserve army for home defence. In the early months of the First World War the high rates of voluntary enlistment in the Dominions were quite surprising to the British government and people (Offer 1989: 313–16). The protection of food and raw material exports from the Empire was part of the Britain's pre-war military plans but so too was the independent United States (Offer 1989: 215–317). Eventually, the United States joined the Allied military effort for two reasons which probably would have drawn the Dominions into combat if they also had been independent: their cultural links with Britain; and the German submarine campaign which was aimed at choking off Britain's food and raw material imports. Thus, perhaps only the quick troop and financial support from the Dominions and the colonies might be thought the irreducible contribution of Empire to the First World War.

On the 'marginal standard' of non-imperialism, it thus seems plausible to treat the actual Empire contribution to the First World War as an upper-bound estimate of what Britain would have had to provide without Empire. Great Britain spent $44.029 billion on the First World War; the Empire spent $4.494 billion (Bogart 1921: 105). Thus, Great Britain's direct expenditures might have been 10.2 per cent higher without Empire support. From 1915 to 1918 British military expenditures absorbed 25–30 per cent of British GNP (Mitchell 1988: 833). An upper-bound estimate of the benefit of Empire might then be 10.2 per cent of this share, that is 2.5–3.0 per cent of GNP. More significantly, Britain lost 744,000 persons in military uniform while the Empire lost 225,000 (Mendershausen 1943: 361). British wartime deaths might therefore have been 30.2 per cent higher in the absence of Empire support. How one translates this sacrifice into an annualised cost is too difficult to attempt here. In any event, by the 'marginal standard' of non-imperialism, the distinct wartime benefits of Empire overshadow the gains calculated for the peaceful Empire *c.* 1913 (Table 8.4) and probably would still do so even if we hazard what a hypothetically freed Empire would have contributed if the US's later entry is used as a standard. With regard to the 'strong' standard of non-imperialism, the growth of the British Empire across the modern era bulks so large in the origins of the First World War as to make calculation implausible.

9 Enterprise and management

TOM NICHOLAS

Contents

INTRODUCTION

The argument that defects in the performance of the British economy can be best explained by lacklustre enterprise and management and a general weakness of the industrial spirit has a long history. Assertions of entrepreneurial failure remain both seductive and appealing, particularly for those who favour cultural explanations. However, in their celebrated 1971 essay on late Victorian business performance Donald McCloskey and Lars Sandberg countered this conventional wisdom. On the basis of the neoclassical conceptual and empirical literature, they found limited evidence for significant and economically relevant instances of failure.

Not all theoretical advances have favoured British entrepreneurs. Institutional approaches reinforce the perspective that entrepreneurs need to be judged against their operating environment. Entrepreneurs interact with institutions, which can both reduce transaction costs and facilitate benefits from exchange, or act as a brake on economic development if 'institutional rigidities' are present. Advocates of this approach claim that competing industrial nations displaced Britain from economic pre-eminence by performing better in respect of labour relations, education, industrial organisation, corporate finance and government policy towards enterprise. Thus, institutional writers have challenged the argument of entrepreneurial redemption deeply rooted in the neoclassical analysis of business behaviour.

Cultural approaches to entrepreneurship broadly agree with this challenge; they explain performance differences between countries by reference to a capacity for enterprise and initiative. In Britain, it is claimed, a rigid social structure and the persistence of gentlemanly capitalism eroded the industrial spirit. Advocates of conventional cultural approaches hail 'the limits of economic explanation' (Wiener 1981: 167). Scholars writing historically on culture have been reluctant to use formal methods or economic theory as analysis tools, preferring casual empiricism as a framework for explanation. In a departure from this conventional method, new approaches use quantitative and conceptual methods to add weight to the viewpoint that culture is a critical determinant of economic behaviour and performance.

This survey proceeds in four stages. The second section describes Britain's economic growth record. The third, fourth and fifth sections discuss neoclassical, institutional and cultural analyses of entrepreneurship as research programmes. These approaches are neither entirely discrete nor confined to specific areas of enquiry. However, delimiting the literature in this way is a useful navigational device, and facilitates the integration of new methods of analysis that build on older vintages of research. Much has been written since the publication of McCloskey and Sandberg's seminal essay, but the emphasis here is on the most recent contributions. Promising avenues of enquiry are highlighted. The main argument is that advances in economic theory offer an improved framework for both macro- and micro-level investigations. Endogenous theories of growth lead to a clearer understanding of international differences in entrepreneurial performance. The evolving literature on the dynamics of technological change elaborates on the neoclassical analysis of constrained optimisation and rational technology choices. Research on institutions highlights the broader economic environment in which entrepreneurs operate. Conceptual and empirical examinations of culture lead away from an unproductive emphasis on casual empiricism. These new approaches, among the others discussed in this essay, enhance our understanding of British entrepreneurial history.

UNDERSTANDING THE GROWTH RECORD

Researchers in the field of growth accounting have confronted difficult measurement problems in establishing informative data on the relative performance of countries in the late nineteenth and early twentieth centuries. Proponents of the entrepreneurial failure hypothesis point to historic indices that emphasise the weakness of the British economy. These data are summarised above in Tables 1.1 to 1.7. In 1870 British GDP growth stood at approximately 2.4 per cent per annum, but had slowed to 1.4 per cent per annum by 1913 (Table 1.3). In 1900 Britain still had the highest *level* of gross domestic product (GDP) per person, but the United States and Germany experienced higher rates of *growth* (Crafts 1999: 19–20). There is nothing in the output series to suggest a break in trend, or 'climacteric' (such as was alleged by some earlier writers); however, unlike competing industrial nations, Britain failed to achieve 'trend acceleration' (Greasley and Oxley 1995; Crafts and Mills 1996b). American GDP per person increased from 75.3 per cent to 131.4 per cent of the British level between 1870 and 1929. Germany also established a large lead over Britain during this period (Crafts 1998: 200, 1999: 20).

Which aspects of decline were to be expected, and which aspects were attributable to the actions of entrepreneurs, is one of the overarching issues in this debate. Contemporary commentators argued that Britain's international economic displacement was indicative of entrepreneurial failure (Shadwell 1909). Cases of weak entrepreneurship were identified in the traditional staple industries – steel, coal and textiles – as well as in some of the newer industries – chemicals, motor cars and electrical engineering (Clapham 1938). Economic history research in the 1950s and 1960s concurred with this view. In 1964 Aldcroft levelled a multi-pronged attack on the British entrepreneur who, among other things, did not invest sufficiently in research and development (R&D), was reluctant to adopt best-practice high-throughput innovations, and was slow to embrace the newer technologically dynamic industries of the second industrial revolution. More sanguine views took it to be expected that the newer industrialising nations would leapfrog Britain, given their natural resources and market conditions. Yet entrepreneurs did not escape blame. According to Marshall although 'it was inevitable that [Britain] should cede much . . . it was not inevitable that she should lose so much of it as she has done' (Marshall 1920: 298).

Contemporaries warned that too much capital was being sent abroad for the good of the British economy, reducing the supply of entrepreneurial investment funds at home. The rate of savings in late nineteenth- and early twentieth-century Britain was similar to the rising industrial nations of Germany and the United States, yet domestic investment in Britain was almost half the level of these countries. However, analysis of the risks and returns associated with domestic and overseas investment shows that investors were acting rationally by channelling funds abroad where higher returns were available to augment British national income (Edelstein 1982). According to Clemens and Williamson (2001) British capital was attracted overseas by fundamentals – human capital, natural resources and demography – which made the New World an attractive investment opportunity. With a diminishing marginal product of capital a substantial diversion of funds from foreign projects to new home investment would have lowered returns domestically. In addition, the marginal efficiency of capital will be lower the greater the amount of capital already possessed. As McCloskey (1979: 539) famously quipped, late Victorian Britain did not need 'two Forth Bridges, two Bakerloo Lines, two London housing stocks, two Port Sunlights'.

McCloskey (1970) used a neoclassical model of exogenous growth to attempt to show that the late Victorian entrepreneur did not fail; rather he was doing the best he could with available resources according to the economy's resource endowments and prevailing technology. First, McCloskey tackled concerns that a slowdown in Britain's late Victorian economic growth was due to an inefficient allocation of resources. The basic ingredient of his model is an aggregate production function with constant returns to labour, and diminishing returns to the accumulation of capital. With a constant level of labour supply, and a given state of technological knowledge, how much output is produced by an economy then depends on the aggregate level of the capital stock. McCloskey calculates that the economy could have only grown at a more rapid rate if capital and labour were substitutable and if capital growth had been substantially higher. Both of these factors were improbable, and in any case, would not have sustained a permanently higher rate of *long-run* growth. Had Britain saved more, or reversed its decision to send capital abroad during this period, more investment at home would have driven the marginal product of capital close to zero unless technology had changed for other reasons. To the extent that entrepreneurs were choosing the most efficient technologies, and that competition was eradicating uneconomical practices, the British economy was 'growing as rapidly as permitted by the growth of its resources and the effective exploitation of the available technology' (McCloskey and Sandberg 1971: 459).

The notion that entrepreneurs were optimising, subject to constraints beyond their control, receives support from research which seeks to explain differences in the adoption of technology and in comparative growth rates between Britain and America. Habakkuk (1962) maintained that in Britain labour was cheaper than capital, which meant that entrepreneurs naturally persisted with labour- rather than capital-intensive methods of production. In America, by contrast, scarcity of labour encouraged the widespread use of capital and mass-production methods to meet the demands of a larger market. David (1975) reformulated this thesis to stress the evolutionary properties of technological change, whereby the initial, often random, choice of technology sets in motion a process of cumulative learning and expansion. Rosenberg (1982) pointed out that, in America, specialisation and hence larger firms were facilitated by the simultaneous growth of several industries sharing certain technical processes. A few firms, each reaping considerable economies of scale, could then satisfy demand.

British entrepreneurs may be further exonerated by branches of the new growth literature (e.g., Aghion and Howitt 1998). Although the forces of endogenous growth are difficult to identify, induced-technological change, as opposed to exogenous technology in traditional neoclassical growth economics, occupies a central role in Crafts' (1998) explanation of late Victorian comparative economic performance. While resource endowment, market size and institutional constraints fettered the British economy, competing nations offered a more favourable platform for endogenous innovation and learning. Because of the different environments in which entrepreneurs operated there were fewer opportunities for international technology spillovers, such as the transfer to Britain of American mass-production techniques. Since British entrepreneurs could do nothing about the hand they were dealt by history, 'the developments in endogenous growth theory may offer additional lines of defence for those wishing to absolve British business of any failure' (Crafts 1998: 206).

The issue of absolution may also be approached from Broadberry's (1997c, 1998) perspective of sectoral productivity rates (see also chapter 3 above). His research questioned whether a weak performance in manufacturing was really at the heart of Britain's economic faltering. Productivity statistics have traditionally reinforced pessimistic assessments regarding British long-run economic development (aggregate British productivity growth advanced at 0.45 per cent per annum between 1873 and 1913, slowing to just 0.05 per cent per annum over the period 1899–1913). However, Broadberry's data reveal that the British experience when set against the United States and Germany was different when analysed sector by sector. In fact, differences between Britain and these benchmark nations arose not so much through performance in manufacturing, as by Britain's comparative loss of labour productivity in services (see Table 1.2).

Explaining why labour productivity in services – transport and communications, distribution, finance, personal and professional services and government – was so high in the late nineteenth century, but relatively low by the end of the twentieth, is problematic because the literature on enterprise and management structure during this period is unduly centred on manufacturing. Although services have not been neglected entirely 'the full explanation of these trends will require [more] detailed investigation at the level of individual service sectors' (Broadberry 1998: 393). Thus, business histories of retailing enterprise document the pioneering role of British firms in product development, branding, distribution, industrial relations and multinational expansion (e.g. Chapman 1984; Fitzgerald 1995), but there are no micro-level comparative studies which may explain the reasons for cross-country productivity differentials. It is often claimed that the social cohesion of the British banking elite epitomised Britain's cultural shortcomings, but it may also have had a positive effect on productivity through enhancing network effects and facilitating informal 'relational contracts' within and between firms. The performance of the service sector is one of the least understood aspects of Britain's comparative economic decline.

NEOCLASSICAL *HOMO ECONOMICUS*, TECHNOLOGY AND PATH DEPENDENCE

Against this backdrop of debate over the growth record, economic historians continue to debate whether Britain's sluggish late nineteenth-century growth performance was due to a slowdown in the rate of technological progress. Britain's comparative advantage during the nineteenth and early twentieth centuries rested in the traditional staple industries (Crafts 1998: 201). Competing nations were stronger in the newer industries, and often made technology choices that did not prevail in Britain. Micro-level research has tried to uncover the causes and consequences of Britain's differential industrial structure and methods of production.

Endogenous growth theorists place innovation at the heart of economic development. Productivity growth derives from the rapid replacement of obsolete knowledge by new discoveries. This process, analogous to Schumpeter's notion of 'creative destruction', is stimulated by incentive structures that facilitate the development of new technologies. Advocates of endogenous growth theory argue that they can develop more flexible models, which embrace a truer vision of economic activity. Unlike the preceding neoclassical paradigm their theory does not assume that technology is universally available at no cost, nor treat entrepreneurs as operating within the constraints of existing technological possibilities.

Scholars of the industrial revolution, however, point out that Britain's mid-nineteenth-century success came from a capacity to create and diffuse new technologies which might be best regarded as exogenous 'macro-inventions' (Mokyr 1990) rather than the continuous technological change implied by such theories. Indeed O'Brien *et al.* (1996) doubted whether endogenous theories could be applied to leading technological innovations of this period, especially those in cotton textiles. Micro-research on British industries has illustrated the power of the neoclassical paradigm to explain technology choices in leading industries for later epochs. Case studies of the adoption of late Victorian technology consider whether entrepreneurs were making economically rational choices; this is a natural starting point from the rational choice perspective, which argues that entrepreneurs do not generally ignore opportunities for profit.

Most research of this type has been devoted to explaining technology choice in the cotton textile industry. The crux of the issue is whether Lancashire entrepreneurs were rational in their decision to install mule spindles at a time when New England entrepreneurs were switching to a newer technology – ring spinning. In the US ring spindles comprised 62 per cent of all spindles by 1890 and 87 per cent by 1913. In Britain, by contrast, only 19 per cent of all spindles were ring spindles on the eve of the First World War. In a pioneering article, Sandberg (1969) argued that demand and factor costs explain the Lancashire decision to persist with mules, rather than a reluctance to embrace new technology. Leunig's (2001) re-examination of Sandberg's classic argument confirmed that demand- rather than supply-side constraints were the dominant force reducing ring spinning adoption rates. This research challenges the view that mule spindles were a necessary response to the industry's inefficient organisation into vertically specialised units which increased transport costs between spinning and weaving facilities (Lazonick 1981b). It suggests that production of high-quality goods supported by a large export trade determined Lancashire's predisposition towards mules.

According to Saxonhouse and Wright (1984) the cotton technology debate ignores the most salient characteristic of the industry during this period – new competition. They sided with the view that Lancashire's reliance on the mule compared with ring spinning was the outcome of a decentralised vertically disintegrated industrial structure which was inimical to technological change. However, they also maintained that a switch to rings would not have given rise to a favourable outcome for the industry. Protectionism and economic development in low-wage countries, combined with a high British wage rate, caused decline. During the late nineteenth and early twentieth centuries Britain was not well placed to be the leading cotton economy.

There are conflicting interpretations of whether domestic supply and demand conditions were equally significant in other sectors of the economy. The British iron and steel industry faced slower-growing demand than its major industrial competitors during the late nineteenth and early twentieth centuries. Differences in demand, according to Temin's (1966) calculations, gave German and American producers a 15 per cent productivity advantage over their British counterparts. Taking account of measurement error, McCloskey's (1973) revisions to these estimates reduces the gap from 15 per cent to 1 per cent, thus questioning the extent to which demand was a source of decline in this industry. None the less, for McCloskey, Britain's late nineteenth-century iron and steel industry should be considered as a case study of economic maturity rather than entrepreneurial deficiency. In 1890 British productivity in iron and steel was at least equal to the American rate. Assertions that the industry did not take advantage of ores in East Midlands districts – a cost-reducing metallic input – are rejected by McCloskey in favour of the argument that entrepreneurs were rational to concentrate on existing areas of production in the north-east. At a time when transport costs were high, East Midland ores were too distant from product and factor markets to be viable. Entrepreneurs were optimising subject to geological and transport cost constraints.

Allen's (1977, 1979) comprehensive analysis of Britain's relative decline as an iron and steel exporter in the late nineteenth century broadly concurred with the view that geological and transport cost constraints were significant, but suggests that 'vigorous entrepreneurs could have overcome . . . these disadvantages'. Germany and America surpassed Britain in productivity because of lower-cost raw materials and superior technical efficiency; American and German producers were approximately 15 per cent more efficient than British producers between 1907 and 1909. Although lower-cost production was hindered by a high British wage rate more investment in integrated plants producing basic steel from north-east ores could have driven costs at least as low as German levels. Without systematic investment in high-efficiency plants, British producers could not (and did not) match the prices of their German counterparts.

Lindert and Trace (1971) found evidence for entrepreneurial-induced decline in the history of the chemicals industry. Their research showed that British dyestuff firms could have secured higher profits by switching from the Leblanc system of alkali production to the superior Solvay production process which was utilised by German and American firms. The Solvay system was patented in 1861, yet by 1894 65 per cent of soda output in Britain still came from the Leblanc method; for competing producers the share was no more than 22 per cent. British firms should be indicted for not taking advantage of the new knowledge, which chemical engineers had predicted would revolutionise the industry. Rather than adopting new and more efficient technologies, manufacturers responded by merging into the United Alkali Company in 1890 in order to protect existing streams of rent. The chemicals industry is used as evidence in the broader debate on the reluctance of British entrepreneurs to take hold of the new innovations associated with the second industrial revolution (Mokyr 1990: 266).

A variety of other industries have been used as case studies to test the hypothesis of entrepreneurial rationality in the late nineteenth and early twentieth centuries (McCloskey 1971). One of the main contributions of this work has been the application of economic theory to a previously qualitative debate. The study of entrepreneurial activity has been transformed from a research programme characterised by arbitrary performance judgements to one in which measurable variables are analysed within a theoretical framework. However, critics have argued that the assumption of rational choice which underlies neoclassical investigations is not well suited to the analysis of entrepreneurial behaviour. Entrepreneurs have no capacity for seizing opportunity or taking strategic action within the neoclassical assumptions of objectivity of information, autonomy of preferences and cost-less optimisation. The case studies discussed above show that this criticism is misplaced. The neoclassical approach is substantive and facilitates empirical tests to determine whether entrepreneurial actions are economically optimal. Rationality is the benchmark against which both success and failure can be judged.

However, alternative frameworks can enhance our understanding. Static neoclassical analysis cannot fully explain the dynamics of technological change and its evolution. The theory of 'path dependence', which provides a conceptual framework for explaining why the economy can be locked in to a specific technology because of technical interrelatedness, scale economies, learning and habituation, has been used to glean fresh insights into British industrial organisation and business performance. In a recent debate Van Fleck (1999) and Scott (1999) used the evolving literature on path dependence to address the oft-cited Veblen–Kindleberger hypothesis that older vintages of industrial equipment placed a burden on the efficiency of railways. Van Fleck's central argument is that the British system of utilising small coal wagons was an efficient method of distributing coal to local markets when compared with road transportation. Larger wagons would not have yielded substantial operating cost savings – 'the little coal wagon was exactly the right type of technology to employ'. Scott, on the other hand, calculates that economies foregone were considerable and that the initial choice of small privately owned coal wagons proved to be a significant constraint on the efficiency of coal distribution by rail. The high costs tied up in existing rolling stock and infrastructure prevented reorganisation of the industry to take advantage of larger cost-minimising wagons under a system of common ownership.

According to the path dependence literature every technology has a history, and the evolution of a technology can depend critically on its own past (Arthur 1989; Liebowitz and Margolis 1995; David 1997). In the case of the British rail industry (and from Scott's perspective) investment in best-practice larger wagon technology was blocked by complementarities between smaller wagons and the industry's infrastructure. Fragmented ownership of the railways and rolling stock created and, through feedbacks, reinforced these 'network effects'. Under a changed set of investment circumstances a different cost-minimising technology – larger wagons – might have been forthcoming. Counterfactual worlds can be contemplated; path dependence is consistent with a multiplicity of equilibria. From Van Fleck's perspective, the historical evolution of rail wagon technology was due to initially efficient entrepreneurial decision making. The small wagon distribution system was cost-effective and exhibited increasing returns to owners. Although Van Fleck has less to say on whether this level of lock-in gave rise to sub-optimality, the literature on path dependence does entertain this possibility. How historical events exert an influence upon subsequent outcomes is just one side of the debate. Whether historical accidents give rise to inferior equilibria is perhaps the more salient other side.

INSTITUTIONS AND BRITISH SCLEROSIS

One of the recurrent criticisms of the highly stylised view of entrepreneurial behaviour which is embodied in the neoclassical approach is that it is of only limited use in explaining the significance of institutions. Institutions surely have to play a part within explanations of long-run growth and development (Acemoglu *et al.* 2001). By reducing transaction costs and facilitating potential gains from exchange, institutions can be a significant source of productivity growth (North 1989). Pointing to a fusion of institutional constraints that undermined British economic competitiveness, Elbaum and Lazonick (1984) put forward a challenge to the neoclassical paradigm of constrained optimisation. Drawing together case studies of leading industries, Elbaum and Lazonick concluded that a common factor – 'institutional rigidity' – explains why entrepreneurs were slow to adapt to international competition during the early twentieth century. British entrepreneurs failed to unlock pre-existing paths of development and this limited the capacity of the economy to respond to a new economic environment. British businessmen did not challenge institutional constraints and therefore were responsible for the country's comparative economic failure. This research was buttressed by Olson's (1982) notion of 'institutional sclerosis', which refers to the economic and social constraints that hold back the modernisation of industry. Britain did not experience the institutional destruction and replacement of self-interested elites that occurred in several European nations. Interest groups colluded to protect their privileged positions, contributing to Britain's economic plight.

Yet to a large extent the interaction of entrepreneurs with institutions is driven by government policy. Baumol (1988, 1990) postulated a link between productive and unproductive entrepreneurship and the structure of payoffs in the economy. According to his theory policy makers are more able to influence the allocation than the supply of entrepreneurship. For example, revisions to the patent laws during the nineteenth century are said to have reduced opportunities for undue appropriation by affording inventors legal protection of their intellectual property rights (Dutton 1984). Company law, on the other hand, may have worked in the opposite direction. Poor information on the stock exchange precluded would-be predators from obtaining knowledge about target enterprises. It was not until 1948 that firms were forced to disclose systematic information concerning their assets and profits. Although American company law was also lax before the formation of the Securities and Exchange Commission in 1934, independent investor services like Moody's and Standard and Poor's provided an antidote to problems of asymmetric information. Lax information disclosure in Britain created opportunities for corruption and malpractice. Over 30 per cent of companies formed between 1856 and 1883 ended in insolvency (Jobert and Moss 1990). It is perhaps no accident that the careers of the unscrupulous company promoters appear frequently in nineteenth- and twentieth-century British entrepreneurial history (Armstrong 1990).

In an attempt to explain the significance of institutions and policy making, revisions to the neoclassical paradigm incorporate more flexible assumptions that allow market imperfections and transaction costs to be determinants of entrepreneurial performance. Theories building on the basic conceptual premise of the neoclassical *homo economicus* have established a more informative predictive theory of entrepreneurship. Bowles and Gintis (1993: 84) have commented that the entrepreneur is 'not satisfied with calculating marginal substitutions while shopping for groceries, [H]e now optimises while deciding how hard to work for his employer, how truthfully to transmit information to his exchange partners and whether the costs exceed the benefits of defaulting on a loan.'

Advances in economic theory have also been used to address the recurrent argument that British entrepreneurs were starved of investment funds as a consequence of imperfections in capital markets. If banks allocate credit according to information on prospective borrowers, informational asymmetries can lead to potentially successful entrepreneurs being denied credit. Liquidity constraints can either exclude individuals with insufficient funds at their disposal from entrepreneurship or prevent those who do enter into entrepreneurship from exploiting the opportunities available. If would-be entrepreneurs cannot borrow on the credit market, or find the cost of capital too high, they may continue in wage work or start an enterprise with a lower level of capital.

Individual case studies of credit rationed entrepreneurs are not sufficient to confirm or reject the hypothesis that capital markets constrained the supply of entrepreneurship. Even the most successful entrepreneurs face problems in accessing capital (Mokyr 1990: 262). Capie and Collins (1996) approached the issue by assembling comprehensive data on lending practices from commercial bank archives. In a study of 453 separate cases of banks refusing to lend to industrial clients, they showed that the decision not to invest was motivated by the desire instead to fund longstanding clients on whom more information was available, who were in competition with risky new investments with highly uncertain outcomes. Although 'the yardstick on adequacy of capital was a severe one when applied to new firms and it seems to have severely hindered their chances of raising bank loans' (1996: 43), this was a natural response to the problems of adverse selection and moral hazard. Contrary to common perceptions, British banks did provide long-term loans to industrial clients in addition to their role as suppliers of short-term credit and working capital (Collins and Baker 1999).

However, we do not know from the Capie–Collins study whether German and American banks treated their clients differently. The central issue about British banking and economic growth is whether or not the system could support sustained economic development following the industrial revolution, and this can be best understood from a comparative perspective. It is commonly argued that British commercial banks were reluctant to develop close relations with industry between 1870 and 1914, in contrast to Germany where formal ties between banks and firms mitigated agency costs and enhanced corporate governance practices. (Gerschenkron 1962; Kennedy 1987). The view that banker influence on a firm's supervisory board was beneficial is also supported from studies of the United States (e.g. De Long 1991). In addition to facilitating access to investment finance adding liquidity, monitoring debt and providing signals to investors, formal bank relationships with firms made possible the rapid replacement of bad managers. In Britain, where such relationships were much less common, bad managers may have been more likely to survive.

On the other hand, such generalisations may be unwarranted. Several studies (Edwards and Ogilvie 1996; Collins 1998; Fohlin 1999) have questioned the alleged inefficiency of British banking in a European context. Taken together, this work suggests that a much smaller weight should be placed on comparative banking systems in accounts of Britain's relative economic decline. Guinnane's (2002) analysis provided a properly stratified account of the benefits and costs of Germany's banking system in relation to growth. Germany's universal banks were able to 'foster and support firms at an earlier stage and more effectively than could other types of banking institutions' (2002: 119), but they also created problems by restricting competition in banking and fostering cartel arrangements in industry. Moreover, universal banks may have played a more limited role than conventionally thought in providing start-up capital for entrepreneurship (Kleeberg 1988). To the extent that smaller private banks were more effective as institutions for venture capital finance, some scholars may have overstated the contribution of universal banking to German economic growth.

British and American industrial relations in the early twentieth century have frequently been subjected to cross-cultural analysis. For example, Lazonick (1994) pointed to employment relations in manufacturing as a source of entrepreneurial failings. Such studies argue that British manufacturers, unlike their American counterparts, faced industrial relations scenarios which inhibited the introduction of advanced production methods. This was symbolised by the reluctance of British manufacturers to invest in the American system of mass-production. The exemplar case is the motor vehicle industry. The strength of organised labour in Britain impeded the introduction of Henry Ford's assembly line technology that reaped considerable economies of scale for the American motor vehicle manufacturer. Lewchuk (1993) has shown that industrial relations strategies in the Ford motor company were effective at extracting surplus labour effort. However, because of the unproductive British bargaining environment, Ford was reluctant to impose American methods of job control on British labour. American entrepreneurs were better placed to undermine craft control and trade unionism, which gave rise to a more favourable technological trajectory.

Different development trajectories were also characteristic of British and American enterprise overseas. By 1914 Britain was by far the largest exporter of capital, approximately 40 per cent of which took the form of direct investment. By 1939 there were more than 350 British manufacturing firms engaged in multinational enterprise (Nicholas 1983). Successful overseas expansion depended on a firm's ability to internalise market transactions. During the 1920s and 1930s British firms relied heavily on the security of Empire, while American firms increasingly invested in Europe. Although the 'safety' of Empire markets provided British firms with more favourable conditions for appropriating profits and rents, lack of competition may also have stifled entrepreneurship. American direct investment in Europe, by contrast, built on a combination of technological superiority and organisational capabilities. As exemplified by American pre-eminence in the motor vehicle industry (Foreman-Peck 1982), these advantages gave rise to a different and crucially productivity enhancing course of development.

CULTURE, WEALTH AND THE ENTREPRENEURIAL SPIRIT

In addition to economic factors Britain's rigid class structure and a system of social and cultural attitudes is said to have inhibited economic development. Wiener's (1981) prominent thesis on culture and economic retardation envisages a cultural *cordon sanitaire* of aristocratic attitudes and aspirations encircling British society. Industrialists pursued gentrification as a means of achieving social status. Cultural forces set in motion an anti-industrial, even anti-capitalist, spirit.

The thesis of culturally led decline has been heavily criticised. Wiener's account has been castigated as presenting a selective array of poetry, English literature and the views of selected opinion makers rather than comprehensive and systematic evidence on business performance. Furthermore, anti-business attitudes can be found in Britain before, during and after the industrial revolution. An intellectual tradition of hostility towards business can be extracted from historical and political literature in Germany and the United States, both of which are traditionally contrasted with the British model (Collins and Robbins 1990). Coleman and Macleod (1986) commented that the 'industrial spirit', like Max Weber's 'spirit of capitalism', floats nebulously in the air with no hard evidence to show that it motivated business decisions. Behind the rhetoric of entrenched middle-class values the cultural thesis moulds the Victorian philosophy of 'self-help' into a schema in which individualism, vigour and entrepreneurial drive are dominated by the desire for material prosperity in the form of gentlemanly pleasures. Although it remains a fair deduction that the pursuit of wealth was linked to the pursuit of social status this need not have been inextricably bound within an anti-capitalist ethos.

This point is central to the recurrent cultural debate concerning the propensity of businessmen in the late nineteenth century to be engaged in the market for land. A preference for social cachet, or leisure, is alleged to have weakened the industrial spirit as businessmen moved their resources from profitable business investments into loss-making landed estates. Pseudo-aristocratic values replaced entrepreneurial drive. A pre-existing landed elite continued to dominate society for much of the nineteenth century and the desire for assimilation was absorbed into the ideology of business culture. It then follows from this argument that, if businessmen were integrated into high society through land purchase, they could devote less time and energy to their businesses.

But landownership by businessmen did not necessarily involve accommodation to the gentlemanly ideal. According to Gunn (1988: 29) we should not comply with

> a simple correlation between social behaviour, ideology and economic practice. It was perfectly possible for a Victorian industrialist to ride with the local hunt, build himself a castle in the country and adopt a 'neo-feudal' pose of paternalist employer without consciously compromising in any way the imperatives of capitalist production or class commitment.

Furthermore, research by Rubinstein (1981a, 1981b, 1996) and by Nicholas (1999a, 2000a) questions whether businessmen held land on a large scale in the late nineteenth century, or indeed whether landed assets comprised a significant element of a businessman's wealth portfolio. Contrary to conventional wisdom (Thompson, 1963, 1990a, 1992, 1994) this research finds that large-scale landownership by businessmen was not a broad avenue of assimilation between old and new wealth. This is not to say that British entrepreneurs ignored the pursuit of gentlemanly fashions and the trappings of high society. Relatively small plots of land, such as those that Habakkuk (1994: 613–14) describes as 'mini-estates' of 200 acres or less, could be bought for residence with a view to social status. Additionally the growth of London and the provincial districts as social centres in the late nineteenth century created an alternative form of urban gentrification. The acquisition of a country mansion or landed estate was only one expression of cultural decadence in Victorian society (Nicholas 2000b).

Given the difficulties inherent in assigning a causal link between cultural variables and business performance, Nicholas (1999b) attempted to establish an objective criterion for analysing entrepreneurship by utilising lifetime rates of wealth accumulation as an index of success.

Profit seeking defines the entrepreneurial function in Nicholas' work; this leads to a model which utilises rate of return calculations to distinguish between wealth due to inheritance and wealth stemming from entrepreneurship. The application of this method to a large sample of British entrepreneurs revealed that industry, region and religious dissent cannot explain performance differences. By contrast, education and entrepreneurial type are the important predictors. Third generation entrepreneurs (and more generally those who inherited firms) experienced relatively low lifetime rates of wealth accumulation compared to entrepreneurs who founded firms. An education at a public school or Oxbridge college was also associated with an inferior business performance. Despite the difficulties in empirically estimating lifetime rates of wealth accumulation, this method does reveal robust insights into aspects of culture and entrepreneurship. An application of this method to a data set of French entrepreneurs (Foreman-Peck *et al.* 1998) highlights opportunities for further research in this area and a potential for cross-national comparisons.

The four aspects of culture studied by Nicholas – firm type, education, religion and type of industry/region – are central to the hypothesis of culturally induced economic decline in Britain. All of these areas have been extensively studied in economic and business history, though not without controversies. The following sections detail how the cultural argument has been advanced through observation, case study evidence and the application of economic theory to historical problems.

Family firms

Cultural explanations of Britain's relative economic decline often assume a connection between family capitalism and entrepreneurial failure. Businessmen, it is alleged, were fundamentally conservative and reluctant to try new and untested methods. The typical firm in the late nineteenth and early twentieth centuries was family owned and controlled and characterised by patronage and nepotism in recruitment patterns. Most references to this view cite Landes' (1969) classic account of European industrialisation in which late nineteenth-century Britain was plagued by a combination of entrepreneurial lethargy, complacency and cultural conservatism. According to Landes, British entrepreneurs were like their French counterparts in that they lacked drive, initiative and imagination. The problems of industry were reflected in distaste for competition and a preference for leisure pursuits. Firm founders and their families continued to shape resource allocation decisions in a way that significantly handicapped the economy.

However, studies of individual family dynasties show that family firms were not always badly managed or profitless. The Gregs of Styal maintained the entrepreneurial drive into and beyond the third generation as cotton industrialists (Rose 1977). Barker's (1977) study of Pilkingtons, the glass manufacturer, documents the history of a largely family owned and controlled business in the vanguard of technological advance. Alistair Pilkington, born in 1920 and educated in mechanical sciences at Trinity College Cambridge, was the inventor of the float process that established Pilkingtons' advantage over foreign rivals in the manufacture of glass. Foreign manufacturers using the more expensive grinding and polishing process were eventually forced to purchase licences from Pilkingtons. The float process was developed over a ten-year period which required sustained funds for investment. According to Barker, family ownership and control facilitated the provision of investment capital that might not have been forthcoming had the directors of the company been accountable to a series of outside shareholders.

Family firm studies document the view that success often depended on the right combination of management and personality rather than on a specific form of corporate structure. The success of Rowntree (the York producer of chocolate and confectionery) in the 1920s and 1930s was accompanied by the recruitment of new managerial personnel, although leading family members retained control of the firm. Arnold Rowntree developed the firm's advertising strategy based on market research, product development and branding. Seebohm Rowntree, the famous social scientist and activist, introduced a 'functional' structure to the company in 1921, and was a prominent management theorist. Rowntree contradicts the classical stereotype of family-based entrepreneurial lethargy (Fitzgerald 1995).

Recent work on family firms, however, has reinforced the conventional viewpoint that inherited business ownership and control more often acted as a brake on the growth of firms and the development of the economy. Mark Casson (1999) identified a trade-off between a positive effect of dynasty – trust between family members and a concomitant reduction in transaction and agency costs – and a negative effect, the reluctance to recruit outside professionals. Whether the economy benefits or suffers depends on the distribution of economic activity. While 'dynastic firms are well-suited to craft-based industries where the optimal scale of production is small' this form of industrial organisation is 'inappropriate for science-based industries in which the optimal scale of production is large' (1999: 11). This standpoint provides an important explanation for the success of family firms in Britain's industrial take-off, while explaining why Britain was slow to adjust to the world of corporate capitalism, which was associated with newer technologically dynamic industries.

Chandler's (1990) treatise on the *Dynamics of Industrial Capitalism* points to an unwillingness to embrace new managerial strategies as a specific cause of entrepreneurial failure in Britain. The peculiar British institution – the family firm – and its concomitant conservatism inhibited investments in manufacturing, marketing and management. Consequently, British firms failed to capture economies of scale and scope inherent in new technologies, particularly those associated with the industries of the second industrial revolution. The Germans and the Americans seized these opportunities both domestically and internationally. There are several case studies of British intransigence in the Chandlerian thesis, but in the light of recent research the electrical equipment industry stands out. David and Wright (1999) attributed America's impressive manufacturing productivity growth rate of 5.5 per cent per annum between 1919 and 1929 to multiple causal factors driven by the diffusion of electrification as a general purpose technology. Between 1924 and 1937 total factor productivity in British manufacturing advanced at a comparatively slow rate of 1.9 per cent per annum. Through individuals like Joseph Swan and Sebastian Ferranti Britain possessed the inventive capacity to develop electrification technology. Yet British firms were unable to build up organisational capabilities such as those of George Westinghouse in the United States or Werner Siemens in Germany. While both of these firms could draw on pools of university-trained engineers, there was a shortage of such human capital in Britain (see chapter 3 above).

Indeed, Broadberry and Crafts (1992a) have argued that more attention should be given to the environment in which firms operated rather than to managerial strategies *per se*. The American labour productivity lead in manufacturing predates the emergence of the large-scale Chandlerian corporation. Although the forces envisaged by Chandler are relevant to the Anglo-American productivity gap, they do not explain a large part of it. Rather, a confluence of factors, including collusion between firms, deficiencies in human capital and an unproductive bargaining environment, explain Britain's comparatively weaker productive potential. Mercer (1995) has shown that market structure was a pervasive influence on productivity performance. During the interwar period British firms, under the patronage of government policy, chose to collude and cartelise as a means of regulating domestic competition. According to Broadberry and Crafts (1992a: 554), 'competitive forces were so weak as to allow degrees of freedom for managers to fail'. Economic theory suggests that competition policy would have had a favourable impact on technological development in interwar Britain because of the preponderance of conservative firms in which managers were reluctant to introduce costly (in terms of effort) but performance-enhancing technologies. The preferred option, industrial policy that subsidised incumbent firms, provided a greater scope for entrepreneurial slack (Aghion and Howitt 1998: 205–32). There is little evidence of a positive relationship between market power and innovation in interwar Britain. Policy makers prevented shifting the allocation of entrepreneurship away from rent-seeking activities.

Education

Education also takes a prominent role in the historical debate concerning the role of culture in influencing entrepreneurial performance. G. C. Allen (1979) suggested that the public (fee-paying) school bestowed gentility to the detriment of the late Victorian business community. Public schools instilled fine and noble values, but this was not conducive to commercial and industrial success. More specifically, the slow pace of technical advance, especially in the old staple industries, is ascribed to the near total exclusion from the public school curriculum of science and technology studies. According to Ward (1967: 38), 'one reason for [businessmen's] failure in the late nineteenth century lay in the growth of the public schools'.

A number of studies have questioned the validity of such claims. Rubinstein's (1994) detailed investigation of entrants to eight public schools – Eton, Harrow, Winchester, Rugby, Cheltenham, St Pauls, Dulwich and Mill Hill – showed that very few public school boys passed their later days as gentlemen. Comparatively few businessmen, compared with fathers active in the professions, sent their sons to a fee-paying school. Of those that did, their sons were not filtered out of business careers; indeed, they followed their fathers into business. Where the sons of businessmen did enter into non-business careers, Coleman (1973) has pointed out that this trend may have removed less gifted sons from the family firm before they could do any damage to it. The public school may not have functioned as an adverse influence on the supply of entrepreneurs. Rather it may have acted as an effective safety net for the redirection of bad businessmen into non-business careers. If successful businessmen withdrew their sons from the business world by sending them to a public school, this may have cleared the way for a succession of newcomers with the requisite skills and drive necessary for successful entrepreneurship.

Furthermore, it is not clear that a classical curriculum was always detrimental to a business career. Berghoff (1990) maintains that it is difficult to understand the willingness of the upper class to place their savings into financiers' hands without taking account of bankers' social integration. In commerce and finance it is possible that the determination to recruit the 'English Gentleman' was a focus of competitive success. An implicit training in leadership qualities, a high level of self-confidence and connections through the social pecking order may have been advantageous. High social status among bankers was a function of political ties, kinship, intermarriage and education. In Cassis' (1985) study of Victorian bankers, 45 per cent had been to Eton, and 26 per cent to Harrow, which contributed to the forming of a cohesive banking elite.

Sanderson (1988) further challenged the idea that a high social status education exclusively involved the study of classics, demonstrating how an education at a public school, or Oxbridge, was not unchanging from the late nineteenth century onwards. The nature of scientific and technical education improved radically in the 1890s and 1900s in response to institutional pressures. At Oxford, the Honours School of Natural Science was introduced in 1852 and the Natural Sciences Tripos began at Cambridge in 1848. A chair of engineering was founded at Cambridge in 1875. Outside Oxford and Cambridge, the London and civic universities were closely integrated with industry, either in origins and development or in the provision of scientific and technical instruction. University College London opened in 1826 giving priority to science and engineering and King's College London was founded in 1828 with a similarly progressive attitude towards vocational studies. The state was not actively engaged in the finance of the civic universities until 1889 which meant that private benefactors, often from commerce and industry, played an invaluable role in the early development of provincial higher education. For example, Sheffield University resulted from the merger of institutions including colleges founded by the steel masters Mark Firth and Sir Frederick Mappin.

However, differences between British and European education systems are invariably invoked to explain comparative economic growth rates. In Britain the most esteemed schools and universities taught classics. Education was liberal in outlook pursuing classics as part of an educational philosophy. By contrast, the French education system was biased towards technical education. The *Ecole Polytechnique* in Paris was one of the earliest and most prestigious technical schools. The German education system in the late nineteenth century was largely state controlled and emphasised science, empiricism and a critical approach to knowledge. In 1902 there were 1,433 engineering students in British universities compared with 7,130 in the six leading *Technische Hochschulen* in Germany (Roderick and Stephens 1972). Britain maintained a much smaller stock of university-trained engineers than rival nations, which constrained British competitiveness in high-technology sectors such as chemicals and electrical engineering.

However, other research questions the claim that comparative differences in educational backgrounds explain entrepreneurial performance more generally. Pollard (1989: 213) compared British and German education systems, arguing that by 1914 British education and science 'was a not unworthy component of what was still the richest and most productive economy in Europe'. Berghoff and Möller's (1994) comparative analysis of British and German businessmen highlights continuity in cultural characteristics, disputing the common perception that British entrepreneurs were tired pioneers relative to their dynamic German counterparts. The majority of businessmen in their German sample had received a classical education at the prestigious *Gymnasium*. Only a small minority attended the *Realschule* with its bias towards science, technology and modern languages. Although Cassis (1997) has identified superior education characteristics among a sample of French business leaders, he claims that this did not translate into a superior entrepreneurial performance. The French system was highly technical, but the abstract nature of the syllabus did little for the businessman or the entrepreneur.

Religion

The third prominent aspect of the cultural thesis is the link between religion and entrepreneurship. Many commentators have followed Max Weber's theory of 'ascetic Protestantism' and have seen nonconformist religious dogmas and patterns of behaviour as a major reason for early industrial success in Britain. Religious persuasion was second only to kinship in eighteenth-century life, according to Ashton (1955). For Kindleberger (1964), religious outgroups – or the lack thereof – were at the hub of the industrial process: 'why did not new enterprises elbow their way to the forefront in Britain after 1880? . . . the hungry outsiders – immigrants, Quakers, Jews and lower class aspirants to wealth diminished in numbers or in the intensity of their drive' (1964: 133).

A number of studies have made empirical connections between nonconformism and entrepreneurial success. Foster's (1974) study of class and the industrial revolution identified a fundamental split between an older more conservative sector, predominately Anglican, and a new liberal section, mainly nonconformist. Prior and Kirby (1993) have shown how Quakers active in the north-east developed mutual systems of support whereby access to information and trading patterns proved a catalyst for the growth of firms.

However, strong religious beliefs could be a mixed blessing for business enterprise. The case of Rowntree, the Quaker chocolate and confectionery manufacturers, provides an example. Quakerism engendered paternalism towards workers and enhanced Rowntree's reputation for product quality. Yet an antipathy towards advertising arising out of Quaker religious values also hindered the company's development. Joseph Rowntree (in office as chairman between 1897 and 1923) opposed mass-marketing, which led to a crisis in the company's fortunes. In an age when branded consumer products were promoted through advertising, Rowntree was less able to compete in the mass-consumer market (Fitgerald 1995).

On the other side of the religion and entrepreneurship debate, researchers have questioned the accuracy of studies that cite seemingly large shares of nonconformists within the business community as evidence for a connection between religion and entrepreneurship. Howe (1984) discovered that the religious composition of a sample of Lancashire cotton manufacturers in the middle of the nineteenth century did not deviate substantially from the denominational structure of the region implied by service attendance figures. Rubinstein (1981a) has pointed out that Hagen's (1962) study of social change, which identifies a large share of dissenters in a sample of eighteenth-century industrial innovators, does not provide evidence to show that dissenters were overrepresented compared with their total percentage in the British population. His own research into Britain's wealth holders identified a small proportion of nonconformists at the top of the British wealth structure. Only 15 per cent of his top wealth holders were nonconformists in religious affiliation.

Berghoff's (1995) research in turn refutes the Howe and Rubinstein hypotheses. Berghoff identified a comparatively large share (61.3 per cent) of nonconformist first generation entrepreneurs in a sample of leading provincial businessmen, providing evidence for the notion that nonconformists substantially strengthened entrepreneurship in Britain. Berghoff is careful to point out, however, that statistical facts are not fully informative because 'there are numerous examples of pleasure-loving dissenters and frugal Anglicans alike' (1991: 235). The overrepresentation of nonconformists among first generation businessmen may not have reflected disproportionately strong business acumen and entrepreneurial drive, but social constraints on entry to alternative career paths. Nonconformist theology was not the handmaiden of entrepreneurial success; rather with external constraints imposed, networks and mutual support systems facilitated the movement of nonconformists into relatively open business careers.

Region and industry

The final strand of the cultural thesis is the postulate that Britain is a country whose comparative advantage has always rested in commerce and finance, so that modern British history is seen as a conflict between commercial and industrial capitalism. Hobsbawm (1968: 151) explains: 'as her industry sagged . . . her finance triumphed, her services as a shipper trader and intermediary in the world's system of payments became more indispensable'. Cassis (1985) shows that bankers and merchant bankers were from privileged sections of society and predominantly educated at socially elite institutions. These traits supposedly culminated in Britain's relative industrial decline, yet were the same traits that sustained Britain's competitive commercial and financial success.

According to Rubinstein's (1977, 1981a, 1994) analysis of the British wealth structure, the economy was oriented towards commerce and finance. Success in these fields militates against traditional declinist allegations, which focus on manufacturing and industry. Rubinstein (1994: 35) views the industrial revolution through the other end of the looking glass as 'no more than a brief interruption of factory capitalism'. However, data on the estates left by top British wealth holders reveal significant regional and occupational differences. London society was dominated by links with commerce and finance. Of those leaving more than £500,000 at death between 1809 and 1939 a larger share were engaged in commerce and finance than in industry and manufacturing. London was the centre of wealth in nineteenth- and early twentieth-century Britain, and there was a general subordination of industrial to commercial and financial wealth.

But how deep-seated was the influence of the City elite on the British social structure? Chapman's (1984) list of merchant banks with a capital exceeding £1 million before 1914 shows that firms with aristocratic connections like the Grenfells, Barings and Rothschilds formed only a minority of the British banking community. Several authors argue that Rubinstein's methods of indexing the fortunes of top wealth holders in Britain do not support his claims that London commerce and finance dominated wealth making. According to Pahl (1990: 231), Rubinstein 'reifies this notion of a wealth structure into some kind of sociological concept without making clear what this particular notion is supposed to show or to do'. Wealth is just one determinant of class; the central importance placed by Rubinstein on the fortunes of a few large wealth makers may be misplaced. Economic development does not take place in a vacuum characterised by a dualism of the City and industry. Indeed the emergence of multi-plant firms and multinational operations makes it difficult to pinpoint the geographical and occupational sources of wealth. Ludwig Mond in the chemicals industry established branch-manufacturing units in Sandbach, Cheshire, Clydach near Swansea, and Brimsdown, Hertfordshire. The Shell Transport and Trading Co., the British holding company of the Shell Group from 1907, maintained central offices in London but exploited oil reserves from Russia to Borneo acquiring production and distribution outlets all over the world. The economic sources of wealth cannot be neatly separated into regional and occupational groupings.

Some critics have used Rubinstein's groupings in order to test his hypothesis, resulting in strong evidence to suggest that commercial and financial fortunes did not overshadow industrial ones. Berghoff (1995) has identified almost equivalent proportions of 'big' industrialists (the owners or managers of firms with 1,000 or more employees) and elite City bankers within wealth ranges including the millionaire class. The industrial revolution created a new stratum of wealthy individuals in provincial districts, which did reduce the significance of London as a location of great wealth. Nicholas' (1999c, 2000b) investigation of wealth holders in the upper echelons of British society, as well as those lower down the scale, concurs with this view. Analysis of the distribution of wealth for a group of 790 businessmen born between 1800 and 1880 reveals that industrial and provincial wealth was not inferior to wealth generated in commerce and finance and in London. Industrialists, manufacturers and entrepreneurs active in provincial districts played an equally important role in the wealth-making process. Although London was distinctive in terms of the social and political ties of its wealth elite, as shown by estate-size, there was no regional or occupational dichotomy.

SUMMARY AND CONCLUSIONS

To determine the factors that contribute to the efficiency of entrepreneurial activity is to study one of the central elements of economic growth and performance. Marshall (1920) made entrepreneurship a fourth factor of production differing fundamentally from land, labour and capital. Schumpeter's (1911) work, upon which branches of modern growth theory rest, attributes to the entrepreneur a vital role in introducing new goods, developing new methods of production, opening up new markets and creating a different type of industrial organisation. In the Schumpeterian schema the entrepreneur is the primary source of creative destruction, disrupting equilibrium through innovation.

To what extent were British entrepreneurs active in seeking out and exploiting profit-making opportunities? Did they drive the economy on to new paths of development? The neoclassical answer to these questions is that entrepreneurs were performing as well as they possibly could have done given resource endowments and exogenous technological possibilities. With an infinite supply of entrepreneurial talent and people, all opportunities presented by an economy will be exploited; competition drives poorly performing entrepreneurs out of business. Supporters of the neoclassical paradigm claim that entrepreneurs did not generally overlook opportunities for profit. Isolated examples of failure in making technological choices must be weighed against more frequent cases in which decisions embodied a rational response to economic conditions. Taken together, neoclassical research refutes the hypothesis of entrepreneurial failure in Britain.

But do entrepreneurs operate in a neoclassical world of perfect competition and exogenous technological change? The new growth literature seeks to model the economic environment more realistically by taking account of how entrepreneurs interact with institutions, how competition, financial intermediation, property rights and the legal framework affect entrepreneurial decision making and the allocation of resources towards innovative activities. To the extent that America and Germany benefited from technology trajectories conducive to endogenous innovation and learning, the first industrial nation's falling behind could be predicted. A combination of resource endowments, market size and institutional advantages created a favourable platform for growth in the newly industrialising economies. The British economy could neither parallel the developments taking place in these countries, nor benefit from international technology transfers.

If structural adjustment was a problem for the British economy, the reasons for economic decline need to be considered over a long time horizon. The high sunk costs of existing technology and infrastructure, which represented 'best practice' during the epoch of the industrial revolution, may have blocked the introduction of new equipment and more efficient production processes later on. Moreover, the knowledge acquired for one fundamental technology might be of limited relevance to the next (Redding 2002). One theoretically appealing mechanism for understanding propagation along these lines is Broadberry's (1994) 'cycles of technological leadership'. Britain's early industrial development was based on low throughput technologies that took advantage of skilled labour. Incremental improvements to this system of production made it hard for Britain to adopt more modern high throughput methods which characterised the American system of manufacturing. Yet it is also important to remember that 'the moral suggested by these historical experiences [is] not at all about "mistakes"' (David 1970: 20). The dynamic process of economic growth embodies multi-linear development trajectories. A different history of investment decisions could have produced an alternative path of cost-minimising technologies, and therefore Britain's incapacity to benefit from mass- production and organisational developments may not be synonymous with entrepreneurial failure.

On the other hand, the Schumpeterian model envisages entrepreneurs as agents of creative destruction whose role is to upset the *status quo* by unlocking predetermined paths of development. The task of the entrepreneur is to establish new opportunities as well as to exploit existing ones. While traditional staple industries such as cotton were fettered by initial technology choices and competition from overseas, the more salient issue is perhaps why resources were kept in unprofitable areas of development. Mokyr (1990: 266) comments that 'British society as a whole clearly lost its knack for taking advantage of the innovations associated with the Second Industrial Revolution'. In America, electricity was tantamount to a 'leading sector', facilitating a productivity surge with its knock-on effects throughout broad sectors of the economy. The British failure in the dyestuffs branch of the chemicals industry is notable, and provides a lens through which to view more general weaknesses in the economy. Due to pioneering inventions relating to processes for making dyes by chemical synthesis, Britain held a mid-nineteenth-century lead in this industry. Yet a failure to devote resources to new systems of production and scientific education and research caused Britain to lose out to German industrialists who made the necessary investments. Germany's comparative advantage was based on better institutions. High-technology industries gave rise to synergies, cumulative expansion and learning. The interaction between science, human capital and organisational capabilities became a driving force for rapid economic development.

Inferior institutions reduced the capacity of the British economy to respond to new competition. Notwithstanding differences in the character and size of markets, the strength of organised labour inhibited the transfer to Britain of American mass-production methods. The ability of firms to benefit from economies of scale and scope depended not only on the visible hand of managerial hierarchies, but more significantly on whether the operating environment was conducive to absorbing new techniques. While financial systems in America and Germany mitigated agency costs and informational asymmetries by providing venture capital and supervisory advice, capital markets and corporate governance practices stood as barriers to the growth of enterprise in Britain. Government policy further undermined the efficiency of firms by failing to establish a legal infrastructure for the development of large corporations. During the interwar years policy was lenient towards restraints of trade at a time when competition policy should have been invoked to compel firms to innovate in order to survive. Entrepreneurship can both generate and retard economic growth. Government policy has an important part to play by encouraging the allocation of entrepreneurship away from rent-seeking activities (Baumol 1988).

Whether there was more or less rent-seeking in Germany and America is not known, but what did distinguish these countries, according to a number of authors, was their cultural attitude towards entrepreneurship. British cultural decadence supposedly negated individualism and drive through the pursuit of social status and gentlemanly pleasures, which hampered performance in manufacturing and industry. Attempts to refute this explanation of decline have reinterpreted modern British economic and social development as being primarily commercial and financial in locus. This hypothesis has typically floundered for lack of supporting evidence. Conventional wisdom suggests that culture is an important determinant of entrepreneurship, and supporting evidence comes from conceptual and empirical research linking cultural variables with a measure of performance – lifetime rates of wealth accumulation. Even though firm inheritors tended to run down their assets over generations, privileged access to the entrepreneurial labour market gave inefficient heir-controlled firms the opportunity to survive. Such links between entrepreneurship and culture critically impact upon a country's economic performance. For Schumpeter (1939: xi) the 'circular flow' was useful 'even beyond the boundaries of economics, in what might be called the theory of cultural evolution'. McCloskey (1998: 300) confirms that 'we need culture' to understand the character of economic growth.

Drawing together the literature on entrepreneurship and wealth accumulation, one central, but still elusive, question remains – did British entrepreneurs fail? It has become an orthodoxy in economic history that Britain's economic pre-eminence as the first industrial nation was short-lived; during the late nineteenth and early twentieth centuries British entrepreneurs could not keep pace with the competition. Yet opinion is divided on performance standards, and therefore success and failure are not homogeneous entities in the literature. British entrepreneurship was subject to a confluence of factors, economic, social and cultural. The American economist Frank H. Knight, who wrote extensively on entrepreneurship in the early twentieth century, explains that 'the ownership of personal or material productive capacity depends on a complex mixture of inheritance, luck, and effort, probably in that order of relative importance' (1923: 598). In Britain there was too much inheritance as social structure and family capitalism preserved the *status quo*, insufficient luck in terms of resource endowments and market size, and too little effort on the part of entrepreneurs to break out of existing paths of development.

10

Domestic finance, 1860–1914

P. L. COTTRELL

Contents

AN IMPERFECT FINANCIAL MARKET?

At the opening of the twentieth century (Joseph 1911), it was implied that the financial sector had the face of Janus, a characterisation many historians have subsequently adopted and further developed. While the markets facilitated a mounting volume of foreign borrowing from the mid-1850s, domestic clients were, it has repeatedly been maintained, increasingly ill served, to the detriment of investment at home (see also chapter 8 above).

The charge laid against financial institutions largely relates to industrial finance (Saville 1961), and to the argument that an imperfect capital market primarily directed savings into overseas securities. These yielded less than 5 per cent immediately prior to the First World War, while total capital invested at home returned more than 10 per cent. This comparison, however, greatly overstates the apparent illogical bias in the financial sector's workings, since much overseas investment comprised publicly marketed and fixed-interest bonds whereas a significant proportion of domestic returns was generated by privately held unsecuritised equity (McCloskey 1970: 451–5). When analogous domestic and overseas financial assets are compared, foreign securities either carried only somewhat higher coupons or distributed slightly greater dividends, reflecting the rather bigger risks that their ownership entailed (Cairncross 1953:

227–31); these risk and return relationships were confirmed by Edelstein (1976). He also found that, although returns on both home and overseas publicly issued securities fell secularly as their respective marketed volumes increased, during periods of domestic boom such as the mid-1890s, the small differential favouring foreign stocks diminished. However, when overseas investment began to mount again – as from 1897 – the 'risk premium' on comparable foreign securities once more increased.

Although overseas securities generated only slightly higher returns than their comparable domestic counterparts, it has been argued that investors much preferred the paper – primarily fixed-interest securities – issued for foreign borrowers (Kennedy 1974). This predilection had considerable adverse macroeconomic effects since, when the volume of overseas issues ebbed, the economy's overall investment rate fell markedly. During periods of high overseas lending – the 1880s and 1903–13 – investment stood at 13.5 per cent and 15.2 per cent of gross national product (GNP), respectively, but during the 1890s home boom it was merely 11.4 per cent (1891–8). Consequently, investors' collective behaviour continues to be considered a factor which adversely affected the economy's growth.

Those without particular business contacts – 'blind' investors – could only respond to security issues placed before them by prospectuses, circulars, etc. This may have led to another bias: the conditions for small- and medium-sized domestic issues, adversely commented upon for nearly more than a century (Foxwell 1917; Lavington 1920: 212–19). Leading institutions generally undertook security issues only for established, creditworthy borrowers. Furthermore, their managements were solely interested in making very sizeable flotations, for which they developed mass-selling techniques and whose preliminary expenses, comprising legal fees, underwriting commissions, etc., were proportionately small. Few domestic issues before the late 1880s were of this size and nature. Consequently, the impersonal market's bias was not so much related to the borrower's nationality – towards foreign as opposed to British issues – as to the volume of individual issues, which did negatively affect many potential domestic flotations.

Small- and medium-sized domestic issues and those for new types of home companies exploiting innovations, when they were offered nationally, were generally undertaken by self-styled, London-based company promoters. They filled the 'gap' in the market. However, promoters, more often than not, were primarily interested in their own personal gains rather than embryonic companies' prospects. Furthermore, their predations, which watered the capital of nascent companies, went largely uncurbed by the law. Following the general introduction of limited liability in the mid-1850s, the British corporate code was the most permissive in Europe (Cottrell 1980: ch. 3). If a company survived such a flotation, it faced further problems because, generally, investors preferred securities quoted on the London Stock Exchange. However, the metropolitan secondary securities market was primarily concerned with trading shares and bonds that existed in volume since this guaranteed their liquidity, which, in turn, allowed deals to be readily cleared. Consequently, the secondary market's partiality went hand in hand with that of London's premier issuing houses, each mutually reinforcing a preference for issues that, individually, were large in size – and therefore primarily foreign.

Domestic borrowers not only looked for finance to the capital market but also to banks. These have also been subject to criticism – over their managements' attitudes to, and facilities for, domestic clients. There is alleged to have been an adverse change in bankers' accommodation of their customers. Some historians have related an onset of a restriction in clients' facilities to their bankers reacting to the impact of crisis. It is argued that the searing experience of a financial panic led bankers to maintain thereafter a higher level of liquidity as a cushion against any further outbreak of market turmoil. Rather than regarding rising liquidity as a secular trend as the 'art of banking' was progressively learned, these critics have maintained that a particular crisis constituted a major, adverse turning point in banking practice – either 1866 (Landes 1960: 113) or 1878 (Kennedy 1976; Best and Humphries 1986: 227–8; Kennedy 1987).

An alternative critical thread gives primacy to bank amalgamations. It is argued that the resultant growth of bureaucratised and centralised control from the 1890s gave branch managers less, if any, discretion with regard to customers' accounts. This led to the dying out of the provision by banks of long-term industrial loans (Cottrell 1980: 236–41). Furthermore, head offices of nationwide banks increasingly placed their respective institutions' funds in liquid assets readily available within the metropolis, such as foreign bills and call money to either the money market or the Stock Exchange. This, in turn, produced the irony that the considerably greater individual resources of the larger Edwardian banks were not mobilised within a framework of greater risk taking which was potentially permitted by their significantly enhanced statures (Watson 1996: 60).

Condemnation of increasing conservatism within banking, whether induced by crisis or organisational change, forms part of an overall stricture, arising from what has been perceived as a contrast with the German credit banks' support of, and direct links with, industry. It has been maintained that Germany's rapid industrial transformation from the 1880s was in part due to the assistance and guidance that its bankers gave to manufacturers, including transforming their undertakings into public companies and taking seats on their boards. This received view of German practice has led to the contention that there was a great deal of difference in a firm's financial position depending upon whether it was either within a German credit bank's Konzern or a customer of a progenitor of the British 'Big Five' banks.

All these long-running and deep-seated criticisms of the financial sector, alleging market failure, have primarily been concerned with industrial finance. However, similar charges have been made with respect to funds available to local government, which have led to the persisting adverse urban environmental impact of the 'industrial revolution until late into the nineteenth century' (Williamson 1990: 294–8).

These are all supply-side arguments: 'If the financial sector had responded to a greater extent, from some time during the last quarter of the nineteenth century, with regard to domestic customers, then things would have been different' – possibly to the extent of the economy growing more rapidly and coming to possess an industrial sector more akin to that of Germany. The counter argument is that, if domestic demand for formally mobilised capital and credit had been greater, then existing financial institutions would have responded accordingly, while new institutions would have emerged to meet any unsatisfied demand, albeit at a profitable price (Kirby 1992: 650). Such a refutation can logically be made, but it also has to be acknowledged that 'an unsatisfied' demand for finance is, by its very nature, difficult to find within the available patchy historical record, which is principally made up of firms of considerable longevity. One of the few and, consequently, much-quoted, cases of capital starvation experienced by a domestic industrial enterprise seeking to augment its scale and product range is that of a cycle maker, F. Hopper & Co. (Harrison: 1982). Although Hopper experienced many of the problems that subsequent critics of the financial sector have highlighted, he also compounded them by his own attitudes towards finance and financial intermediaries.

This is not to dismiss almost out of hand the voluminous and long-running critical literature addressing domestic finance.[1] Indeed, it will be appraised in this review's following sections. Yet, much of that scholarship, especially broadly cast contributions seeking to explore and explain detected fallings in the economy after 1870, treats the financial sector, particularly the capital market, as a monolith. Scholars have frequently neither taken account of its nature during the mid-century, nor traced its subsequent evolution as it responded to almost entirely new demands for funds. Indeed, some have gone as far as to date institutional sclerosis with regard to finance to the late Victorian period, while others have confidently claimed that provincial capital markets were integrated with those of the metropolis by the close of the eighteenth century (Buchinsky and Polak 1993).

[1] There is no overall synthesis of domestic finance, while the dates of the references cited indicate that this is an intense and continuing area of scholarly exploration, especially with respect to bank behaviour. Useful starting points are the relevant chronological sections of Michie 1992; Collins 1995; and Wilson 1995.

INSTITUTIONAL DEVELOPMENT: BORROWERS, THE CAPITAL MARKET AND INVESTORS

The capital market formally coalesced at the end of the seventeenth century in response to the state's new policy of war finance; its pattern was then set for at least a further century and a half. Up to and during the 1860s, it mainly dealt in the national debt, comprising funded, fixed-interest securities, such as Consols, which were specifically designed to appeal to investors. However, the volume of the national debt began to decline from the mid-1850s due to the prevalence of peace, 'Gladstonian finance' and redemption; this led investors to seek substitute securities for their portfolios. To meet this demand, many foreign issues were modelled on Consols, as were those of domestic railway companies after the 1866 crisis and of local authorities from the 1870s. These two important domestic developments will be considered in some greater detail within the context of the decline in the volume of Consols.

In 1860, the state's funded debt amounted to £782.9 million nominal, and the securities composing it constituted the focus of London Stock Exchange dealings (domestic railway stocks and shares at £245.2 million nominal comprising in aggregate its next largest market). More jobbers – market makers – dealt in the national debt than in any other securities (Attard 2000: 7), and their firms tended to have greater resources, so making them more prepared to 'take a position'. They expressed this by quoting a narrower spread between buying and selling prices than for other securities, while brokers charged a lower commission on transactions in Consols. All this made for a highly liquid market in the national debt – the basis for an efficient secondary securities market (Morgan and Thomas 1962: 117–18; Brown and Easton 1989; Michie 1999: 66–8).

The last major issues of Consols financed British involvement in the Crimean War; thereafter sinking funds progressively reduced the national debt. This marked a watershed in the capital market's development. However, the experience of the previous 150 years – perhaps particularly the absence of inflation during peacetime – had accustomed investors to take up secured, fixed-interest bonds, establishing and inculcating a preference that was to persist. The 'cult of equity' was, by contrast, a late twentieth-century development, arising from the unique experience of sustained and marked inflation during peacetime.

The 'Old Sinking Fund' was established in 1829; from then, particularly with William Gladstone as Chancellor, the nominal size of the national debt was progressively cut back, most markedly from £790.5 million in 1859 to £723.5 million in 1874. However, the yield on Consols (coupon divided by the stock's market price), was already falling; it fell to 3.4 per cent during the mid-1850s, to cause a 'social problem' for middle-class

England. What close substitutes were available to investors who sought a higher return from a financial investment (Cottrell 1980: 46–7)? Their dilemma became even greater in 1875, when Sir Stafford Northcote initiated the 'New Sinking Fund', which worked in tandem with the 'Old' to reduce the size of the funded debt to *c.* £640 million by the mid-1880s. The dilemma was made more intense, and felt by institutional investors, because of concomitant falls in the yields from other 'safe' domestic investment outlets: in house prices, and the returns from mortgages and agricultural rents (Treble 1980).

The national debt's redemption went along with its conversion – the permanent reduction in the coupon (interest payments) – made to its holders in order to cut debt service charges for government. High nominal interest rates for nearly three decades after 1853 prevented government from reducing further its debt service charges. However, when stock exchange prices for Consols rose above their par – above £100 per unit of stock – during early 1881, it became clear that conditions for a further conversion were being established. In 1888, Goschen reduced the servicing costs of 'New Three per Cents', then amounting to £500 million nominal, through the creation of a conversion stock, which bore a $2\frac{3}{4}$ per cent coupon until 1903 but only $2\frac{1}{2}$ per cent thereafter (Harley 1976).

Redemption steadily reduced the outstanding volume of gilt-edged securities from the 1860s, while Goschen's 1888 grand conversion brought fully home again to investors the falling return – the diminishing income – obtainable from Consols. The more adventurous may have turned to higher-yielding issues of foreign securities, many modelled on Consols to suit investors' nurtured tastes. Otherwise, it was a question of domestic borrowers developing closely analogous securities to attract investors, as was undertaken by railway companies from the late 1860s and, then, by local authorities to finance urban improvement.

The mid-1840s railway mania, together with the inability of many surviving companies to pay dividends, resulted in many investors shying away from railway shares. Indeed, construction was almost halted until the late 1850s due to the difficulties of publicly raising finance. The railway companies' turn to perpetual debt was one consequence of changes in the finance of further construction from the 1850s – a switch to credit – that, ultimately, led to the 1866 crisis.

The third building boom added over a thousand miles to the railway system between 1857 and 1872, and, initially, was financed by methods developed during the 1830s and 1840s. Yet, investors would only readily take up preference shares and debentures on which a return was stipulated and guaranteed; these were some of the attributes of Consols. Furthermore, as construction gained momentum, there was a return to, and further development of, the practices employed in the aftermath of the 1840s 'mania'. These centred upon the contractor acting as his own financier (Pollins 1957–8; Cottrell 1975). This reversion to 'private' finance was forced by the relative attractiveness of other securities, especially as many of the new lines were rightly perceived as marginal by a variety of criteria.

The financing methods of contractors varied substantially, but many involved discounting bills backed by railway securities received in payment for their work. However, the contractors' use, or rather misuse, of bills of exchange to sustain their activities became increasingly difficult from autumn 1865 as interest rates rose. Unable to raise further credit, many went bankrupt, with the greatest shock produced by the failure of Peto & Betts, major contractors. Their collapse triggered on 'Black Friday', 10 May 1866, the closure of Overend, Gurney, the biggest London discount house, causing the City's worst panic since 1825. The 1844 Bank Charter Act was suspended for a third time, and Bank rate remained at the crisis level of 10 per cent for no less than three months. The 1866 crisis had lasting consequences both for railway finance and for, more generally, the London money market. When Landes (1960: 113) highlights its long-term domestic financial impact, he is thinking not so much of bank advances to industrial customers but of the resultant decline in the use of finance bills that had been so prevalent during the booms of the mid-1860s and the mid-1850s.

The 1866 crisis threw many railway companies' finances into complete disarray, with some forced 'into Chancery'. Others, from small, new lines to major companies were also severely affected. The prime issue concerned the solidity of railway debentures. Until 1866 these had seemed almost riskless investments and they were, consequently, acquired by not only what the *Economist* called the 'timid public' but also by the Bank of England and other bankers and trustees. Before 1866, they had been issued with terms of seven years. With the crisis, and the resulting substantial fall in prices for railway securities, questions arose over whether railway companies could either roll forward their debentures or even redeem outstanding issues. From 1867, beginning with the Great Eastern, medium-term debentures were replaced by perpetual debentures, closely comparable in nature to Consols. This capital restructuring was arduous, and prices of domestic railway securities did not once more appreciate until spring 1870. The increasing volume of domestic railway stocks quoted thereafter on the London Stock Exchange demonstrates the rehabilitation of domestic railway finance. Their nominal value rose from £347 million in 1873 to £854.8 million, 1893, and to £1,217 million, 1913. In 1889 they gained trustee status and so, by inference, were deemed fit again for the savings of the 'timid public' (Morgan and Thomas 1962: 110 and Table V).

The tailoring of long-term, securitised debt – producing securities closely analogous to Consols – to meet the preference of the market and investors was also undertaken from the 1870s by municipalities. In the early 1870s their aggregate funded debt amounted to £10.3 million but considerable difficulties had been encountered in obtaining these funds – particularly over the term of loans and their respective issue prices. A wider, more effective market only developed following major issues by Mersey Docks & Harbour Board and Metropolitan Board of Works, the latter floating £2.6 million $3^1/_2$ per cent stock in 1869.

Pressures upon local authorities to raise capital increased with their greater responsibilities following the 1870 Education Act and the Public Health Acts of 1872 and 1875. The largest towns with the largest capital needs chose the path blazed by the Metropolitan Board of Works in London, issuing stocks under powers obtained by private acts of parliament. Middling-sized towns continued to face a financial problem as the markets, even the provincial ones, shunned small-scale corporation issues. A solution came through gaining the permission of the Local Government Board, although the Treasury was able to insist that resultant borrowings, usually mortgages, could only have a term of thirty years.

Municipal issues surged from the 1870s; by 1884, £50 million worth had been floated on regional markets which had at their centre a provincial stock exchange (Thomas 1973: 184). By 1888, local authority loan stocks and mortgages were established as safe, reliable securities, alternatives to Consols, while providing a somewhat higher yield. Investors' repugnance towards Consols following Goschen's 1888 conversion, together with the collapse of foreign investment after the 1890 Baring crisis, enabled local authorities to borrow heavily again, taking advantage of the decade's extremely low nominal interest rates. This second major wave of municipal stock issues reached a peak in 1905. By 1914, local authority indebtedness in all its forms totalled £652.6 million – in size almost on a par with the national debt, which stood at £706 million (Wilson 1997). Such very considerable borrowings refute the contention that overseas lending took place at the cost of the improvement of British urban infrastructure. None the less, it is apparent that municipal issues largely occurred when foreign lending was at low levels – during the mid-1870s and, again, over the 1890s home boom.

To sum up, the capital market could therefore readily meet the needs of domestic borrowers when they utilised securities comparable to those to which investors had long been accustomed – Consols. This led to the domestic market's further and greater development as, first, the national debt's volume declined through redemption and, second, the income from Consols was cut by Goschen's grand conversion of 1888. Investors reacted by seeking close alternatives to Consols. The investors were first satisfied by domestic railways companies' perpetual debentures and then by the flotation of municipal loan stocks from the 1870s. All were secured and bore fixed-interest coupons to put them alongside Consols; furthermore, they were issued in large blocks to give them liquidity on the secondary financial market. As such they met the long-expressed preferences of investors and fulfilled jobbers' requirements for active trading – to the extent that market makers in Consols increasingly turned to municipal stocks as the volume of Consols continued to decline. These issues of domestic long-term debt also benefited from the secular fall in prices for a quarter of a century after 1873 since their holders, as creditors, accrued a real gain on their capital. However, foreign securities modelled on Consols also gave a somewhat higher running return, reflecting a risk premium, and, in that respect, might have a somewhat greater attraction for investors. Consequently, railway companies and local authorities tended to benefit as borrowers when a dark shadow was cast over overseas securities – as after either the collapse of the foreign-loan boom in the mid-1870s or following the Baring crisis of 1890.

LIMITED LIABILITY: INITIAL ADOPTION, 1855–85

A further aspect of the greater development of the domestic capital market over the second half of the nineteenth century arose from the unfettered freedom to establish limited liability companies, given by acts passed in 1855, 1856 and 1862 (Shannon 1930–3, Shannon 1932–3; Hunt 1936; Cottrell 1980: 45–54). This permissive legislation allowed, potentially, a very significant change in the finance and organisation of British capitalism. Hitherto, partners (except proprietors of joint-stock companies established or recognised by legislation) had been individually liable for all the debts of their partnerships; mismanagement or ill-fortune could lead to personal bankruptcy, a staple of Victorian novels. Limited liability companies had shareholders instead of partners, with their individual liability restricted to the nominal value of the shares that they held. Thus they might, in the event of business failure, lose the value of their shareholding but they were not liable for the debts of the company except, rarely, in the event of fraud.

The coming of limited liability led to two persistent developments. One was the formation of what would be later termed 'private companies' arising, generally, from the conversion of partnerships without any public appeal for capital. Limited liability was used in these cases primarily by family firms, either to restrict their risk exposure or to divide up property between former partners. Although these companies' distinct nature gained no legal recognition until 1900 and 1907, they became increasingly numerous from at least 1866. They were established throughout the various sectors of the economy, accounting in manufacturing after 1875 for four out of every ten registrations of limited companies that subsequently resulted in an active business undertaking.

The other trend was the use of limited liability to raise capital. Attracting shareholders was undertaken in various ways. These ranged from confidentially soliciting family members, friends and business acquaintances, a not very great step away from forming a 'private' limited company, to employing either local and regional contacts or the impersonal mechanisms of the London market.

The basic procedure was to publish a prospectus. Its local circulation built upon past proven methods of raising capital for constructing canals, turnpikes and railways. Furthermore, employing a lawyer to draw up the documentation, and particularly the memorandum of association, could lead to a company's founders being brought into contact with his clientele, some of whom might be interested in backing a new venture. With the office of the Registrar of Joint-Stock Companies being located in London (along with separate establishments in Edinburgh and Dublin responsible for Scottish and Irish registrations), it was frequently convenient to turn to a metropolitan lawyer, some handling the financial affairs of other clients. Beyond the roles of lawyers (and accountants), in privately mobilising finance through their own particular personal networks, there were those of stockbrokers and company promoters, acting in either provincial or London markets. Available evidence points to the very great importance of locally mobilised funds, with 76 per cent of companies' capitals being raised within a 10-mile radius of their registered offices in 1860, and 61 per cent in 1885.

The continuing significance of local finance was, in part, due to many companies being established within business fields where 'external' capital had an established role. During the 1860s and 1870s there was a further wave of joint-stock bank formations, accompanied by the promotion of discount and finance companies (Cottrell 1988; Cottrell and Newton 1999). Another major strand of early registrations comprised nonferrous metal mining companies, arising out of the context of the costbook company in Cornwall and Devon and the pay–share partnership in the Pennines. Furthermore, in terms of continuity, there was a rapid adoption of limited liability within shipping.

As with the mining of non-ferrous metals, shipping had a long tradition of fractional ownership (Jarvis 1959). The risks and costs attendant to the development of the iron steamship had resulted from the 1820s in the employment of various corporate forms but ownership and therefore financing patterns varied greatly between ports. In the early 1850s, while 217 of the 334 steam vessels registered at London were owned by joint-stock companies, the great majority of Liverpool's steamers – seventy-three out of ninety-two – were in the hands of partnerships based upon sixty-fourth 'ship-shares' (Palmer 1972; Cottrell 1981).

Over the quarter of a century from 1856, 413 limited shipping companies were effectively established, primarily to operate steamers. Some, along with earlier chartered companies, came to constitute the industry's core. During the early 1880s nineteen joint-stock companies, with an aggregate capital of £15 million, controlled 20 per cent of the national steamship fleet (Green 1985: 225–7). Until the late 1870s, most operated fleets and, in the case of the forty-five companies established on Merseyside, it was primarily local residents with knowledge of the industry–merchants and shipowners – who supplied their capitals. The continuing importance of regional and industry-based capital markets during the transition from sail to steam is pointed up by the fact that only one Merseyside company had a London Stock Exchange quotation during the late 1870s.

From 1879 'single-ship' companies joined 'fleet' companies. Their formation was initiated on Merseyside but also rapidly taken up at Cardiff and, although to a lesser degree, London. Their registrations dominated all applications made to the Registrar of Joint-Stock Companies during the early 1880s. It has been suggested, drawing on the activities of Cunard and Currie, that this sudden change in shipowning finance was due to traditional shipowners, who, armed with superior information made divestments in anticipation of poor trade (Boyce 1992). Yet, although Cunard adopted limited liability in 1878, its fleet was not turned into a suite of subsidiary 'single-ship' companies. Furthermore, and more generally, the flood of 'single-ship' company registrations commenced precisely as freight rates rose after the mid- and late 1870s depression. Rather, it would appear that shipowners turned to the 'single-ship' limited company as a result of Plimsoll's campaign over the loss of life at sea, the legal ramifications of a collision or comparable misadventure, and because of contractual and accounting advantages. All resulted in the ownership of fleets of sailing vessels, as well as of steamers, being turned over to 'single-ship' limited companies, although with continuity maintained through each vessel being run respectively by the same managing agency.

Last, but not least, the 'single-ship' limited company was used to a degree for obtaining fresh capital. But, in the case of the first wave of Merseyside 'single-ship' companies, only eight had more than fifty shareholders, a strong pointer to this particular type of limited company not generally being employed to widen the catchment area for funds. Rather, the 'single-ship' company continued the old ship partnership, albeit in new corporate clothes (Cottrell 1992b: 194–6). In some instances, shipbuilders took shares as part payment for new vessels, just as their predecessors had taken sixty-fourths 'ship-shares'. Further, numerous single-ship companies were formed during the 1880s and 1890s, their capitals subscribed, as previously, predominantly either through informal channels or within the industry. Some of these financial conduits arose from the personal networks of the two great marine markets of the Baltic Exchange and Lloyds, while William Lithgow appears to have had a special talent in acting as a broker for shares in 'single-ship' companies (Green 1985: 227–9).

Within manufacturing, cotton spinning constituted a major area of the early take-up of limited liability, building upon the foundations established by co-operative production in Lancashire and the West Riding (Farnie 1979). However, the 'Cotton Famine' and the long, post-1866 business depression brought this development temporarily to an end. It got underway again from 1873, producing three different types of company. One strand comprised private conversions. Alongside these were public conversions, attracting funds largely supplied by banks and bankers, friendly societies, engineers and mill architects, Liverpool cotton brokers and Manchester merchants. The third strand – the so-called 'Oldham Limiteds' – made a major mark. Thirty-three were established between 1873 and 1875, motivated by constraining overhead costs through increasing the size of the spinning mill. Cheaper suburban land made the Oldham area the focus, while factory legislation favoured the larger employer since, it was claimed, the full development of the self-acting mule had made the management of spinning 'simpler'. The first 'Oldham Limiteds' were promoted within the trade. Their shares, usually £5, but on which only a small deposit was called up, 1s. in some cases, were nearly all taken up locally, largely by wage earning manual labourers. In this respect, the 'Limiteds' were the inheritors of the tradition of co-operative production. However, within a year of the registration of the first Oldham mill-building company, forty sharebrokers were active in the town, forming four loosely organised markets sited in public houses, also the venues for launching new companies.

The rapid rise of a local, informal stock market facilitated a change in the composition of the companies' shareholders. Attracted by the initial success of the 'Limiteds', shopkeepers and mill owners took the place of worker shareholders. Furthermore, the late 1870s' cyclical trade depression resulted in working-class subscribers being unable to meet calls for further capital and, consequently, being forced to sell their shares. None the less, workers continued to finance the companies through supplying loan capital, which comprised over 50 per cent of the aggregate funds of the 'Limiteds' in 1879. Each concern acted almost as a savings bank. Local retail traders and workers held their 'pass books,' and earned between 4 and 6 per cent interest on the small sums deposited. The substantial employment of loan capital was a cachet of the 'Oldham Limiteds' but had its origins in the 1830s, when private spinners commenced taking small loans from workers and others. It resulted in the companies of the 1870s being highly geared.

The cotton trade's cyclical revival led to the establishment of a further 141 limited companies between 1880 and 1884. Nearly all were new concerns, promoted by groups comprising a financier, an architect, a builder and a manufacturer of cotton machinery. These were enticed by a fall in building costs, of the order of 40 per cent since the early 1870s, and were even more dependent on loan capital than the first 'Oldham Limiteds'. The increasing number of 'Limiteds' went hand in hand with a greater formalisation of Oldham's share market. The town's sharebrokers formed their own association in 1880 and it had its own premises by 1883. By 1886 Oldham was the greatest centre of joint-stock enterprise within Britain, while its 'Limiteds' accounted for two-thirds of the increase in Lancashire's cotton spindles, 6.75 million, 1870–87.

Iron and steel was the other industrial branch where limited liability had some early impact. By the early 1880s, two-fifths of blast furnace capacity was owned by limited companies, and the London Stock Exchange gave quotations for 102 coal, iron and steel companies with an aggregate capital of £36.9 million, primarily comprising ordinary shares. However, the marked transformation of ownership and finance largely related to plants located in the north-east or Sheffield area. This regional transformation was primarily brought about by David Chadwick, a Manchester accountant, who, with the general availability of limited liability, became a London financial agent (Cottrell 1980: 113–40).

Between 1862 and 1874, Chadwick undertook the formation of forty-seven limited companies amongst which were major concerns; many, such as John Brown, Charles Cammell, Ebbw Vale, Palmers Shipbuilding and Vickers, Son & Co. were to remain household names until well into the twentieth century. Each conversion had its own circumstance but, generally, they appear to have been motivated by cyclical upswings in the demand for iron together with the need to meet the adoption costs of the Bessemer process. Chadwick's conversions began with Ashbury Railway Carriage in 1862, which may have brought him into contact with Sheffield firms, such as John Brown and Charles Cammell, producers of railway rolling-stock parts. During his previous business career in Salford and Manchester, he had built up a group of acquaintances who later invested in his conversions, some to the extent of becoming directors with a significant stake in the companies that they guided. This investment group took between a fifth and a quarter of the shares arising from his various conversions, and for thirty years after 1862 constituted an integrated management block within the iron and steel industry.

The local and regional promotion of limited companies led to a resurgence of the provincial stock exchanges. As already noted, an entirely new market was established in Oldham and likewise at Newcastle and Dundee, although the latter was primarily a product of Tayside investment in the United States. Chadwick's conversions played a substantial part in reviving activity on the Manchester and Sheffield exchanges as did steam shipping companies in the case of the Liverpool and Glasgow markets, the latter very markedly so with the number of brokers involved increasing from 31 in 1873/4 to 124 in 1881/2.

London initially played a minor role in publicly mobilising funds for new limited companies. The aggregate subscribed capital of domestic industrial and commercial companies only accounted for 1 per cent of the total value of all securities quoted on the London Stock Exchange in 1883. Even this is misleading since, as the *Stock Exchange Year Book* pointed out, although concerns like Muntz's Metal and Young Paraffin Light & Mineral Oil had London quotations, most dealings in their shares took place on the provincial exchange close to where the company operated – Birmingham in the case of Muntz's.

The barrier to entry to the London market arose from the relatively small size of most domestic issues before the late 1880s. The problems involved are pointed up by Jay & Co.'s flotation of the South Staffordshire Iron Works during the early 1870s, for which they charged £10,000,

14.3 per cent of the company's nominal capital as opposed to Chadwick's fee of 1 per cent (which would have been £700, if he had acted for this company). High promotional charges were one constraint, but court cases and parliamentary inquiries indicated a range of others, arising from unscrupulous promoters being more interested in their own profits than insuring a successful conversion into a limited company.

There were two main strands of financial malpractice (Cottrell 1980: 147–51). One was to transfer the vendor's assets to a number of third and fourth parties connected to the promoter before their acquisition by the limited company, with, at each stage, their value increasing. Consequently, the company had overvalued assets, the promoter having largely pocketed the difference. Some attempt to stop this abuse was made in the 1867 Companies Act, which required every contract entered into by a company, or its promoters or directors or trustees, to be disclosed in its prospectus. However, the clause was imprecise because of hurried drafting and caused great difficulties over what had to be disclosed. The only effective, albeit small, step towards shareholder protection made by the act was the requirement that a company had to call a general meeting within four months of its registration.

The other main area of abuse stemmed from the courts interpreting the 1862 Companies Act to preclude underwriting since it involved the issue of shares at a discount; this was not remedied by legislation until 1900. Consequently, to ensure that an issue was fully subscribed, some promoters manipulated the stock market so that an embryonic company's shares were quoted at a premium – at a price above their par value. A share at a premium price brought in subscriptions from 'blind' investors – 'well-to-do tradesmen, clergymen, females of independent means and so forth'. Attracting their subscriptions involved dealings before allotment, which required the promoter to have connections with sharebrokers (Kynaston 1991: 46–76). The London Stock Exchange had no house rules preventing its members from trading in anything, while newspapers reported the prices of shares of new companies. During the late 1870s, it was estimated that artificial premium creation had been a feature of 75 per cent of all, domestic and foreign, company formation. The London Stock Exchange reacted on 7 April 1864 by no longer recognising share dealings before allotment, but the rule only lasted a year. Its effect had been undercut by promoters turning to the 'outside market' and having 'grey' prices for nascent securities reported in the press, while Stock Exchange members ignored the regulation.

Some promoters went further by subsequently allotting only a few shares to maintain their premium price. They then gradually unloaded the shares, reaping the bonus. The defence made was that this was a legitimate riposte to the activities of 'stags' (speculative applicants solely subscribing for a company's shares to reap a short-term gain), or 'guinea pigs' (who covered for 'stags').

In making investment choices, 'blind' investors appear also to have given undue credence to London Stock Exchange procedures for admitting securities to regular market dealings – the fortnightly account. The Exchange's Committee undertook the grant of a special settlement. However, its members, when they examined a prospectus, share applications and allotment book, were only concerned with a company's technical origins as opposed to its solvency or soundness. 'Blind' investors gave even greater weight to companies that had also gained a quotation – an entry in the Stock Exchange List. Although quotation rules were more stringent, they were primarily designed to ensure that an issue was sizeable in order to give it liquidity. The emphasis on 'sufficient magnitude' meant that many domestic issues did not receive a quotation, which deterred investors.

The small volume of the securities of those domestic companies that obtained a quotation on the London Stock Exchange resulted in there being no specialist jobbers who regularly dealt in them. Instead, they constituted the so-called 'miscellaneous market' spread right across the Exchange's trading floor. As a result, it could be almost impossible to trade in such securities, as a broker forcibly pointed out in 1877. He considered that 1,082 out of the 1,367 securities which had a quotation, amounting to £562.8 million, were unmarketable, including those of East & West India Dock, National Provincial Bank and gas, water and insurance companies. The only method of trading was through indicating an interest on a notice board.

London's very modest role before the mid-1880s was also due to the predominant pattern of local company promotion, which meant, except for the largest concerns, that their shares remained largely concentrated within the localities where they undertook their businesses. This was aided by provincial share markets which took up these securities, while trading in railway stocks and bonds increasingly migrated to London, with the rehabilitation of railway finance after the 1866 crisis. Local marketability was also assisted by the different way that the provincial markets conducted their business – an auction call-over system. If a company's securities were not traded on a local market, of which there were fifteen by the early 1880s, from Aberdeen to Bristol, then dealings in them could only take place through its respective secretary, which in the case of 'well-established and profitable concerns' was considered a sufficient medium.

LIMITED LIABILITY: WIDER TAKE-UP, 1885–1914

By 1913, domestic industrial, commercial and shipping companies accounted for nearly 10 per cent of the nominal value of all securities quoted on the London Stock Exchange – collectively almost on a par with the national debt (Michie 1999: 89). London's growing role in domestic commercial and industrial finance over the thirty years before 1914 was due to a variety of factors. One of the most important was the conscious tailoring from the 1880s of securities to meet investor preference. There was a greater use of preference shares, which had priority in dividend distributions up to a specified rate, and the increasing employment of debentures, a form of fixed-interest loan capital analogous to Consols. By 1913 preference shares comprised 30 per cent of London quoted companies' securities, and debentures and comparable loan stocks a further 22.4 per cent (Jeffreys 1971: 458, Appendix E).

As discussed above, domestic public industrial and commercial companies had turned to securities which were comparable in nature to Consols. These had been the mainstay of the London market until the 1860s and had subsequently been imitated by domestic railway companies, local authorities and foreign borrowers. Preference shares and debentures gave a guaranteed return that appealed to risk-averse 'blind' investors but at the cost to the issuing companies of having subsequently to generate sufficient annual net revenues to meet their servicing. However, set against this was the advantage that preference shares and debentures normally carried no voting rights. This maintained control of the enterprise in the hands of the founding family and its immediate associates, who generally held a substantial proportion of the company's equity – its ordinary shares.

Iron and steel concerns had made some use of preference shares and debentures from the earliest conversions undertaken by Chadwick. As more became public companies from the turn of the century, their number quoted in London rising from 49 in 1895 to 106 by 1910, preference shares as a proportion of their capitals increased from 8 to 26 per cent and debentures from 15 to 19 per cent (Watson 1995: 233, Table 10.8). More dramatic than the steady trickle of iron and steel preference shares and debentures on to the market were the two waves of security issues, primarily of debentures, which were made by brewers, both large and small, during the late 1880s and again a decade later. These were issued primarily to finance the acquisition of tied houses ('pubs' owned by brewers which generally sold only the beer brewed by the owner), which provided the security backing their debentures. The low interest rates prevailing during the 1890s made debentures a relatively cheap way of acquiring capital finance to the extent that they, along with preference shares, were issued at a premium, with the extra funds acquired employed to bolster the reserves of the brewery companies (Cottrell 1980: 168–70; Watson 1996: 63–6). In the process, the number of London-quoted brewery companies rose from 17 to 316 between 1885 and 1905 and, in the latter year, preference shares constituted 27 per cent of their publicly traded capitals and debentures 43 per cent (Watson 1995: 233, Table 10.7). The cost of the brewers' use of fixed-interest securities to finance retail market expansion only became clear after 1900, when beer consumption began to decline and, as a result, capitals had to be written down and dividends passed (not paid).

Iron and steel and brewery issues were relatively large with some being handled by the City's premier institutions: Barings dealt with the Guinness flotation and Glyn, Mills acted for Reid and Bass. Home flotations in general were given a further edge by the collapse of foreign issues in the wake of the 1890 Baring crisis and the low nominal and real interest rates of the 1890s, which led to domestic issues being made in considerable numbers from 1895. One stream was for the finance of merger activity, with 650 firms valued at £42 million involved in 198 separate mergers between 1898 and 1900; the public were offered the related issues of preference shares and debentures (Hannah 1976: 17, 22–3). Merger activity embraced provincial centres as well as the London market, Manchester benefiting from this activity in the textile preparatory and finishing trades and Bristol from the emergence of tobacco giants.

Small companies in the new cycle and motor car industries were less well served, although their promotion was also a feature of the 1890s. Over three-quarters of the cycle companies had capitals below £60,000, and any concern of less than £100,000 was regarded as 'small'. They were self-promoted, or had to pay substantially in effect for underwriting; 'professional' promoters like E. T. Hooley or H. J. Lawson attempted to attract investors through prestigious, titled directors who were rewarded with handsome fees. None the less, most of their share issues were undersubscribed, particularly those of £30,000 or less, which resulted in flotations being abandoned or vendors being forced to supply necessary working capital or the new company having but a brief existence. Otherwise, it was a question of 'second best solutions' through the company gaining funds by trade credit, or turning to its bank, or mortgaging its property or privately issuing debentures (Harrison 1981). Hooley handled both large and small promotions during the 1890s, regarding each as a personal milch cow. He extracted at least £325,000 from his re-launch of Bovril Co. in 1896, which he re-capitalised at £2.5 million (Armstrong 1986). To attract investors, Hooley not only raised funds through the market by employing a variety of differentiated securities but also suborned the press, paying £17,000 to the *Financial News* in connection with his flotation of the Beeston Cycle Co.

The *Financial News*, a London daily, was the most successful title of the new financial journalism that developed from the mid-1880s. Harry Marks moulded it on American lines, the paper being noted for its sprightly and humorous style. Initially, Marks acted as the small investors' friend, uncovering fraud, but from 1888 and the Ashley Bottle Co., his commentaries became increasingly the disguised 'puffing' of shares (Porter 1986). Although the British financial press numbered some 109 titles by 1914, supplemented by yearbooks and specialist handbooks, the quality of information that investors gained with respect to both home and foreign issues must be questioned. Marks' roguery was particularly related to South African mines. Directly related was the standard of promotional practice; Payne's claim (1967) that 'professional' promoters stood behind the merger boom of the late 1890s can be severely questioned. One late nineteenth-century promoter, Osborne O'Hagan, can be directly compared with Chadwick's earlier high standards but alongside him were the likes of Horatio Bottomley, Hooley and Lawson (Cottrell 1980: 185–6; Armstrong 1990).

The lack of established market facilities for small- and medium-sized undertakings was a concern – the so-called 'Macmillan gap' – that was to be explored and debated during the 1930s and again after 1945. These companies faced very considerable difficulties when attempts were made to float them on the London market in order to tap a national catchment area of savings. This continuing experience from the coming of limited liability contrasted greatly by 1900 with both the ability of large domestic companies to make rights issues and the success of private flotations, as in the cotton industry, where funds were supplied locally by directors and their friends (Lavington 1921: 208). His near-contemporary assessment receives some confirmation from an analysis of the proprietors of London-quoted public companies established between 1883 and 1907. This found that members of the non-mercantile home business community preferred domestic shares over those issued by either foreign or imperial concerns, with manufacturers in particular holding three domestic shares for every foreign share in their portfolios. Shares of incorporated home enterprise drew savings from throughout the United Kingdom but London residents were three times more likely to invest overseas. This suggests that the nation had two financial markets rather than one, at least with respect to equity capital, during the thirty years before the First World War (Davis and Huttenback 1986: 195–217).

BANKS AND BORROWERS

Understanding of the behaviour of the commercial banks of late Victorian and Edwardian Britain has been greatly advanced through studies of particular institutions (Cottrell 1980: 212–36; Holmes and Green 1986; Wale 1994; Ackrill and Hannah 2001), of their activities in particular regions (Newton 1996), of their role in the finance of a number of industries (Watson 1996; Cottrell 2002) and of their aggregate activity (e.g., Capie and Collins 1996).

As with the capital market, domestic commercial banking underwent substantial structural changes. From the early 1870s, the inland bill of exchange – previously the 'bread and butter' of most bankers' businesses – entered secular decline and, consequently, clients were increasingly accommodated by overdrafts. This fundamental transformation was assisted by the growth of deposits to the extent that, by the 1890s, few banks were 'over lent' – had ratios of discounts+advances: deposits greater than 100 per cent (Nishimura 1971). The disuse of bill finance was a product of the maturation of the economy's transport systems that also facilitated the expansion of branch banking, particularly within England (Munn 1997; Newton and Cottrell 1998). Lastly, following the failure of the City of Glasgow Bank in 1878, the pace of amalgamations quickened as joint-stock banks acquired private houses (Capie and Rodrik-Bali 1982).

The outcome was initially to maintain the collective position of provincial, joint-stock institutions within the English and Welsh banking system. These particular banks together held 30.2 per cent of total deposits and controlled 37.7 per cent of branches in 1871, with their shares thirty years later being 27.2 per cent of deposits and 35.2 per cent of branches (calculated from Capie and Webber 1985: 432 and Appendix III, 567–8). As a result, the late Victorian period marked the apogee of 'country banking', albeit that it was now corporate as opposed to private enterprise. The concentrating effects of amalgamations within the industry were offset before 1910 by the growth of deposits experienced by smaller banks, both unit and branching. In particular, the share of deposits held collectively by the sixth to the tenth largest banks increased from 7.8 per cent in 1870 to 21.7 per cent in 1910. Furthermore, existing banks were not threatened by the creation of new institutions after 1880 as banking was not a contestable market because of difficulties in gaining entry to the all important London Clearing House (Capie 1988).

A second wave of organisational change began in the mid-1880s but was not to have a major effect until 1909. Birmingham-based Lloyds acquired a London bank to gain entry to the Clearing House, followed by its local competitor, Midland, in 1891, moves approved by the financial markets as shares of 'London and provincial banks' appreciated in the wake of the Baring crisis whereas those of 'London banks' fell. Stock market endorsement went hand in hand with dispensing with expensive London agency costs during a period of exceptionally low nominal and real interest rates. Midland's management found that acquiring existing banks was a cheaper way of gaining a greater market position than opening new branches. Midland's pursuit of a deliberate amalgamation strategy from 1898 produced reactions and counters from within the industry as its constituents increasingly competed solely on the basis of size and, therefore, market presence. The reaction of competitors reached a pre-war climax from 1909, when London & Westminster merged with London & County. In riposte, Lloyds acquired Wilts & Dorset Bank in 1914, while Midland took over Metropolitan Bank, thereby increasing its deposits to £125 million to make it the largest bank in the United Kingdom (Cottrell 1992a: 47–50). The very large commercial banks of Edwardian England formed an oligopoly from which their shareholders benefited, receiving dividends of the order of 14 to 16 per cent, but the climax of the amalgamation movement 'may have rendered banks less efficient as allocators of capital' (Grossman 1999: 344).

The ways that commercial banks generally mobilised their deposits have been investigated by Baker, Capie and Collins; they employed a sample of 3,000 industrial accounts held by the branches of twenty banks located in the Midlands, the north and South Wales (predominantly future constituents of Lloyds and Midland), over the period 1860–1914. Their investigations found that bankers seldom refused to meet requests for facilities from industrial customers, though this may have been due to the fact that those seeking credit knew the terms on which it would be forthcoming. Nearly a quarter of the relatively few refusals made by bankers were given to approaches from new firms that in particular were considered to have insufficient capital and so to be uncreditworthy. Bankers' doubts on this score went along with low profitability and the inability of those soliciting credit to provide sufficient security with which to back the facility being sought. Indeed, with all refusals from banks, it was usually a question of the customer's business inexperience or the approach for credit being made in desperation so that the approach to the bank was a matter of last resort. Otherwise, bankers turned down customers' requests because they were to finance the purchase of capital assets or involved facilities that would run for too long a period of time. This examination of why banks refused loans confirms the received view of banking behaviour – that bankers saw their primary role as providing short-term facilities to proven creditworthy customers (Capie and Collins 1996).

None the less, this survey of bankers' responses to customers' approaches found the somewhat surprising result that over 50 per cent of credits were supplied either without requiring the provision of a formal security or against solely the customer's personal guarantee. This can be explained in terms of credit being granted primarily to established clients in whom the banker had trust and confidence through having either experience of how they had previously conducted their accounts or knowledge of their wealth. With joint-stock companies, the latter information could be established through discovering who were the directors and shareholders (available from the annual returns to the Registrar of Joint-Stock Companies), and examining balance sheets and annual reports, if published. However, the increasing number of joint-stock companies, private and public, led to a decline in the proportion of unsecured bank loans – from 64.6 per cent in the early 1880s to 27.3 per cent during the quinquennium before 1914. None the less, directors' personal guarantees to a considerable degree took the place of the personal guarantees previously proffered by sole proprietors and members of partnerships while joint-stock companies' debentures provided an entirely new form of security (Capie and Collins 1999).

The size of bank credits varied with the amount of security that a borrower could put forward, along with the purpose for which it was being sought and the period for which it would be outstanding. In the case of Lloyds, the turnover of a customer's account was also a factor; this provided a guide to the extent of both the customer's business and the account's earning power for the bank, since commissions were an important source of bank income. The security proffered for loans by customers acted as, in effect, the pricing for bank facilities since bankers' charges – commission and interest rates – were common to all. In the provinces, bankers extended overdrafts at the fixed rate of 5 per cent. During the 1890s, when interest rates were so low, this procedure made 'country' banks targets for takeover. This was especially the case because the cost of metropolitan advances from at least the mid-1850s was directly related to the level of Bank rate with a margin of 0.5 or 1 per cent. The cost of bank loans was only increased in exceptional circumstances, as when a greatly increased overdraft line was negotiated due to a proven customer being in distress. However, commission charges levied on an account's turnover were subject to greater variation: higher when an account was considered by the banker to be inactive, and lower when it was large.

The size of individual loans increased markedly over the quarter century before 1914, the mean rising from £10,824 to £19,816, and the median from £2,000 to £5,500. This reflected both the greatly increasing size of the fewer banks that constituted the system on the supply side, and the growing importance of joint-stock companies as customers, with these forms of business organisation enjoying bigger loans, six times the average (Capie and Collins 1999). Bank loans were formally extended for six to eight and a half months but in practice ran for eight to twelve months (median) or thirteen to nineteen months (mean). Indeed, overdrafts were routinely renewed, and bankers would support established customers when they were in difficulties, although not to the extent of becoming enmeshed with such clients' enterprises (Baker and Collins 1999). None the less, bankers saw their prime role as providing trading or working capital, or assisting customers' cash flows. From the late 1880s, the relatively small proportion of facilities granted to assist capital expenditure dwindled further. However, bankers were prepared to assist such outlays in the short term until they could be refinanced from within the customer's circle of friends, or by mortgage or by the issue of equity and/or debentures, with, in the latter instances, the banker recommending contacts for arranging their flotation (Capie and Collins 1999).

In the case of brewers, bank credit financed interest payments on debentures, beer duty payments or deposits for the acquisition of tied houses. The major brewers generally held their accounts with London banks and obtained loans on 'London' terms – at Bank rate plus 0.5 or 1 per cent. At such a price, bank credits were competitive, yet, during the late 1880s and 1890s, brewers could tap abundant funds on the capital market through issues of either preference shares or debentures. These circumstances gave brewers the opportunity to play off banks and, in response, bankers attempted to meet brewers' approaches as far as their own interests permitted. The major advantages of approaching a bank for a brewer, or any other customer, were the potential opportunity of quickly gaining funds together with the lack of publicity that, otherwise, would be attendant upon an issue on the capital market (Watson 1996: 73–9).

Reports from the research of Baker, Capie and Collins strongly suggest continuity in banking behaviour from the 1860s until 1914, apart from the growth in the size of individual loans. However, their methodology provides little indication of how bankers coped with the substitution of overdrafts (unsecuritised assets) for bill discounts (securitised assets that could be liquidated on the London money market), although banking records in general are stubbornly reticent over the question of discounting and its extent. Furthermore, to date, their work concerned with long-run trends has provided little general direct indication of any changes in banking behaviour that came with the amalgamation movement, either during its first phase from 1878 or its second phase from 1909/10. None the less, it has contributed to the understanding of the wider ramifications of the collapse of the City of Glasgow Bank.

The importance of the 1878 City of Glasgow Bank failure has recently been reappraised. It has long been seen as resulting in commercial banks adopting limited liability via 'reserved liability', and accelerating amalgamations. There is still debate over whether it initiated a crisis, comparable to those of 1866 or 1890, through administering a short-term liquidity shock of sufficient magnitude to produce a long-term shift in banking assets, arising from bankers being less willing after 1878 to lend 'long' for customers' capital expenditures. Two contextual reasons for the discussion over whether the episode merits the term 'crisis' is that few other banks failed in 1878 while, as there was no foreign pressure, the Bank of England was readily able to act as lender of last resort. Yet, available evidence strongly suggests that, as a result of the experience, bankers raised their cash ratios to a new, and permanent, higher level, possibly of the order of 17 per cent. Furthermore, the City of Glasgow Bank collapse appears to have been the crystallising event in the slowing of the growth of bank deposits not only in Scotland but also in England and Wales from 4 per cent per annum over the mid-century to 2.7 per cent during the late 1870s and early 1880s (Collins 1989).

The Midland Bank in Birmingham required its managers from autumn 1878 to refer overdraft requests greater than £200 to its directors (Holmes and Green 1986: 63), while the City of Glasgow Bank failure may also have raised the question of the continuing ability of a group of banks in Cumberland, Westmoreland and Yorkshire to assist manufacturers in the long term. The businesses of six banks of varying sizes in these northern counties were closely intertwined with a small number of industrial customers (Collins 1990). However, the events of autumn 1878 did not produce a major change in the lending policy of one of the largest – Cumberland Union. Its management was new to 'industrial banking', consequent upon the local, greater growth of the iron and steel industry, which led, unusually, to their bank becoming 'over lent' during the mid-1880s. Manufacturers still accounted for 60 per cent of the bank's provision of overdrafts totalling £0.488 million at the close of 1885, with the West Cumberland Iron & Steel Co. the dominant borrower. The bank continued to support these customers to its ultimate cost – a loss of £0.25 million on the West Cumberland's accounts alone in 1894. Over the latter 1890s, Cumberland Union's management was able to reduce these illiquid assets, and it was unrelated fraud and the collapse of a debtor client bank that led to its demise by amalgamation in 1901 (Cottrell 1980: 233–8).

Although another of this group, York City & County, received a setback during the late 1870s to its management's newly initiated policy of industrial lending, it led to no reversal of strategy. Indeed, the bank developed to be the largest provincial bank in late Victorian England, either by acquiring banks or by opening new branches in the industrial north-east and the Sheffield area. As a result, for instance, it was lending during the mid-1890s to shipping companies involved in the relatively new business of carrying oil and oil-based products, and to other ship owners and shipbuilders by advancing sums ranging from £100 to £40,000 on securities variously comprising debentures, directors' guarantees, a mortgage on a new steamer, shares, ship owners' acceptances and trade debts (Cottrell 2002: 239–46; see also Ollerenshaw 1997: 54–5).

The 1878 crisis did have an effect, albeit temporary, on the lending of the small Hull Bank but its management's decision to 'get out of all securities upon fishing smacks' was as much related to a sudden marked fall in the profitability of fishing. Within eighteen months, the bank was lending again on smacks and, at the end of the 1880s, a new branch was opened at Grimsby to sustain its engagement with the fishing trade. This went along from 1886 with providing facilities to enable customers to acquire the new steamer trawlers that on average cost £4,700 compared with £1,600 for a sailing smack (Cottrell 2002: 221–42).

Such case study evidence is supported by general, quantitative data. They show that from the late 1870s until the early twentieth century provincial banks as a group were less liquid – at 35 per cent – than London banks (45–50 per cent). During this period, provincial banks made the largest commitment to private sector credit through loans and overdrafts, whereas London bank managements preferred to invest in bills, which increasingly meant foreign trade acceptances after the secular decline in the use of the inland bill of exchange. This has the implication that, from the latter part of the amalgamation movement, as London-based institutions acquired provincial banks, there was a consequent, relative decline in the system's overall supply of private sector credit. Loans and overdrafts to clients fell following an amalgamation (Collins and Baker 2001).

The current direct evidence for the impact of amalgamation upon lending is relatively slight. Mergers of provincial banks, as with York City & County's acquisition of Hull Bank in 1894, seem to have caused no major change in lending policy. In the case of the second phase of amalgamations, available evidence points in opposite directions. After 1900 Midland branch managers enjoyed higher discretionary limits while large corporate customers could deal directly with the bank's London board. However, its metropolitan directors became more concerned about the overall balance of loans granted to industrial customers – discriminating against colliery accounts (Holmes and Green 1986: 115, 117). Discrimination also seems to have occurred when Midland, the most managerially centralised of the progenitors of the post-1918 'Big Five', acquired provincial joint-stock banks. In the case of Huddersfield Banking Co. during the late 1890s, the overdraft limits of substantial borrowers were reduced and requests were made for alterations in the securities that backed them. If these customers were unresponsive, their existing securities were to be sold at their cost, with the Midland's London directors being prepared to go as far as placing nominees on their respective boards to enforce these changes. This stern approach led to a loss of custom and a decline of morale amongst the Huddersfield's former managers (Ziegler 1997: 191–2). The Huddersfield experience coincides with Lavington's early twentieth-century opinion that amalgamations would result in a decline of 'long' loans with bank assets coming consequently to comprise 'advances both secured and more readily recoverable' (1921: 145). Midland's London management also requested from the 1890s that managers of absorbed banks refrained from accommodating customers by bill discounts – direct discrimination against the inland bill (Goodhart 1972: 151).

By the 1890s every town of any size in the United Kingdom had branches of a number of banks. Their managers provided overdrafts to creditworthy customers that were rolled over to comprise lines of credit which could continue for decades. In this way English banks, and their Irish and Scottish counterparts, behaved in a comparable manner to continental European institutions, whose main form of lending also comprised short-term credits that were, likewise, rolled over and renewed (Collins 1998). Their primary, day-to-day businesses were the same. The difference was that some major continental banks were prepared from the 1890s to act as issuing houses but only for their major industrial customers. This led in Germany to a concentration upon iron, steel and coal to the detriment of the Mittelstand and the economy as a whole (Neuberger and Stokes 1974; Tilly 1986). However, British commercial banks would nurse for a time, sometimes for a considerable time, prized industrial accounts when these ran into difficulties, and would provide advice, or even short-term bridging finance, when a customer required capital funds. The holdings of industrial shares and bonds by major German banks were only slightly higher as a proportion of their assets than were those of their English counterparts. This was primarily a reflection of the lack of depth in the German home capital market for such securities (Fohlin 1997; 2001: 2, 12; and see Edwards and Fischer 1994; Edwards and Ogilvy 1996).

AN EVOLVING FINANCIAL MARKET

There certainly were flaws in domestic finance but these arose primarily from a permissive company code, substantially unreformed until 1900 and 1907, which allowed self-styled company promoters to have full sway. In this situation, 'blind' investors were not assisted substantially by the growth of the financial press from the 1880s, especially the new style of market reporting. Otherwise, it was largely a question of the coalescence of long-established and largely effective provincial markets for credit and capital, at least a century old in 1860, with the metropolitan market of equally long, if longer, standing.

That integration was constrained by a number of factors. One was the continuing importance of personal capitalism, which gave primacy to the partnership, to the private limited company and, when required, and if profits were inadequate, to raising capital from immediate business, filial and religious circles, and to dealing with a local banker. Personal small and medium-scale enterprises – the family firms – only began to wane at the beginning of the twentieth century. Another factor was the internationalisation of the London markets for credit and capital from the mid-nineteenth century as both the national debt and the inland bill of exchange entered secular declines at the same time as the British economy became an even greater globalising force.

Some historians have concluded that the absence of financial panic after 1866 is a strong indicator of the maturity of the markets and, thereby, of their respective member institutions (e.g., Habakkuk 1962). However, while major crises were less a recurring feature, none the less they continued to be experienced – in 1878 and 1890. The degree of maturity achieved is also questioned by the subsequent series of official inquiries over the twentieth century maintaining that there were gaps – the most well known being the 'Macmillan gap' – in the provision of domestic facilities. This implies that the financial sector's coverage was not complete by 1914 – a half-century after many had assumed that it had matured. Furthermore, some credence is given to this conclusion by measures of Goldsmith's financial interrelations ratio (FIR), namely, the ratio of financial assets to national wealth. Goldsmith's comparative studies indicate that this ratio rises with economic modernisation to reach a ceiling band with a range of 1 to 1.5. Available data point to the British economy being on the verge of financial maturity during the decades before 1914 but not clearly achieving full maturity according to this measure until thereafter, with FIR reaching 1.3 (1929) and 1.6 (1938) (Goldsmith 1966, 1969; Cottrell 1992a: 43–4).

The markets in general before 1900 were not so much imperfect as still evolving. That process was shaped in the capital market by 'blind' investors' preferences; these had previously been shaped by issues of the national debt so that they would only readily take up domestic issues that had analogous characteristics – railway perpetual debentures from the late 1860s, municipal stocks from the 1870s and industrial debentures and preference shares from the mid-1880s. None the less, railway companies apart, Britain in 1906 had eight times more joint-stock companies than Germany – 40,995 compared with 5,061 – and they collectively had three times more capital – £2,000 million as opposed to £685 million (Michie 1988a: 51–2). Furthermore, although the London Stock Exchange, like any other financial market, required stocks and shares in volume to guarantee their liquidity – their tradability – its conditions for a quotation were far less strict than those of the New York Exchange, and it largely dealt in time bargains which New York had given up in 1857 (Michie 1986: 180, 185).

By 1908 London quoted 200 domestic industrial and commercial companies in which trading was regularly conducted. Furthermore, it was integrated with the provincial markets through ten member firms employing private telephone lines to undertake arbitrage business – 'shunting' as it was known. However, this business raised the question of 'dual capacity' in London that was not to be resolved until the 'Big Bang' of the late twentieth century (Michie 1985: 72–81). Although new companies pioneering new technologies found difficulties in raising capital with the assistance of the London Stock Exchange, in part because the market could not measure the risks involved, some of its members provided networks whereby syndicates and other like associations could obtain the funds to prove or otherwise the commercial possibilities of a patent (Michie 1981; 1988b). However, it is probably straining this line of argument to claim that, other operative factors apart, the relatively slow adoption of new technologies within Britain from the 1880s was due more to legislative restraints than the lack of responsiveness of financial institutions.

It is difficult to assess the number of 'blind' investors within late Victorian society. One estimate is that they numbered 300,000 and a survey in 1907 maintained that at least 60 per cent were risk-averse. It is perfectly understandable why small investors should take a conservative stance, particularly when only 18 per cent of new joint-stock companies survived for more than ten years (albeit this was an improvement on the 1860s, when nearly all collapsed within three years) (Michie 1981: 147–9). The related question of how far 'stock and bond' capitalism penetrated downwards through society is equally difficult to assess. The floor might be people with an income of £160 per annum, who numbered 280,000 in 1860 and 1.2m by 1913. What is clearer is the geography, at least of those willing to subscribe to shares as opposed to bonds, which shows the continuing vibrancy of provincial and intra-industry markets, formal and informal, where investors had direct knowledge of, and contact with, companies seeking equity funds.

In the case of credit, provincial joint-stock banks remained the backbone of the market. However, when these were absorbed during the second phase of the amalgamation movement, their customers may have been accommodated on more stringent terms as London-based managements preferred to maintain higher levels of liquid assets than their 'country' counterparts. The dominance of the oligopoly of the 'Big Five' was only fully established in 1918 but had already begun to coalesce from 1909. It was only from 1909 that Lloyds, Midland and the Westminster individually had assets on a par with major continental banks such as Crédit Lyonnais and Deutsche. Their London senior managements would rightly point out that they had responsibilities to their depositors as well as borrowing customers. Furthermore, all banks were called upon by the Chancellor, in the wake of the Baring crisis, to publish balance sheets and increase reserve holdings; and the transparency that this gave to cash ratios and liquidity ratios led to the somewhat dubious practice of 'window dressing'. Within this context, by 1900 London bank managements preferred to maintain advances: deposits ratios below 55 per cent, any rise above 60 per cent calling for immediate remedial action (Goodhart 1972: 158–9).

Greater liquidity gave the overall system greater stability, a not inconsequential asset. It was obtained through the interconnections between the overall financial system, home and external. In June 1914, at the time of the publication of half-year balance sheets (in which allowance has to be made for window dressing), the London joint-stock banks collectively placed £90 million at call and short notice, of which £45 million comprised very short-term facilities extended to the London and provincial stock exchanges. Otherwise, liquidity was controlled by variations in open market purchases by banks of bills payable in London, paper primarily generated by the finance of international trade and the movement of short-term capital between major financial centres – the daily workings of the classical gold standard. Although the financial sector was characterised by functional specialisation, each component was integrated and increasingly integrated into the whole.

11 Living standards, 1860–1939

GEORGE R. BOYER

Contents

INTRODUCTION

The trend in working-class living standards from the Great Exhibition to the eve of the Second World War has generated relatively little controversy compared to the debate over living standards during the industrial revolution. Most economic historians agree that real wages increased significantly from 1851 to 1913, and continued to increase during the interwar period. However, despite these achievements, the social surveys of the late Victorian and Edwardian eras revealed high rates of urban poverty and 'a working-class stunted and debilitated by a century of industrialism' (Hobsbawm 1968: 137). This suggests that, as with the period 1780–1860, one might reach a different conclusion about trends in and levels of working-class living standards depending on what type of information is examined.

Economic historians measure movements in living standards in various ways, by examining trends in real wage rates or incomes of workers (or more rarely households), national income per capita, life expectancy at birth (or at other ages), infant mortality and height by age. These measures can to some extent be grouped into economic indicators of material living standards – real wages, per capita income – and biological indicators – life expectancy, infant mortality and height by age, which are sometimes said to measure 'quality of life'. Biological measures suggest a somewhat less optimistic assessment of the trend in working-class living standards than do wage series, at least up to 1900. In order to determine the extent to which living standards improved from 1860 to 1939, it therefore is necessary to examine trends in both economic and biological indicators for the working class as a whole and also for occupational subgroups of the working class.

The fact that different measures of living standards do not always move together has led economists and economic historians to develop more comprehensive measures of the quality of life. The 1990 *Human Development Report* presented a new approach to examining movements in living standards, the human development index (HDI), which combined measures of income, longevity and knowledge into a single indicator of 'well-being'. Dasgupta and Weale (1992) created an even broader index of well-being by expanding the HDI to include measures of political and civil rights. While these attempts at more comprehensive indices of living standards are to be applauded, they are not without problems. In particular, the weighting schemes for the components in the indices appear to be somewhat arbitrary, and changes in relative weights can lead to different conclusions regarding trends in well-being (Crafts 1997a).

Living standards were also affected by the vast rural–urban migration that took place during this period. From 1851 to 1911 the rural districts of England and Wales lost over 4 million people as a result of migration. During the same period London and the eight largest northern cities gained 1.6 million people through migration, 118 other towns gained over 370,000, and the colliery districts gained 568,000; 1.5 million persons emigrated (Cairncross 1949: 83). Workers who migrated from rural to urban areas typically experienced significant real wage increases but deterioration in other aspects of living standards. In 1861–70 life expectancy at birth was 46.5 years in rural England and Wales, 37.7 in London and 33–4 in other large cities (Woods 2000: 369). Did workers who migrated from relatively healthy rural areas to large cities experience an increase or a decline in well-being? The answer depends on how one weights income relative to longevity and other urban disamenities. Williamson (1981, 1990) estimated how high urban workers' wages had to be to offset the high death rates and crowding in large cities, and concluded that rural workers who migrated to industrial cities experienced a significant increase in living standards. Other historians have reached less optimistic conclusions. Floud and Harris (1997: 97) concluded that the wage increases of the mid-nineteenth century 'were bought at a high price in terms of health and mortality'.

The examination of long-term movements in economic or biological indicators of living standards tells us little about workers' ability to cope with periodic losses of income. The British economy experienced several cyclical downturns between 1860 and 1939, during which 10 per cent or more of the male industrial labour force were thrown out of work. Even in prosperous times, workers lost their jobs because they were injured or sick or too old to work. The extent to which income loss led to economic hardship was determined in part by how much workers saved, and by whether they were eligible for insurance benefits through membership of friendly societies or trade unions. Relatively few workers had the resources to withstand a prolonged period of income loss, so that during such periods some share of the working class was forced to turn to other sources for income assistance. The living standards of these workers was determined by the extent of the safety net provided by local governments or private charities.

This chapter focuses on the living standards of the working class, roughly the bottom 75–80 per cent of the occupied population (Baxter 1868: 15; Routh 1965: 4–5). Middle-class living standards have generated little controversy, and are ably discussed elsewhere (Trainor 2000). The emphasis here is on movements in quantifiable aspects of living standards. There is little discussion of how increases in income affected the daily lives of particular working-class families, or of what it meant to such families for the household head to be sick or out of work.[1]

WORKERS' LIVING STANDARDS

Britain at the beginning of our period had completed its industrial revolution and was the wealthiest country in Europe. Table 11.1 presents five measures of the standard of living in 1870 for Britain and nine other countries. Gross domestic product (GDP) per capita was about $3,260 (in 1990 US dollars) in Britain, nearly 20 per cent greater than that of its closest European rivals and 25 per cent greater than that of the United States. One might guess from Britain's wealth that its workers had higher living standards than workers elsewhere, but the other indicators of well-being show that this might not have been the case. Real wages were higher in Britain than elsewhere in Europe, but they were significantly

[1] There is a large literature on the day-to-day living of the working class. Several of the social surveys of late Victorian and Edwardian England contain detailed discussions of family budgets, leisure activities, etc. See, for example, Rowntree 1901: 222–94, 306–32; Bell 1907; and Pember Reeves 1913. Other useful accounts of working-class life, both fictional and non-fictional, include Morrison 1894; London 1903; Williams 1915; Greenwood 1933; Orwell 1937; Tressell 1955; Ashby 1961; and Roberts 1971.

Table 11.1 Measures of living standards for Britain and other countries, 1870

	GDP per capita ($1990)	Real wage index	Life expectancy at birth	Literacy rate (%)	HDI
Britain	3,263	100	41.3	76	0.496
Belgium	2,640	90	40.0	66	0.429
Netherlands	2,640	85	38.9	78	0.450
United States	2,457	172	44.0	75	0.466
Denmark	1,927	54	45.5	81	0.448
Germany	1,913	87	36.2	80	0.397
France	1,858	75	42.0	69	0.400
Sweden	1,664	42	45.8	75	0.412
Canada	1,620	148	42.6	79	0.411
Italy	1,467	39	28.0	32	0.187

Note: The construction of the human development index is discussed in Crafts 1997b: 301–5.

Sources: GDP per capita: Maddison 1995; Real wage: Taylor and Williamson 1997: 36; Life expectancy, Literacy rate, HDI: Crafts 1997b: 306, 310.

below wages in the United States and Canada. Britain fared even worse in the non-material measures of living standards, ranking sixth in life expectancy and fifth in literacy. The final column gives the HDI estimate for each country, which is a combination of per capita GDP, life expectancy and literacy and schooling. On this measure Britain ranks first, followed by the United States, the Netherlands and Denmark. However, if income were measured using real wages rather than per capita GDP, the United States would rank ahead of Britain.

Per capita GDP is a blunt instrument for measuring the standard of living of the working class. It includes income from sources other than labour, and it says nothing about the distribution of income among different groups of workers. Real wage rates or earnings provide a more precise measure of workers' command over resources, although aggregate wage data, like per capita GDP, reveal nothing about income differences across groups of workers. Wage data are available for several major (male) occupations, so that it is possible to examine trends in real wage rates from 1860 to 1939 for the working class as a whole and for different occupations.

Trends in real wages

Pioneering work in the construction of time series for nominal (money) wages and the cost of living for the period up to 1914 was done by Arthur Bowley and George Wood. Bowley (1904, 1937) constructed time series of the average rate of wages and the cost of living for 1860–1913, and Wood (1909) constructed time series of average money wages and retail prices for 1850–1902. While Bowley's series in particular has been widely used by economic historians, it omits several important sectors of the economy.

Table 11.2 Trends in nominal and real wages, 1856–1938 (annual percentage growth rates)

(a) Wage trends 1856–1913	1856–1913	1856–73	1873–82	1882–99	1899–1913
Bowley					
Nominal wages	0.91	2.03	−0.98	1.01	0.76
Cost of living	−0.19	0.40	−2.01	−1.01	1.23
Real wages	1.11	1.62	1.03	2.03	−0.46
Feinstein					
Nominal wages	1.07	1.85	−0.41	0.92	1.26
Within sectors				0.61	0.95
Between sectors				0.31	0.30
Cost of living	−0.17	0.04	−1.41	−0.66	0.97
Real wages	1.24	1.81	1.02	1.58	0.29
Real GDP per worker	1.01	1.32	0.90	1.49	0.09
(b) Wage trends 1913–38	**1913–38**	**1913–24**	**1924–38**	**1920–38**	
Feinstein					
Nominal wages	2.98	6.43	0.36	−1.58	
Cost of living	1.74	5.08	−0.80	−2.54	
Real wages	1.21	1.28	1.17	0.98	

Sources: Wage and cost-of-living data for Bowley are from Bowley 1937: 30, 122, 1904: 459. For 1856–9, nominal wage data from Wood 1909: 102 were spliced to the Bowley series. Wage and cost-of-living data for Feinstein are from Feinstein 1995a: 263–5,1990d: 344. Real GDP per worker from Feinstein 1990d: 337.

Charles Feinstein (1990c, 1995a) has reworked several of the sectoral series used by Bowley, and has added further manufacturing series as well as series for transport, distribution, domestic service and government. Ian Gazeley (1989) and Feinstein (1991a) also constructed new cost-of-living indices, which include several items not in the Bowley index. Whereas Bowley's budget weights assume that the typical working-class household spent 95.5 per cent of its income on food, rent, clothing and fuel and light, Feinstein (1991a: 169–75) assigns these items a combined budget weight of 69.4 per cent, and adds 18.0 per cent for alcohol and tobacco, 3.0 per cent for furniture, 0.9 per cent for cleaning materials and 8.7 per cent for travel and other services.

Panel (a) of Table 11.2 presents estimates of the average rate of growth of nominal and real wages for 1856–1913 and for four subperiods using data series constructed by Bowley and Feinstein. The subperiods distinguish four distinct phases of growth – differences across subperiods in the rate of growth in labour productivity (GDP per worker) are given in the final row of panel (a). The Bowley and Feinstein cost-of-living series are quite similar for the period as a whole, while Feinstein's nominal wage series grows at a faster rate than Bowley's, leading to a slightly faster growth rate for real wages in Feinstein's estimates.

There are, however, significant differences in rates of wage growth across subperiods. Real wages grew faster during periods of rapid growth in labour productivity, 1856–73 and 1882–99, than during periods when productivity slowed. The most pronounced differences between the Bowley and Feinstein wage series are for the final two subperiods. In Bowley's series, real wages increased at a very rapid rate from 1882 to 1899, then declined from 1899 to the eve of the First World War. The differences in wage growth between 1882–99 and 1899–1913 are much less dramatic in Feinstein's series. Most significantly, Feinstein's estimates suggest that real wages continued to rise after 1899, albeit at a very slow pace.

Average wage rates increased over time partly because workers shifted from low-wage to higher-wage occupations. Agriculture, a low-wage sector, lost over 300,000 workers from 1881 to 1911 while coal mining, a high-wage sector, gained nearly 700,000 workers. Table 11.2 shows for 1882–1913 Feinstein's estimation of the increase in nominal wages due to rising wages within sectors and that due to movements of workers between sectors. He finds that 24–34 per cent of the increase in wages was a result of intersectoral shifts in the labour force. If the wage structure had remained the same after 1881, nominal wages would have increased by 0.61 per cent per year from 1882 to 1899 and by 0.95 per cent from 1899 to 1913.

Feinstein's estimates of the average rate of growth of nominal and real wages for 1913–38 are given in panel (b) of Table 11.2. Nominal wages and the cost of living both increased sharply during the First World War, then declined from 1920 to 1938. Real wages increased from 1913 to 1938 at about the same rate as they had in 1856–1913, and at a much more rapid rate than in 1899–1913.

The estimated rates of growth in Table 11.2 are for weekly wages. They underestimate the increase in hourly wage rates, because the number of hours worked per week declined over time. Economists maintain that workers gain satisfaction from leisure as well as income, and there is plenty of evidence from the twentieth century that workers desire reductions in hours as well as increases in wages. Reductions in weekly hours of work were quite discontinuous; much of the decline occurred during the boom of 1872–4 and in 1919–20, in the aftermath of the First World War (Bienefeld 1972: 82; Dowie 1975). The average number of hours worked per week declined from 65 in 1856 to 56 in 1873, remained constant until 1913, fell to 46.6 in 1924, then increased slightly to 48.2 in 1937 (Matthews *et al.* 1982: 65).

The data in Table 11.2 also mask significant differences in the rate of growth of wages across sectors of the economy. Table 11.3 presents estimates of annual full-time wage earnings for sixteen industries for 1881, 1896, and 1913, and of the percentage change in wages between years. Looking first at the level of earnings, three well-known differentials stand out. Skilled workers earned more than unskilled workers, men earned more than women and urban workers earned more than rural workers. In 1881, when average annual full-time earnings were £48.2, general

Table 11.3 Annual full-time nominal wage earnings 1881–1938; (£s)

				Percentage change			
	1881	1896	1913	1881–96	1896–1913	1881–1913	1922–38
Iron and steel	63.1	70.3	116.7	11.4	66.0	84.9	28.3
Coal mining	50.5	65.2	94.3	29.1	44.7	86.8	6.6
Engineering	56.5	65.3	76.9	15.5	17.8	36.1	13.0
Clothing (male workers)	53.4	62.7	75.2	17.3	20.0	40.8	−1.8
Building	62.4	68.0	74.2	9.0	9.1	19.0	3.0
Railways	56.2	60.8	70.7	8.3	16.2	25.8	−2.9
Furniture	61.0	63.0	66.5	3.2	5.6	9.0	−1.0
Printing	54.8	59.6	65.0	8.7	9.1	18.6	−2.9
Footwear	52.4	51.8	56.4	−1.1	8.9	7.7	−1.0
Cotton	38.1	43.3	51.8	13.6	19.6	36.0	−8.0
Agriculture (Eng. and Wales)	39.6	39.8	48.2	0.6	21.0	21.7	25.3
Domestic service (females)	37.6	37.1	46.4	−1.3	25.0	23.4	
Wool and worsted	38.3	37.7	45.5	−1.5	20.7	18.9	−11.0
General labour	34.0	37.0	43.3	8.6	17.1	27.2	
Linen, hosiery, silk	36.3	36.0	40.0	−0.8	11.0	10.1	−10.5
Clothing (female workers)	29.3	29.3	29.3	0.0	0.0	0.0	−5.3
All sectors	48.2	51.6	61.4	7.1	19.0	27.5	
Cost of living				−12.8	17.6	2.6	−14.5

Notes: Occupations are ranked by earnings in 1913. Of the seven lowest-paid occupations, five (cotton, domestic service, wool and worsted, linen, hosiery and silk and female clothing workers) were dominated by females. The other two (agriculture, general labour) were low-skilled male occupations.

Sources: Data for 1881–1913 from Feinstein 1991b: 161. Data for 1922–38 from Ramsbottom 1935: 665–6, 1939: 289–90.

labourers earned £34.0, agricultural workers £39.6, female domestic servants £37.6, and female clothing workers £29.3. Workers in cotton, wool and worsted and linen, hosiery and silk industries employing large numbers of women, all had annual earnings below £40. Thirty-two years later, in 1913, wage earnings in these industries were still significantly below the average for all manual workers. Similarly, most of the industries with above average earnings in 1881 also had above average earnings in 1913.

From 1881 to 1913 the rate of wage increase varied from 86.8 per cent in coal mining and 84.9 per cent in iron and steel manufacture to 0.0 per cent for females in clothing and 7.7 per cent in footwear. For each industry, the percentage increase in nominal wage earnings for 1896–1913 was as great or greater than the percentage increase for 1881–96. However, the cost of living fell by 12.8 per cent from 1881 to 1896, then increased by 17.6 per cent from 1896 to 1913. Thus, real earnings increased for workers in each industry in the earlier period, but declined for workers in eight of the industries from 1896 to 1913. The economic slowdown of the Edwardian period clearly affected some industries and occupations more than others.

What caused these sharp differences in wage growth across occupations? In most of the industries where wage growth was the slowest, workers were adversely effected by the introduction of steam powered machinery. Female workers in clothing were hurt by the introduction of new technologies which led to the mass-production of ready-made clothing, and workers in the boot and shoe industry suffered from the introduction of machinery and mounting competition from American factories. Workers in the building trades had above-average wage increases from 1881 to 1896, but were hurt by a serious slump in the construction industry in the first decade of the twentieth century. In contrast, there were no significant technological changes in either coal mining or iron and steel manufacture, the industries where wage increases were the largest. Miners were greatly aided by the buoyant demand for coal, which caused the price of coal to increase at a time when most prices were stagnant or falling. Iron and steel workers also benefited from a sharp increase in the world demand for manufactured iron and steel, particularly after 1896 (Feinstein 1991b: 162–9).

The last column of Table 11.3 presents estimates of the percentage change in nominal wages from 1922 to 1938. Wage rates increased by 28.3 per cent in iron and steel, 25.3 per cent in agriculture, and 13.0 per cent in engineering, but fell in nine of fourteen industries. The largest declines were in textiles, where wages fell by 8.0–11.0 per cent (Ramsbottom 1935, 1939). The cost of living fell by 14.5 per cent over the period, so real wages increased in all fourteen industries; the size of the increase varied from 4.1 per cent in wool and worsted to 50.0 per cent in iron and steel. The average wage differential between skilled and unskilled workers narrowed during the interwar period. Wage rates for unskilled males in manufacturing were on average about 60 per cent of skilled wage rates in 1880–1914, and 70–5 per cent of skilled wage rates in the interwar years (Robertson 1960).

Industries not only differed in their rates of wage growth, they also differed in the frequency and volatility of wage changes. Coal mining and the metal trades experienced large year-to-year fluctuations in wages, while in the building trades wages often remained constant for several years in a row, and there were few years in which nominal wages declined (Pollard 1954; Gourvish 1979: 26–9; Feinstein 1991b: 156–60). The average length of time a wage rate remained unchanged was about 5 months in iron and steel, 6 months in coal mining, 2.9 years in cotton, 3.8 years in engineering, 4.8 years in building and 14.5 years in printing (Wood 1901: 152). The frequency of wage changes in iron and steel and in coal was a result of the use of sliding scales or conciliation or arbitration procedures which linked wages to product prices (Porter 1970; Treble 1987). The volatility of wages created a higher level of uncertainty in miners' and steel workers' households than existed in the households of many lower-paid skilled workers.

For many occupations the examination of full-time earnings is misleading, because few workers were employed fifty-two weeks a year. Many workers were hired by the job, the week or even the day, and those with a greater degree of job security were often sick or unemployed, during which time they were not compensated by their employers. A system of casual employment existed in low-skilled occupations that were subject to sudden and irregular fluctuations in the demand for labour (Beveridge 1909: 77–110; Jones 1971: 52–126). Some degree of casualisation existed in many occupations, including the building trades, land transport, menial services and certain manufacturing trades, but the prototypical casual occupation was dock labour. Dockworkers were hired by the day or half-day, chosen by foremen each morning and afternoon from groups of workers at 'calling-on stands'. While firms employed a number of 'permanent' men full time, foremen often gave out the remaining work in rotation rather than hiring the same men every day, in order to retain a reserve of labour about equal to their expected maximum demand. Thus, even though the hourly wage rate for dockworkers was relatively high, the irregularity of employment meant that many suffered chronic distress (Beveridge 1909: 106–7). In the building trades, workers were hired by the job, which often was as short as a week. Hiring was done by foremen at job sites, typically on a first-come first-served basis. This led to the creation of a 'casual fringe' of painters and unskilled labourers 'drifting perpetually about the streets' in search of work (Dearle 1908; Beveridge 1909: 96–8). There are no estimates of the extent of casual labour in Britain, but Stedman Jones (1971: 54–6) estimated that in London in 1891 casual workers and their families totalled about 400,000 persons, or one tenth of the population.

Cyclical downturns, and the resulting threat of unemployment or a reduction in weekly hours worked, created additional uncertainty for workers. From 1870 to 1913, the average unemployment rate for male industrial workers was 6.6 per cent; it exceeded 8 per cent in 1878–9, 1885–7, 1893–5, 1904–5, and 1908–9 (Boyer and Hatton 2002: Table 4). From 1921 to 1938, the average unemployment rate among workers covered by the unemployment insurance system was 14.2 per cent; it exceeded 20 per cent in 1931–2 (Garside 1990: 5). Unemployment rates varied greatly across industries. The average unemployment rate for 1870–1913 (broadly defined to include hours lost from short-time working) ranged from 11.3 per cent in coal mining and 8.7 per cent in shipbuilding to less than 4 per cent in woodworking, printing and bookbinding and clothing and footwear. At the peak of the depression in 1932, the unemployment rate was 62.0 per cent in shipbuilding, 34.5 per cent in coal mining, 15.7 per cent in railway service and 11.0 per cent in printing and bookbinding (Mitchell 1988: 129).

Figure 11.1 presents wage series (adjusted for unemployment) for coal mining, building and printing for 1870–1913. The differences across industries are a result both of differences in the frequency and volatility

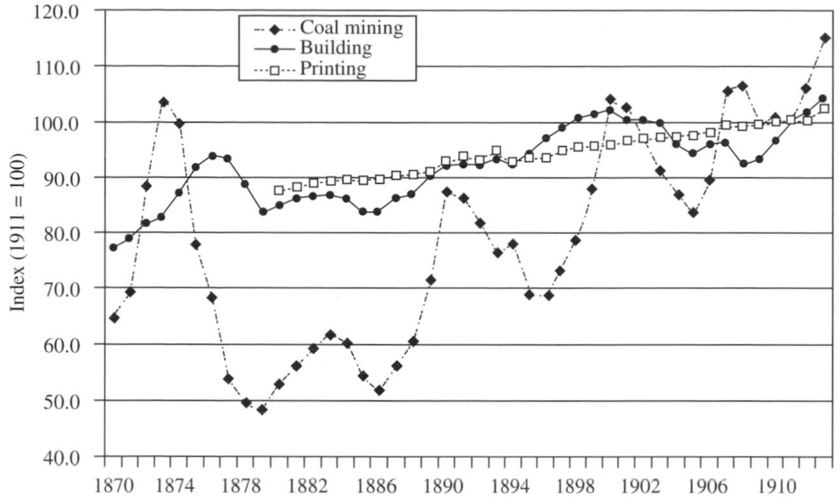

Figure 11.1 Unemployment adjusted wage trends, 1870–1913

Sources: Wage data for coal mining and building from Feinstein 1995: 260–1. Wage data for printing from Feinstein 1990c: 610–11. Unemployment data for coal mining, building and printing from Boyer and Hatton 2002.

of nominal wage changes and of differences in the volatility of unemployment. The series for coal mining is highly volatile while that for printing is remarkably stable; the series for building is moderately volatile. There were costs to income instability, one of which was the cost of defaulting on debts. The income volatility of coal miners was matched by high fluctuations in the number of local court cases initiated for the recovery of small debts (Johnson 1993). Miners' high wages did not protect them from periodic times of economic distress.

Wages and unemployment rates for workers in any particular occupation varied across locations. F. W. Lawrence (1899) found 'marked' differences across cities and regions in artisans' wages in the building, printing and iron industries. In 1886, the average weekly wage in summer for carpenters was 39.4s. in London, 36.0s. in Birmingham, 29.9s. in Bradford and 22.5s. in Bristol. These differences had declined somewhat by 1913, but they had not been eliminated (Hunt 1973, 1986; Boyer and Hatton 1994). Regional wage dispersion in agriculture was large throughout the period, and might have increased from 1860 to 1900 (Boyer and Hatton 1997: 726–8; Dewey 2000: 830–3). Agricultural wages varied sharply within as well as between regions. Wages were high in farming areas near cities or coalfields. There were steep wage gradients around London and other large cities throughout the nineteenth century (Hunt 1973; Boyer 1998). Some wage differentials were due as much to custom as to supply and demand – in south Warwickshire in the early 1890s, weekly wage differentials of 1.5–2s. could be found in adjacent villages (Ashby and King 1893: 5).

There were similar variations in regional unemployment rates. During most downturns, unemployment was higher in the industrial cities of northern England, Scotland and Ireland than it was in London and the south. In 1909, the unemployment rate for engineers was 24.0 per cent in the east of Scotland, 19.5 per cent in the north-east coast, 7.1 per cent in Birmingham and West Midlands towns and 6.4 per cent in London (Southall 1988). In 1932, unemployment rates ranged from 36.5 per cent in Wales and 28.5 per cent in the north-east to 13.5 per cent in London (Garside 1990: 10). Data on fluctuations in county court debt also suggest that the timing and magnitude of economic cycles 'varied considerably' across regions, and that the labour market was spatially segmented up to the First World War (Johnson 1993).

Information on average full-time wage earnings for the working class as a whole, while valuable, is not sufficient to determine workers' material living standards. Wage earnings for some industries were far above average, while earnings for others were far below average. In some industries there were large year-to-year fluctuations in full-time earnings, and some experienced quite volatile cyclical fluctuations that resulted in high unemployment rates. In those sectors where average (unemployment adjusted) wage earnings were highly volatile, workers' material living standards could change significantly from one year (or one month) to the next. A skilled worker who enjoyed a respectable standard of living when employed could find his savings depleted and his living standard greatly reduced if he was unemployed for several months during a prolonged downturn.

Trends in biological measures of living standards

Many economists and historians believe that real wages are not an adequate measure of the standard of living. In their view, income is a measure of command over resources; it is an input to well-being rather than an indicator of well-being, which is better measured by life expectancy, health, level of nutrition, education and voluntary leisure time (Sen 1987; Floud *et al.* 1990; Anand and Ravallion 1993). In recent years there has been an outpouring of research measuring trends in biological indicators of well-being, in particular life expectancy and height by age. The value of life expectancy as a measure is clear: increased longevity typically is assumed to be a good thing in and of itself, and longevity also is a proxy for the state of health of those living. Height is 'a function of net nutritional status, that is, the amount of food taken in by children and adolescents net of demands made on their bodies by labour and diseases' (Mokyr 1993: 127). There are potential problems associated with the use of height as a measure of well-being; for one thing, the precise 'relationship between food input and height' is not known (Engerman 1997: 34–8; Riley 1994: 5–6). Still, height is an output measure rather than an input to well-being, and it clearly should be examined along with other indicators of living standards.

While height is an indicator of nutritional status or health during childhood, a person's body mass index (BMI) measures his or her current nutritional status. The BMI is a measure of weight for height; it is

Table 11.4 Life expectancy and infant mortality: England and Wales, 1851–1932

(a) Life expectancy at birth (years)

	1851–60	1861–70	1871–80	1881–90	1891–1900	1901–10	1910–12	1920–2	1930–2
England/Wales	41.1	41.2	43.0	45.3	46.1	50.9	53.5	57.6	60.8
Rural areas	45.5	46.5	47.7	51.0	53.5	56.5			
Small towns	37.2	38.0	41.4	44.0	44.8	50.5			
Large cities	32.3	33.0	36.6	39.0	39.6	46.3			
London	38.0	37.7	40.4	42.6	43.7	49.4			
Manchester	32.0	31.0	34.0	37.0	36.0				
Liverpool	31.0	30.0	34.0	36.0	38.0				
Birmingham	37.0	37.0	39.0	42.0	42.0				
Leeds	36.0	35.0	38.0	40.0	41.0				
Sheffield	36.0	35.0	37.0	40.0	42.0				
Newcastle	35.0	35.0	38.0	41.0	43.0				
Bristol	39.0	40.0	42.0	46.0	47.0				
Portsmouth	40.0	42.0	44.0	45.0	46.0				

(b) Infant mortality (infant deaths per 1,000 live births)

	1851–60	1861–70	1871–80	1881–90	1891–1900	1901–10	1911–13	1921–30	1931–9
England/Wales	153.1	154.1	148.8	141.8	153.5	127.3	111.0	71.0	58.9

Sources: Life expectancy estimates for England and Wales, rural areas, small towns, large cities and London for 1851–1910 from Woods 2000: 365, 369. Life expectancy estimates for England and Wales for 1920–32 from Great Britain, Office of Population Censuses and Surveys 1987: 25. Life expectancy estimates for other cities from Szreter and Mooney 1998: 88, 106. Infant mortality rates from Mitchell 1988: 57–9.

calculated as weight in kilograms divided by the square of height in metres (Fogel 1991: 47–50; Floud 1998: 4–5). The BMI has been shown to be a good predictor of risk of mortality. Those with BMIs of 20–9 are at significantly lower risk than those with BMIs under 20 or over 29. Historical weight data are not as readily available as height data, but Floud (1998) offers provisional estimates of trends in average BMI for Britain since 1820.

Table 11.4 reports estimates of life expectancy at birth and infant mortality rates for England and Wales from the 1850s to the 1930s. Over this period average longevity increased sharply in all types of locations. From 1851 to 1910 life expectancy increased by eleven years in rural areas and London, by thirteen years in small towns and by fourteen years in large cities. Much of the increase in urban longevity occurred in the first decade of the twentieth century. In London, life expectancy increased by 5.7 years from 1891–1900 to 1901–10; in large provincial cities it increased by 6.7 years over the same period. Despite the significant increase in urban longevity, rural areas remained much healthier than cities – in 1901–10 life expectancy was 7–10 years longer in rural areas than in London and other large cities.

One of the major determinants of life expectancy at birth was the infant mortality rate. Panel (b) of Table 11.4 reports infant mortality rates for England and Wales. In 1851–60 there were, on average, 153.1 deaths of infants under 1 year old per 1,000 live births. The infant mortality rate fell to 141.8 in 1881–90, before rising again in the 1890s. A sharp and continued decline began in the first decade of the twentieth century; the infant mortality rate fell from 127.3 in 1901–10 to 58.9 in 1931–9. If infant mortality were used as a proxy for health, one would conclude that the health of the population of England and Wales remained roughly constant from 1851 to 1900, then increased sharply from 1900 to 1939.

Table 11.4 also gives estimates of average longevity for London and eight other cities. The most unhealthy cities were Manchester and Liverpool. The healthiest cities were Bristol and Portsmouth, southern cities with relatively low shares of their populations employed in manufacturing. London came in between.

Life expectancy was significantly lower, and infant mortality rates higher, in working-class districts of cities than in middle-class districts. In 1895–7 the infant mortality rate was 114.5 for the upper and middle classes, 139.3 for skilled workers and 157.7 for unskilled workers. Moreover, while infant mortality rates declined significantly for all social classes from 1895–7 to 1910, both the absolute decline and the percentage rate of decline were higher for the upper and middle classes than for the working class (Woods 2000: 264). These results suggest that aggregate data for trends in life expectancy and infant mortality exaggerate the improvement in health enjoyed by the working class in the decades leading up to the First World War.

The increase in life expectancy was largely a result of sharp declines in deaths from tuberculosis, cholera, diarrhoea, dysentery, typhoid, typhus, scarlet fever and diphtheria – declines in these infectious diseases accounted for nearly 80 per cent of the decline in deaths from 1848–54 to 1901 (McKeown 1976: 54–5, 58). Declines in mortality can come about because of improvements in health technology, changes in the virulence of diseases or the resistance of the population, improvements in nutrition and housing and improvements in public health. There is some disagreement as to which of these played the most important role in the mortality decline from 1850 to 1914. McKeown and Record (1962) conclude that improvements in nutrition, a result of increasing real wages, was the major cause of the decline in mortality, while Szreter (1988, 1997) contends that improvements in sanitation and water supply played the largest role in reducing death rates. The reasons for the mortality decline are discussed in detail in chapter 2.

The trends in life expectancy and infant mortality suggest that the health of the population in England and Wales improved substantially from 1851 to 1939, but that a large share of this improvement occurred after 1900. While the mortality data suggest a somewhat different trend in well-being from the real wage data, the estimates of movements in height, weight and body mass given in Table 11.5 present an even less optimistic picture. Recent studies by Floud *et al.* (1990) of the heights of military recruits and by Johnson and Nicholas (1995) of the heights of

Table 11.5 Trends in height, weight and body mass in England and Wales, 1840–1939

Year measured	Birth cohort	Mean height (cm)	Mean weight (kg)	BMI
(a) *Data for army recruits age 20*				
1860–4	1840–4	167.0	59.8	21.4
1876–80	1856–60	167.0		
1880–4	1860–4	165.9	60.0	21.8
1885–9	1865–9	166.5	59.6	21.5
1890–4	1870–4	167.0	59.8	21.5
1895–9	1875–9	167.6	59.7	21.3
1900–4	1880–4	167.0	58.6	21.0
1905–9	1885–9	168.1	59.5	21.0
1910–13	1890–3	168.2	59.2	20.9
(b) *Data for army recruits ages 20–4*				
1910–13	1886–92	168.4	61.1	21.5
1951–4	1927–34	172.6	63.8	21.4
1955–9	1931–9	172.7	64.8	21.7
1960–4	1936–44	173.0	65.4	21.9
(c) *Data for males ages 19–25*				
	1840–59	171.0	63.3	21.5
	1860–79	171.0	61.9	21.1
	1880–99	173.0	66.0	22.0
	1900–19	173.0	63.5	21.1
	1920–39	175.0	66.1	21.5

Sources: Height data in panel (a) are from Floud *et al.* 1990: 143–4; Rosenbaum 1988: 282. Weight data are from Rosenbaum 1988: 284. BMI calculations are by the author. Data in panel (b) are from Rosenbaum 1988: 282, 284, 293. Data for 1910–13 are for ages 21–4. Data in panel (c) are from Floud 1998: 34–6.

petty criminals have shown that the average height of the British population, after increasing at the beginning of the nineteenth century, began to decline with the birth cohort of the 1830s and continued to decline through the birth cohort of the 1850s. The estimates for army recruits in panel (a) show that those born in 1880–4 were no taller than recruits born forty years earlier. The vast majority of recruits were drawn from the working class, and most were unskilled or semi-skilled labourers (Floud *et al.* 1990: 86–111). Thus, the height data in panel (a) suggest that the nutritional status of the working class, at least during childhood, remained roughly constant throughout the second half of the nineteenth century. The data for army recruits aged 20–4 in panel (b) show that those born in 1927–39 were taller than those born in 1886–92, which suggests that workers' nutritional status improved during the interwar period.

Floud (1998) constructed the height estimates for males aged 18–25 reported in panel (c) from data obtained from a variety of published sources. The data probably include middle-class as well as working-class individuals, and might not be consistent over time (Floud 1998: 6–7). The estimates show that heights increased slightly in the last two decades of the nineteenth century, maintained this higher level in the years leading up to the First World War and then increased again during the interwar period.

The estimates of the body mass index are, if anything, more sobering. The average BMI for recruits born between 1880 and 1893 was slightly lower than that for recruits born between 1840 and 1874. The data for recruits aged 20–4 in panel (b) suggest that body mass increased only slightly during the interwar period. The data in panel (c) indicate that the mean BMI for males aged 18–25 who were born in 1880–99 was slightly higher than that of males born in 1840–59, but that body mass declined in the early twentieth century. Average BMI increased significantly in the 1940s and 1950s; its current mean value for adult British males is 24.3 (Floud 1998: 9). While it is not possible to calculate the distribution of BMI for the data in Table 11.5, if it was similar to a modern distribution of BMI, then a mean value of 21–21.5 suggests that a third of the distribution had a BMI of less than 20 (Floud 1998: 15). That is, perhaps a third of young working-class males in the first decade of the twentieth century were underweight by enough to significantly raise their risk of death.

In sum, the biological indicators do not yield consistent results regarding the trend in well-being from 1851 to 1939. Average life expectancy increased by nearly twenty years from 1851–60 to 1930–2, while height increased slightly and BMI barely increased at all. It seems reasonable to conclude that, overall, the health of the British population improved from the 1850s to the 1930s, although the extent of the improvement is overstated by simply looking at trends in life expectancy. On average people lived significantly longer in the 1930s than did their ancestors eighty years earlier, but the population still contained a significant number of 'stunted' and undernourished individuals.

Broader measures of living standards

How does the trend in health suggested by the biological indicators compare with the trend in material living standards suggested by the real wage series? Both real wages and life expectancy increased significantly from the 1850s to the 1930s. However, as in 1780–1850, longevity and income did not always move together over shorter periods. In particular, the greatest improvement in life expectancy occurred in the first decade of the twentieth century, a time when real wages grew slowly if at all. The somewhat different trends in longevity and income have troubled some historians, but they should not. Workers' command over commodities is only one of many determinants of mortality. In the twenty years before 1914, mortality rates in general, and infant mortality in particular, declined in British cities largely in response to increases in spending on sanitation and water supply (Szreter 1988, 1997). Moreover, the sharp decline in infant mortality during the interwar years was 'a result of extensions of public health services and their greater . . . utilization' by women (Winter 1979: 460).

Table 11.6 Measures of living standards for Britain and other countries, 1913

	GDP per capita ($1990)	Real wage index	Life expectancy at birth	Literacy rate (%)	HDI
Britain	5,032	100	53.4	96	0.730
Belgium	4,130	92	49.6	86	0.621
Netherlands	3,950	81	56.1	97	0.676
United States	5,307	179	51.6	92	0.733
Denmark	3,764	104	57.7	99	0.677
Germany	3,833	92	49.0	97	0.632
France	3,452	75	50.4	92	0.611
Sweden	3,096	105	57.0	98	0.628
Canada	4,213	216	52.5	94	0.682
Italy	2,507	53	47.2	62	0.441

Sources: GDP per capita: Maddison 1995; Real wage: Taylor and Williamson 1997: 36; Life expectancy, Literacy rate, HDI: Crafts 1997b: 307, 310.

If income and life expectancy measure different aspects of well-being, then both should be included in a measure of living standards. Table 11.6 presents the component parts of the human development index, as well as real wage estimates, for Britain and nine other countries in 1913. A comparison with Table 11.1 shows that from 1870 to 1913 Britain's HDI score improved from 0.496 to 0.730, as a result of significant improvements in each of the components – income per capita, longevity and education. How well off was the average person in 1913? Britain's HDI score for 1913 was higher than that for any other country in the world except the United States, Australia and New Zealand. It was about equal to that for Ireland and Austria in 1950, higher than that for Italy, Spain and Japan in 1950 and higher than that for Taiwan, South Korea and Turkey in 1973 (Crafts 1997b: 310–11).

It is possible to combine income and longevity data to calculate a measure of movements in living standards over time. Usher (1980) developed a method for adjusting the rate of growth of GDP per capita to take account of changes in mortality, and Williamson (1984) used a version of Usher's model to estimate health-augmented rates of income growth for Britain. Some share of the increase in life expectancy was endogenous; that is, it was caused by increases in income, which led workers to spend more on food and housing. In order to avoid double counting when estimating health-augmented growth rates in living standards, it is important to include only the gains in longevity due to exogenous factors, such as changes in the virulence of diseases and investments in public health. Williamson assumed that 50 per cent of the gains in longevity were due to exogenous factors. He estimated that the 'true' rate of growth in living standards – real earnings growth augmented to take account of the exogenous increase in longevity – was 1.24 per cent per year from 1851 to 1911, and 1.95 per cent per year from 1911 to 1931. For the same periods, real earnings of manual labourers increased at annual rates of

1.06 per cent and 1.44 per cent, respectively. Thus, the conventional measure of income/earnings growth underestimated the true growth in living standards for 1851–1911 by 14.5 per cent and for 1911–31 by 26.2 per cent (Willliamson 1984: 167–8).

It was noted above that full-time weekly (and thus annual) hours of work declined sharply during this period. The decline in hours meant an increase in leisure time for workers. Nordhaus and Tobin (1973) and others contend that the value of this increased leisure should be included in estimates of the rate of economic growth. Crafts (1997b) estimated leisure-augmented growth rates of GDP per capita for Britain in 1870–1913 and 1913–50. Unadjusted GDP per capita increased at an annual rate of 1.0 per cent from 1870 to 1913. Adjusting for the increase in life expectancy raised the annual rate of growth to 1.6 per cent, and further adjusting for the increase in leisure raised the annual growth rate to 1.8 per cent. For 1913–50, unadjusted GDP per capita increased at an annual rate of 0.8 per cent; when improvements in mortality and increased leisure are taken into account, the adjusted annual growth rate rose to 1.8 per cent (Crafts 1997b: 315–17).

The work by Williamson and Crafts indicates that, on average, the British population was much better off in 1913 or 1938 than it had been in 1851 or 1870. However, similar adjustments done with different indicators for health lead to less optimistic conclusions. The 'true' rate of growth in living standards from 1851 to 1931 would have been lower if income/earnings growth had been adjusted for changes in average height or BMI rather than changes in life expectancy. In sum, while almost all indices point to improvements in living standards from the Great Exhibition to the Second World War, the extent of improvement varies greatly depending on which indicators are used. There will continue to be disagreement among economic historians as to the trend in living standards until there is agreement on how best to measure well-being.

THE EXTENT OF POVERTY

The fact that, on average, material living standards improved from 1860 to 1939 tells us little about changes in well-being for the bottom 10–20 per cent of the income distribution, the very poor. In the absence of wage and unemployment data for the very poor, economic historians have tended to assume that their material living standards moved in line with those of more regularly employed unskilled workers, such as building labourers. However, William Beveridge (1909: 26) maintains that the very poor were a distinct stratum below that of unskilled labourers in regular employment, and Mary MacKinnon (1986: 299–300) contends that the incomes of the 'submerged tenth' were 'only tenuously related' to the wages of unskilled workers.

Table 11.7 Numbers receiving poor relief in England and Wales, 1850–1939

	Number on relief (000s)	Percentage on relief	Corrected number on relief (000s)	Corrected percentage on relief	Percentage relieved indoors	Able-bodied males on indoor relief (1911 = 100)	Vagrancy rate (1911 = 100)
1850	1,009	5.7	2,260	12.9	12.3		
1855	898	4.8	2,012	10.8	13.5		
1860	845	4.3	1,893	9.6	12.7	40.1	22.4
1865	951	4.6	2,130	10.2	13.1	41.1	47.6
1870	1,033	4.7	2,314	10.4	14.4	65.6	56.0
1875	801	3.4	1,794	7.6	17.3	35.7	32.8
1880	808	3.2	1,810	7.1	21.5	50.5	66.0
1885	769	2.9	1,723	6.4	23.3	51.0	45.6
1890	775	2.7	1,736	6.1	23.9	55.5	47.1
1895	797	2.7	1,785	5.9	26.0	94.8	100.5
1900	797	2.5	1,785	5.6	27.3	57.3	66.0
1905	879	2.6	1,890	5.6	30.5	100.0	105.0
1910	916	2.6	1,969	5.6	33.7	104.2	105.5
1913	784	2.2	1,686	4.7	39.1	82.1	62.6
1920	563	1.5	1,210	3.2	37.8		
1925	1,229	3.2	2,642	6.8			
1930	1,183	3.0	2,543	6.4			
1935	1,529	3.8	3,287	8.1			
1939	1,208	3.0	2,597	6.3			

Sources: Columns 1, 2 and 5 from Williams 1981: 158–61; columns 3 and 4 from Lees 1998: 180; columns 6 and 7 from Great Britain, Board of Trade 1915: 332–3; MacKinnon 1984: 118, 337, 1986: 306–7.

The major source of information on changes over time in the well-being of the very poor is the poor law. All destitute individuals were eligible for relief from their local Poor Law Union. Those granted assistance were either given cash or in-kind payments in their homes (outdoor relief) or were relieved in workhouses (indoor relief). Columns 1 and 2 of Table 11.7 report the number receiving relief and the share of the population on relief at five-year intervals from 1850 to 1939. The numbers in column 1 give the average of the number relieved on two days a year, January 1 and July 1. Studies conducted by poor law administrators in 1892 and 1906–7 indicate that the number recorded in the day counts was less than half the number assisted during the year. Columns 3 and 4 report 'corrected' estimates of annual relief recipients, assuming that the ratio of actual to counted paupers was 2.24 for 1850–1900 and 2.15 for 1905–39. The revised estimates suggest that about 10 per cent of the population was assisted by the poor law each year from 1850 to 1870. Given the temporary nature of most relief spells, over a three-year period as much as 25 per cent of the population made use of the poor law (Lees 1998: 180–2).

The percentage of the population on relief declined almost continuously from 1870 to 1913, by which time it was less than half its 1870 level. This might suggest that the share of the population living in poverty declined throughout the period. Such a conclusion is not warranted, however, because there were significant changes over time in how relief was administered and in the attitudes of the poor towards relief. The Crusade Against Outrelief ushered in a major change in relief administration in the 1870s. Poor Law Unions throughout England and Wales curtailed outdoor relief for all types of paupers, but especially for able-bodied males and the elderly (MacKinnon 1987). The effect of the Crusade can be seen in column 5 of Table 11.7. In the 1850s and 1860s, 12–15 per cent of paupers were relieved indoors; by 1880 the share relieved indoors had increased to 21.5 per cent, and it continued to rise until by 1913 nearly 40 per cent were relieved indoors. The strong deterrent effect associated with the workhouse – many of those offered indoor relief removed themselves from the relief roles – led to a sharp fall in numbers on relief. From 1870 to 1880, the number of paupers receiving outdoor relief fell by 256,000, while the number receiving indoor relief rose by only 18,000. The last third of the century also witnessed a change in the attitude of the poor towards relief. Prior to 1870, the working class regarded access to public relief as an entitlement, although they rejected the workhouse as a form of relief. However, by the end of the century most within the working class viewed poor relief as stigmatising and went to great lengths to avoid applying for relief (Lees 1998: 162–5, 294–301).

In sum, it is not possible to determine what share of the decline in numbers on relief from 1870 to 1913 was caused by a decline in poverty, and what share was caused by changes in relief administration and working-class attitudes towards relief. While the time series for the share of the population on relief reveals little about trends in poverty, the time series for able-bodied males receiving indoor relief is more informative (MacKinnon 1986, 1988). Most able-bodied male inmates of workhouses were from the bottom of the income distribution. The number of male able-bodied indoor paupers was small at all times – in 1905 they made up 3.3 per cent of all paupers – but it was responsive to economic conditions. MacKinnon (1986: 305, 330–4) contends that the rate of male able-bodied indoor pauperism is a reasonable indicator of the state of the labour market for the bottom 10 per cent of the income distribution.

Column 6 of Table 11.7 reports the trend in male able-bodied indoor paupers as a share of the male population aged 15–64. The series presents a very different picture from that of columns 2 and 4. While the overall pauperism rate declines almost continuously after the onset of the Crusade Against Outrelief, and appears to be independent of the trade cycle, the series for male able-bodied indoor pauperism follows a pattern that corresponds to the trade cycle. The long-term trend in able-bodied male pauperism remained roughly constant (except for cyclical fluctuations) from 1860 to the early 1890s, then increased sharply after 1900. There is no reason to believe that workhouse relief became more attractive for healthy able-bodied males at this time. Column 7 reports the trend in the vagrancy rate. Vagrants typically were adult males under the age of 60, many of whom were unemployed and searching for work (Crowther 1981: 252–5). Various attempts were made during the late nineteenth century to make the casual wards of workhouses more deterrent. Despite these attempts to reduce the number of vagrants, the vagrancy rate, like that for male indoor paupers, increased in the 1890s and again after 1900.

The data for male able-bodied indoor pauperism and vagrancy suggest that material living standards for the very poor improved little if at all from 1860 to the early 1890s, and then deteriorated in the first decade of the twentieth century. If a large share of military recruits were drawn from the bottom of the income distribution (Floud *et al.* 1990: 82), then the height and weight data reported in Table 11.5 give further support to the notion that living standards for the very poor stagnated in the two decades before 1914. The rising tide of late Victorian and Edwardian economic growth apparently did not raise all ships in the labour market.

Pauperism rates were especially high for the elderly. In 1906, 24.5 per cent of persons aged 70 and over in England and Wales received either indoor or outdoor relief (Williams 1981: 207). For both males and females, non-able-bodied outdoor pauperism rates declined sharply, and indoor pauperism increased, from 1860 to 1910. The increase in the number of elderly paupers accepting indoor relief was largely due to improvements in workhouse medical facilities, and should not be interpreted as evidence that living standards for the elderly were declining (MacKinnon 1988).

During the interwar period the poor law served as a residual safety net, assisting those who fell through the cracks of the recently established social insurance programmes. The number of relief recipients rose by 157 per cent from 1920 to 1922, mainly as a result of the sharp increase in unemployment. The official count of numbers relieved averaged 1,379,800 from 1922 to 1938, and peaked at 2,064,000 (5.3 per cent of the population) in 1927. A large share of those on relief were unemployed workers and their dependants, especially in 1922–6. The vast majority were given outdoor relief; from 1920 to 1923 the number of outdoor relief recipients increased by 1,100,000 while the number receiving indoor relief increased by 33,000.

The poor relief data in Table 11.7, while useful for determining the trend in living standards for the very poor, cannot be used to determine the absolute level of poverty at any point in time. For such estimates of poverty rates we need to turn to the social surveys of late Victorian, Edwardian and interwar Britain, beginning with Charles Booth's investigation of poverty in London in the late 1880s. Booth classified the population of London into four groups – very poor, poor, comfortable working class and middle and upper classes. He defined as poor those with an average weekly income of 18–21s.; those with incomes below 18s. he defined as very poor (Booth 1892: I, 33). Booth estimated that 8.4 per cent of London's population was very poor and 22.3 per cent was poor. Altogether, 1,293,000 persons, representing 30.7 per cent of the population and 37.4 per cent of the working class, were living in poverty (Booth 1892: II, 21).

Booth's pioneering work was followed by B. Seebohm Rowntree's (1901) survey of working-class York in 1899 and Arthur Bowley and A. R. Burnett-Hurst's (1915, 1920) investigations of Reading, Northampton, Warrington, Stanley and Bolton in 1912–14. Rowntree determined the 'poverty line' for families of various sizes, by calculating the income required 'to provide the minimum of food, clothing, and shelter needful for the maintenance of merely physical health'. Families whose income was below the minimum level were described as living in 'primary poverty'. He defined a second category, 'secondary poverty', as consisting of families whose income would have been above the minimum level necessary to maintain physical efficiency 'were it not that some portion of it is absorbed by other expenditure, either useful or wasteful' (Rowntree 1901: 86–7). Bowley and Burnett-Hurst defined a family to be living in poverty if its total income was 'insufficient for the maintenance of physical health' – their definition of poverty was Rowntree's definition of primary poverty. They admitted that, since few families spent their income solely for the purpose of maintaining physical health, their estimates represented the minimum number of families living in poverty in the towns they investigated (Bowley and Burnett-Hurst 1915: 36–7). P. H. Mann (1904) and Maude Davies (1909) used methods similar to Rowntree's to estimate poverty rates in the rural villages of Ridgmount, Bedfordshire, and Corsley, Wiltshire.

Table 11.8 presents estimates of poverty rates for the six English towns and two agricultural villages for which pre-war data are available. The percentage of the working class living in primary poverty varied greatly across towns, from a high of 29.0 per cent in Reading, in the south, to 6.1 per cent in Stanley, a small north-eastern mining town. While most contemporaries focused on urban poverty, the estimates for Ridgmount and Corsley suggest that rural poverty rates, at least in the south of England, were as high or higher than urban poverty rates (Freeman 2000).

A comparison of the numbers in Table 11.8 with the number of paupers shows the extent to which poor law data underestimate the level of poverty. From 1899 to 1913 the share of the population of England and Wales receiving poor relief ranged from 2.0 per cent to 2.7 per cent – or, using Lees' revised estimates, 4.4 per cent to 5.9 per cent – significantly below the poverty rates for every town or village except Stanley. In York, 3,451 persons, 4.5 per cent of the population, received poor relief in 1900 (not counting lunatics in asylums), less than half of the 7,230 persons living in primary poverty (Rowntree 1901: 112, 365–7). The significant differences between poverty rates and pauperism rates indicate that large numbers of poor people either did not apply for public assistance or had their applications turned down by local relief officials.

The authors of the social surveys tried to determine the causes of poverty. Booth concluded that nearly two-thirds of the poor were in

Table 11.8 Poverty rates and causes of poverty, 1899–1914

	York 1899	Northampton 1913	Warrington 1913	Reading 1912	Stanley 1913	Bolton 1914	Ridgmount Bedford 1903	Corsley Wiltshire 1905–6
Population	75,812	90,064	72,100	87,693	23,294	180,851	467	824
Major industry	Railways and cocoa	Boots and shoes	Various	Various	Coal mining	Cotton textiles	Agriculture	Agriculture
(a) *Percentage in poverty*								
Working-class households								
Primary poverty	12.7	8.4	12.8	23.2	6.0	7.8	38.5	17.8
Working-class population								
Primary poverty	15.5	9.3	14.7	29.0	6.1	8.0	41.0	
Secondary poverty	27.9						9.0	
Town/village population								
Primary poverty	9.9	7.2	12.2	17.5	4.8		34.3	17.5
Secondary poverty	17.9						7.1	15.5
(b) *Causes of primary poverty (%)*								
Chief wage earner:								
Dead or absent	27.5	25.0	6.0	14.0		35.0		14.3
Ill or old	10.0	14.0	1.0	11.0		17.0		25.0
Out of work	2.6	3.5	3.0	2.0		3.0		
Irregularly employed	3.5	9.0	3.0	4.0		6.0		
In full work but:								
Low wages	43.7							60.7
Second adult dependent		3.5						
Wage insufficient for 3 children								
3 children or less		16.0	22.0	33.0		20.0		
4 children or more		7.0	38.0	16.0		9.0		
Wage sufficient for 3 children but more than 3 children	12.8	22.0	27.0	20.0		10.0		

Sources: York: Rowntree 1901: 26, 111–12, 117–20; Northampton, Warrington, Reading, Stanley and Bolton: Bowley and Burnett-Hurst 1920: 237, 240; Bowley and Hogg 1925: 18, 78, 104, 128, 158; Ridgmount: Mann 1904: 177, 185; Corsley: Davies 1909: 105–7, 142–3, 147.

poverty because of employment – low wages or lack of work. The majority of these were poor because of the casual or irregular nature of their employment. About one fifth were in poverty because of circumstance – large families or sickness, and one seventh were poor because of habit – idleness, thriftlessness, or drunkenness (Booth 1892: I, 146–9).

Rowntree's classification of the causes of primary poverty was somewhat different to that of Booth; most later studies followed Rowntree's scheme. Panel (b) of Table 11.8 shows the causes of poverty in five towns and one rural village. The numbers reported are the percentages of households living in poverty due to each cause. Those for Northampton, Warrington, Reading and Bolton are from a later study by Bowley and Hogg (1925), and are slightly different from those reported by Bowley and Burnett-Hurst (1915). In all five towns the principal cause of poverty was low wages, or low wages combined with large families. In York, 43.7 per cent of households in poverty (and 52.0 per cent of persons in poverty) were poor because the household's earnings were not large enough to support a moderately sized family of four or fewer children. In 73 per cent of these households the head was a general labourer. The average weekly wage of a labourer, allowing for 'broken time', was 18–21s., while the minimum necessary weekly expenditure for a family consisting of a husband, wife and three children was 21s. 8d. (Rowntree 1901: 130–3). Unless the wife or at least one child was working, the family was living in poverty. Similarly, in 60 per cent of poor households in Warrington, and 49 per cent of poor households in Reading, the chief wage earner, although regularly employed, did not earn enough to support a family of three children. Bowley and Burnett-Hurst (1915: 41–2) concluded that a 'great part' of poverty was 'not accidental or due to exceptional misfortune, but a regular feature of the industries of the towns concerned'. The other major causes of poverty were large families and the death or illness of the chief wage earner. Each of the town surveys was undertaken at a time of low unemployment; as a result, unemployment or irregularity of work was the major cause of poverty in only 6–12.5 per cent of poor households.

The numbers in Table 11.8 show the percentage of the population living in poverty at a point in time. However, the share of the working class who experienced poverty at some point in their lives was much higher than the share in poverty at any particular time. Rowntree (1901: 136–8) maintained that a labourer's life was marked by 'alternating periods of want and comparative plenty'. A typical labourer would live in poverty at three points in his life: in childhood; in early middle age, when he had three or more children too young to work; and in old age, when he could no longer work.

Rowntree (1901: 198–221) examined the relationship between poverty and health by selecting three sections of working-class York – representing the poorest workers, a middle group and the best-paid workers – and comparing infant and child mortality, the height and weight of children and the general physical condition of children across the sections. For each measure, he found a strong negative correlation between health and poverty. From section 1 (the poorest section) 13-year-old boys were $3\frac{1}{2}$ inches shorter, and $11\frac{1}{4}$ pounds lighter than working-class boys from section 3. The physical condition of a majority of both the girls and boys from section 1 was classified as 'bad', while only 11–12 per cent of the children from section 3 were in bad physical condition. Maud Pember Reeves (1913: 193–4) also concluded that poverty led to a low standard of health from her study of poor families in Lambeth, south London. To her, 'the outstanding fact about the children was . . . their puny size and damaged health . . . whatever the exact causes are which produce in each case the sickly children so common in these households, the all-embracing one is poverty'.

Several other similar poverty surveys were undertaken during the interwar period. Table 11.9 presents estimates of poverty rates for London and the ten provincial towns covered in these surveys. All the studies except those for York and Bristol calculated poverty rates using the methodology developed by Bowley for his pre-war town surveys (Gazeley 2003). While there are minor differences in definitions, the poverty lines for these cities are reasonably comparable.

The percentage of working-class households living in poverty varied from 21.3 per cent in Southampton in 1931 to 4.0 per cent in Northampton in 1923–4. One of the major reasons for the high poverty rates in Southampton and Sheffield was that the towns were surveyed during a period of very high unemployment. Ford (1934: 118) estimated that if the Southampton survey had been done in 1928 or 1929, the poverty rate would have been 13–15 per cent, about two-thirds of its 1931 level. For York and the five towns studied by Bowley, it is possible to compare poverty rates in the interwar period with those before 1914. In each town except Stanley, poverty rates were much lower in the interwar years than they had been before the war. Bowley and Hogg (1925: 20–1) attributed the decline in poverty mainly to an increase in the wage rates of low-skilled workers and a decline in family size. Similarly, Rowntree (1941: 454) attributed the fall in poverty to a reduction in the size of families, a 35 per cent increase in real wages and 'the remarkable growth of social services' from 1899 to 1936.

Rowntree calculated two distinct poverty lines for York in 1936. One of these represented 'a standard of bare subsistence', and was comparable to his 1899 poverty line. This yielded the poverty rate of 6.5 per cent given in Table 11.9. The second and more generous poverty line, which he referred to as a 'human needs standard', represented the income necessary to secure 'a healthy life'. For a family consisting of a husband, wife and three children, the poverty line under the first standard was 30s. 7d. per week in 1936; under the second standard it was 43s. 6d. When the 'human needs'

Table 11.9 Poverty rates and causes of poverty, 1923–37

	Northampton 1923–4	Warrington 1923–4	Reading 1923–4	Stanley 1923–4	Bolton 1923–4	London 1929–30	Merseyside 1929–30	Southampton 1931	Sheffield 1931–2	York 1936	Bristol 1937
(a) *Percentage in poverty*											
Working-class households	4.0	7.9	11.3	7.5	4.9	9.8	16.1	21.3	15.4	6.5	10.7
Working-class population	4.2	7.9	11.9	7.2	4.3	9.1	16.0	21.5	17.1	6.8	11.8
All households[a]	2.8	6.6	7.9	7.0	3.7	7.1	10.9	15.0	12.6	4.0	7.8
Working-class households[b] (Rowntree's 'human needs' standard)	8.6	17.2	24.2	16.1	10.7	22.2	37.1	42.9		31.1	10.7
(b) *Causes of poverty (%)*											
Chief wage earner											
Dead or absent	21.9	11.8	27.2	38.3	13.6	24.5	13.6[c]	2.8	10.0	9.0	13.3
Ill or old	21.9	9.2	16.3	14.9	34.1	8.5		14.6	18.2	23.5	24.2
On strike	3.1	7.9	3.3								
Out of work	18.8	30.3	19.6	14.9	38.6	48.0	39.9	63.8	66.6	44.5	32.0
Irregularly employed	25.0	10.5	5.4		4.5		23.3	2.3		5.9	
Self-employment or hawking											6.5
In full work but:											
Low Wages									5.2	9.2	
Second adult dependent		3.9	2.2					4.7			0.2
Wage insufficient for 3 children											
3 children or less		3.9	7.6	2.1	4.5	5.25		4.7			8.1
4 children or more	3.1	6.6	2.2			2.25		4.7			9.0
Wage sufficient for 3 children but more than 3 children	6.3	14.5	12.0	29.8	4.5	11.5		2.3		8.0	4.0
Other members unemployed		1.3	4.3								
Other											2.7

[a] The estimates for the percentage of all households in poverty are from Hatton and Bailey 1998: 376.
[b] Rowntree's 'human needs' poverty line is much more generous than his 1899 'bare subsistence' poverty line. The sources for the poverty rates obtained using the human needs standard are as follows: York: Rowntree 1941: 11, 34–6; London: Hatton and Bailey 1998: 584–5; Northampton, Warrington, Reading, Stanley, Bolton, Merseyside, Southampton: Linsley and Linsley 1993: 103. Tout's 1938: 25 estimate for Bristol is based on a poverty line similar to that constructed by Rowntree.
[c] The data on causes of poverty in Merseyside do not sum to 100 per cent.

Sources: Northampton, Warrington, Reading, Stanley, Bolton: Bowley and Hogg 1925: 17–18, 78, 104, 128, 158, 197; London: Smith 1930–5: III: 87–8, 108; Merseyside: Jones 1934: 164, 166, 174; Southampton: Ford 1934: 119, 129; Sheffield: Owen 1933: 24, 28; York: Rowntree 1941: 108, 110; Bristol: Tout 1938: 25, 37, 44, 46.

poverty line was used, Rowntree found that 31.1 per cent of working-class households in York were living in poverty in 1936 (Rowntree 1941: 28–32, 102). Hatton and Bailey (1998) applied the human needs scale to London in 1929–30, and obtained a poverty rate of 22.2 per cent. The estimates for York and London, along with rough estimates of the 'human needs' poverty rate for other cities calculated by Linsley and Linsley (1993: 102–3) are given in row 4 of Table 11.9. Under the more generous standard, the poverty rate ranges from 42.9 per cent in Southampton to 8.6 per cent in Northampton.

Panel (b) gives the causes of poverty in each town. A comparison of Tables 11.8 and 11.9 shows that the principal causes of poverty in the interwar years were significantly different from those found by the pre-war surveys. Before 1914, the major causes of poverty were low wages, large families and the death or illness of the chief wage earner. The increase in wage rates and the decline in family size during and after the war greatly reduced the importance of these factors as causes of poverty. Bowley and Hogg (1925) found that, in four of the five towns they surveyed, unemployment or underemployment (short time), the death or illness of the chief wage earner and old age were the principal causes of poverty. Unemployment was the main cause of poverty in each of the towns surveyed after 1928; in Merseyside, Southampton, Sheffield and York, a majority of the households in poverty were poor because the chief wage earner was unemployed or underemployed. The other major causes of poverty were the death or illness of the chief wage earner and old age – these factors accounted for about a third of the households in poverty in London, York and Bristol. As we will see below, the number of households living in poverty because of unemployment, sickness or old age would have been even higher were it not for the interwar social security system.

FRIENDLY SOCIETIES, TRADE UNIONS AND SELF-HELP

The high rates of poverty revealed by the social surveys indicate that, despite the improvements in material living standards from 1860 to 1939, a large proportion of manual workers experienced economic difficulties at some point in their lives (Johnson 1985: 3). Workers' lives were dominated by insecurity – as Hobsbawm (1975: 221) put it: 'the worker was rarely more than a hair's breadth removed from the pauper'. How did workers cope with this uncertainty? Those who could afford to opened savings accounts and insured themselves against income loss by joining friendly societies and trade unions that offered insurance benefits. Those who could not save, or whose income loss was prolonged enough to exhaust savings or insurance benefits, were forced to turn to friends and neighbours, public relief or private charity for assistance.

Mid-Victorian Britain saw the rise of an ethic of respectability and self-help, preached by middle-class reformers such as Samuel Smiles, and widely accepted by the working class. Smiles (1886: 325–6) argued that workers should set aside money to provide for 'want of employment, sickness, and death', and in the years after 1851 they began to do just that. In particular, there was a sharp increase in the membership of friendly societies – mutual help associations providing sickness and death benefits. There were two main types of friendly society: ordinary societies, typically small, local organisations, some of which offered only burial insurance; and affiliated societies, large regional or national organisations, with individual branches. The two largest affiliated societies, the Independent Order of Oddfellows, Manchester Unity, and the Ancient Order of Foresters, had between them 506,000 members in 1861 and 1,012,000 members in 1881 (Gosden 1961: 30, 38; Johnson 1985: 50). In 1901, there were 5.47 million members of ordinary and affiliated friendly societies in England and Wales, which was 54.5 per cent of adult males; in 1931, membership totalled 8.38 million, nearly 60 per cent of adult males. Not all members were eligible for sickness benefits. In 1901 about 4.14 million persons belonged to friendly societies providing sickness insurance. The number of workers buying sickness insurance grew more slowly after 1901 than did total friendly society membership, so that the share of adult males eligible for sickness benefits declined from 41.2 per cent in 1901 to 32.2 per cent in 1931 (Johnson 1985: 57).

The occupational makeup of friendly societies has been a source of debate. Most contemporaries and historians concluded that friendly societies were dominated by skilled workers, largely because few labourers could afford the premiums (Johnson 1985: 57–63). However, Riley (1997: 31–4) contends that the records of individual clubs show that many poorly paid workers joined friendly societies. Affiliated societies typically offered more benefits, and charged higher premiums, than did ordinary societies, and it is possible that lower-paid workers were more likely to join ordinary societies, some of which were little more than burial clubs. One point on which historians agree is that the urban poor could not afford to join friendly societies paying sickness benefits (Gilbert 1966: 166–7).

The average weekly sickness benefit paid by friendly societies was 8s. in the 1860s and 1870s, rising to 10s. in 1880 and 12s. by 1900; the average benefit remained at 12s. until the 1920s, and perhaps throughout the interwar period (Riley 1997: 280–1). Sickness benefits were reduced during prolonged illnesses, usually to half benefits after six months, and to quarter benefits after a year. Members were also entitled to death benefits to cover their funeral expenses, and sometimes smaller benefits upon the death of a wife or child. Most societies also contracted with doctors to provide medical services to members at reduced fees, and many of the affiliated societies provided quarter benefits to elderly members unable to work. In return for these benefits, workers paid weekly premiums of 4–8d., which came to £0.87–1.73 per year. Rowntree's subsistence calculations suggest that benefit payments were about high enough to feed a moderate sized family in 1900, but not high enough also to pay for rent, fuel, clothing and sundries. They had to be supplemented 'by the earnings of wife and children, by private saving, by assistance from fellow-workmen and neighbours, by running into debt, by pawning and in other ways' (Beveridge 1909: 225).

The provision of mutual insurance policies by trade unions spread rapidly in the third quarter of the nineteenth century. A strong emphasis on mutual insurance was one of the characteristics of the 'New Model' unionism, which began in 1851 with the formation of the Amalgamated Society of Engineers, and by 1870 included craft unions in several trades. The rapid union growth after 1870 was accompanied by a spread of insurance benefits to a broader range of occupations. Unions provided their members with insurance against unemployment, sickness and accidents, pensions for retired members and death benefits to ensure workers and their wives a proper funeral. In 1908, 1.47 million members (70 per cent of male union members, 14 per cent of manual workers) were eligible for unemployment benefits, and 729,000 for sickness benefits (Boyer 1988: 320). Many unions continued to provide insurance benefits during the interwar period despite the institution of government-provided welfare policies (Johnson 1985: 76–80).

The availability of mutual insurance benefits differed markedly across occupations. They were widespread in metals, engineering, shipbuilding and the building trades, where most unions provided unemployment, sickness, accident, old age and funeral benefits. Most mining and textile unions provided funeral benefits, and several provided unemployment benefits under certain conditions (when a mine or factory was shut down), but few provided sickness or old age benefits. Unions of low-skilled workers typically provided funeral and accident benefits only (Boyer 1988).

Benefit levels were, on average, similar to those offered by friendly societies. In 1892, the Amalgamated Engineers paid an unemployed member 10s. per week for the first fourteen weeks of unemployment, then 7s. for the next thirty weeks, and 6s. for another sixty weeks. A sick worker received 10s. per week for twenty-six weeks, then 5s. per week until recovery. The benefits replaced at most a third of members' lost wages, and they declined as the duration of time out of work increased. Benefits grew slowly if at all from 1892 to 1908, when the typical unemployment or sickness benefit was 10s. per week. Union members received these benefits for a weekly contribution of 9d.–1s. 3d., with the typical premium being 1s., double the usual friendly society premium. The high cost is a major reason why most unions of low-skilled workers did not offer unemployment, sickness or old age benefits, although a few had optional sickness funds.

Parliament attempted to encourage working-class saving with the establishment of Trustee Savings Banks in 1817, but as late as 1864 William Gladstone estimated that fewer than one in ten working-class households 'had any deposits in a savings bank' (Fishlow 1961: 36). Private savings increased after 1860, with the establishment of the Post Office Savings Bank (POSB). In 1870 there were over 2.5 million depositors in the POSB and in Trustee Savings Banks. The number of depositors increased to 11 million in 1913 and 14 million in 1939. In 1899, 83 per cent of all POSB accounts had balances of less than £25; the median balance of these accounts was under £4. In 1929, 75 per cent of accounts had balances under £25 (Johnson 1985: 89–102). The typical manual worker had very few savings, and most unskilled workers were unable to save at all.

In sum, a large proportion of skilled and semi-skilled manual workers belonged to friendly societies or to trade unions that offered mutual insurance benefits. These workers were afforded some protection against income loss when sick or unemployed, although the benefits needed to be combined with other sources of income and savings. The situation was very different for unskilled workers, few of whom were members of friendly societies paying sickness benefits or of unions providing anything more than funeral benefits. In times of distress, large numbers of low-skilled workers continued to apply for public or private assistance.

GOVERNMENT SOCIAL POLICY

The middle years of the nineteenth century have been called 'the age of laissez-faire', and governmental attempts to improve working-class living standards were sporadic at best in the third quarter of the century. The Crusade Against Outrelief of the 1870s led to a decline in public assistance, which reduced the well-being of some proportion of the very poor, especially the elderly and widows with children (Thomson 1984; MacKinnon 1987). However, the 1870s was also a period of increased government intervention in public health, housing and the labour market. While the governments of the 1880s and 1890s did little to extend social policy, there was an explosion of social welfare legislation in the decade before the First World War.

Public health and urban housing

The rapid and unplanned growth of cities in the nineteenth century created serious health problems for the urban working class. Parliament responded to the lack of sanitation, impure water and overcrowding in cities with the Public Health Act of 1848, which empowered local authorities to establish boards of health to manage sewer and drainage systems and water supplies. However, many cities made little investment in public health before the late 1860s, largely because of the enormous expense of constructing sewer and water systems, and the determination of shopkeepers, landlords and other small tradesmen to keep their regressive property taxes as low as possible (Hennock 1963, 1973; Briggs 1963). The Reform Act of 1867 and the Municipal Franchise Act of 1869, which extended voting rights to most urban working-class males, reduced the political power of the 'shopocracy' and increased the power of those most likely to benefit from investments in public health. In addition, after 1870 cities began to acquire new sources of revenue, such as gas works and tramways, which enabled them to fund projects without significantly raising taxes. The availability of loans, and after 1888 grants, from the central government also helped to finance investment. As a result, there was a sharp increase in urban public health expenditures after 1870, which led to a reduction in death rates due to cholera, typhus, typhoid and infant diarrhoea, and improved the quality of life of the working class (Szreter 1997: 709–12; Hennock 1963).

Parliament attempted to deal with the problems of overcrowding and slums in 1875 through the Artisans' and Labourers' Dwellings Act, which empowered local officials to take over areas of unsanitary housing, demolish slum property and then sell the land to developers willing to build new working-class housing. The law proved to be expensive and ineffective, and in the short run probably reduced the housing stock in many cities – much of the land cleared of slums remained vacant for years (Jones 1971: 199–203). In 1890 parliament adopted the Housing of the Working Classes Act, which enabled local authorities to use tax revenue to construct working-class housing. However, outside London there was little construction of public housing, and many cities still had serious shortages of working-class housing in 1914.

Labour market policies

Parliament adopted a variety of acts regulating the employment of women and children in the second half of the nineteenth century. The Factory Extension Act of 1867 extended government regulation of child labour to factories employing over fifty workers in a number of trades, including metalworking, printing, paper, tobacco and glassworks. In the same year parliament passed the Hours of Labour (Workshops) Regulation Act, which regulated the labour of children, young people and women in establishments with fewer than fifty workers. The Factory Act of 1874 set a ten-hour workday for women and young persons, and effectively established a ten-hour day for adult males. The Workmen's Compensation Act of 1897 made employers liable for workplace injuries to their employees. In 1906 the act was extended to cover certain occupational diseases.

The decline of outdoor relief after 1870 did not signal the end of local government involvement in assisting unemployed males. In 1886 the Local Government Board issued the Chamberlain Circular, which encouraged cities to set up temporary work relief projects when unemployment was high. The work provided was outside the poor law and did not involve 'the stigma of pauperism'. The forms of work relief included road repairing, road sweeping, sewerage work, snow removal and planting trees. Those employed were paid below market wages and typically given only two or three days work per week (Harris 1972: 75–8; Boyer forthcoming). The 1905 Unemployed Workman Act established in all large cities distress committees to provide temporary employment to 'deserving' applicants who were temporarily unemployed because of a 'dislocation of trade', although most applicants for relief were general or casual labourers (Beveridge 1909: 154–91; Harris 1972: 157–210).

Liberal welfare reforms

Between 1906 and 1914 parliament passed several pieces of social welfare legislation which collectively are known as the Liberal welfare reforms (Hay 1975). The first of the welfare reforms concerned the health of children, and was in response to the poor physical state of army recruits during the Boer War and the subsequent recommendations of the 1904 Report of the Interdepartmental Committee on Physical Deterioration. The 1906 Education (Provision of Meals) Act allowed local authorities to use tax revenue to provide free school meals for needy children. This was followed a year later by the Education (Administrative Provisions) Act, which implemented school medical inspections; beginning in 1912 government grants were provided for medical treatment of children.

Parliament attacked the problem of poverty among the elderly with the 1908 Old Age Pension Act, which granted weekly pensions of 5s. to persons aged 70 and over whose annual income was less than £21, and smaller pensions to those with slightly higher incomes. The pensions were non-contributory, and were paid through the Post Office. The number of elderly persons who qualified for pensions in 1909–13 was far greater than the number receiving poor relief in 1906. The moral stigma of the poor law apparently kept thousands of poor elderly persons from applying for relief (Thane 2000: 226–8).

The keystone of the Liberal welfare reforms was the National Insurance Act of 1911, Part I of which established a system of compulsory health insurance covering all manual workers. The system was contributory – workers paid 4d. per week, their employers 3d. and the state 2d. In return, an insured man received 10s. per week when sick (a woman 7.5s.), payable from the fourth day of illness, for up to thirteen weeks. Thereafter, weekly benefits for both men and women were 5s. Insured workers also received free medical treatment from a doctor, although their dependants did not. Part II of the act established compulsory unemployment insurance (UI) in a limited number of industries – building, construction of works, shipbuilding, mechanical engineering, ironfounding, construction of vehicles and sawmilling. A total of $2\frac{1}{4}$ million workers were covered – about 20 per cent of employed males. Workers and their employers each contributed $2\frac{1}{2}$d. per week to the UI fund, and the state contributed $1\frac{2}{3}$d. Unemployed workers received a weekly benefit of 7s. for a maximum of fifteen weeks in any twelve-month period.

In 1909 parliament responded to the low wages paid in 'sweated industries' by adopting the Trade Boards Act, which established boards to set minimum hourly wages in four trades – ready-made and wholesale bespoke tailoring, paper box making, chain making and machine lace-finishing. Each of the trades contained both men and women, but far more women than men earned wages below the minimum. Available evidence suggests that the boards significantly raised wages for low-paid workers (Tawney 1915; Sells 1923; Hatton 1997). In 1913 boards were set up in five additional trades: sugar confectionery and food preserving, shirt making, hollow ware making, tin box making and linen and cotton embroidery.

Interwar welfare reforms

The 1918 Trade Boards Act empowered the minister of labour to establish boards in trades where 'no adequate machinery exists for the effective regulation of wages'. By December 1922, forty-four trade boards were in place. Few additional boards were established thereafter; in 1937 there were forty-seven boards in operation, covering 1.14 million workers, 73 per cent of whom were women (Sells 1939: 366; Hatton 1997). Minimum wage rates for agricultural labourers were established in 1924 by the Agricultural Wages (Regulation) Act (Gowers and Hatton 1997).

The Unemployment Insurance Act of 1920 extended compulsory unemployment insurance to virtually all workers except the self-employed and those in agriculture or domestic service; a separate insurance scheme for agricultural workers was established in 1936. The generosity and maximum duration of benefits were raised at various points during the 1920s. In 1931, the weekly benefit for an unemployed man with a wife and two children was 30s.; the maximum duration of benefits was twenty-six weeks. The Unemployment Act of 1934 established the Unemployment Assistance Board to provide for those among the unemployed who were outside the unemployment insurance system or who had exhausted their benefits.

The 1925 Widows', Orphans' and Old Age Contributory Pensions Act provided insured workers and their wives with a weekly pension of 10s. after age 65; the act also established benefits for widows and children under age 14. Housing Acts of 1919, 1923 and 1924 provided subsidies for the construction of low-cost housing. From 1919 to 1939, about 4 million new houses were built, 39 per cent either by local authorities or with the aid of state subsidies (Burnett 1986: 226–49).

What effect did the interwar social security system have on poverty rates? Using records from the 1929–30 London survey, Hatton and Bailey (1998) examined the importance of social security by deducting from household income all state benefits and then recalculating the poverty rate. They concluded that, under the 'bare subsistence' standard used by Bowley and Llewellyn Smith, the poverty rate would have been 17.2 per cent in the absence of social security benefits; under Rowntree's 'human needs' standard, it would have been 25.6 per cent. The elderly benefited the most from the social security system; without it, half of those 65 and older would have had incomes below the bare subsistence level. Moreover, while social security reduced the poverty rate by a relatively small amount, it greatly reduced the intensity of poverty. The average income deficit of those in poverty was 21 per cent of minimum needs (using the bare subsistence scale); without social security, the average deficit would have been 60 per cent of minimum needs (Hatton and Bailey 1998: 586–90). The importance of social security in alleviating poverty was also noted by Rowntree (1941: 117), who found that two-thirds of the income of families in 'primary poverty' came from social benefits, and by Ford (1934: 132–3), who estimated that 76 per cent of families living in poverty received at least half of their income from social services.

Overall, social transfer spending in Britain – welfare and unemployment compensation, and pension, health and housing subsidies – increased from 0.86 per cent of national product in 1880 to 1.39 per cent in 1910, and 2.61 per cent in 1930. How did Britain's level of transfer spending compare with that of other countries? In 1880 Britain ranked third in the percentage of income devoted to social spending, behind Norway and Denmark; in 1910 Britain was second, behind only Denmark. Despite a sharp increase in social spending during the interwar period, by 1930 Britain ranked fifth in percentage of income devoted to social spending, behind Germany, Ireland, Denmark and Finland (Lindert 1994).

CONCLUSION

On average, British workers in the 1930s had significantly higher living standards than their grandfathers had experienced in the 1860s. Their spending power was much greater – from 1860 to 1938 real wages for manual workers increased by 158 per cent (Feinstein 1995a: 263–5). Workers spent some of their larger incomes on a more varied diet, in part because food prices declined faster than the overall cost of living (Feinstein 1991b: 170–1). Per capita consumption of meat and bacon, fresh milk, butter, tea and sugar increased greatly from 1860 to 1934–8 (Mackenzie 1921: 224; Mitchell 1988: 713). Some of workers' higher incomes was spent on better housing. The share of the population living in overcrowded conditions – defined as more than two adults per room, with children aged 1 to 9 counting as half an adult – was 11.2 per cent in 1891; it fell to 7.8 per cent in 1911 and to 6.9 per cent in 1931, although in some north-eastern towns it was 25 per cent or higher (Carr-Saunders and Jones 1937: 16; Burnett 1986: 144–5). The reduction in overcrowding was to some extent a result of workers moving from the centre of cities to suburbs. London working-class suburbs developed in the 1880s and 1890s, helped by the passage of the Cheap Trains Act in 1883. From 1901 to 1911, the population of the county of London fell by 14,000, while the population of London's 'outer ring' increased by nearly 700,000 (Coppock 1976: 373; Hall 1976: 436–45). The cities were healthier places to live than they had been in the early nineteenth century, partly because of better housing for workers and partly because of sharp increases in public health expenditures after 1870 (Millward and Bell 1998).

Bowley's study of five English towns in 1912–14 and 1923–4 found that, on average, 11 per cent of urban working-class households were living in poverty in 1912–14, and 6.5 per cent were in poverty in 1923–4 (Bowley and Hogg 1925: 16–17). While some contemporaries and historians have found the numbers for 1912–14 to be surprisingly high, they are lower than urban poverty rates in Britain in 1850 or poverty rates in most, if not all, European countries in 1913. Using methods similar to those used by Rowntree and Bowley, Anderson (1971: 30–2) estimated that 20 per cent of working-class families in Preston in 1851 were living in poverty, and Foster (1974: 95–9) estimated that 20–33 per cent of working-class families in Oldham, Northampton and South Shields were living in poverty in 1849. Similar calculations have not been done for other European countries, but one can get some idea of the extent of poverty, relative to that in Britain, by comparing real wages of unskilled labourers across countries. Throughout the period 1860–1913 real wages were higher in Britain than in other European countries, which suggests that British poverty rates were lower than poverty rates elsewhere in Europe (Williamson 1995: 178–80).

As a result of the adoption of national old age pensions, sickness and unemployment insurance and other social welfare policies, workers in the interwar period had a much better social safety net than had workers in the 1860s. The extension of the Factory Acts and the Trade Boards Act offered more protection to children, women and some males in the labour market, and the reductions in the average work week gave workers more leisure time. The insecurity of work did not diminish much, but, on the whole, the growth of the private economy and government social policy from 1870 to 1938 improved the well-being of the working class.

12 The British economy between the wars

BARRY EICHENGREEN

Contents

INTRODUCTION

The 1920s and 1930s were years of transition, most obviously between the First and Second World Wars. But they were also years of transition between the long nineteenth century, when Britain was the world's leading creditor nation, its leading trading nation and the producer of a third of the world's manufactured exports, and the years after 1945, when the country was overtaken in terms of per capita incomes, productivity and growth rates by many of its European competitors. The story of the interwar period is thus the story of how this transformation came about. It is the story of Britain's loss of economic pre-eminence.

The interwar years were troubled not just for Britain, of course, but for the entire world. Growth slowed in virtually every industrial country. Growth was also slower everywhere than the post-Second World War norm. The 1920s were dominated by political disputes and inflations that disrupted economic growth throughout Europe, the 1930s by a business cycle downturn of exceptional depth and duration, a downturn that came to be known as the slump in Britain and the great depression in the United States. All market economies were affected. Thus, any critique of Britain's economic performance in this period is more compelling if it

Table 12.1 Output per worker, 1913–50 (normalised to 100 in 1913)

										Memo Item		
	Belgium	Denmark	France	Germany	Italy	Holland	Norway	Sweden	Switzerland	UK	Canada	US
1913	100	100	100	100	100	100	100	100	100	100	100	100
1929	199	116	137	96	126	130	141	102	147	122	112	147
1938	124	119	126	122	145	125	159	128	156	144	104	136
1950	150	146	146	124	153	134	191	171	175	159	167	177

Source: Maddison 1995: Tables 2–7(a).

can be shown that the country performed poorly not just in an absolute sense or in comparison with the golden age of growth after the Second World War, but also relative to other advanced industrial economies.

Evidence on this question does not speak clearly. Table 12.1 presents the growth of output per worker, a simple measure of labour productivity, between 1913 and 1950 – what some authors have called 'the trans-war period'. Starting in 1913 rather than in 1920 avoids biasing the comparison in Britain's favour, since other countries suffered more severe disruptions during the Great War and their recoveries were initiated later, allowing them to grow more quickly in so far as they began at a lower starting point (Aldcroft 1970). Considering 1950 rather than 1945 similarly avoids biasing the comparison in Britain's favour, since France, Belgium and Germany all suffered relatively severe disruptions in the immediate aftermath of the Second World War. It means that we are comparing output per worker roughly at the time of two cyclical peaks.[1] In the resulting table, Britain does not stand out. Output per worker rose over this period by 59 per cent. The United States and Canada did better (output per worker in these two countries rose by 77 per cent and 67 per cent), but these were the countries where the destruction of the two wars was least. Similar explanations apply in the cases of Norway, Sweden and Switzerland, three other countries that outperformed Britain as measured here. But – surprisingly, given the pessimistic interpretation of Britain's economic performance that is so pervasive in the literature – output per worker rose over these thirty-seven years faster than in Belgium, Denmark, France, Germany, Italy and the Netherlands. This fact is more striking still in so far as the dates bracketing these estimates bias the comparison against Britain.[2]

[1] Although whether the peaks in question occurred in 1913 or 1914 and in 1950 or 1951 depends on the country concerned.

[2] Alternative measures are somewhat less favourable to the country. When we consider GNP per worker hour rather than per worker, Italy creeps ahead of the UK. When we consider GNP per person, France and Denmark also surpass the UK as a consequence of their relatively low population growth rates. But Table 12.1 makes the essential point.

If 1913–50 was a turning point, then, it was not because this was when the British economy began dramatically to underperform its continental European and North American rivals. Rather, these years were a turning point in the sense that this was when the institutions and policies that conditioned economic performance after the Second World War were put in place, or at least when their seeds were sown. Some of those changes, like the adoption of more flexible and stabilising monetary and fiscal policies, had favourable effects on the business cycle and therefore, indirectly, on growth. Others, however, limited competition, stifled technical progress and slowed structural change, creating problems that came home to roost after the Second World War. At the centre of any account of British economic history between the wars, therefore, is the story of how these changes came about.

LOOKING CLOSER

Before considering that history in more detail, it is worth taking a closer look at our summary measures of economic performance. To this end, Table 12.1 also presents data for the period from 1913 through 1938, which removes growth during the Second World War, and distinguishes the periods before and after 1929.[3] Evidently, Britain did better during the First and Second World Wars than the European continent, which served as the main theatre for hostilities. Its performance compares less favourably with Europe's in the 1920s, when it persistently lagged its continental rivals, than in the 1930s, when it closed much of the gap that had opened up in that earlier decade. Figure 12.1 suggests a number of other respects in which Britain's growth record was distinctive – for example, the severity of the post-First World War recession and the relatively mild nature of Britain's post-1929 slump. These variations in turn provide pointers to the policies and factors that rendered the economy's performance distinctive.

The growth of output per worker can be decomposed into that part due to the growth of inputs per worker (effectively, the growth of the capital/labour ratio) and that part due to the growth of labour productivity (the share of output growth that cannot be accounted for by the deepening of the capital stock). Table 12.2 shows that the rate of growth of net non-residential capital per employed person was above the arithmetic average for the four other countries in the comparison group.[4] This may seem surprising in so far as Britain was hardly a high-investment economy in the 1920s and 1930s – to the contrary, the failure to sustain a higher investment rate is frequently cited as one of its shortcomings.

[3] Conveniently, 1929 and 1938 are also cyclical peaks.
[4] These are the four countries for which consistent figures are available.

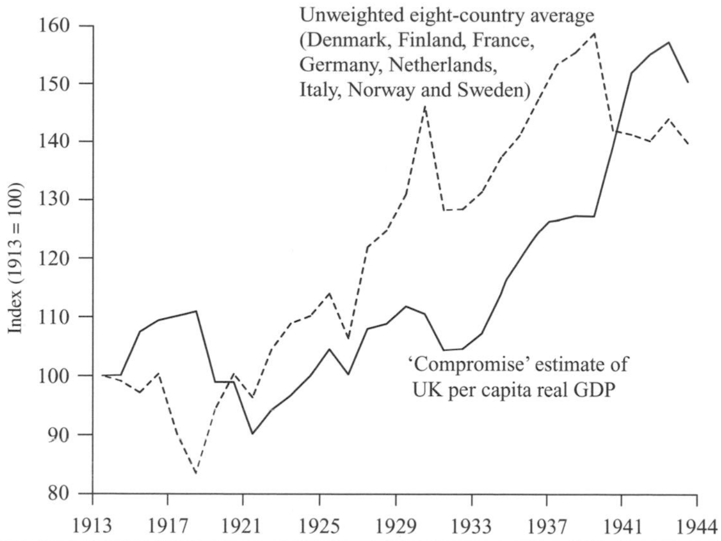

Figure 12.1 Per capita GDP for eight European countries and the UK, 1913–44

Note: 1913 = 100
Sources: Maddison 1982; Mitchell 1988.

But the two world wars were less disruptive in Britain than on the continent, and the depression of the 1930s was shorter and milder. It follows that over the long period considered in Table 12.2 the per worker non-residential capital stock grew faster than in these other countries. But since there was no guarantee that Britain would again display respectable rates of capital formation in the future – and, in fact, a relatively low investment rate turned out to be a chronic problem after the Second World War – respectable growth rates sustained by better-than-average investment rates are hardly reassuring, especially in so far as the latter reflected not the intrinsic strengths of the British economy but rather the greater disruptiveness of the two wars on the continent and the gravity of other countries' macroeconomic blunders.

The other side of this coin is the rate of total factor productivity (TFP) growth. Since we already know that overall growth in Britain was unexceptional but the contribution of factor accumulation was above average, we therefore also know that the contribution of TFP growth must have been below average. The second column of Table 12.2 shows the relevant estimates, obtained by subtracting from output growth the contribution not just of the accumulation of non-residential capital but also the contributions of additional residential capital and of the growth of the labour force. The results reveal that the growth of TFP was scarcely half the arithmetic average for the other

Table 12.2 Annual average rate of growth of net non-residential capital stock per person employed and total factor productivity, 1913–50

	Non-residential capital	Productivity
France	1.18	0.67
Germany	0.51	0.28
Netherlands	0.88	0.34
US	0.42	1.26
UK	1.04	0.35
Average excluding UK	0.75	0.64

Source: Derived from Maddison 1991.

countries. Clearly, that shortfall is heavily driven by the exceptional productivity performance of the United States, the country that pioneered the methods of modern mass-production in this period. But British industry's failure to emulate the US example is disturbing. TFP growth, and factors like the organisation of production that enter into its determination, are the products of deeply embedded socio-economic structures that develop slowly over time and are resistant to change. This implies that lagging productivity growth was likely to remain a problem after the Second World War.

Statistics like these, while helpful for sketching the outlines of Britain's economic performance between the wars and pointing to their proximate determinants, do not identify its underlying sources. For these we must consider the history.

THE IMPACT OF THE FIRST WORLD WAR ON THE BRITISH ECONOMY

On the eve of the First World War, Great Britain was the world's leading trading and lending nation. Her merchandise imports and exports were nearly a third larger than Germany's and half again as large as those of the United States. More international trade was invoiced in sterling than in any other currency. Foreign producers and merchants held bank deposits in London to settle their accounts with British importers and exporters and with one another. London's financial district, the City, was the world's leading financial centre. Half of all the foreign currency reserves of central banks and governments was held in the form of bank deposits and other assets denominated in sterling (Lindert 1969). Britain's stock of overseas investments, valued at as much as £4 billion in 1914, far exceeded that of other nations and loomed large even relative to the country's formidable gross domestic product (GDP) (£2.3 billion).

Given the country's dependence on international transactions, it is not surprising that the British economy was shaken by World War I. The decline of trade relative to gross national product (GNP) implied profound changes for an economy that had exported a third of national product (re-exports included). Declining trade reflected import controls on the continent and domestic measures designed to redeploy productive capacity to other uses, but it also reflected the special costs and risks of oceanic shipping in a hostile environment. At the same time, the demand for imports in South America and South Asia did not evaporate. As Britain withdrew from these markets, the United States and Japan moved to fill the void. US exports to Latin America rose by more than 75 per cent in 1916, while Japan, building on her expertise in silk production and trade, expanded textile exports to India, China, the United States and even Britain itself (Clavin 2000: 10). This 'beachhead effect' was not easily reversed; following the conclusion of hostilities, British producers found themselves face to face with new competitors.

Another legacy of the war was the impact on Britain's international financial position. Though war debts were less of a burden for Britain than for its European Allies (the government having lent on to France and the other Allied powers much of the money it borrowed from the United States), private debts were another matter. A considerable portion of Britain's wartime trade deficit was financed by selling off the foreign securities of British citizens, which the government had requisitioned. Morgan (1952) estimates that perhaps a tenth of British foreign assets was liquidated. This implied roughly a 10 per cent decline in interest income from abroad following the war, requiring a corresponding improvement in the balance of trade (in the absence of other changes in international payments). Given the intensification of American and Japanese competition, this shift proved difficult to achieve.

Compared to the far-reaching nature of these developments, the impact on the gold standard, the institution symbolising the country's commitment to the international economy, was limited, or so it appeared. Britain was not forced to suspend gold convertibility during the war (although suspension did take place in 1919, requiring years of hard work to restore convertibility at the pre-war parity, a task that was finally completed in 1925). With the declaration of war, the exchange rate actually strengthened, as British investors repatriated funds held abroad. But once shipping tonnage was diverted to military uses and U-boat warfare intensified, exports of manufactures fell off, while imports of grain and war matériel from North America rose dramatically. By 1915 sterling had begun to fall against the dollar. But even then the authorities were able to peg the currency at a 10 per cent discount against the dollar, using a combination of moral suasion and intervention in the foreign exchange market (financed by a loan from the United States). There sterling remained for the duration of hostilities.

That sterling could be held fairly stable against the dollar even in these exceptional circumstances encouraged the belief that the pre-war parity (the pre-war sterling price of gold, and by implication the exchange rate against the dollar) could be restored quickly following the war and that the British economy would have little difficulty in adjusting to the policy. But, as events were to reveal, the wartime stability of the sterling–dollar rate had more to do with US financial support and with restrictions, both formal and informal, on the ability of individuals to engage in foreign exchange market transactions than with any intrinsic compatibility of the gold standard with changed economic conditions.

As the battle against Germany widened, the War Office contracted for a growing share of imported supplies, to the point where it controlled 90 per cent of British imports at the end of the war. This expansion of direct government purchases of imported goods may have been temporary (trade was quickly restored to private hands following the war's conclusion), but the expansion of direct government involvement was not. A case in point is the McKenna Duties, import taxes imposed in 1915 on luxury items such as cars, clocks and musical instruments to prevent the latter from taking up scarce cargo space, which were Britain's first tariffs on imported manufactures in nearly a century and provided a precedent for the Key Industries Duties imposed in 1921. In effect, the first step down the road from free trade to protection was taken during the First World War.

In other economic realms, change was dramatic but temporary. By the end of the war the government marketed about 80 per cent of the food consumed at home and controlled the vast majority of consumer prices. But within four years of the conclusion of hostilities the entire control apparatus had been abandoned. As shortages of strategic products became increasingly pervasive, the government took over management of firms producing munitions, coal and flour. But this too was temporary; wartime control was not the platform for a wave of enterprise nationalisation like that which would follow the Second World War. Thus, when the government asserted its control of the railways, it left their day-to-day operation in private hands, facilitating the process of turning them back to the private sector following the war. The Sankey Commission set up to review the problems of the coal mining industry in 1919 came down narrowly for nationalisation, but its recommendation found little support in government or outside – aside, that is, from the miners.

Where government's expanding role had a durable impact was in attitudes and policies toward competition. Manufacturers were encouraged to collaborate under the watchful eye of a government whose controls prevented the price mechanism from playing its co-ordinating role. Producers were encouraged to share expertise and information. As always, collaboration provided a fertile environment for collusion. It led to the formation of trade associations that facilitated the efforts of producers to lobby more effectively for tariff protection, tax concessions and government support for arrangements that were used to restrict output and 'rationalise' production in the 1920s and 1930s.

Among the most dramatic impacts of the war was on labour. This refers not just to the tragic death of more than 600,000 servicemen and the wounding of 1.6 million others, many so seriously that they would never work again, but also to profound changes in work organisation. For the first time, scientific management techniques – time-and-motion studies, for example – were applied in the effort to maximise efficiency. Machine tools were imported from the United States and installed in factories where they were previously unknown. Automatic welding spread through the shipyards. As skilled workers were conscripted, unskilled labour was substituted in a process known as 'dilution'.[5] The installation of automatic machinery allowed a growing number of operations to be undertaken by workers with minimal training. In this way, British industry took a first tentative step down the road that led to modern mass-production as in the United States.

Whether these new modes of shopfloor organisation and their consequences would be accepted by an increasingly assertive labour movement once the latter was freed of wartime restraints was another matter. During the war, workers had been encouraged to join unions as a matter of public policy, in order to give the authorities a body with which to negotiate in the effort to discourage strikes and slowdowns. Trade union membership more than doubled from 4 million in 1913 to more than 8 million in 1919. A third to half of all British workers were covered by collective bargaining in the 1920s, a much larger share than before 1913. Small unions formed larger federations. Joint Industrial Councils were established to negotiate wages industry wide; in 1925 some 3 million workers were covered by their deliberations. Unions and the Parliamentary Labour Party applied pressure to expand the coverage of an unemployment insurance system that had been established on a limited basis before the war. (When established in 1911 the insurance system had covered only seven cyclically sensitive industries, barely a sixth of the industrial labour force.) Labour pushed for the Trade Boards Act of 1918, which extended the coverage of a set of labour-management councils established in 1909 to set minimum wages and regulate hours and working conditions for 'sweated labour' (low-wage workers, mainly women and juveniles, in tailoring, paper box making, machine made lace-finishing and chain making). Whether these interventions enhanced or reduced the efficiency of the British labour market became the subject of contention almost immediately and has remained the subject of enduring scholarly debate.

Given the hardships and suffering endured during the war, the desire to restore normal pre-war arrangements was understandable. But this instinct confronted conditions that were very different from those of 1913. The country's financial position was weaker: its foreign assets had been run down, while the government's debts had been run up. Competition in Britain's export markets had grown more intense. Levels of unionisation had risen. The labour market had grown more structured and, there was reason to think, less flexible. The question was thus whether these new twentieth-century circumstances were compatible with the nineteenth-century policy framework that politicians and officials now sought to restore.

[5] By raising the demand for unskilled relative to skilled labour these innovations reduced the wage premium commanded by the trained. In turn this encouraged the entry into industrial employment of inexperienced workers, including women and juveniles.

REINTEGRATION INTO THE WORLD ECONOMY

There was considerable scope for growth in the early 1920s simply by redeploying resources to peacetime uses. Demobilised soldiers could return to private employment. Resources could be used for building ships rather than sinking them, for producing motor vehicles rather than disabling them. The greater had been the wartime destruction of productive capacity and the diversion of resources from peacetime uses, the greater now was the scope for raising output through repair, reconstruction and reconversion. Every percentage point by which GNP had fallen between 1913 and 1920 increased the growth rate by 1920 and 1927 by half a percentage point. This estimate comes from a regression using the cross-country data depicted in Figure 12.2 (the numbers in parentheses are t-statistics):

$$GNP_{1927}/GNP_{1920} = \underset{(8.36)}{182.23} - \underset{(2.30)}{0.52}[GNP_{1920}/GNP_{1913}]$$

This is the regression line shown in the figure.[6]

Because wartime destruction was less than elsewhere, it was perhaps natural that the British economy recovered relatively slowly in the 1920s. But Figure 12.2 also gives reason to think that Britain was exceptional. British growth between 1920 and 1927 was slower than one would predict from the decline in GNP between 1913 and 1920 and the performance of other European countries. The observation for the UK is in other words far below the line that summarises typical performance. A dummy variable for Britain, when added to the equation reported above, enters with a coefficient of −22.12 and a t-statistic of 2.09. This means that British GNP rose in these seven years by 22 percentage points less than predicted for a country in its position, and that the difference is statistically significant.[7]

Why did Britain lag? Realised levels of output, in interwar Britain as everywhere, reflect the interaction of aggregate supply and demand. On the demand side, the government set the stage for the events that followed by cutting spending by fully 75 per cent between 1918 and 1920,

[6] These results should be taken with a grain of salt, since any error in measuring GNP in 1920 will exaggerate the precision of the estimated negative relationship (because the 1920 value appears both in the denominator of the variable on the left-hand side and the numerator of the variable on the right). But there is every indication of a positive relationship between the extent of wartime dislocation and the speed of post-war recovery.

[7] It is hard to argue that this reflects the 1919–21 recession, which was more severe in Britain than elsewhere (as discussed momentarily), or the fact that GDP per capita rose in Britain during the war while falling on the continent. In 1920, the year chosen for the start of this comparison, GDP per capita was almost exactly back at 1913 levels both in Britain and on the continent (where the figure for the latter is the unweighted average for eight countries shown in Figure 12.1). It is not obvious, in other words, that intervening events bias the comparison one way or the other. It is clear from Figure 12.1 that Britain still underperforms its European competitors if one starts the comparison in, say, 1921, when the country's post-war recession was over, and extends it through 1929.

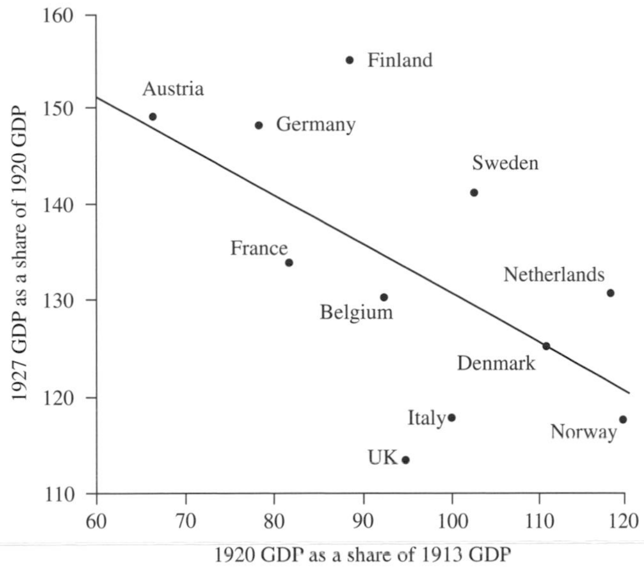

Figure 12.2 Post-war growth and the wartime setback, 1913, 1920 and 1927

Source: See Appendix.

in an effort to restore its finances and the British economy to a peacetime footing. To stem the inflation that boiled up as price controls were relaxed and pent-up consumption demands were released – an inflation that jeopardised the goal of restoring the pre-war sterling parity at an early date – the Bank of England raised its discount rate from 5 to 6 per cent in November 1919 and then to 7 per cent in April 1920. With both monetary and fiscal policies becoming sharply contractionary, it is no surprise that the economy turned down. In contrast, since many European countries had not yet marshalled the political will to undertake fiscal consolidation and price stabilisation, no such negative demand shock was evident on the continent.

The only surprise about the 1920–1 recession was its severity. Some observers such as Glynn and Booth (1992) have argued that the hike in interest rates had burst the unsustainable financial bubble that developed following the armistice. Firms freed to use their wartime profits to invest in additional capacity scrambled to acquire their industrial competitors in what critics saw as an orgy of speculation. These financial excesses raised demand to unsustainable heights, from which it now needed to fall very considerably in order to reach sustainable levels. Those same uneconomical investments saddled firms with weak balance sheets, rendering many of them unwilling or unable to invest. On the 'real' (that is to say, non-financial) side of the economy, these earlier speculative investments manifested themselves in a problem of chronic excess capacity, particularly in the so-called staple trades where much of the earlier speculative activity had been concentrated. In this view, the post-war recession was unusually deep because the preceding boom had bequeathed both real and financial burdens.

Other authors, like Dowie (1968) and Broadberry (1986), have emphasised instead developments in the labour market. Labour leaders, demanding a land fit for heroes, pressed for and succeeded in obtaining employers' agreement to a reduction in the length of the average working week from fifty-four to forty-seven hours. This was the period when levels of unionisation were highest, reflecting organised labour's wartime gains, and when its bargaining power was consequently greatest.

The cut in weekly hours was not matched, however, by a cut in weekly wages. Nor was the increase in effective hourly labour costs offset by any immediate increase in hourly labour productivity. Employers responded by laying off some of their now more expensive employees, thereby adding to the severity of the recession.

If the 1920–1 recession was purely a supply-side phenomenon, then there was no reason to expect the economy to bounce back with special vigour. The current level of output had fallen, and the economy would presumably expand from that lower level at its customary pace; no more and no less. But if the post-war recession also reflected, at least in part, a one-time negative demand shock, then there was reason to hope for unusually rapid growth once normal demand conditions were restored.[8] From this point of view, the failure of the economy to grow more rapidly in the 1920s was particularly disturbing.

The popular explanation for this failure emphasises the return to gold, together with the decision of the chancellor, Winston Churchill, to resume at the pre-war parity, and the deflationary consequences of the policies needed to bring this about. A significant rise in US prices might have relieved Britain of the need to endure a long and arduous deflation, but the hoped-for US inflation failed to materialise. (There was even a proposal, never implemented, to ship £100 million of gold to the United States in payment of Britain's war debts in an effort to force up American prices.) Instead, the Federal Reserve System (the 'Fed'), anxious to demonstrate its anti-inflationary resolve, sterilised much of the gold that flowed toward the United States as a result of the country's strong competitive position. For four long years until April 1925, when gold convertibility was finally restored, the Bank of England and the Treasury were thus forced to pursue restrictive monetary and fiscal policies with the goal of pushing down British prices and pushing up sterling to its pre-war level of $4.86.[9] Moreover, once the currency had been restored to that level,

[8] The inclusion of 'also' in this sentence should indicate that the Dowie–Broadberry and Glynn–Booth interpretations of this period need not be mutually exclusive.

[9] Even before the decision to resume gold convertibility was taken, speculators bid up the currency, aware that the act of parliament suspending the gold standard would expire in 1925 and that extending it would embarrass the government (Miller and Sutherland 1994). This handicapped British exporters, whose overseas sales stagnated in 1924–5 (coincident with the sharp appreciation of sterling). British exporters' loss of world market share reflected the fact that this strengthening of the currency was not accompanied by a commensurate fall in prices and costs.

it was still necessary to keep it there. This meant keeping interest rates high, which increased the burden of servicing the public debt, requiring high taxes that stifled consumption and investment. Thus, in much the same way that demand was curtailed in 1918–20, it remained depressed for much of the subsequent decade.

While this tale of sterling's overvaluation is found in every textbook, among specialists there no longer exists a consensus on by how much – or even, for that matter, whether – sterling was overvalued. Keynes' famous conclusion had been that British prices had risen by 10 per cent relative to American prices between 1913 and 1925, thereby pricing British goods out of international markets. But Moggridge (1969) showed that this calculation hinged on the particular price indices used; specifically, Keynes had measured the change in US prices using a retail price index for the state of Massachusetts with some rather unusual properties. Other price indices, by comparison, showed the deterioration in the British position to be less. Another problem with Keynes' calculation (which, it turns out, biased the conclusion the other way) was that he failed to consider the position of third countries. Britain did not trade exclusively with the United States, and the exports of some of its other partners had been rendered much more competitive by the wartime and post-war depreciation of their currencies. To the extent that the exports of other countries had become more competitive, the deterioration in Britain's relative position was correspondingly greater. Redmond (1984) took this into account by computing real effective exchange rates for a variety of European countries. He found that British prices had been pushed up relative to the prices of Britain's principal trading partners between 1913 and 1925 by 5 to 10 per cent in the case of wholesale prices and by 15 to 20 per cent in the case of retail prices. The wholesale price comparison is probably more relevant, since the components of this index are more heavily traded across borders.

Given the imprecision of such calculations, 5 to 10 per cent is not a large margin. Can it be confidently asserted, then, that sterling was overvalued, pricing British goods out of international markets? Other factors simultaneously affected the pattern of trade. Recall that US companies had established footholds in Latin America and elsewhere during the war, creating distribution networks, extending letters of credit and cultivating customers for the branded, standardised products of America's mass-production industries. In order for British products to regain their traditional market share, their prices now had to fall relative to those charged by the competition, and not just hold steady. Moreover, given the decline in interest income after the war, a stronger balance of trade was required than before, which implied the need for a yet further expansion of exports and a further decline in prices.

The obvious place to look for the effects of an overvalued currency, it follows, is in the behaviour of overseas trade. Figure 12.3 is consistent

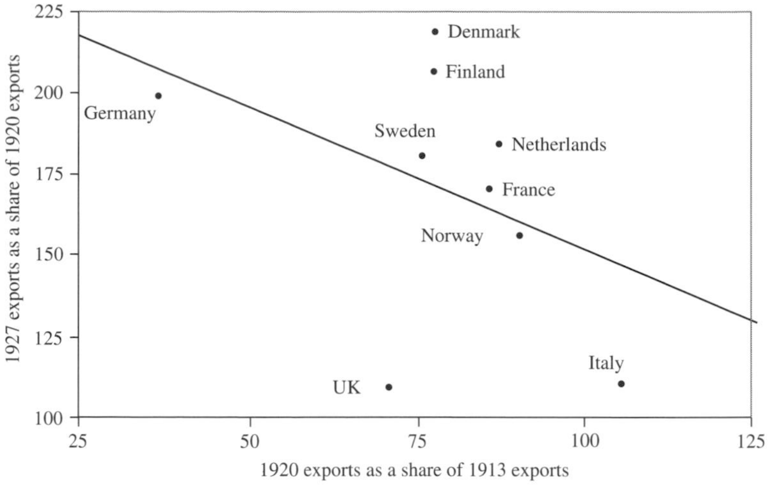

Figure 12.3 Exports as a share of GNP in Britain and Europe, 1920 and 1927

Source: See Appendix.

with the view that British exporters laboured under serious handicaps. It shows, not surprisingly, that where merchandise exports had been most severely disrupted by the war, there was the most scope for their subsequent growth. But, again, Britain is an outlier: her exports grew more slowly between 1920 and 1927 than the wartime setback and the average performance of other European countries would predict. A regression using the data in Figure 12.3 yields the equation:

$$\text{Exports}_{1927}/\text{Exports}_{1920} = \underset{(6.07)}{266.25} - \underset{(2.07)}{1.11}[\text{Exports}_{1920}/\text{Exports}_{1913}] - \underset{(2.60)}{78.54}\text{UK}$$

suggesting that British exports grew by 78 percentage points less between 1920 and 1927 than predicted by their wartime shortfall and the performance of other European exporters.

DECLINING INDUSTRIES AND RISING UNEMPLOYMENT

A high exchange rate and high costs may not be the only – or, for that matter, even the principal -- explanation for Britain's disappointing export performance in this period. Another view (see chapters 4 above and 14 below) is that the economy suffered from having specialised in the wrong industries, notably coal, iron and steel, textiles and shipbuilding, sectors where demand was weak and whose products were consequently in chronic oversupply. These were the sectors in which Britain had invested in the nineteenth century and in which it naturally continued to specialise, but also the sectors where subsequent industrialisers found it easiest to compete. Moreover, with the development of new products based on advances in chemical, electrical and mechanical engineering (rayon, radio and the internal combustion engine being three examples), these staple goods commanded a shrinking share of final expenditure. Even had wartime inflation and post-war exchange rates not elevated British costs of production, in other words, there is reason to think that exports of the traditional staples would have remained chronically depressed.

As demand weakened and foreign competition intensified, a market economy should have begun to reallocate resources out of these uses. So it did; employment in chemicals, electrical engineering, vehicles, electricity (including gas and water), silk, rayon and hosiery expanded by fully a quarter between 1920 and 1929, this in a period when employment in industry and mining was falling by 9 per cent. The share of total employment accounted for by the new industries rose from 11 to 15 per cent between 1920 and 1929, while the share accounted for by the basic industries (coal, cotton, woollens, shipbuilding and iron and steel) declined from 30 to 25 per cent.

The question is why this transformation did not occur more quickly. Some scholars interpret the resulting rigidities in terms of the handicap of an early start. The skills and the attitudes toward the pace and organisation of work of English cotton spinners, Welsh coal miners and Scottish shipyard workers, imparted by socio-economic institutions developed for an earlier era, were ill suited to the more technologically sophisticated new industries of the 1920s and 1930s (Heim 1984b). These workers could not move overnight to the growing chemical and motor vehicle industries. The old and new industries were located in different places; moving between them required access to information about employment opportunities far away and involved non-negligible costs (Dimsdale *et al.* 1989a). British financial institutions and markets, developed for an age when the financial needs of industry were modest and the export of capital was big business, were ill suited for underwriting the activities of newborn small firms (a phenomenon contemporaries referred to as the Macmillan gap, echoing the chairman of the expert committee that emphasised its existence).

The basic industries also had a considerable installed base of old-vintage machinery. So long as this remained viable it posed additional competition for anyone who contemplated investing in more up-to-date equipment. As a result, the knowledge gains from familiarity with the latest technology were correspondingly less. Reflecting the sluggishness of demand and investment, the average vintage of the capital stock was slow to change. This problem was naturally greatest for a country which had made such a large investment in its installed base in prior years.

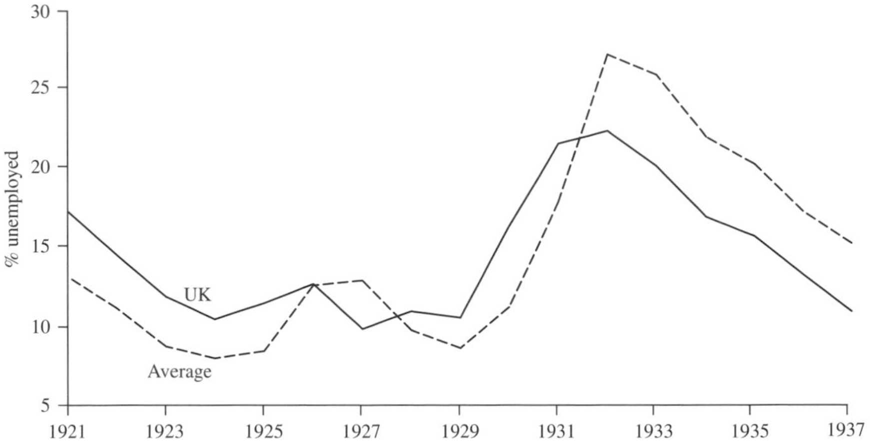

Figure 12.4 Unemployment rate in industry in Britain and Europe, 1921–37

Source: See Appendix.

In addition, the basic industries were entrenched interests; the Federation of British Industries (founded in 1916) and the National Confederation of Employers' Organisations (formed in 1919) were well placed to lobby for government subsidies and support. The 1921 Key Industries Duties, adopted following the sharp collapse in the value of textile, iron and steel and shipbuilding enterprises, provided limited amounts of tariff protection and, more importantly, held out the promise of more. (They were extended to the motor vehicle and parts industries in 1926.) Policy thus encouraged producers who might have otherwise contemplated exit to hold on in the hope of better times. The Bank of England, not obviously the public agency best suited to the task, became heavily involved in efforts to encourage co-operation among steel, textile and shipbuilding firms in the orderly elimination of excess capacity, rather than allowing market forces to winnow the weak (Garside and Greaves 1996). Given the Bank's interest in the stability of the financial system, bankruptcies were the last thing it wanted; cotton firms understood this, which relieved them of pressure to pursue painful rationalisation measures.

That more workers did not move between the old and new industries seems even more disturbing when so many remained out of work. Recorded unemployment hovered above 10 per cent throughout the 1920s (as described and analysed further in chapter 13 below). While unemployment was not exclusively a British problem, Figure 12.4 suggests that it was even more widespread than elsewhere in Europe.[10] Economic historians agree that unemployment in the 1920s and 1930s reflected the

[10] Except in 1927, when unemployment on the continent rose to exceptional heights due to post-stabilisation recessions in France and Italy. Note that these comparative unemployment rates must be taken with several grains of salt, since the accuracy with which they measure the phenomenon is questionable (see Baines and Johnson 1999 and Hatton in this volume).

failure of wages to keep pace with the downward march of prices.[11] High real wages were the mirror image of a high exchange rate: in the same way that the latter priced British goods out of international markets, the former priced British workers out of employment.

But while there may be widespread agreement on the existence of this problem, there is no agreement on its causes. Dimsdale (1984) and Newell and Symons (1988), among others, argue that Britain's chronic double digit unemployment stemmed from the high exchange rate, which forced down prices and put intense pressure on the equilibrium level of wages, a harsh adjustment that the institutions of the labour market found difficult to carry out. Wholesale prices fell by 25 per cent between 1921 and 1929. Given the reluctance of workers to see their pay packets shrink, not even a relatively well-functioning labour market could have easily accommodated this shift. To be sure, half of that deflation occurred at the beginning of this period, when a large part of the wartime inflation was unwound (causing unemployment to shoot up to double digits). But wholesale prices (as measured by the Sauerbeck–Statist index) continued to fall, by a cumulative 13 per cent between 1922 and 1929 – that is, by almost 2 per cent a year. Economists like Akerlof, Dickens and Perry (2000) argue that a little inflation can play a large role in lubricating the labour market. It follows that deflation in the 1920s, even if modest, could have contributed to the machinery seizing up.

Other like Matthews (1986) and Beenstock and Warburton (1986) insist that the problem stemmed from undue upward pressure on wages and ran from there to higher prices and an overvalued exchange rate. A well-functioning labour market should have had no trouble, they argue, in accommodating the return to gold. But trade unions were more militant than before 1913; they were unwilling to accept a dramatic cut in money wages. With the growth of the Parliamentary Labour Party, they could hope for political support for labour action. Like the coal miners in 1926, they engaged in work stoppages rather than accepting lower wages.

But it is important to recall that the great coal strike of 1926 was in fact a defeat for the miners. They slunk back to work, their wages cut. Episodes like this hardly enhanced the reputation of unions for delivering the goods: the share of workers subject to collective-bargaining agreements, after rising sharply during the First World War, fell back equally sharply in the 1920s. Attempts to discern a clear connection between high levels of unionisation and inflexible wages have been unsuccessful (see e.g. Dimsdale *et al.* 1989b).

[11] It is no coincidence that studies of this problem proliferated in the 1980s, when unemployment again became a serious problem in Britain and not a few economists diagnosed it in similar terms.

If there were new obstacles to wage adjustment, then, they presumably lay elsewhere. The obvious candidate is Britain's unemployment insurance system, established before the war but greatly extended following its conclusion. In the 1920s the ratio of average weekly benefits to average weekly wages hovered around 50 per cent, arguably encouraging leisurely job search. Payments were independent of wages; thus, workers in low-wage industries were supported generously when out of work, with benefits that might rise to 80 or even 90 per cent of their previous wages. Benjamin and Kochin (1979) argued that this one factor by itself could explain the high level of British unemployment in the 1920s and 1930s. They based their conclusion on the observation that there was a significant time-series correlation between the replacement rate (the ratio of average benefits to average wages) and unemployment between 1920 and 1938.

A large literature arose in response to these results. Ormerod and Worswick (1982) questioned the direction of causality: unemployment could be positively correlated with the replacement rate even if it was simply a reflection of weak domestic demand (since weaker demand for labour would put downward pressure on wages and therefore raise the replacement rate). Hatton (1985) showed that the mechanism posited by Benjamin and Kochin – more time spent in search, reflecting the benefit-induced rise in the reservation wage – did not find reflection, as it should have, in a positive relationship between the ratio of unfilled vacancies to unemployed workers on the one hand and the ratio of benefits to wages on the other. Eichengreen (1987) showed that data for individual workers suggest a weaker impact of benefits on unemployment.

All this suggests that the unemployment insurance system was only part of the story. As Loungani (1991) showed, the benefit/wage ratio by itself can 'explain' only 16 per cent of the variance of interwar unemployment (and this leaves aside questions about the direction of causality). Clarke's (1996: 153) conclusion seems judicious, that 'There is no reason to suppose that large numbers of people started living off the state as a preferred way of life, though there is evidence that clients maximised the support they could obtain from the competing agencies.'

MONETARY POLICY IN SLUMP AND RECOVERY

Also important for the evolution of output and employment, this broader perspective suggests, were shocks to aggregate supply and demand. The principal negative supply shock, as we have seen, occurred in the early 1920s, when there was a 13 per cent fall in the normal working week without any compensating adjustment in the weekly wage. The most powerful shock to aggregate demand was the slump that began in 1929. That slump was global; it did not originate in Britain. The UK was not

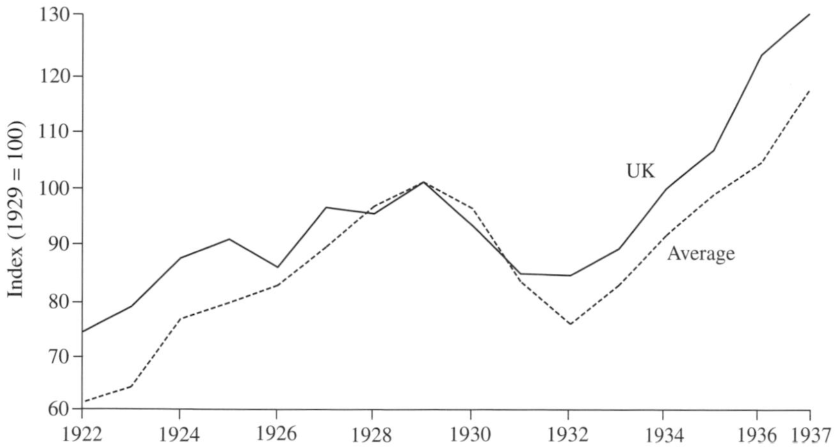

Figure 12.5 Industrial production in Britain and Europe, 1922–37

Source: See Appendix.

among the countries where financial excesses had run out of control in the 1920s and where the tighter monetary policy initiated by the Federal Reserve System in 1928 found a significant bubble to prick. Britain was less dependent on capital exports from the United States than were Argentina, Australia, Brazil, Poland and Germany. It was not as sensitive to Federal Reserve policy as the United States. But the weakness of the balance of payments left no room for an outflow of financial capital. Consequently, the Bank of England had no choice but to follow the Fed when US monetary policy makers began raising interest rates in response to what they perceived as speculative excesses on Wall Street. Tighter money of course did nothing to sustain Britain's fragile expansion.

Figure 12.5 shows that industrial production fell more quickly in Britain than in the rest of Europe between 1929 and 1930 but more slowly between 1930 and 1931. The behaviour of exports suggests that the early decline of British industrial output reflected the deterioration of conditions in important British export markets such as Australia, Argentina, Brazil and the United States. But all differences between Britain and the rest of Europe before 1932 pale in comparison to those which opened up subsequently. British industrial production stabilised in 1932 while continuing to fall precipitously – by 10 per cent in a single year – on the continent. The stabilising impulse came not from conditions abroad but from policy at home, specifically from the country's abandonment of the gold standard in September 1931 and from the changes in policy – mainly a sharp reduction in the Bank of England's discount rate – facilitated by this event (Figure 12.6). The decision to stop defending the sterling parity in 1931 is the most closely studied policy decision of the interwar years – along of course with Churchill's decision to restore that parity in 1925. From the perspective of investors, it was not obvious that Britain

Figure 12.6 Central bank discount rates, 1921–37

Source: See Appendix.

should be the first European country to throw in this towel. It had not been among those countries with an overheated economy in the 1920s; consequently there were fewer accumulated excesses to complicate the maintenance of financial stability. As we have seen, the downturn was not more severe than elsewhere; if anything, the opposite was true. The financial system was in reasonably good shape – British banks had more foreign assets than liabilities, in contrast to banks in Germany and the rest of central Europe.

To be sure, there were other problems, such as the decline in the dividends paid by foreign companies and in the interest paid by foreign governments on monies borrowed previously on the London market, which led to a deterioration in the current account of the balance of payments (Moggridge 1970). But Britain's singular weakness was her high level of unemployment, which created a reluctance on the part of the politicians to defend the exchange rate using policies that might imply further increases (which would have undermined the position of the Labour government by cutting into its working-class support). The policies in question were high interest rates and cuts in public expenditure, which threatened to exacerbate unemployment. Knowing that the government had little stomach for such measures, investors began selling sterling, and the authorities, as expected, showed themselves to be either unable or unwilling to respond (Eichengreen and Jeanne 2000). It took a National Government formed on 24 August, dominated by Conservatives but led by the holdover Labour premier, Ramsay MacDonald, to push through limited cuts in unemployment benefit and public sector salaries, but even these were too much for the affected to bear (leading to the famous 'mutiny' of seamen at the naval base at Invergordon). Confidence, rather than being rebuilt, was dashed. With the Bank of England's reserves approaching exhaustion, the decision was taken to abandon the sterling parity on 19 September.

This was arguably the most important economic policy decision of the 1930s. What is surprising, in retrospect, is that the Bank of England and the government did not do more to defend the sterling parity in which they had so heavily invested. An increase in the Bank's discount rate was considered on 16 July but rejected. The rate was raised by one point to 3.5 per cent on 23 July and by another point a week later. But, remarkably, this was the last increase prior to the suspension of gold convertibility in mid-September. For its part, the Labour government pushed through modest budgetary economies, but it was unable to agree on significant cuts in unemployment benefit, ultimately resigning over the issue. Its effort was modest by the standards of, say, France, where the economy was put through a deflationary wringer for five additional years in a desperate effort to preserve the gold standard.

This comparative perspective helps one to understand why the Bank of England and the British government responded as they did. Open unemployment was much higher in Britain; unlike France, there was virtually no agricultural sector for jobless workers to retreat to. Interest rate hikes and cuts in public spending that further weakened domestic demand thus threatened to aggravate an already intolerable problem. 'At the onset of the Great Depression', Janeway (1995–6: 255) writes, 'Britain had already suffered nearly a decade of unemployment in excess of one million insured workers. This was the central economic fact that constrained monetary policy throughout the period.'

Not just the Bank of England but the British government was constrained. The government in office from 1929 through mid-1931 was beholden to labour; its French counterpart had a more diversified constituency. Writing of the political impact of high unemployment, Fraser (1933: 113) observed that 'A democratic government cannot shut its eyes to such things, and, consciously or unconsciously, the British Government were influenced by them, and so they chose the policy that would minimise social unrest.'

Finally, in Britain, unlike France and other European countries, there was no searing experience with high inflation in the 1920s to look back upon. To be sure, there were fears that cutting the golden anchor might augur runaway inflation, but these were less immediate, and hence less of a deterrent, than on the continent where there had been first-hand experience with high inflation.

In the three months following its departure from gold, sterling fell from 4.86 to around 3.40 against the US dollar. While the currency's decline enhanced the competitiveness of British goods, the positive effects were limited, given that international markets were not exactly firing on all cylinders. At least British exports stabilised in 1932, as Figure 12.7 shows, while continuing to fall elsewhere at an alarming

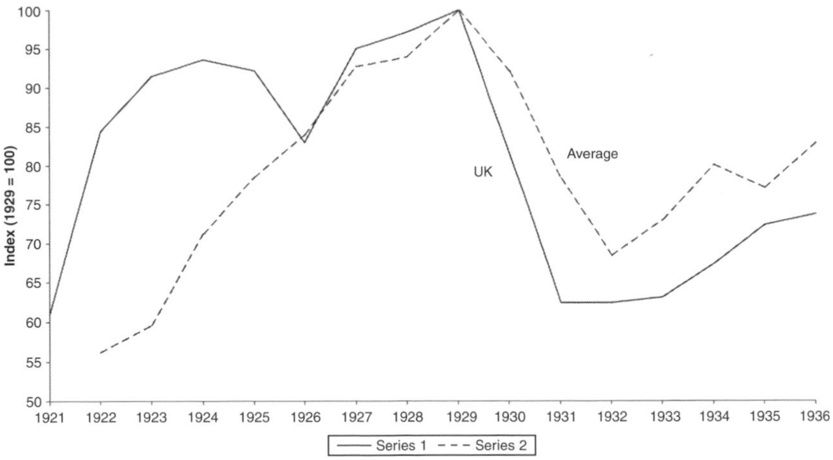

Figure 12.7 Volume of British and European exports, 1921–36

Source: See Appendix.

rate. This much is explained by the depreciation of sterling. But what went down could also go up: starting in 1933, sterling appreciated on an effective basis as a result of depreciation abroad (mainly depreciation of the US dollar), reversing the preceding competiveness gains. Whether they were completely or only partially neutralised depends on whether one prefers the effective exchange rate index of Dimsdale (1981) or that of Redmond (1984), which differ by their choice of trade and country weights. Either way, the question becomes how British exports could continue to expand through 1936 despite their continued stagnation on the continent.

The answer lies in the relatively early and robust recovery of the British economy, powered by a more accommodating monetary policy (Dimsdale 1984; Worswick 1984). The Bank of England responded to the removal of the gold standard constraints by cutting interest rates to 2 per cent and keeping them there. The banks were helped by this decline in funding costs. Since their liabilities were denominated in sterling, their balance sheets were not compromised by depreciation of sterling, in contrast to the situation in other countries (Grossman 1994). With no bank failures to destroy the value of financial assets, consumption remained stable by international standards (Richardson 1967; Broadberry 1988). Bond yields were also pushed down, enabling the government in the summer of 1932 to convert the 5 per cent War Loan to an issue yielding a more economical 3.5 per cent, in turn allowing its limited fiscal resources to be redeployed to other uses like support for the unemployed and salaries for public servants which had a more immediate impact on aggregate demand.

Cheap money, as this policy came to be known, thus supported domestic demand, the demand for interest-sensitive consumer durables and housing services in particular. Average monthly mortgage payments on

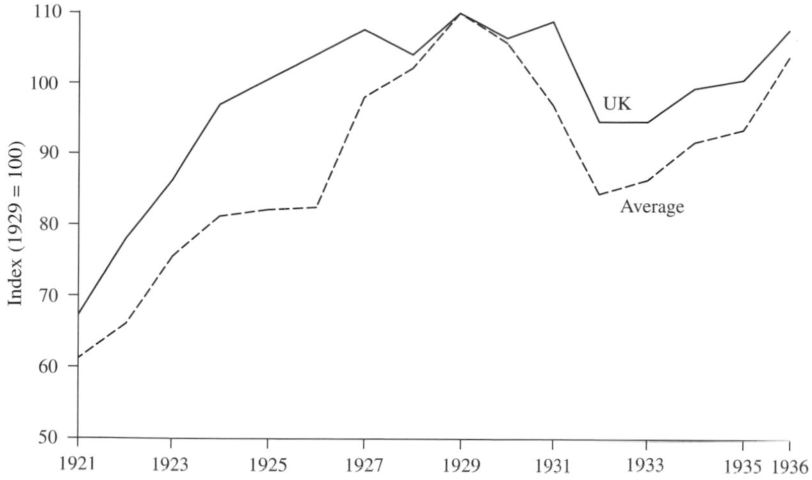

Figure 12.8 Volume of British and European imports, 1921–36

Source: See Appendix.

new homes declined by 9 per cent between 1931 and 1933. Residential construction stabilised and recovered robustly. The increase in house building accounted for 17 per cent of the increase in GNP between 1932 and 1934. Together with the associated sectors (those producing bricks, tiles, pipes and other construction materials), it accounted for 30 per cent of the increase in employment in the first three years of recovery. The impact of the housing boom did not stop there; residential construction stimulated the demand for the products of industries producing everything from electric irons to radios. Broadberry (1987) finds that cheap money accounted for roughly half of the cumulative increase in housing investment, with rising incomes and falling construction costs accounting for the remainder. Bowden (1988) finds similar effects of cheap money on the demand for and production of consumer durables.

As activity recovered, led by the construction sector, so did the demand for imports (Figure 12.8). And, as Britain's productive capacity came back on line, more traded goods were produced and exported to pay for raw material and consumer goods imports demanded by firms and households. But fewer than one in ten of all new jobs was in an export-linked sector. This is all by way of saying that economic recovery in the 1930s was led by domestic demand and that the recovery of exports was a corollary. Other countries that abandoned the gold standard in the early 1930s recovered from the depression in similar fashion: the rate of growth was similar to Britain's, the role of cheap money was similar and the dominance of domestic demand was similar. In contrast, the economies of the gold bloc (France, Belgium, the Netherlands, Switzerland) continued to stagnate under the burden of high exchange rates and high interest rates (Figure 12.9).

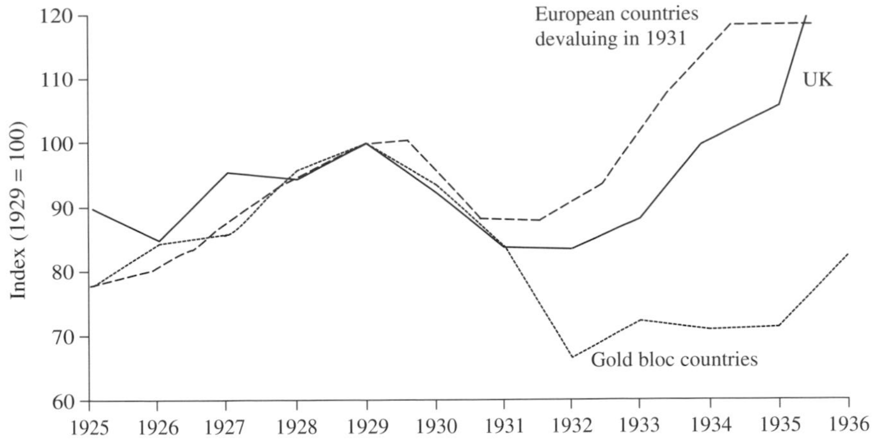

Figure 12.9 Industrial production of gold and non-gold countries, 1925–36

Source: See Appendix.

FISCAL POLICY

Compared to cheap money, fiscal policy played little role in the recovery. This may come as a surprise to students of Keynesian economics, who are taught that fiscal policy is particularly effective for fighting depressions and that Keynes' followers had demonstrated this in the 1930s. To be sure, Keynes and others had elaborated the case for a countercyclical fiscal policy (one in which fiscal policy becomes more stimulative as the economy weakens) to both the Macmillan Committee investigating the connections between trade and industry and the Economic Advisory Council advising the government. But there remained obstacles to its implementation. Adherents to the 'Treasury view' warned that an increase in deficit spending might raise questions about the prudence of a government with a history of budgetary problems and thereby undermine confidence and investment. A £500 million increase in government spending, which Thomas (1976) and Dimsdale and Horsewood (1995) estimate would have been required to put even a tenth of the unemployed back to work, would have radically transformed a central government budget amounting to less than twice that amount, even if the additional spending had been spread out over a number of years.[12] Middleton (1985) exaggerates when he writes that such a programme would have required the socialisation of investment and the nationalisation of industry, but

[12] Matthews (1989) argues that a public spending programme of this magnitude would have put a much larger number of the unemployed back to work but via a mechanism that most economists would regard as fantastic. He assumes that the fiscal expansion would have been financed by printing money – hardly plausible behaviour for a central bank constrained to defend a fixed exchange rate for the first three years of the period under consideration – and that increased deficit spending would have induced an outward shift in labour supply by pushing up prices and reducing the real value of unemployment benefits, not a mechanism that most economists would regard as the major transmission channel for fiscal policy.

he is right that it would have represented a very significant expansion of the role of government in the economy, something that did not yet command public support.

Although the budget swung from a surplus of 0.4 per cent of GNP in 1929/30 to a deficit of 1.3 per cent of GDP in 1932/3, the constant employment budget (which corrects the actual budget for changes induced by the business cycle) in fact increased rather than decreased – from a surplus 0.4 per cent of GDP in 1929/30 to a surplus 3.0 per cent of GDP in 1932/3 (Middleton 1981) – as the authorities raised taxes and cut spending in a desperate attempt to keep the deficit from widening further. Only in 1936–7 did the constant employment surplus decline significantly. This reflected not any putative influence of the Keynesian revolution on economic policy but diplomatic and military storm clouds. Defence spending rose from 2.7 per cent of GDP in the fiscal year 1935/6 to 7.7 per cent in 1938/9. A radical break with traditional fiscal policy had finally taken place but without forcing the socialisation of the British economy or undermining investor confidence, due more to Mr Hitler than Mr Keynes. Thomas (1983) shows that spending on rearmament stimulated output and employment not just in defence-related industries such as iron, steel and engineering but economy wide. He estimates that it created 445,000 jobs already in 1935, reabsorbing some 15 per cent of the unemployed, and that by 1938 the number of jobs so created had risen to 1.5 million. Together with the monetary flexibility that a floating exchange rate conferred, rearmament spending mitigated the severity of the 1937–8 downturn, which proved modest by the standards of both 1920–1 and 1930–1. Note the contrast with the rest of Europe, in Figure 12.1. While rearmament spending was well underway in Germany, with analogous macroeconomic effects (Silverman 1988), the same was not yet true in other European countries.

PROTECTION AND COMPETITION

The other innovation in fiscal policy was the tariff. No one suffered more from the slump than producers of internationally traded goods; by the early 1930s producers in a variety of other sectors had joined the basic industries in blaming import competition for their plight. The political setback suffered by the Labour party, which had the bad luck of occupying Downing Street when the 1931 financial crisis struck, allowed the Conservatives finally to push through the general tariff they had long espoused. It was shepherded in by a new chancellor of the Exchequer, Neville Chamberlain, son of the long-time Conservative champion of protection. Adopted in 1932, the general tariff applied a 10 per cent tax to imports, exempting only raw materials, and established an Import Duties Advisory Committee to consider applications for higher rates. To prevent the tariff from disrupting relations with the Commonwealth countries, the government met with their representatives in Ottawa and negotiated an agreement to extend preferential treatment to their exports in return for concessions on their treatment of British goods.

Most historians are sceptical that the tariff was a major factor in recovery. To the extent that it strengthened the balance of trade, the tariff would have induced an appreciation of sterling, since the exchange rate was now floating. That stronger exchange rate would have neutralised any tendency for the tariff to switch expenditure toward domestic goods.

To be sure, sterling's float was less than free. An Exchange Equalisation Account was established to intervene in the foreign exchange market and prevent sterling from appreciating excessively. Given this, most observers agree that the tariff pushed up prices, which was helpful in a period when prices worldwide were collapsing. Higher prices stimulated aggregate supply and were good for profitability. As a result, there was probably some modestly positive macroeconomic effect.

Still, the impact was almost certainly small; with unemployment in excess of 20 per cent of the labour force, a modest increase in the relative price of imported goods could not solve the underlying problem. Foreman-Peck (1981a) estimates that the tariff raised British output by 3 per cent; Okun's Law suggests that this might have reduced the unemployment rate by $1\frac{1}{2}$ percentage points. Kitson and Solomou (1990) argue that the tariff may have had a larger impact in so far as it shifted resources toward sectors characterised by economies of scale and consequently gave a relatively powerful boost to output and productivity. Other historians remain more sceptical.

Where the tariff may have mattered most was in slowing the transfer of resources to new uses and creating a cosy environment sheltered from the chill winds of competition. In both the 1920s and 1930s, the rate of change of the sectoral allocation of resources (as measured by Matthews *et al.* 1982) was considerably slower than it would become after the Second World War. To be sure, employment in the staple trades, which felt the pressure of import competition most intensely and received the most generous tariff protection, continued to fall in the 1930s (by almost a quarter in the nine years ending in 1938). But it would have fallen even faster in the absence of the tariff. Employment in the new industries continued to rise (by more than a quarter over the same nine-year period), but it would have risen even faster without the tariff. One indication of the limited pace of adjustment is that on the eve of the Second World War the number of workers employed in the new industries still only barely surpassed the number working in the staple trades.

The effects of this delayed transformation were not immediately catastrophic; there remained productivity gains to be ground out of the basic industries by raising capital/labour ratios. For instance, 61 per cent of all coal was cut by machinery by 1939, while 54 per cent was mechanically conveyed, up from just 8 and 2 per cent respectively in 1913. As a result, output per man-shift rose by 14 per cent (Court 1945). Increases in labour productivity of 0.5 per cent a year were hardly grounds for self-congratulation, but they were enough to keep British coal mines in business. Moreover, given the unemployment and idle capacity with which the economy entered the 1930s, there was an argument for any policy that might put underutilised resources to work and at any task, not just those with the brightest prospects. And, yet, with the benefit of hindsight it can be argued that Britain would have been better off after the Second World War had she been faster to reallocate resources to sectors that were technologically more dynamic and where demand was more buoyant – and had she not hindered the process in the 1930s by imposing a tariff. The fact that countries where pre-1945 economic arrangements were more extensively disrupted by the Second World War grew faster and more persistently in its aftermath is consistent with this view.

The effects of the tariff were more pernicious to the extent that they interacted with other policies of encouraging industrial consolidation and concentration. Looking to the experience of the United States, officials and industrialists concluded that the economies of scale associated with large firm size were the key to raising efficiency. This belief had already led to a first wave of mergers during the First World War and the 1920s, the most spectacular being the creation of ICI, the British chemicals giant, in 1926. Following this lead, large enterprises appeared in a variety of industries including motor vehicles, retailing and electrical engineering (Hannah 1983).

This process of merger and amalgamation accelerated sharply in the 1930s due to government intervention. The state's involvement reflected experience during the First World War, when intervention had coincided with (contemporaries would have said 'produced') considerable productivity growth. Subsequent interventions in the affairs of industry by the Treasury and the Bank of England were inspired by this episode and reflected the perception that the economic crisis of the 1930s was an emergency tantamount to war. The shipbuilding industry, with government encouragement, established the National Shipbuilders' Security Ltd to buy poorly equipped, outdated yards. The British Iron and Steel Federation worked hand in glove, or hand in pocket, with the state to merge complementary firms and regulate the supply of raw materials. State control went furthest in the Coal Mines Act of 1930, which gave workers shorter hours in return for their acceding to the cartelisation of production and empowered the government to compel the amalgamation of competing firms.

If economies of scale were the promise held out from consolidation, high levels of industrial concentration were the danger. Sheltered from import competition, a handful of firms commanding the lion's share of the domestic market could raise prices at will. They could reach market-sharing agreements (a practice encouraged by the government as a way of facilitating orderly competition), which removed the incentive to develop and adopt new technologies and to otherwise reduce costs in the effort to gain market share. They could threaten a price war against firms tempted to invest in new technologies or to undercut cartel prices. The tendency for the tariff to inhibit competition was reinforced by the practice of the Import Duties Advisory Committee, the body that set rates, to extend more generous protection to industries that demonstrated a willingness to reduce excess capacity through merger and consolidation. The idea may have been to encourage British producers to reduce costs, but the effect was to enable them to raise mark-ups.

In contrast to the situation in the United States, collusion by producers was not restrained by a modern anti-trust act until the second half of the 1950s. This allowed as much as half of manufactured output to be produced by cartel members in the mid-1930s (Crafts 1999), leading one contemporary pessimistically to observe that 'as a feature of industrial and commercial organisation free competition has nearly disappeared from the British scene' (Lucas 1937: 64).

The results are not hard to see. In the 1930s the interindustry correlation between mergers and productivity growth was negative, not positive as the mergers-as-a-response-to-scale-economies hypothesis would lead one to predict. This is unsurprising in so far as measures to limit competition were felt most strongly in sectors such as food, drink, tobacco and textiles, where scale economies were hardly pronounced. Broadberry and Crafts (1990b, 1990c) find that more concentrated industries had larger productivity gaps vis-à-vis their American counterparts. The shortfall was largest in long-established sectors like hosiery and lace, railway rolling stock, iron and steel, leather, china, glass and clothing that enjoyed the most generous effective rates of tariff protection.

Policy toward these sectors, these authors conclude, permitted the preservation of inefficient firms, incompetent managers and anachronistic practices (Gourvish 1987). In an environment sheltered from competition, with rents available even to inefficient firms, there was less pressure to replace poor managers. The persistence of family control and, in the case of joint-stock companies, the dispersal of shareholdings (reflecting the divorce of banks from industry) rendered the hostile takeover as a source of market discipline virtually unknown. All this limited the incentive to invest in the capital-intensive manufacturing techniques pioneered by large American corporations, to reorganise factory layout to permit use of the electric unit drive, to reorganise the firm along multidivisional lines and to invest in research and development (R&D). To be sure, this cosy collusive environment is not the entire explanation for the reluctance of British firms to invest in American-style mass-production methods; also important, as Broadberry (1997c) has emphasised, was the relatively small size of final-goods markets, which made it difficult to exploit economies of scale. But here too policy mattered; the policy of imperial preference pursued after Ottawa linked Britain's sales to slowly growing Commonwealth markets, a problem that became increasingly evident after the Second World War.

Also weakened was the incentive to rationalise labour relations and for firms to install new technologies over the objections of workers. Lazonick (1981c) and McKinlay and Zeitlin (1989) show that cotton textile and engineering firms continued to use labour-intensive low-speed techniques in order to avoid incurring high capital costs and incurring the wrath of their workers. The reluctance to install new technologies was evident even in new industries such as motor vehicles; Lewchuk (1987) shows that British vehicle producers shunned Henry Ford's capital-intensive mass-production methods in order to limit their vulnerability to slowdowns, something which they could afford as a result of the protection afforded by the tariff and an oligopoly dominated by Morris Motors. Admittedly, high levels of unemployment, by eroding the bargaining power of unions, may have enhanced the ability of firms to push for organisational and technical change, but the rise of cartelisation and protection diluted the incentives for doing so.

This litany of woes runs the risk of overstating the case. By the end of the 1930s some 250 British firms had adopted modern techniques of managerial control (including the multidivisional form). Modern cost accounting had been installed, and top management was being professionalised. Spending on research and development tripled over the course of the decade. New products and processes proliferated, fuelling hopes of the emergence of a 'development bloc' of modern industries. But quantitative analyses of British productivity are damning. Rostas' (1948) pioneering study found that net output per worker in manufacturing in the second half of the 1930s was 11 per cent higher in Germany than in the UK. Germany may have suffered from some of the same collusive practices as Britain, but she none the less had an advantage in heavy industry where plant size was larger (Broadberry and Fremdling 1990). And worker productivity was an astounding 125 per cent higher in the United States. These discrepancies would have been less disturbing had the gap closed quickly after the Second World War. But in the late 1940s US labour productivity was still 150 cent higher in heavy industry and 67 per cent higher in light industry (Frankel 1957; Broadberry and Crafts 1990a), and Britain did little to narrow the gap over the three subsequent decades. Evidently, the problems that developed in the interwar period proved remarkably persistent.

Thus, the interwar period had conflicting implications for short-run macroeconomic stabilisation and long-term growth. This was true in particular of the policies pursued in the 1930s, which developed out of the expanding role of government in the economy during the Great War and in

Appendix table 12.1									
	Figure number								
	12.1	12.2	12.3	12.4	12.5	12.6	12.7	12.8	12.9
France	*	*	*	*	*	*	*	*	*
Germany	*	*	*	*	*	*	*	*	*
Italy	*	*	*	*		*	*	*	*
Denmark	*	*	*	*	*	*	*	*	*
Norway	*	*	*	*	*	*	*	*	*
Finland	*	*	*		*	*	*	*	*
Sweden	*	*	*	*	*	*	*	*	*
Switzerland				*	*	*	*	*	
Austria		*		*					*
Netherlands	*	*	*	*	*	*	*	*	*
Belgium		*		*	*	*	*	*	*

the decade that followed. In a strongly deflationary environment like that of the 1930s, anything that pushed up prices and boosted demand was good for employment, profitability and financial stability. This included cheap money, the tariff and even inducements to industrial collusion that prevented disastrous bankruptcies and disorderly exit that might have destabilised financial markets. But by creating an anti-competitive environment and reducing the incentive for firms to make hard choices, these same policies slowed the pace of structural and organisational change, which prepared Britain poorly for participation in the more intensely competitive world economy that emerged after the Second World War. The same policies that helped with the immediate economic crisis thus positioned Britain poorly to compete in the long run.

Statistical appendix

The data underlying Figures 12.2 and 12.3 come from Maddison 1982. The one exception is GDP figures for Britain; these are Feinstein's revised estimates as reported in Mitchell 1988. Most other data were drawn from League of Nations publications which collected figures published by national statistical offices. All industrial production indices used in this chapter, for example, were taken from the League of Nations' *Monthly Statistical Bulletin* and *Statistical Year-Book*. Data on the volume of merchandise imports and exports were taken from the League's *International Trade and Balance of Payments* and *Memoranda on Balance of Payments and Foreign Trade Balances*, except for export and import volumes for Britain, which are from Mitchell 1988. These publications list the value as well as the volume of imports and exports; the ratio of value to volume was the implicit price deflator used to compute the international terms of trade. Central bank discount rates came from the *Year-Book* and the *Monthly Statistical Bulletin.* Contemporary unemployment statistics are from Eichengreen and Hatton 1988. Since many national statistical offices were only set up in this period, there are significant gaps in the material available to historians. The strategy followed in constructing the figures here was to include only countries for which continuous series could be constructed. The main omissions are Germany and Austria in the early 1920s, for which estimates of economic activity and its components are difficult to reconstruct in the period of the hyper-inflation. In many cases two graphs were drawn, one starting in 1921 but omitting Germany and Austria, another starting in 1925. I have used the first such figure where the early 1920s feature prominently in the discussion, the second where the experience of Germany and Austria seems particularly relevant. Appendix table 12.1 denotes with an asterisk countries that are included in each figure.

13 Unemployment and the labour market, 1870–1939

TIMOTHY J. HATTON

Contents

THE UNEMPLOYMENT PROBLEM

Unemployment is an enduring feature of industrial market economies – indeed it is often seen as one of the most unfortunate side effects of the capitalist system.[1] Between 1870 and 1939 the understanding of unemployment, attitudes and policies towards it, and the scale and structure of unemployment itself, underwent considerable change. Before the 1890s the problem was perceived as one of personal deficiencies and lack of industrial quality among the workers concerned; by the turn of the century it was understood as reflecting lack of organisation in the labour market; and by the 1930s it was seen by many as a problem of the malfunctioning of the entire economic system.

In mid-Victorian times, middle-class observers saw unemployment as the result chiefly of indigence or incapacity and largely a feature of the lowest stratum of society. For steady and respectable workmen thrown out of work by cyclical downturns, unemployment was temporary and its effects were ameliorated by self-help or mutual aid. But fact and circumstance conspired to alter these perceptions as awareness of, and concern

[1] For helpful comments on an earlier draft I am grateful to V. Bhaskar, George Boyer, George Chouliarakis, Emmett Sullivan and participants at the contributors conference.

about, unemployment increased. One ingredient was the findings of social investigators such as Charles Booth whose social survey of London revealed poverty and deprivation even among the families of relatively respectable workers. Another was the series of official inquiries ranging from the Royal Commission on Labour (1892–4) to the Royal Commission on the Poor Laws and Relief of Distress (1905–9), which took evidence on unemployment and the workings of the labour market. Such discussions were accompanied and informed by a widening range of labour market statistics collected by the Labour Department of the Board of Trade, which was formed in 1892.

The new view that emerged from these inquiries is best exemplified by William Beveridge's book *Unemployment: A Problem of Industry* (1909). Although the 'personal factor' in unemployment was not eliminated, the stress was placed firmly on larger and more impersonal forces. Studies like this highlighted periodic cycles in unemployment, which permeated the entire labour market. They also distinguished very different patterns of unemployment across industries and by skill level. While cyclical unemployment was most severe in export industries such as engineering and shipbuilding and in construction, in other cases the organisation of the labour market was seen as faulty. In sectors where casual engagement was the norm such as unskilled building labour, and most notably on the docks, lack of co-ordination produced a pool of permanently underemployed labour. This diagnosis was clearly reflected in legislation enacted just before the First World War. The National Insurance Act (Part II) of 1911 was designed to provide workers with unemployment benefit during depressions in trade, while the Labour Exchanges Act of 1909 was aimed at reducing wasteful frictions between labour supply and labour demand.

Legislation reflected not only contemporary understanding of the unemployment problem but political imperatives too. From the turn of the century the increasing clamour of the unemployed and the growing strength of labour representatives in parliament pushed the Liberal government into action (Brown 1971: ch. 8; Harris 1972: ch. 5). Further extension of the franchise in 1918, the demobilisation crisis and the emergence of mass unemployment in 1921 provided the background to a substantial expansion of the system beyond the small group of trades covered before the war. The emergence of mass unemployment in the 1920s and its persistence into the 1930s transformed the unemployment question from one problem among many to *the* problem for economic and social policy during the interwar period.

The experience of mass unemployment provided the background for a new view of the causes of unemployment that emerged during the 1930s. Keynes' *General Theory of Employment, Interest and Money* (1936) laid the blame on deficient aggregate demand for goods and services and placed the onus for remedial action firmly at the door of the government.

As in the pre-war period the emerging consensus was best summarised by Beveridge, this time in his book *Full Employment in a Free Society* (1944: 89):

> The central problem of unemployment between the wars was not what it had seemed to be before the First World War. It was not a problem of cyclical unemployment reducing demand for a time, or of disorganisation of the labour market wasting men's lives in drifting and waiting. It was a problem of persistent weakness of demand for labour.

This new consensus was reflected in the White Paper on Employment Policy of 1944 and in policies designed to maintain full employment in the 1950s and 1960s.

Since Beveridge wrote, opinion on the character, causes and ultimate remedies for unemployment in the interwar period has ebbed and flowed. For a while, the Keynesian demand-side analysis held sway. But with unemployment rising again in the 1970s new theories revived views that had previously been sidelined. One view is that interwar unemployment was essentially a structural problem caused by the decline of the so-called staple industries. More prominent still is the idea that the system of unemployment benefits, designed to cope with the effects of unemployment, in fact became its cause. Some see the emerging strength of labour in collective bargaining as impeding labour market adjustment while others associate the emergence of mass unemployment with shocks to the supply side of the economy. These arguments will be reviewed in what follows, but it is important first to explore more fully the dimensions of unemployment.

UNEMPLOYMENT STATISTICS

The level of unemployment recorded in the statistics depends upon how unemployment is defined and measured. The distinction between those who are counted as unemployed and those who are not is always somewhat blurred at the margins. Among the most difficult areas are: how far those with weak labour force attachment are counted as part of the labour force; whether those on short time or temporary layoff are counted as employed or unemployed; and whether those who are self-employed or in informal employment are included in the statistics at all. In practice the definition of unemployment reflects the structures for the administration of assistance to the unemployed. As a result the definitions tend to be narrower than might otherwise be desirable. More important still, the scope of the administrative structures through which unemployment is measured changes dramatically over time (see Garside 1979: chs. 1, 2).

For the interwar period we have relatively comprehensive statistics that result from the joint operation of the labour exchanges and the unemployment insurance system. On becoming unemployed an insured worker would register at the exchange and at the same time apply for benefit (a small number of uninsured workers also registered). The rate of unemployment among insured workers averaged 14.2 per cent between 1921 and 1938. But only two-thirds of all workers were covered by unemployment insurance. Unemployment was much lower among those in occupations that were not covered, such as farm workers, domestic servants, certain public employees and white-collar workers. Estimates of the unemployment rate among all employees therefore yields a somewhat lower average unemployment rate of 10.9 per cent (Feinstein 1972: T128)

Pre-First World War statistics are much less satisfactory. Before the advent of labour exchanges and unemployment insurance there were no comprehensive administrative statistics upon which to base an estimate. Even those relating to the years 1913 to 1920 are restricted to relatively few sectors of the economy. However, the Board of Trade compiled an index of unemployment from 1888 onwards, based on the records of trade unions that paid some form of benefit to their unemployed members. On the basis of a small number of unions, that index was extended back to 1860 in order to provide a reasonably long perspective on the course of unemployment. This index reflects unemployment among unionists chiefly in engineering, building and metal trades although the number of trades covered increases over time. It largely excludes unskilled workers and those in service sector trades and agriculture. And it does not include as unemployed those on short time or temporary layoff even among the sectors that were covered by the index.

From 1870 to 1913 the Board of Trade's unemployment rate fluctuates between 0.9 per cent and 10.7 per cent, with an overall average of 4.5 per cent. Although this index has been widely referred to as a key indicator of the state of the labour market in the era before 1914, its narrow base makes comparisons with later periods difficult.[2] On the basis of his knowledge of the labour market Beveridge guessed that pre-war unemployment averaged about 6 per cent, and following from this, that during the interwar years unemployment was 'between two and three times as severe as before the First World War' (1944: 336).

Recently a new index has been derived that attempts to remedy some of the deficiencies inherent in the Board of Trade index (Boyer and Hatton 2002). This new index includes an allowance for short-time working in certain key industries, it includes unskilled labour, it uses labour force weights and it is adjusted on to an economy-wide basis. It is therefore as consistent as possible with later periods. This new series is plotted in Figure 13.1 together with the (adjusted) figures for the interwar period. The average unemployment rate for 1870–1913 is 5.8 per cent; somewhat

[2] Officals of the Board of Trade were well aware of the deficiences of the index. They recognised that unemployment in the trades covered by the index fluctuated more widely than unemployment in other sectors, but they suggested that the index was a good barometer of the direction of change in labour market conditions (Garside 1979: 21).

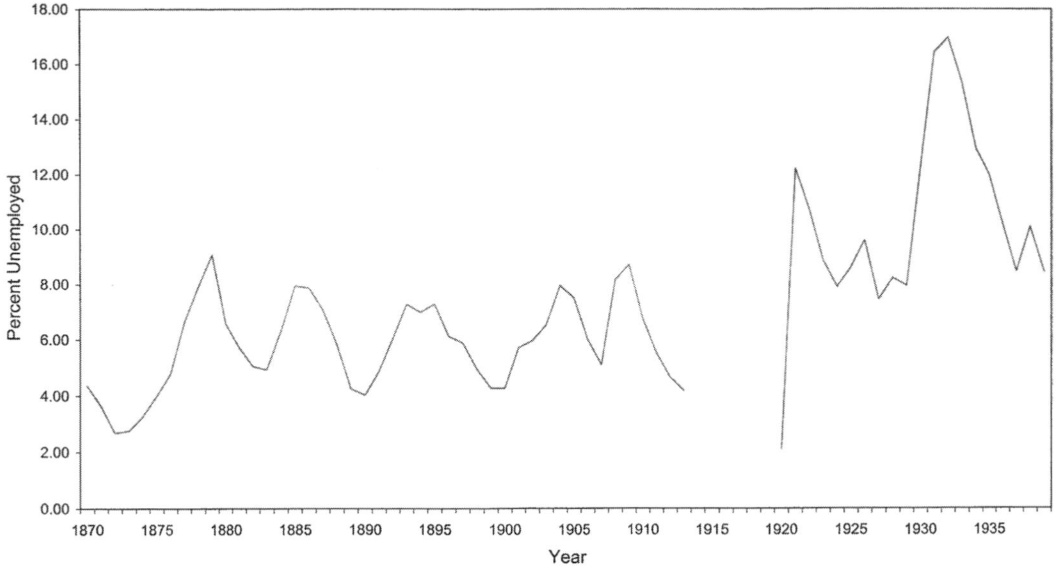

Figure 13.1 Unemployment rate, 1870–1939

Source: Boyer and Hatton 2002.

higher than that of the Board of Trade's index. During the interwar period the average unemployment rate was 10.9 per cent; nearly twice as high as the pre-war average. Thus the rise in the average unemployment rate between the pre-war and interwar periods is at the lower end of the range suggested by Beveridge.

Figure 13.1 shows that before 1914 there was a fairly regular cycle, consistent with other cyclical indicators, with unemployment rates reaching 6 to 8 per cent in depressions and falling to 3 or 4 per cent in booms. By contrast, after the intense boom of 1918–20, the years when unemployment was lowest in the interwar period were comparable with the years when it was highest in the pre-war period. The sharp increases in unemployment which occurred in 1920–1 and in 1929–31 have almost no parallel before the war. This highlights the most important feature revealed by the new pre-war estimates: that unemployment was far less volatile from year to year than the Board of Trade's estimate suggested. The coefficient of variation of the new index is 0.23 compared with 0.55 for the Board of Trade index. Thus the new estimates, while confirming that unemployment was significantly lower before 1914 than in the interwar period, also suggest that it was less volatile before the First World War than it was in the ensuing decades.

PATTERNS OF UNEMPLOYMENT

Unemployment varied greatly across time, place, industry and occupation. Industries such as metals, engineering, shipbuilding, construction and mining were among the most volatile before 1914. These were industries connected with the production of goods for investment or export, which were the least stable components of aggregate demand. Thus, for example, in shipbuilding the unemployment rate ranged between 0.7 and 22.7 per cent and in construction it varied between 0.6 and 12.4 per cent. In other trades where demand varied less the range of unemployment rates was correspondingly smaller: 1.3 to 6.3 per cent in printing and bookbinding and 2.9 to 8.6 per cent in transport. Nevertheless, changes in unemployment rates were strongly correlated across different industrial sectors. This reflects the fact that, although fluctuations were more intense in some sectors than others, periodic booms and slumps were pervasive across the economy as a whole. In booms unemployment rates tended to be close together while in slumps the most volatile industries suffered much higher unemployment rates than the others.

In the interwar period, a pattern reminiscent of pre-war booms and slumps can be observed but on an altogether different scale. Unemployment in engineering, shipbuilding and construction and other heavy industries fluctuated more widely than the average. But the pattern typical of a pre-war slump was intensified, persisted throughout the period and saw higher unemployment in virtually all industries. Thus the average unemployment rate for 1923 to 1938 was 23.1 per cent in mining and 24.3 per cent in the metal trades as compared with 6.7 per cent in paper and printing and 9.5 per cent in food, drink and tobacco. These differences reflect the sharp and permanent decline in employment in the great staple industries of the late nineteenth century. Because they were located disproportionately in the north of England, Wales, Scotland and Northern Ireland, these differences in unemployment rates were also reflected in persistent regional variations in unemployment. Across the nine regions distinguished by the Ministry of Labour average rates varied from 8 per cent in London and the South-East to around 22 per cent in the most hard-hit regions of Wales and Northern Ireland.

The regional pattern of unemployment is illustrated for three interwar years in Table 13.1. Some observers have suggested that this persistent regional pattern was the reverse of that which typically prevailed before the First World War. The first column of Table 13.1 reports unemployment rates in the second half of 1913 for the limited range of trades that were covered by unemployment insurance at that time. However, this was a time of low unemployment overall. Using the records from trade unions in the engineering and building trades Southall (1988) shows that during economic slumps unemployment rates among unionists were substantially higher in Scotland and the north of England than they were in the south.

This persistent maldistribution of unemployment during the interwar period has led some observers to argue that unemployment during the interwar period was largely structural in nature (Booth and Glynn 1975). In this view unemployment should be understood more in terms of the

Table 13.1 Regional unemployment rates, 1913–36

Region	1913	Region	1929	1932	1936
London and South-East	5.8	London	4.7	12.6	6.4
		South-East	3.3	12.0	5.0
South-West	4.4	South-West	6.0	14.8	7.1
West Midlands	2.6	Midlands	9.5	21.2	8.6
Yorkshire and East Midlands	1.9	North-East	12.6	29.8	17.5
North-West	2.5	North-West	12.8	26.8	16.4
Scotland and north	2.0	Scotland	10.9	25.9	15.8
Wales	2.4	Wales	18.1	37.3	29.0
Ireland	7.6	N. Ireland	13.7	25.9	19.6

Source: Southall 1988: 241; Hatton 1986: 63.

problems of specific industries and regions than as a general macroeconomic failure. The structural view implies that policies aimed at moving workers to jobs or jobs to workers would have been more effective than the management of aggregate demand. There is some evidence that structural turbulence was greater in the interwar period than it was before 1914 (see further below). Nevertheless, the pattern of interwar unemployment was similar to that in pre-war slumps, with the important difference that it persisted for twenty years. It therefore seems likely that an increase in economic activity, however it arose, would have tended to narrow the differences in unemployment rates across industries and regions. Such tendencies can be observed at the end of the 1930s when, with war approaching, regional and industrial differences began to melt away as aggregate unemployment fell (Hatton 1986: 75).

If labour mobility between regions, industries and occupations was low, then demand shocks or structural change would have resulted in higher and more persistent unemployment than otherwise. Between 1870 and 1914, the growth of the industrial cities of the north of England, the shipbuilding centres of the north-east and Scotland, the coalfields of South Wales and the commercial, financial and service industries of London attracted migrants from other urban areas and from the rural hinterland. Both internal migration and emigration were responsive to relative wage rates and, especially, to variations in unemployment (Southall 1991; Boyer and Hatton 1997). In the interwar period, too, a substantial redistribution of the labour force took place. The share of the insured labour force in southern England and the Midlands rose from 46.8 per cent in 1923 to 52.3 per cent in 1938. Meanwhile the gap in unemployment rates was almost unchanged. Thus, although migration did respond to differentials in wage rates and unemployment it was not sufficient to even out the regional imbalance in unemployment rates.

It is far from clear whether labour mobility was lower in the interwar period than before 1914. In the late nineteenth century rural areas provided a reservoir of labour which drained more rapidly in booms and less rapidly in slumps, as to some extent did international migration. By the interwar period these sources of flexibility had diminished. But there still remains the question of why greater numbers did not move south during the interwar period. One argument is that the new jobs which were being created in light industries and the service sector did not recruit displaced workers from the staple industries but sought 'new' labour in the form of juveniles, women or workers previously in non-industrial occupations (Heim 1984). Another is that unemployment in the south was simply not low enough to make migration a risk worth taking. From 1928 an industrial transference scheme was operated by the Ministry of Labour to find vacancies in the south for the unemployed in the depressed areas and to help with removal expenses. With the intensification of unemployment after 1929, the number of transferees declined and many returned home.[3] The limited success of the scheme suggests that it was largely the poor job prospects, rather than unwillingness to move, that limited geographical mobility.

Periodic downturns in the economy were met with different forms of adjustment. In coal mining much of the adjustment took the form of reducing the number of days the pits worked, sharing the burden across the workforce. In textiles too, short-time working or temporary layoffs were a common response to a downturn in activity before the First World War. From 1926 the Ministry of Labour distinguished three types of unemployed on the register: the wholly unemployed, the temporarily stopped and casuals. The wholly unemployed were those with no job, who were looking for new employment. The temporarily stopped were those who had been laid off by their employers but with a definite promise of re-employment within six weeks. They accounted for almost a fifth of recorded unemployment between 1928 and 1938. The number of temporarily stopped tended to increase at the beginning of a downturn in economic activity but then decreased as a share of all unemployment when, as in the 1930s, the decline became more permanent. They were also concentrated in certain industries. Among men, in September 1929, over half the temporarily stopped were in mining, metals, engineering and textiles. Among women, nearly 80 per cent were in textiles and clothing.

Casuals were those for whom normal employment was for a day or a few days at a time, interspersed with frequent days of unemployment. Unskilled labourers on the docks, in construction and in a variety of other trades were hired by the day from a crowd at the factory gates, each gaining a few days employment in any week. Before 1914 these

[3] Over the period 1928–38 about 30 per cent of transferees returned. It has been suggested that, although transferees were given preference for jobs at the receiving labour exchanges, partly for this reason, they faced a somewhat hostile social environment in the towns to which they moved (Scott 2000: 347–9).

formed a substantial core of workers in a state of what might be called rotating underemployment. As with the temporarily stopped, pre-war patterns of unemployment persisted into the interwar period (Whiteside and Gillespie 1991). But from 1928 to 1938 casuals formed only 4.5 per cent of insured unemployment and, like the temporarily stopped, they were overshadowed in terms of sheer numbers by the much larger volume of the wholly unemployed.

In the interwar period those who suffered the highest unemployment rates were the unskilled, whichever industry or region they belonged to. Among males in 1931 the unemployment rate for clerical workers, supervisors and foremen was 5.4 per cent; for skilled and semi-skilled manual workers it was 12 per cent; and for unskilled manual workers 21.5 per cent (Thomas 1988: 123). But this was not new. Although there are no firm estimates of unemployment rates among the unskilled before the First World War, there was a growing recognition of the intermittent nature of unskilled work. And the rising rate of pauperism suggests that it was becoming more intense, especially from the early 1890s. In his pioneering investigations in east London Charles Booth (1892: 36) found that about 12 per cent of the male labour force in the East End of London, typically the least skilled and least able, were chronically unemployed or underemployed.[4]

The problem of the so-called residuum of the chronically unemployed drew special attention in the years before 1914. It was often associated with the hiring practices of firms in trades with high volatility in demand for labour from day to day or month to month where no centralised employment exchanges existed. Lack of skills and low industrial quality were seen as part cause and part effect of the structure and dynamics of the labour market. As Beveridge remarked ‘casuals by necessity are always on the way to become casuals by inclination’ (1930: 130–1). Furthermore, unemployment and underemployment perpetuated themselves from one generation to the next. Unskilled jobs were abundant for young workers but, on reaching the age of 18 or 21, opportunities for unskilled labour at adult wage rates diminished sharply. For children in poor households the immediate rewards of a job often outweighed the longer-term rewards of acquiring skills which would ensure a lower probability of unemployment in the future (Stedman Jones 1971, ch. 4). To some observers this was part of a cycle of urban degeneration in which poverty and unemployment in one generation led to among other things, poor physique, low expectations and lack of labour market quality in the next.

Contemporary observers, both before and after the First World War, repeatedly found that unemployment was associated with individual characteristics (see, for example, Rowntree and Lasker 1911; Pilgrim Trust 1938). Not only were the unemployed more often unskilled than the

[4] For a discussion of living standards and poverty, see chapter 11.

employed, they also comprised the least motivated and the least physically fit and able part of the labour force. Workers over the age of 50, with declining health and efficiency, were more often unemployed and for longer periods than younger workers. A significant proportion of these had once been in regular skilled or semi-skilled employment and had slipped into the ranks of the chronically underemployed. Nevertheless, very few could be described as unemployable.[5] Rather they were among the last to be employed when demand for labour was increasing, and among the first to be released when it was declining.

THE UNEMPLOYMENT PROCESS

Unemployment rates alone can tell us little about the dynamics of unemployment flows. For example an annual unemployment rate of 10 per cent could arise from ten workers in every hundred being jobless for the whole year, twenty being jobless for six months each, or sixty each with two months of unemployment. In the first case unemployment is a 'stagnant pool' in which the faces change only slowly. At the other extreme it is a 'rushing stream' with individuals flowing in and out rapidly. Which of these characterisations is correct matters both for assessing the hardships borne by the unemployed and for understanding the causes of their unemployment. Though it may seem odd at first sight, both of these characterisations were evident in some degree.

Before 1914 evidence from the unemployment books of trade unions indicates that between 20 and 40 per cent of members became unemployed in an average year, roughly five to eight times the number who were unemployed at any one point in time (Beveridge 1909: 71). From this, the average duration of an unemployment spell can be calculated. Between 1894 and 1903 average duration was 10.2 weeks for the London Compositors, 4.8 weeks for the Amalgamated Mill Sawyers, 8.4 weeks for the Associated Blacksmiths and 6.7 weeks for the London Bookbinders. The vast majority of the unemployment spells in these and other unions was for less than three months. A small minority nevertheless experienced repeated spells of unemployment. Thus, although long spells of continuous unemployment were rare, a disproportionate share of all unemployment was concentrated among a small minority of members.

From the early 1920s, the working of the labour exchanges and the unemployment insurance system provide us with a much richer statistical picture. Even among the wholly unemployed (excluding the temporarily stopped and casuals), the vast majority did not stay on the unemployment

[5] The Pilgrim Trust's survey of men who were long-term unemployed in the 1930s found that while 64 per cent were fully employable, 30 per cent were mentally or physically restricted, but only 6 per cent were totally unemployable (1938: 432).

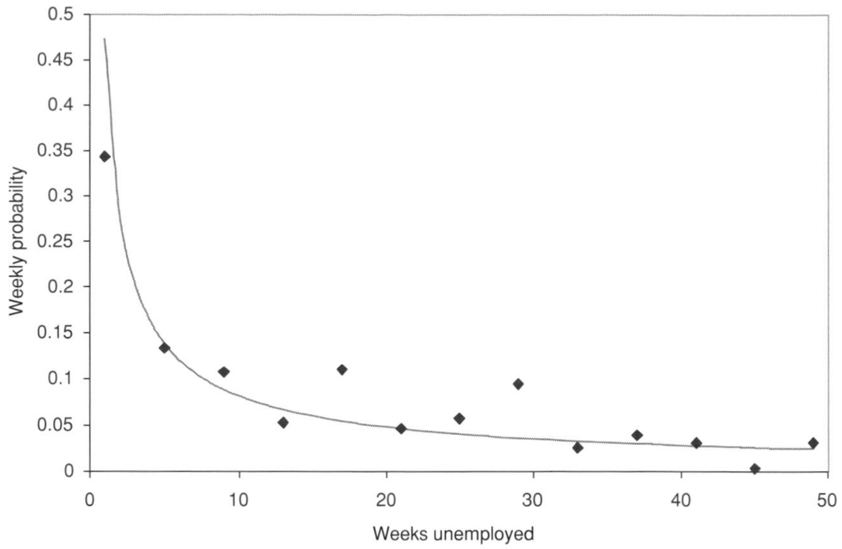

Figure 13.2 The probability of leaving unemployment, 1929

Source: Calculated from *Ministry of Labour Gazette*, 1930.

register for long. Among those who regained employment it is estimated that a third were returning to their previous employer (even though they were not classified as temporarily stopped). Others accepted jobs that were notified to the exchanges. But about four times as many moved into jobs that had not been advertised at the exchanges. Taking these into account it can be estimated that, during the 1930s, the average monthly flow into jobs was equivalent to nearly two-fifths of the average number wholly unemployed on the register. This means that if all the unemployed had an equal chance of finding a vacancy, that chance would be two in five of finding a job within a month.

Given this rapid rate of outflow from unemployment one might expect that, at any given time, there must have been a large stock of vacancies waiting to be filled. This was not the case. A crude estimate for the 1920s (there are no data for the 1930s) indicates that there was on average one unfilled vacancy for every eight of the wholly unemployed. So why was the stock of unfilled vacancies so small compared with the monthly flow of workers into jobs? Evidently the new vacancies were taken up almost immediately; 95 per cent were taken up within a week of being posted (Hatton 1985). As a result the number outstanding at any moment in time was small. This implies that the unemployed queuing at the exchanges were eager to take up the jobs offered; they were not as choosy as some would suggest.

Who were those that were most fortunate in finding vacancies quickly? In 1929 the Ministry of Labour conducted a special analysis of the durations of unemployment among benefit claimants. We can use the results to estimate the chance of leaving the register at different unemployment durations, as shown in Figure 13.2. This relationship is best illustrated

Table 13.2 The duration of unemployment, 1929–38 (wholly unemployed only)

	Percentage of unemployed with durations of:		Estimated completed average duration of a spell (weeks)	Estimated uncompleted duration of average unemployed worker (weeks)
	Less than three months	More than one year		
1929	43.7	7.2	–	15.4
1932	40.8	22.0	19.5	34.1
1933	38.9	28.4	17.9	43.6
1934	41.3	29.0	16.6	45.8
1935	41.6	28.5	14.4	45.6
1936	42.9	29.5	13.9	49.1
1937	46.2	28.1	14.2	48.7
1938	48.3	23.2	13.1	39.0

Source: Thomas 1988: 112.

by the curve fitted to the scatter of points. It reveals a dramatic decline in the probability of leaving unemployment in the first month on the register, followed by a more gentle decline. Although the weekly probability of leaving the register was nearly a half during the first week of unemployment, after a year it falls to one in fifty. Even those who had been on the register for three months were likely to go on being unemployed for a long time. This pattern has led some to describe the interwar labour market as 'bifurcated' (Thomas 1988). Those who were most likely to regain employment were those who had spent the least time unemployed. It is as if most of those joining the queue joined it at, or near, the front. For those towards the back, the chance of re-employment became increasingly remote as their unemployment duration increased.[6]

With the sharp increase in layoffs in the early 1930s the chances of re-employment declined for all the unemployed. It was this that gave rise to what was perhaps the most sombre legacy of the depression: the host of the long-term unemployed that persisted into the late 1930s. The share of the wholly unemployed who had been unemployed for less than three months and for more than a year is shown in the first two columns of Table 13.2. In the worst years of the 1930s over two-fifths of the unemployed had been on the register for less than three months. At the other extreme, the proportion of long-term unemployed rose to over 20 per cent and stayed there until 1938. Information on the numbers in different duration categories can be used to estimate the average length of a completed spell of unemployment. The third column of the table shows

[6] There are two reasons why re-employment probabilities decline with the duration of unemployment. One is that individuals entering unemployment have different characteristics that affect their chances of re-employment. Those with the best chance leave the register quickly so that those remaining on the register for long periods are typically the ones with the lowest chances of exit. The other is that, for any given individual, the chance of re-employment declines with duration due to the atrophy of skills and/or motivation.

that the average length of unemployment spells reached twenty weeks in 1932 before declining to thirteen or fourteen weeks in the late 1930s.

It is important to be aware of the difference between the duration of a typical spell of unemployment and the duration faced by the average worker on the unemployed register at any one time. Because of the rapid turnover of the short-term unemployed, most spells were short. But because of the sharply diminishing chances of re-employment illustrated in Figure 13.2 the typical worker observed on the register would be undergoing a much longer spell. Following Crafts (1987) column 4 of the table shows the average uncompleted duration of unemployment of those on the register. This was between ten and eleven months for most of the 1930s. Because the unemployed are observed, on average, half-way through a spell of unemployment, their average completed durations would have been about twice as long. Hence, on a conservative estimate, the average unemployed worker in the 1930s was enduring a spell of unemployment that would last a year and nine months.

Even this figure is likely to underestimate the concentration of unemployment if repeated spells are taken into account. Among those observed as unemployed at a particular date, perhaps with a relatively short duration, some would have experienced a previous spell of unemployment in the recent past. Of a sample of wholly unemployed applicants for benefit in 1932, the average length of the current spell of unemployment, up to two years, was twenty-three weeks. But the average number of weeks spent unemployed over the preceding two years was fifty-three weeks. Thus the burden of unemployment fell very unevenly. Some of the unemployed experienced single spells of unemployment, others experienced repeated spells, while the least fortunate experienced long durations of continuous unemployment.

UNEMPLOYMENT AND INSURANCE

The unemployment insurance system, introduced on a limited scale in 1911 and substantially expanded in 1920, marked a sharp break with the past. Before this, support for the unemployed was limited to benefit from trade unions, charity or the poor law. As we have seen, the expansion of unemployment insurance coincided with higher average unemployment in the years after 1920 as compared with before the First World War. On the one hand this might be seen as rather fortuitous, since it helped to avert even greater poverty and destitution that might otherwise have occurred among the families of the unemployed. But on the other hand it has been forcefully argued that generous unemployment benefits were the *cause* of persistently high unemployment. In their important article Benjamin and Kochin (1979) sought to overturn the previously accepted view that mass unemployment was largely the result of demand-side failure. Instead, they argued that 'the army of the unemployed standing watch at the publication of [Keynes'] *General Theory* was largely a volunteer army' (1979: 474). In this view, it was not that too few jobs were available but that too few workers were willing to accept offers of employment. The implication is that, with the exception of sharp cyclical downturns, there was relatively full employment for those who wanted to work, in spite of the high unemployment figures.

Benjamin and Kochin argued that the abnormally high levels of unemployment in the interwar period were largely the result of high rates of benefit provided by the unemployment insurance system (relative to prevailing wage rates), combined with the liberal eligibility conditions under which these benefits were administered. For such disincentive effects to occur benefits need not have been as high as wages, since the unemployed would have gained additional leisure from not working. Benefits could be claimed for periods as short as one day provided that that day's unemployment could be linked to a spell of unemployment in the recent past.[7] Once a claim to benefit had been established, benefit could be drawn almost indefinitely, although, from 1931, continuation after six months was contingent on a means test.[8] Thus, according to this view, a significant proportion of the unemployed spent longer searching for new employment and were more choosy in accepting offers, or were content to live on benefits without the burden of having to work.

Benjamin and Kochin argued that during the interwar period 'benefits were on a more generous scale than ever before or since' (1979: 442). Using the rate of benefit for an adult male claiming for a wife and two children, they estimated that the benefit to wage ratio averaged 0.49 over the period 1920–38 with a peak of 0.57 in 1936. But their use of a wage index that includes women and young workers exaggerates this ratio, as does the assumption that the typical adult male had three dependants. A more realistic figure for the average benefit to wage ratio in the 1930s would be around 0.4 (Table 13.3). Nevertheless, when examining benefit to wage ratios, averages can be misleading. The average ratio could be quite

[7] Normally there was a waiting period of six days between first registering as unemployed and receiving benefit. Any three days of unemployment within six working days could be counted as continuous unemployment. Under the 'continuity rule' spells of unemployment less than ten weeks apart could be connected together without having to serve further waiting days. It has sometimes been argued that these rules encouraged firms to engage in temporary layoffs, rotating their labour force so that the workers involved could maintain continuous entitlement to benefit on the days or weeks they were unemployed.

[8] From 1921 onwards the system of unemployment benefit consisted of two distinct elements. Unemployment insurance benefit could be claimed as a right by those who could meet the qualifying conditions. For those who could not or who had exhausted their insurance benefit claims, support was provided under a supplementary system where there was generally a greater element of discretion. There was a sequence of these schemes, representing slightly different sets of rules, under the titles uncovenanted benefit, extended benefit, transitional benefit, transitional payments and, from January 1935, unemployment assistance. Full details of the evolution of the insurance and supplementary systems can be found in Burns 1941.

Table 13.3 Benefit to wage ratios for claimants to insurance benefits, 1937 (cumulative percentage)

B/W ratio greater than	Men aged 18–20	Men aged 21–64	Women aged 18–20	Women aged 21–64
1.0	2.6	0.5	3.4	0.9
0.8	6.5	2.0	8.2	4.4
0.6	17.1	11.7	23.1	17.5
0.4	48.0	50.6	78.8	82.8
0.2	97.6	98.8	99.8	100.0
Average B/W	0.38	0.43	0.48	0.50

Source: Calculated from HMSO 1937: 55–9.

low, but if benefits were high relative to wages for a substantial minority, there could be a significant effect on unemployment in total. In the late 1930s, the Ministry of Labour conducted surveys of the unemployed to investigate precisely this issue. As Table 13.3 shows, among insurance benefit recipients, hardly any had benefits in excess of the wage in their last job. Only 2.0 per cent of adult men and 4.4 per cent of adult women had benefits higher than four-fifths of their last wage. Among recipients of unemployment assistance (those who did not qualify for insurance benefits), few had benefits in excess of their last wage but a larger proportion had benefits in excess of four-fifths of it: 15 per cent of men and 18 per cent of women.

The evidence for benefit-induced unemployment rested principally on the results from an econometric equation estimated on annual observations from 1920 to 1938. From the results, Benjamin and Kochin calculated that, had the benefit to wage ratio remained at a relatively low level (specifically, 0.27), then the unemployment rate among insured workers would have averaged between 9.6 and 6.9 per cent between 1921 and 1938 rather than the 14.2 per cent actually observed. But the basis of this calculation has been severely criticised on two grounds. First, the empirical estimate of the effect of the benefit to wage ratio on unemployment is not robust to small changes in specification (Ormerod and Worswick 1982). Second, the model itself does not provide an appropriate framework with which to measure the effect of benefits on unemployment (Broadberry 1983; Hatton 1983).

Benjamin and Kochin viewed unemployment in the interwar period as the result of individual behaviour rather than of collective action. Thus individuals or groups, who would have received high benefits if unemployed relative to their wages if employed, are more likely to be observed as unemployed. But hypotheses about the *incidence* of unemployment across different individuals can only be tested with individual level data. And simply knowing the benefit to wage ratios of different individuals or groups is not enough. There are a variety of other personal characteristics and circumstances, in addition to benefits, that make some individuals more likely to become unemployed. In a pioneering study Eichengreen (1987) examined data for 3,000 adult males from the *New Survey of London Life and Labour* (*NSLLL*), a survey of working-class households in London in 1929–31. He found that the effect of benefits on the probability of unemployment was modest overall and that household heads were less susceptible to benefit-induced unemployment than were non-heads.

The development of a larger and richer set of data from the same source makes it possible to conduct a fuller analysis than was feasible with Eichengreen's 10 per cent sample (see Hatton and Bailey 2002). For adult males aged 25–64, econometric estimates on these new data indicate that the effects of the benefit to wage ratio on the probability of unemployment were close to zero. But it is important also to allow for the effects of the individual's skill level and industry on the probability of being unemployed. The unskilled were significantly more likely to be unemployed than skilled or semi-skilled workers – an effect that could otherwise be falsely attributed to the benefit to wage ratio. (Since the unskilled had lower wages on average, they also had higher benefit to wage ratios.) Among men aged 25 to 64 (mainly household heads) a small positive effect of the benefit to wage ratio disappears once these characteristics are taken into account.

Two groups not previously examined are young workers and females. Benefit rates increased in a number of steps between first entry into insurance at the age of 16 and receiving the full adult rate at the age of 21. Benjamin and Kochin suggested that this could largely explain why unemployment rates gradually increased with age among these younger workers. But wages also increased with age and so, for young males, there was very little increase in the benefit to wage ratio between the ages of 17 and 23. Estimates using the *NSLLL* confirm that the benefit to wage ratio does not explain why the incidence of unemployment increased with age. An alternative is the argument mentioned earlier that young men often entered dead-end jobs, finding themselves laid off and without skills by the age of 21. If so, then the effect of being unskilled on the incidence of unemployment should have increased with age. Surprisingly, no such effect could be found: unemployment incidence did increase sharply with age but this does not seem to be due to the changing effects of skill.

Among young women, the benefit to wage ratio did increase with age but unemployment incidence did not rise appreciably. For women over the age of 24 the average benefit to wage ratio was higher than for adult males, but their unemployment rates were only half those of males. In neither case could significant benefit effects be found. However, the Anomalies Regulations introduced in October 1931 tightened the conditions for receiving benefit, particularly for married women. As a result the unemployment rate among women fell relative to that among men (Beveridge 1936: 359). But this was because fewer unemployed women bothered to register at the exchanges rather than that they had found jobs.

Overall, studies of the most detailed evidence available suggest that the *direct* effects of unemployment benefits on unemployment were minimal. This is consistent with the qualitative findings of contemporary observers, one of whom commented that 'The behaviour of the unemployed in searching for employment gives no evidence that the possibility of drawing Unemployment Insurance benefit has retarded the efforts of the unemployed to get back to work. It has removed the cutting edge of the desperation that would otherwise attend that search' (Bakke, 1933: 143). But it is important to stress that benefits could still have generated unemployment more *indirectly*. If, for example, unemployment benefit levels were used as reference points in wage negotiations, then the effect could have arisen though the collective action of unions and employers rather than as a result of the direct incentives facing individual workers.

DEMAND, SUPPLY AND REAL WAGES IN THE INTERWAR PERIOD

The high unemployment of the interwar period has often been associated with aggregate demand shocks, leading, as Beveridge put it, to 'persistent weakness of demand for labour' (1944: 89). As Figure 13.1 implies, the shocks to the labour market were much greater in the interwar period than in the period before 1914. In the pre-war period there were recurrent cyclical downturns such as the deep slump of the late 1870s and the sharp but short downturn of 1907–9, both of which saw unemployment rise to 8 per cent. In the former period there were contractions in domestic and foreign demand while the latter was associated with financial crisis abroad. But unemployment soon fell again, partly due to the revival of demand and partly due to adjustments in the labour market itself, which helped push unemployment back down towards its long-run average.

By contrast, demand shocks were much larger in the interwar period, and in their wake the unemployment rate soared to new heights. Within the space of a decade there were three major demand shocks. The post-war boom, driven by pent-up demand for investment and consumer goods, collapsed dramatically at the end of 1920. The return to the gold standard (both the anticipated and the actual increase in the sterling exchange rate) continued to hold back demand for the rest of the 1920s. Finally, the great depression, initiated by a fall in exports as world trade contracted, sent unemployment up to two-digit levels. Thus the story of persistently high interwar unemployment could be told in terms of a series of large and unanticipated negative demand shocks followed by incomplete recovery. But the fact that prices and wages fell only slowly after 1922 suggests that the equilibrium level of unemployment had also increased. Otherwise one might have expected continued deflation with wages falling faster than prices until the real wage had declined sufficiently to cause employment to recover and unemployment to rebound to levels approaching those typical of the pre-war period.

Lack of downward flexibility in real wages is seen by many as the heart of the interwar unemployment problem, and the wider debate about the relationship between real wages and employment stems from that time. The questions are whether fluctuations in employment are determined by real wages and, in turn, what determines the real wage. Keynes (1936: 17) predicted, on the basis of marginal productivity theory, a clear inverse relationship between the real wage and employment. But further investigation during the late 1930s cast doubt on this as an empirical proposition (Dunlop 1938; Keynes 1939). The course of the real wage (the nominal wage divided by the average price of output) and employment is shown for the whole economy and for the manufacturing sector in Figure 13.3. On trend, both the real wage and employment grew strongly over the interwar period. But even relative to trend, the sharp fall in employment in 1929–31 and the subsequent recovery has little parallel in real wage movements at the economy-wide level. For the manufacturing sector, however, there is some evidence of inverse movements in the early 1930s and especially towards the end of the decade.

In order to identify the downward sloping demand curve relating employment to the real wage, other effects on employment must also be taken into account. There have been a series of econometric studies, using different specifications and different types of data, that have examined the employment demand relationship. Broadly speaking, three different views have emerged. One is that an inverse relationship between real wages and employment can be identified, at least for manufacturing, in the absence of variables representing demand shocks (Beenstock and Warburton 1991). A second view is that aggregate demand, as represented by its underlying determinants such as the money supply and world trade, had strong and permanent effects on employment. In the presence of these variables, a downward sloping real wage–employment relationship can be observed in aggregate (Dimsdale 1984) but not consistently across individual industries (Turner and Bowden 1997). A third view emerging chiefly from studies of quarterly (rather than annual) data suggests that although short-run demand effects can be identified, their effects are small and they diminish, or even disappear in the long run (Hatton 1988b; Dimsdale *et al.* 1989b).

The real wage elasticities that have been derived are sensitive to the specification used and they generally fall in the range between zero and minus one. A number of them are clustered in the middle of this range, suggesting a 'consensus' estimate of about −0.5. It is tempting to conclude from this that, had the real wage been set 10 per cent lower, then most of the abnormally high unemployment of the interwar period could have

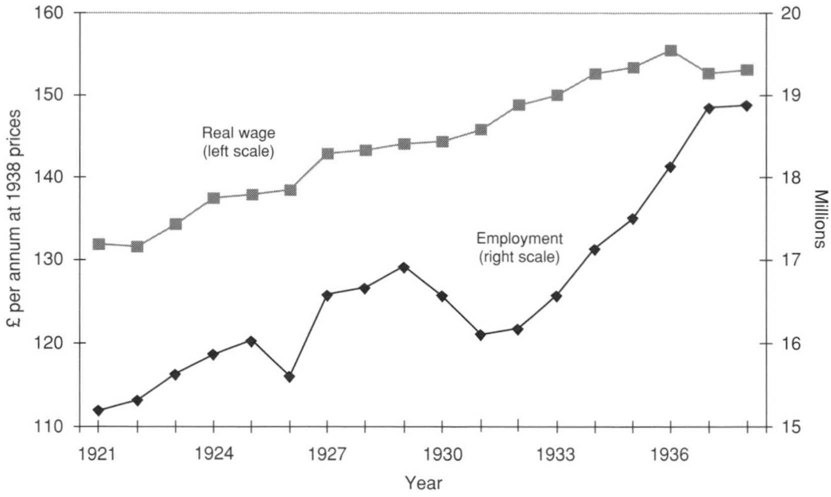

Figure 13.3a The real wage and employment, 1921–38: whole economy

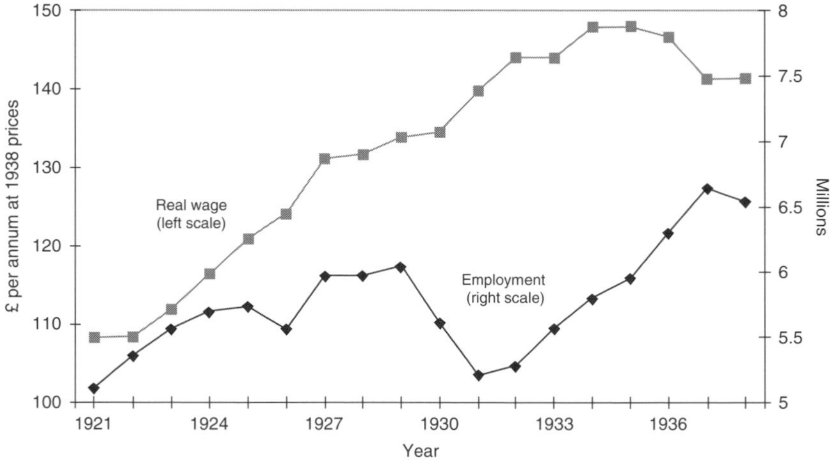

Figure 13.3b The real wage and employment, 1921–38: manufacturing sector

Source: Real wage from Dimsdale 1984: 95–7; employment from Chapman and Knight 1953: 18.

been eliminated. Indeed, some have taken the view that high real wages were *the* major cause of unemployment, even during the depression of the 1930s. But the real wage is itself the outcome of economic forces and cannot therefore be treated as a truly independent cause of high unemployment.

To understand real wage movements it is useful to use the 'competing claims' framework laid out by Layard *et al.* (1991), which has been widely used in the analysis of post-war unemployment. The key relationships are depicted in Figure 13.4. The upward sloping line reflects the behaviour of imperfectly competitive firms in setting prices as a markup on wage costs. Its position represents the 'feasible' real wage: the real wage that is consistent with the profit-maximising behaviour of firms. This could

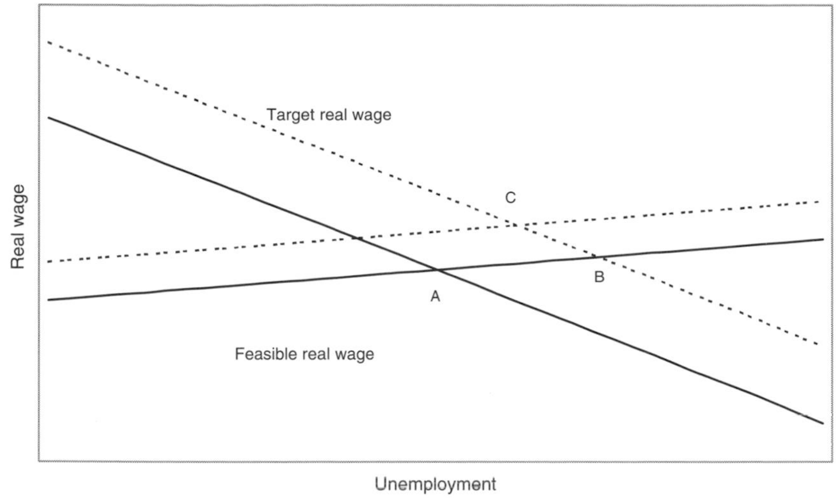

Figure 13.4 The competing claims model

shift upwards in the long run with a rise in productivity or a fall in raw material costs. In the short run it could increase if prices turned out to be lower than expected. The downward sloping line represents the 'target' wage that emerges from collective bargaining. This reflects conditions in the labour market: higher levels of employment lead to higher 'target' real wages. The target real wage schedule could shift upwards as a result of an increase in labour's bargaining power in wage negotiations, or of higher wage aspirations. These aspirations will in turn be affected by alternative incomes (such as unemployment benefits), and by the degree of competition and mobility in the labour market.

Equilibrium in the labour market is the intersection between the feasible wage schedule and the target wage schedule. At this point the two are reconciled and there is no unexpected inflation or deflation. The level of employment that emerges gives the Non-Accelerating Inflation Rate of Unemployment (NAIRU). A fall in demand for labour pushes employment below the NAIRU; prices and wages fall until the original equilibrium is restored. In this framework demand shocks, even if they are permanent, will depress employment for a while but their long-run effects on the level of unemployment will be temporary and the original real wage will be restored. During the period of adjustment, the real wage could either rise (if wages are less responsive to shocks than are prices) or fall (if prices are more sticky than wages). By contrast, a permanent upward shift in the target wage schedule would lead to a permanent rise in the NAIRU. The long-run result would be a higher real wage but lower employment.

This framework can be used to explain the course of real wages during the 1930s. As Figure 13.5 shows, both the nominal wage and the price level declined from 1929 to the mid-1930s and then recovered. Between

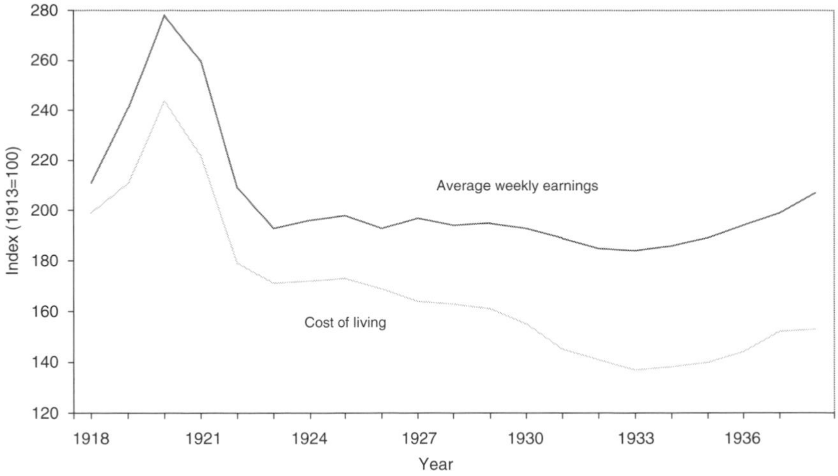

Figure 13.5 Wage rates and the cost of living, 1918–38

Source: Feinstein 1972: table 65.

1929 and 1931 the demand shocks arising from the worldwide slump in world trade and the fall in world prices caused employment to contract. Downward pressure on the real wage due to the fall in employment was more than offset by increased labour market turbulence and especially by the sharp fall in the prices of basic commodities (Dimsdale *et al.* 1989b: 288). This is illustrated in Figure 13.4 by the move from point A to point B. Over the longer term the feasible real wage shifted upwards as productivity increased, but there was also an upward shift in the target real wage. The situation in the mid-1930s is represented by the new equilibrium, with a higher real wage and slightly higher unemployment, at point C in Figure 13.4.

A number of factors have been identified that determined wage pressure over the longer term and which, by shifting up the target wage relative to the feasible wage, kept the NAIRU in the interwar period above pre-1914 levels. These include unemployment benefits, which are seen here as influencing unemployment indirectly by setting a floor to wage bargaining, rather than directly through individual work incentives. They also include trade union density as a proxy for labour's bargaining strength in wage negotiations (with higher unionism raising the target wage). In addition, the marginalisation of some groups of workers weakened labour market competition so that wage pressure decreased by less than the high unemployment levels would suggest. 'Mismatch' between the characteristics demanded by new jobs and those possessed by the existing labour force, marginalising those with obsolete skills, is one example (Dimsdale *et al.* 1989b). And, as we have seen, the long-term unemployed, drifting to the back of the queue, were unable to compete effectively for jobs. The evidence suggests that they exerted very little downward pressure on wage rates (Crafts 1989a) and that this factor helps to explain the *persistence* of high unemployment in the 1930s.

Estimates of the relative magnitude of these effects on the unemployment percentage vary, but most of them are based on analysing data from the early 1920s to the late 1930s – a period when variations in the underlying NAIRU were relatively small. The years between 1918 and 1921 are usually excluded from the analysis and they are very different from the rest of the period. Prices and wages first rose dramatically in the aftermath of the war and then spiralled downwards until 1922. As we have seen, unemployment was very low until 1920 and then increased sharply, never recovering its former level until the Second World War. In part this was due to severe demand shocks, first positive and then negative, which far exceeded the contractionary impulse between 1929 and 1931. Unemployment was clearly below the NAIRU in 1919–20 and above the NAIRU by 1921. But the NAIRU itself seems to have increased sharply during these crucial years – perhaps by about 4 percentage points (see Table 13.4 below).

This rise in the NAIRU could have been accounted for, at least in part, by the sharp rise in unemployment benefit rates in 1920, associated with the dramatic extension in the share of the labour force covered by unemployment insurance. Perhaps more important was the sharp fall in average weekly hours of work of about 13 per cent in the first half of 1919 (Dowie 1975), which was not accompanied by a proportionate reduction in the weekly real wage. As a result average output per worker fell in proportion to the cut in hours, and the feasible wage fell relative to the target wage, leading to a sharp increase in the NAIRU (Broadberry 1986). This would be enough to account for the rise in the NAIRU and there is evidence that unemployment was strongly correlated with the divergence between output per worker and the real wage (Hatton 2002). The results suggest that the productivity shock raised unemployment – by as much as 4 percentage points in 1922 – but that the effect had largely disappeared by the end of the 1920s as the real wage gradually adjusted.[9]

By contrast with these effects, trade union membership *fell* sharply, by 1.7 million between 1920 and 1922, with an effect that should, on the face of it, have been lowering the target real wage. Nevertheless, it is often suggested that the hand of labour had been decisively strengthened during and immediately after the war – a view that was shared by many contemporary observers. Typical of these was the economist Henry Clay who argued in 1929 that:

> Before the war the policy of maintaining wage rates in spite of unemployment could be practised only by the organised minority of wage-earners. The majority were unable to resist reductions that were needed to maintain employment; and any workers excluded by the policy of the stronger unions could compete

[9] It is interesting to note, however, that the somewhat smaller reduction in hours in the early 1870s was also followed by a fairly deep recession.

> for employment in industries in which wages were not held above absorbtion level. Today there are no unorganised industries in this sense; wages are held up, either by trade-union or Government support, generally, and workers excluded by a *general* holding up of wage rates above absorbtion level have no resort except unemployment relief. (1929: 332)

In this view it was the changing balance of power in the labour market and in the structure of organisation within the labour market, buttressed by government intervention, that gave rise to high unemployment.

INSTITUTIONS AND WAGE SETTING

It is widely believed that the outcome of the wage setting process is influenced by the structure of collective bargaining, which, in turn, determines the position of the target real wage schedule in Figure 13.4. The most influential accounts stress two features: the degree of centralisation in the wage bargaining structure and/or co-ordination across sectors in wage bargaining, and the relative bargaining strengths of workers and employers (Calmfors and Driffill 1988; Soskice 1991). Systems of industrial relations that are either very decentralised or very centralised lead to target wage schedules that are located towards the left in Figure 13.4 while intermediate structures produce a target wage schedule displaced to the right. Thus there is a hump shaped relationship between the NAIRU and the degree of centralisation. When wages are set at the level of the individual firm, wage bargainers take into account the effect on employment of the relatively high elasticity of demand faced by the individual firm in an industry. The effect of wage increases on job losses tends to moderate wage claims. When wage setting is co-ordinated through an economy-wide 'encompassing' institutional structure a wage increase affects all firms relatively equally. But centralised (or co-ordinated) wage agreements would more likely take into account the negative economy-wide effects on employment of the implied increase in the aggregate price level. In the intermediate case, where bargaining takes place at the industry level, negative direct employment effects are smaller and the effects on the price level are small for each industry but large for the economy as a whole. Thus the combination of market power and lack of co-ordination increases the NAIRU. These stylised cases provide useful benchmarks for the assessment of bargaining structures between 1870 and 1939.

In 1850 trade unionists numbered about a quarter of a million, rising to three-quarters of a million by 1888 and two and a half million by 1913 by which time they comprised 23 per cent of the labour force. The phase of 'new unionism' in 1889–92 saw a permanent extension of organisation in the docks and gasworks, and the birth of several unions of unskilled workers – a pattern that was further extended in the years before 1914. But, even so, union strength remained concentrated in relatively few sectors. Only in mining were a majority of workers union members in 1910, though in other industries or occupations such as shipbuilding, cotton textiles, printing and among government employees union density exceeded a third (Clegg *et al.* 1964: 468). Sharp bursts in the growth of organisation in the early 1870s, 1889–92 and 1910–13 are often seen as marking changes in labour's bargaining strength, and this brought about a countervailing response from employers, and promoted institutional change in the wage setting process (Clegg *et al.* 1964: ch. 2). By 1914 there were 1,500 employers associations, varying greatly in size, strength and coherence. These can be seen in part as a response to the extension of union influence. The rising temperature of industrial relations is reflected in the Taff Vale case of 1900 and the Osborne judgement of 1909, both of which undermined the legal status of trade unions, and both of which were subsequently reversed (Pelling 1987: ch. 7).[10]

Before 1890 collective bargaining was largely confined to craft occupations in the major export industries and in industries such as building and printing and it was organised on a local or regional basis. But the scope and influence of collective agreements grew. By 1910 there were 1,696 formal agreements covering an estimated 2.4 million workers, and the number whose wages were effectively set by these agreements was 'very materially in excess' of this (Board of Trade 1910). With the official encouragement of the Conciliation Act of 1896, the number of industrial conciliation boards grew from 64 in 1894 to 162 in 1905 and 325 by 1913 (Pelling 1987: 142), and the scope of individual boards also expanded. According to one historian, 'whereas in 1890 few joint negotiating agreements covered employment beyond a city and its environs, by 1914 numerous trades negotiated upon a county or regional basis and some boards governed an entire industry' (Hunt 1981: 327). But even by 1914 the national agreements were largely procedural in nature and only in a few industries were wages set at the national level.

Before 1914 market forces were often used as criteria in collective bargaining. The boards of conciliation and arbitration that emerged in the 1860s and 1870s often referred to the current 'state of the trade' when setting wage rates (Porter 1970). In those industries with relatively homogeneous products, the best available index of prosperity was the price of key products and 'it was a short step from this to save argument by agreeing to a scale by which wages should change with prices' (Hicks 1930: 37; see also Treble 1987). Sliding scales were found predominantly

[10] In the legal case concerning a strike and picketing by the Amalgamated Society of Railway Servants at the Taff Vale Railway, the House of Lords determined that a trade union was liable for damages inflicted by the actions of its officials. This was reversed by the Trade Disputes Act of 1906. In the Osborne judgement the House of Lords held that union funds could not be used for contributions to political parties. This was modified by the Trade Union Act of 1913 which provided that individual members could opt out of a political levy.

in the iron and steel industry and in coal mining, but in other major industries such as textiles and engineering the alternative machinery produced rather similar results. In engineering, for example, 'cyclical fluctuations provided the context for numerous struggles, yet these were played out according to mutually accepted ground rules like the "state of trade" or "what the industry could afford"' (Burgess 1975: 4). The repudiation of sliding scale agreements by the miners at the turn of the century is often associated with growing resistance to the idea that wage rates should be closely tied to demand conditions and with the emerging claim that they should be set more by reference to living standards.

The First World War saw the transformation of the system of collective bargaining. In the effort to maintain production and minimise disputes, the regulation of wages by War Ministries and tribunals spread to virtually every section of industry (Wrigley 1987a). In the face of economy-wide excess demand for labour, wage rates were increasingly set on the grounds of fairness (resulting in a narrowing of skill differentials) and with reference to changes in the cost of living. Wartime government intervention was a major factor accelerating the trend towards industry-wide collective bargaining and under the Committee on Production national agreements became standard. It was also fostered by the Whitley Committee, which was set up in 1917 to consider the appropriate framework for collective bargaining after the war. The committee recommended a three-tier system of Joint Industrial Councils, with the industry-level national councils being the most important (Charles 1973: ch. 5). In industries with little formal organisation, Trade Boards were established under the 1918 Act expressly to promote collective bargaining between the representatives of employers and workers (in contrast to the 1909 Act, which was aimed specifically at eliminating exploitation of workers in the so-called sweated trades; see Hatton 1997).

Although the conclusion of the war saw a return to voluntarism in most areas of wage setting, it left behind a system of collective bargaining that had been transformed and vastly extended. By 1921, seventy-four Whitley Councils had been established and although a number subsequently went out of existence, these were cases where there was a reversion to pre-existing machinery for collective bargaining. Union density climbed to a peak of 45 per cent in 1920, subsequently declining to below 30 per cent after 1925. But the scope of collective bargaining, underpinned by government intervention, had permanently expanded. It included statutory wage regulation in sectors covered by the Trade Boards, and agriculture (under the Agricultural Wages (Regulation) Act of 1924). Estimates of the share of employees covered by industry-level wage agreements vary, but recent estimates suggest that it reached 60 per cent in the mid-1920s, before declining to around 40 per cent in the mid-1930s (Milner 1995: 82).

These centralising forces underpinned the establishment of national level bargaining over wages in a wide range of industries. In terms of the three-part classification set out above, the British labour market can be seen as having evolved from local-level to industry-level bargaining but not to a fully centralised system. Wage rates were set industry by industry or trade by trade rather than co-ordinated across the entire labour market. In this respect it is worth noting Keynes' comment a year before the general strike of 1926.

> Our export industries are suffering because they are the *first* to be asked to accept the 10 per cent [wage] reduction. If *every one* was accepting a similar reduction at the same time, the cost of living would fall, so that the lower money wage would represent nearly the same money wage as before. But, in fact, there is no machinery for effecting a simultaneous reduction. (1925: 29)

Attempts to foster more co-operation and co-ordination in wage setting largely failed during the interwar period. Attempts at co-operation such as the National Industrial Conference in the early 1920s and the Mond–Turner talks of 1927–8 collapsed due to the diversity of aims and philosophies and the mutual suspicion among the participants, as well as the unwillingness of the government to provide co-ordinating intervention (Lowe 1987). It was not until after 1945 that a greater degree of co-ordination was achieved.

UNEMPLOYMENT IN THE LONG RUN

In evaluating the causes of unemployment it is worth taking a long-term perspective and, in particular, one that includes the early post-Second World War period. The top panel of Table 13.4 shows average unemployment rates in four periods, each of twenty years or so, and the variation within each period. While the average unemployment rate rose sharply between the pre-1914 period and the interwar years, it fell even more dramatically between the interwar and the early period after the Second World War. These large differences between periods provide a sharper focus that should help to discriminate between 'grand' theories of the long-run causes of unemployment. While the ups and downs in the unemployment rate *within* each period reflect a variety of short-term shocks, mainly on the demand side, the long-term averages more closely reflect the NAIRU for each period. The NAIRU is the unemployment rate that, in the absence of short-term shocks, is consistent with a constant rate of inflation. As Table 13.4 illustrates, prices and wage rates drifted down in the two decades after the early 1870s and again in the interwar period, while they rose gradually in the other eras. But there was no progressive acceleration or deceleration in inflation within each period and hence average unemployment rates should reflect the underlying NAIRU for each period.

The second panel of Table 13.4 presents period averages of variables that might be expected to influence the NAIRU. The slight rise in average unemployment from the 1890s could, perhaps, be associated with the increasing strength of labour organisations. There are a number of potential explanations for the persistently higher unemployment of the interwar period. As we have seen, the increase in union density, the widening scope of collective agreements and the shift to industry-level bargaining underpinned by the advent of unemployment insurance, were decisive changes from the pre-war era. There is some evidence as well that structural turbulence (year-to-year structural change) was greater during the interwar period than before – offering some support for the structural or mismatch view of unemployment. The rise in direct taxes could also have added to wage pressure in the interwar period although the improvement in the terms of trade is likely to have worked in the opposite direction.

By contrast, there seem to be too few explanations to account for the even larger drop in the NAIRU between the interwar and the early post-war periods. Although there was some decline in structural turbulence, there is nothing in the other indicators to suggest a dramatic fall in the NAIRU across the Second World War. For example, the benefit to wage ratio was only marginally lower after 1945 than it was during the interwar period. It follows that this factor alone cannot account for both the high unemployment of the interwar years, as compared to before 1914, *and* the low unemployment of the early post-war period (Metcalf *et al.* 1982). Similarly, the terms of trade worsened slightly and the tax take increased. More important, union density in the early post-war period was 62 per cent higher than it was during the interwar period and more than three times the average for 1892–1913. On the basis of these determinants of the target wage, it is difficult to see why unemployment was so much lower after 1945 than it was in the interwar period.

This puzzle could be resolved in two possible ways. One would be to say that there is something missing – something that overwhelmed the other influences on the NAIRU. The other is to say that the forces which kept unemployment at a historically high level during the interwar period had much smaller effects after the Second World War. One possibility is that the institutional structure of wage bargaining became more centralised and this made for greater co-ordination in wage setting, taking greater account of the economy-wide effects of wage bargains, shifting the target wage schedule to the left, and lowering the NAIRU. Some observers see the 'post-war settlement', which emerged after 1945, but broke down from the late 1960s, as the key to twenty years of low unemployment. The post-war settlement is characterised as an implicit agreement or consensus between the government, organised employers and unions.

Table 13.4 Unemployment in four economic eras, 1871/91 to 1947/65

	1871–91	1892–1913	1921–38	1947–65
Unemployment and inflation				
Average unemployment rate (%)	5.48	6.18	10.91	1.80
Standard deviation of unemployment rate	1.83	1.31	2.98	0.43
Average rate of price increase (% p.a.)	−0.43	0.52	−2.45	3.96
Average rate of wage increase (% p.a.)	0.95	1.16	−1.60	6.36
Wage pressure variables				
Benefit to wage ratio	–	–	0.41	0.39
Structural turbulence index	2.26	1.97	4.04	2.51
Union density (%)	–	13.0	27.1	43.8
Coverage of national collective bargaining (%)	–	10.4	42.3	72.0
Share of direct tax in national income (%)	1.1	1.8	10.3	18.0
Terms of trade (1913 = 100)	92.3	97.9	133.1	126.7
Productivity and the NAIRU				
Deviation from trend of labour productivity (%)	1.32	2.02	−5.99	3.45
Growth rate of labour productivity (% p.a.)	1.07	0.77	1.55	2.10
Estimated period-average NAIRU	5.42	6.41	9.82	3.01
Counterfactual NAIRU with productivity growth = 1.3%	5.22	5.85	9.80	5.66

Sources and notes: *Unemployment*: from Boyer and Hatton 2002. *Prices and wage rates*: GDP deflator from Feinstein 1972: T132–3; average earnings from Feinstein 1995: 264–6. *Benefit to wage ratio*: from Metcalf *et al.* 1982. *Structural turbulence*: (defined as $S_t = \Sigma_i w_i |g_{i,t} - g_t|$, where w_i are value added weights, g_i and g are one-year growth rates of individual sectors and GDP respectively) calculated across twelve sectors from Feinstein 1972: T24–5, T111–13, T116–17. *Trade union density*: membership from Bain and Price 1980: 38–9; labour force from own calculations based on Boyer and Hatton 2002. *Coverage of national collective agreements*: calculated from five-year averages in Milner 1995: 82. *Direct tax share*: defined as income tax and national insurance contributions as a share of nominal GDP, calculated from Feinstein 1972: T35. *Terms of trade*: Feinstein 1972: T139. *Labour productivity*: Feinstein 1972: T51. Deviation from trend productivity is calculated as the average percentage deviation from a logarithmic trend calculated for 1870–1965. *NAIRU*: based on estimated coefficients of equations for the real wage and the unemployment rate estimated over 1871–1999 in Hatton 2002. The NAIRU for different periods is calculated from period-averages for the growth rate of productivity and the terms of trade, and period-specific dummies.

The government guaranteed full employment, and employers acquiesced in restrictive practices and shopfloor control of production processes by unions, in exchange for wage restraint on the part of workers (see Eichengreen 1996).

Union leaders gained influence in government during and after the war; new, more encompassing, institutions were set up and a series of incomes policies were introduced (Flanagan *et al.* 1983; Jones 1987). Yet these policies are often seen as relatively ineffective because the institutional structure was inadequate to make them stick for more than very short periods. As Table 13.4 shows, as compared to the interwar period, the coverage of national agreements (including statutory agreements such as those under the Wage Councils) increased even more in absolute terms than did union membership. These developments might be viewed as offering greater scope for economy-wide wage moderation. But the structure of collective bargaining remained chiefly at the industry level, and to the extent that these national wage bargains reflected the post-war consensus they were increasingly undermined by a second tier of bargaining at local or plant level. Thus it is hard to believe that changes in the structure of wage setting alone were sufficient to deliver two decades of spectacularly low unemployment.

In a rare comparison between the interwar and the early post-war period, Broadberry (1994b) found that the effect on the target wage of factors such as union density and unemployment benefits had, if anything, increased. On the other hand, the entire target wage schedule seems to have shifted to the left as compared with the interwar period. While this could have been the effect of the post-war settlement, it suggests that other influences, omitted so far, mattered too. One of these is the level and growth rate of labour productivity. As the third panel of Table 13.4 shows, labour productivity was below its trend in the interwar period and above its trend during the post-war period, and its growth rate also increased sharply across the Second World War. As we have seen, productivity fell sharply after the First World War and it subsequently grew at a rate close to the long-term trend. So having shifted down relative to the target wage, the feasible wage grew modestly, returning only slowly to its long-term growth path. By contrast, productivity fell less across the Second World War and it subsequently grew faster than ever before.

The effect of productivity on unemployment is controversial but a recent analysis of long-run experience from 1870 right up to the present suggests that the NAIRU is inversely related to productivity growth (Hatton 2002). Because wage setting follows productivity with a lag, faster productivity growth raises the *level* of productivity relative to the real wage, causing a fall in the NAIRU. This effect seems to have been more powerful after 1945 than it was in earlier eras, partly as a result of greater inertia in wage setting. The NAIRU estimated using this framework is shown in the penultimate row of Table 13.4. For each period it is fairly close to the average unemployment rate. The final row gives the NAIRU that would have emerged in different periods if productivity growth had been constant at 1.3 per cent per annum. Slower productivity growth after the Second World War would have led to a NAIRU of 5.7 per cent rather than 3.0 per cent, cutting the gap between the interwar and post-war periods by nearly half.

Although the exact magnitudes are still uncertain it appears that a consistent story is emerging that can explain long-run shifts in average unemployment. It goes as follows. Before the First World War institutional forces in the labour market were weak and, in response to demand shocks, unemployment reverted fairly quickly to the long-run equilibrium level. But as a result of the growing strength of labour organisations after 1890, and a slowdown in productivity from the turn of the century, there was a modest increase in the NAIRU towards the end of the period. In the interwar period an increase in structural turbulence, the growth of union power, changes in the structure of collective bargaining and the advent of unemployment insurance all served to raise wage pressures, increasing the NAIRU and leading to much higher average unemployment rates than before. Together, these forces more than offset the effects of higher productivity growth and improving terms of trade. In the post-1945 period the greater centralisation and co-operation in collective bargaining that was engendered by the post-war settlement introduced greater inertia in wage setting. The lower unemployment that resulted was underpinned by a fall in structural turbulence and, above all, by faster productivity growth than ever before.

Moving closer to the present, it is worth noting that in the early 1970s these conditions were sharply reversed: the Organisation of Petroleum Exporting Countries (OPEC) oil shocks raised industrial turbulence, productivity growth slowed down and industrial unrest increased as the post-war settlement fell apart. As a result of these developments (among others) the NAIRU increased sharply between the early 1970s and the early 1980s. Under the Thatcher reforms, union power was weakened, unemployment benefit conditions were tightened, and the benefit to wage ratio fell. In addition there was some revival in productivity growth, which, taken together with the labour market reforms, helps to account for the fall in the NAIRU during the 1990s.

14 British industry in the interwar years

SUE BOWDEN AND DAVID M. HIGGINS

Contents

OVERVIEW AND INTRODUCTION

> Private enterprise has achieved great results. If present economic conditions are often bad, it is incontestable that past conditions have been very much worse. The nineteenth century was an age of unequalled material progress . . . There has been, and still is, an energy and resourcefulness in our industry and commerce which it would be harmful to impair and fatal to destroy. The problem is how to cure what is unhealthy in the economic body without injuring the organs which are sound. (Liberal Industrial Inquiry 1928: xviii)

Thus concluded an inquiry into Britain's industrial performance and her future industrial prospects in 1928: it aptly captures the picture of industry in the interwar years as having both positive and negative aspects, sound characteristics but equally constraints on its ability to realise its full potential. As indicated in chapters 1 and 4 above, industry before the war was not without its problems: shares of world trade slipped as other nations industrialised; new industries born of the new technology of electricity, motor power and chemicals were relatively slow to develop; Britain's productivity performance seemed less impressive than that of its main rivals. However, these concerns were small compared to the chorus of predictions of gloom which characterised the interwar years: a collapse in international trade, and with it our export markets, signalled a picture of doom to contemporary commentators.

There was, however, another side to industrial performance in these years: a story of successful industries, firms adapting to change, technological innovation and entrepreneurial energy. How do we explain this? Which industries and firms prospered, and which did not? Why were some industries able to adapt to change, but others not? What were the implications for the long-run performance of the economy? Insights from industrial economics help us to identify constraints on change and provide the theoretical framework for this chapter.

MANUFACTURING WITHIN THE ECONOMY

Despite the very serious difficulties (which we detail later) confronting manufacturing, this sector not only consolidated but actually increased its share of national income in the interwar years. Manufacturing's share of national income (at constant prices), increased from 29 per cent in 1913, to 31 per cent in 1924 and to 35 per cent in 1937 (Matthews *et al.* 1982: Table 8.1). Manufacturing continued to be of central importance to the economy.

Within the manufacturing sector, however, the importance of particular sub-sectors and of particular industries varied enormously during the interwar period. If we compare 1907 with 1935 (Table 14.1), the chemicals and allied trades and engineering sectors increased their contribution to total manufacturing output. The performance of particular industries within these growing sectors was not uniform, however. Within the engineering sector, for example, there were noticeable declines in the importance of mechanical engineering and shipbuilding.

Table 14.1 Net output (%) by sector 1907–35

	1907	1924	1930	1935
Chemicals and allied	5.00	6.10	6.60	7.00
Metal manufacture	8.40	6.60	5.90	7.00
Engineering, of which	26.60	25.70	29.10	27.30
Mechanical engineering	9.60	7.00	7.30	7.70
Instrument engineering	0.40	0.40	0.70	0.60
Electrical engineering	1.40	2.90	4.30	4.90
Shipbuilding	4.40	3.40	3.80	2.30
Vehicles	5.60	7.70	8.40	6.70
Other metal goods	5.20	4.30	4.60	5.10
Textiles and clothing, of which	29.30	27.30	20.60	19.90
Textiles	19.80	18.10	12.40	12.30
Leather and fur	1.20	1.30	1.20	1.20
Clothing and footwear	8.30	7.90	7.00	6.40
Miscellaneous, of which	16.00	18.10	20.10	21.10
Bricks, pottery, glass, cement	3.50	3.90	4.20	4.80
Timber and furniture	3.10	3.10	3.80	4.20
Paper, printing and publishing	6.80	8.20	9.20	9.30
Other manufacturing	2.60	2.90	2.90	2.80

Source: Broadberry 1997c: 33, Table A2.4.

Table 14.2 Consumers' expenditure at constant prices, 1920–38

	1920–4 £m	% total	1925–9 £m	% total	1930–4 £m	% total	1935–8 £m	% Total
Food	1,002.3	*29.84*	1,116.7	*30.24*	1,231.1	*30.98*	1,285.9	*29.38*
Alcoholic drink	351.8	*10.47*	320.5	*8.68*	264.6	*6.66*	286.4	*6.54*
Tobacco	113.0	*3.36*	123.6	*3.35*	137.8	*3.47*	163.3	*3.73*
Rent, rates and water	368.3	*10.96*	393.4	*10.65*	428.9	*10.79*	471.7	*10.78*
Fuel and light	138.7	*4.13*	155	*4.20*	163.7	*4.12*	182.7	*4.17*
Clothing	356.7	*10.62*	388.8	*10.53*	403.1	*10.14*	434.8	*9.93*
Durable household goods	176.9	*5.27*	218.0	*5.90*	258.5	*6.51*	289.4	*6.61*
Transport and communications	188.5	*5.61*	241.9	*6.55*	258.2	*6.50*	326.1	*7.45*
Other goods	204.3	*6.08*	219.9	*5.95*	243.6	*6.13*	293.4	*6.70*
Other services	458.5	*13.65*	515.4	*13.96*	584	*14.70*	643.4	*14.70*
Total	3,359.0	*100.00*	3,693.2	*100.00*	3,973.5	*100.00*	4,377.1	*100.00*

Note: Values given in constant 1938 prices.

Source: Stone and Rowe, 1966: 125, Table 56.

By contrast, there was a growing role for instrument, electrical and motor vehicle engineering. This was the age which witnessed the growth of private motor ownership, and the spread of electrical supply to homes which permitted its use for a wide range of domestic purposes (Bowden and Offer 1994). The overall increase in the contribution made by the miscellaneous industry group was made up by the growing importance of bricks and allied trades, timber and furniture and the paper industries. The first two sub-sectors reflected the increase in public and private house building, the latter the growth of commerce and the increased propensity of the British public to buy newspapers, magazines and, to a lesser extent, books.

The interwar years saw a marked increase in consumers' expenditure on a range of goods. After the First World War, the rate of growth of expenditure on durable goods far exceeded that for any other class of good. Two sectors accounted for the bulk of this increased expenditure: transport and communications and durable household goods (Table 14.2).

In sharp contrast, the textiles and metal manufacturing sub-sectors, the mainstay of the nineteenth-century economy, made a declining contribution to manufacturing output. In other words, the interwar years were characterised by marked structural change within the manufacturing sector. A particularly pronounced aspect of this was the declining importance of industries which had dominated the Victorian and Edwardian economies.

These structural changes within the manufacturing sector led some observers to characterise the interwar years as being dominated by structural change between the 'old' and the 'new' industries. Cotton textiles, coal mining, shipbuilding and mechanical engineering constituted the former, whilst chemicals, vehicles and electrical engineering constituted the latter (Aldcroft and Richardson 1969; Landes 1969). These authors took an essentially optimistic line, arguing that the housing boom of the 1930s acted as a stimulus to certain sectors of the economy. Building created a demand for bricks, pottery, cement and glass. The new homes in turn created a demand for timber and furniture. The creation of the National Grid led to an extension of electrical supply throughout the country, and with it a demand for and supply of a range of electrical consuming goods (wiring, cookers, irons, kettles, etc.). The fact that many of the new homes were fitted with electricity added to the multiplier effect. The final ingredient in the argument was the fact that many of the new homes were built in 'suburbia'. This, so it was claimed, created a demand for the motor vehicles which duly ferried the occupants of the new homes to and from their places of work.

It took nearly two decades for economic historians to question the validity of this interpretation of the interwar years. (The challenge to the previous orthodoxy is best seen in Dowie 1968; Hannah 1976; Buxton and Aldcroft 1979; von Tunzelmann 1982). There were too many holes in the 'optimistic' argument: the problem of assigning industries to 'new' or 'old' categories, the constraints on change in the new industries and the failure to recognise the limits to the multiplier effects of the housing boom. Synthetic fibres, for example, became increasingly popular in these years: were they to be assigned to the 'new' chemical or the 'old' textile industries? It was not obvious that sales of the products of electrical and motor vehicle engineering could be associated with 'new' housing in suburbia. Structural change, it seemed, had little to do with any multiplier effect. (For a further analysis of the limits of the multiplier during this period see Garside and Hatton 1985; Thomas 1994).

THE STRUCTURE OF INDUSTRY

How, then, can we explain the very different performances of particular sectors and industries within manufacturing? One explanatory framework is the structure–conduct performance model. In traditional forms of this, structure determines conduct which determines performance, but in some forms of this model conduct is downplayed. Whichever form is chosen, there is thought to be a clear link between structure and performance (Reid 1987: 12–13). This framework potentially provides an easy explanation for differences between 'old' and 'new' industries. If new industries performed better than old industries, then they must have benefited from a superior (more competitive) structure. Conversely, if the old industries performed badly it was because they had an inferior (less competitive) structure.

Table 14.3 Merger activity in British manufacturing industry, 1920–38

	Number of firm disappearances by merger	Values (at 1961 share prices of firm disappearances) (£m)	Merger values as a proportion of total investment expenditure (%)
1920	336	317–59	29
1921	78	110–25	11
1922	67	73–93	16
1923	124	121–49	30
1924	129	62–77	18
1925	116	202–20	36
1926	153	301–32	51
1927	180	154–75	37
1928	270	155–80	39
1929	431	159–76	38
1930	158	120–36	30
1931	101	88–105	25
1932	86	49–57	16
1933	92	67–82	23
1934	121	66–75	18
1935	187	67–75	20
1936	274	98–124	26
1937	174	63–75	14
1938	127	84–104	18

Source: Hannah 1976: 212–13, Appendix Table A.1.

A major aspect of industrial structure is the number and size of firms. The interwar years (and especially the 1920s) were characterised by high levels of merger activity (Table 14.3). In fact, between 1920 and 1939 more firms disappeared as a result of merger than the total number of firm disappearances caused by merger between 1880 and 1919. The number of firm disappearances during one decade, the 1920s, was not exceeded until the 1960s (Hannah 1983: Table A.1). Table 14.3 also shows that this merger activity accounted for a large share of total investment expenditure.

Enhanced concentration was the natural outcome of this merger activity. When industries become highly concentrated it is the major firms which determine the nature of competitive behaviour by, for example, price maintenance schemes. Pricing agreements are more easily implemented and monitored in an industry with high degrees of concentration.

However, there is no sign that competitive behaviour was greater in the new industries. Merger activity was as pronounced in some of the 'new' industries as it was in the 'old'. In addition, the degree of industrial concentration was equally as high in 'new' industries as it was in the 'old'. In chemicals, the formation of ICI (1926) and in the electrical industry, the formation of AEI (1928) were central in increasing the five-firm concentration ratio (the share of an industry's output produced by the five biggest firms) in each industry from 76.7 and 42.1 in 1919 to 93.2 and 48.6 in 1930 (Hannah and Kay 1977: 69–70). Rising concentration in new industries had its counterpart in the old industries: in Lancashire cotton spinning the formation of the Lancashire Cotton Corporation (1929) and Combined Egyptian Mills (1929) accelerated concentration in the coarse and fine spinning sections respectively. Similar trends were apparent in the heavy engineering and armaments industries with the merger in 1927 of Vickers and Armstrong Whitworth.

The conduct of industry

Structure, therefore, does not seem to provide a satisfactory explanation of performance. What about conduct? Analyses of how and why manufacturing industries responded to the changed economic conditions of the interwar years (and the long-run consequences of the responses) have come to dominate the literature. Recently, many have emphasised collusion and the adoption of a wide range of anti-competitive practices (Broadberry and Crafts 1990b, 1990c, 1992a, 1996).

The argument is that the interwar years were characterised by uncertainty, specifically uncertainty as to when international trading conditions would improve and, consequently, uncertainty as to when exports to overseas markets would be regained. Firms assumed that good times *would* return, the only question being when. It was for this reason, understandably, that many firms chose a defensive reaction to the changed economic environment.

Across a wide range of industries, both 'old' and 'new', large proportions of output were covered by formal price agreements. In shipbuilding, the share of output governed by cartel agreements was 100 per cent; in cement, iron and steel smelting, tobacco and typewriters, it was in excess of 95 per cent; the book printing, glass, glue, photographic goods, wireless and wireless apparatus industries enacted price agreements covering 90 per cent or more of their industries, while in drugs and electric lamps, cartel agreements covered 80 per cent of industrial output (Mercer 1989: Appendix 2).

The structure of industry allowed firms to adopt conduct which avoided competition; the economic environment convinced many that a defensive reaction was appropriate. Firms may decide not to compete on price or on price-quality factors. The idea that firms may adopt noncompetitive behaviour is standard in basic microeconomics and industrial economics. In the interwar period, changes in the structure of industries, particularly growing concentration, facilitated the adoption of anti-competitive practices. This was not, however, because structural variables in themselves alone determined this behaviour. Exogenous factors such as greater volatility and risk in the environment were equally strong in determining that a wide range of industries would adopt collusive practices. But did the changes in structure and conduct together affect or even determine performance or was it the case that performance was determined, in whole or in part, exogenously?

The performance of industry

The implications of structural change (caused in part by the decline of former staple industries which relied on now-collapsed export markets) and of defensive conduct which witnessed industries in both 'old' and 'new' sectors avoiding competition certainly go a long way to explaining the performance of British industry in the interwar years. The period witnessed a marked decline in Britain's share of world export trade in manufactured goods: from 27.5 per cent in 1911–13, to 23.8 per cent in 1921–5 and 18.5 per cent in 1931–8. Exports declined as a proportion of national income from 33 per cent in 1907, to 27 per cent in 1924 and 15 per cent in 1938 (Pollard 1983: 116). Iron and steel, coal mining, shipbuilding and cotton textiles, those stalwarts of the Victorian economy, were particularly badly affected (Figure 14.1). Between 1913 and 1937, exports of cotton manufactures and of cotton yarn declined by 71 and 24 per cent respectively (Robson 1957: Table 14.1). The principal explanation for cotton's precipitous decline was the loss of the Indian market and Japanese competition in third markets. India had been the greatest single market for Lancashire's goods; out of a total British production of about 700 million yards of cotton piece goods in 1913, 43 per cent by quantity and 36 per cent by value were exported to India (Burnett-Hurst 1932: 410). As international trade collapsed, so too did demand for the ships which carried trade and the demand for boats built in Britain. In 1913, the value of new ships and boats exported at current prices was £11 million; by 1925 the value had fallen to £6.3 million and by 1932 to £3.9 million (Mitchell and Deane 1962: 305–6). But the problem for this country was exacerbated as new competitors, namely Japan and the United States, built up their own merchant fleets.

The 'new' industries were unable to replace the old industries. The ratio of exports to output of manufactures declined substantially between 1913 and 1937. Taking 1929 as the base year equal to 100, this ratio declined from 132 in 1913, to 59 in 1937 (Matthews *et al.* 1982: 436–7). Although Britain increased her exports of motor cars from 15,700 in 1924 to 65,000 in 1938, thereby exceeding the exports of motor cars from Germany (36,200), Italy (11,800) and France (21,400), these volumes were not sufficient to compensate for the decline in overseas demand for our 'old' industries (Bowden 1991). The 'new' industries were less dependent upon export markets for their success than the 'old' industries.

But this was not a story of untold misery. Britain appears to have had a comparative advantage in terms of world market share in woollen and worsteds, cotton spinning, tobacco, rubber tyres and tubes, matches, soap

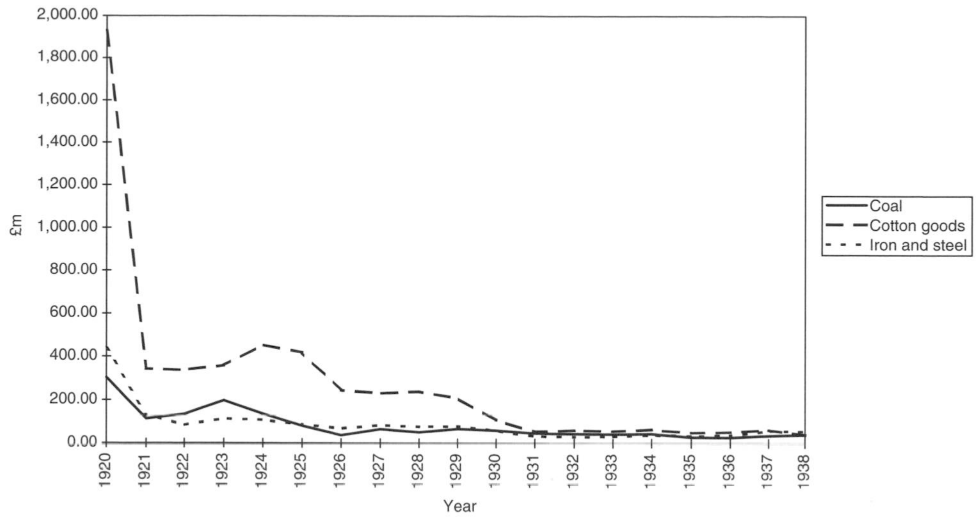

Figure 14.1 Value of exports at constant prices, 1920–38

Source: Mitchell and Deane 1962: 305–6, Table 5.B (output) and 477, Table 5.C (Board of Trade price indices).

and boots and shoes (Broadberry and Crafts 1990a: 380). This is a list in which some 'old' industries dominated. It is also a list which brings out some important features of the interwar economy, of which a key case study is that of the woollen and worsted industry.

For Chandler, British industry failed because of its bias for small-scale operation and personal management. Woollen and worsteds in the interwar years, however, disprove the Chandlerian thesis that success belonged to those industries which invested in production, distribution and management, all of which were essential to exploit economies of scale and scope (Chandler 1990: 286). The woollen and worsted industry appears to have succeeded in terms of its comparative advantage in world trade in the interwar years, despite its small-scale operation, personal management and the absence of large-scale investment in production (Bowden and Higgins 2000).

In 1925, Britain exported 60 per cent of the combined exports of woollen goods of the United States, France and Germany. Even when we make allowance for countries such as Italy, Belgium and Czechoslovakia (which had gained ground in export markets before the war), Britain's share of total exports was 46 per cent in 1925, slightly higher than in the years before the war. Exports of wool, moreover, maintained their importance in relation to other British exports and in the years before the Second World War were still 9 per cent of the total – the same proportion as in 1907 (Working Party Reports 1947: 6–7).

The industry achieved this success, not by adopting the three-pronged Chandlerian route to success, but by pursuing a policy based on supply to high-quality, niche markets abroad and on cultivation of the domestic market. As world demand shifted in the more highly developed countries from lower-grade goods to those of a higher class, wool adapted its production strategy. In these terms, wool behaved according to the predictions of product cycle theories of trade. Exports of low-grade goods declined, to be replaced by those of finer-grade goods. Product ranges were extended and new styles introduced. Overseas, many old markets were retained and new ones developed, largely as a result of market niche specialisation in finer goods sold to the more highly developed countries. Although exports to China and Japan fell, those to the developed economies of Europe, South Africa and the USA held up well. Trade with Portugal, the Netherlands and Sweden grew in these years (Bowden and Higgins 2000).

Export markets could be and were cultivated, not through the adoption of 'modern' mass-production methods or the introduction of professional management, but by the pursuit of a flexible reaction to changed market conditions. Why other industries were unable to follow this route is one of the major themes of the sections which follow in this chapter: we will find that there were underlying reasons which enabled wool (but not other industries) to adopt this strategy.

PRODUCTIVITY

Exogenous factors such as falling demand for exports were clearly important, but was the problem compounded by weakness within the manufacturing sector? In other words, was British industry becoming increasingly non-competitive? The most important data relevant to this question are comparative figures on labour productivity. These data suggest that some of the problems were of Britain's own making. If we compare output per employee in Britain and the USA (Table 14.4), the productivity gap was larger in manufacturing than for the economy as a whole. In 1937, British productivity in finance and services was superior to that of the USA, but noticeably lower in manufacturing (Broadberry 1997c: Table 5.3; and see chapters 1, 3 and 4 above). Clearly, manufacturing in the UK was outperformed by our main competitor.

We should add three riders here, however. The first is that the US–UK productivity gap in manufacturing was longstanding and was not born of the interwar years (Broadberry 1997c). Second, there were signs of a catch-up towards the end of the period. Finally, whilst it is true that if we compare this country with 'the best', there are reasons to believe that the interwar British economy was underperforming, if we compare Britain with 'the rest', then the comparisons seem less depressing. Recent research has shown that we did not lag behind Germany in

Table 14.4 Comparative US/UK output per employee in manufacturing and the whole economy, 1870–1938 (UK = 100)

	Manufacturing	Whole economy
1870	192.0	85.9
1913	212.9	115.5
1929	249.9	139.0
1938	191.6	130.5

Source: Broadberry 1997: 66, Table 5.2.

manufacturing productivity *as a whole* until after the Second World War (Table 14.5; Broadberry 1997c: 211). British industry was superior in food, drink, tobacco and textiles, but by the mid-1930s Germany was superior in chemicals and engineering (Table 14.5).

Table 14.5 Comparative labour productivity by industry, 1935/7 (UK = 100)

	US/UK 1937/1935	Germany/UK 1935
Chemicals and allied trades	227	123
Metal manufacture	192	116
Engineering, of which	289	120
Motor vehicles	294	141
Textiles and clothing, of which	145	97
Cotton	150	135
Food, drink and tobacco	204	41
Miscellaneous industries	211	102
Total manufacturing	218	102

Source: Broadberry 1997: 28–30, Table A2.1, and 31, Table A2.2.

Does superiority in the level and growth rate of productivity generate commercial success? It is notoriously difficult to estimate productivity at the firm level, especially for the purposes of generating interfirm comparisons. This is largely because the data are insufficiently reliable to yield meaningful results. In addition, productivity growth does not necessarily guarantee commercial success because it is just one of many determining factors. In the first place, of course, the firm must have a product which attracts sales. But revenue from those sales does not necessarily guarantee commercial success either. Success also depends on the balance between revenues and costs if profits are to be generated and on the reinvestment of some of those profits to ensure renewal of capital and the launch of new products.

The key inputs to the productivity equation are the quantity and quality of labour and capital. There is a large literature which argues that the superior productivity of manufacturing in the USA owed much to its capital-intensive technology. Output per worker in Britain was dragged down by the relatively poor capital-labour ratio. This, in turn, was the outcome of technical choices made in the nineteenth century. In that period, America was resource rich, but poor in terms of the amount of skilled labour at its disposal. The UK, along with Europe, was, in sharp contrast, resource poor but rich in skilled labour (Broadberry 1997c: 77–89).

From these resource endowments, technological choice followed with the USA adopting capital-intensive production methods. In addition, American demand tended to be more homogeneous, whereas the British market tended to be more differentiated (Payne 1967). The former allowed standardised products, the latter encouraged product differentiation which, in turn, precluded standardised production. Given the resources available, the technical choices made by both countries were economically rational because they allowed both to utilise most efficiently the resources at their disposal.

The problem with the above interpretation is that it is essentially static: it traces the misfortunes of the interwar years to technical choices made in the previous century which depended upon specific supply- and demand-side factors. It presumes that demand can be taken as given and that supply adjusted accordingly, rather than allowing for the possibility that supply-side changes may create new demands. It lacks the possibility of change, of adaptation to different conditions and changes in resource constraints.

We need to ask whether British industry could have done better and, if so, how and whether the decisions made in the nineteenth century held us forever to poor relative performance. The concept of comparative advantage allows for change over time, for economies to make the best uses of the resources available and, of crucial importance, to overcome any constraints they face (Porter 1990). The economy which survives best in the long run is that which adapts, which regenerates its industrial structure and which allows failing industries to be replaced by new more dynamic ones.

The case for the prosecution therefore is that Britain failed to adapt to the changed conditions of the interwar years and that it allowed relative productivity levels to fall, underinvested in new machinery (and hence production processes), failed to modernise its management, underequipped its labour force with relevant skills and embodied a myriad of restrictive practices which prevented industry from realising its potential. We take each in turn and consider the evidence.

Investment

When economists write of capital as being an essential ingredient of productivity, they usually have machinery in mind. In addition, it is often not so much machinery *per se* which is important, but the intensity with which it is used. We need, therefore, to look not only at investment in fixed assets (to include plant and machinery and vehicles), but also at the efficiency with which capital assets were used, differentiating of course between manufacturing industries.

It is apparent that capital as an input to the production process did grow in the interwar years, albeit with marked differences between industries. In textiles, the annual rate of growth of the capital stock between 1924 and 1937 was −0.4 per cent; in mechanical engineering it was 0.6 per cent, in bricks, pottery, glass and cement it was 0.1 per cent. Industries with high growth rates of the capital stock over the same period were electrical engineering (2.4 per cent), vehicles (3.1 per cent) and clothing (2.1 per cent) (Matthews *et al.* 1982: Table 8.7). However, the bulk of this investment was not directed towards plant and machinery. In fact, the annual growth rate of plant and machinery in manufacturing was zero between 1924 and 1937. Instead capital was directed towards buildings and works in industry and commerce, which grew by 1.2 and 1.5 per cent respectively per annum, and to road vehicles, which grew at 4.4 per cent per annum between 1924 and 1937 (Matthews *et al.* 1982: Table 11.2). This meant that by 1938, nearly 29 per cent of the buildings, plant and

Table 14.6 Ratio of actual to potential electricity consumption in manufacturing, 1924 and 1930

	% 1924	% 1930
Food, drink and tobacco	57.6	55.1
Chemicals	68	68
Iron and steel	27.9	31.5
Other metal-users	23.9	22.5
Textiles, leather and clothing	44.3	45.8
Paper, printing and publishing	52.6	59.5
Other manufacturing	42.9	48.7
Total manufacturing	34.3	37.5

Source: Matthews *et al.* 1982: 153, Table 5.8.

machinery used in manufacturing and construction (excluding textiles) was the result of investment which had taken place between 1930 and 1939 (Matthews *et al.* 1982: Table G.2).

Did this new investment incorporate best practice and the use of up-to-date technology? In this period, the ratio of actual to potential electricity consumption is a reasonable proxy for the uptake of modern technology. The evidence suggests that there was little real improvement in the interwar years: indeed, some sectors indicate a fall-back (Table 14.6). Recent research, moreover, has found that horsepower per worker was far higher in the USA than in Britain, whereas Germany and France used roughly the same amount as Britain (Broadberry 1997c: 108). What evidence is there to suggest that we should have acquired more machinery – and used it more efficiently? The question is perhaps best illustrated by the cases of cotton textiles and motor vehicle engineering.

The cotton textile industry is the subject of heated debate. On the one hand, Lazonick and others have argued that productivity growth and long-run competitiveness foundered on the industry's propensity to favour short-run profit maximisation over investment in technological change (Lazonick 1981a, 1981b, 1983, 1986; Mass and Lazonick 1990). On the other hand, a number of authors have been highly sceptical of this interpretation of decline.

Lazonick and others have argued that the cotton textile industry should have modernised by re-equipping with ring spinning and automatic looms. However, the pattern of the industry's development in the nineteenth and early twentieth centuries placed apparently insuperable constraints on the modernisation process. The 'usual suspects' which received most condemnation were the absence of any major vertical integration, and its adverse consequences for co-ordinated investment decision making, transport costs and managerial ability. These negative forces were exacerbated by the behaviour of formal associations representing the interests of employers and employees. The overall consequence of these factors was fatally low levels of capacity utilisation and throughput.

If we focus on the technology that was used, the case appears overwhelming. By the interwar years, a large proportion of British cotton spinning machinery was technically obsolete. By 1920, for example, 36.7 per cent of the industry's mule spinning capacity was pre-1900 vintage; by 1930, 77.5 per cent of this capacity was pre-1910 vintage (Political and Economic Planning 1934: 54). In comparative terms, despite owning approximately 33 per cent of world total spinning capacity between 1924 and 1933, the UK accounted for just 13 per cent of world ring spinning capacity. During this period, whereas ring spinning capacity was the dominant spinning choice in the world (accounting for approximately two-thirds of total spinning capacity), in the UK the relative importance of rings remained unchanged at around 23 per cent (Political and Economic Planning 1934: 53).

The motor vehicle engineering industry has been criticised for the failure to invest in 'Fordist' production methods which embody capital, the mass-production process and full capacity utilisation. Fordist production methods were characterised by the use of high cost, specially designed machines arranged in sequence such that output flowed smoothly and in sequence from one work station to another. The end result was high-volume production of standardised products. The British motor vehicle industry did not adopt Fordism in the interwar years. For this it has been deemed by critics, such as Lewchuk, to have 'failed' (Lewchuk 1987).

Prima facie, the evidence of the investment policies in two of our major industries seems to suggest that they 'failed' during the interwar years: opportunities to increase productivity by investing in the latest machines and production processes were neglected. But is the evidence so clear-cut? In each case, there were good reasons why British industry chose not to invest.

In the case of cotton spinning, a number of robust criticisms have been levelled at the Lazonick interpretation. One set of criticisms has focused on the undue emphasis given to transport costs and the implications these allegedly had for the slow pace of ring adoption (Saxonhouse and Wright 1984, 1987; Leunig 2001). Another set of criticisms have shown that the financial incentives to adopt ring spinning were lacking (Toms 1998). It has been shown that the alleged benefits of vertical integration rarely manifested themselves in terms of superior profitability. In other words, there appear to have been few financial incentives for businessmen to pursue vertical integration (Higgins and Toms 1997). Moreover, the financial legacy of the refinancing and reflotation of many cotton firms in 1919–20 was a high level of debt which impeded investment in new equipment (Higgins and Toms 2001). One should also note that large sections of the American industry suffered as badly as Lancashire firms (Rose 2000: 209–14).

In the automobile industry, the 'failure' to invest on a large scale in capital-intensive, asset-specific machinery, as required by Fordism, was a rational decision, born of an appreciation of the market conditions that British manufacturers faced. Fordism involved mass-production for a mass-market. No such mass-market existed in Britain during these years: demand was limited to the middle and upper classes, who required a large variety of cars, were less concerned with price constraints and who also placed a high premium on the performance and quality of their motor vehicles. Mass-production was not viable, hence the decision not to invest in Fordism was entirely rational (Bowden 1991; Bowden and Turner 1993: 144–258).

Nor is it fair to allege failure because the industry chose not to follow a certain route. The interwar years did witness significant investment in the industry, and the fact that it was not 'Fordist' does not invalidate it. The annual growth rate of capital in the vehicle industry, at 3.1 per cent, was among the highest in British industry in the interwar years (Matthews *et al.* 1982: 240) and by 1935, investment in plant and machinery in the motor vehicle industry amounted to £12.4 million and constituted 77 per cent of investment in plant and machinery in the vehicle sector (Board of Trade 1950: 9–10). The industry had invested heavily throughout the interwar period and, relative to other sectors, had not experienced any investment shortfall.

The interwar years had witnessed large investment programmes undertaken by the major motor vehicle producers, with the gradual introduction of mechanised production techniques, notably moving assembly lines and machines which were used to produce individual items on a continuous basis. In 1923, for example, a major investment programme in continuous flow production began at Longbridge as a result of which this site became the first motor works in the country with a moving assembly line for the production of chassis and car bodies (Church 1979: 100). By 1938, Morris' total net assets of £11,464,000 were the highest among the major car-producing companies, with additions to net assets achieved by this company between 1934 and 1938 being valued at £3,617,000 (Overy 1976: 56; Bowden 1991).

This section has shown that the fierce criticism directed at two of Britain's major manufacturing industries for their 'failure' to invest is not fully justified. As we shall observe later, new insights from the theoretical literature on investment show that in conditions of uncertainty it may be rational to *delay* expenditure.

Human capital

There is an increasing awareness amongst economists of the integral link between economic growth and the capabilities of human beings (Sen 1999; United Nations Development Programme, *Human Development Reports*). Growth is a function not only of physical capital but of the quality of human capital. An educated, healthy labour force, whose training and work skills are augmented over its working life, is an essential ingredient of a 'successful' economy. No longer do economists look only to time spent in formal education, they look also to the health of the labour force, and to the commitment of industry to up-date constantly the skills of its workers, at all occupational levels from the shop floor to the boardroom.

In 1934, 93 per cent of the population of England aged between 6 and 10 attended public elementary schools. In 1935, of the 662,532 who left elementary school, just over 83 per cent left for employment and just under 16 per cent continued into full-time education. Within that 16 per cent, only 0.4 per cent eventually reached university (Sanderson 1987: 34). In terms of formal education, less than a quarter of the population was receiving secondary or tertiary education, which is hardly the basis for a highly skilled labour force (see chapter 3 above).

Formal education, however, was not the only route by which skills could be acquired. Many learned their trade and its requisite skills through the apprenticeship system. The evidence suggests that in this respect Britain was outperformed by Germany. In 1933, apprentices made up just over 12 per cent of employees in the German metals and engineering industries, but only 8.2 per cent of employees in British engineering. Germany enjoyed a larger stock of skilled workers. For an economy that had enjoyed a comparative advantage through its skilled workforce, this was not good news. In the USA, by contrast, just 0.7 per cent of employees in 1930 in manufacturing and mechanical engineering had served apprenticeships (Broadberry 1997c: Tables 8.4, 8.6, 8.9; and chapter 3 above).

Skill enhancement in the workplace was also obtained through learning-by-doing on the shop floor. Learning-by-doing, however, assumes employment. The conditions of the interwar period, with endemic unemployment and short-time working, created a bi-partite system of 'insiders' who could enhance their skills by experience on the shop floor, and 'outsiders' denied such possibilities. Outsiders, moreover, experienced skill diminution: the more they were unable to work, the more work skills they lost. Unemployment, therefore, reduced the stock of skilled workers available to British industry (see chapter 13 above).

In addition, it is increasingly recognised that a healthy labour force is a productive labour force. Many industries in interwar Britain were plagued by occupational illness and injury. Textile workers, coal miners and those employed in the pottery industries, endured dust-induced respiratory illnesses which at best reduced their efficiency and at worst led ultimately to death (Meiklejohn 1952a, 1952b; McIvor 1995; Tweedale, 2000). Carcinogenic pathogens were commonly used in industry: oil used to clean machinery in cotton textiles, for example, led to certain forms of cancer, whilst occupational injury remained a common hazard of industrial life.

The British workforce was not a healthy workforce and, in human development terms, may not have had the capabilities to be a productive labour force, let alone lead a productive life. Future scholars must explore in more detail occupational health and its effects on the well-being of the workforce and on industrial output. Much research is waiting to be done on the development of the labour force in this country, not only in the interwar years but in the decades before and after.

Institutional constraints

In the 1980s, it became fashionable to attribute the decline of the British economy to a range of institutional rigidities (Olson 1982; Elbaum and Lazonick 1986; Feinstein 1990a). It was argued that although business people may have acted rationally in economic terms (i.e., they performed well subject to the constraints which existed), they never attempted to overcome these constraints. Problems, in other words, were taken as given. Few entrepreneurs, it seemed, had the wherewithal, the energy or the vision to grasp and overturn problems. Provided the firm made profits, there was no real reason to think how a different production method, or system of labour relations, or product or management style might make those profits even higher. 'Satisficing', rather than entrepreneurial behaviour, was, allegedly, endemic.

In many case studies of such constraints, scholars have focused on labour relations, in particular the reluctance of either side to move from entrenched standpoints. Thus, in motor vehicles, it has been argued that the main barrier to the introduction of Fordist production methods was the reluctance of managers to manage, their propensity to cede control of shopfloor working practices to shop stewards and their aversion to switching pay methods which might have prompted union resistance (Lewchuk 1987). Similar concerns have also been voiced over the Lancashire cotton textile industry (Lazonick 1986: 24–27).

Two problems arose from this analysis. The first related to disputed historical facts. Lewchuk, for example, was criticised for overemphasising the strength of unions in the motor industry during the interwar years and for ignoring demand-side constraints (Bowden 1991). Lazonick attracted fierce criticism for his failure to encompass the evidence on the introduction of ring spinning in cotton textiles, and his reluctance to appreciate the reasons why ring spinning was not always a viable way forward (Higgins and Toms 1997: 212–14; Toms 1998; Higgins and Toms 2001: 53–6).

The second problem is that adherents of the institutional school underplay the reality of constraints. In their view, constraints are there to be overcome: the entrepreneurial spirit requires only an ability to acknowledge and then deal with problems. In these terms, there is no real reason why constraints should explain away defensive behaviour. However, as we demonstrate in a later section of this chapter, defensive, risk-averse behaviour may be optimal, especially when large-scale investment expenditures are being contemplated. From this perspective, apparent lack of entrepreneurship can be explained by the need to acquire sufficient market information to minimise risk and thereby justify expenditure. Industries which and entrepreneurs who evaluate risk and make rational decisions based upon that evaluation are the successful ones. To make a mistake is a costly option which may 'lock-in' industries and firms to sub-optimal paths for long periods.

Research and development

Was Britain nostalgic, spending more time looking back to (and regretting) the demise of the glories of the Victorian era? Did the country devote insufficient time (and monies) to research and development that might have underpinned industrial regeneration? One argument is that the more an economy spends on research and development, the greater its ability to produce new goods with more favourable long-term market potential.

Research and development, though twinned together in the same phrase, mean distinct things. Research is concerned with the time, effort and expertise that go into creating a new product or process, whereas development relates to the time, effort and expertise that translates research into a marketable commodity. One does not necessarily need both within the same economy: the success of the Japanese in buying patents from abroad and translating these into marketable products in the post-war period, for example, is now part of business and economic folklore.

What of British industry in the interwar years? It is generally agreed that British industry spent far less on research and development than did the USA before the war: Britain's research and development expenditure, as a percentage of net output, was 0.43 per cent, compared to 0.98 per cent in the USA (Broadberry 1997c: 122). There is, however, a problem in determining causation here, since higher rates of research and development generate higher levels of national output, but higher levels of national output permit more resources to be devoted to research and development.

Government policy

Standard growth theory stresses the importance of the quality and quantity of labour and capital as key inputs to economic growth (Solow 1956, 1988; Romer 1986, 1990; Lucas 1988, 1990). Endogenous growth theory is based on the assumption that the rate of growth will depend on both the rate of technological progress and its diffusion. These, in turn, will depend on institutions, incentives and the role of government.

Traditionally, two forms of government policy which may affect industry and its performance have been identified. There are policies which reduce restrictions on the operation of the market (which it is thought increase aggregate supply) and those which involve an interventionist government agenda (which is thought to counteract deficiencies in the market). In terms of government policy to assist industrial growth in the interwar years, we can discern a mixture of policies which do not fit neatly into either of these approaches. These, in turn, undoubtedly reflected the uncertainty within government as to how best to deal with the economic problems at the time.

One such policy which, if anything, enhanced restrictions on the operation of the market was the introduction of tariffs. Tariff protection acted to insulate the domestic market from foreign competition and was an international phenomenon at this time (Capie 1978; see also chapters 7 and 12 above). UK-imposed tariffs may have benefited the motor industry (Bowden 1991), but externally imposed tariffs undoubtedly made it more difficult for other industries, especially cotton textiles, to export their products (Burnett-Hurst 1932).

Nor did the government take real action to deal with the growing tendency of firms and industries to adopt collusive practices. We have already noted how the conduct of industry was informed by collusion. In contrast with modern-day practice, governments in the interwar years were remarkably lenient in their toleration of collusion. Trusts and cartels were not new during this period and, indeed, there had been a creeping tendency for them to grow before the First World War. What distinguished the interwar years was an acceleration of this gradual tendency towards collusive practices (Levy 1927: 177), and a reluctance by governments to reverse this trend. The Balfour Committee in 1929 noted the 'tendency of undertakings to associate themselves . . . with a view to regulating output, prices, marketing or other matters' (Balfour 1929: 176). However, these trends were not viewed as a problem. On the contrary, the consensus view amongst Liberal, Labour and Conservative politicians at the time was to emphasise the negative aspects of competition which might lead to destructive price cutting (Lucas 1937: 30–3). In addition, as Hannah has demonstrated, there was an almost complete acquiescence by successive governments in the move toward higher industrial concentration, the maintenance of trusts and cartels and the practice of monopolistic pricing (Hannah 1983: 41–53).

When intervention into private business did occur it was not always conducted *directly* under government auspices. Where mergers and amalgamations were thought to be desirable the government was keen that these should be enacted by the banks. Accordingly, following the initiative of the Bank of England, the Bankers Industrial Development Company (BIDC) was established in 1929. The BIDC appears to have been primarily an attempt to *prevent* government intervention in the financing and reorganisation of industry (Hannah 1983: 64).

In some instances, the operation of the BIDC can be viewed as an attempt to *reduce* competition. Active support from the Bank of England and the BIDC in the rationalisation of the cotton spinning and shipbuilding industries are two such examples. In both cases, there was recognition that substantial excess capacity was undermining the financial health of each industry. By the late 1920s there was growing recognition, both officially and unofficially, that some rationalisation was necessary in these industries. As far as the cotton spinning industry was concerned two major investigations endorsed the beneficial effects of such measures. The Economic Advisory Council was convinced that 'it will be of the utmost importance to the industry that . . . large scale amalgamations should take place in the spinning section' (Economic Advisory Council 1930: 21). Greater amalgamation would facilitate rationalisation and would allow the smaller number of remaining firms to achieve maximum firm level economies (e.g. bulk buying), as well as making them strong enough to generate the necessary finance required to re-equip and modernise their mills. Greater amalgamation in spinning, if accompanied by greater amalgamations in other sections of the industry (especially weaving and marketing), would facilitate co-ordination between the different sections of the industry and make it easier to effect policies which would benefit the industry as a whole (Economic Advisory Council 1930: 27).

The creation of the Lancashire Cotton Corporation (LCC) in 1929 was, perhaps, the most visible of the activities undertaken by the BIDC. The LCC was specifically set up to acquire some of the most uneconomic mills in the cotton spinning industry. Although it was successful in scrapping around 4.5 million spindles, the managerial diseconomies it confronted precluded any major cost savings and the possibility of integration into weaving (Bamberg 1984: 39–72, 136–52, 1988: 88–97; Greaves 2000: 106–9).

A similar but more successful picture emerges in the case of the British shipbuilding industry. This industry had experienced a substantial increase in capacity during the First World War and by 1919 its capacity was thought to be around 40 per cent higher than in 1914. In order to be viable, this extra capacity required an expanding market. However, the presence of surplus carrying capacity in the world fleet, together with slow growth in world trade and the limited orders for warships, meant that the market prospects for British shipbuilders were very uninspiring during the interwar years (Slaven 1995: 1130–1).

As in the cotton industry the presence of high levels of excess capacity encouraged bouts of cut-throat competition which threatened further the financial health of the industry. The incentive of individual firms to seek orders at unremunerative prices meant that the existence of excess capacity was prolonged. In these circumstances there was an urgent need for the industry to act collectively to reduce excess capacity. With the support of the Bank of England, the National Shipbuilders Security Ltd (NSS) was formed in 1930 to purchase redundant and obsolete shipyards and their contents. While the initial plan was to sterilise approximately 170 berths, both naval and liner, by 1939, the NSS had acquired 216 berths, representing a capacity of about 1.4 million tons (Slaven 1995: 1135).

Investment in infrastructure is a third area in which governments can affect industrial performance. The building of the National Grid (1926), which brought electric power to most homes and businesses throughout the country, was one such development. By 1932, 32 per cent of homes in England and Wales were wired for electricity; by 1938, this figure was 65 per cent whilst average domestic consumption of electricity grew at 10 per cent per annum through the 1930s (Bowden 1988: Tables 14.1 and 14.2). Road building helped increase motor car ownership, although the benefits of better roads were largely offset by a particularly unenlightened taxation policy which meant British consumers paid far more in tax on motor car ownership than did their counterparts in Europe and America (Bowden 1991) (Table 14.7).

Table 14.7 International comparison of private car taxation on 8,000 miles per annum on the average class of car in use, mid-1930s (£)

	France	Germany	USA	UK
Average tax per 1,000cc	1.1	0.9	0.2	1.67
Total annual taxation	19.29	15.75	7.05	25.05

Source: Society of Motor Manufacturers and Traders 1937: 130, Table 71.

'NEW' EXPLANATIONS FOR INDUSTRIAL PERFORMANCE

Two questions still follow from the preceding analysis: could the 'old' industries have done anything else to withstand the effects of the economic downturn? Alternatively, and, perhaps more importantly, could the 'new' industries have done any better? New theories in industrial economics suggest some complex, dynamic processes which better explain industrial performance. They point to explanations as to why industries in Britain seemed unable to react to the economic environment of the period. These theories focus on constraints to change and the importance of risk evaluation, and point us toward a greater understanding of the role of technological change, investment, research and development and labour utilisation in industry.

These approaches also adopt a more thematic approach in which economic historians have much to offer to our understanding of long-run industrial change. In the following sections, we consider 'new' perspectives on these questions and assess their ability to explain limited structural change and the tendency to collusive practices.

Thus far we have *suggested* that manufacturing industry may have performed reasonably well in the circumstances and that the decisions and strategies of firms in different industries were both satisfactory and understandable. But where was the vigour and dynamism that characterised the USA? Were other factors in operation which might explain why British industry behaved in such a defensive and cautious manner? In the following sections we speculate on the wider, more fundamental explanations which *may* lie behind the performance of British industry during the interwar years.

Path dependency

New technologies are rarely immediately and easily adopted. However, as experience of operating the new technology accumulates, businesses and workers become more receptive: businesses because they become more willing to invest in new technology and workers because they become more willing to acquire the skills necessary for its operation. But, as investment of financial and human capital in a particular technology increases so, too, does the degree of 'lock-in' (David 1985; Arthur 1988; Sull *et al.* 1997). At this juncture, 'lock-in' generates further problems of inflexibility and path dependency, as individuals and firms are heavily constrained by their history and the decisions that they have already taken. It becomes increasingly difficult for new, competing, technologies to be adopted.

We can view the interwar economy as being 'locked-into' technology which, although appropriate for the nineteenth century, was inappropriate for the twentieth. Industry had incurred 'sunk costs' from the technological choices of the nineteenth century. To change these choices required investment, a labour force prepared to acquire the new relevant skills, and management capable of innovation. Of central importance to all of these issues was the *perception* of risk and uncertainty and the fear of making the wrong decision. Uncertainty as to when export markets would recover, and uncertainty about the growth prospects of the domestic market, would act to limit investment in new technology in 'old' and 'new' industries respectively. The greater the perceived level of risk associated with investment expenditure, the greater the potential payoffs necessary to justify expenditure. However, as trading conditions became more depressed during the interwar years the less likely it became that these high payoffs would be achieved.

Path dependency can also result from inherited human rather than financial capital. The characteristics and strategies of organisations can be attributed to the pre-eminence of particular professional groups such as research and development, production, accounting or marketing staff (Dietrich 1997). This dominance may come about as a result of chance opportunities for a particular group to gain influence; however, once it does so, its aims and objectives can dominate the organisation. When this happens, the area of expertise of the group will be defined as the norm and success will be measured in terms which maximise the group's interests. Eventually, the dominance of a core competence can create learning and co-ordination effects and expectations which lock the firm into a unique path of growth or decline. If and when the ethos of the dominant group is no longer appropriate for economic conditions, professional lock-in to the core expectations and success criteria of the dominant group may impede the ability of firms and industries to respond to changes in the market environment.

For Chandler, it was Britain's 'lock-in' to gentlemanly capitalism which underpinned her industrial problems (Chandler 1990: 235–392). Many industries in Britain were dominated by small-scale undertakings, with the large majority being privately owned and personally managed. In the early 1920s, for example, 56.4 per cent of the 1,384 companies in wool textiles were private firms and, of these, 78.6 per cent employed less than 100 people (Committee on Industry and Trade 1928: 175–6).

But was it the case that *all* industries were 'locked-in' to nineteenth-century technology? If we widen our understanding of technology away from fixed capital in industry to infrastructure, then the evidence suggests that 'lock-in' did not apply to all industries. The case of the electrical engineering industry is the key example in this respect. The interwar years witnessed a marked increase in electrical lighting in the home and the acquisition of a range of electrical goods. The use of lighting and appliances depended on access to electrical power. Industry's ability to market its goods (from light bulbs to vacuum cleaners) depended on electricity supply to the home. Hence the fundamental importance of the development of the National Grid and the activities of local authorities and private companies who, at that time, supplied the electricity. Massive investment in electricity supply did take place, premised on the correct assumption of a growing domestic demand for electrical goods (Bowden 1988, 1990; Bowden and Offer 1994).

The concept of risk is central to much of this analysis. Indeed, it seems to have been an abiding characteristic and determining factor of business behaviour during the interwar years. The defensive reaction to competitive behaviour during this period may be traced to an aversion to risk; the decision not to invest in mass-production or new technology can similarly be explained by the catastrophic consequences of investment when market conditions were more volatile than anything previously experienced. Below, we discuss 'new' theories of investment, which provide a framework within which the investment behaviour of much of British manufacturing may be explained.

Investment under uncertainty

Dixit and Pindyck refined the notion of risk for our understanding of decisions governing investment (Pindyck 1988; Dixit 1992; Dixit and Pindyck 1994) showing that investment, whilst being rational and desirable in theory, may be 'mistaken' in practice in conditions of uncertainty. Their approach suggests some key insights for our understanding of the dynamic and long-run implications of the timing of investment decisions in different industries. Investment expenditures usually involve sunk costs, that is costs which cannot be fully recovered (if at all), even if a decision is made to scrap the project soon after it is initiated. This means that 'mistimed' investment, by saddling firms with sunk costs which cannot be recouped, may constrain the range of strategic options available to them. In addition, this approach emphasises the importance of the trading environment in which these decisions are made. Uncertainty is endemic in the economic environment and the decision to incur sunk costs is made within the prevailing economic mood of uncertainty. A misreading of the environment can create long-run problems for industry (Bowden and Turner 1998).

In addition, in a dynamic environment, firms may adjust their investment decisions on the basis of other firms' investment behaviour. This approach thus emphasises the competitive environment in which firms operate and the possibility that 'lemming-like' behaviour may lead firms to behave in a similar manner (i.e., incurring large sunk costs), leading all firms in a given industry into strategic rigidities should optimistic assessments of the *future* trading environment turn out to be wrong. This applies not only to investment in capital goods (machinery) but to the whole range of financial assets including, for example, stocks and shares. Finally, this approach offers important insights into our understanding of two key themes which were of particular importance in the interwar period: why the exit process failed to work and why collusion characterised industrial strategy.

The relevance of this approach to our understanding of industrial performance can best be illustrated by reference to the experiences of the cotton and wool textile industries. Based on (excessively) optimistic beliefs about future trends, the former industry decided to embark upon a heavy reflotation process at grossly inflated prices. The latter industry adopted an entirely different route: reflotations were very largely foregone (Bowden and Higgins, 2000: 98–100).

In the cotton textile industry, the immediate 'post-war scramble for goods' generated high prices and profits. These profits were used mainly to pay high dividends and support reflotation. Owners of spinning firms issued new shares in their companies and these were bought by speculators at high prices in the expectation of making profits in the future. The total number of firms in the spinning industry which underwent reflotation accounted for 46 per cent of the industry's capacity (Daniels and Jewkes 1928: 174).

The situation was exacerbated by the methods employed to finance the boom. Shareholders were called upon to provide only 55 per cent of the finance, the remainder being raised by loans, bank overdrafts and debentures. This finance incurred fixed interest which had to be paid irrespective of profitability. Effectively, the method by which reflotation was financed augmented the debt of the industry. The very high levels of debt accumulated as a direct result of the 1919–20 boom, together with their high fixed interest charges, meant that it was no longer sufficient only to cover variable costs in order to remain viable. When the post-war boom collapsed, the new owners of the industry were saddled with massive, fixed interest-bearing debt (Higgins and Toms 2001).

In marked contrast, profits in the wool textile industry in the immediate post-war years were not read as a signal for large-scale reflotation. Although some joint-stock companies were formed, it was not on such a scale that it disturbed the existing pattern of organisation and ownership. Reflotation would have involved a switch away from privately owned and managed firms on which the industry was run – but the owners decided it was in their best interests to keep the *status quo*. Whilst profits were being made there was no incentive to alter traditional ownership patterns in the industry. Privately owned and managed firms remained the dominant method of organisation in the industry throughout the interwar years. The absence of any significant move to joint-stock status reflected an accurate reading of the economic returns from any such change. Evidence available at the time did not suggest the superior efficiency of the large over the small firm and, as such, there was no overriding incentive for owners to float firms on the market in any attempt to build large-scale units.

What were the implications for the strategies pursued within these two industries? Badly timed investment expenditures and/or too much expenditure can generate hysteresis in an industry.[1] Industries which suffer from hysteresis are at a comparative disadvantage compared to those which do not. If all firms in an industry are saddled with large sunk costs at a time when markets are collapsing, it follows that all firms are in a precarious financial position. Should such conditions apply, it may be in the short-term interests of an industry to pursue anti-competitive practices in order to protect its current financial position. In other words, collusion may be the natural, though undesirable, outcome of adverse financial conditions. Viewed from this perspective, the different strategies of the cotton spinning and wool textile industries can perhaps best be appreciated (Bowden and Higgins 1998; Bowden and Higgins 2000; Higgins and Toms 2001).

The second round effect of adverse financial conditions may be that the exit process is unlikely to operate. The emphasis is on short-run survival, albeit at the expense of long-run change. In cotton textiles, new owners could not easily exit because their financial resources were intricately tied up in the fortunes of the industry. Exit would have required owners to forego any opportunity they had of recovering their investments should the trading environment improve. In addition, the highly

[1] Hysteresis is a form of path-dependency in which short-term shocks have persistent impacts.

depressed conditions on the Oldham stock market meant that it was impossible to reverse wealth transfers by selling cotton shares (Higgins and Toms 2001).

The only option available to the new owners of the industry was to continue to operate fully depreciated machinery in the hope of making some surplus which could be used to retire debt. Mistimed recapitalisation thus precluded the normal exit process. As a result, abnormal and prolonged levels of excess capacity were maintained and this increased financial fragility and uncertainty in the industry. In any case, such were the financial burdens experienced by firms in the cotton spinning industry that the choice of exit was no longer their own: the banks were just as keen that heavily indebted firms should continue, in order to safeguard their previous lending (Bamberg 1984).

In marked contrast, the exit process appears to have functioned much more successfully in the wool textile industry. By the turn of the decade, 476 firms had exited the industry and 55 mills had ceased operation. Because the financial condition of this industry was less precarious than that in cotton spinning, firms in the former industry did not need to pursue collective defensive arrangements, and this reinforced the lack of any incentive to keep financially weak firms in business. There was no price fixing in the wool textile industry and therefore no mechanisms such as those which applied in cotton to preserve the most inefficient firms. In wool textiles, competition existed and the price mechanism operated to weed out the inefficient.

These two industry examples explain how different responses to the post-war boom fed through into financial decisions which locked them into very different growth trajectories. The absence of debt overhang allowed wool textiles to compete, adopt flexible specialisation and to exploit market niches thereby confirming its comparative advantage in international markets. In cotton spinning, debt overhang prevented it from moving away from its nineteenth-century heritage. How widespread was this problem? This is an area which requires further research.

Principal agent analysis

The previous sections emphasised the importance of mistimed investment expenditure and their implications for industrial response to the changed economic conditions of the interwar years. We have further emphasised the importance of including in the definition of investment, expenditure on reflotation and have shown how reflotations created conditions which made it difficult for the cotton textile industry to compete effectively in the interwar years. In so doing, we have introduced into our discussion the interrelationships between industry and financial markets.

The interwar years were characterised by an increase in the number of limited liability companies and in the number of people who sought to acquire shares for investment or speculative purposes. By 1937, there were 149,000 limited liability companies registered in England and Wales at Bush House in London, of which 17,500 were public and 131,500 private. Prior to 1930, the number of new companies registered annually ranged between 8,000 and 9,000. After 1930, this number increased, with approximately 14,000 being newly formed and registered in 1936 alone (Report of the Departmental Committee 1937: 6). Of these one of the more famous was Morris Motors. Previously owned and managed by one individual, William Morris, the company was floated in 1935 on the London Stock Exchange (Hannah 1976: 62).

The amount of capital bound up in these companies was considerable. In 1928, for example, the total amount subscribed for the capital issues (shares and debentures) of 284 companies was £117 million (Macmillan 1931: 166). Seven years later, the paid-up capital of *all* joint-stock companies was £5,640 million (Florence 1953: 10).

Ownership of publicly quoted companies rested in the hands of shareholders (principals) but the management of these companies was in the hands of individuals (agents) who did not necessarily hold shares in them. However, the ownership of equity was distributed amongst a large number of principals. In 1925, for example, ICI and Imperial Tobacco had 124,690 and 106,900 ordinary shareholders respectively. Just over ten years later, Lever Brothers had about 210,000 shareholders (Florence 1953: 178).

What were the characteristics of these share owners? Florence was somewhat dismissive of the quality of shareholders in British industry, describing them as 'either ignorant, business-shy, or too busy – or any two of them or even all three'. He noted that many (nearly half) were women 'many of them shy (with or without reason) of business'; and many 'retired and living away from business centres' (Florence 1953: 179). The interwar years witnessed some growth in equity ownership by institutional investors, but the typical investor remained the private individual. None the less, institutions such as insurance companies, investment trusts and banks were developing equity portfolios. Just after the war an analysis of holdings of over 10,000 shares in thirty large companies found that insurance companies held 5.6 per cent, investment trusts 5.3 per cent and banks 2.9 per cent of the capital. Private individuals accounted for 36.4 per cent (Florence 1953: 180).

What real influence did these shareholders have on the industries in which they held equity? Where ownership is spread amongst large numbers of shareholders, the answer is: little; no one shareholder has sufficient equity to affect the market price. But what if blocks of shareholders held large numbers of shares which were sufficient to affect the market price of a company? What proportion of the voting shares in British companies were held by the twenty largest shareholders? An analysis of the eighty-two largest British companies just after the war suggested a wide range of experience; compared with the USA,

> more English companies have a concentration so low that the twenty largest owners hold less than 10 per cent of shares (examples of this being Harrods Stores and Dunlop Rubber both of which in 1936 had no individual shareholding greater than 0.6 per cent of all voting shares). At the other extreme, though, more English companies have a concentration so high that the twenty largest owners hold 50 per cent or more. (Florence 1953: 189–99).

None the less, the average holding of capital remained small: only £301 at the end of the 1920s (Committee on Industry and Trade 1927: 128).

In many instances, 'large' control was exerted not by anonymous financial institutions, but by families. Thus, just after the war, three out of twenty English companies analysed had among their twenty largest shareholdings members of one or two families. Perhaps the best-cited example of this was Tate and Lyle Ltd which in 1935 had six Tates among the largest shareholders (they held between them just over 27 per cent of all voting shares) and three Lyles who held between them just over 15 per cent of all voting shares (Florence 1953: 196).

There is, therefore, evidence both for an increase in company capitalisation and for an enhanced propensity on the part of British institutions and individuals to own equity. The phenomenon of the divorce of ownership from control, first noted by Berle and Means, has led to a growing and as yet unresolved debate as to its effects on industrial performance (Berle and Means 1933). The controversy centres on the extent to which underperformance in British industry in the twentieth century may be attributed to the structure of share ownership and to the conflicting priorities of owners and managers. Ownership of shares by many separate individuals may promote a lack of responsibility on the part of the equity owners: no one individual has a realistic chance of affecting performance. This was the position in interwar Britain, although it was mitigated both by the presence of large shareholders and by the presence of majority family shareholdings.

If a company is perceived to be underperforming, it is argued that shareholders will sell their shares; they will 'exit' rather than make any attempt to intervene and help turn its performance around by 'voicing' their discontent (Hart 1995; Hirschmann 1970). This suggests that financial markets are principally interested in short-term returns on their equity investment, place too much weight on current profits and dividends and mark down the share prices of companies which allocate resources for future projects (Nickell 1995). Both create pressure on management to prioritise dividends (Milner 1996).

Were interwar companies under pressure from their shareholders? What evidence is there of speculative behaviour on stock markets? There is evidence of a very considerable increase in the number of share transactions recorded on all stock exchanges, although the majority of these transactions were of quite modest amounts (Report of the Departmental Committee 1937: 6). To that extent, industry during the interwar years was under pressure from speculative behaviour on the stock exchanges. There is also empirical evidence to suggest that some firms felt *undue* pressure to prioritise dividends. Investment in new capacity by the major automobile manufacturers, Morris and Austin, for example, came second to the higher claims of dividends (Bowden 1991: 262). In contrast, Singer, the maker of sewing machines, opted for reinvestment rather than the payment of large dividends.

In many respects, however, the jury is still out. We need more evidence on the behaviour of share transactions before we can determine whether shareholders demonstrated a propensity to exit from 'underperforming firms'; we need to identify what prompted any such sales (for example, in the post-war years, strike activity prompted massive selling in motor vehicle companies) and finally, we need to assess whether certain financial institutions were more or less likely to sell (for example, in the post-war years, investment trusts were more likely than insurance companies to sell). At the moment, the links between stock markets and individual companies remains a sorely neglected research area.

What we do know is that, among contemporaries, the more vocal complaints came from independent shareholders who believed that they had been sold shares at inflated values by share promoters. In the short run, at least, they had a case: £117 million was raised for 284 companies in 1928 but the total market value of these issues had fallen to £66 million, by 31 May 1931, representing a loss of about 44 per cent (Macmillan 1931: 166).

CONCLUSIONS

In this chapter we have tried to evaluate the performance of British manufacturing industry during the interwar period. Our focus on key performance indicators, such as exports, productivity growth, research and development and investment in human capital, reflects the importance of these measures in much of the current historiography. In addition, we have also tried to link these performance indicators to some of the key explanatory frameworks which exist in the fields of industrial economics, growth theory and the theory surrounding investment expenditure.

We have indicated that there existed a very wide dispersion in performance between the manufacturing industries. Much of this dispersion does not appear to have been determined by the structural characteristics of these industries. In other words, simple structure–conduct performance models appear inadequate. Much more emphasis, we believe, needs to be given to non-structural factors which determined the success, or otherwise, of industrial response to the changed economic environment. In this respect, the role of financial markets, the reflotation excesses of 1919–20, and collusive behaviour appear to have been paramount.

Unfortunately, while these variables have considerable power in explaining differences in performance between individual industries, some uncertainty still exists about whether they can be generalised across the manufacturing sector as a whole. In assessing the contributory role of a wide range of factors to industrial performance during the interwar years, the distinction between core and secondary explanations is still a little elusive; but perhaps therein lies its fascination?

15 Industrial and commercial finance in the interwar years

DUNCAN M. ROSS

Contents

INTRODUCTION

The relationship between industry and the financial system in the interwar years has been extensively discussed, almost always with a perspective of seeking to allocate some kind of blame for poor performance. This approach stems from two closely related fundamental positions. The first of these, inspired by the work of Hilferding (1910), postulates a hegemony of financial capital over the needs of productive industry. Authors such as Newton and Porter (1988) have argued that the interwar years can be seen as a period in which the core institutional nexus of the Bank of England, the Treasury and the City of London exercised a malign influence on policy making – the return to the gold standard at an inappropriate exchange rate being the prime example. The needs of manufacturing were systematically ignored by a banking and financial system obsessed with liquidity and unattainable standards of creditworthiness (Ingham 1984).

The second approach is located in the general institutional understanding of the decline of the British economy. This takes the view that, by the interwar years, the set of institutions and ways of doing things, which had delivered so much economic success and prosperity to Britain in the nineteenth century, were no longer appropriate to the new environment of international competition in the industries of the second industrial revolution (Chandler 1990). Adherents of this view suggest that the financial system, as it had developed over the previous century, acted as a constraint on the reallocation of resources from the declining staple industries to the newer, high-technology, growth-oriented sector (Best and Humphries 1986; Mowery 1992). In addition, when granted the opportunity to engage constructively with the rationalisation process in large sections of British industry, the anti-industrial bias of much of the banking system led it to adopt a decidedly half-hearted position, dominated by the need for extrication and self-preservation (Elbaum and Lazonick 1986; Tolliday 1987).

Both of these views, then, see the financial system as in some sense 'failing' British industry in the interwar period (Capie and Collins 1992). It is important to their arguments that this is seen and understood to be a supply-side failure; they both hold it to be a truth self-evident that it is in some ways the job of the financial system to supply finance to industry and commerce and that, whenever there is an inability or failing on the part of the manufacturing sector, the existing financial institutions should do whatever they can to provide the appropriate remedy in the form of additional capital. Such a perspective, it should be noted, is at variance with the conclusion of Arthur Thomas who, in his review of the financing of British industry over much of the twentieth century, felt it important to justify the inclusion of two chapters on the role of the banking system, there being 'no duty on the banking system to provide finance for industry' (Thomas 1978: 53; Ross 1990). One element which has perhaps been insufficiently stressed in the literature so far is the extent to which the banks operated in the context of a well-developed set of financial and capital markets and institutions.

Any review of industrial and commercial finance in the interwar years must, then, address a number of crucial issues. These range from whether it is the function of financial institutions to supply finance for industry, to whether the particular financial institutions which existed in Britain in this period did provide finance for industry. Assessment of these issues requires, however, an understanding of the nature and processes of financial intermediation.

FINANCIAL INTERMEDIATION

The process of financial intermediation involves the bringing together of individuals or institutions who have some spare money with those who do not have enough. By creating the conditions in which these surplus and deficit economic actors come together, the financial intermediary performs an extremely important role, since it allows the funds of those in surplus to be put to productive economic use. Financial intermediaries thus contribute to economic welfare. They are able to do this because they have information about those who need to borrow (those in deficit), those who need to lend (those in surplus) and the various terms and conditions under which they are willing to enter into an agreement. The institution is then able to bring them together in a mutually satisfactory way.

Such introductory services have sometimes been called brokerage, rather than intermediation (Dowd 1996). The difference between these two concepts lies in what the financial institutions do with the information at their disposal: if they make it available to others, and then leave the borrowers and lenders to get on with the business of sorting out the contracts between themselves, then that is brokerage. Brokers may sell information, but they do not themselves make use of it to purchase financial assets or to issue claims based on their specialist information. Lewis and Davis (1987) liken the activities of these information brokers to a marriage bureau or a computer dating service. Individuals will happily pay a fee in order to gain access to the pool of information on potential partners retained by the broker. The fees charged will be made up of two related elements: first, the savings in transactions and search costs made by the participants, and second, the costs of creating and maintaining the pool of information.

Financial intermediation, however, usually involves the development of further activities, such as the giving of advice on potential and appropriate partners. Transactions costs are further reduced by this process, but it is in the transformation of portfolio wants and needs that the real contribution of financial intermediation lies. This is the process by which the financial institution itself makes loans to or investments in the deficit actors and issues some kind of financial claim on themselves to those in surplus. It does this because lenders and borrowers often want very different things. It is generally in the borrower's best interests to have access to long-term loans, but it is in the best interests of the lenders to insist on repayment after a short period. Similarly, borrowers might want large loans, when lenders only have a small amount of spare funds at their disposal, or borrowers may be unable to convince the lender that they are able to make good use of the funds and therefore repay the loan after the stipulated length of time. Financial intermediation, therefore, brings the various surpluses and deficits together in a financial institution, which in turn takes responsibility for ensuring that the divergent demands of the borrower and lender are met satisfactorily. It is a process based, therefore, not just on the accumulation of information, but on its efficient use (Goodhart 1989).

Information is, then, the key to understanding financial intermediation. Financial intermediaries which engage in asset transformation – that is, those institutions which gather together the financial assets of borrowers and lenders and transform them into different sets of assets which they themselves issue – are able to do this because they make use of the information about the borrowers and lenders which they have previously gathered. There are at least two kinds of financial institution which operate in this way. On the one hand, there are mutual funds, which issue liabilities and use the proceeds to buy income-earning assets (Dowd 1996). By doing so, the mutual fund is providing an insurance service to depositors: faced with uncertain consumption needs over the long run, they will purchase financial assets which allow them to take advantage of the transactions and search costs reductions made possible by the institution's specialisation in this activity. Mutual institutions, however, only issue one kind of liability – usually an insurance policy, or a pension fund, but they purchase a diverse range of assets in order to ensure a steady flow of income. The depositors, therefore, gain access to considerable economies of scale in the processing and production of the information, and are able to reap the benefits of diversification which would otherwise be unavailable. The value of the asset will reflect in part the efficiency and the skill with which the diversification and management of the collected funds are carried out.

The second kind of financial intermediary is a bank. Banks similarly specialise in the reduction of transaction and search costs, and pass these on to depositors. But what separates banks from other financial intermediaries is that they issue loans as well as equity instruments (Dowd 1996). That is, the amount which they promise to repay to the ultimate lenders does not vary with the performance of the investments which they make. They gather as much information as they can about the ultimate borrowers, and then – because they agree to repay depositors whatever happens to the money which they lend – they bet on their ability to make better use of that information than any other institution. Banks are able to operate in this way because they specialise in overcoming asymmetric information – the situation where one party (the borrower) knows more about what he or she intends to do with the money and the likelihood of repayment, than the other (the lender) – within loan contracts (Leland and Pyle 1977). The way in which banks transform the (short-term, repayable on demand) assets of depositors into (longer, fixed-term) loans to borrowers is by taking responsibility for ensuring that the latter are creditworthy and will use the money sensibly and for the purposes established. Banks become what are known as 'delegated monitors' (Diamond 1984). If banks perform this function effectively, depositors will feel safe and be willing to make their surplus funds available. If they do not perform this function effectively, banks will suffer significant losses on their loan portfolio, but will still have to repay their depositors. If depositors begin to think that the bank is not performing well, they will withdraw their money as quickly as possible, and a bank run will develop. Either way, the bank will very quickly be forced out of business.

Financial intermediation, then, is the process by which borrowers and lenders are brought together. Individuals can make their surplus funds available to companies in a number of ways. They can engage directly in transactions, for example, by purchasing shares in the new issue market. Secondly, they can make use of vehicles such as insurance companies, investment trusts and pension funds which specialise in bringing lenders and borrowers together, and which offer a variety of brokerage and intermediation services designed to satisfy the needs of both parties. Third, they can place their funds at the disposal of their bankers, who will then exploit their own specialist skills in screening and appraising applicants for loans, and who will promise to repay the depositor from their own funds, regardless of the performance of the borrower.

It is clear that the policies, skills and abilities of the various financial intermediaries will play an enormous role in determining the success or otherwise of an economy. Examination of Britain's poorly performing economic system in the interwar years has for this reason often focused on the role of the financial institutions – and in particular the banks. Criticism of the financial system has been located in the belief that the supply-side process of intermediation somehow failed British industry in this period: the gathering, exploitation and application of information by the financial sector was, it is argued, inefficient, or at least ineffective, in bringing together ultimate lenders and borrowers.

THE CLEARING BANKS AND THE RATIONALISATION OF INDUSTRY

Involvement of the major clearing banks with the staple trades in the 1920s had its roots in the amalgamation of the banking sector in the period prior to 1914, but more particularly in the expansion of lending in the post-war boom of 1919–20. There were two closely linked main characteristics of commercial banking in England in the period before 1914. The first was increasing concentration. The series of banking and commercial crises in the second half of the nineteenth century encouraged the banking sector to pursue a process of amalgamation and concentration, with head offices centralised in London (Capie and Rodrik-Bali 1982; Collins 1994; Cottrell 1997). Some loss of the close and symbiotic relationships between local banks and firms was the inevitable result, and Collins and Baker (2001) have noted the marked rise in balance sheet liquidity across the whole sector in the period prior to 1914. Bank financing of industry began to be dominated by short-term and repayable on demand overdrafts, rather than by long-term investments or loans. Liquidity is important to banks, since only by being in a position to off-load their assets quickly will they assure their depositors of their safety. It has been suggested (Alborn 1998) that the large joint-stock banks were able to justify their size and cartelised relationship by pointing to the safety and security which they offered in return.

This focus on liquidity was not maintained in the post-war years. Attracted by the opportunity to expand their lending to fast-growing sectors, clearing bank advances rose from £580 million in 1919 (38.4 per cent of deposits) to £832 million (or 48.4 per cent of deposits) one year later. Tolliday (1987) suggests that in the case of steel it was the high profits to be made in the post-war rebuilding programme which encouraged bankers to jettison their policies of caution and prudence, and that many very large overdrafts were granted after only cursory investigation of the prospects of the borrowers. The economic downturn which hit this sector after 1921 then resulted in many of these overdrafts turning into frozen loans, which the bankers had to renew continually in the hope of regaining at least some of their funds.

The story of the cotton industry is very similar (Bamberg 1988; see also chapter 14 above). In 1919–20, many cotton mill owners borrowed heavily from their bankers for the purposes of investment and expansion. The bankers, who had previously been very little involved in financing the Lancashire industry (Toms 1998), were attracted by considerably inflated post-war prices and lent freely. The loans were to be repaid from the proceeds of stock market flotation. When the boom broke, some of the banks were caught with substantial outstanding advances made to companies which could not be refloated at anywhere near the value at which they had been bought. Two matters made the situation worse; the loss of markets and profits meant that the cotton companies were unable even to service the debt which they had taken on, and the Lancashire banks, having largely spurned the pre-1914 merger activity in the sector, were caught with very large and poorly diversified loan portfolios. The indebtedness of the cotton spinning industry became concentrated in the banking system which served it, and the two became inextricably linked. It was this which eventually required intervention from the Bank of England, in the famous words of Sayers (1976: 319) 'partly to help the cotton industry, partly to keep the question away from politics, but more especially to relieve certain of the banks from a dangerous position'.

What was required in both of these sectors – and in many others – became known as rationalisation, and a full-scale movement developed in the 1920s and 1930s. Although never fully defined, even by those who were its strongest advocates (Hannah 1983), this notion brought together many of the elements which might equally have been defined as modernisation – concentration of profitable productive units, closure of excess capacity, reorganisation of competitive relationships and investment in new technology. It also entailed the application of techniques of scientific management and the removal of old, family-dominated, paternal capitalism. It was, in short, a collective term for the ways in which many of the real or imagined problems of the staple industries in Britain could be resolved. Two things about rationalisation were abundantly clear: it would be expensive and it required some guiding force to develop policy and drive change through the recalcitrant and fragmented staple industry sector. The criticism of British business in this period, of which Chandler (1990) was to become an exemplar, clearly holds that firms and industries not only failed to make the three-pronged investment in manufacturing, management and marketing, which he identified as crucial to American business success in the years between 1880 and 1930, but that they were unable to do so. The staple industries in particular lacked market leaders with sufficient influence or power to act as organisers and rationalisers of the individual sectors, and it was the banks that came to be seen as the biggest failures in this regard. It is ironic, therefore, that the one sector which did rationalise, professionalise and create vertically integrated managerial organisations in this period was the banking industry itself (Collins 1994; Wardley 2000).

It is this failure to act as an external, modernising force which is emphasised by Best and Humphries (1986: 230), whose work represents the high point of criticism of the bankers' actions. They note that the frozen loans incurred in the immediate post-war years were nursed throughout the 1920s and into the 1930s, when some improvement in industrial profitability allowed the banks to extricate themselves. It is this extrication from industry 'with a minimum of loss' which they see as perhaps the most serious indictment of all, since 'the highly concentrated structure of the clearing banks in the interwar years could have produced credit policies that were in the interests of an industry as a whole'. Elbaum and Lazonick (1986: 8), take a similar position, and criticise the banks for adopting a policy aimed more at 'salvaging their individual financial positions than at developing a coherent plan for industry revitalization'.

This view suggests that the banks should have taken responsibility for the sectors in which they were represented and that they should have developed some kind of national industrial and economic policy. Not all contemporary observers agreed, however: one source of advice to businessmen seeking capital warned against asking their bankers for long-term loans as 'he is the custodian of other people's money' (Finnie 1931: 6). Dudley Docker, the arms manufacturer and one of the greatest industrial leaders of the day (Davenport-Hines 1984), wrote in January 1930 that the banks 'are just as much trading concerns as anyone else, and by reason of their deposits it behoves them to be ten times more careful' (Docker, MRC 1930). The force of this evidence is that it was the depositors, rather than the borrowers, that the banks had to satisfy, even – or perhaps especially – in difficult times.

Nevertheless, the potential for the clearing banks to have played at least some role in helping to restructure industry in the interwar years is one of the powerful strands which runs through the deliberations and report of the Macmillan Committee, established to investigate the relationship between finance and industry in the period (Macmillan 1931). It should be allowed, however, that not all the criticism directed at the banks in the course of the investigation concerned their remoteness from their industrial clients. Sir James Lithgow, vice-president of the Federation of British Industries, wrote that 'there is, to my mind, far too great a tendency both for labour and industry to seek to put the blame on some third party, the popular scapegoat at the moment being the bankers' (Lithgow, MRC 1930). The Balfour Committee had recently come to the conclusion that the economy was in need of a shakeout of inefficient and unprofitable firms. The banks, however, in nursing their loss-making clients, had been tempted 'to do too much rather than too little to keep weak concerns in being' (Balfour 1929: 52). The National Chamber of Trade voiced concern about maintenance of the 'highest standards of wise and conservative finance' (evidence to Macmillan 1931: para. 5), while Thomas Balogh noted that the sharp rise in bank lending recorded after the war was a result of credit policies which were 'not conservative. Many advances were granted which should never have been permitted' (Balogh 1947: 47). Perhaps unsurprisingly, the *Bankers Magazine* (Feb. 1930: 165) took a similar approach: 'If bankers are to be criticised for their general attitude towards the past ten difficult years, it has been rather that they have been too ready to stand by industry in the matter of banking facilities.'

The clear assumption in these discussions, that any departure from the principles of conservative financing was by definition unwise, is important and can be understood in two ways. First, it can be interpreted as a defence of the various banks against the general criticism that, concerned more with liquidity than with making loans, they provided little support to their industrial customers. Second, it could be seen as adding weight to the view that the banks failed in their duty to make effective use of the position in which they found themselves. The bankers themselves, of course, preferred the former interpretation in their evidence before the Macmillan Committee, which was impressive in its consistency (Ross 1990). They made three arguments. First, industrial policy was not part of their remit, and they should not be held responsible for the structure and shape of British industry. This was 'not one of the functions of our English joint-stock banks' (evidence to Macmillan 1931: Q2203). Second, the bankers held that overdrafts were made available to all who could meet the required standards of creditworthiness. To act in any other way would of course have been to limit their opportunities for making money, since advances were the most profitable element in the balance sheet, but it is clear that definitions of creditworthiness or of what constituted a reasonable risk could vary between institutions. The third element of the bankers' 'defence' before the Macmillan Committee was that they lent only for working capital, not for purposes of long-term investment. Again, this was dictated by the nature of their own liability structures:

> The sort of applications that we should most favourably consider would be those from our trading customers who want temporary accommodation in connection with their ordinary in and out business – not applications for capital expenditure, but just temporary advances that in the course of a few weeks or possibly a few months would liquidate themselves.
>
> (evidence to Macmillan 1931: Q889)

Such short-term, liquidity-preserving purity was a policy developed for public consumption. It is not how the banks habitually operated. Through the process of regional concentration, the Midland Bank had become a major creditor of the Lancashire cotton industry, and Hewit of the Calico Printers Association described how the District Bank of Manchester had 'Advanced money in all directions to the mills; they put one man on to the work and in a few years that man knew more than the mill owners and told them where to buy their cotton etc.; and worked the whole thing on overdrafts' (Hewit, MRC 1930). By the same token, Lloyds was heavily involved in financing the coal industry of north-east England, and the steel industry in South Wales, while the National Provincial was heavily committed to iron and steel and the Yorkshire woollen trade. Holmes and Green (1986) discuss the commitment of the Midland Bank to a wide range of their customers, concluding that to have made such relationships public would have been contrary to the best interests of both the bank and the customers involved. The closeness of the ties and the willingness to support industrial customers through periods of difficulty had for long been the standard mode of operation of the Scottish banks; Munn (1988) has shown how the Clydesdale Bank actively sought to provide both funding and assistance to a broad range of its industrial clients engaged in engineering, textiles, shipbuilding and the retail, service and motor car sectors. Saville's (1996: 537) history of the Bank of Scotland discusses 'the long-established Scottish practice of helping firms in difficulty', and the evidence of the Scots bankers before the Macmillan Committee that they were willing to suggest or even 'insist upon some measure of reorganisation'.

Further work on the relationship between two of the main English clearers and their clients has been reported by Ross (1990). Based on an admittedly small sample, a number of conclusions are suggested. First, it is clear that the banks were often involved in negotiations leading to merger, restructuring, the issuance of new capital or even closing down. This involvement took many forms and could last for a considerable length of time. The requirement that a bank functionary was placed on the board of companies in distress was not unusual; sometimes no cheques or payments could be made without the express approval of such an official. Banks often encouraged firms to become involved in merger activity or took the lead role in reorganising indebtedness and the balance sheet. This was true even where the bank's exposure presented no immediate danger or difficulties. What emerges from that discussion is that 'pragmatism and consideration of each case on its merits characterized the attitude of the banks' (Ross 1990: 64). There was no evidence of a consistent policy approach dominated either by involvement or non-involvement. Indeed, such an approach would have been counterproductive, since it would undoubtedly have resulted, in the former case, in considerable losses for the banks, and in the latter, the demise of many good and long-established customers, with the concomitant serious impact on localised economic and employment conditions (Foreman-Peck 1981b). Bank funding of industry was, therefore, a vital component of the recipient company's overall financial situation (Collins 1991). Bank credit, often long term, in substantial amounts and relatively easily available, was crucial in this period to the liquidity of British industry. The banks, in turn, took their role as providers of this credit seriously, and displayed considerable willingness and ability, when necessary and appropriate, to engage in the process of company restructuring.

These conclusions are now not in dispute: there is enough case study evidence from particular companies to buttress the view from the bank archives that involvement and close relationships were important in dictating the response of bankers to the difficulties and problems of their industrial customers (Mathias 1967; Church 1971; Wilson 1977; Tolliday 1987). Two further issues require to be examined, however. First, we must explore the question of liquidity – since it is possible that bank involvement with any particular company may have been predicated on the availability of sufficient liquidity to ensure that the bank's exposure represented no real risk of loss. Collateral security is the means by which this was usually achieved. Secondly, we will examine the criticism of banks' extrication from industrial lending in the 1930s, so that we may assess the extent to which the involvement, support and the provision of managerial assistance in times of exigency was a question of the banks being pulled along as unwilling partners in order to ensure repayment of the loans which had been made. The insight here is that even if the criticism of non-involvement in industrial affairs is seen to be unfounded, the real failure – as developed by Elbaum and Lazonick (1986) – is that the banks did not fully utilise their potential for restructuring British industry in the improving economic conditions of the 1930s.

One of the key characteristics of bank loans is that they are subject to very high levels of asymmetric information. Because banks make fixed-interest loans rather than equity investments, and since they know little about the characteristics or prospects of a loan or an applicant, they are exposed to the very considerable prospect of loss. Banks can reduce this risk of loss in three ways: first they can raise the level of interest, in order to discourage all but the most sure of success from borrowing. The theory of credit rationing (Stiglitz and Weiss 1981), however, implies that making loans or overdrafts available only to those willing to pay high interest rates is counterproductive, since it will result in good-quality borrowers going elsewhere, and bad-quality borrowers who are willing to pay any price being attracted (because they have a low expectation of success, and therefore of having to repay the loan). Second, banks can demand high levels of collateral and security for all loans. This is an important element in loan contracts, but it cannot be applied with any precision for a number of reasons – most obviously the cost and difficulty involved in appraising the value of such collateral and in disposing of it when necessary. Third, banks can reduce their risk of loss by attempting to overcome the information asymmetries inherent in the loan contracts. This is derived from one of the fundamental positions established above – their role as delegated monitors – in which they take on the responsibility from ultimate lenders (depositors) of ensuring that the borrowers are creditworthy and will repay the loans. Their job is to find out as much as they possibly can about the borrowers, in order to ensure the safety of the depositors' funds.

Table 15.1 Percentage of overdraft secured by collateral, 1930s

Percentage of overdraft secured	Percentage of firms in sample
0	29.3
1–20	6.7
21–40	5.3
41–60	6.7
61–80	6.7
81–99	5.3
100 and above	40.0

Source: Ross 1995.

Collateral is a key element in the relationship between banks and their customers, but there is some evidence that firms were able to borrow extensively from their bankers without offering any security whatsoever (Ross 1995). Table 15.1 reports these results, but there are a number of caveats. First, the sample is small (n = 75). Second, the extent of security will be overstated, because in many cases only the nominal value of collateral was available – clearly, in many cases the personal guarantee of a firm's proprietor will be worth less than face value in times of firm distress. More generally, the greater the element of asset specificity attached to a mortgage or charge over physical assets, the lower will be the ultimate value. Third, unless explicitly carried out by the bank concerned, there have been no adjustments made for the substantial costs involved in taking control of and liquidating collateral security.

Table 15.1 suggests that much bank lending in this period was carried on with very limited or no security. The bankers themselves were clear about this. Sir Ralph Anstruther, reporting the Bank of Scotland's results for 1930, pointed to a total of £13 million lent on security to 6,800 customers and a further £3 million to 3,900 with no collateral whatsoever, 'the bank relying, in accordance with banking principles in Scotland, upon its knowledge of the character and resources of its customers' (Saville 1996: 574). Such principles were not only applied in Scotland, and not only in the interwar years: Capie and Collins (1999) have noted a similar result for a much larger sample in the (famously conservative) pre-First World War period.

Such illiquidity and risky practices can only be maintained, of course, by developing the close contacts and in-depth knowledge of customers which is a hallmark of good banking. In those cases in which assistance was required by customers, the banks were able to provide it. This is because they were good at what they did – reducing asymmetric information and moral hazard in the loan contract, securing a steady stream of valuable information about their customers and the industry in which they operated, taking calculated risks about the potential of individual customers to repay or default on loans, and intervening as and when necessary to maintain an acceptable level of risk. Only by doing this were the banks likely to win the bet on themselves (outlined above) to undertake financial intermediation more effectively than other institutions.

There remains, however, the criticism of extrication: that the banks only supported their industrial customers and engaged in restructuring to protect their narrowly defined best interests, and that the reduction in bank lending in the 1930s represents a missed opportunity to prosecute a radical policy of restructuring and rationalisation. Bank lending did fall in the 1930s. Between 1924 and 1929, the clearing banks reported a ratio of advances to total assets of between 41 and 48 per cent, while between 1933 and 1937, the range fell to 34–6 per cent. The *Economist* (1934: 6) concluded that 'it is obvious that the bankers must have a coherent policy on industrial and financial matters, but in the absence of any exposition of it, the man in the street finds it all too easy to believe that it consists of the word "No" '.

Others took a more sanguine view: Balogh (1947) argued that the peak was reached in 1929 as a result of the frozen loans of the 1920s, and that a secular decline in the advances ratio had set in in the 1930s. One analyst in the *Banker* (1936: 124) took the view that 'there is good reason to believe that the decline in the demand for advances is, to some extent at any rate, of a permanent nature'. The crucial element here is that the focus was on the demand for advances, rather than supply. The Midland Bank, clearly deeply concerned about the failure of bank advances to respond to improving economic conditions in the 1930s, monitored their industrial lending throughout the decade, and instituted a careful sectoral and geographical analysis in 1936. The results are presented in Table 15.2.

The period covered in this table is very short, but important. It allowed W. F. Crick, the bank's economist, to note that the failure of bank advances to recover along with industry was as marked in the prosperous regions and sectors as in those less prosperous. Although this did change somewhat later in the decade, the implication is clear. The problem was identified as one of demand, rather than of supply, and both the National Provincial and Lloyds Banks in this period encouraged their branch managers to expand their lending and accept loan applications which they might otherwise have rejected (Ross 1995). Barclays adopted an alternative strategy: they concentrated on offering better service to customers in

Table 15.2 Midland Bank advances to industrial groups and areas, 1934–5 (£m)

Industry	November	London	Midlands and east	Yorkshire and north-east	Lancashire and north-west	south and west
Textiles	1934	2.5	1.6	7.3	4.2	0.1
	1935	2.4	1.4	6.1	2.7	0.1
Heavy industry	1934	2.2	3.8	1.8	1.4	0.8
	1935	1.8	3.5	1.5	1.2	1.2
Agriculture and fishing	1934	0.6	3.8	1.8	1.4	0.8
	1935	0.5	3.5	1.5	1.2	0.7
Food, drink and tobacco	1934	3.6	2.2	1.2	1.5	0.9
	1935	3.5	2.0	1.2	1.3	0.9
Leather and chemicals	1934	1.8	1.4	1.1	0.4	0.1
	1935	1.5	1.4	0.9	0.3	0.1
Building	1934	3.4	3.2	1.7	2.1	0.7
	1935	3.4	3.4	1.6	1.9	0.7
Misc. and others	1934	10.2	7.2	4.5	3.4	2.7
	1935	9.5	7.3	4.6	3.4	2.7

Source: Midland Bank Archives, Intelligence Department Files, Memorandum on Analysis of Advances, November 1935; Ross 1992.

order to expand their share of the market in advances from 18 per cent in 1929–30 to 21 per cent in 1938–9 (Ackrill and Hannah 2001).

Analysis of the relationship between bank lending and industrial production in this period supports the conclusion that bank advances to industry failed to recover in the 1930s because businesses sought other forms of finance (Ross 1992). Encouraged by low long-term interest rates, many companies sold their holdings of securities and used the proceeds to repay bank advances. Similarly, the rescheduling of long-term indebtedness to lower interest rates provided increased liquidity to many firms. A number of institutions which had previously not engaged in this activity began to move into the market for industrial lending (see below) and many firms took a conscious decision to reduce their exposure to their bankers. The banks tried hard to expand their lending, but were unable to do so, although Capie (1995) suggests that the banks' loss of market share in the 1930s was at least in part due to the protected and cartelised position that they had created for themselves. The suggestion here is that price was an issue, and that the banks were either too conservative or too myopic to engage in competition with new entrants in the capital and credit markets. Ackrill and Hannah (2001: 97), however, conclude that 'Almost all the evidence points instead to absence of new demand.'

The role of the banking system in encouraging and participating in rationalisation can, then, be defined in the following terms. First, the banks took an active and interventionist stance when necessary and appropriate to protect their own lending and to support their customers. Managerial advice and consultation were intrinsic components of this relationship, although it should be stressed that the banks' policy was essentially pragmatic. As Capie and Collins (1992: 59) conclude 'It is not obvious why deposit banks should be expected to take on the responsibility for industrial rationalisation.' Second, this pragmatism was built on the close relationships and deep connections which the banks developed with their clients, as a result of having to overcome the difficulties and information problems common to all bank lending. The implication here is that the amalgamation and concentration movement of the pre-war era did not entirely erode the local relationships between banks and their industrial clients. Third, bank lending did not recover to the same extent as the economy more generally in the 1930s; this has been explained at least partly as a problem of demand, but there may also have been an element of the banks pricing themselves out of the market. Best and Humphries (1986) suggest that the banks were insufficiently entrepreneurial in seeking out new markets when the level of advances to traditional sectors failed to recover, and cite the expansion of building societies as an example. Another suggestion is that the banks did not have sufficient skills to make sensible and informed judgements about the potential for success of applicants for loans in the new, technology-based industries (Ackrill and Hannah 2001).

PUBLIC SECTOR INSTITUTIONS AND RATIONALISATION

The failure of private sector institutions to adopt the mantle of modernisers and to coax and cajole the staple industries into a more modern, rational economic structure meant that the public sector had to take up the challenge. The involvement of the Bank of England in rationalisation is a well-known story (Sayers 1976; Tolliday 1987; Bamberg 1988; Garside and Greaves 1996). It was noted above that the Bank of England was pulled inexorably into the difficulties of the Lancashire cotton spinning sector, as it sought to protect the banking industry from the impact of an insufficiently diversified portfolio of non-performing loans. Because it retained some ordinary industrial clients into the interwar years, the Bank was exposed to enormous losses (£6.5 million in the case of Armstrong-Whitworth, a north-east of England steel and armaments manufacturer) and it adopted the leading role in organising mergers in the industry. With little in the way of rationalisation of the staple trades being achieved in the 1920s, Montagu Norman, the Bank's governor, began to pursue the issue more energetically, first through his financing of the National Shipbuilders Security Ltd, which was to remove excess capacity from shipbuilding (Johnman and Murphy 2002) and then by organising the Securities Management Trust (SMT) and the Bankers Industrial Development Company. The first of these was designed to oversee and advise the Bank on matters relating to its industrial holdings and to develop policy on reorganisation of particular industries. The latter was a fund, subscribed by the SMT and other financial institutions, which supplied capital to particular industrial schemes presented to it (Thomas 1931; Lucas 1932).

Garside and Greaves (1996) note that there were two main areas of difficulty in driving forward this programme of industrial rejuvenation from the governor's office. First, it was extremely difficult to get firms to agree on specific projects which would yield rationalisation benefits. Payne (1979) came to the conclusion that the steel industry in Scotland could not agree on an effective way forward simply because the ruling families had a long history of hating each other. Second, even when a scheme could be agreed on in principle, the details and operational aspects were difficult to nail down. Continued and long-term commitment from shareholders, creditors and others involved was elusive. The general conclusion on the role of the Bank of England in the rationalisation process is that, first, it was motivated by a desire to maintain the general structure of institutional relationships between politicians, industry and the financial institutions; second, that it was more concerned with playing to an audience beginning to think about the powers of politicians to intervene in the private sector economy than with the real industrial difficulties; and third that it had correspondingly limited ambitions. It was not successful because it was insufficiently radical. It is a moot point whether a policy of much more radical intervention would have brought greater success in the face of hostility and lack of demand for the imposition of reorganisation schemes on the part of a staple industrial sector resolutely unable and unwilling to devise solutions to its own difficulties.

Public sector assistance to industrial firms was also made available via the operation of regional policy (Ross 1997). Persistent, regionally concentrated unemployment and the consequent social and economic difficulties which came in its wake led the government to adopt a number of strategies aimed at providing assistance to individuals and firms in the depressed areas in the 1930s. One of these led to the creation of the Special Areas Reconstruction Association (SARA) (Heim 1984a, 1986). This body was established by the Bank of England to provide funds for small companies in the Special Areas, and its £1 million capital came equally from the City, insurance companies and large industrial companies. Its specific aim was to assist small, existing companies, but it was under very great pressure to avoid the appearance of subsidy. It therefore charged market rates of interest and applied standard tests of creditworthiness, thus greatly reducing its impact as an additional source of funding for industry. The Treasury Fund, which was created in March 1937 to make loans to larger enterprises than those envisaged in SARA's operation, suffered the same difficulties, as did the Nuffield Trust, a private bequest under which Lord Nuffield made £2 million available for the benefit of firms working in the depressed regions. Heim's (1984a: 550) conclusion on these bodies is that they were 'relatively small and ineffective'. The Treasury Fund, for example, assisted a total of twenty-four firms, paying out £1.16 million. Political and Economic Planning, the quasi-official think-tank, agreed: 'many more institutions of this type are needed' (Political and Economic Planning 1939: 73–4).

But whether they would have helped is a question worth asking. Heim (1986) is clear that both SARA and the Treasury Fund, as well as being small, were hamstrung by the powerful message from both the Treasury and large industrialists that they had to operate in a manner as close as possible to ordinary banking business. The Nuffield Trust, as a private body, had fewer restrictions of this sort and was accordingly seen by contemporaries as having been more successful. The key point, however, is that a private bequest such as Nuffield could afford to take more risks, while the other bodies had to adhere to strict standards of creditworthiness and avoid the allegation of subsidy, since they were using either public or investors' money. To depart from established notions of creditworthiness would, by definition, be to embrace more risky applicants and therefore reduce the returns to the investors. We need, therefore, to assess the extent to which the standard tests of creditworthiness were appropriate or overly conservative.

THE MACMILLAN GAP AND THE UNSATISFIED FRINGE OF BORROWERS

Perhaps the most famous statement with regard to industrial finance in the interwar years is the following one by the Macmillan Committee: 'it has been represented to us that great difficulty is experienced by the smaller and medium sized businesses in raising the capital which they may from time to time require even when the security offered is perfectly sound' (Macmillan 1931: para. 404). The committee went on to stress that this difficulty referred to long-term investment capital rather than the overdraft finance with which banks were most concerned – they saw no reason to request a change in 'the character of present banking practice' (Macmillan 1931: para. 403) but the mud has stuck and the notion of the Macmillan gap has been used to construct a view of bank bias against lending to small companies as well as the problems of raising investment funds. This view has continued to be put forward in discussions of industrial policy and small- and medium-sized enterprises (SMEs) into the twenty-first century.

One way of understanding this is to consider the market for industrial and commercial finance. In a competitive (or contestable) market, any systematic bias on the part of existing institutions would be eroded by entry of new services and products. If this does not happen, we have to conclude either that the market was competitive and no bias existed, or that the incumbent institutions in the market exerted very powerful constraints on entry so that their oligopolistic position and profits could not be eroded. It is clear that the banks did operate a powerful oligopoly in the interwar years, reinforced by the activities of the London Clearing House in England and the General Managers' Committee in Scotland. The smaller banks essentially followed the big banks' pricing and service policies. Yet, as Ackrill and Hannah (2001) have noted, contestability at the margins did exist, and market entry was not impossible. It was noted above, however, that the public sector attempts to augment the financial architecture in this period were less than wholly successful, since they foundered mostly on their inability to identify sufficient good-quality applicants for loans or investment when applying standard creditworthiness criteria. The private sector fared little better.

The most famous examples of this are the various institutions which were established by a number of merchant banks in an attempt to take advantage of the Macmillan gap. Some of these even went so far as to mention the Macmillan gap in their prospectuses, so making a very clear statement of intent. Schroeders established Leadenhall Securities with a capital of £250,000 in 1935 and the Charterhouse Industrial Development Trust was set up by Charterhouse, with the participation of the Prudential, Lloyds and the Midland in 1932. The United Dominions Trust (a hire purchase company 50 per cent owned by the Bank of England) created a body called Credit for Industry which, unlike the others, sought to make loans rather than investments in small companies. Others which entered the field include the London Industrial Finance Trust, the New Trading Co., Ridgeford Industrial Developments and the Whitehead and Lonsdale Investment Trusts (Balogh 1947; Grant 1967). None of them made any impact, and all found difficulty in identifying good-quality opportunities. Charterhouse received 9,000 applications in their first week of operation, which seemed to indicate that there was indeed a significant unsatisfied demand for financing, but only twelve of these were worthy of serious consideration (Dennett 1979). Another investment trust established to deal with small companies was estimated by its director to have taken on perhaps 1 in 400 of cases referred to it (Kinross 1982).

It seems therefore that neither public nor private sector attempts to deal with the Macmillan gap had any significant success in funding large numbers of projects which had been excluded either by the banks or by existing investment institutions. Keynes (1930) referred to the existence of these excluded projects as the 'fringe of unsatisfied borrowers' and pointed out that it would clearly be unrealistic to expect financial institutions to fund everyone who came to them asking for loans or investments, since many of them will be deluded dreamers or charlatans, and, as pointed out above, one of the key roles of financial intermediation is to reduce the level of risk to which individual investors are exposed. It makes sense, therefore, for financial institutions to exclude those whom they consider untrustworthy and/or uncreditworthy. The fringe of unsatisfied borrowers will always exist, because there will always be small, new or growing firms anxious to secure funding. That financial institutions subject them to some form of screening process (in which they specialise, and for which their depositors are generally happy to pay a proportion of the gross return on all loans and investments) and reject many, should be seen as evidence not of market failure, but of sensible market operation. There is no substantial evidence that the fringe of unsatisfied borrowers in Britain could have been significantly reduced by market entry (Ross 1996b). In other words, the existing financial institutions, given the prevailing rates of interest and levels of return required, were largely proved to be right in their estimation of poor risks.

This is not to suggest, of course, that the financial institutions were right in each and every case, merely that the costs and difficulties involved in identifying sufficient numbers of good risks outweighed the estimated returns which could be made from them. Banks and financial institutions could have invested significantly in the additional expertise required to appraise the small and new technology firms which, it is alleged, dominated the fringe of unsatisfied borrowers especially in the 1930s, and they would therefore have been in a better position to identify the good risks and exclude the high-risk applicants. Such investment, however, was simply too expensive and would have compromised the level of interest or dividends which they would have been able to pay to their depositors and investors. It was not until after 1945 that such an institution was created, and the evidence suggests that this was only successful because it was protected by the Bank of England and allowed to operate at a loss for a number of years until its expertise had been sufficiently established (Coopey and Clark 1995; Ross 1996b; Carnevali and Scott 1999).

There is a second way of understanding this position, however, and it is that rather than there being very little evidence of market failure in the size of the fringe of unsatisfied borrowers, the threshold of creditworthiness had simply been set too high. This approach suggests that the bankers' cartel made the market uncompetitive, and prices were kept artificially high. Market entrants were kept out not by the efficiency of the incumbents, but by their power to set prevailing prices. The evidence on this is unconvincing. Ackrill and Hannah (2001) suggest that British banks in the interwar years had an efficiency and productivity record as good as those in the United States, and superior to most areas of British industry. More importantly, perhaps, is the observation that the single most important asset of the British financial system in the 1920s and 1930s was its stability. There were no liquidity crises of the sort which devastated the banking systems of many European countries as well as the United States in those years, stemming from higher levels of competition in the banking sector, less conservative lending policies and a deterioration in the quality of bank assets (Jonker and Van Zanden 1995).

The British banking market may have been a cartel, but the stability it offered meant that at least no one lost their savings, and this achievement should be recognised.

THE GERMAN COMPARISON AND THE MARKET-ORIENTED FINANCIAL SYSTEM

The British banking system may have been both stable and efficient, but it is clear that the banks operated as one part of a wider collection of financial institutions. The extent and quality of information about the various assets for sale are the crucial determinants of efficiency in a financial market. Ross (1996) argues that the banks in interwar Britain operated in the context of a market-oriented financial system. The implications of this argument are important, since they address the issue of rationalisation and the extent to which the banks could be expected to construct a national industrial policy, and take the lead in investing and reorganising the declining staple trades. The Macmillan Committee and many others have suggested that this was not the job of the banks, since they must first look after their depositors. But the banks were only part of the financial architecture, and there were other institutions well suited to such a task. Financial markets – and for this purpose we are concentrating on the stock market – deal in assets which represent ownership of companies. If a firm is in crisis, its assets will be sold in the stock market, and the new owners are those responsible for undertaking an overhaul of the business. Two questions arise from this. The first is, why should banks, rather than the stock market, lead the rationalisation process? This question has most often been posed with regard to the situation in Germany, where the great banks were in the 1920s and have subsequently been seen as capable of arranging mergers, organising cartels and encouraging rationalisation in a way that the British banks were incapable of doing. The second question is whether the financial assets being sold in the stock market in the interwar years sufficiently reflected the true position of companies to encourage investors to respond appropriately.

The comparison with Germany is a longstanding one. Foxwell, Professor of Economics at the University of London, argued in 1919 that

> The financing of industry and trade should be the main business of banking . . . This is precisely what the German banks have done. They have done it with such conspicuous success, and by methods and machinery so radically different from our own, that a study of their methods is perhaps the best way by which we Englishmen can approach the subject. (Foxwell 1919:113).

The Macmillan Committee (1931: para. 376) noted that 'the relations between the British financial world and British industry . . . have never been so close as between German finance and German industry'. The nature of the comparison is an interesting one. On the one hand, there are the British commercial banks, who had developed a specialism in short-term overdraft financing and the deep personal and corporate relationships which made this possible. On the other, there are the German Universal banks which offered not only banking but also issuing and underwriting services, which took long-term equity positions in industrial firms and which often had representatives on their boards of management. Gerschenkron (1962: 67) noted that the German banks were capable of dominating their industrial clients to the extent that they 'refused to tolerate fratricidal struggles among their children', and the macroeconomic benefits were thought to be clear in the larger, more technically advanced and more efficient industrial combines which came to dominate in Germany in both the pre- and post-war years.

This dichotomy between the distant and aloof British banks and the closely integrated, managing and assisting German banks has been shown to be greatly exaggerated, however. The evidence described above suggests that in the British case at least, the characterisation has been somewhat overdrawn; many of the English and Scottish banks took very great care to nurse their industrial customers through periods of difficulty, exploiting as they did so the accumulated expertise of long-term close relationships which recognised the mutual benefits of continued co-operation. Collins (1998), in a broad overview of the development of banking systems in Europe, notes the similarities rather than differences across the continent. Recent reappraisals of the German banking system have come to a similar conclusion; the benefits of Universal banks seem to have been overstated by those most keen to draw lessons from Britain's great industrial and military rival of the early twentieth century. Edwards and Fischer (1993) have suggested that the German economy gained very little from the existence of Universal banks, by pointing out that they worked only with the very largest firms and that many of these did not, in any case, make use of them. Fohlin (2001) has argued that the German banking system, in the pre-First World War period at least, was equally focused on maintaining liquidity, and may have underinvested in risky projects. Her conclusion that differences in banking structure were not the cause of differential economic performance – either before or after the 1920s – is important and convincing.

OTHER FINANCIAL INTERMEDIARIES

The above discussion has focused on banks. But as we have seen, the word 'bank' can refer to very different types of institution (Ross and Ziegler, 2000). While Universal banks emerged in many countries in continental Europe because of the absence of efficient or extensive financial markets

(Gerschenkron 1962; Tilly 1986), this did not apply in Britain, where the specialist deposit and commercial banking system developed in the context of a sophisticated financial environment. By the 1920s there was a variety of markets and institutions, apart from banks, which together afforded an extensive set of opportunities to companies seeking to raise funds. Grant (1967) stressed the importance of the new issue market as a vehicle for industrial companies in search of finance, especially in the immediate post-war years. The amount of capital raised in 1920 (£263 million for domestic industry, trade and transport) was not to be surpassed until just before the resumption of hostilities in 1939. Much of this represented grossly inflated asset values and contributed to the difficulties, noted above, in a number of industries throughout the subsequent decades (Macrosty 1927; Bamberg 1988). Nevertheless, the ease with which companies could turn to the market underlines its importance as a first port of call for capital raising.

The number and sophistication of institutions operating in the new issue and secondary stock markets increased considerably throughout the interwar years. This happened in response to the decline in overseas investment opportunities after the First World War, as savings and investment vehicles increasingly turned their attentions to the domestic market. Investment trusts such as Charterhouse and Gresham began to offer their services as underwriters to companies from the middle 1920s, but they concentrated on large issues, in excess of £200,000 (Chapman 1984; Diaper 1986), although their investments in individual companies tended to be considerably smaller, as they sought to diversify their risks. Between 1920 and 1933, such trusts grew faster than any other group of financial institutions (with the exception of building societies), more than trebling their capital from £90 million to £295 million. In 1923, approximately 65 per cent of their funds were invested overseas, but by 1939 – by which time some sixty-one companies were being reported – this had fallen to 45 per cent (Corner and Burton 1963; Cassis 1990). One estimate of the sectoral distribution of this investment has 16.2 per cent of their funds being directed towards British industry in 1928, and Cassis (1990: 148) concludes that 'there was no particular relationship between the investment trusts and British industry'. As sources of capital in the market, however, it is clear that they were far from insignificant and steadily growing in importance.

One of the most interesting aspects of Cassis' analysis of investment trusts is the extent to which famous banking names and very well-informed and connected individuals played a role in this industry. The decline of London private bankers and the need for merchant banks also to find profitable outlets for their funds meant that the investment trust movement became an important avenue by which the old, private and exclusive City came into contact with industrial and domestic financing. The extensive involvement of bankers, lawyers, accountants and stock brokers, the rising professionalism of the investment trust movement in the 1920s and 1930s and the fact that many individuals held directorships in a number of trusts led to the notion of investment groups, in which these people worked together and shared information on investment opportunities. They therefore contributed to greater sophistication and ease of information flow in the growing domestic capital markets.

Merchant banks also began to play some role in the domestic financial markets in the 1920s. Traditionally these institutions had avoided financing domestic industry, preferring to concentrate on foreign loans and government finance. Declining opportunities in those directions in the interwar years, however, encouraged them to move towards both domestic issues and the provision of loans to industrial enterprises. Morgan Grenfell, who are considered to have been the leaders of this movement, were instrumental in the General Motors' purchase of Vauxhall in the 1920s, and were also intimately connected with the steel industry, a relationship which lasted well into the era after the Second World War (Burk 1989). Lazards played an active role in the merger discussions in the British electrical industry throughout the interwar years (Jones and Marriott 1970), Kleinworts became engaged with the shipping and shipbuilding industries on the Tyne in the 1920s (Diaper 1990) and Barings moved into railway and underground financing as well as brewery takeovers in the 1930s. These merchant bank activities were clearly focused at the peak level of industrial financing, and represent very large amounts of capital being mobilised for large companies, but they also indicate a growing complexity and variety of financing options in the capital market over this period.

This is an important conclusion in understanding the market-oriented financial system which existed in Britain in this period, since there has been some dispute over its extent. Some authors have suggested that the capital markets in Britain – or at least the information attaching to financial assets traded in the markets – were insufficiently developed to generate demand among institutional investors until at least the 1950s (Mowery 1992; Roberts 1992; Lazonick and O'Sullivan 1997). This position has focused on the limited divorce of ownership from control in British industry in the interwar years and the related supposedly laggard development of high-technology industries, but it pays little attention to two factors: first, British business history stresses the appropriateness of the business and institutional structure of ownership in this period (Wilson 1995) and, second, the emergence and growth of significant relationships between industry and financial institutions outlined above. A recent study of the emergence of insurance companies as investors in corporate securities in the interwar years suggests that 'a well-diversified and efficient market in industrial and commercial equities' had emerged prior to the First World War and that many of the companies responded to this by developing specialist equity and strategy appraisal capabilities (Scott 2002: 88).

A number of pressures from the First World War onwards led the large life insurance offices, which traditionally focused on safety and security of capital values, to reappraise their position and begin to include considerable amounts of corporate securities in their portfolios (Scott 2002). The first of these pressures was inflation in the war years and immediately afterwards, which drastically eroded the value of the large holdings of government stocks which they had been compelled to hold. The second element was heightened competitiveness in the insurance market from the 1920s, as individuals sought to use life insurance polices as a means of investment and companies began to offer higher returns in order to entice customers. Third, the cheap money policies of the 1930s and the decline of foreign bond issues reinforced the companies' attempts to locate alternative investment outlets.

The Prudential led the movement into industrial equities (Williams 1935). Keynes, as chairman of the National Mutual, and closely aligned with the Provincial, developed a powerful conviction that equity investment – and with it active portfolio management – was the answer to many of the industry's difficulties (Westall 1992). The Provincial held 4.3 per cent of its portfolio in ordinary shares in 1922, 14.2 per cent by 1928 and 30 per cent in 1937. The National Mutual had 18.7 per cent of its assets invested in ordinary shares in 1924, while the industry average the following year was 4.3 per cent (Keynes 1928). Influenced partly by the work of Raynes (1926, 1937), the industry followed Keynes' lead. Standard Life's holdings of ordinary shares rose from less than 1 per cent of its total portfolio in 1922 to over 20 per cent in 1936 (Moss 2000). As part of a definite strategy of shifting towards marketable securities, the company improved the quality of its market information, developed expertise in appraising stock brokers' advice and adopted careful monitoring techniques. These information and monitoring capabilities were put to good use when the company became involved in the rationalisation of the steel industry in the late 1920s. Similar approaches to appraising the market and improving their information flows were adopted by the Pearl Insurance Company and by Equity and Law, which delegated wide powers to its investment committee.

As well as developing the managerial systems, financial information appraisal techniques and monitoring mechanisms which an active investment policy required, many companies also began to play a significant role as underwriters, and contributed significantly to the development of the new issue market in the 1920s and 1930s. The Prudential, for example, moved aggressively into industrial finance, through its investment trusts, its underwriting business and by establishing the Industrial Finance and

Investment Corporation Ltd. Among the Prudential's activities were the financing of Marks and Spencer and the Mayfair Hotel in the 1920s (Scott 2002).

Overall, it is clear from this discussion that the insurance companies – along with many of the other financial intermediaries which turned their attention to the domestic capital market in the 1920s and 1930s – contributed enormously to the credibility of the instruments being traded and thus to the efficiency of the market itself. A market-dominated financial system, in which the prices of the securities traded reflected the quality of the underlying assets, had clearly developed sufficiently by the 1930s to entice institutional investors, who in turn contributed greatly to the flow of information in that system. This context helps us understand the role of the commercial banks more clearly, since, as the examples of many of the merchant banks, the investment trusts, of Standard Life and the Prudential make clear, there were many other avenues and sources to which industry and commerce could turn when they sought finance for investment or for rationalisation.

CONCLUSIONS

This chapter has focused on the mechanisms by which industry and commerce were able to raise finance in the interwar years for the purposes of rationalisation or investment. It has addressed the question of whether the banking system failed its industrial customers by adopting a policy of liquidity and security above assistance and commitment. It suggests that many of the criticisms of the banking sector's reluctance to engage with their industrial and commercial customers have been based on a faulty understanding both of the nature of that relationship and the market context in which the banks operated.

There are two fundamental conclusions. First, banks in Britain clearly supported their customers and became involved in industrial reorganisation where it was sensible for them to do so, based on the close and long-term relationships which characterised their approach to banking. It is not, however, the banks' job to formulate industrial or macroeconomic policy, nor should they be held responsible for failing to drive forward schemes of rationalisation in the staple industries. Rather, the approach taken here – in which the banks are seen very clearly in the context of a market with a sophisticated set of institutions offering a variety of financial services and options from the 1920s onwards – requires us not to think exclusively in terms of banking, but rather to focus on the impact of the financial system as a whole.

The second conclusion is that there is little evidence that the banks – or the rest of the financial system – failed to meet an overwhelming level of demand for finance in this period. Demand for bank loans fell in the

1930s, and the new issue market and institutional investors were able to respond when necessary to requests for capital investment. The fringe of unsatisfied borrowers identified by the Macmillan Committee represented a significantly smaller pool of potentially profitable firms than has been suggested. The evidence of overwhelming demand is not convincing, so criticism of the supply mechanisms is misplaced.

16 Scotland, 1860–1939: growth and poverty

CLIVE H. LEE

Contents

SCOTLAND AND INDUSTRIALISATION

The period from the beginning of Queen Victoria's reign to the Second World War was a good one for the history of the Scottish economy. It was characterised by flourishing heavy industry, based on iron and steel manufacture that generated a diversity of engineering products and was fuelled by coal. This was the era when the railway network spread throughout the economy, even to remote parts of the Highlands, and when British finance and technology played a leading part in fostering economic progress throughout the world. Scotland was a full participant in that process, providing more than its fair share of inventors, scientists, industrialists and financiers. Indeed, for Scotland, the Victorian era produced much to support the claim that it was the country's greatest era of innovation and growth. Industrialisation proceeded on a scale hitherto unsurpassed and created a continuous urban sprawl in the central belt, along the valleys of the Clyde and the Forth. It was an era in which Scottish goods were traded throughout the world, and in which Scottish finance helped underwrite the expansion of the international economy.

In popular perception, too, the great period of Scottish economic advance took place in Queen Victoria's reign. As Devine observed in his survey of Scottish history, in the formal opening of Glasgow City Chambers by the Queen in 1888, and in hosting the 1901 International Exhibition in Kelvingrove Park, an event attended by 11.5 million visitors, Glasgow had established its position as a great international centre of industry and as the second city of the Empire. Other superlatives could be claimed. By the eve of the First World War, the industrial complex based on Glasgow, Lanarkshire and Renfrewshire accounted for the production of half of British marine engine horsepower, for one third of railway locomotive and rolling-stock production, and of shipping tonnage, together with one fifth of steel output. Clydeside was recognised as one of the great shipbuilding and engineering centres of the world (Devine 1999: 249–50).

The economic expansion of the Victorian years did not continue through the interwar decades. High and persistent unemployment, social deprivation and widespread poverty were the familiar characteristics of that era. The pattern was broken only by the preparations for the Second World War that revived the shipyards.

In both Victorian growth and interwar recession, Scotland shared a common experience with other parts of the United Kingdom. But the central hypothesis of this chapter is that Scotland differed in responding to that experience in two key respects. First, Scotland was unable to retain and employ its population increase; outward migration became a pervasive feature of Scottish life. Second, the fruits of economic advance were unevenly distributed so that many sectors of society were largely excluded from the enjoyment of their benefits. As a consequence, many Scots remained in poverty, and eventually sought political solutions to their economic and social problems. In so doing, they were able to exploit political opportunities that were available by virtue of the semi-autonomous position that Scotland held within the United Kingdom as a consequence of the Union of 1707. The outcome was that the Scots evolved a distinctly critical response to the free market, and embraced a much greater enthusiasm for state intervention in economic affairs than was evident south of the border. These differences placed Scotland on a distinctive and different developmental path to that taken by its southern neighbour. This divergence eventually placed considerable stress on the cohesiveness of the United Kingdom, and raised fundamental questions about Scotland's place within it.

DEMOGRAPHIC CHANGE, MIGRATION AND DECLINE

The most obvious characteristic of economic growth in Scotland was manifest in its demographic change. The population of Scotland grew from about 1 million in 1700 to reach almost 3 millions by the middle of the nineteenth century, and 5 million by 1951. This overall rate of growth was

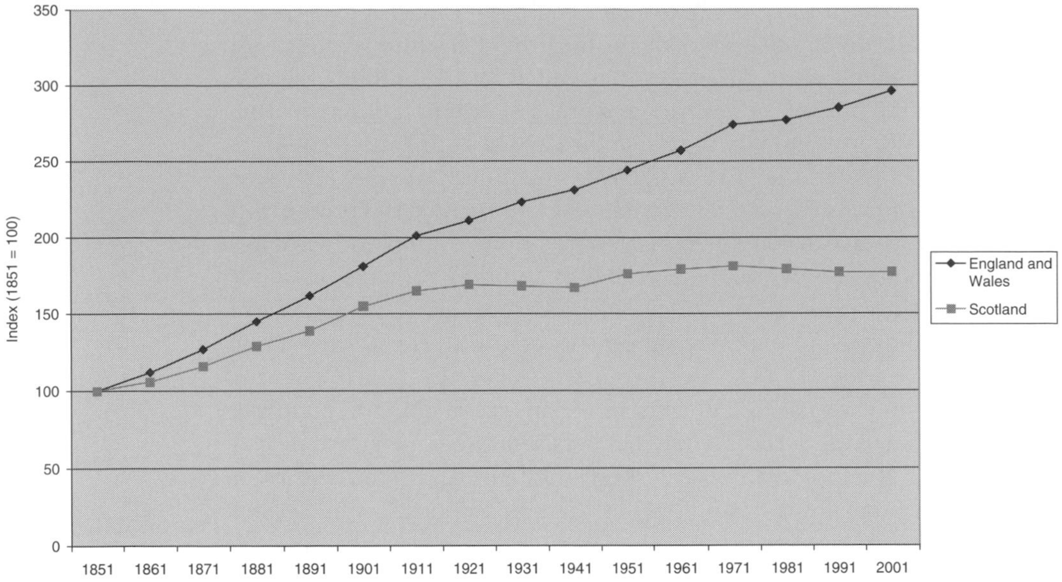

Figure 16.1 Index of population growth, Scotland and England and Wales, 1851–2001

Source: HMSO 1961, 2001.

relatively modest compared to England and Wales where a much higher rate of growth was sustained, and additional population retained, than in Scotland. Indeed, through much of the twentieth century Scottish population remained almost static (Figure 16.1).

The process of population change exhibited a number of clearly delineated characteristics. The most obvious of these was the difference between the central belt and the rural periphery. In this chapter the central belt has been defined as comprising Strathclyde, Lothian, Central and Fife regions. The rest of Scotland, that is Dumfries and Galloway and the Borders in the south, plus the Tayside, Grampian and Highland regions in the north, has been defined as the rural regions.

The demographic experience of the rural regions was consistent throughout this period as net natural increase, adding births and subtracting deaths, was almost exactly balanced by net outward migration. The loss of population through migration did not occur as the result of the decline of a few particular areas; it was pervasive and endemic. Every region experienced net outward migration in every decade between 1861 and 1938. Only a handful of the twenty-one counties experienced any net inward migration and only on rare occasions. Loss of population through net migration was persistent through successive decades and virtually universal throughout rural Scotland, even though this area included two of the four major Scottish cities, Aberdeen and Dundee, within its bounds.

The persistent loss of population was no novelty in the Highland counties. Temporary and seasonal migration from the Highlands to supplement income had been a common practice since the late seventeenth

Figure 16.2 Major Scottish regions

century. Young women found work in domestic service, textile manufacture and fish processing, while men undertook seasonal agricultural work and employment on railway construction. These additions to family income were essential for crofters (small-scale tenant farmers, see below). The low productivity of farming was compounded by the practice of dividing land on the occasion of marriage, while the potato blight that caused the great famine induced a massive temporary migration in 1846–7. The fragility of this way of life was also threatened by the small size of holdings, by the encroachment of sheep farming, by insecurity of tenure and by high rents. All these weaknesses were identified by the investigations of the Napier Commission in the 1880s (Withers 1998: 30–2, 46).

The outflow of population from the rural areas was cumulative in its effects. Migration disproportionately affects the young, able and ambitious. The loss of eligible males leads to an excess of marriageable women and a decline in the marriage rate. There was a steady stream of young men away from the Highland counties throughout the nineteenth century marked by the depletion of successive cohorts of population (Anderson 2000: 116–17). As population left the rural regions, the rate of natural increase fell, principally as a consequence of falling birth rates. For example, Inverness-shire recorded an average birth rate per thousand of population of 27.6 in the 1860s that fell to 15.6 by the 1930s, while in Shetland the average birth rate fell from 25.7 to 13.1 (Flinn 1977: 318, 338–9). By the 1930s this process had advanced to the stage that several counties, including Argyll, Bute, Orkney, Peebles, Ross and Cromarty, Selkirk, Shetland and Sutherland, experienced a net loss in natural increase, as deaths exceeded births. Ageing populations exacerbated the problems of economic regeneration. As a result of emigration and increased longevity, the proportion of Scots aged over sixty-five rose from 4.9 per cent of the population in 1861 to 7.3 per cent by 1931, although these ratios tended to be higher in the rural counties.

Many of those who left their rural homes headed towards the central belt, often in several stages or subsequent to earlier temporary migrations. The central belt counties enjoyed a modest net increase from migration in the 1860s, 1870s and 1890s. Much of this increase represented additions to Lanarkshire, including Glasgow, and its adjacent counties of Renfrew and Dunbarton, and to Midlothian, including Edinburgh. In addition there was a surge of migration in the 1900s into Stirling, Fife and West Lothian as new coalfields expanded production. Net inward migration into the central belt was sharply reversed after the turn of the century with three decades of massive population loss through net outward migration. As a result, the population of the central belt increased by less than 20 per cent between 1901 and 1938. Between 1861 and 1938 the central belt managed to retain about 75 per cent of its natural increase in population, a much higher rate than that of the rural regions but distinctly less than in England and Wales where little more than 5 per cent of natural increase was lost in net outward migration. The Scottish economy between the mid-nineteenth century and the Second World War was dominated and shaped by outward migration that cost a net loss in excess of 1 million people. Many of these migrants went south to England, the majority between 1861 and the turn of the century, although

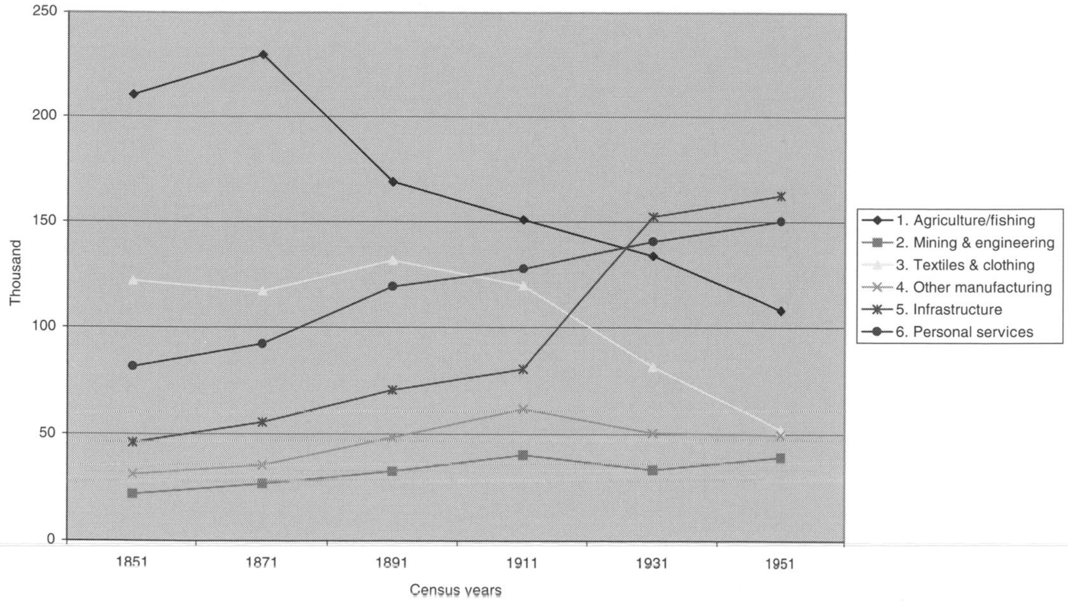

Figure 16.3
Employment in rural regions in Scotland, by employment sector, 1851–1951

Source: Lee 1979.

the large outflow in the early twentieth century moved primarily overseas (Flinn 1977: 441ff).

There can be little doubt that the loss of population in the first half of the twentieth century represented a response to severe economic dislocation. But the same thesis fits many characteristics of the Victorian era, and the ubiquity of population loss throughout the rural regions suggests decline. Some authorities have stressed the positive aspects of migration, and depicted enterprising Scots seeking their fortunes throughout the world, often with great success. There is certainly substance to this claim, as evidenced by the many Scots who prospered abroad (Devine 1999: 471–73). Furthermore, the open plains of the United States and Canada offered abundant compensation to those denied access to small patches of infertile land in the Highlands. The historical literature of the Highlands has blamed landlords for the clearances that destroyed traditional society. It might be more accurate to argue that the most significant contribution made by the lairds was to stimulate population growth in the late eighteenth and early nineteenth centuries by offering prospects of employment, based on crofting and kelp production. Unfortunately, it was a combination that could not be sustained in the long term (Anderson 2000: 112, 128).

It is quite clear that the rural regions of Scotland were struggling to provide employment sufficient to sustain population growth in the first half of the nineteenth century and that their capacity to do so was virtually exhausted by mid-century (Figure 16.3). The decline in employment in agriculture and fishing between 1851 and 1951, by almost one half,

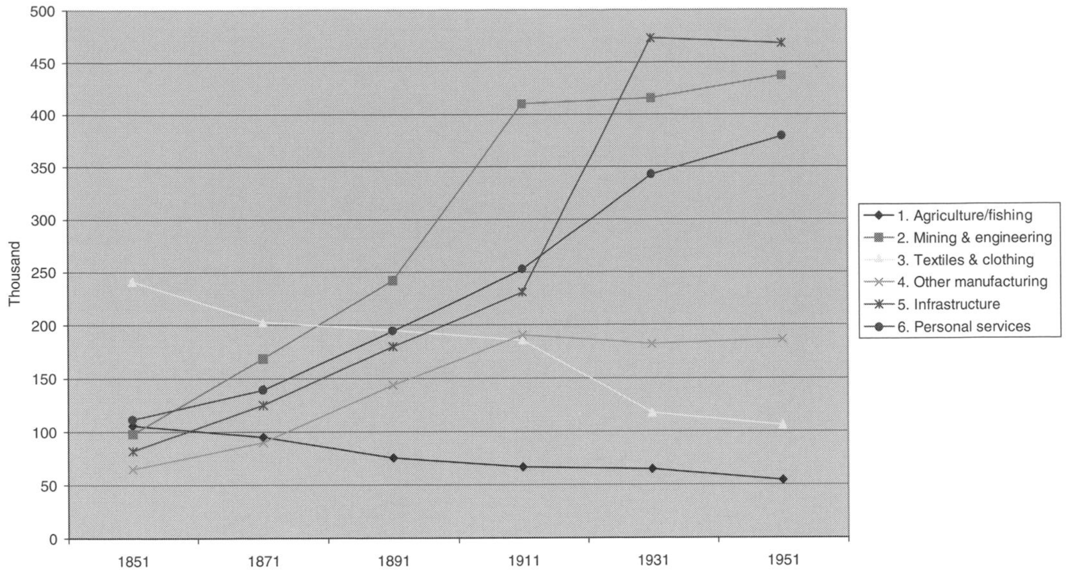

Figure 16.4 Employment in the central belt of Scotland, by employment sector, 1851–1951

Source: Lee 1979.

was the same relative decline as that suffered by the central belt, as was the scale of decline in textiles and clothing, by a little more than half. The difference between these two regions of the Scottish economy lay not in the loss of employment resulting from this structural change, but in their relative ability to generate new kinds of employment. The rural areas experienced much greater difficulty in creating employment in sectors such as construction, distribution, transport and utilities, lumped together as 'infrastructure' in Figures 16.3 and 16.4, and in personal and professional services, than did the central belt. Nor could they replicate its industrialisation. The absorption of Highlanders into the central belt in the second half of the nineteenth century provided only a temporary palliative. The massive outward flows of population suffered in the first half of the twentieth century were not the manifestation of temporary economic recession, they were the measure of rural Scotland's continuing and increasing difficulty in coping with the consequences of the natural increase of population.

EXCESS LABOUR AND THE LOW-WAGE ECONOMY

The fact that Scottish emigration per head of population represented one of the largest outflows recorded in western Europe, comparable only to those of the Norwegians and the Irish, indicates an obvious lack of opportunity at home. Since the labour market was profoundly influenced by the growth of population that relationship is of fundamental importance. The main issues may be expressed as two questions. Did the loss of population through migration prevent an oversupply of labour, even creating shortages in particular locations or industries through the loss of workers with particular skills? Alternatively, was the scale of emigration insufficient to prevent the process of population growth from creating an excess supply of labour? There are several ways in which answers to these questions might be found, most obviously in wage rates, in the level and prevalence of unemployment or underemployment and in industrial relations.

Roy Campbell's seminal investigation of Scottish industry paid close attention to wage rates, and he argued that Scotland secured a comparative advantage by paying lower wages than those that prevailed in England. There is evidence that suggests that, for much of the nineteenth century, Scottish wages remained substantially below rates paid south of the border. In the 1860s, estimates indicate that the gap ranged from 16 to 19 per cent according to trade, and it remained at 9–13 per cent in the 1890s. By the time of the 1886 wage census, Scottish rates were below the national average in most textile manufactures, including a deficit in excess of 20 per cent in the cotton industry, while the gap in iron and steel and in shipbuilding was 8 per cent, and in brewing it was 13 per cent. By the next wage census of 1906, Scotland had closed the gap and exceeded the national average in most industries, thereby apparently losing the comparative advantage identified by Campbell (Campbell 1980: 191–4). While many estimates of wage rates show the west of Scotland, in particular, converging on rates paid in other labour markets in the later nineteenth century, this does not necessarily represent improving prospects for the workers. Piecework grew rapidly in many trades, thereby linking payment to work completed. In engineering, the proportion of workers paid in this way increased from 5 per cent in 1886 to 46 per cent of fitters and 37 per cent of turners by 1914 (McIvor 2001: 69–70). Riveters in the Clydeside shipyards received incomes that varied greatly around the average payment, fluctuations being determined by absenteeism, absence through illness or injury and by the availability of work. Some incomes were reduced by the introduction of machinery that left the workers to undertake residual and unskilled tasks (Price 1981: 59).

Treble's studies of the Glasgow labour market in the late Victorian period also identified characteristically low pay. In 1903, it was estimated that labourers in iron foundries in Glasgow earned less than £1 per week, as did railway platelayers and machinists in tailoring workshops (Treble 1978a: 129–30). The average weekly pay of labourers, when in employment, was also less than £1, a sum that was reckoned insufficient to provide either a proper home or the basic necessities of life. While some workers did rather better, such as builders' and plasterers' labourers who earned 24s. (£1.20p) per week, their pay fell between 10 and 30 per cent below the wages of their counterparts in Birmingham and Leeds (Treble 1979: 21). Gray argued, in the context of Edinburgh, that each specific labour market contained a hierarchy of workers, ranging from those whose skill secured high wages and security of employment to those with limited skills who were most exposed to the vagaries of fluctuating availability of work (Gray 1976: 88–90).

There is ample evidence to suggest that, even in the main urban labour markets, unemployment was frequent and underemployment was endemic. In 1907 the *Glasgow Herald*, referring to underemployment, stated that 'the evil is too familiar to require proof'. The Rev. J. C. Pringle's report, three years later, described a pattern of employment in which short periods of work were interspersed with long intervals of idleness, demonstrating the surplus of available labour (HMSO 1910; Treble 1978b: 149, 167). Many jobs were affected by seasonal variations, usually with underemployment occurring in the winter months as it did, characteristically, in building, dock working and tailoring. Some industries relied heavily on casual employment as a matter of policy. Bakeries in Glasgow preferred to employ a limited number of full-time staff that could be supplemented by casual workers at weekends. Some industries, such as the finishing trades in the clothing industry, were characterised by highly variable payments without any standard accepted rate. Certainly, Scotland possessed a fair share of industries that were prone to cyclical variations in activity. Estimates for unemployment in shipbuilding and engineering between 1902 and 1914 placed Scotland above the United Kingdom average. In engineering, the average rate of unemployment in the Glasgow area was 7.7 per cent compared to 9.2 per cent in eastern Scotland and to the United Kingdom average of 5.4 per cent. Unemployment rates in the shipyards, for the same three areas respectively, were 10.5, 15.6 and 11.0 per cent (Southall 1988: 246–7).

While historians have argued about the significance of 'Red Clydeside', there is greater agreement about the major characteristics of the Victorian labour market. The extent to which Scottish employers were more anti-trade union than their peers in other industrial areas of Britain has been a prominent theme. Clydeside employers have often been depicted as autocratic and hostile to organised labour, and they certainly appear to have enjoyed the best of industrial disputes. The engineering employers imposed successful lock-outs in 1898 and 1922, while the shipbuilders were similarly successful in 1865 and 1877. The Clyde Shipbuilders' Association shunned negotiation, used non-union labour when it preferred and did not recognise trade unions until late in the nineteenth century. It was claimed that the Lanarkshire Coalmasters' Association also ignored trade unions, victimised their representatives and called out the cavalry to disperse strikers. The success of periodic lock-outs imposed by employers increased their control over the labour market. Perhaps, as a consequence of this environment, trade unionism grew relatively slowly in Scotland. In 1892 only 3.7 per cent of adults were members compared to 4.9 per cent in England (Johnston 2000: 135–6, 173).

The widespread and persistent loss of population from all parts of Scotland through migration suggests that labour shortages would be unlikely to occur except in unusual and infrequent circumstances. In the Victorian era, many industries were characterised by casual semi-skilled and unskilled work, such as construction, and were subject to bouts of unemployment and underemployment. Erratic employment, casual work and poor wages combined to ensure that, for many citizens, life was a perpetual struggle against poverty and destitution. A small disaster, such as the loss of work for a few weeks, or the loss of a spouse or a parent from death or desertion, could be sufficient to plunge a family into an irresistible spiral of decline. Furthermore, surveys conducted by the Board of Trade, in 1905 and in 1912, found that prices were higher in Scotland for foodstuffs such as flour, butter, cheese, eggs, tea and beef, indicating a real wage disadvantage for urban Scots of about 10 per cent (Rodger 1989a: 32). The near universal loss of population from migration after 1900, and the prolonged recession that followed the Great War, confirmed a state in which surplus labour supply was characteristic of all markets for labour throughout the first half of the twentieth century except in time of war.

THE LABOUR-INTENSIVE STRUCTURE OF PRODUCTION

The characteristics of demographic change and the structure of labour markets had a profound effect on both the productive process and the distribution of benefits within Scottish society. Availability of labour was an important requirement for Scottish industrialisation, the most familiar and prominent aspect of which was the emergence of the industrial complex in the western Lowlands, centred upon Glasgow and its hinterland. Industrialisation spread through much of the central belt where Scottish coal reserves were concentrated (see Figure 16.4 for the changing employment structure in this central belt). It brought together a cluster of strongly interlinked manufactures. The shipyards and the engineers relied upon steel and iron producers for essential inputs while they, in turn, needed coal and iron ore. Since all these raw material inputs were heavy and expensive to move, spatial proximity of the sequences of the productive process, and the geological configuration of raw material deposits, were important. The principal market for the output of much of this activity, a vast array of both mercantile shipping and warships, was the expanding international market, although Admiralty contracts accounted for 45 per cent of the tonnage ordered from Clydeside yards in the quarter of a century before the Great War. Approximately one third of the shipping tonnage launched from British yards between 1870 and 1914 came from the Clyde, and in 1913, the final year of peace,

18 per cent of world shipping tonnage was launched on the river (Peebles 1987: 1–2).

As in many British industries, Scottish producers relied on skilled manual workers. Data from John Brown's yard showed that labour accounted for between 31 and 49 per cent of the total cost of manufacturing the hulls for a sample of thirty vessels built in the 1880s and 1890s (Campbell 1980: 16–17). Reliance on skilled manual work was combined with extreme specialisation of function, and craft-based trade unions were vigilant in defending their particular contributions (Knox *et al.* 1993: 200–9). This form of productive structure had advantages when order books were full. Dependence on skilled labour, together with a lack of standardisation, enabled shipyards to adjust production to meet highly specific requirements of their customers for individual vessels. In times of economic recession, however, such flexibility led to underutilisation of capacity, increasing production costs and prices, and a consequent loss of competitiveness (Slaven 1977: 194). Labour-intensive production allowed firms to limit their investment in capital equipment. In 1913 the Clydebank shipyard of John Brown & Co., with a capital value of £3.4 million, stood at the peak of the industrial hierarchy, while Beardmore & Co., general engineers, was valued at £2 million. The rest of the Clydeside shipyards failed to reach a valuation of £1 million (Pollard and Robertson 1979: 81, 127). The limited scale of investment in capital equipment was reflected in the fact that, as late as 1910, the value of machinery in John Brown's yard was worth only £200,000.

The modest commitment of capital investment supported a structure that could comfortably be defended against change. On the eve of the Great War, membership of the board of directors in more than one quarter of the principal Scottish shipbuilding firms was confined to a single family. Reliance on skilled labour rather than on capital equipment limited investment to sums affordable by a small group of co-owners. A plethora of small firms, each able to resist amalgamation, was a weakness that ran throughout heavy industry. The historians of the British shipbuilding industry drew attention to the manifest need for large-scale yards, standardised production and effective managerial co-ordination of successive processes. All were contrary to the traditions of British shipyards and to the vested interests of both employers and their workers (Lorenz and Wilkinson 1986: 118–19). Even so, there were some signal indications of approaching difficulty. At the beginning of the twentieth century, Beardmore, the largest steel manufacturer and engineering company in Scotland, had to seek rescue from its financial problems by entering into partnership with Vickers & Co. of Barrow-in-Furness (Hume and Moss 1979: 56, 90). Salvation, albeit temporary, appeared in the demand for military equipment in the two world wars.

The preferred response to business problems between the wars was to create larger entities through merger. The shipbuilders, anticipating a replacement boom after the Great War and anxious to protect their supplies of steel, carried out a series of mergers with steel producers. As a result, the largest industrial units in Ulster and the west of Scotland became concentrated into two massive combines. But the depressed market for shipping in the 1920s undermined the rationale of merger. As debts increased, further change was resisted through fear of increased liability. Lloyds Bank, a major shareholder in the Lanarkshire Steel Co., blocked its sale to Colville & Co. at a price that would have incurred losses (Tolliday 1987: 94). Furthermore, the process of merger did not lead to the rationalisation of productive practices. Even though Colville & Co. had acquired control of 80 per cent of Scottish steel making capacity by 1936, the newly enlarged company continued to manufacture on the basis of its unreformed constituent operations. Hence Tolliday's persuasive judgement that the rationalisation process in the Scottish steel industry, as a means to improving production and productivity, was largely a sham. Even so, by the 1930s the steel and shipbuilding complex, focused on Colville and Lithgow interests, had achieved domination over heavy industry in Scotland. The Second World War brought a strong surge of demand and a temporary postponement of inherent difficulties.

The weaknesses of the industrial structure were increasingly exposed after the First World War. The expansion of wartime iron production had brought the natural resource base close to exhaustion. Given the unsuitability of local iron ore for steel production, an alternative strategy emerged whereby malleable iron production was mixed with scrap and imported iron. This enabled Scottish manufacturers to produce steel, but it restricted output to a scale of operation that prevented the introduction of the best technology or the achievement of economies of scale. The inefficiency of production was compounded by the location of steel manufacture in central Lanarkshire, adding transport charges to production costs as raw materials and finished products moved to and from the Clyde. These difficulties were sufficient to induce one major manufacturer, Stewart & Lloyd, to transfer its entire steel manufacture to Corby (in the English Midlands), a location with easy access to raw materials, seaports and markets. At the end of the 1920s the Brassert Report, commissioned from a leading American engineering consultancy, offered a radical blueprint for the redevelopment of the Scottish steel industry. The key recommendation proposed the establishment of a new integrated iron and steel works close to the Clyde. The industry declined to adopt the strategy. Payne emphasised antipathies between rival firms, while Tolliday explained the decision in terms of weak market conditions and doubts that some of the proposed savings could actually be realised (Payne 1979: 316, 418; Tolliday 1987: 105).

There were other inherent and unavoidable weaknesses that increased the vulnerability of Scottish production. It relied on natural resources that were finite, and those limitations were becoming evident before the nineteenth century closed. The iron industry depended on splint coal and iron ore deposits that were high in phosphorus content. They were not well suited for making the malleable iron required for steel production. Scottish supplies of iron ore fell from a peak level of output in 1880 to near extinction by the First World War. By that date some of the older coalfields had exploited their best and most easily accessible reserves. Furthermore, output per man was declining in the western coalfields, and while new reserves were being exploited they were some distance away from the main iron making regions, in West Lothian, Fife and Clackmannan. The eve of the Great War marked the peak of Scottish coal production with almost all coalfields recording declining output thereafter. Between the wars, Scottish coal mines operated on a scale that was substantially smaller than other coalfields. The average size of the British coalfield increased from 408 to 427 workers between 1913 and 1938, while in Scotland the average fell from 301 to 255 (Supple 1987: 364–5).

Labour-intensive production was a defining characteristic of Scottish heavy industry as an alternative to capital-intensive production that would have required greater investment and possible loss of managerial control by owners. Excess labour confirmed the superior negotiating position of employers in the labour market. But the exhaustion of limited natural resources, increasingly competitive international markets and inefficient production methods eventually destroyed much of the central belt's industrial capacity.

THE CREATION AND OWNERSHIP OF WEALTH

While heavy industry might rightly claim pre-eminence in the industrialisation of the central belt, it was neither unique nor pre-eminent in the creation of wealth. A diversity of other manufactures prospered in central Scotland. The largest was the Coats textile manufacture in Paisley that had a capital value of £42 million in 1904/5, greater than all other Scottish manufacturers (Wardley 1991: 278). But the greatest companies that were established before 1914 were the railways and the financial institutions. By the beginning of the twentieth century they had coalesced into complex structures bound by a multiplicity of commercial links. The Edinburgh network brought together the Royal Bank of Scotland, the Linen Bank and the North British Railway, while the Glasgow network was centred upon the Clydesdale Bank, the Caledonian Railway and the Tennant family's extensive business connections (Scott and Hughes 1980: 42–3).

From the early eighteenth century, the Scottish financial system had grown steadily, encompassing commercial banks and insurance companies. Their business lay initially outside manufacturing, and focused on the commercial and personal transactions of prosperous landowners and merchants. The financial services sector produced some of the largest economic institutions in Scotland, such as Standard Life that was to become the largest mutual life company in Europe. Its annual revenue rose from £169,000 in 1850 to £1.6 million in 1913 and £3.9 million in 1938. Scottish financial institutions possessed a number of advantages that their manufacturing contemporaries lacked. Finance was not constrained by having to operate in specific locations, and the increase in affluence throughout the world offered many new opportunities. Standard Life soon established a network of outposts such that half of its business was conducted outside the United Kingdom by 1914. At home, it pioneered company pension schemes, establishing a programme for Brunner Mond in 1910, a branch of business that was extended to other client organisations after the Great War. Like other insurance companies, Standard Life used income from premiums to build an investment portfolio. In 1880 the company had assets worth £5.5 million, almost 75 per cent of which were held in mortgages. By 1914, the company's international business had been restructured to focus on farm mortgages in the American west, so that 45 per cent of the company's assets were invested in the United States and Canada. By 1938 assets were worth £36.1 million, held mainly in gilts and equities (Moss 2000: 171, 376, 386–7).

Other suppliers of financial services were swift to exploit opportunities in international markets, such as the investment trusts that drew upon private wealth. Profits generated in the Dundee jute industry provided the finance for the pioneer investment trusts that became closely associated with the city. Many of the best investment opportunities open to Victorian financiers lay overseas, in the establishment of the infrastructure of the growing international economy, in telegraph and telephone links, in railways and in the exploitation of natural resources. In contrast, there were relatively fewer, and less attractive, opportunities in Scotland for accumulated capital that was seeking profitable investment outlets. The Dundee investment trusts put money into railways, ranching and mining in the United States. Edinburgh financial interests were soon involved, and by the beginning of the twentieth century there existed a substantial number of investment syndicates with overlapping memberships (Scott and Hughes 1980: 28–9).

The difficulties experienced by Scottish industry during the interwar period were not replicated in the financial sector. Indeed, all the major banks recorded very healthy profits (Saville 1996: 982–3). Mergers and takeovers increased the links between banks and insurance companies, while the continued expansion of life assurance further enhanced their role as corporate investors. Standard Life built up a substantial portfolio of investments, including housing developments in suburban Glasgow, at Kelvinside, and included railways, hospitals, prisons and docks throughout the United Kingdom. The company was also drawn into the complexities of the heavy industry network and, between the wars, contributed to the financial package required to save the Harland and Wolff shipyard

(Moss 2000: 198). By the close of the 1930s, financial companies had assumed a central role in the Scottish business community. They possessed a flexibility of product, a capacity to operate unconstrained by location and the supportive framework of increasing demand for finance from both companies and individuals that grew with economic progress and rising income. By the late 1930s the major characteristic of the structure of Scottish business comprised an intensively connected network of financial companies and a series of smaller industrial groupings. The fact that 370 directorships were confined to 132 individuals confirmed the closeness of the ties and the concentration of wealth (Scott and Hughes 1980: 94–7).

The success of Scottish business, both manufacturing and financial, relied heavily on international markets. The manufacturing sector comprised a set of interrelated activities whose outlet was the shipyard, supplying vessels for international trade. Similarly, investment networks required the scope of the international economy to exploit market opportunities wherever they occurred. These businesses were thus located in Scotland, but relied on international markets for their successful operation. This limited the multiplier effects of their activities within Scotland such that most of the benefit went to employers, financiers, investors and other captains of industry. For employees, however, the prevalence of low wages created a substantial inequality to their disadvantage in the distribution of the benefits. It was the international economy, and not demand generated in the domestic economy, that provided the platform for successful Scottish business. The home market provided a more restricted and relatively less prosperous platform, and the effects of this imbalance were painfully exposed by the international depression after 1918.

The greatest fortunes that were accumulated in Scotland in the nineteenth century were created in industry. William Baird, owner of the fifth in rank of all estates bequeathed before 1914 in the United Kingdom, made his money in manufacturing iron. But his death in 1864 marks his contribution as belonging to the earlier decades of the century. Four other Scottish manufacturers managed a place in the list of the largest forty estates, three of them occupying the last three places. They were Sir Charles Tennant, chemical manufacturer, Peter Coats and Sir James Coats of the Paisley textile dynasty and William Weir, whose fortune came from coal mining and iron manufacture. The list of the elite included two landed magnates with strong Scottish interests, the Duke of Sutherland and the Marquis of Bute. Apart from the landed aristocracy, the primacy of Clydeside in generating Victorian fortunes is clear. Indeed outside London, with its massive preponderance in British wealth creation, Clydeside's tally of fourteen millionaires surpassed all other provincial regions. But both Manchester and Merseyside produced more half-millionaires than Clydeside (Rubinstein 1987: 25–6, 31–2). Great individual fortunes were amassed and impressive personal achievements recorded. William Lithgow, from modest beginnings, left an estate worth over £1 million in 1908, and was credited with accumulating a fortune of £2.2 million in his career in shipbuilding. Edward Tennant, first Lord Glenconner, inherited great wealth from the family chemical business, including 5,000 acres in Perthshire, plantations in Trinidad, the family industrial empire and directorships in five gold mining companies. He devoted time and effort to looking after the family art collection, and to public service as lord lieutenant of Peebles (Slaven and Checkland 1986: 227–9, 289–90).

The financial services industry generated a number of fortunes. Robert Fleming started the Dundee-based Scottish American Investment Trust in 1873, and was subsequently involved in forming other trusts in London, Edinburgh and Glasgow. He left an estate worth £2.2 million and, in the fashion of Victorian philanthropists, gave money to Dundee City Council to finance slum clearances as well as to University College, Dundee. Sir Francis Norie-Miller became chief officer of the two-year-old General Accident and Employers' Liability Association in 1887. The company pioneered integrated insurance and became a major provider of motor vehicle insurance after the First World War. Norie-Miller also played a prominent part in civic affairs in Perth, the home of the company (Slaven and Checkland 1990: 401–2, 416–17).

INCOMES, WEALTH AND INEQUALITY

The substantial fortunes accumulated by a relative few stand in sharp contrast to the widespread indicators of poverty, such as outward migration, poor pay and unreliable employment opportunities that provided the working environment for the majority of Scots. While the Scottish economy created considerable wealth in the process of modern industrialisation, the distribution of its benefits among its citizens was very unequally divided. This became the most important influence shaping both the economics and politics of twentieth-century Scotland. The inequality of the distribution of income and wealth both hampered economic progress and fostered discontent.

The first plausible estimate of a national income for Scotland covered the period 1924–49, and suggested that Scottish per capita income ranged between 87 and 96 per cent of the United Kingdom average during that period (Campbell 1955: 231). As might be expected, until the mid-1930s Scotland appeared to fare increasingly less well than the rest of the United Kingdom, recovering thereafter as war became imminent and rearmament stimulated the recovery of heavy industry. Rather more significant are Campbell's estimates for the composition of the Scottish national income in terms of wages, salaries and property income. The latter category, which included company profits, non-agricultural rents and investment incomes from abroad, comprised a substantially higher share of income in Scotland than it did in the United Kingdom as a whole. Conversely, wages and salaries contributed relatively less in Scotland. The importance of investment income from abroad is particularly noteworthy. One estimate reported that, by 1914, overseas investment was equivalent to £110 for every Scot compared to an average of £90 per head for the United Kingdom as a whole (Harvie 1994: 70). Lenman also observed the unusually large overseas investment undertaken by Scots in the late nineteenth century, and characterised it as an indicator of a mature economy (Lenman 1977: 192). But such heavy investment overseas, while representing excellent opportunities for subscribers, meant that capital was lost to possible investment in the domestic economy. Such a massive and sustained outflow of capital suggests that there was a lack of opportunities at home, a sign of weakness rather than strength. Furthermore, capital invested abroad on behalf of the most prosperous members of society would obviously exacerbate inequalities in income by confining benefits to share owners. Interpreting his estimates, Campbell attributed the relatively weaker contribution of wages and salaries in Scotland to a combination of low pay and an employment structure that emphasised activities that did not pay well, like textiles and engineering.

A complementary indicator of relative prosperity is provided by the liability to pay income tax, a duty restricted to a very small proportion of the most affluent members of society throughout the nineteenth century. These data suggested that the liability of Scottish incomes was highest in 1851/2 with a share that was estimated at 15.7 per cent of the national total. It subsequently fell to a share of 9–11 per cent at which it remained stable through the final four decades of the century. The proportion of Scottish incomes assessed as liable to pay income tax, at each of three different levels of income, fell progressively between 1860/1 and 1900/1, suggesting that Scotland's growth in income was falling behind the rest of the United Kingdom (Rubinstein 1987: 92–5, 112–13).

The scarcity of data relating to Scottish national income is matched by the limited information available about the distribution of income. However, one annual report published by the Inland Revenue does provide disaggregated data for taxable incomes and their aggregation into each of eighteen income categories, and with separate data for every county for the tax year 1949/50. As indicated in Figure 16.5, a much greater share of Scottish taxable income was concentrated in the lower-income categories, under £350 per annum. England and Wales, in contrast, had a much greater share of its income in the middle ranges between £350 and £999, while above £3,000 there was no difference between them. The concentration of Scottish incomes in the lower-income categories, together with equity at the highest level, indicates that Scotland exhibited a greater inequality in the distribution of income compared to England and Wales.

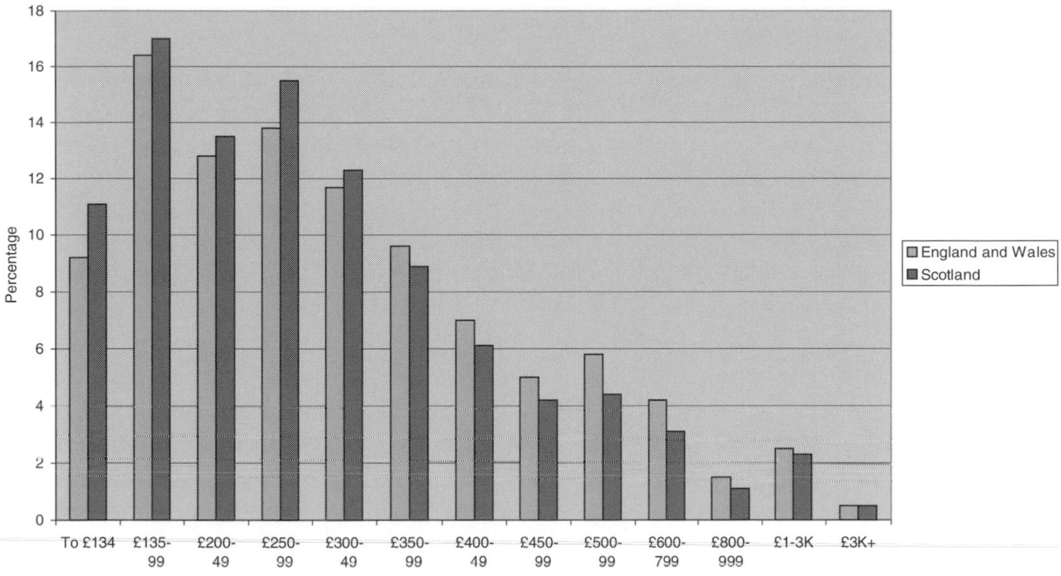

Figure 16.5
Distribution of taxable incomes, Scotland and England and Wales, 1949/50

Source: As Table 16.1.

The income tax data for 1949/50 provide a rare glimpse of the distribution of taxable incomes, and of the aggregate value of those incomes at county level. This makes it possible to set Scotland, and its component regions, within the wider context of the rest of Britain. Information relating to the total workforce was used to estimate that group of workers who were employed at incomes below the threshold of £135 at which liability to income tax commenced. The figure for Scotland was 226,300 or 11.1 per cent of the total workforce, compared to 9.2 per cent for England and Wales, thus further confirming the low-income bias of the Scottish economy. The data in Tables 16.1 and 16.2 relate to taxable income only. They were divided into three income groups to indicate the relative importance of the middle group, covering incomes between £500 and £999 as an indicator of an emergent middle class. By 1950, this range of incomes included skilled manual workers, clerks and managers, and women in the lower professions (Routh 1979: 120–1). Scotland had a relatively low share of such incomes, several percentage points below the industrial regions of England and higher only than the rural regions of East Anglia and the South-West. With regard to the distribution of all taxable income, as opposed to individual incomes, Scotland also contributed weakly to the middle category. However in the very highest group, the rural regions of Scotland had a relatively large percentage, reflecting the enduring importance of the prosperous laird. The same data may be expressed, as in Table 16.2, as income generated per thousand head of population. The index shows that Scotland again fell well below the average for Great Britain, especially in the middle-income group. These data clearly support the hypothesis that Scotland was relatively weak in generating middle-class

Table 16.1 The distribution of taxable income, 1949/50

	Number of incomes (%)			Taxable income (%)		
	£135–499	£500–999	£1,000+	£135–499	£500–999	£1,000+
South-east	81.9	13.9	4.2	55.7	20.4	23.9
East Anglia	89.6	7.2	3.2	66.1	12.5	21.4
South-West	87.9	8.9	3.2	65.5	15.4	19.1
West Midands	83.1	14.3	2.6	62.2	22.4	15.4
East Midlands	84.4	13.1	2.5	63.3	20.6	16.1
North-West	85.8	11.6	2.6	64.8	19.1	16.1
Yorkshire & Humberside	85.1	12.2	2.7	63.1	19.1	17.8
North	86.2	11.6	2.2	67.9	19.3	12.8
Wales	88.1	10.1	1.8	71.3	17.6	11.1
Scotland	87.3	9.6	3.1	65.1	16.1	18.8
Great Britain	84.3	12.4	3.3	61.1	19.8	19.1
Scotland: central belt	86.8	10.1	3.1	65.6	16.6	17.8
Scotland: rural regions	88.3	8.1	3.6	63.3	14.3	22.4

Source: HMSO 1952.

Table 16.2 Income generated per 1,000 population, 1949/50

					Index: Great Britain = 100			
	Total (£)	£135–499	£500–999	£1,000+	Total	£135–499	£500–999	£1,000+
South-east	171,578	95,569	35,002	41,007	116	106	119	145
East Anglia	132,264	87,294	16,665	28,305	89	96	57	100
South-West	133,650	87,541	20,582	25,527	90	97	70	90
West Midlands	155,432	96,678	34,817	23,937	105	107	119	85
East Midlands	154,334	97,693	31,793	24,848	104	108	108	88
North-West	151,802	98,368	28,994	24,440	102	109	99	86
Yorkshire and Humberside	153,284	96,568	29,431	27,285	103	107	100	96
North	136,391	92,609	26,323	17,459	92	102	90	62
Wales	121,478	86,614	21,380	13,484	82	96	73	48
Scotland	135,261	88,055	21,777	25,429	91	97	74	90
Great Britain	148,200	90,550	29,344	28,306	100	100	100	100
Scotland: central belt	140,497	92,166	23,323	25,008	95	102	80	88
Scotland: rural regions	120,790	76,460	17,273	27,057	82	84	59	96

Source: As Table 16.1.

incomes. The clustering of both individual incomes and aggregate income in the lower part of the distributions reflects both poverty and inequality that was especially marked in the rural regions.

These data may be compared to the first official estimate of the distribution of wealth in Scotland. Although it relates to 1973, it is consistent with the data for earlier years in showing greater inequality in Scotland than in England and Wales. The top 5 per cent of Scottish wealth holders enjoyed 30.6 per cent of the national wealth, while the top 10 per cent enjoyed 79.3 per cent. Equivalent figures for England and Wales were 22.8 and 66.1 per cent respectively. Only one third of adult Scots were identified as wealth holders as compared to half of the adults in England and Wales (HMSO 1975: 123). It seems improbable that inequality would have been substantially greater in 1973 than it had been fifty or even one hundred years earlier, and there is no strong reason to hypothesise a trend towards greater inequality in the Scottish wealth distribution during that period. It is likely therefore that this difference reflects a long-term phenomenon, possibly exacerbated by the stronger trend towards owner-occupation of property in England and Wales that constituted a major cause of wealth redistribution. These limited but varied data are consistent with the thesis that Scotland experienced a marked inequality in the distribution of income and wealth as an effect of an excess supply of labour. The phenomenon is further evidenced by the widespread existence of poverty and deprivation.

POVERTY, DEPRIVATION AND MARKET FAILURE

The worst effects of social deprivation were manifest in extensive poverty that was barely tackled at all before the First World War and on a limited scale thereafter. Deprivation was evident in a variety of important indicators, most obviously in infant mortality and housing conditions. Infant mortality has long been recognised as a very significant measure of social progress. While English infant mortality rates were falling by the later decades of the nineteenth century, in Scotland they were actually rising. Although Scottish rates also began to fall after the turn of the century, the decline was slower than in England and convergence was not achieved until well into the twentieth century (Lee 1991: 57–8). In the four Scottish cities infant mortality was particularly high and declined very slowly. Historical studies have found that various forms of deprivation are strongly associated with high infant mortality, most especially high-density occupation of housing and the proximity of heavy industrialisation and mining. These conditions provide a suitable environment for a diversity of contagious diseases, and excellent conditions for spreading infection. Cage's study of Glasgow confirmed the pattern of high mortality linked to overcrowding and poor living conditions that greatly increase the probability of death in infancy or childhood. The highest rates of infant mortality in Glasgow in 1911 were found in 'single ends', houses with one room within a building divided into a large number of separate occupancies (Cage 1994: 87).

Housing represents a major economic, social and political phenomenon in which the Scottish experience has been radically different from the rest of Britain. It also offers a graphic illustration of extreme and widespread deprivation. Scottish housing was notoriously poor in quality. Sanitary facilities were often limited, there was chronic overcrowding and the practice of subdividing buildings to create many tenancies diminished the quality of life. Improvement, throughout the Victorian years, started from a very low base and proceeded tentatively. By 1921, 68.7 per cent of Scots lived in accommodation comprising three rooms or less compared to 29.6 per cent of the population of England and Wales. Almost half the Scottish population lived in overcrowded conditions, a situation exacerbated by migration into the industrial areas of the central belt. In England, in 1921, only London and the mining counties of Durham and Northumberland housed over half of their respective populations in three rooms or less. But such overcrowding was virtually universal in Scotland. Only Dumfries and Galloway and the Highlands housed less than half of their populations in accommodation comprising three rooms or less while from Lanarkshire to Tayside, throughout central Scotland, levels ranging between 65 and 80 per cent of the population living in such conditions were the norm (Lee 1991: 64). This form of deprivation, graphically described and explained in the Royal Commission on Scottish Housing, forced Scotland to depend very heavily on the public sector for housing after the First World War. Contemporary estimates suggested that Scotland needed between 100,000 and 250,000 new dwellings at the end of the Great War. The Royal Commission described the dreadful housing conditions prevailing throughout the country and drew the radical conclusion that market forces would be unable to provide sufficient houses at affordable prices to rectify the situation. It thus provided an official endorsement for the provision of public sector housing (HMSO 1917: 292).

The reasons for the unusually poor state of housing lay in limited demand, itself the result of low incomes and, it has been suggested, by a low preference for spending on accommodation (Melling 1989: 60). It was also the product of Scottish legal controls on land tenure that substantially influenced the construction industry. When land was sold, the vendor relinquished the title to the land but retained the right to receive an annual income in perpetuity, known as feu duty. This system had an obvious influence on the buying and selling of land. Vendors were encouraged to wait until the price was high, as a means of ensuring a high feu duty that, once set, could not be changed. This created a market for land where supply was restricted and prices kept high. Furthermore, the entitlement to feu duty was passed through the sequence of owners in a chain of obligation. The need to ensure that there was sufficient cover for default by one of the parties provided a further incentive to keep feu duty values at a high level. It has been estimated that this system added 10–14 per cent to the gross rent of Victorian tenements (Rodger 1989a: 33). The high cost of land thus necessitated intensive use, and produced the high-rise tenements characteristic of urban Scotland. The high cost of property had the further effect of ensuring that rents were commensurately high, and consequently beyond the incomes of many potential tenants. This produced a hierarchy of accommodation in which families moved up in the world by occupying properties abandoned by those immediately above them in the economic order, sometimes after they had been further subdivided. The existence of 13,000 untenanted properties in Glasgow at the outbreak of the Great War was a clear indication that there existed a disjuncture in the property market between the rents affordable by potential tenants and the rents required by landlords (Damer 1980: 90).

Government legal controls, modified periodically through the Victorian years, announced the awareness of the authorities of the housing problem. But the specific response in each area was devolved to the local authority. Many were active in destroying and clearing slums. In Aberdeen the strongly interventionist medical officer of health, Matthew Hay, successfully pressed reluctant councillors to fulfil their duties. But, like many other authorities, Aberdeen City Council was very slow to embark on the construction and lease of property (Williams 2000: 299–306). Hay himself described the housing problem at the turn of the century, noting that properties identified for slum clearance had sometimes been allowed to remain in use because there were no alternatives. Private landlords and builders were unwilling to risk providing accommodation for the poorest, and often the most troublesome, tenants. The poverty of Scottish housing was the most obvious and widespread manifestation of deprivation. It became a particular focus for discontent, and for industrial and political action, that reflected the view held in some sections of Scottish society that the operation of the competitive market was loaded against them.

ECONOMIC PROBLEMS AND POLITICAL SOLUTIONS

The extremes of affluence and poverty, existing in close and visible proximity, provided an ideal context for the growth of industrial unrest and the politics of protest. The inequity of the distribution of the products of economic growth, as allocated by market forces, led to attempts to curb them. Some of the sharpest disputes focused, unsurprisingly, upon the housing market. One of the principal sources of discontent was the Scottish practice of annual leases, often requiring that a substantial part of the rent be paid in advance. This was far less satisfactory, for people with limited means and who were liable to experience periodic unemployment, than the English practice of contracting weekly rents. Public meetings to protest about rents and contracts were frequent from the 1880s onward. Support for change came from the Scottish Trades Union Congress and, in 1904, a deputation of Scottish MPs placed these grievances before the Lord Advocate. The Scottish Housing Council was formed in 1900, two years after the establishment of the Workmen's National Housing

Council, to press for lower rents. In Glasgow, the support of the Trades Council and numerous trades unions for the provision of housing by local authorities, was added to that of the Independent Labour Party (ILP). In 1914 the Glasgow Women's Housing Association joined the fray. The opposition was equally active and articulate. Bodies such as the Glasgow Citizens' Union and the local branch of the Charity Organisation Society defended the contractual rights of landlords, and worried about the provision of unjustified financial support for the 'loafer class' (Treble 1978b: 155–6).

Legislation, enacted in 1911, introduced monthly lets for cheaper housing, although this provided landlords with additional opportunities to increase rents by revising contracts. The outbreak of war immediately exacerbated the potential conflict as recruitment for the munitions industry grew rapidly, adding some 20,000 workers to the labour force of Glasgow and district (Damer 1980: 91; Lee 1999: 22–4). Housing in the shipbuilding districts became fully occupied as the shipyards also responded to increased wartime demand. The growth in demand for housing coincided with a decline in construction, discouraged by rising interest rates. Landlords took advantage of the housing shortage to increase rents (Melling 1980a: 147ff). By the summer of 1915 rent strikes had spread throughout Glasgow and, by the autumn, some 20,000 tenants were withholding payment. Attempted evictions, even when supported by the authorities, frequently resulted in public disorder and the evictions were thwarted. There were many demonstrations and marches as the balance of advantage in the labour market shifted in favour of the workers. Such disturbances threatened to disrupt the war effort so that the government responded swiftly with the Rents and Mortgage Interest (War Restrictions) Act in December 1915. This curbed rent increases, and introduced a highly significant intervention to restrain the free operation of the housing market. But it did not mark the end of rent strikes. In 1920 the government allowed a 15 per cent increase in rents. The Scottish Housing Association, in conjunction with the ILP, organised a rent strike that by 1922 included 22,000 tenants in the Glasgow area. Thereafter, rent control became an important political tool as the public housing programme took several years to make serious progress in alleviating overcrowding and replacing slum dwellings.

The rent strikes and subsequent legislation represented the first serious successes of the campaign, waged in various theatres, against the failure of market forces with regard to housing provision. Perhaps only a serious threat to the war effort could have induced such change. Rent restrictions remained in force after the Great War, many until the 1930s. The political pressure to improve housing was further increased by the promise of 'homes fit for heroes' for members of the armed forces returning from the conflict. But rent control diminished the capacity of the private market to provide cheap housing for the lowest echelons of society. The combination of restricted rents, high interest rates, increased building costs and rising local authority rates acted as a substantial deterrent to the private landlord (Melling 1980b: 15).

The political and social pressure for public sector housing became overwhelming after the Great War. The only mechanism that could seriously realise the aim of producing such a stock of housing was subsidy from central government, and this appeared soon after the end of hostilities. The housing programme of the interwar years represented a major intrusion by the state into the operation of the free market, and a substantive and highly effective policy for the redistribution of income. The scale of public sector housing was far greater in Scotland than in any other part of Great Britain. In the interwar period, the public sector in Scotland was responsible for 67 per cent of the new houses built, as compared to 25 per cent of equivalent construction in England and Wales. Even so, a large deficit in decent housing still remained in Scotland after 1945, and the greatest expansion in public sector housing construction came in the three subsequent decades. The proportion of Scots living in public sector houses became one of the most obvious differences between themselves and their southern neighbours in the twentieth century. The provision of public sector housing was not simply a vehicle for removing slums and providing habitable accommodation. It brought together a number of agencies and interests that combined to produce an economic, social and political structure in Scotland that was, and remains, distinctly different from that found elsewhere in Great Britain. First, the programme of public sector housing always relied on central government subsidy. By relying on this form of provision to a greater extent than the rest of the country, the Scots benefited relatively more than others from the subsidy. By the early 1920s, the system that was to endure for the next fifty years had been established. Local authorities built the houses and claimed a subsidy on each dwelling from HM Treasury. The size of the subsidy, special allowances for slum clearance, incentives to reduce overcrowding and the size of dwellings, all varied from time to time (Lee 1995: 198–9). Subsidies contributed a significant proportion of the total cost. One estimate, made in the early 1950s, suggested that 42.3 per cent of the construction cost of a four-apartment house, built for Glasgow City Corporation, was being borne by the subsidy. The local rates contributed 14.3 per cent, leaving a balance of 43.4 per cent to be paid in rent. However, the second peculiar feature of the Scottish housing system was its evolution as a political tool. From the late nineteenth century trades councils, trades unions, the Labour party and various radical groups campaigned for cheap rents and public sector housing. The provision of new housing increased the political success of sponsoring and supporting agencies, and improved their political representation. In due course, it also delivered control of local government in the major cities. Thus, in the 1950s, rents in Glasgow covered only 18 per of the cost of housing, leaving a deficit of some 25 per cent of the total cost unpaid. The deficit was often covered by an overdraft. Not surprisingly, Glasgow City Corporation had a deficit on its housing account in excess of £1 million in the 1950s (Cramond 1966: 39).

Overriding the market mechanism was not confined to local government. Since the establishment of a secretary of state for Scotland in 1885, political pressure had secured the establishment of a Scottish Office with responsibility for several aspects of Scottish affairs by 1914. The Scottish Office was not located in Edinburgh until 1935 but, by then, it had become a powerful and influential department of government. It had begun to assemble the skills and networks that were so effective after 1945, including control over the Scottish Special Housing Association, an agency for public sector construction established in 1937. By the 1950s, the Scottish Office had established its competence, both in negotiating an extremely generous share of resources for Scotland from HM Treasury, and in running the Scottish economy with steadily increasing intervention.

The disparity in prosperity within Scottish society, the inherent conflict of interests and the prevalence of destitution and poverty that contributed to the generation of civil unrest and support for radical political action was not confined to 'Red Clydeside'. In the crofting counties, conflict was long established and, as in the industrial heartlands, it stemmed from dissatisfaction with the outcome of market forces. The western Highlands covered a very large area, although much of the land was difficult to cultivate. Ownership was highly concentrated, and a small number of proprietors enjoyed extremely large holdings. The greatest of these, the Duke of Sutherland, owned over 1.3 million acres by the 1870s, while Sir James Matheson owned the Isle of Lewis, and Alexander Matheson owned over 220,000 acres in Kintail and Lochalsh. The whole of the Outer Isles from the Butt of Lewis to Barra Head covered only five estates, while Tiree, Iona and the Ross of Mull belonged to the estate of the Duke of Argyll (Hunter 1976: 120). Ironically, the main source of conflict was the result of land shortages, at least on the part of the crofters.

Landowners devised the economy based on the cultivation of the croft. They needed to attract a labour force to the western Highlands to make kelp for soap and glass manufacture, activities that flourished in the Napoleonic Wars. By combining the cultivation of a croft with kelp manufacture the tenant could just make a livelihood, so that the offer of supplementary employment was hard to refuse. The decline of kelp manufacture deprived the crofter of that additional employment until the herring fishing boom in the middle decades of the nineteenth century. But the landowner did find alternative uses for the land, in sheep rearing and, later, for recreational shooting as favoured by the Victorian gentry.

Considerable resources were invested in the creation of over 150 deer forests in the Highlands in the second half of the nineteenth century, employing a modest number of ancillary workers, but providing a blatant demonstration of the relative acreage devoted to sport and cultivation (Orr 1982: 147). It was the conversion of land usage to sheep grazing and deer forests that necessitated the clearances whereby many evicted Highlanders either chose, or were obliged, to start new lives beyond the Highlands.

The festering problem of land availability eventually came to a head in the 1880s in the land war that started as a rent strike, and subsequently turned to violence as arrests were successfully resisted. In 1882 rent strikes were confined to Skye, but by 1885 they threatened to encompass the entire crofting region. The combination of agricultural depression and rent strikes threatened to destroy the economy of the Highlands. The radical Highlands Land Law Reform Association exploited its growing power and support in pressing for legislative change. The Crofters Act of 1886 guaranteed security of tenure to crofters, and compensation for any improvements that had been made to a croft when a tenancy was relinquished. A land court was established to fix fair rents that were to be subjected to review every seven years. The extent to which this legislation favoured the crofter was reflected in its description by the *Scotsman* as a great infringement on the rights of property and by Fraser of Kilmuir as a portent of approaching communism (Hunter 1976: 161–2).

While the legislation benefited the crofters, it did not address the question of land shortage, nor did it make any provision for the landless labourers, cottars, who themselves aspired to become crofters and wanted land. In consequence, the conflict continued, and direct action extended from rent strikes to the mass slaughter of deer and eventually to land seizures. Military intervention was needed to restore law and order. The Congested Districts Board, established in 1897, was hailed as a serious attempt to deal with the shortage of land and consequent overcrowding. The Board was allowed to buy land to sell to smallholders, but was inhibited by financial constraints as it was not permitted to borrow to fund its activities. Essentially this structure, based on the Irish land settlement where farmers had been keen to become owners of their land, foundered upon the reluctance of the crofters to become landowners as opposed to tenants. Nor did the Board have the authority to assist the crofter to buy stock. For these reasons the success of similar strategies in Ireland was not reproduced in the Highlands (Hunter 1976: 185). The lack of a satisfactory resolution led to land seizures, and the occupation of properties with intent to cultivate the land, a threat sometimes realised. This type of disruption lasted until the end of the 1920s, despite the Land Settlement (Scotland) Act 1919 that greatly extended the financial powers of the Board of Agriculture, and gave it authority to offer loans to new tenants.

THE DEPENDENCY CULTURE

It is a characteristic of economically backward and poor societies that wealth and income are inequitably distributed, and that subsequent economic development is expected to modify such inequalities. In Scotland, economic progress generated income and wealth but was less successful in reducing inequality. The fundamental reason for the economic and political disjuncture lay in Scotland's incapacity to provide employment for the additional population that resulted from demographic change. Despite substantial net emigration, the labour market in Scotland remained in a state of excess supply. As a consequence employers, landowners and investors prospered while wage earners fared much less well. The resultant concentration of prosperity in few hands stifled the 'trickle-down' process of growth by which spending power is spread increasingly widely within the community. The juxtaposition of extreme wealth and extreme poverty created distrust of the market as a mechanism for allocating resources; it soured industrial relations, and gained support for non-economic and interventionist political strategies among those who felt disadvantaged.

The path followed by the Scottish economy through the second half of the twentieth century was distinctive and often at variance with that of its southern neighbour. The existence of the Scottish Office proved to be extremely advantageous, providing a facility for special pleading and, through its links with Whitehall, a conduit to political influence that neither English provincial regions nor Wales could rival. Only the unusual political circumstances in Ulster enabled that part of the United Kingdom to attract the attention of central government to similar effect. The semi-autonomous authority of the Scottish Office allowed it to follow effectively interventionist policies, as in sponsoring public sector housing construction. It was responsible for the establishment of the Highlands and Islands Development Board in 1965, designed to revive the depressed Highlands, some two decades after the North of Scotland Hydro-Electric Board had been established for the same purpose (Mackay and Buxton 1965; Payne 1988). Scotland also benefited from national regional policy, securing an embryonic, albeit short-lived, motor industry transferred from the industrial Midlands of England.

Not surprisingly, Scotland became strongly attached to the fruits of government intervention as public expenditure (consistently at higher levels than in England and Wales) confirmed and embedded structures for economic support. Heavily subsidised council house rents secured political support for Labour administrations, and allowed trade unions and workers to tolerate low wages. The dependency culture became firmly established in the central belt, especially as the effects of industrial decline became more painful. The Conservative administrations that held office between 1979 and 1997 maintained a strong belief in free market competition, combined with a strong commitment to reduce public expenditure. In Scotland their policies received a bitterly hostile reaction, as manifest in demonstrations against the poll tax and the widespread refusal to pay it. This discontent reflected growing disenchantment with Scotland's situation within the United Kingdom. Scottish nationalism emerged from the fringes of the political landscape to offer a serious threat and, for a large minority, an increasingly attractive alternative to the *status quo*.

As the twenty-first century began, the gulf between Scotland and the rest of the United Kingdom did not appear to have been closed by the establishment of a Scottish parliament in Edinburgh, furnished with some powers devolved from Westminster. The propensity of the new parliament to choose policies different from those adopted by central government, albeit one representing the same political party, reinforced the apparent divergence. Governmental support in Scotland for increases in public expenditure, to help students and to fund residential care for elderly citizens, reinforced the differences. The perspectives that determined those policy preferences emerged from a different experience of economic progress, and from fundamentally different reactions to it on the part of the Scots, compared to their cousins in many other parts of the United Kingdom.

17 Government and the economy, 1860–1939

ROGER MIDDLETON

Contents

INTRODUCTION

The period between the mid-nineteenth century and the eve of the Second World War is often represented as one of transition for the British state: from small, *laissez-faire* government to embryonic modern government, that of the managed-mixed economy and welfare state which has endured – albeit much changed – to the present day. This transition necessarily entailed a transformation in terms of government's scale, scope and impact upon the economy, which, in turn, was underpinned by a transformation in the accepted role of government in the economy. The proper role of government is a perennial of political and economic discourse, but from the classical economists onwards it has been understood in terms of the cardinal choice that all societies must make: that concerning 'the degree to which markets or governments – each with their respective flaws – should determine the allocation, use and distribution of resources in the economy' (Wolf 1993: 7). For the classical economists, as for mainstream economists today, this cardinal choice between government or market starts from the presumption that markets are instrumentally superior and then proceeds by way of politics and history to investigate how and why in practice there occurred shifting conceptions of markets' and governments' capabilities which justified disturbing the *status quo* and which resulted in this long-term trend towards big government.

In a telling phrase, Okun (1975: 119) noted that 'the market needs a place, and the market needs to be kept in its place'. The primary purpose of this chapter is to establish how and why those boundaries were set, at what level of government and with what consequences for efficiency and equity, the twin benchmarks by which government's economic role is routinely assessed. This topic is, of course, potentially vast: it has attracted a huge and varied literature (summarised in Middleton 1996: ch. 2), whilst in addition almost all public policies impact upon efficiency and equity. However, the central issues for an economic history are the scale, scope and impact of government on the economy and explanations of the historical dynamic of changes therein. These can be distilled into three interrelated types of questions: first, matters empirical, namely what the size of government was, what it did and how it grew; secondly, matters of causality, why and when size and scope changed, where attention can be given to periodisation and to comparison with other advanced economies; and thirdly, matters of policy impact, which combine traditional concerns about efficiency and equity with more recent literatures relating institutional quality to national economic performance.

We preface our exploration of these questions with two important caveats. First, following Einstein's maxim that 'What counts cannot necessarily be counted; what can be counted does not necessarily count', some aspects of what government did and of its impact are inevitably more visible and measurable than others. Thus, for example, we can measure the tax take but can be far less certain about the compliance costs of government regulation, although in a welfare sense and in the historical context of relatively low effective tax rates the latter may have been more important than the former. None the less, we do in the following analysis of government growth initially emphasise fiscal aspects, for the budget can be taken as representing the clearest expression of society's preferences and the results of interest groups' competition for resources. Secondly, in an epoch in which 'progressive' opinion coalesced around bigger government as the preferred modernising instrument for effecting economic and social change, we must be attentive to matters of omission (what government did not do) as well as commission (what government did do). Much of the historical debate concerns the economic implications of too little government regulation and of low spending/taxing, and we have thus an added complication in assessing the significance of what was actually done.

UNDERSTANDING THE GROWTH OF GOVERNMENT

Theories of government growth

The growth of government and the implications of that growth for the real economy can be analysed using a number of different approaches which reflect the diverse techniques and theories that historians and varieties of social scientists adopt towards understanding state dynamics. History, sociology, political science and economics thus all have something to offer. What unites recent work in all of these disciplines, and efforts to integrate these diverse academic approaches to government growth, is the finding that the modern British state has eighteenth-century rather than more recent origins (Harling 2001). Beyond this we distinguish between the highly aggregated analyses of most sociologists and political scientists, who focus upon the influence of long-run changes within the structure of society (such as ideology, institutional structures and constitutional rules) on government growth; the often highly abstract analyses of economists when they apply their toolkit of the theory of market failure; and the more microeconomic approaches (often known as the economics of politics) adopted by public choice theorists who model those factors that influence the demand for, and supply of, public policies.

These approaches generally share the common position that 'Public expenditures are the recorded outcomes of the interaction of the demand of voters, as consumers-citizens, for publicly provided goods and services and the supply response of politicians and bureaucrats' (Jackson 1993: 122), and with various degrees of emphasis ground government growth in terms of changing demand and supply conditions in which the process of choice and policy process, and thus politics, matters intensely. It is the particular demand and supply characteristics of non-marketed production of goods and services which create the opportunities for different interpretations of the motives for government growth and of their distributional impacts. Thus, when on the demand side consumers do not pay in direct proportion to their consumption, and on the supply side the quality and quantity of services provided may not match exactly the demand preferences of consumers, we have the potential for under/overspending, allocative inefficiencies and debate. Does, for example, greater government activity represent legitimate responses to market failures by benign governments and bureaucracies or potential excess supply and inequality by a Leviathan, that is government and bureaucracy by and for vested interests? A detailed study of each of these distinct approaches is not possible here, and what follows is a very abbreviated account of the main writings on Britain (for a fuller account and bibliography, see Middleton 1996: 112–32) which highlights and to some extent contrasts the economists' rationale for government with recent historical research on the British case.

A long-run perspective

Our starting point is with the mid-Victorian consensus of small government and *laissez-faire* in economic and social policy, which had prevailed during the 'first' industrial revolution. This was to be challenged by two long-run developments and two contingent set of events, all acting to augment a pre-existing challenge to this *status quo*: the realisation, as Williamson (1990: 273) later put it, that Britain had by the 1830s 'accumulated an enormous deficit in [its] social overhead [capital] stocks by pursuing seventy years of industrialisation on the cheap. It cost her dearly, as the social reformers were about to point out.' Such was the challenge posed by rapid urbanisation, let alone the investment arrears already accumulated, that the *status quo ante* was not an option for a small and, increasingly crowded island experiencing largely unregulated industrialisation and development (see chapter 11 above).

These critical long-run developments were, first, the advent of democracy, in particular the rise of organised labour and the evolutionary path to a full democratic franchise, which changed fundamentally the nature of political competition; and, second, developing anxieties about British economic hegemony as other countries industrialised. The latter interacted with these concurrent political changes and promoted an agenda in which the state (that is central and local government and their agents) was once more capable of being viewed as a potential instrument for economic and social modernisation. The contingent events were, first, and principally, the shocks of war, namely one expensive imperial conflict (the Boer War, 1899–1902), one ruinously expensive world war (1914–18) and preparations for another even more expensive total war (1939–45); and, secondly, and not unconnected, the experience of mass unemployment for a generation after the First World War. Both these long-run and contingent sets of factors were, moreover, operating in an environment of rapid technological progress and economic-structural change which *inter alia*, through their effects on transport and communication costs and the ever more specialised division of labour, reduced transactions costs and thus impacted upon the demand/supply schedules for private and public goods.

These developments bring us to the heart of British political economy. Their net effect during these years was to highlight fundamental aspects of the operation of the market economy and of the polity in responding to deficiencies (real, imagined or constructed) in that market economy. The cardinal choice of government *versus* the market, or sometimes government *and* the market, was thereby highlighted as never before, with intense debate thereafter about the legitimacy of the classical economists' case for the instrumental superiority of the market with respect to its dynamism, stability and equity in *all* circumstances. The resulting changes in how that choice was perceived and resolved during this period can be understood in terms of how both market and government as institutions evolved in response to:

1. changes in the world, especially the shocks of war and new technologies;
2. changes in the understanding of that world, in particular assessments of the circumstances in which markets/governments were instrumentally superior; and
3. changes in normative values about that world (notably shifting preferences with respect to dynamism, stability and equity), these in turn being *inter alia* a function of changes in the world and society's understanding of that world.

Table 17.1 gives a broad schema and evolutionary path for the scale and scope of the economic functions of the British state. These evolved from having in *c.* 1860 a largely classical agenda (contained within panel A, but excluding macroeconomic management) to having important intermediate functions (panel B) with respect to addressing market failures and some activist functions (panel C) for co-ordinating private activity, to the point that by the eve of the Second World War Britain had a modern managed economy in all but name. From the provision of minimal basic services at the beginning of the period – defining and enforcing property rights and the maintenance of defence, law and order and financial probity (Fry 1979: 117–28) – British governments thus came to assume a broader role in the allocation of resources, in the provision of public and merit goods, in guiding the market to reduce income and wealth inequalities and in economic management. All three of Musgrave's (1959) functions of the public economy – allocation, distribution and stabilisation – thus expanded, although to differing degrees and at varying times, although the stabilisation function remained underdeveloped in the period up to 1939.

Public sector growth

Demographic changes, which are discussed in chapter 2 above and which form the background to the demand side of public sector growth, provide a natural starting point for our assessment which begins here with total public expenditure (TPE). In money terms, TPE increased from approximately £87 million in 1860 to £1.96 billion in 1939, or at constant

Table 17.1 Functions of the state

		Addressing market failure		Improving equity
A Minimal functions		*Providing pure public goods:*		*Protecting the poor:*
		• Defence		• Anti-poverty programmes
		• Law and order		• Disaster relief
		• Property rights		
		• Public health		
		• Macroeconomic management		
B Intermediate functions	*Addressing externalities:*	*Regulating monopoly:*	*Overcoming imperfect information:*	*Providing social insurance:*
	• Basic education	• Utility regulation	• Insurance (health, life, pensions)	• Redistributive pensions
	• Environmental protection	• Anti-trust policy	• Financial regulation	• Family allowances
			• Consumer protection	• Unemployment insurance
C Activist functions		*Coordinating private activity:*		*Redistribution:*
		• Fostering markets		• Asset redistribution
		• Cluster initiatives		

Source: World Bank 1997: Table 1.1.

Table 17.2 Summary indicators of public sector size, selected years, 1860–1939

	1860	1890	1900	1913	1920	1929	1937	1939
A *Public sector employment as % of total employment*[a]								
Armed forces	1.7	1.7	2.5	1.8	2.4	1.7		1.7
Civil central government	0.4	0.7	1.0	1.5	2.6	2.1		2.6
Local government	0.3	1.2	2.3	3.6	5.0	5.9		5.6
Total	2.4	3.6	5.8	6.9	10.0	9.7		9.9
B *Public expenditure as % of GDP*[b]								
1 *By economic category:*								
Fixed capital formation	0.5	0.7	1.8	1.2	1.7	2.6	3.3	2.9
Current expenditure on goods/services	6.2	5.8	9.3	8.1	8.2	9.2	11.7	19.8
Transfer payments	4.5	1.9	2.2	2.7	10.7	12.7	11.0	10.5
Total (TPE)	11.2	8.4	13.3	11.9	20.5	24.5	26.0	33.2
2 *By functional classification:*								
Public administration and other	n.a.	n.a.	0.7	0.8	0.8	1.0	1.0	n.a.
Debt interest	3.2	1.6	1.6	1.7	5.7	7.7	5.4	5.0
Law and order	n.a.	0.6	0.4	0.6	0.2	0.6	0.5	n.a.
Defence	3.3	2.4	6.0	3.1	6.1	2.6	4.9	15.0
Social services	n.a.	1.9	2.3	3.7	4.9	9.2	10.5	n.a.
Economic services	n.a.	1.0	1.6	1.4	2.4	2.7	2.7	n.a.
Environmental services	n.a.	0.3	0.5	0.6	0.3	0.7	0.9	n.a.
Total (TPE)	11.2	8.4	13.3	11.9	20.5	24.5	26.0	33.2
C *Public sector receipts as % of GDP*[b]								
Taxes on income	2.7	1.1	1.0	1.8	10.2	6.2	6.2	7.4
Taxes on capital	n.a.	0.5	1.0	1.1	0.8	1.7	1.8	1.3
Taxes on expenditure	5.4	5.8	6.6	7.0	8.3	10.6	11.6	11.5
Other	2.9	1.1	1.1	2.5	1.6	5.3	4.9	4.7
Total[c]	11.0	8.5	9.7	12.4	20.9	23.8	24.5	24.9
D *Income tax, year ending 5 April*								
Standard rate (%)	2.08	2.50	3.33	5.80	30.00	20.00	23.75	27.50
Highest marginal rate (%)	2.08	2.50	3.33	8.33	52.50	50.00	61.25	75.00
No. chargeable (m)[d]	n.a.	n.a.	n.a.	1.13	3.81	2.20	3.60	4.00
E *Ratio of outstanding national debt to GDP*, year ending 5 April								
	0.98	0.43	0.31	0.26	1.26	1.59	1.56	1.41

[a] Nearest dates: 1851 for 1860; 1891 for 1890; 1911 for 1913; 1921 for 1920; 1931 for 1929; 1938 for 1939.
[b] Pre-1900 estimates for main components are approximate, and more so for 1860 than for 1890 when Peacock and Wiseman's (1967) series becomes available.
[c] Pre-1900 estimated to track the expenditure ratio subject to known movements in outstanding national debt and the balance of the central government budget as then defined; see Buxton 1888: II, 335–6; and Mallet 1913: 356–9.
[d] After abatements and allowances.

Sources: A: Abramovitz and Eliasberg 1957: Table 1; and Parry 1985: Table 2.1; B: 1860–90: Veverka 1963: Table 1; Peacock and Wiseman 1967: Table A-15; Feinstein 1972: Tables: 2, 39; and Mitchell 1988: 832–3; 1900–39: Middleton 1996: Table 3.2; C: Middleton 1996: App. I and author's rough approximations for 1860 and 1890 (see note c); D: Mitchell 1988: 645 and Board of Inland Revenue; and E: Mitchell 1988: 645.

1900 prices from approximately £72 million to £934 million.[1] Total UK population increased from 28.8 million to 47.8 million between 1860 and 1939, equivalent to an annual average growth rate of 0.6 per cent as against a growth rate for real gross domestic product (GDP) of 1.6 per cent.[2] Thus GDP outpaced population growth, and, given the trend rise in the expenditure ratio (the ratio of TPE to GDP), TPE outpaced GDP growth. TPE per capita at constant prices increased from approximately £2.50 in 1860 to £19.55 in 1939 (£15.10 in 1937). Part of the reason for this lies in the changing age structure of the population (chapter 2 above), in particular the rise in the proportion of the population aged 65 and over from 4.7 to 8.9 per cent. Concomitant developments included intensive urbanisation, with accompanying challenges to the infrastructure, public health and the social order; an increase in life expectancy at birth; an increase in the average years of formal educational experience of the population, together with a shifting balance towards secondary schooling; and a reduction in fertility and thus average family size. All of these developments have implications for the demands for public policy and, through the electoral process, what politicians felt impelled to supply.

Table 17.2 widens our coverage of the public sector to provide the standard summary measures of governmental activity, with the dates selected on grounds of data availability and to illustrate our chosen periodisation. These phases are described initially in terms of the expenditure ratio which rose from approximately 11.2 per cent of GDP in 1860 to 33.2 per cent in 1939, although the long-term trend might better be calculated over the non-war business cycle peaks 1860–1937, at which terminal date the expenditure ratio stood at 26 per cent of GDP. Accordingly, over our period the expenditure ratio approximately doubled, having developed as follows through five phases.

1. 1860–90: although the expenditure ratio fell by approximately 3 percentage points (from 11.2 to 8.4 per cent of GDP), once adjustments have been made for above average defence expenditures in 1860–1, this is better represented as a phase of approximate stability.
2. 1890–1913: a phase of gentle growth (from 8.4 to 11.9 per cent of GDP) and with important compositional changes.
3. 1913–20: the First World War and its immediate aftermath (from 11.9 to 20.5 per cent of GDP). The expenditure ratio peaked in 1918 at 43.6 per cent, before beginning to fall back but not to its pre-war level,

[1] Since the figures for 1939 were much affected by intense rearmament, for trend purposes the nearest business cycle peak provides a better terminal date, with money and constant price figures for 1937 of £1.3 billion and £713 million respectively.

[2] TPE from Veverka 1963: Table 1; Peacock and Wiseman 1967: Table A-5; and Middleton 1996: App. I, with 1939 from author's calculations; GDP and population from Mitchell 1988: 12–13, 838, 840; and age structure from Feinstein 1972: Table 56.

thereby giving rise to the Peacock and Wiseman (1967: xiii–xv, 27–8) hypothesis that war had a 'displacement effect' on the public economy.
4. 1920–37: a period of historically significant but irregular growth (from 20.5 to 26 per cent of GDP).
5. 1937–9 and beyond: a final phase of belated but intensive rearmament and then the Second World War (in which the expenditure ratio peaked at 60.4 per cent of GDP in 1944).

The trend of public expenditure after 1890 was very different from that of the preceding century in two important respects. First, over the century 1790–1890 the elasticity of TPE with respect to GNP was consistently below unity as the cumulative rate of growth of public expenditure was 1.9 per cent per annum, compared with 2.3 per cent per annum for GNP, and 0.9 per cent per annum for population (Veverka 1963: 116). Secondly, until 1910 or thereabouts it was local government which was increasing its share of TPE; thereafter, there was a concentration of expenditure by central government with local government increasingly assuming client status in financial matters. This concentration process is characterised by Peacock and Wiseman (1967: xxxiv–xxxv) as one in which arguments for the efficiency of central provision and responses to demands for national standards and equality of treatment overrode the political tradition of local government autonomy. British government growth thus coincided with a significant centralisation process set against a background, particularly but not exclusively before the First World War, of local initiative and vigour initiating new spending programmes in health, sanitation, anti-poverty and housing which were later adopted, adapted and then extended by the centre.

Public sector growth decomposed

After 1890, government's greater scale and scope was reflected in the changed composition of TPE, with trend increases in all three main economic categories (panel B.1, Table 17.2), although the space for fiscal adjustments was always conditioned by the resource demands of war, either directly or indirectly through the debt burden of past and current conflicts. Public sector capital formation was concentrated before 1914 at municipal level as the shortfalls in urban infrastructure identified by Williamson began to be addressed (Millward and Sheard 1995; Wilson 1997), with such spending mirrored in the employment trends (panel A). As early as 1910 some 5 per cent of the net stock of domestic reproducible fixed assets were in the public sector, with the capital employed in the local authority controlled network industries particularly significant and, indeed, greater than that employed in manufacturing (Foreman-Peck and Millward 1994). Interwar trends saw central government become active in state trading, notably in transport, communications and the media, with again spending mirrored in employment trends.

Whilst current expenditure on goods and services also rose on trend, and exhibited high variability according to the weight of its principal component (defence expenditures), this was dwarfed by the rise in transfer payments which became the largest category in peacetime. Until 1913 the largest element in transfers was debt interest, and whilst the burden of the debt increased substantially in weight because of the First World War, it was social expenditures which emerged to become the single most important expenditure category, rising from approximately 1.9 per cent of GDP in 1890, to 3.7 per cent in 1913, 4.9 per cent in 1920 and onward to 10.5 per cent in 1937, by which point it exceeded outlays on defence and debt interest combined. Social welfare spending thus drove government expenditure growth, and whilst some of the institutional foundations for this were lain by the reforming Liberal governments immediately before the First World War, it was not manifest in significant additional spending until after that war. Accordingly, over the period as a whole, the expansion of public expenditure was a reflection of government assuming new tasks, and particularly with respect to increasing equity (Table 17.1).

Growth in expenditure was made possible by, but also compelled, a transformation on the supply side in terms of increased taxation (see Daunton 2001, 2002). As can be seen from panel C, the receipts ratio tracked the expenditure ratio very closely and until the First World War there was no tendency towards deficit finance, merely temporary borrowing to cover imperial wars and public sector capital formation. Comparative studies suggest that, relative to other major industrial countries and particularly Germany, Britain's tax receipts were elastic with respect to GDP (Schremmer 1989), but over the longer term, and especially from the 1890s onwards, there was a widening of the tax base and higher rates on existing taxes which raised the effective rates of taxes on income, capital and expenditure.

Tax innovation included new taxes to tap prevailing trends in consumers' expenditure (especially on the motor car) and the introduction of national insurance (employers' and employees') contributions to part fund social welfare programmes; a universal sales tax did not come until 1940. Nevertheless, these developments were overshadowed, quantitatively and politically, by the transformation of the income tax which occurred, first with the introduction of progression in 1909, and second with the First World War which required that the immense scope offered by progression be harnessed to meet the financial exigencies. As a consequence, British income tax payers, numbering a million or so in 1913/14 and enduring a standard rate of less than 6 per cent, were only five years later trebled in numbers and suffering a standard rate of 30 per cent with marginal rates peaking in excess of 50 per cent.

Progression in income tax, which built upon major structural reforms to death duties in 1889, introduced the principle that tax should be related (to a greater or lesser degree) to the ability to pay, rather than be based on the extent to which the tax payer benefited from the activities of the state (Musgrave 1985). Although generating intense political debate at the time, this was less a dramatic change and more the beginnings of a process which would eventually have profound consequences as the most important supply-side prerequisite for big government. The twentieth-century expansion of the income tax thus vindicated Gladstone's original rationale for wanting to abolish it (a hope he had entertained and thought nearly realisable as late as 1874), namely that the tax contained enormous potential for revenue raising and thus, if it were to become more than a temporary expedient, it would be capable of financing a huge expansion in expenditure (Baysinger and Tollison 1980: 209–10).

But wartime rates were to be no temporary expedient. Indeed, since Peacock and Wiseman (1967: viii) introduced the concept of the displacement effect, it was normal to ascribe to war the responsibility for a permanent upward shift in society's tolerance of higher taxation, thereby increasing taxable capacity and lessening the constraint on government growth. Whilst the First and Second World Wars were associated with sharp upward shifts in the receipts and expenditure ratios, the displacement effect does not, however, explain the secular upward trend in periods of peace and prosperity. Moreover, it is not compatible with the international experience of big government in the twentieth century which is invariant to participation in those conflicts. Accordingly, attention has turned back to a much older demand-side explanation of government growth, that of Wagner's law, whereby an upward trend to the expenditure ratio derived from responses to market failures:

1. the expansion of the administrative and protective functions of the state which stemmed from both the substitution of public for private regulatory activity and additional demands generated by industrialisation, which had increased the complexity of legal and economic arrangements;
2. the growth of cultural and welfare expenditures, especially on education and the redistribution of income; and
3. changes in technology and the scale of investment which created conditions of monopoly requiring government regulation or production.

Wagner's law, like the displacement effect, has proved to have weak empirical foundations (Middleton 1996: 114–18). None the less, both concepts are useful organising frameworks for Britain, experiencing as it did in short succession the twin shocks of war and depression.

Table 17.3 General government expenditure and revenue as a percentage of GDP in OECD countries, selected years, c. 1870–1937

	Expenditure				Revenue			
	c. 1870[a]	1913	1920	1937	c. 1870[a]	1913	1920	1937
Australia	18.3	16.5	19.3	14.8	17.8	16.7	19.4	14.9
Austria	10.5	17.0	14.7	20.6[b]	–	–	9.0[b]	15.7[b]
Belgium[b]	–	13.8	22.1	21.8	11.6	–	17.0	–
Canada	–	–	16.7	25.0	4.1[b]	5.5[b]	16.6[b]	22.6[b]
France	12.6	17.0	27.6	29.0	15.3	13.7	17.9	20.5
Germany	10.0	14.8	25.0	34.1	1.4[b]	3.2[b]	8.6[b]	15.9[b]
Ireland	–	–	18.8	25.5	9.6	11.8	23.2	26.3
Italy	13.7	17.1	30.1	31.1	12.5	14.7	24.2	31.1
Japan	8.8	8.3	14.8	25.4	9.5	–	–	–
Netherlands[b]	9.1	9.0	13.5	19.0	–	6.4	11.8	11.9
New Zealand	–	–	24.6[b]	25.3[b]	–	–	24.7	27.0
Norway	5.9	9.3	16.0	11.8	4.3	7.7	11.5	10.9
Spain[b]	–	11.0	8.3	13.2	9.4	10.3	5.8	11.9
Sweden	5.7[b]	10.4	10.9	16.5	9.5[b]	6.7[b]	7.2[b]	8.5[b]
Switzerland	16.5	14.0	17.0	24.1	–	2.5[b]	3.8[b]	6.0[b]
UK	9.4	12.7	26.2	30.0	8.7	11.2	20.1	22.6
US	7.3	7.5	12.1	19.7	7.4	7.0	12.4	19.7
Unweighted average[c]	10.8	13.1	19.6	23.8	10.6	11.8	19.2	21.6

[a] Or closest year available for all columns.
[b] Central government only.
[c] For those countries and dates for which general government data are available.

Source: Derived from Tanzi and Schuknecht 2000: Tables I.1, III.1.

Public sector growth compared

It remains to compare getting and spending in Britain with the experience of comparable states. Table 17.3 gives such evidence as we have for the expenditure and receipts ratios for the Organisation for Economic Co-operation and Development (OECD) countries and shows that there was little at aggregate level that was distinctive about Britain's public sector before the First World War. Thereafter, the expenditure ratio rose in all of these states. However, this and other evidence (assessed in Middleton 1992: App. Table 2) suggests that the proportionate rise was greatest for Britain between 1913 and 1929; other G-7 economies experienced their critical phase in public sector growth in the 1930s.[3] The most likely explanation is the differential experiences of unemployment as between Britain and the other advanced industrial economies, with the 1920s

[3] The G-7 group of leading economies comprises Canada, France, Germany, Italy, Japan, the UK and the USA.

being relatively worse than the 1930s in the case of the former, and the British downturn beginning in 1929 being far less severe than was generally the case elsewhere (see chapter 12 above). In terms of public sector size the interwar period can be characterised as exhibiting a process of catch-up and convergence with a lower coefficient of variation for the OECD expenditure ratios in 1938 than in 1929 or 1913.

It was noted earlier that TPE growth since 1900 was dominated by the expansion of transfer payments, principally welfare expenditures. The question naturally arises whether there was anything distinctive about the pattern and composition of British expenditure growth relative to comparators. It is extremely difficult to provide a satisfactory answer to this as there is only very fragmentary cross-country evidence about the functional classification of public expenditure. Cross-country data for social transfers have, however, been constructed by Lindert (1994). These reveal that by 1910 Britain had the second highest rate of social expenditure, and was well ahead of all its immediate economic competitors. There is also evidence that, whilst in terms of the implementation of social welfare programmes it was the newly unified German state that was in the vanguard in Europe, Britain was distinctive in having a phase of very rapid expansion rather than a period of more steady growth and, with the exception of Sweden, had developed social programmes with the widest coverage in Europe by the eve of the First World War (Flora and Alber 1981: Figure 2.4). The sums involved, however, were minute, and even after the First World War they remained small in relation to the growth that would be exhibited in all advanced economies after the Second World War. None the less, by the late 1930s Britain had one of the most developed welfare sectors of these countries, though as is well known there had been no underlying grand design, 'policy [having] evolved, like the British empire, in a fit of absence of mind' (Gilbert 1970: 308). It was thus during the interwar period that the pattern was set of a state committed, in so far as the burden of defence permitted, to the easing of social tensions created by unemployment and structural adjustment. This now involved, in budgetary terms, very substantial welfare programmes: some 10.5 per cent of GDP by 1937 (panel B.2, Table 17.2). Thus a new balance between social equity and economic efficiency had emerged by the outbreak of the Second World War.

On the revenue side, there again appears little that was distinctive at aggregate level. Although the excessive nature of British taxation was a staple of budgetary debate, with the lower tax burdens of other major countries often claimed by participants in those debates, in practice such international evidence as we have shows that the tax ratio in Britain was broadly comparable to comparators and competitors, albeit with a tax mix more biased towards taxes on income and social security contributions (Middleton 1992). The domestic politics of this tax mix are significant. Thus Cronin (1991: 97) argues that by the late 1920s 'The social compromise embedded in the tax system . . . was delicate – a careful mix of progressive and regressive elements whose distributional consequences were finely adjusted to the balance of power.' The immediate pre-war characteristic of the tax system, with its pronounced progression at the upper level of incomes and steep regressive impact at the opposite end of the income distribution, was sustained throughout the interwar period, and little affected by the two short periods (1924 and 1929–31) when Labour was in office. Whilst conservative opinion undoubtedly sought more of a balance between direct and indirect taxation, the budgetary position provided but limited room for manoeuvre. The bias of the tax mix towards direct sources, which are more visible than taxes on expenditure, was seen by the Treasury as an important means of educating the public about the mounting cost of public (particularly social) expenditures. Cronin (1991: 77, 93) argues that:

> The specific contours of the tax system closely reflected the peculiar features of British society. It was overall a monument to fiscal responsibility, itself largely a product of the combined influence of the Treasury, City and the Bank of England. It was a system whose lineaments were highly visible and whose incidence spread the burden of taxation fairly widely among classes. This guaranteed an intense public scrutiny of tax policy and an equally sustained mobilisation of interests, particularly middle- and upper-class interests, around tax policy-making . . . They were ordinarily arrayed against increases and in favour of decreases in tax and were prolific in generating proposals to shift the burden onto some other interest. The effect was to make it hard to move tax policy in any direction other than towards a general reduction [which] . . . was extremely difficult to achieve in the face of a massive debt, a deepening depression and a mounting military threat. The tax system therefore proved very resilient throughout the late 1920s and 1930s.

FROM *LAISSEZ-FAIRE* TO MANAGED ECONOMY

The economic analysis of the role of government

Having established changes in the getting and spending of government along the path to its modern form of a large public sector and interventionist economic role, we now turn to consider how that growth can be explained. Economists typically ground the case for government intervention in a market economy in terms of correcting market failures, with government growth the cumulative result of responses to such market failures. Concomitantly, those opposing such interventions invoke the theory of government failure and argue that in practice the limitations of government typically exceed the market failures that are supposedly to be remedied. Separating these two camps is a theoretical gulf, between very different economic approaches to the economic analysis of market and government, and a chasm, more contingent, historical and empirical in character, about the strengths and limitations of these two institutions in practice, and in particular whether government must always be Leviathan or whether it can ever act for the public good.[4]

The cardinal choice of government or market, however, is not simply a contest between theoretical and non-theoretical assessments of the properties of these competing allocative mechanisms. In practice, theoretical economic assessments often proceed by way of comparison between ideal-type perfect markets (governments) and an alternative of stereotypical imperfect governments (markets), when they ought to proceed from the standpoint of a choice between 'imperfect markets and imperfect governments, as well as imperfect combinations between them' (Wolf 1993: 1). Similarly, the parallel, more empirical and historical dimension of that choice is often imperfectly pursued because of confusion between means (instrumental arguments about market efficiency) and ends (liberty and welfare). This in turn occurs because the economic and political cases for markets/governments are often conflated and misunderstood. This stems from the corrupting influence of ideology and the reality of democratic politics that personal and societal expectations about the capacity of markets and/or governments to deliver favourable results in practice narrow unrealistically the time-horizons in which these results are expected. As a consequence, in political discourse, the balance of arguments in favour of government and market through time has a cyclical as well as a trend character, as for example in the Hirschman (1982) thesis: that the relative popularity of individualist and collectivist ideas and solutions conforms to a cycle in which both solutions arouse expectations which, given the human condition, can never be satisfied. Thus as the disappointments with one are amassed, so are the attractions of the other, until in turn a new body of disappointments are generated and the cycle moves into its alternate phase.

Between 1860 and 1939 the cardinal choice was transformed by changing perceptions of market failure and government potential to remedy those failures together with a reconfiguration of the 'biggest' of all the socio-economic trade-offs (Okun 1975: 2), that between efficiency and equity. In some quarters such a trade-off is viewed as illusory (or largely illusory), its existence is seen as an artefact invoked by market liberals pursuing a distinctly political agenda, such that the question of how much (or indeed how little) efficiency can safely be traded for an improvement in equity (however defined) forms a core question of the political debates of this period. Figure 17.1 shows two possible conceptions of this relationship: the first is a stylised trade-off, a neoclassical position of a simple inverse relation between efficiency and equity; the second is a

[4] This section draws extensively upon Middleton 1996: ch. 2; see also Stiglitz 1998 for a good, concise and broadly optimistic view of a positive economic role for government; and Stiglitz *et al.* 1989 for a wide-ranging debate with much scepticism on that role.

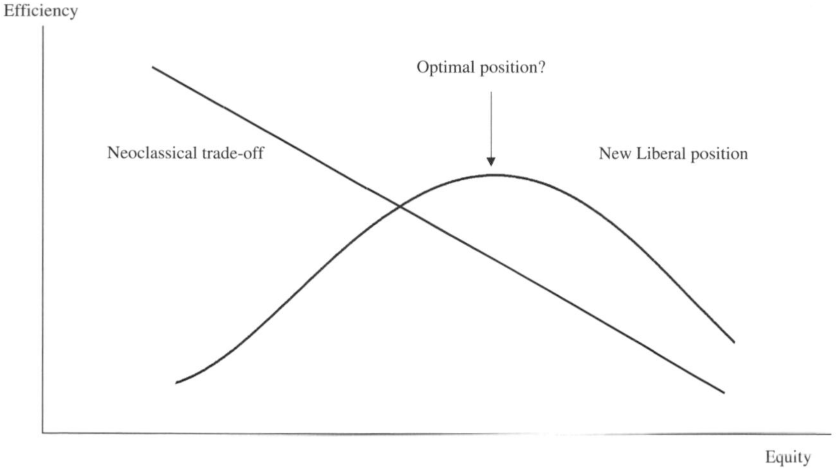

Figure 17.1
Efficiency–equity trade-off(s)

New Liberal position. It is based on the view that, because the burden of social market failures is not felt equally across the population, appropriately designed egalitarian policies may promote economic efficiency in two ways: directly by the impact of improvements in health, housing and education on the quality of the labour input in the growth process, and indirectly by enhancing political and economic stability and social cohesion. We term this latter position New Liberal to indicate its origins in New Liberalism, a term which

> describe[s] significant developments in liberal theory and practice in the last two decades of the nineteenth and first decade of the twentieth centuries which not only adapted the traditional concerns of liberalism to changing economic, social and political circumstances but also provided a dynamic framework in which those circumstances could be analysed and acted upon.
>
> (Pearson and Williams 1984: 144)

In practice, New Liberalism's espousal of more egalitarian spending, taxation and broader governmental policies differed little from the progressive, interventionist case put by the Labour party (established 1900) or, indeed, some interwar Conservatives. This trade-off between efficiency and equity, if indeed it is a trade-off in the range that was under discussion during this period, sets the parameters for contemplating adjustments to the scale and scope of government, with the positions adopted necessarily in part a function not so much of the instrumental claims for market superiority but of political conceptions of liberty, justice and individual rights and how they impact upon the construction of the equity issue (Checkland 1983; Meadowcroft 1995).

Market failure is traditionally analysed at two levels: technical market failure, that is problems of allocational inefficiency, generated by monopoly, externalities and asymmetric information, which are inherent to the system; and social market failure, where technically efficient markets may none the less 'produce results – that is, prices, income distributions, or conditions of competition – that are not accepted by a smaller or larger proportion of the population' (Lehner and Widmaier 1983: 241). Alternatively, and more pungently, as Sen (1985: 10) puts it: 'If the utility of the deprived cannot be raised without cutting into the utility of the rich, the situation can be Pareto optimal but truly awful.' Social market failure, which is grounded in equity considerations, is central to advanced politico-economic systems, and has been the principal motor of government growth in Britain as elsewhere. (It is noteworthy also that Adam Smith's case for the instrumental superiority of the market was tempered by reservations about its results for social justice: see O'Brien 1975: 31–2.)

The analysis of technical market failure was transformed during this period as economists developed what is now known as welfare economics at the beginning of the twentieth century (Middleton 1998: ch. 4), but on the whole changing conceptions of the acceptability of market failure were largely driven by developing concerns about social market failure. As we have seen this was reflected in expenditure trends. None the less, these would have come to little or nought had there not been a contemporaneous lessening of the mistrust of government as always and inevitably Leviathan. From research in the history of economic thought we now understand more clearly why the classical economists, from which this antipathy stemmed, assumed the pessimistic stance on government that they did (O'Brien 1975). Accordingly, they 'were not, as a group, extreme advocates of laissez-faire. Such extreme advocacy was mainly confined in Britain to popularisers' (Fry 1979: 36). For the economists, *laissez-faire* was a pragmatic philosophy providing benchmarks for government; it was not a dogma. None the less, flexibility in policy was accompanied by a deep mistrust of government for its tendency to authoritarianism and susceptibility to rent-seeking sectional interests. To overcome this tendency required improvements in governance which lessened these risks of Leviathan; these came from the mid-nineteenth century onwards with electoral reform, civil service reform and the development of more rigorous and accountable parliamentary scrutiny of the executive and its expenditure activities (Fry 1979: 114–15; Peden 2002).

It is helpful here to distinguish between governing as a process and government as an agent, one institution amongst a number embracing markets and hierarchies (Gamble 2000). From this perspective improvements in institutional quality were a precondition for government growth. They lessened elite anxieties about the potential welfare losses of greater governmental scale and scope at the very time when various reform-minded groups and individuals, proclaiming technical expertise and the 'sovereignty of the facts' of British social and economic malaise (Harris 1990a), were seeking to establish the modernist view which believed that greater efficiency and equity were jointly and simultaneously attainable. Moreover, a governance approach permits of a more nuanced account of the dynamic of these changes, one which progresses beyond a dichotomy of government or market to an appreciation that whilst the

> two principles sometimes clashed head-on . . . , more often and less obtrusively they advanced in tandem at the expense of other more traditional social arrangements, such as philanthropy, the family and the local community . . . Indeed, it would not be implausible to argue that the growth of the collectivist state was largely facilitated by the advent of the market – by the latter's erosion of the stable communities, charitable relationships and autonomous organisations upon which the Victorian constitution relied so heavily.
>
> (Harris 1990b: 113)

Such an approach, in turn, cuts through the old debate about nineteenth-century government as a transitional phase, from individualism to collectivism, by emphasising instead that it was both and neither. This fluidity is then used to explain why there never emerged a dominant political philosophy of public purpose and intervention in Britain, but instead an expediency founded upon a very elastic interpretation of legitimate public action when certain conditions were fulfilled with respect to technical and social market failure. We have thus a 'self-expanding' process of government growth 'which, acquiring its own momentum, carried state intervention forward despite ideological and political resistance [from] the middle years of the nineteenth century' (Thane 1990: 19).

These trends towards greater confidence in governmental capacity, born of improved governance, were then intensified by the First World War and the subsequent reconstruction phase (Burk 1982), mirroring a displacement effect of sorts in the public finances more generally. Although many have argued that the war had but a delayed effect on state capability and the impulse to intervene (notably Tawney 1943), this first total war is now seen as a more critical event in British state growth, transforming what had been a minority into a majority demand for a developmental state (Cronin 1991: ch. 4). Lowe (1995: 50) develops the point thus:

> In the short term, the rapid abandonment of many wartime innovations was indeed remarkable and, to this extent, the war can be portrayed as a lost opportunity for the modernisation of British government. However, in a longer-term perspective stretching from the 1870s to the 1930s and embracing the political culture underpinning both central and local government, the war can be seen as the occasion that forced choices to be made from a wide range of options long debated but largely evaded during late Victorian and Edwardian Britain. The structure of both central and local government was at last rationalised and made responsive to new political demands arising from the greatly increased electorate.

The traditional defences of the minimalist state under siege

Whilst the state's unique capacities – its powers to tax, to prohibit, to punish and to demand participation – would appear to imbue it with a potentially unlimited capability, in practice democratic politics imposed severe constraints – even during wartime – such that consent and credibility for its activities were critical. We now explore growing government capability, which made possible increased scale and scope, in terms of the traditional defences of the minimalist state and the pressures to which they were subjected over this period. This also provides a vehicle to broaden our analysis to include the institutions, instruments and objectives of economic policy where we detect both significant developments but also a remarkable continuity of belief and action.

We begin with what Checkland (1983: 174) aptly termed the 'three pillars of the anti-collectivist temple': the gold standard, the balanced budget rule (more correctly, the minimal balanced budget rule, MBBR) and free trade. These were the foundation of classical liberal political economy, an interlocking policy regime which enmeshed policy instruments and objectives – so much so that Tomlinson (1990: 14) calls them institutions. They derived from a common body of economic and political principles: that there needed to be constitutional disciplines to prevent oversupply of public goods; that 'automatic' regimes of monetary control were preferable to ones that granted discretion to politicians; and that adherence to free trade removed much scope for rent-seeking behaviour. In short, and using the terminology of public choice theory, they constituted an unwritten 'fiscal constitution' which had evolved to restrain potential political abuse of the economy and to maximise the ambit of the efficiency-enhancing market economy.

We here stress the evolutionary nature of this policy regime which underpinned the minimalist state, and we should also preface this part of our discussion with an important reminder that, certainly before the First World War, few contemporary policy actors actually conceived of what they were doing as economic policy in the sense that we would understand it today. Accepting no responsibility for economic management, they saw no need for objectives to be made explicit, nor for instruments and objectives to be identified, matched and co-ordinated, whilst policy trade-offs were an as yet undreamed of complication. Rather, and adopting Tomlinson's (1990: 10–11) terminology, the agencies of policy operated primarily in terms of doctrines, and more particularly the three pillars of the anti-collectivist temple. For pre-1914 governments the objectives were thus: 'To maintain the gold standard and with it the free flow of capital, the value of money, and the stability and strength of the financial system. To maintain free trade in Britain and as far as possible in the Empire. Finally, to keep the budget small and in balance.'

The desire immediately after the First World War to return to some (idealised) pre-war normality meant that, initially and affecting most but not all of the policy elite, interwar policy makers would have liked to have done the same. They were frustrated by radically altered circumstances, so much so that the war and its aftermath challenged and eventually destroyed two of the three pillars of that pre-war policy regime, with only the third (the MBBR) remaining but, arguably, fatally compromised.

The gold standard, having been suspended during the war, and then succeeded by a basically unmanaged float (1919–25), was eventually (and controversially) re-established in 1925 at the pre-war parity (Moggridge 1972). However, notwithstanding supporting deflationary monetary and fiscal policies, that parity could not be defended and sterling was forced once more off gold in September 1931 amidst the storms of an international financial crisis which was part and parcel of the world depression. Thereafter, a managed float was pursued which, at the time and subsequently, has generally been seen as permitting a liberalisation of macroeconomic policies which contributed to the strong cyclical recovery of the British economy from 1932 onwards (Howson 1975). It also marked a new stage in the development of discretion in policy for the Treasury which after 1932 had *de facto* operational control of fiscal, monetary and exchange rate policy.

The MBBR was subjected to ever more intense strains by a combination of a cyclically highly sensitive fiscal system, an unstable economy, intermittently very high unemployment and – as the advent of democracy generated a new phase of political competition – tax resistance, but also intensified pressures for greater public expenditure. As a pillar of the anti-collectivist temple, indeed the central pillar against excess bias, the MBBR was now confronting the political reality that 'budget[ary] policy [had] replac[ed] the barricades as the area of struggle among group and class interests' (Musgrave 1985: 2). In fact, budget deficits had been far from unusual even before the First World War; they occurred in seventeen out of fifty-four years between 1860/1 and 1913/14, but all but six of these were in years of war, thereby continuing a long-established fiscal characteristic of the British state. Gunter and Maloney (1999) have in fact shown econometrically (for 1841–97) that, relative to Conservative administrations, Gladstonian finance in practice made no statistically significant difference to trends in public expenditure, taxation, the budget balance or national debt. For the period since 1900 it appears also that, even if Keynesian deficit-finance was not yet permissible on stabilisation grounds (functional finance), public sector deficits were far from exceptional: in the thirty peacetime years between 1900 and 1938, the combined balance was in deficit on eighteen occasions, with the current account in deficit in seven of these years. It is clear, therefore, that pre-Keynesian budgetary orthodoxy was often more an aspiration than a reality, even if the desire for strict fiscal balance dominated the policy agenda and the authorities *appeared* to give no ground to the Keynesian challenge (Middleton 1985: chs. 4–5, 1996: 111, Figure 5.1).

The fate of the third pillar, that of free trade, appears dramatic but in fact there was a long pre-history of its breach in practice if not principle, and again with war as the catalyst. Formally, and decisively, the historic abandonment of free trade came in November 1931, two months and for connected reasons – another casualty of the world depression – after the abandonment of gold. In 1913 the overall nominal tariff rate in Britain had been about 5 per cent, but the tariff structure and design was not protectionist. However, in that year, for strategic reasons, a subsidy was granted to the sugar beet industry; this was an important turning point in commercial policy. Thereafter, under pressure of war, and then with peacetime as parts of British industry and other interests lobbied for protection to assist the reconstruction of British industry, strategic, infant-industry and revenue-raising arguments were used to secure an end to the historic commitment to free trade (Capie 1983). Finally obtained in 1931–2, the new tariff system contained the potential for additional protection if industries could demonstrate an adequate case, thereby increasing the potential for rent-seeking. This marked a new stage in government–industry relations, although the origins of the modern engagement of the state in industry, and vice versa, ought properly to be located in the needs of both parties during the First World War.[5]

Our account hitherto has stressed the role of war and then interwar unemployment in these developments, but there were broader, longer-running challenges to the minimalist state which would eventually overwhelm the three pillars of the anti-collectivist temple. We can explain the eventual triumph of a managed economy in Britain as a consequence of three interrelated developments arising from these further challenges. First, beginning in the 1870s, the demands for government growth 'now involved dual criticism of the structure and the values of the English political order, both being viewed as a reflection of Society's economic basis whose justice and efficiency were alike disputed' (Emy 1972: 104). Secondly, the passage of the third Reform Act in 1884 and the advent of a comprehensive (although not universal) male franchise resulted in the manual working class for the first time forming the greatest single element in the electorate. However, the unitary nature of the British state, and the comparative absence of regional, ethnic and religious interests, produced exceptional stability in Britain's social structure before the Second World War, if not a little later (Harris 1990b), which ensured that the main political parties competed 'as national parties appealing on a national basis, putting forward programmes and policies in the national interest, claiming to speak for the whole national community. It also

[5] See the important thesis by Middlemas (1979) on the origins of British-style corporatism.

forced them to compete for the votes of the working class, and gradually made the concerns of the working class the central concerns of domestic politics' (Gamble 1990: 86–7). Thirdly, and at the same time as the advent of democracy, the British ruling elites began to feel that military and political hegemony were being threatened by the rise of the emergent industrial economies and a new wave of social discontent appeared, at least in the industrial field, to be adding to Britain's difficulties. New vested interest groups, demanding both representation and state responses, were also arising, all challenging the minimalist state. All of this was to have consequences for the perception of, and significance granted to, market failures and the pressures upon government.

Policy space and national policy style

In emphasising these challenges to the minimalist state, through shocks superimposed upon systemic forces for government growth, we follow the dominant strand of the literature which portrays the path to a managed economy as *ad hoc* and unplanned (Middleton 1996: chs. 6, 9; Tomlinson 1994: 132). However, against the fluidity and policy innovation permitted by the flexibility of the *laissez-faire* inheritance, we need to emphasise how limited in practice was the institutional setting and thus the policy space, the parameters of what was possible (Middleton 1998: 59–60). The policy space is a useful concept designed to capture the interplay of past policies, choices and inherited institutional structures and the way in which they influence the definition of current problems, the perception of the range and efficacy of potential policy instruments and the resulting space for manoeuvre. This is path-dependency (see chapter 4 above) dressed up in different (political) clothing. Thus, for Hall (1986), Gamble (1990) and many other writers sympathetic to interpretation of economic decline which ascribes it to institutional rigidity, Britain's political system and the scale and scope of government were shaped, as was its economy, by the formative influences of early industrialisation and empire.

A limited policy space had its counterpart in a distinctive national policy style, characterised as follows. First, in Britain, and notwithstanding the almost universal charge of institutional conservatism, the state has exhibited very considerable institutional and ideological flexibility, particularly in respect of accommodating the challenges posed by organised labour and the demand for full democratic rights (Gamble 1990). The imperative of flexibility, upon which the continuance of the nation state rested, led to a British policy style of consultation and a bias against policy actions which challenged well-entrenched interests. Radical change was, thereby, precluded and policy tended to be reactive rather than initiatory (Jordan and Richardson 1982). Secondly, there is a distinctive policy community which initially generated and then sustains this policy style, a nexus of interests whereby co-operation flows from a sense of mutual advantage, assisted no doubt by politicians and civil servants having attended the same public schools followed by an Oxbridge education. Thirdly, as has long been recognised, policy may well have its own causes rather than being due to policy evaluation or new problems. Rose and Karran (1984: 44) put it starkly: 'Governing . . . is not so much about making fresh choices; it is principally about living with the consequences of past choices. Most activities of government do not reflect today's decisions, but decisions made yesterday.' Inertia thus limits the policy space, while the unintended effects of policy, particularly in respect of fiscal instruments and their consequences for incentives and resource allocation, are typically as important as the intended effects. Fourthly, if there are few opportunities to start afresh in policy terms it might be argued that the policy space was none the less very wide at the beginning of the century because government was small, there was a widespread expectation about the possibility of beneficial economic and social reform and entropy had not yet the opportunity to establish itself at the institutional level. However, in Britain the *laissez-faire*, minimalist state provided no such clean slate.

The consequences of Britain's limited policy space and distinctive policy style can be encapsulated in a set of preferences that guided policy, both in the negative sense (when not to intervene) and the positive (when and how to intervene). Thus, first and foremost, the primary focus was maintaining the vitality of the market order: 'to "keep the ring" round industry, to let men compete and fight it out, and only to ensure that they did not break the rules' (Florence 1957: 24). This preference for non-intervention in factor and goods markets implied that if intervention was required to secure efficiency potential, government should introduce competition where that was attainable and efficient regulation where elements of natural monopoly remained (Foreman-Peck and Hannah 1999; Millward 2000). However, in Britain, in contrast to the USA (Dobbin 1994), the dominance of the principle of individual sovereignty (stemming from a dominant political tradition of maximising individual as against community liberty) often resulted in policies which protected industry from both market and government.

Secondly, efficient regulation was interpreted within the *laissez-faire* spirit, of government as referee rather than as participant in commerce and industry, long after *laissez-faire* itself had ceased to prevail. This produced a very British policy style of voluntarism (for example, in industrial relations), the promotion of self-regulation in industry and commerce long after there was clear-cut evidence of market failures, and support for intermediate organisations. If direct intervention could not be avoided then its potential costs could at least be lessened by using arms-length bodies, as for example in the activities of the Bank of England in promoting the rationalisation of the staple industries in the 1920s and 1930s (see chapters 14 and 15). This was the institutional foundation for the anti-competitive environment that has been identified for the 1930s.

Thirdly, Gladstone's axiom that 'money should be left to fructify in the pocket of the taxpayer' (cited in Middleton 1996: 185), the economic basis of which derived from concerns about potential disincentive effects and risks to competitiveness, placed an important supply-side constraint on government growth. Notwithstanding known regressive effects, this implied a preference for indirect over direct taxation. Although fiscal doctrine did develop, with ability-to-pay principles making some considerable headway against the classical economists' benefit principle (Musgrave 1985), fiscal conservatism was very evident through to the end of the period (Middleton 1985: ch. 4).

Fourthly, matching the commitment to domestic liberalism was a commitment to international liberalisation of trade, payments and factors of production, albeit one stressed to breaking point by the world depression and always qualified in important respects by the British Empire. However, strategic national interests did extend beyond this and an important exception to any consideration of attitudes towards government and the market was the latitude that was afforded the defence sector. Finally, in keeping with our conclusion that it was responses to social market failure that were the principal impetus to government growth, we find that as the period progressed government was prepared to countenance many efficiency losses to compensate for the social costs of the market, whether as unemployment, income distributions or health and housing conditions. Thus from the 1920s onwards we can identify a systematic bias in policy towards considerations of short-term economic management and the amelioration of the social distress occasioned by structural changes in Britain's productive base. This was at the expense of longer-run structural adjustments because the form of policy tended to entrench opposition to such changes and to lessen the market's capacity to act towards a more optimal resource reallocation. Mottershead (1978: 483) describes well the broad stance of policy in his assessment of the period 1960–74, though it is equally applicable to the interwar period; he concluded that 'governments have intervened against market forces, rather than trying to improve the functioning of the market', with industrial policy being 'limited to a peripheral role of tidying up at the edges of the economy, rather than providing any central thrust to alter and improve industry's performance and that of the economy as a whole'.

POLICY IMPACT

Benchmarks for assessment

To investigate the economic impact of government and of its growth in scale and scope we must first establish some benchmarks for assessment.

A natural starting point is to measure outcomes in relation to policy objectives, but as we have seen until the First World War if not later what we would now conceive of as macroeconomic policy was pursued through the three pillars which enmeshed policy instruments and objectives, and with policy goals typically more implicit than explicit. Policy objectives were characteristically more explicit for what we would now term microeconomic and regulatory policies, but here there has been much less research to ground a thorough appraisal. There is the further problem of what comprises economic policy in the sense that, even when professing non-intervention, greater governmental size and scope often had unintended economic consequences. The classic example is that of fiscal leverage over aggregate demand after the First World War; this was an inevitable consequence of the greatly enlarged public sector, and meant that the Treasury had to consider the fiscal stance even when it was, in its efforts to maintain the discipline of the MBBR, resisting Keynes and other economic radicals' call for deficit-financing to remedy high unemployment.

Various efforts have been made to infer policy objectives for this period (for example, Moggridge 1972: 98–9; Middleton 1996: 215–25, 352–73). Without too much risk of anachronism it is possible to apply as a benchmark the modern conception of macroeconomic policy as seeking to achieve simultaneous internal and external balance in the short run with some concern – not yet an explicit objective of growth – for living standards in the longer term. In such a policy regime, internal balance might be defined as the lowest possible rate of unemployment consistent with stable prices, and external balance as some desirable level of the current account balance of payments (typically a significant surplus to finance overseas investment and to sustain London as a leading financial centre), with living standards viewed increasingly through the filter of social market failure and thus conceived with an eye to distributional issues.

Such an approach, which emphasises stabilisation, efficiency and equity, then forms a natural basis against which to judge microeconomic objectives. These were the dominant preoccupation and conception of the national economy and of government's role until the shocks of war and unemployment brought macroeconomic concerns to the forefront. The principal benchmark thus becomes the impact of government on economic efficiency and equity through its activities in addressing technical and social market failure. A modern, but not inappropriate, conception of this benchmark would then highlight: first the efficiency, appropriateness and responsiveness of governmental activities with respect to the issues of competitiveness, non-market provision of goods and services and, second, and commensurate with the new emphasis on institutional quality, the establishment and maintenance of the infrastructure of an efficient market economy. This provides a very full potential agenda and in the following we can only be highly selective. Fuller accounts are available elsewhere (Tomlinson 1990, 1994; Middleton 1996), with many of the topics also considered in other chapters in this volume.

Government and the macroeconomy

With a relatively small public sector, a broadly balanced budget, an independent central bank, a fixed exchange rate and international capital mobility, the scope for government to exert an impact on the macroeconomy before the First World War was limited. In any case, government had no such inclination, although the desirability of a stabilisation function was being discussed by some economic radicals. After the First World War, in terms of both scope and inclination the situation was radically different in all respects, save for the independence of the Bank of England (which was not nationalised until 1946), and even there its sensitivity to political priorities was greatly enhanced by the 1930s. The enlarged national debt produced by the war resulted in enormous funding problems which dominated monetary policy for the remainder of the period; the cyclical sensitivity of the budget, itself greatly enlarged and buffeted by a business cycle also greatly magnified compared with pre-war, resulted in fiscal policy often being destabilising as the authorities sought to maintain the MBBR in these changed circumstances; the failed international efforts to reconstitute a durable multilateral trade and payments system resulted in instability in exchange rate arrangements, and eventually autarchy in the 1930s; and all of this lay alongside major changes to the structural characteristics of the British economy which lessened its resilience to aggregate demand and supply shocks.

The interwar period epitomised macroeconomic instability (of prices, output and employment), as the pre-war period had epitomised stability. The renewed demand for a stabilisation function for government was thus well founded, but just because the scope for governmental macroeconomic impact was small before 1914 does not signify that it was insignificant. This was a period of growing stability of the monetary system, with no major banking crises after 1870 and with broadly stable long-term interest rates themselves reflecting stable inflationary expectations. Solomou (1994) has pointed to episodes in which there were deleterious effects for the real economy of changes in interest rates and monetary growth, but over 1870–1914 there appears no clear relationship between money and the business cycle (Capie 1992: 93). Claims have been made by Pollard (1989) that Britain suffered from a significant appreciation of sterling, and consequent 'Dutch disease',[6] but Solomou and Catao (2000)

[6] 'Dutch disease' refers to the problem encountered by export industries when the exchange rate appreciates because of the value of raw material exports. The issue first attracted the attention of economists in the 1960s, when Dutch exports of natural gas drove up the relative price of the Dutch guilder, thereby raising the price of Dutch manufactured goods in overseas markets, and thus reducing Dutch manufactured exports and employment in the manufacturing sector.

calculate real effective exchange rates to be trendless albeit variable in this period. It is possible that there were episodes in which fiscal policy was destabilising before 1914, with these associated with wartime and its immediate aftermath, but we await a detailed study. Finally, at the macroeconomic level the continuing commitment to free trade has generated a big literature; this broadly concludes that it was welfare-enhancing compared to contemporary alternatives (Pollard 1989: 243–4, 267–8).

Assessments become more complex and contested as we turn to the interwar period. The role of demand and supply shocks, and the contribution of policy to generating and mitigating those shocks, has been much debated in relation to the downturns of 1920–1, 1929–32 and 1937–8. For the 1920s the major focus has been the desirability of returning to gold at the pre-war parity in 1925; for the 1930s it has been the extent to which the recovery beginning in 1932 can be explained by the new policy regime of cheap money and tariffs that was made possible by the abandonment of gold in 1931, and whether that recovery would have been fuller and faster if the Keynesian solution of deficit-finance had been adopted. Unemployment was much higher between the wars than before, and the price level was characterised by a much larger variance (a post-war inflation followed by sustained deflation). Further, the huge current account balance of payments surplus of pre-war (approaching 10 per cent of GDP) had become a deficit by the 1930s. Given these factors, we might conclude that macroeconomic policy was an unmitigated disaster. However, trend GDP growth was higher than before the war, and these macroeconomic characteristics were not uncommon experiences at the time (see chapter 12 above).

Given the enormity of the problems facing the leading industrial economies after the First World War, the particular characteristics of Britain's unemployment problem, the structural adjustment crisis confronting its industries and the initially limited policy objectives of the British authorities – essentially to return to pre-war normalcy – the question arises of what alternative and credible policy could have delivered improved macroeconomic performance. For contemporaries, the alternatives were between, first, an even stricter interpretation of economic orthodoxy (reduced public sector size, debt funding, a challenging real exchange rate, wage and social security benefit cuts) and, second, the emerging Keynesian solution. However, after the general strike there was something of a political impasse on wage cuts. It was increasingly seen that public works programmes on sufficient scale were administratively difficult. At the same time, in any case, they never obtained sufficient political approval. Thus when an expanded policy space did come it was only as a consequence of what had not been sought (the abandonment of gold) and the authorities were unsurprisingly reluctant to take further risks with the public finances thereafter until rearmament compelled deficit-finance. Ironically, it was public works in the form of rearmament which ultimately resolved interwar unemployment. As we now know, whatever the force of the 'Treasury view' on the inexpediency of deficit-finance in peacetime, officials had by the eve of the war come to understand how the budget could be used to stimulate demand and had learned much about the more effective timing of intervention, choice of policy instruments and co-ordination (Middleton 1985: ch. 8). Passivity in face of the business cycle was thus no more, and government had assumed by the eve of war, if not a formal stabilisation function, then something very closely resembling a managed economy, albeit that they remained severely handicapped by the scarcity and poor quality of economic data available to them, for which Treasury parsimony must bear some responsibility.

Contrasting the 1930s with the 1920s, and even more so with 1913 and before, the authorities clearly used the expanded policy space to conduct more explicitly macroeconomic policies, and with increasing success. Much has been claimed for the beneficial effects of the new policy regime of a floating exchange rate, cheap money and protective tariffs, with particular advocacy for the last of these (Solomou 1996: ch. 6). Whether a more Keynesian public works programme ought to have been implemented, or Britain not returned to gold in 1925 at a lower rate, no longer excites the same debate as it once did since recent writings tend to emphasise the supply as much as the demand side (Dimsdale and Horsewood 1995). Concurrently, Broadberry and Crafts (1990c, 1996) have begun to develop the thesis that, while the policy framework that emerged in the 1930s was understandable and quite effective in ameliorating the worst effects of macroeconomic shocks, it established microeconomic and regulatory policies and behaviours which were potentially harmful to longer-term growth.

Government and the microeconomy

The Keynesian bias in the historiography of British government growth, combined with the sheer breadth of potential policy areas that could be researched, results in the literature on microeconomic impact being far less developed. An indication of the scale and diversity of these potential impacts is given by an enumeration of legislation of an economic and social character passed during this period.[7] Approximately 200 acts of parliament were passed which had the capacity to affect the quality, quantity and price of the factors of production; to generate compliance costs; to alter the rules under which market exchange was conducted; and, generally, to affect the myriad of economic transactions and behaviours

[7] The legislation enumerated here is taken from the indexes of standard works on government growth: Florence 1957: 20–1; Grove 1962: 505; Checkland 1983: 426–9; and Greenleaf 1983: 332–3.

that underpin resource allocation and distribution. The following discussion confines itself to the core concerns for economic performance of industrial policy and product market intervention and labour policy and factor market intervention. Thus, for reasons of space, we do not here address the economic impact of environmental regulation, food standards, land and physical planning controls, regional policy, etc., but we must not discount – even if we cannot yet measure – their significance for costs and economic behaviour. Recent work in these important areas includes Sheail (1993; 1997) on organised capital's resistance to growing air pollution and water management legislation; French and Phillips' (2000) wide-ranging study of food hygiene legislation, which demonstrates how, as so often, social reformers pursuit of the 'public interest' resulted in legislation and enforcement procedures which amounted to regulatory capture by the industry; McLean and Johnes' (2000) further case study of regulatory capture, that of the Board of Trade by the shipping lobby after the dramatic loss of the *Titanic*; and Bartrip (1998), one of a series of his studies of industrial health and safety.[8]

Current economic orthodoxy considers that policies affecting product market competition and labour market adaptability can greatly influence economic performance through their impact *inter alia* on the incentives to improve efficiency and the costs of so doing. Consequently an easing of product market regulation and employment protection enhances productivity, while policies that favour competition spur the innovative efforts of firms. Whilst that orthodoxy may generally be appropriate for today's advanced industrial economies (for example, OECD 2002: ch. 7), to what extent might those policy preferences have reduced welfare before 1939 when state intervention was far less developed? A strong case has been made that the delay in developing an active and statutory competition policy may well have had enduring negative effects for the British economy (Freyer 1992; Mercer 1995). Similarly, there has been much recent interest in how the various efforts, often state-assisted, to rationalise the staple industries between the wars undermined the competitive order by raising barriers to entry, delaying the exit of inefficient firms and strengthening pre-existing constraints to achieving X-efficiency.[9] These are further examples of the national policy style generating unintended policy consequences and policy immaturity which had potentially negative effects on efficiency.

The enforcement of property rights is now seen as a central task of government in relation to the promotion of growth, with a particular

[8] Regulatory capture occurs when economic agents that the state wishes to regulate exercise a significant degree of influence over the regulatory process because of their control of information about and access to the relevant economic activities.

[9] X-efficiency refers to the effectiveness with which a given set of inputs are transformed into outputs. When a firm is producing the maximum output it can, given the resources it employs, then it is said to be X-efficient. X-inefficiency occurs when X-efficiency is not achieved.

focus for this period on developments in company law and the legal immunities of trade unions. Broadly, as with competition policy, the legal environment with regard to business organisation and finance was extremely permissive. Although there were efforts at reform, these were successfully resisted by powerful interests with the result that 'company law still remained unsatisfactory' to 1914 (Cottrell 1980: 75, 270). Some of these deficiencies were remedied between the wars. The ability of the capital market to monitor company performance was much enhanced by the Companies Act, 1929, which required that accounts be 'true and correct', a novel idea in Britain (Foreman-Peck 1994: 391).

Government also had the capacity strongly to affect product markets through greater public ownership and the provision of certain public goods and services. Foreman-Peck and Millward identify five phases in British state policy towards the all-important network industries of which the first three relate to our period:

1. the competitive era (1820–60s): when regulation was absent or largely ineffective and intense competition between producers led eventually to amalgamations and local private monopolies;
2. regulation and municipalisation (1860s–First World War): characterised by closer railway regulation, the nationalisation of telegraphy and much increased local authority ownership of electricity, gas, tram and water undertakings; this new regulatory phase was a response to the previous ineffectiveness of regulation and the ubiquity of environmental spillovers, together with the desire of local authorities to augment rate income through the possibilities offered by enhanced trading profits; and
3. state-sponsored rationalisation (interwar period): in response to the collapse of the staple export industries and technological weaknesses revealed by the war, government intervened in industrial organisation to promote rationalisation, but resisted nationalisation of coal, 'dabble[d] hesitantly with manufacturing, fail[ed] to overcome stubborn local intervention in gas and water, but ha[d] some success with the electricity grid and broadcasting' (Foreman Peck and Millward 1994: 4–7).

The increased scale of public ownership and state trading caused many anxieties about the efficiency of non-market activities. Much contemporary evidence is tainted by ideological views concerning the superiority of private over public provision and vice versa. Later empirical work, especially for the network industries, has given state trading a largely clean bill of health relative to the known deficiencies of the private sector. It has identified important instances (interwar electricity supply) where regulation reduced costs and helped to close the productivity gap with the United States and where the decision not to nationalise a key sector (railways, post-First World War) was to its detriment and that of the wider economy it served (Foreman-Peck and Millward 1994). Accordingly, there is no evidence of widespread non-market failure here (Middleton 1996: 241–2, 401–3). The preconditions for non-market failure on both the demand and supply side were being established before the First World War as the scale and scope of government grew. However, there is very little actual evidence, save perhaps with defence procurement, where special conditions prevailed in a unique relationship between government and a small number of armaments producers.

It is generally agreed that in no other advanced industrial economy has the law played a less significant role in shaping industrial relations than in Britain (Clegg 1970: 343); it was voluntary dealings between capital and labour, variously organised, that determined the form and pace of developments. This voluntarist tradition dictated a non-interventionist stance by successive governments and suggests that, so far as economic performance is concerned, it is what governments did not do rather than what they did do that may be critical. The legal immunities enjoyed by trade unions were established just before the First World War and broadly endured thereafter. Historians debate the extent to which threats to the British state by organised labour were successfully diffused but with longer-run costs for the labour process and for government's capacity to impose its authority upon the market.

As we lack a full-scale economic study of the growth of government regulation we do not know the extent of compliance costs for firms with respect to the myriad of areas that were becoming regulated, nor the efficiency of such regulation, nor how it compared with the experience of competitor economies. More is known about the labour market. Some interventions were clearly beneficial to its operation, such as labour exchanges; others have been seen as detrimental, as for example with the strong claims made for how unemployment insurance increased interwar unemployment. The thesis that the excess of interwar unemployment was induced by the level of benefits has not stood up to scrutiny (see chapter 13 above). However, there is clearer evidence that minimum wage legislation, much strengthened in 1918, did have a negative effect in some sectors, and especially agriculture (Gowers and Hatton 1997). Rent controls, also a product of the war, can also be expected to have lessened labour's geographical mobility. However, the implications for the labour market of what government did not do has also received attention, as for example in the supposed deficiencies of investment in human capital. The available cross-country data suggest that Britain was a relatively low spender on public education at the beginning of our period but had caught up to become a middle-ranking spender by 1913 and an above average spender by 1937 (Tanzi and Schuknecht 2000: Table II.5). Given this profile, those who now look for connections between deficiencies in educational provision and Britain's relative economic decline need, as Sanderson (1999) has done recently, to look beyond the quantity dimension of publicly funded education to issues of structure and quality (see chapter 3 above).

The microeconomic impacts of taxation have not been much explored. However, since effective rates of tax on expenditures and on income, both personal and corporate, were at least twice as high between the wars as in 1913 (Middleton 1996: Figure 3.13), they can be assumed to be significant. Certainly, there is evidence of company and household portfolio behaviour being affected, with policy makers much concerned about 'high' taxation impacting on savings and investment. The counterpart to higher corporate taxation after the First World War was the growth of subsidies, the foremost of which was to agriculture which emerged in the 1930s as one of the most highly protected, heavily subsidised and organised of all British industries. Financial and other assistance to this sector (comprising but 5.7 per cent of the employed labour force in 1938) dwarfed that of assistance to industry (44 per cent) (calculated from Feinstein 1972: Table 59), which was itself in receipt of a growing volume and variety of subsidies, many strategically motivated (Middleton 1996: 365, 369). In this, like much else, it was the war which established business–government relations on a new footing and created the possibilities for greater engagement for sectional or national benefit. Such had been the eventual highly regulated nature of the economy during that war (see Hurwitz 1949) that it acted thereafter as an exemplar, according to ideological predisposition, both of what was possible and of what to avoid.

Government and equity

Using comparative data on the distribution of pre-tax incomes, Lindert and Williamson (1983: 96) conclude that 'mid-Victorian England and Wales was among the most unequal of modern societies . . . exceed[ing] those of all advanced countries since World War II'. They estimate a Gini coefficient[10] for 1867 of 0.538, at which point the top decile of income earners had 46.8 per cent of incomes and the bottom four deciles some 15.2 per cent. The Gini coefficient had fallen to 0.423 by 1938/9, with the shares of the top and bottom four deciles now 31.5 and 19.1 per cent respectively (Middleton 1996: Table 1.9). Since there was an increase in average real earnings of approximately 260 per cent between 1861 and 1938 (Feinstein 1995: Table 1.7), the result was both material advance for the generality and some lessening of the grosser material inequalities. How far these changes were a consequence of public policy and how much a reflection of the evolution of the market economy remains largely unexplored, but it has been calculated that by 1937 some 5–6 per cent of national income was being redistributed from rich to poor (Barna 1945:

[10] The Gini coefficient is a summary measure of distributional equality. A coefficient of 0 indicates complete equality (the top 1 per cent and the bottom 1 per cent, and all percentiles in between each receive 1 per cent of total income), and a coefficient of 1 indicates complete inequality (the top 1 per cent receive all the income, and the rest get nothing).

233). Very recent research, using micro survey evidence, is beginning to show that the social security system was an important mechanism for poverty reduction before the Beveridge welfare reforms of the late 1940s (Hatton and Bailey 1998). Accordingly, although income redistribution through public finance was not an explicit policy objective before the Second World War, the interaction of the evolving social security system and the now more progressive taxation system was producing that result with significant implications for equity.

CONCLUSIONS

It is generally agreed that, in the middle of the nineteenth century, the British state was an exemplar of non-intervention amongst the industrial economies; that by 1914, 'the intervention of the state in economic affairs was important, but restricted' (Tawney 1943: 1); and that by 1939, in policy objectives and instruments, in size and in scope, Britain had a recognisably modern managed economy if not yet a coherent and agreed philosophy of economic management. It had by then no longer become a question so much of whether the state ought to intervene, but to what extent it should and how.

The origins of the managed economy thus lie between the wars, with the First World War accelerating the momentum to greater state intervention provided by the systemic forces for government growth. This was so even if, in the short term, with the rolling back of the state in the early 1920s, it appeared that it was *laissez-faire* and not policy activism and an enlarged state which would endure. Such was the nature of that conflict, one that embodied a perpetual tension, being 'at once a catalyst for reform and an obstacle to change' (Gilbert 1970: 1). The post-1945 period is therefore that of the consolidation of big government, although such a conclusion must depend upon a judgement about the criteria for locating the crucial discontinuity. Higgs (1987), in his study of US government growth, stresses the ratchet effect of the First World War and the 1930s depression and asks whether that crucial discontinuity was the phase in which the institutions of government intervention were conceived, made or fully implemented. Asking the question in this way is important because it helps to focus on the essence of big government which is as much about state authority over economic decision making as the enlargement of the public sector.

The First World War thus has a central role in long-run government growth. There is no consensus about the economic effects of that conflict, nor about the economic impact of government. But for too long there has been a presumption that the principal economic effects of government operated at the microeconomic level before the First World War and the macroeconomic level between the wars. Such a presumption is no longer sustainable: fiscal and monetary policies were having discernible macroeconomic effects before the First World War, whilst between the wars government policies, by design or by ignorance, were having important microeconomic effects. Whilst economics furnishes no hard and fast answers about the optimal size and scope of government, and is typically on stronger ground about what governments ought not to do than what they can usefully do, it remains the case that there is still much to be researched about government growth and its impact during this period. This applies particularly to the efficiency of non-market production of goods and services and to the impact of growing regulation. Offer's (2002) recent model of British public sector growth is also likely to prove particularly fertile for researchers; he argues that for a century or so from 1870, collective provision evolved to overcome consumers' myopia and to facilitate long-term commitment.

The *laissez-faire* inheritance is now seen as more complicated than was hitherto thought. It was less a dogma and more a pragmatic approach to the cardinal choice between government and market, albeit one with clear preferences, producing a very British policy style in which economic and social equilibrium was not disturbed too substantially. But, as we have seen, disturbance was the norm. Beginning with the enormous stresses generated by having industrialised on the cheap, the traditional defences of the minimalist state were overwhelmed by the advent of democracy, the first stirrings of concern about maintaining economic hegemony, the shock of the First World War and then the challenge of mass unemployment. All of these disturbances heightened awareness of social market failures, and made them less politically sustainable, whilst making it more urgent that government intervene to improve both efficiency and equity. However, such was the attachment to a particular negative version of *laissez-faire* by political elites and opinion-formers, and such was the fragmented nature of the British state, and its limited authority, that even if there was the appearance of a modern managed economy, greatly enlarged in size and scope, this does not equate to the development of effective big government by 1939. Good governance is the key to high economic policy capability and low policy distortion (World Bank 1997). It is thus the quality as much as the quantity of government that matters.

References

Place of publication is London unless otherwise stated. All references to the *Economic History Review* are to the 2nd series, unless otherwise stated.

Abramovitz, M. 1993. The search for the sources of growth: areas of ignorance, old and new. *Journal of Economic History* 53: 217–43.

Abramovitz, M. and David, P. A. 1996. Convergence and delayed catch-up: productivity leadership and the waning of American exceptionalism. In R. Landau, T. Taylor and G. Wright, eds., *The Mosaic of Economic Growth*. Stanford.

Abramovitz, M. and Eliasberg, V. F. 1957. *The Growth of Public Employment in Great Britain*. Princeton, NJ.

Acemoglu, D., Johnson S. and Robinson, J. 2001. The colonial origins of comparative development: an empirical investigation. *American Economic Review* 91: 1369–401.

Ackrill, M. and Hannah, L. 2001. *Barclays: The Business of Banking 1690–1996*. Cambridge.

Afton, B. and Turner, M. E. 2000. The statistical base of agricultural performance in England and Wales. In Collins 2000b.

Aghion, P. and Howitt, P. 1998. *Endogenous Growth Theory*. Cambridge, MA.

Aghion, P., Bloom, N., Blundell, R., Griffith, R. and Howitt, P. 2002. Competition and innovation: an inverted u-shape. Institute for Fiscal Studies, London, working paper.

Aghion, P., Dewatripont, M. and Rey, P. 1997. Corporate governance, competition policy and industrial policy. *European Economic Review* 41: 797–805.

Akerlof, G., Dickens, W. and Perry, G. 2000. Near-rational wage and price setting and the long-run Phillips curve. *Brookings Paper on Economic Activity* 1: 1–60.

Alborn, T. L. 1998. *Conceiving Companies: Joint Stock Politics in Victorian England*.

Aldcroft, D. H. 1964. The entrepreneur and the British economy 1870–1914. *Economic History Review* 17: 113–14.

1970. *The Inter-War Economy: Britain, 1919–1939*. New York.

1975. Investment in and utilisation of manpower: Great Britain and her rivals, 1870–1914. In B. M. Ratcliffe, ed., *Great Britain and her World, 1750–1915*. Manchester.

Aldcroft, D. H., ed. 1968. *The Development of British Industry and Foreign Competition*. Glasgow.

Aldcroft, D. H. and Richardson, H. W. 1969. *The British Economy 1870–1939*.

Alexander, D. 1970. *Retailing in England during the Industrial Revolution*.

Alford, B. W. E. 1973. *W. D. & H. O. Wills and the Development of the U. K. Tobacco Industry, 1786–1965*.

1977. Penny cigarettes, oligopoly, and entrepreneurship in the UK tobacco industry in the late nineteenth century. In Supple 1977.

1996. *Britain in the World Economy since 1880*.

Allen, G. C. 1951. *British Industries and their Organisation*.

1979. *The British Disease: A Short Essay on the Nature and Causes of the Nation's Lagging Wealth*.

Allen, R. C. 1977. The peculiar productivity history of American blast furnaces, 1840–1913. *Journal of Economic History* 37: 605–33.
1979. International competition in iron and steel, 1850–1913. *Journal of Economic History* 39: 911–37.
Ames, E. and Rosenberg, N. 1968. The Enfield arsenal in theory and history. *Economic Journal* 78: 827–42.
Anand, Sudhir and Ravallion, Martin. 1993. Human development in poor countries: on the role of private incomes and public services. *Journal of Economic Perspectives* 7: 133–50.
Anderson, M. 1971. *Family Structure in Nineteenth Century Lancashire*. Cambridge.
1985. The emergence of the modern life cycle in Britain. *Social History* 10: 69–87.
1990. The social implications of demographic change. In Thompson 1990b.
2000. Population growth and population regulation in nineteenth-century rural Scotland. In T. Bengtsson and O. Saito, eds., *Population and Economy: From Hunger to Modern Economic Growth*. Oxford.
Anderson, M., ed. 1996. *British Population History: From the Black Death to the Present Day*. Cambridge.
Argles, M. 1964. *South Kensington to Robbins: An Account of English Technical and Scientific Education since 1851*.
Armstrong, J. 1986. Hooley and the Bovril Company. *Business History* 28: 18–34.
1987. The role of coastal shipping in UK transport: an estimate of comparative shipping movements in 1910. *Journal of Transport History* 8: 158–74.
1990. The rise and fall of the company promoter and the financing of British industry. In van Helton and Cassis 1990.
Armstrong, W. A. 1981. The trend of mortality in Carlisle between the 1780s and the 1840s: a demographic contribution to the standard of living debate. *Economic History Review* 34: 94–118.
Armytage, W. H. G. 1970. *Four Hundred Years of Education*, 2nd edn. Cambridge.
Arnold, A. J. 1999. Innovation, deskilling and profitability in the British machine-tools industry: Alfred Herbert, 1887–1927. *Journal of Industrial History* 1: 50–71.
Arthur, W. B. 1989. Competing technologies and lock-in by historical small events. *Economic Journal* 99: 116–31.
Arthur, W. B. 1988. Competing technologies: an overview. In G. Dosi, C. Freeman and R. Nelson, eds., *Technical Change and Economic Theory*.
Ashby, J. and King, B. 1893. Statistics of some Midland villages. *Economic Journal* 3: 1–22.
Ashby, M. K. 1961. *Joseph Ashby of Tysoe, 1859–1919: A Study of English Village Life*. Cambridge.
Ashton, T. S. 1955. *An Economic History of England: The Eighteenth Century*. Manchester.
Attard, B. 2000. Making a market: the jobbers of the London Stock Exchange, 1800–1986. *Financial History Review* 7: 5–54.
Bagwell, P. and Armstrong, J. 1988. Coastal shipping. In Freeman and Aldcroft 1988.
Bain, G. S. and Price, R. 1980. *Profiles of Union Growth*. Oxford.
Baines, D. 1985. *Migration in a Mature Economy: Emigration and Internal Migration in England and Wales, 1861–1900*. Cambridge.
1991. *Emigration from Europe, 1815–1930*.
1994. European emigration, 1815–1930: looking at the emigration decision again. *Economic History Review* 47: 525–44.
Baines, D. and Johnson, P. 1999. Did they jump or were they pushed? The exit of older men from the London labor market, 1929–1931. *Journal of Economic History* 49: 949–72.
Bairoch, P. 1982. International industrialization levels from 1750 to 1980. *Journal of European Economic History* 11: 269–333.
1989. European trade policy, 1815–1914. In Mathias and Pollard 1989.

Baker, M. and Collins, M. 1999. English industrial distress before 1914 and the response of banks. *European Review of Economic History* 3: 1–24.
Bakke, E. Wight. 1933. *The Unemployed Man*. New Haven, CT.
Balfour 1929. *Report of the Balfour Committee on Industry and Trade*.
Bamberg, J. H. 1984. The government, the banks, and the Lancashire cotton industry. Unpublished PhD thesis, University of Cambridge.
1988. The rationalisation of the British cotton industry in the interwar years. *Textile History* 19: 83–102.
Barker, T. C. 1977. *The Glassmakers: Pilkington: The Rise of an International Company, 1826–1976*.
Barna, T. 1945. *Redistribution of Incomes through Public Finance in 1937*.
Barnett, C. 1986. *The Audit of War: The Illusion and Reality of Britain as a Great Nation*.
Barro, R. J. 1999. Notes on growth accounting. *Journal of Economic Growth* 4: 119–37.
Barro, R. J. and Sala-i-Martin, X. 1995. *Economic Growth*. New York.
Bartrip, P. W. J. 1998. Too little, too late? The Home Office and the asbestos industry regulations, 1931. *Medical History* 42: 421–38.
Baumol, W. J. 1967. Macroeconomics and unbalanced growth. *American Economic Review* 57: 415–26.
1988. *Entrepreneurship, Management and the Structure of Payoffs*. Cambridge, MA.
1990. Entrepreneurship: productive, unproductive and destructive. *Journal of Political Economy* 98: 893–921.
Baxter, R. D. 1866. On railway extension and its results. *Journal of the Statistical Society of London* 29: 549–95.
1868. *National Income: The United Kingdom*.
Baysinger, B. and Tollison, R. D. 1980. Chaining Leviathan: the case of Gladstonian finance. *History of Political Economy* 12: 206–13.
Bean, C. and Crafts, N. 1996. British economic growth since 1945: relative economic decline . . . and renaissance? In Crafts and Toniolo 1996.
Beenstock, M. and Warburton, P. 1986. Wages and unemployment in interwar Britain. *Explorations in Economic History* 23: 1653–72.
1991. The market for labor in interwar Britain. *Explorations in Economic History* 28: 287–308.
Beilby, O. J. 1939. Changes in agricultural production in England and Wales. *Journal of the Royal Agricultural Society of England* 100: 62–73.
Bell, Lady Florence. 1907. *At the Works: A Study of a Manufacturing Town*.
Bellerby, J. R. 1953. The distribution of farm income in the UK, 1867–1938. *Journal of the Proceedings of the Agricultural Economics Society* 10: 127–44. Reprinted in Minchinton 1968.
1959. National and agricultural income in 1851. *Economic Journal* 69: 95–104.
Benjamin, D. K. and Kochin, L. A. 1979. Searching for an explanation of unemployment in interwar Britain. *Journal of Political Economy* 87: 441–78.
Berghoff, H. 1990. Public schools and the decline of the British economy. *Past and Present* 129: 148–67.
1995. Regional variations in provincial business biography: the case of Birmingham, Bristol and Manchester, 1870–1914. *Business History* 37: 64–85.
Berghoff, H. and Moller, R. 1994. Tired pioneers and dynamic newcomers? A comparative essay on English and German entrepreneurial history, 1870–1914. *Economic History Review* 47: 262–87.
Berle, A. A. and Means, G. C. 1933. *The Modern Corporation and Private Property*. New York.
Best, M. H. and Humphries, J. 1986. The City and industrial decline. In Elbaum and Lazonick 1986.
Beveridge, W. H. 1909. *Unemployment: A Problem of Industry*.
1930. *Unemployment: A Problem of Industry*. 2nd edn.
1936. An analysis of unemployment (part I). *Economica* 3: 357–86.
1944. *Full Employment in a Free Society*.
Bienefeld, M. A. 1972. *Working Hours in British Industry: An Economic History*.

Board of Trade. 1910. *Report on Collective Agreements between Employers and Workpeople in the United Kingdom*, Cd 5366.

1947. *Working Party Reports: Wool.*

1950. *Census of Production.*

Bogart, E. L. 1921. *War Costs and their Financing: A Study of the Financing of the War and the After-War Problem of Debt and Taxation.* New York.

Booth, A. 1987. Britain in the 1930s: a managed economy. *Economic History Review* 40: 499–522.

Booth, A. E. and Glynn, S. 1975. Unemployment in the interwar period: a multiple problem. *Journal of Contemporary History* 10: 611–37.

Booth, Charles. 1892. *Life and Labour of the People in London.*

Bowden, S. 1988. The consumer durables revolution in England, 1932–1938: a regional analysis. *Explorations in Economic History* 25: 42–59.

1990. Credit facilities and the growth of consumer demand for electric appliances in England in the 1930s. *Business History* 32: 52–75.

1991. Demand and supply constraints in the inter-war British car industry: did the manufacturers get it right? *Business History* 33: 241–67.

Bowden, S. and Higgins, D. M. 1998. Short-time working and price maintenance: collusive tendencies in the cotton-spinning industry, 1919–1939. *Economic History Review* 51: 319–43.

2000. Quiet successes and loud failures: the UK textile industries in the interwar years. *Journal of Industrial History* 3: 91–101.

Bowden, S. and Offer, A. 1994. Household appliances and the use of time: the United States and Britain since the 1920s. *Economic History Review* 47: 725–48.

Bowden, S. and Turner, P. 1993. The UK market and the market for consumer durables. *Journal of Economic History* 53: 244–58.

1998. Uncertainty and the competitive decline of the British motor industry, 1945–1975. *New Political Economy* 3: 103–20.

Bowles, S. and Gintis, H. 1993. The revenge of homo economicus: contested exchange and the revival of political economy. *Journal of Economic Perspectives* 7: 83–102.

Bowley, A. L. 1904. Tests of national progress. *Economic Journal* 14: 457–65.

1937. *Wages and Income in the United Kingdom since 1860.* Cambridge.

Bowley, A. L. and Burnett-Hurst, A. R. 1915. *Livelihood and Poverty: A Study in the Economic Conditions of Working-class Households in Northampton, Warrington, Stanley and Reading.*

1920. *Economic Conditions of Working-class Households in Bolton, 1914: Supplementary Chapter to 'Livelihood and Poverty'.*

Bowley, A. L. and Hogg, M. H. 1925. *Has Poverty Diminished?.*

Boyce, G. 1992. 64thers, syndicates and stock promotions: information flows and fund-raising techniques of British shipowners before 1914. *Journal of Economic History* 52: 181–205.

Boyer, G. R. 1988. What did unions do in nineteenth-century Britain? *Journal of Economic History* 48: 319–32.

1997. Labour migration in southern and eastern England, 1861–1901. *European Review of Economic History* 1: 191–215.

1998. The influence of London on labour markets in southern England, 1830–1914. *Social Science History* 22: 257–85.

Forthcoming. The evolution of unemployment relief before the adoption of National Insurance: Great Britain, 1834–1911. *Journal of Interdisciplinary History.*

Boyer, G. R. and Hatton, T. J. 1994. Regional labour market integration in England and Wales, 1850–1913. In G. Grantham and M. MacKinnon, eds., *Labour Market Evolution.*

1997. Migration and labour market integration in late nineteenth-century England and Wales. *Economic History Review* 50: 697–734.

2002. New estimates of British unemployment, 1870–1913. *Journal of Economic History* 62: 643–75.

Brassley, P. 2000. Plant nutrition. In Collins 2000b.

Briggs, Asa. 1963. *Victorian Cities.*

Broadberry, S. N. 1983. Unemployment in interwar Britain: a disequilibrium approach. *Oxford Economic Papers* 35: 463–85.

Aggregate supply in interwar Britain. *Economic Journal* 96: 467–81.

1987. Cheap money and the housing boom in interwar Britain: an econometric appraisal. *Manchester School* 87: 378–91.

1988. Perspectives on consumption in interwar Britain. *Applied Economics* 20: 1465–79.

1993. Manufacturing and the convergence hypothesis: what the long-run data show. *Journal of Economic History* 53: 772–95.

1994a. Technological leadership and productivity leadership in manufacturing since the industrial revolution: implications for the convergence debate. *Economic Journal* 104: 291–302.

1994b. Why was unemployment in postwar Britain so low? *Bulletin of Economic Research* 46: 241–61.

1997a. Anglo-German productivity differences 1870–1990: a sectoral analysis. *European Review of Economic History* 1: 247–67.

1997b. Forging ahead, falling behind and catching-up: a sectoral analysis of Anglo-American productivity differences, 1870–1990. *Research in Economic History* 17: 1–37.

1997c. *The Productivity Race: British Manufacturing in International Perspective, 1850–1990.* Cambridge.

1998. How did the United States and Germany overtake Britain? A sectoral analysis of comparative productivity levels, 1870–1990. *Journal of Economic History* 58: 375–407.

2003. Human capital and productivity performance: Britain, the United States and Germany, 1870–1990. In P. A. David and M. Thomas, eds., *Economic Challenges of the 21st Century in Historical Perspective.* Oxford.

Broadberry, S. N. and Crafts, N. F. R. 1990a. Explaining Anglo-American productivity differences in the mid-twentieth century. *Oxford Bulletin of Economics and Statistics* 52: 375–401.

1990b. The impact of the depression of the 1930s on the productive potential of the United Kingdom. *European Economic Review* 34: 599–607.

1990c. The implications of British macroeconomic policy in the 1930s for long run growth performance. *Rivista di Storia Economica* 7: 1–19.

1992a. Britain's productivity gap in the 1930s: some neglected factors. *Journal of Economic History* 52: 531–58.

1996. British economic policy and industrial performance in the early post-war period. *Business History* 38: 65–91.

2001. Competition and innovation in 1950s Britain. *Business History* 43: 97–118.

Broadberry, S. N. and Crafts, N. F. R., eds. 1992b. *Britain in the World Economy: Essays in Honour of Alec Ford.* Cambridge.

Broadberry, S. N. and Fremdling, R. 1990. Comparative productivity in British and German industry, 1907–1939. *Oxford Bulletin of Economics and Statistics* 52: 403–21.

Broadberry, S. N. and Ghosal, S. 2002. From the counting house to the modern office: explaining Anglo-American productivity differences in services, 1870–1990. *Journal of Economic History* 62: 967–98.

Broadberry, S. N. and Wagner, K. 1996. Human capital and productivity in manufacturing during the twentieth century: Britain, Germany and the United States. In van Ark and Crafts 1996.

Broadbridge, S. 1970. *Studies in Railway Expansion and the Capital Markets in England 1825–1873.*

Brown, A. J. 1972. *The Framework of Regional Economics in the United Kingdom.* Cambridge.

Brown, K. D. 1971. *Labour and Unemployment, 1900–1914*. Newton Abbot.

Brown, M. 1966. *On the Theory and Measurement of Technological Change*. Cambridge.

Brown, R. L. and Easton, S. D. 1989. Weak-form efficiency in the nineteenth century: a study of daily prices in the London market for 3 per cent Consols, 1821–1860. *Economica* 56: 61–70.

Brownlee, J. 1916. The history of the birth and death rates in England and Wales taken as a whole from 1570 to the present time. *Public Health* 19: 211–22 and 228–38.

Buchinsky, M. and Polak, B. 1993. The emergence of a national capital market in England, 1710–1880. *Journal of Economic History* 53: 1–24.

Burgess, K. 1975. *The Origins of British Industrial Relations*.

Burk, K. 1989. *Morgan Grenfell, 1838–1988: The Biography of a Merchant Bank*. Oxford.

Burk, K., ed. 1982. *War and the State: The Transformation of British Government, 1914–1919*.

Burnett, John. 1986. *A Social History of Housing 1815–1985*. 2nd edn.

Burnett-Hurst, A. R. 1932. Lancashire and the Indian market. *Journal of the Royal Statistical Society* 95: 395–440.

Burns, E. M. 1941. *British Unemployment Programs, 1920–1938*. Washington DC.

Buxton, N. K. and Aldcroft, D. H. 1979. *British Industry between the Wars*. Whitstable.

Buxton, S. 1888. *Finance and Politics: An Historical Study, 1783–1885*. 2 vols.

Cage, R. A. 1994. Infant mortality rates and housing: twentieth century Glasgow. *Scottish Economic and Social History* 14: 77–92.

Cain, P. J. 1988. Railways 1870–1914: the maturity of the private system. In Freeman and Aldcroft 1988.

1998. Was it worth it? The British empire, 1850–1950. *Rivista de Historia Economica*, Ano XVI, No. 1, Invierno, 351–76.

Cain, P. J. and Hopkins, A. G. 1987. Gentlemanly capitalism and British expansion overseas II: new imperialism, 1850–1945. *Economic History Review* 40: 1–26.

1993. *British Imperialism: Innovation and Expansion, 1688–1914*.

2001. *British Imperialism, 1688–2000*. 2nd edn.

Cairncross, A. K. 1949. Internal migration in Victorian England. *Manchester School* 17: 67–87.

1953. *Home and Foreign Investment, 1870–1913*. Cambridge.

Cairncross, A. K. and Eichengreen, B. 1983. *Sterling in Decline*. Oxford.

Calmfors, L. and Driffill, J. 1988. Bargaining structure, corporatism and macroeconomic performance. *Economic Policy* 6: 13–61.

Cameron, R. 1961. *France and the Economic Development of Europe*. Princeton.

Campbell, A. D. 1955. Changes in Scottish income 1924–1949. *Economic Journal* 65: 225–40.

Campbell, R. H. 1980. *The Rise and Fall of Scottish Industry 1707–1939*. Edinburgh.

Cantwell, J. 1991. Historical trends in international patterns of technological innovation. In Foreman-Peck 1991.

Capie, F. H. 1978. The British tariff and industrial protection in the 1930s. *Economic History Review* 31: 399–409.

1983. *Depression and Protectionism: Britain between the Wars*.

1988. Structure and performance in British banking 1870–1939. In Cottrell and Moggridge 1988.

1992. British economic fluctuations in the nineteenth century: is there a role for money? In Broadberry and Crafts 1992b.

1995. Commercial banking in Britain. In Feinstein 1995b.

Capie, F. H. and Collins, M. 1992. *Have the Banks Failed British Industry?*

1996. Industrial lending by English commercial banks, 1860s–1914: why did banks refuse loans? *Business History* 38: 26–44.

1999. Banks, industry and finance, 1880–1914. *Business History* 41: 37–62.

Capie, F. H. and Rodrik-Bali, G. 1982. Concentration in British banking, 1870–1920. *Business History* 24: 280–92.

Capie, F. H. and Webber, A. 1985. *A Monetary History of the United Kingdom, 1870–1982.*

Carnevali, F. and Scott, P. 1999. The Treasury as venture capitalist: DATAC industrial finance and the Macmillan gap. *Financial History Review* 6: 47–66.

Carrier, N. H. and Jeffery, J. R. 1953. *External Migration: A Study of the Available Statistics, 1815–1950*. General Register Office, Studies in Medical and Population Subjects No. 6.

Carr-Saunders, A. M. and Jones, D. Caradog. 1937. *A Survey of the Social Structure of England and Wales: As Illustrated by Statistics*, 2nd edn. Oxford.

Carr-Saunders, A. M. and Wilson, P. A. 1933. *The Professions*. Oxford.

Cassis, Y. 1985. Bankers in English society in the late nineteenth century. *Economic History Review* 38: 210–29.

1990. The emergence of a new financial institution: investment trusts in Britain, 1870–1939. In van Helten and Cassis 1990.

1997. *Big Business: The European Experience in the Twentieth Century*. Oxford.

Cassis, Y., Feldman, G. D. and Olsson, U., eds. 1995. *The Evolution of Financial Institutions and Markets in Twentieth Century Europe*. Aldershot.

Casson, M. 1999. The economics of the family firm. *Scandinavian Economic History Review* 47: 10–23.

Chandler, A. D. 1977. *The Visible Hand: The Managerial Revolution in American Business*. Cambridge, MA.

1990. *Scale and Scope: The Dynamics of Industrial Capitalism*. Cambridge, MA.

Chapman, A. assisted by Knight, R. 1953. *Wages and Salaries in the United Kingdom, 1920–1938*. Cambridge.

Chapman, S. D. 1984. *The Rise of Merchant Banking.*

Charles, R. 1973. *The Development of Industrial Relations in Britain, 1911–1939.*

Checkland, S. G. 1983. *British Public Policy, 1776–1939: An Economic, Social and Political Perspective*. Cambridge.

Church, R. 1979. *Herbert Austin: The British Motor Car Industry to 1941.*

Clapham, J. H. 1932. *An Economic History of Modern Britain: Free Trade and Steel, 1850–1886*. Cambridge.

1938. *An Economic History of Modern Britain: Machines and National Rivalries, 1887–1914*. Cambridge.

Clark, C. 1940. *Conditions of Economic Progress.*

Clarke, P. 1996. *Hope and Glory: Britain 1900–1990.*

Clavin, P. 2000. *The Great Depression in Europe 1929–1939*. New York.

Clay, H. 1929. The public regulation of wages in Great Britain. *Economic Journal* 39: 323–43.

Clegg, H. A. 1970. *The System of Industrial Relations in Great Britain*. Oxford.

Clegg, H. A., Fox, A. and Thompson, A. F. 1964. *A History of British Trade Unions since 1889*, I.

Clemens, M. A. and Williamson, J. G. 2001. Wealth bias in the first global capital market boom, 1870–1913. Revised. NBER, Cambridge, MA, working paper 8028.

Coale, A. J. and Cotts Watkins, S., eds. 1986. *The Decline of Fertility in Europe.*

Cohen, D. and Soto, M. 2001. Growth and human capital: good data, good results. CEPR, London, discussion paper 3025.

Cole, G. D. H., ed. 1935. *Studies in Capital and Investment.*

Coleman, D. C. 1973. Gentlemen and players. *Economic History Review* 26: 92–116.

Coleman, D. C. and Macleod C. 1986. Attitudes to new techniques: British businessmen, 1800–1950. *Economic History Review* 39: 588–611.

Collins, B. and Robbins, K., eds. 1990. *British Culture and Economic Decline.*

Collins, E. J. T. 1975. Dietary change and cereal consumption in Britain in the nineteenth century. *Agricultural History Review* 23: 97–115.

2000a. Agriculture in the industrial state. In Collins 2000b.

Collins, E. J. T., ed. 2000b. *The Agrarian History of England and Wales*, VII: *1850–1914*. Cambridge.

Collins, E. J. T. and Jones, E. L. 1967. Sectoral advance in English agriculture, 1850–80. *Agricultural History Review* 15: 65–81.

Collins, M. 1989. The banking crisis of 1878. *Economic History Review* 42: 504–27.

1990. English bank lending and the financial crisis of the 1870s. *Business History* 32: 198–224.

1991. *Banks and Industrial Finance in Britain, 1870–1939*. Basingstoke.

1994. The growth of the firm in the domestic banking sector. In Kirby and Rose 1994.

1995. *Banks and Industrial Finance in Britain, 1800–1939*. Cambridge.

1998. English bank development within a European context, 1870–1939. *Economic History Review* 51: 1–24.

Collins, M. and Baker, M. 1999. English industrial distress before 1914 and the response of the banks. *European Review of Economic History* 3: 1–24.

2001. Sectoral differences in English bank asset structures and the impact of mergers, 1860–1913. *Business History* 43: 1–28.

Committee on Industry and Trade, 1927. *Report*.

1928. *Survey of the Textile Industries*.

Constantine, S. 1990. *Emigrants and Empire: British Settlement in the Dominions between the Wars*. Manchester.

Coopey, R. and Clarke, D. 1995. *3i: Fifty Years Investing in Industry*. Oxford.

Copeman, G. H. 1955. *Leaders of British Industry*.

Coppock, D. J. 1956. The climacteric of the 1890s: a critical note. *Manchester School of Economic and Social Studies* 24: 1–31.

1961. The causes of the great depression, 1873–1896. *Manchester School of Economic and Social Studies* 29: 205–32.

Coppock, J. T. 1976. The changing face of England: 1850–circa 1900. In Darby 1976.

Corner, D. L. and Burton, H. 1963. *Investment Trusts and Unit Trusts in Britain and America*.

Cottrell, P. L. 1975. *British Overseas Investment in the Nineteenth Century*.

1980. *Industrial Finance, 1830–1914: The Finance and Organization of English Manufacturing Industry*.

1981. The steamship on the Mersey, 1815–80: investment and ownership. In P. L. Cottrell and D. H. Aldcroft, eds., *Shipping Trade and Commerce: Essays in Memory of Ralph Davis*. Leicester.

1988. Credit, morals and sunspots: the financial boom of the 1860s and trade cycle theory. In Cottrell and Moggridge 1988.

1992a. The domestic commercial banks and the City of London, 1870–1939. In Y. Cassis, ed., *Finance and Financiers in European History 1880–1960*. Cambridge.

1992b. Liverpool shipowners, the Mediterranean, and the transition from sail to steam during the mid-nineteenth century. In L. Fischer, ed., *From Wheel House to Counting House: Essays in Maritime History in Honour of Professor Peter Davies*, Research in Maritime History, 2.

1997. Finance and the germination of the British corporate economy. In Cottrell et al. 1997.

2002. Britannia's sovereign: banks in the finance of British shipbuilding and shipping, c. 1830–1894. In L. M. Akveld, F. R. Loomeijer and M. Hahn-Pedersen, eds., *Financing the Maritime Sector: Proceedings from the Fifth North Sea History Conference, Rotterdam 1997*. Esbjerg.

Cottrell, P. L. and Moggridge, D. E., eds. 1988. *Money and Power: Essays in Honour of L. S. Pressnell*.

Cottrell, P. L. and Newton, L. 1999. Banking liberalization in England and Wales, 1826–1844. In R. Sylla, R. Tilly and G. Tortella, eds., *The State, the Financial System and Economic Modernization*. Cambridge.

Cottrell, P., Teichova, A. and Yuzawa, T., eds. 1997. *Finance in the Age of the Corporate Economy*. Aldershot.

Court, W. H. B. 1945. Problems of the British coal industry beween the wars. *Economic History Review* 15: 1–24.
Crafts, N. F. R. 1979. Victorian Britain did fail. *Economic History Review* 32: 533–7.
1985. *British Economic Growth during the Industrial Revolution*. Oxford.
1987. Long-term unemployment in Britain in the 1930s. *Economic History Review* 40: 85–101.
1988. The assessment: British economic growth over the long run. *Oxford Review of Economic Policy* 4: 1–21.
1989a. Long-term unemployment and the wage equation in Britain 1925–1939. *Economica* 56: 247–54
1989b. Revealed comparative advantage in manufacturing, 1899–1950. *Journal of European Economic History* 18: 127–37.
1995. Exogenous or endogenous growth? The industrial revolution reconsidered. *Journal of Economic History* 55: 745–72.
1997a. Some dimensions of the 'quality of life' during the British industrial revolution. *Economic History Review* 50: 617–39.
1997b. The human development index and changes in standards of living: some historical comparisons. *European Review of Economic History* 1: 299–322.
1998. Forging ahead and falling behind: the rise and relative decline of the first industrial nation. *Journal of Economic Perspectives* 122: 193–210.
1999. Economic growth in the twentieth century. *Oxford Review of Economic Policy* 15: 18–34.
2002. *Britain's Relative Economic Performance, 1870–1999*.
Crafts, N. F. R., Leybourne, S. J. and Mills, T. C. 1989. The climacteric in late-Victorian Britain and France: a reappraisal of the evidence. *Journal of Applied Econometrics* 4: 103–17.
Crafts, N. F. R. and Mills, T. C. 1996a. Europe's golden age: an econometric investigation of changing trend rates of growth. In van Ark and Crafts 1996.
1996b. Trend growth in British industrial output, 1700–1913: a reappraisal. *Explorations in Economic History* 33: 277–95.
Crafts, N. F. R. and Thomas, M. 1986. Comparative advantage in UK manufacturing trades, 1910–1935. *Economic Journal* 96: 629–45.
Crafts, N. F. R. and Toniolo, G., eds. 1996. *Economic Growth in Europe since 1945*. Cambridge.
Crafts, N. F. R. and Venables, A. J. 2001. Globalization in history: a geographical perspective. CEPR, London, discussion paper 3079.
Craigie, P. G. 1883. Statistics of agricultural production. *Journal of the Royal Statistical Society* 46: 1–47.
Cramond, R. D. 1966. *Housing Policy in Scotland 1919–1964: A Study in State Assistance*. Edinburgh.
Crisp, O. 1967. Russia, 1860–1914. In R. Cameron, ed., *Banking in the Early Stages of Industrialization*. Oxford.
Cronin, J. E. 1991. *The Politics of State Expansion: War, State and Society in Twentieth-Century Britain*.
Crouch, C. 1993. *Industrial Relations and European State Traditions*. Oxford.
Crouzet, F. 1982. *The Victorian Economy*.
Crowther, M. A. 1981. *The Workhouse System 1834–1929: The History of an English Social Institution*.
Damer, S. 1980. State, class and housing: Glasgow 1885–1919. In Melling 1980b.
Daniels, G. W. and Jewkes, J. 1928. The post-war depression and the Lancashire cotton industry. *Journal of the Royal Statistical Society* 91: 153–206.
Darby, H. C., ed. 1976. *A New Historical Geography of England after 1600*. Cambridge.
Dasgupta, P. and Weale, M. 1992. On measuring the quality of life. *World Development* 20: 119–31.
Daunton, M. J. 2001. *Trusting Leviathan: The Politics of Taxation in Britain, 1799–1914*. Cambridge.

2002. *Just Taxes: The Politics of Taxation in Britain, 1914–1979*. Cambridge.
Daunton, M. J., ed. 2000. *The Cambridge Urban History of Britain, III: 1840–1950*. Cambridge.
Davenport-Hines, R. P. T. 1984. *Dudley Docker: The Life and Times of a Trade Warrior*. Cambridge.
David, P. A. 1975. *Technical Choice, Innovation and Economic Growth*. Cambridge.
1985. Clio and the economics of QWERTY. *American Economic Review* 75: 332–7.
1997. Path dependence and the quest for historical economics: one more chorus of the ballad of Qwerty. University of Oxford, discussion papers in economic and social history 20.
David, P. A. and Wright, G. 1997. Increasing returns and the genesis of American resource abundance. *Industrial and Corporate Change* 6: 203–45.
1999. Early twentieth century productivity growth dynamics: an inquiry into the economic history of 'our ignorance', University of Oxford, discussion papers in economic history 33.
Davies, M. F. 1909. *Life in an English Village*.
Davis, L. E. 1966. The capital markets and industrial concentration: the U.S. and the U.K., a comparative study. *Economic History Review* 19: 255–72.
Davis, L. E. and Gallman, R. E. 2001. *Evolving Financial Markets and International Capital Flows*. Cambridge and New York.
Davis, L. E. and Huttenback, R. A. 1986. *Mammon and the Pursuit of Empire: The Political Economy of British Imperialism, 1860–1912*. Cambridge.
Davis, L. E., Hughes, J. R. T. and McDougall, D. M. 1969. *American Economic History*, 3rd edn. Homewood, IL.
De Long, B. 1991. Did Morgan's men add value? In P. Temin, ed., *Inside the Business Enterprise: Historical Perspectives on the Use of Information*. Chicago.
Dearle, N. B. 1908. *Problems of Unemployment in the London Building Trades*.
Dennet, L. 1979. *The Charterhouse Group, 1925–1979: A History*.
Dent, H. C. 1970. *1870–1970: Century of Growth in English Education*.
Devine, T. M. 1999. *The Scottish Nation 1700–2000*.
Dewey, P. E. 1975. Agricultural labour supply in England and Wales during the First World War. *Economic History Review* 28: 100–12.
1989. *British Agriculture in the First World War*.
1991. Production problems in British agriculture during the First World War. In Holderness and Turner 1991.
2000. Farm labour. In Collins 2000b.
Diamond, D. W. 1984. Financial intermediation and delegated monitoring. *Review of Economic Studies* 51: 393–414.
Diaper, S. 1986. Merchant banking in the interwar period: the case of Kleinwort, Sons and Co. *Business History* 28: 56–76.
1990. The Sperling Combine and the shipbuilding industry: merchant banking and industrial finance in the 1920s. In van Helten and Cassis 1990.
Dietrich, M. 1997. Strategic lock-in as a human issue: the role of professional orientation. In L. Magnusson and J. Ottosson, eds., *Evolutionary Economics and Path Dependence*. Cheltenham.
Digby, A. and Searby, P. 1981. *Children, School and Society in Nineteenth-Century England*.
Dimsdale, N. H. 1981. British monetary policy and the exchange rate. *Oxford Economic Papers* 33: 306–49.
1984. Unemployment and real wages in the inter-war period. *National Institute Economic Review* 110: 94–103.
Dimsdale, N. H. and Horsewood, N. 1995. Fiscal policy and employment in interwar Britain: some evidence from a new model. *Oxford Economic Papers* 47: 369–96.
Dimsdale, N. H., Nickell, S. J. and Horsewood, N. 1989a. Employment and wage flexibility in interwar Britain. University of Oxford, Institute of Economics and Statistics, applied economics discussion paper 71.

1989b. Real wages and unemployment in Britain during the 1930s. *Economic Journal* 99: 271–92.

Dixit, A. 1992. Investment and hysteresis. *Journal of Economic Perspectives* 6: 107–32.

Dixit, A. and Pindyck, R. S. 1994. *Investment under Uncertainty*. Princeton.

Dobbin, F. 1994. *Forging Industrial Policy: The United States, Britain and France in the Railway Age*. Cambridge.

Dowd, K. 1996. *Competition and Finance: A Reinterpretation of Financial and Monetary Economics*. Basingstoke.

Dowie, J. A. 1968. Growth in the interwar period: some more arithmetic. *Economic History Review* 21: 93–112.

1975. 1919–20 is in need of attention. *Economic History Review* 28: 429–50.

Drescher, L. 1955. The development of agricultural production in Great Britain and Ireland from the early nineteenth century. *Manchester School* 23: 153–75.

Drummond, I. 1974. *Imperial Economic Policy 1917–1939: Studies in Expansion and Protection*.

Dunlop, J. T. 1938. The movement of real and money wage rates. *Economic Journal* 48: 413–34.

Dunning, J. H. 1983. Changes in the level and structure of international production: the last one hundred years. In M. Casson, ed., *The Growth of International Business*.

Dutton, H. I. 1984. *The Patent System and Inventive Activity*. Manchester.

Easterlin, R. A. 1981. Why isn't the whole world developed? *Journal of Economic History* 41: 1–19.

Ebery, M. and Preston, B. 1972. Domestic service in late Victorian and Edwardian Britain, 1871–1914. *Geographical Papers*, 42. Reading.

Economic Advisory Council 1930. Committee on the Cotton Industry, *Report* Cmd 3615.

Edelstein, M. 1976. Realized rates of return on UK home and foreign investment in the age of high imperialism. *Explorations in Economic History* 13: 283–329.

1982. *Overseas Investment in the Age of High Imperialism: The UK 1850–1914*.

Edgerton, D. E. H. 1994. British industrial R & D, 1900–1970. *Journal of European Economic History* 23: 49–67.

1996. *Science, Technology and the British Industrial 'Decline', 1870–1970*. Cambridge.

Edgerton, D. E. H. and Horrocks, S. M. 1994. British industrial research and development before 1945. *Economic History Review* 47: 213–38.

Edwards, J. D. 1978. *History of Public Accounting in the United States*. Tuscaloosa, AL.

Edwards, J. R. 1989. *A History of Financial Accounting*.

Edwards, J. R. and Fischer, K. 1993. *Banks, Finance and Investment in Germany*. Cambridge.

Edwards, J. R. and Ogilvie, S. 1996. Universal banks and German industrialisation: a reappraisal. *Economic History Review* 49: 427–46.

Eichengreen, B. 1987. Unemployment in interwar Britain: dole or doldrums? *Oxford Economic Papers* 39: 597–623.

1992. *Golden Fetters: The Gold Standard and the Great Depression, 1919–1939*. New York.

1994. The inter-war economy in a European mirror. In Floud and McCloskey 1994.

1996. Institutions and economic growth: Europe after World War II. In Crafts and Toniolo 1996.

Eichengreen, B. and Hatton, T. J., eds. 1988. *Interwar Unemployment in International Perspective*. Dordrecht.

Eichengreen, B. and Jeanne, O. 2000. Currency crisis and unemployment: sterling in 1931. In P. Krugman, ed., *Currency Crises*. Chicago.

Elbaum, B. 1989. Why apprenticeship persisted in Britain but not in the United States. *Journal of Economic History* 49: 337–49.

Elbaum, B. and Lazonick, W., eds. 1986. *The Decline of the British Economy*. Oxford.

Emy, H. V. 1972. The impact of financial policy on English party politics before 1914. *Historical Journal* 15: 103–31.

Engerman, Stanley, 1997. The standard of living debate in international perspective: measures and indicators. In Steckel and Floud 1997.

Erickson, C. 1972. Who were the English and Scottish emigrants in the 1880s? In D. V. Glass and R. Revelle, eds., *Population and Social Change.*

Estevadeordal, A., Frantz, B. and Taylor, A. M. 2002. The rise and fall of world trade, 1870–1939. NBER, Cambridge, MA, working paper 9318.

Fairlie, S. 1965. The nineteenth-century corn law reconsidered. *Economic History Review* 18: 562–75.

1969. The corn laws and British wheat production, 1829–76. *Economic History Review* 22: 88–116.

Farnie, D. A. 1979. *The English Cotton Industry and the World Market, 1815–1896.* Oxford.

Feinstein, C. H. 1965. *Domestic Capital Formation in the United Kingdom, 1920–1938.* Cambridge.

1972. *National Income, Expenditure and Output in the UK, 1855–1965.* Cambridge.

1976. *Statistical Tables of National Income, Expenditure and Output in the UK, 1855–1965.* Cambridge.

1988a. Agriculture. In Feinstein and Pollard 1988.

1988b. National statistics, 1760–1920. In Feinstein and Pollard 1988.

1990a. Benefits of backwardness and costs of continuity. In A. Graham and A. Seldon, eds., *Government and Economies in the Postwar World: Economic Policies and Comparative Performance, 1945–1985.*

1990b. Britain's overseas investments in 1913. *Economic History Review* 43: 288–95.

1990c. New estimates of average earnings in the United Kingdom, 1880–1913. *Economic History Review* 43: 595–632.

1990d. What really happened to real wages?: trends in wages, prices, and productivity in the United Kingdom, 1880–1913. *Economic History Review* 43: 329–55.

1991a. A new look at the cost of living 1870–1914. In Foreman-Peck 1991.

1991b. Variety and volatility: some aspects of the labour market in Britain, 1880–1913. In C. Holmes and A. Booth, eds., *Economy and Society: European Industrialisation and its Social Consequences.* Leicester.

1995a. Changes in nominal wages, the cost of living and real wages in the United Kingdom over the two centuries, 1780–1990. In P. Scholliers and V. Zamagni, eds., *Labour's Reward: Real Wages and Economic Change in 19th- and 20th-century Europe.* Aldershot.

Feinstein, C. H., ed. 1995b. *Banking, Currency and Finance in Europe between the Wars.* Oxford.

Feinstein, C. H., Matthews, R. C. O. and Odling-Smee, J. C. 1982. The timing of the climacteric and its sectoral incidence in the UK, 1873–1913. In Kindleberger and di Tella 1982.

Feinstein, C. H. and Pollard, S., eds. 1988. *Studies in Capital Formation in the United Kingdom, 1750–1920.* Oxford.

Field, A. J. 1985. On the unimportance of machinery. *Explorations in Economic History* 22: 378–401.

Fieldhouse, D. K. 1973. *Economics and Empire, 1830–1914.*

Finnie, D. 1931. *Finding Capital for Business.*

Fisher, A. G. B. 1952. A note on tertiary production. *Economic Journal* 62: 820–34.

Fishlow, Albert. 1961. The Trustee Savings Banks, 1817–1861. *Journal of Economic History* 21: 26–40.

Fitzgerald, R. 1995. *Rowntree and the Marketing Revolution 1862–1969.* Cambridge.

Flanagan, R. J., Soskice, D. W. and Ulman, L. 1983. *Unionism, Economic Stability and Incomes Policies: The European Experience.* Washington DC.

Fletcher, T. W. 1961a. The great depression of English agriculture, 1873–1896. *Economic History Review* 13: 417–32. Reprinted in Minchinton 1968 and Perry 1973.

1961b. Lancashire livestock farming during the great depression. *Agricultural History Review* 9: 17–42. Reprinted in Perry 1973.

Flinn, M. W., ed. 1977. *Scottish Population History from the Seventeenth Century to the 1930s*. Cambridge.

Flora, P. and Alber, J. 1981. Modernization, democratization and the development of welfare states in western Europe. In P. Flora and A. J. Heidenheimer, eds., *The Development of the Welfare States in Europe and America*. New Brunswick, NJ.

Florence, P. S. 1953. *The Logic of British and American Industry*.

1957. *Industry and the State*.

Floud, R. 1982. Technical education and economic performance: Britain 1850–1914. *Albion* 14: 153–71.

1998. *Height, Weight and Body Mass of the British Population since 1820*. NBER, Cambridge, MA, working paper series on historical factors in long run growth, historical paper 108.

Floud, Roderick and Harris, Bernard. 1997. Health, height and welfare: Britain, 1700–1980. In Steckel and Floud 1997.

Floud, R. and McCloskey, D. N., eds. 1981. *The Economic History of Britain since 1700*, 1st edn., Cambridge.

1994. *The Economic History of Britain since 1700*, 2nd edn., Cambridge.

Floud, Roderick, Wachter, Kenneth and Gregory, Annabel. 1990. *Height, Health and History: Nutritional Status in the United Kingdom, 1750–1980*. Cambridge.

Fogel, Robert W. 1991. The conquest of high mortality and hunger in Europe and America: timing and mechanisms. In Patrice Higonnet, David S. Landes and H. Rosovsky, eds., *Favorites of Fortune: Technology, Growth, and Economic Development since the Industrial Revolution*. Cambridge, MA.

Fohlin, C. 1997. Bank securities holdings and industrial finance before World War I: Britain and Germany compared. *Business and Economic History* 26: 463–75.

1999. The rise of interlocking directorates in imperial Germany. *Economic History Review* 52: 307–33.

2001. The balancing act of German universal banks and English deposit banks. *Business History* 43: 1–24.

Ford, P. 1934. *Work and Wealth in a Modern Port: An Economic Survey of Southampton*.

Foreman-Peck, J. S. 1979. Tariff protection and economies of scale: the British motor industry before 1939. *Oxford Economic Papers* 31: 237–57.

1981a. The British tariff and industrial protection in the 1930s: an alternative model. *Economic History Review* 34: 132–9.

1981b. Exit, voice and loyalty as responses to interwar decline: the Rover company in the interwar years. *Business History* 23: 191–207.

1982. The American challenge of the twenties: multinationals and the European motor industry. *Journal of Economic History* 42: 865–81.

1994. Industry and industrial organisation in the inter-war years. In Floud and McCloskey 1994.

Foreman-Peck, J. S., ed. 1991. *New Perspectives on the Late Victorian Economy*. Cambridge.

Foreman-Peck, J. S., Boccaletti, S. E. and Nicholas, T. 1998. Entrepreneurs and business performance in nineteenth century France. *European Review of Economic History* 2: 235–62.

Foreman-Peck, J. S. and Hannah, L. 1999. Britain: from economic liberalism to socialism – and back? In J. S. Foreman-Peck and G. Federico, eds., *European Industrial Policy: The Twentieth-Century Experience*. Oxford.

Foreman-Peck, J. S. and Millward, R. 1994. *Public and Private Ownership of British Industry, 1820–1990*. Oxford.

Foster, John. 1974. *Class Struggle and the Industrial Revolution: Early Industrial Capitalism in Three English Towns*.

Fox, R. and Guagnini, A., eds. 1993. *Education, Technology and Industrial Performance in Europe, 1850–1939*. Cambridge.

Foxwell, H. S. 1917. The financing of industry and trade. *Economic Journal* 27: 502–22.

Foxwell, H. S., ed. 1919. *Papers on Current Finance.*

Frankel, M. 1957. *British and American Manufacturing Productivity*. Urbana, IL.

Frankel, S. H. 1967. *Investment and the Return to Equity Capital in the South African Gold Mining Industry, 1887–1965*. Oxford.

Fraser, H. F. 1933. *Great Britain and the Gold Standard.*

Freeman, Mark. 2000. Investigating rural poverty 1870–1914: problems of conceptualisation and methodology. In J. Bradshaw and R. Sainsbury, eds., *Getting the Measure of Poverty: The Early Legacy of Seebohm Rowntree*. Aldershot.

Freeman, M. J. and Aldcroft, D. H., eds. 1988. *Transport in the Victorian Age*. Manchester.

French, M. and Phillips, J. 2000. *Cheated not Poisoned?: Food Regulation in the United Kingdom, 1875–1938*. Manchester.

Freyer, T. A. 1992. *Regulating Big Business: Antitrust in Great Britain and America, 1880–1990*. Cambridge.

Friedlander, D. 1992. Occupational structure, wages and migration in late nineteenth century England and Wales. *Economic Development and Cultural Change* 40: 295–318.

Fry, G. K. 1979. *The Growth of Government: The Development of Ideas about the Role of the State and the Machinery and Functions of Government in Britain since 1780.*

Gallagher, J. and Robinson, R. 1953. The imperialism of free trade. *Economic History Review* 6: 1–15.

Gamble, A. M. 1990. *Britain in Decline: Economic Policy, Political Strategy and the British State*, 3rd edn.

2000. Economic governance. In J. Pierre, ed., *Debating Governance: Authority, Steering and Democracy*. Oxford.

Garrett, E., Reid, A. Schurer, K. and Szreter, S. 2001. *Changing Family Size in England and Wales: Place, Class and Demography, 1891–1911*. Cambridge.

Garside, W. R. 1979. *The Measurement of Unemployment: Methods and Sources, 1850–1979*. Oxford.

1990. *British Unemployment 1919–39: A Study in Public Policy*. Cambridge.

Garside, W. R. and Greaves, J. I. 1996. The Bank of England and industrial intervention in interwar Britain. *Financial History Review* 3: 69–86.

Garside, W. R. and Hatton, T. J. 1985. Keynesian policy and British unemployment in the 1930s. *Economic History Review* 38: 83–8.

Gartner, L. P. 1960. *The Jewish Immigrant in England, 1870–1914*. Detroit, MI.

Gazeley, Ian. 1989. The cost of living for urban workers in late Victorian and Edwardian Britain. *Economic History Review* 42: 207–21.

2003. *Poverty in Britain, 1900–1965.*

Gemmell, N. and Wardley, P. 1990. The contribution of services to British economic growth, 1856–1913. *Explorations in Economic History* 27: 299–321.

Gerschenkron, A. 1962. *Economic Backwardness in Historical Perspective*. Cambridge, MA.

Gilb, C. L. 1966. *Hidden Hierarchies: The Professions and Government*. New York.

Gilbert, B. B. 1966. *The Evolution of National Insurance in Great Britain: The Origins of the Welfare State.*

1970. *British Social Policy, 1914–1939.*

Glass, D. V. 1938. Changes in fertility in England and Wales, 1851–1931. In L. Hogben, ed. *Political Arithmetic.*

Glucksmann, M. 1990. *Women Assemble: Women Workers and the New Industries in Inter-war Britain.*

Glynn, S. and Booth, A. 1992. The emergence of mass unemployment: some questions of precision. *Economic History Review* 45: 731–8.

Godley, A. 1996. Immigrant entrepreneurs and the emergence of London's East End as an industrial district. *London Journal* 21: 38–45.

Goldin, C. 1998. America's graduation from high school: the evolution and spread of secondary schooling in the twentieth century. *Journal of Economic History* 58: 345–74.

2001. The human-capital century and American leadership: virtues of the past. *Journal of Economic History* 61: 263–92.

Goldin, C. and Katz, L. 1996. Technology, skill, and the wage structure: insights from the past. *American Economic Review, Papers and Proceedings* 86: 252–7.

Goldsmith, R. W. 1966. *The Determinants of Financial Structure*. Paris.

1969. *Financial Structure and Development*. New Haven, CT.

Goldthorpe, J. H. 2000. *On Sociology: Numbers, Narratives, and the Integration of Research and Theory*. Oxford.

Goodhart, C. A. E. 1972 (1986). *The Business of Banking, 1890–1914*.

Goodhart, C. A. E. 1989. *Money, Information and Uncertainty*, 2nd edn.

Gordon, P., Aldrich, R. and Dean, D. 1991. *Education and Policy in England in the Twentieth Century*.

Gosden, P. H. J. H. 1961. *The Friendly Societies in England, 1815–1875*. Manchester.

Gourvish, T. R. 1979. The standard of living, 1890–1914. In Alan O'Day, ed., *The Edwardian Age: Conflict and Stability, 1900–1914*.

1980. *Railways and the British economy, 1830–1914*.

1987. British business and the transition to a corporate economy: entrepreneurship and management structures. *Business History* 29: 18–45.

Gowers, R. and Hatton, T. J. 1997. The origins and early impact of the minimum wage in agriculture. *Economic History Review* 50: 82–103.

Grant, A. T. K. 1967. *A Study of the Capital Market in Britain from 1919–1936*, 2nd edn.

Gray, R. Q. 1976. *The Labour Aristocracy in Victorian Edinburgh*. Oxford.

1981. *The Aristocracy of Labour in Nineteenth-Century Britain, c. 1850–1914*.

Greasley, D. and Oxley, L. 1995. Balanced versus compromise estimates of UK GDP 1870–1913. *Explorations in Economic History* 32: 262–72.

1996. Discontinuities in competitiveness: the impact of the First World War on British industry. *Economic History Review* 49: 82–100.

Great Britain, Board of Trade. 1915. *Seventeenth Abstract of Labour Statistics*.

Great Britain, Office of Population Censuses and Surveys. 1987. *Mortality Statistics: Review of the Registrar General on Deaths in England and Wales, 1985*. Series DH1 no. 17.

Greaves, J. I. 2000. 'Visible hands' and the rationalisation of the British cotton industry. *Textile History* 31: 102–22.

Green, A. and Urquhart, M. C. 1976. Factor and commodity flows in the international economy of 1870–1914: a multi-country view. *Journal of Economic History* 36: 217–52.

Green, E. 1985. Very private enterprise: ownership and finance in British shipping, 1925–1940. In T. Yui and K. Kakagawa, eds., *Business History of Shipping: Strategy and Structure*. Tokyo.

Greenleaf, W. H. 1983. *The British Political Tradition, I: The Rise of Collectivism*.

Greenwood, Walter. 1933. *Love on the Dole*.

Grossman, R. S. 1994. The shoe that didn't drop: explaining banking stability during the great depression. *Journal of Economic History* 54: 654–82.

1999. Rearranging deck chairs on the Titanic: English banking concentration and efficiency, 1870–1914. *European Review of Economic History* 3: 323–49.

Grove, J. W. 1962. *Government and Industry in Britain*.

Guinnane, T. W. 2002. Delegated monitors large and small: Germany's banking system, 1800–1914. *Journal of Economic Literature* 40: 73–124.

Gunn, S. 1988. The 'failure' of the Victorian middle class: a critique. In J. Wolff and J. Seed, eds., *The Culture of Capital*. Manchester.

Gunter, C. and Maloney, J. 1999. Did Gladstone make a difference?: rhetoric and reality in mid-Victorian finance. *Accounting, Business and Financial History* 9: 325–47.

Habakkuk, H. J. 1962. *American and British Technology in the Nineteenth Century*. Cambridge.

1994. *Marriage, Debt, and the Estates System: English Landownership 1650–1950*. Oxford.

Hagen, E. E. 1962. *On the Theory of Social Change*. Homewood, IL.
Hall, A. R. 1963. *The London Capital Market and Australia 1870–1914*. Canberra.
Hall, Peter. 1976. England circa 1900. In Darby 1976.
Hall, P. A. 1986. *Governing the Economy: The Politics of State Intervention in Britain and France*. Cambridge.
Halsey, A. H., ed. 1988. *Trends in British Society since 1900: A Guide to the Changing Social Structure of Britain*, 2nd edn.
Hannah, L. 1974. Takeover bids in Britain before 1950. *Business History* 16: 65–77.
1976. *The Rise of the Corporate Economy*.
1983. *The Rise of the Corporate Economy*, 2nd edn.
Hannah, L. and Kay, J. 1977. *Concentration in Modern Industry: Theory, Measurement and the UK Experience*.
Hardach, G. 1977. *The First World War, 1914–1918*.
Harley, C. K. 1974. Skilled labour and the choice of technique in Edwardian industry. *Explorations in Economic History* 11: 391–414.
1976. Goschen's conversion of the national debt and the yield on Consols. *Economic History Review* 29: 101–6.
1980. Transportation, the world wheat trade and Kuznets cycle. *Explorations in Economic History* 17: 218–50.
1986. Late nineteenth century transportation, trade and settlement. In J. Schneider, ed., *The Emergence of a World Economy, 1500–1914, II: 1850–1914*. Wiesbaden.
1989. Review of William P. Kennedy, *Industrial Structure, Capital Markets and Origins of British Economic Decline*. *American Historical Review* 94: 1380.
1992. The world food economy and pre World War I Argentina. In Broadberry and Crafts 1992b.
1999. The North Atlantic meat trade and its institutional consequences, 1870–1913. Working paper, University of Western Ontario.
Harley, C. K., ed. 1995. *The Integration of the World Economy, 1850–1914*. Cheltenham.
Harley, C. K. and Crafts, N. F. R. 2000. Simulating the two views of the industrial revolution. *Journal of Economic History* 60: 819–41.
Harling, P. 2001. *The Modern British State: An Historical Introduction*. Cambridge.
Harnetty, P. 1972. *Imperialism and Free Trade: Lancashire and India in the Mid-Nineteenth Century*. Vancouver.
Harris, B. 1988. Unemployment, insurance and health in interwar Britain. In Eichengreen and Hatton 1988.
Harris, J. 1972. *Unemployment and Politics 1886–1914: A Study of English Social Policy*. Oxford.
1990a. Economic knowledge and British social policy. In M. O. Furner and B. E. Supple, eds., *The State and Economic Knowledge: The American and British Experiences*. Cambridge.
1990b. Society and state in twentieth-century Britain. In Thompson 1990b.
Harrison, A. E. 1981. Joint-stock company flotation in the cycle, motor-vehicle and related industries, 1882–1914. *Business History* 23: 165–90.
1982. F. Hopper & Co.: the problems of capital supply in the cycle manufacturing industry 1891–1914. *Business History* 24: 3–23.
Hart, O. 1995. *Firms, Contracts and Financial Structure*. Oxford.
Hartmann, H. 1959. *Authority and Organization in German Management*. Westport, CT.
Hartwell, R. M. 1973. The service revolution: the growth of services in the modern economy. In C. Cipolla, ed., *The Industrial Revolution, 1750–1914*.
Harvie, C. 1994. *Scotland and Nationalism: Scottish Society and Politics 1707–1994*.
Hatton, T. J. 1983. Unemployment benefits and the macroeconomics of the interwar labour market: a further analysis. *Oxford Economic Papers* 35: 486–505.
1985. The British labour market in the 1920s: a test of the search-turnover approach. *Explorations in Economic History* 22: 257–70.
1986. Structural aspects of unemployment in Britain between the world wars. *Research in Economic History* 10: 55–92.

1988a. Profit sharing in British industry, 1865–1913. *Journal of Industrial Organisation* 6: 69–90.
1988b. A quarterly model of the labour market in interwar Britain. *Oxford Bulletin of Economics and Statistics* 50: 1–26.
1990. The demand for British exports, 1870–1914. *Economic History Review* 43: 576–94.
1997. Trade boards and minimum wages, 1909–39. *Economic Affairs* 17: 22–8.
2002. Can productivity growth explain the NAIRU? CEPR, London, discussion paper 3424.
Hatton, T. J. and Bailey, R. E. 1998. Poverty and the welfare state in interwar London. *Oxford Economic Papers* 50: 576–606.
Hatton, T. J. and Bailey, R. E. 2002. Unemployment incidence in interwar London. *Economica* 69: 631–54.
Hatton, T. J. and Williamson, J. G. 1998. *The Age of Mass Migration: An Economic Analysis*. Oxford.
Hawke, G. R. 1970. *Railways and Economic Growth in England and Wales, 1840–1870*. Oxford.
Hawke, G. R. and Higgins, J. P. P. 1981. Transport and social overhead capital. In Floud and McCloskey 1981.
Hay, J. R. 1975. *The Origins of the Liberal Welfare Reforms 1906–1914*.
Haydu, J. 1988. Employers, unions, and American exceptionalism: pre-World War I open shops in the machine trades in comparative perspective. *International Review of Social History* 33: 25–41.
Heim, C. 1984a. Limits to intervention: the Bank of England and industrial diversification in the depressed areas. *Economic History Review* 38: 533–50.
1984b. Structural transformation and the demand for new labor in advanced economies: interwar Britain. *Journal of Economic History* 44: 585–95.
1986. Interwar responses to industrial decline. In Elbaum and Lazonick 1986.
Hennock, E. P. 1963. Finance and politics in urban local government in England, 1835–1900. *Historical Journal* 6: 212–25.
1973. *Fit and Proper Persons: Ideal and Reality in Nineteenth-Century Urban Government*.
Herbert, R. 1959. Statistics of live stock and dead meat for consumption in the metropolis. *Journal of the Royal Agricultural Society of England* 1st ser. 20: 473–81.
Herrigel, G. 1996. *Industrial Constructions: The Sources of German Industrial Power*. Cambridge.
Hicks, J. R. 1930. An early history of industrial conciliation in England. *Economica* 10: 25–39.
Higgins, D. M. and Toms, J. S. 1997. Firm structure and financial performance: the Lancashire textile industry, c. 1884–c. 1960. *Accounting, Business and Financial History* 7: 195–232.
2001. Capital ownership, capital structure and capital markets: financial constraints and the decline of the Lancashire cotton textile industry, 1880–1965. *Journal of Industrial History* 4: 48–64.
Higgs, R. 1987. *Crisis and Leviathan: Critical Episodes in the Growth of American Government*. Oxford.
Hilferding, R. 1910. *Finance Capital: A Study of the Latest Phase of Capitalist Development*.
Hilgerdt, F. 1942. *The Network of Trade*. Geneva.
1945. *Industrialization and Foreign Trade*.
Hirschmann, A. O. 1970. *Exit, Voice and Loyalty: Responses to Decline in Firms, Organisations and States*. Cambridge, MA.
1982. *Shifting Involvements: Private Interest and Public Action*. Princeton, NJ.
HMSO 1910. *Report of the Royal Commission on the Poor Laws: Report by Rev. J. C. Pringle*. Cmd 5073.

1917. *Report of the Royal Commission on the Housing of the Industrial Population of Scotland, Rural and Urban*. Cd 8731.
1937. *Report of the Unemployment Insurance Statutory Committee*.
1952. *95th Report of the Commissioners of HM Inland Revenue*. Cmd 8726.
1961, 2001. *Annual Abstract of Statistics*, 98, 138.
1975. *Report of the Royal Commission on the Distribution of Income and Wealth: Report No 1*. Cmnd 6171.
Hobsbawm, E. J. 1968. *Industry and Empire: An Economic History of Britain since 1750*.
1975. *The Age of Capital, 1848–1875*. New York.
Hobson, J. A. 1902. *Imperialism: A Study*.
Hoffman, J. R. S. 1933. *Great Britain and the German Trade Rivalry, 1875–1914*.
Hoffmann, W. G. 1965. *Das Wachstum der deutschen Wirtschaft seit der Mitte des 19. Jahrhunderts*. Berlin.
Holderness, B. A. 1989. Prices, productivity, and output. In G. E. Mingay, ed., *The Agrarian History of England and Wales, VI: 1750–1850*. Cambridge.
Holderness, B. A. and Turner, M. E., eds. 1991. *Land, Labour and Agriculture, 1700–1920: Essays for Gordon Mingay*.
Holmes, A. R. and Green, E. 1986. *Midland: 150 years of Joint Stock Banking*.
Hopkins, A. G. 1973. *An Economic History of West Africa*.
Hounsell, D. A. 1984. *From the American system to Mass Production, 1800–1932*. Baltimore, MD.
Howe, A. C. 1984. *The Cotton Masters 1830–1860*. Oxford.
Howson, S. K. 1975. *Domestic Monetary Management in Britain, 1919–38*. Cambridge.
Hudson, P., ed. 2001. *Living Economic and Social History*. Glasgow.
Hughes, T. P. 1988. *Networks of Power: Electrification in Western Society, 1880–1930*. Baltimore, MD.
Hume, J. R. and Moss, M. S. 1979. *Beardmore: The History of a Scottish Industrial Giant*.
Hunt, B. C. 1936. *The Development of the Business Corporation in England 1800–1867*. Cambridge, MA.
Hunt, E. H. 1967. Labour productivity in English agriculture, 1850–1914. *Economic History Review* 20: 280–92.
1973. *Regional Wage Variations in Britain, 1850–1914*. Oxford.
1981. *British Labour History, 1815–1914*.
1986. Industrialization and regional inequality: wages in Britain. *Journal of Economic History* 46: 935–66.
Hunt, E. H., and Pam, S. J. 1997. Prices and structural response in English agriculture, 1873–1896. *Economic History Review* 50: 477–505.
2002. Responding to agricultural depression, 1873–96: managerial success, entrepreneurial failure? *Agricultural History Review*, 50: 225–52.
Hunter, J. 1976. *The Making of the Crofting Community*. Edinburgh.
Hurwitz, S. J. 1949. *State Intervention in Great Britain: A Study of Economic Control and Social Response, 1914–1919*. New York.
Imlah, A. 1958. *Economic Elements in the Pax Britannica*. Cambridge, MA.
Ingham, G. 1984. *Capitalism Divided: The City and Industry in British Social Development*.
Irwin, D. 1996. *Against the Tide: An Intellectual History of Free Trade*. Princeton, NJ.
2002. Interpreting the tariff-growth correlation of the late 19th century. *American Economic Review* 92: 165–9.
Jackson, P. M. 1993. Modelling public expenditure growth: an integrated approach. In N. Gemmell, ed., *The Growth of the Public Sector: Theories and International Evidence*. Aldershot.
Jaffe, A. B. 1988. Demand and supply influences in R and D intensity and productivity growth. *Review of Economics and Statistics* 72: 431–7.
James, J. A. 1983. Structural change in American manufacturing, 1850–1890. *Journal of Economic History* 43: 433–59.

James, J. A. and Skinner, J. S. 1985. The resolution of the labor-scarcity paradox. *Journal of Economic History* 45: 513–40.

Janeway, W. H. 1995–6. The 1931 sterling crisis and the independence of the Bank of England. *Journal of Post-Keynesian Economics* 43: 263–86.

Jarvis, R. 1959. Fractional shareholding in British merchant vessels with special reference to the 64ths. *Mariners Mirror*, 45.

Jefferys, J. B. 1949. *The Distribution of Consumer Goods*. Cambridge.

1954. *Retailing Trading in Britain, 1850–1950*. Cambridge.

1971. *Business Organisation in Great Britain since 1856*. New York.

Jefferys, J. B. and Walters, D. 1955. National income and expenditure of the United Kingdom, 1870–1952. In S. Kuznets, ed., *Studies in Income and Wealth*, V.

Jenks, L. H. 1927. *The Migration of British Capital to 1875*. New York.

Jobert, P. and Moss, M. S., eds. 1990. *The Birth and Death of Companies: An Historical Perspective*. Carnforth.

Johnman, L. and Murphy, H. 2002. *British Shipbuilding and the State since 1918*. Exeter.

Johnson, P. 1985. *Saving and Spending: The Working-Class Economy in Britain 1870–1939*. Oxford.

1993. Small debts and economic distress in England and Wales, 1857–1913. *Economic History Review* 46: 65–87.

1996. Economic development and industrial dynamism in Victorian London. *London Journal* 21: 27–37.

Johnson, P. and Nicholas, S. 1995. Male and female living standards in England and Wales, 1812–1857: evidence from criminal height records. *Economic History Review* 48: 470–81.

Johnston, R. 2000. *Clydeside Capital 1870–1920: A Social History of Employers*. East Linton.

Jones, C. I. 1995. Time series tests of endogenous growth models. *Quarterly Journal of Economics* 110: 495–525.

1999. Growth: with or without scale effects? *American Economic Review Papers and Proceedings* 89: 139–44.

Jones, D. Caradog, ed. 1934. *The Social Survey of Merseyside*, I.

Jones, E. L. 1964. *Seasons and Prices: The Role of the Weather in English Agricultural History*.

Jones, H. 1994. *Health and Society in Twentieth-Century Britain*.

Jones, M. A. 1973. The background to emigration from Britain in the nineteenth century. *Perspectives in American History* 7: 3–92.

Jones, R. 1987. *Wages and Employment Policy, 1936–1985*.

Jones, R. and Marriott, O. 1970. *Anatomy of a Merger: A History of GEC, AEI and English Electric*.

Jonker, J. and van Zanden, J. L. 1995. Method in the madness? Banking crises between the wars, an international comparison. In Feinstein 1995b.

Jordan, G. and Richardson, J. J. 1982. The British policy style or the logic of negotiation? In J. J. Richardson, ed., *Policy Styles in Western Europe*.

Joseph, L. 1911. *Industrial Finance: A Comparison between Home and Foreign Development*.

Kaldor, N. 1966. *Causes of the Slow Rate of Economic Growth in the United Kingdom*. Cambridge.

Kendrick, J. W. 1961. *Productivity Trends in the United States*. Princeton, NJ.

Kennedy, W. P. 1974. Foreign investment, trade and growth in the United Kingdom, 1870–1913. *Explorations in Economic History* 11: 415–43.

1976. Institutional response to economic growth: capital markets in Britain to 1914. In L. Hannah, ed., *Management Strategy and Business Development: An Historical and Comparative Study*.

Kennedy, W. P. 1987a. *Industrial Structure, Capital Markets and the Origins of British Economic Decline*. Cambridge.

Kennedy, W. P. 1987b. Review of *Britain's Investment Overseas on the Eve of the First World War: The Use and Abuse of Numbers* by D. C. M. Platt. *Economic History Review* 40: 307–09.

1989. The costs and benefits of British imperialism, 1946–1914. *Past and Present* 125: 186–92.

Kennedy, W. P. 2000. Explaining Victorian entrepreneurship: a cultural problem? A market problem? No problem? London School of Economics, working paper in economic history 61.

Kesner, R. M. 1981. *Economic Control and Colonial Development: Crown Colony Financial Management in the Age of Joseph Chamberlain*. Westport, CT.

Keynes, J. M. 1924. Foreign investment and the national advantage. *The Nation and the Athenaeum* 35: 584–7.

1925. *The Economic Consequences of Mr. Churchill*. In Keynes 1963.

1928. Speech to annual meeting of the National Mutual Assurance Co. 25 January 1928. Reprinted in D. E. Moggridge, ed., *The Collected Writings of John Maynard Keynes, XII: Economic Articles and Correspondence, Investment and Editorial*. Cambridge, 1973.

1930. *A Treatise on Money*.

1936. *The General Theory of Employment, Interest and Money*.

1939. The relative movements of real wages and output. *Economic Journal* 49: 34–51.

1963 [1931]. *Essays in Persuasion*.

Kindleberger, C. P. 1964. *Economic Growth in France and Britain, 1851–1950*. Oxford.

1973. *The World in Depression, 1929–1939*.

1975. The rise of free trade in western Europe, 1820–1875. *Journal of Economic History* 35: 20–55.

Kindleberger, C. P. and di Tella, G. 1982. *Economics in the Long View: Essays in Honour of W. W. Rostow*.

Kinghorn, J. R., and Nye, J. V. 1996. The scale of production in western economic development: a comparison of official industry statistics in the United States, Britain, France and Germany, 1905–1913. *Journal of Economic History* 56: 90–112.

Kinross, J. 1982. *Fifty Years in the City*.

Kirby, M. W. 1981. *The Decline of British Economic Power since 1870*.

1992. Institutional rigidities and economic decline: reflections on the British experience. *Economic History Review* 45: 637–60.

Kirby, M. W. and Rose, M., eds. 1994. *Business Enterprise in Modern Britain: From the Eighteenth to the Twentieth Century*.

Kitson, M. and Solomou, S. 1990. *Protectionism and Economic Revival: The Interwar Economy*. Cambridge.

Kleeberg, J. 1988. The Disconto-Gesellschaft and German industrialisation. Unpublished DPhil thesis, Oxford University.

Knight, F. 1923. The ethics of competition. *Quarterly Journal of Economics* 37: 579–624.

Knox, W., McKinlay, A. and Smyth, J. 1993. Industrialisation, work and labour politics: Clydeside c. 1850–1990. In Schulze 1993.

Königlichen Statistischen Bureau. *Statistisches Handbuch für den Preussischen Staat*. Berlin.

Kowakatsu, H. 1998. The Lancashire cotton industry and its rivals. In K. Bruland and P. O'Brien, eds., *From Family Firms to Corporate Capitalism: Essays in Business and Industrial History in Honour of Peter Mathias*. Oxford.

Krueger, A. B. and Lindahl, M. 2000. Education for growth: why and for whom? NBER, Cambridge, MA, working paper 7591.

Kynaston, D. 1991. *Cazenove & Co: A History*.

Länderrat des Amerikanischen Besatzungsgebietes. *Statistisches Handbuch von Deutschland, 1928–1944*. München, 1949.

Landes, D. S. 1960. The structure of enterprise in the nineteenth century: the cases of Britain and Germany. XI Congrès internationale des Sciences historiques, *Rapports*, V, *Histoire contemporaine*. Uppsala.

1969. *The Unbound Prometheus: Technological Change and Industrial Development in Western Europe from 1750 to the Present*. Cambridge.

1998. *The Wealth and Poverty of Nations*. London.

Latham, A. H. J. and Neal, L. 1983. The international market in rice and wheat, 1868–1914. *Economic History Review* 36: 260–80.

Lavington, F. 1968 [1921]. *The English Capital Market.*

Law, C. M. 1980. *British Regional Development since World War I.*

Lawes, J. B. and Gilbert, J. H. 1893. Home produce, imports, consumption, and price of wheat, over forty harvest-years, 1852–53 to 1891–92. *Journal of the Royal Agricultural Society of England* 3rd ser. 4: 77–133.

Lawrence, F. W. 1899. *Local Variations in Wages.*

Layard, P. R. G., Nickell, S. J. and Jackman, R. 1991. *Unemployment, Macroeconomic Performance and the Labour Market.* Oxford.

Lazonick, W. A. 1979. Industrial relations and technical change: the case of the self-acting mule. *Cambridge Journal of Economics* 3: 231–62.

1981a. Competition, specialisation, and industrial decline. *Journal of Economic History* 41: 31–8.

1981b. Factor costs and the diffusion of ring spinning in Britain prior to World War One. *Quarterly Journal of Economics* 96: 89–109.

1981c. Production relations, labor productivity and choice of technique: British and U.S. cotton spinning. *Journal of Economic History* 41: 491–516.

1983. Industrial organisation and technological change: the decline of the British cotton industry. *Business History Review* 57: 195–236.

1986. The cotton industry. In Elbaum and Lazonick 1986.

1994. Employment relations in manufacturing and international competition. In Floud and McCloskey 1994.

Lazonick, W. A. and O'Sullivan, M. 1997. Finance and industrial development, Part 1: The United States and the United Kingdom. *Financial History Review* 4: 7–30.

Leak, H. and Maizels, A. 1945. The structure of British industry. *Journal of the Royal Statistical Society* 108: 142–99.

Lee, C. H. 1979. *British Regional Employment Statistics, 1841–1971.* Cambridge.

1986. *The British Economy since 1700: A Macro-Economic Perspective.* Cambridge.

1991. Regional inequalities in infant mortality in Britain 1861–1971: patterns and hypotheses. *Population Studies* 45: 55–65.

1995. *Scotland and the United Kingdom: The Economy and the Union in the Twentieth Century.* Manchester.

1999. The Scottish economy and the First World War. In C. M. M. Macdonald and E. W. McFarland, eds., *Scotland and the Great War.* Edinburgh.

Lees, L. H. 1979. *Exiles of Erin: Irish Migrants in Victorian London.* Manchester.

1998. *The Solidarities of Strangers: The English Poor Laws and the People, 1700–1948.* Cambridge.

Lehner, F. and Widmaier, U. 1983. Market failure and growth of government: a sociological explanation. In C. L. Taylor, ed., *Why Governments Grow: Measuring Public Sector Size.*

Leland, H. E. and Pyle, D. H. 1977. Informational asymmetries, financial structure and financial intermediation. *Journal of Finance* 32: 371–87.

Lenin, V. I. 1915. *Imperialism: The Highest State of Capitalism.* Moscow.

Lenman, B. 1977. *An Economic History of Modern Scotland.*

Leunig, T. 1997. The myth of the corporate economy: factor costs, industrial structure, and technical choice in the Lancashire and New England cotton industries, 1900–1913. *Business and Economic History* 26: 311–17.

2001. New answers to old questions: explaining the slow adoption of ring spinning in Lancashire, 1880–1913. *Journal of Economic History* 61: 439–66.

Levy, H. 1927. *Monopolies, Trusts and Cartels in British Industry.*

Lewchuck, W. A. 1987. *American Technology and the British Vehicle Industry.* Cambridge.

1993. Men and monotony: fraternalism as a managerial strategy at the Ford Motor Company. *Journal of Economic History* 53: 824–56.

Lewis, M. K. and Davis, K. 1987. *Domestic and International Banking.* Cambridge, MA.

Lewis, W. A. 1978. *Growth and Fluctuations, 1870–1913.*

Liberal Industrial Inquiry. 1928. *Britain's Industrial Future.*

Liebowitz, S. J. and Margolis, S. E. 1995. Path dependence, lock-in, and history. *Journal of Law, Economics, and Organization* 11: 205–26.

Liepmann, K. 1960. *Apprenticeship: An Enquiry into its Adequacy in Modern Conditions.*

Lindert, P. H. 1969. Key currencies and gold, 1900–1913. *Princeton Studies in International Finance* 24, International Finance Section, Department of Economics, Princeton University.

1994. The rise of social spending, 1880–1930. *Explorations in Economic History* 31: 1–37.

2001. Democracy, decentralization, and mass schooling before 1914: appendices. Agricultural History Center, University of California, Davis, working paper 105.

Lindert, P. H. and Trace, K. 1971. Yardsticks for Victorian entrepreneurs. In McCloskey 1971.

Lindert, P. H. and Williamson, J. G. 1983. Reinterpreting Britain's social tables, 1688–1913. *Explorations in Economic History* 20: 94–109.

Linsley, C. A. and Linsley, C. L. 1993. Booth, Rowntree, and Llewelyn Smith: a reassessment of interwar poverty. *Economic History Review* 46: 88–104.

London, Jack. 1903. *The People of the Abyss.*

Lorenz, E. and Wilkinson, F. 1986. The shipbuilding industry 1880–1965. In Elbaum and Lazonick 1986.

Louis, W. R., ed. 1976. *Imperialism: The Robinson and Gallagher Controversy.* New York.

Loungani, P. 1991. Structural unemployment and public policy in interwar Britain. *Journal of Monetary Economics* 28: 149–59.

Lowe, R. 1987. The government and industrial relations. In Wrigley 1987b.

1995. Government. In S. Constantine, M. W. Kirby and M. B. Rose, eds., *The First World War in British History.*

Lucas, A. F. 1932. The bankers' industrial development company. *Harvard Business Review* 11: 273–4.

1937. *Industrial Reconstruction and the Control of Competition: The British Experiments.*

Lucas, R. E. 1988. On the mechanics of economic development. *Journal of Monetary Economics* 22: 3–42.

1990. Why doesn't capital flow from rich to poor. *American Economic Review, Papers and Proceedings* 80: 92–6.

McClelland, C. E. 1991. *The German Experience of Professionalization: Modern Learned Professions and their Organizations from the Early Nineteenth Century to the Hitler Era.* Cambridge.

McCloskey, D. N. 1970. Did Victorian Britain fail? *Economic History Review* 23: 446–59.

1973. *Economic Maturity and Entrepreneurial Decline: British Iron and Steel, 1870–1913.* Cambridge, MA.

1979. No it did not: a reply to Crafts. *Economic History Review* 32: 538–41.

1981. *Enterprise and Trade in Victorian Britain: Essays in Historical Economics.*

1998. Bourgeois virtue and the history of P and S. *Journal of Economic History* 58: 297–317.

McCloskey, D. N., ed. 1971. *Essays on a Mature Economy: Britain after 1840.*

McCloskey, D. N. and Sandberg, L. 1971. From damnation to redemption: judgements on the late Victorian entrepreneur. *Explorations in Economic History* 9: 89–108.

McIvor, A. 1995. Health and safety in the cotton industry: a literature survey. *Manchester Region History Review* 9: 50–7.

McIvor, A. 2001. *A History of Work in Britain 1880–1950.* Basingstoke.

MacKay, D. I. and Buxton, N. K. 1965. The north of Scotland economy – a case for redevelopment? *Scottish Journal of Political Economy* 12: 23–49.

Mackenzie, W. A. 1921. Changes in the standard of living in the United Kingdom, 1860–1914. *Economica* 1: 211–30.

McKeown, T. 1976. *The Modern Rise of Population.*

McKeown, T. and Record, R. G. 1962. Reasons for the decline of mortality in England and Wales during the nineteenth century. *Population Studies* 16: 94–122.
McKinlay, A. and Zeitlin, J. 1989. The meaning of managerial prerogative: industrial relations and the organisation of work in British engineering, 1880–1939. In C. Harvey and J. Turner, eds., *Labour and Business in Modern Britain*.
MacKinnon, Mary. 1984. 'Poverty and policy: the English poor law 1860–1910'. Unpublished DPhil thesis, University of Oxford.
1986. Poor law policy, unemployment, and pauperism. *Explorations in Economic History* 23: 299–336.
1987. English poor law policy and the crusade against outrelief. *Journal of Economic History* 47: 603–25.
1988. The use and misuse of poor law statistics, 1857–1912. *Historical Methods* 21: 5–16.
McLean, D. 1976. Finance and 'informal empire' before the First World War. *Economic History Review* 29: 291–305.
McLean, I. and Johnes, M. 2000. 'Regulation run mad': the Board of Trade and the loss of the *Titanic*. *Public Administration* 78: 729–49.
Macleod, C. 1999. Negotiating the rewards of invention: the shop-floor inventor in Victorian Britain. *Business History* 41: 17–36.
Macmillan. 1931. *Report of the Macmillan Committee on Finance and Industry*. Cmd 3897.
Macrosty, H. W. 1927. Inflation and deflation in the United States and United Kingdom, 1919–1923. *Journal of the Royal Statistical Society* 90: 45–134.
Maddison, A. 1964. *Economic Growth in the West*. New York.
1982. *Phases of Capitalist Development*. Cambridge.
1987. Growth and slowdown in advanced capitalist economies: techniques of quantitative assessment. *Journal of Economic Literature* 25: 649–98.
1991. *Dynamic Forces in Capitalist Development*. New York.
1995. *Monitoring the World Economy, 1820–1992*. Paris.
1996. Macroeconomic accounts for European countries. In van Ark and Crafts 1996.
2001. *The World Economy: A Millennial Perspective*. Paris.
Maddock, R. and McLean, I. W., eds. 1987. *The Australian Economy in the Long-Run*. Cambridge.
MAFF. 1966. *A Century of Agricultural Statistics*.
Magee, G. B. 1997a. Competence or omniscience: assessing entrepreneurship in the Victorian and Edwardian British paper industry. *Business History Review* 71: 230–59.
1997b. *Productivity and Performance in the Paper Industry*. Cambridge.
1999. Technological development and foreign patenting: evidence from nineteenth-century Australia. *Explorations in Economic History* 36: 344–59.
2000. *Knowledge Generation*. Melbourne.
Maizels, A. 1963. *Industrial Growth and World Trade*. Cambridge.
Mallet, B. 1913. *British Budgets, 1887–88 to 1912–13*.
Mann, P. H. 1904. Life in an agricultural village in England. *Sociological Papers* 1: 163–93.
Marks, L. V. 1994. *Model Mothers: Jewish Mothers and Maternity Provision in East London, 1870–1939*. Oxford.
Marshall, A. 1919. *Industry and Trade*.
1920. *Principles of Economics*.
Martin, J. 2000. *The Development of Modern Agriculture: British Farming since 1931*. Basingstoke.
Martin, P. and Rogers, C. A. 2000. Long-term growth and short-term economic instability. *European Economic Review* 44: 359–81.
Mass, W. and Lazonick, W. A. 1990. The British cotton industry and international competitive advantage: the state of the debates. *Business History* 32: 9–65.

Mathias, P. 1967. *Retailing Revolution.*
1983. *The First Industrial Nation*, 2nd edn.
Mathias, P. and Pollard, S., eds. 1989. *The Cambridge Economic History of Europe, VIII: The Industrial Economies: The Development of Economic and Social Policies*. Cambridge.
Matthews, D., Anderson, M. and Edwards, J. R. 1997. The rise of the professional accountant in British management. *Economic History Review* 50: 407–29.
Matthews, K. G. P. 1986. Was sterling overvalued in 1925? *Economic History Review* 39: 572–87.
1989. Could Lloyd George have done it? The pledge reconsidered. *Oxford Economic Papers* 41: 374–407.
Matthews, R. C. O. 1959. *The Business Cycle*. Cambridge.
Matthews, R. C. O., Feinstein, C. H. and Odling-Smee, J. C. 1982. *British Economic Growth, 1856–1973*. Oxford.
Meadowcroft, J. 1995. *Conceptualizing the State: Innovation and Dispute in British Political Thought, 1880–1914*. Oxford.
Meiklejohn, A. 1952. History of lung diseases of coal miners in Great Britain: Part II, 1875–1920; Part III, 1930–52. *British Journal of Industrial Medicine* 9: 93–8; 208–18.
Melling, J. 1980a. Clydeside housing and the evolution of rent control 1900–1939. In Melling 1980b.
1989. Clydeside rent struggles and the making of Labour politics in Scotland 1900–1939. In Rodger 1989b.
Melling, J., ed. 1980b. *Housing, Social Policy and the State.*
Mendershausen, H. 1943. *The Economics of War*. New York.
Mercer, H. 1989. The evolution of British government policy towards competition in private industry, 1940–1956. Unpublished PhD thesis, University of London.
1995. *Constructing a Competitive Order: The Hidden History of British Anti-Trust Policies*. Cambridge.
Metcalf, D., Nickell, S. J. and Floros, N. 1982. Still searching for an explanation of unemployment in interwar Britain. *Journal of Political Economy* 90: 368–99.
Meyer, J. R. 1955. An input-output approach to evaluating British industrial production in the late nineteenth century. In A. H. Conrad and J. R. Meyer, eds., *The Economics of Slavery and Other Studies in Econometric History*. Chicago.
Michie, R. C. 1981. Options, concessions, syndicates and the provision of venture capital 1880–1913. *Business History* 23: 147–64.
1985. The London Stock exchange and the British securities market, 1850–1914. *Economic History Review* 38: 61–82.
1986. The London and New York Stock Exchanges, 1850–1914. *Journal of Economic History* 46: 171–87.
1987. *The London and New York Stock Exchanges, 1850–1914.*
1988a. Different in name only? The London Stock Exchange and foreign bourses c.1850–1914. *Business History* 30: 46–68.
1988b. The finance of innovation in late Victorian and Edwardian Britain: possibilities and constraints. *Journal of European Economic History* 17: 491–530.
1992. *The City of London: Continuity and Change, 1850–1990.*
1999. *The London Stock Exchange: A History*. Oxford.
Middlemas, K. 1979. *Politics in Industrial Society: The Experience of the British System since 1911.*
Middleton, R. 1981. The constant employment budget balance and British monetary policy, 1929–39. *Economic History Review* 34: 266–86.
1985. *Towards the Managed Economy: Keynes, the Treasury and the Fiscal Policy Debate of the 1930s.*
1992. The economic role of the interwar British state. In S. Groenveld and M. J. Wintle, eds., *State and Trade: Government and Economy in Britain and the Netherlands since the Middle Ages*. Zutphen.

1996. *Government versus the Market: The Growth of the Public Sector, Economic Management and British Economic Performance, c. 1890–1979*. Cheltenham.
1998. *Charlatans or Saviours? Economists and the British Economy from Marshall to Meade*. Cheltenham.
Miller, M. and Sutherland, A. 1994. Speculative anticipations of sterling's return to gold: was Keynes wrong? *Economic Journal* 104: 804–12.
2000. State enterprise in Britain in the twentieth century. In P. A. Toninelli, ed. *The Rise and Fall of State-Owned Enterprises in the Western World*. Cambridge.
Millward, R. and Bell, F. N. 1998. Economic factors in the decline of mortality in late nineteenth century Britain. *European Review of Economic History* 2: 263–88.
2001. Infant mortality in Victorian Britain: the mother as medium. *Economic History Review* 54: 699–733.
Millward, R. and Sheard, S. 1995. The urban fiscal problem, 1870–1914: government expenditure and finance in England and Wales. *Economic History Review* 48: 501–35.
Milner, S. 1995. The coverage of collective pay-setting institutions in Britain, 1895–1990. *British Journal of Industrial Relations* 33: 69–91.
Milner, S., ed. 1996. *Could Finance Do More for British Business?*
Minchinton, W. E., ed. 1968. *Essays in Agrarian History*, II. Newton Abbot.
Ministry of Labour. 1928. *Report of an Enquiry into Apprenticeship and Training for the Skilled Occupations in Great Britain and Northern Ireland, 1925–26*.
Ministry of Labour Gazette. Various years.
Mitch, D. F. 1992. *The Rise of Literacy in Victorian England: The Influence of Private Choice and Public Policy*. Philadelphia, PA.
1999. The role of education and skill in the British industrial revolution. In J. Mokyr, ed., *The British Industrial Revolution: An Economic Perspective*. Oxford.
Mitchell, B. R. 1988. *British Historical Statistics*. Cambridge.
Mitchell, B. R. and Deane, P. 1962. *Abstract of British Historical Statistics*. Cambridge.
Moggridge, D. E. 1969. *The Return to Gold, 1925*. Cambridge.
1970. The 1931 financial crisis – a new view. *The Banker*: 832–9.
1972. *British Monetary Policy, 1924–1931: The Norman Conquest of $4.86*. Cambridge.
Mokyr, J. 1990. *The Lever of Riches: Technological Creativity and Economic Progress*. Oxford.
Mokyr, J., ed. 1993. *The British Industrial Revolution: An Economic Perspective*. Boulder.
More, C. 1980. *Skill and the English Working Class, 1870–1914*.
Morgan, E. V. 1952. *Studies in British Financial Policy*.
Morgan, E. V. and Thomas, W. A. 1962. *The Stock Exchange: Its History and Functions*.
Morris, M. D. 1963. Towards a reinterpretation of nineteenth century Indian economic history. *Journal of Economic History* 23: 606–18.
Morrison, Arthur. 1894. *Tales of Mean Streets*.
Moss, M. 2000. *Standard Life 1825–2000: The Building of Europe's Largest Mutual Life Company*. Edinburgh.
Mottershead, P. 1978. Industrial policy. In F. T. Blackaby, ed., *British Economic Policy, 1960–74*. Cambridge.
Mowery, D. C. 1992. Finance and corporate evolution in five industrial economies, 1900–1950. *Industrial and Corporate Change* 1: 1–36.
Mowery, D. C. and Rosenberg, N. 1989. *Technology and the Pursuit of Economic Growth*. Cambridge.
1998. *Paths of Innovation*. Cambridge.
MRC. 1930. Modern Records Collection, University of Warwick, CBI Predecessors Archive, Federation of British Industry, Minutes of Committee on Industry and Finance, MSS200/F/1/1/175
Mukerjee, T. 1972. Theory of economic drain: impact of British rule on the Indian economy, 1840–1900. In K. E. Boulding and T. Mukerjee, eds., *Economic Imperialism*. Ann Arbor.
Munn, C. W. 1988. *Clydesdale Bank: The First Hundred and Fifty Years*. Glasgow.

1997. Banking on branches: the origins and development of branch banking in the United Kingdom. In Cottrell *et al.* 1997.

Musgrave, R. A. 1959. *The Theory of Public Finance: A Study in Public Economy.*

1985. A brief history of fiscal doctrine. In A. J. Auerbach and M. Feldstein, eds., *Handbook of Public Economics*, I. Amsterdam.

Musson, A. E. 1978. *The Growth of British Industry.*

Nelson, R. R. and Wright, G. 1992. The rise and fall of American technological leadership: the postwar era in historical perspective. *Journal of Economic Literature* 30: 1931–64.

Neuberger, H. and Stokes, H. H. 1974. German banks and German growth, 1883–1913: an empirical view. *Journal of Economic History* 34: 710–31.

Newell, A. and Symons, J. S. V. 1988. The macroeconomics of the interwar years: international comparisons. In Eichengreen and Hatton 1988.

Newton, L. 1996. Regional bank-industry relations during the mid-nineteenth century: links between bankers and manufacturers in Shefffield c. 1850–c. 1885. *Business History* 38: 64–83.

Newton, L. and Cottrell, P. L. 1998. Joint-stock banking in the English provinces 1826–1857: to branch or not to branch? *Business and Economic History* 27: 115–28.

Newton, S. and Porter, D. 1988. *Modernization Frustrated: The Politics of Industrial Decline in Britain since 1900.*

Nicholas, S. J. 1983. Agency contracts, institutional modes, and the transition to foreign direct investment by British manufacturing multinationals before 1939. *Journal of Economic History* 43: 675–86.

1984. The overseas marketing performance of British industry, 1870–1914. *Economic History Review* 37: 489–506.

Nicholas, T. 1999a. Businessmen and land ownership in the late nineteenth century. *Economic History Review* 52: 27–44.

1999b. Clogs to clogs in three generations? Explaining entrepreneurial performance in Britain since 1850. *Journal of Economic History* 59: 688–713.

1999c. Wealth-making in nineteenth and early twentieth century Britain: industry v. commerce and finance. *Business History* 41: 16–36.

2000a. Businessmen and land ownership in the late nineteenth century revisited. *Economic History Review* 53: 777–82.

2000b. Wealth making in the nineteenth and early twentieth century: the Rubinstein hypothesis revisited. *Business History* 42: 155–68.

Nickell, S. J. 1995. *The Performance of Companies*. Oxford.

1996. Competition and corporate performance. *Journal of Political Economy* 104: 724–46.

Nickell, S. J., Nicolitsas, D. and Dryden, N. 1997. What makes firms perform well? *European Economic Review* 41: 783–96.

Nishimura, S. 1971. *The Decline of Inland Bills of Exchange in the London Money Market, 1855–1913*. Cambridge.

Nordhaus, W. D. 1972. The recent productivity slowdown. *Brookings Papers on Economic Activity* 3: 493–531.

Nordhaus, W. D. and Tobin, James. 1973. Is growth obsolete? In M. Moss, ed., *The Measurement of Economic and Social Performance*. New York.

North, D. 1989. Institutions and economic growth: an historical introduction. *World Development* 17: 1319–32.

Notestein, F. W. 1945. Population: the long view. In T. W. Schultz, ed., *Food for the World*. Chicago.

O'Brien, A. P. 1988. Factory size, economies of scale, and the great merger wave of 1898–1902. *Journal of Economic History* 48: 639–49.

O'Brien, D. P. 1975. *The Classical Economists*. Oxford.

O'Brien, P. K. 1988. The costs and benefits of British imperialism 1846–1914. *Past and Present* 120: 163–200.

1989. Reply. *Past and Present* 125: 192–9.
O'Brien, P. K., Griffiths, T. and Hunt, P. A. 1996. Theories of technological progress and the British textile industry from Kay to Cartwright. *Revista de Historia Economica* 14: 533–56.
Ó Gráda, C. 1981. British agriculture, 1860–1914. In Floud and McCloskey 1981.
1994. British agriculture, 1860–1914. In Floud and McCloskey 1994.
1999. *Black 47 and Beyond: The Great Irish Famine in History, Economy and Memory*. Princeton.
O'Mahony, M. 1999. *Britain's Productivity Performance, 1950–1996: An International Perspective*.
O'Rourke, K. 1997. The European grain invasion, 1870–1913. *Journal of Economic History* 57: 775–801.
O'Rourke, K. and Williamson, J. G. 1999. *Globalisation and History: The Evolution of the Nineteenth Century International Economy*. Cambridge, MA.
O'Rourke, K. H. 1996. Trade, migration and convergence: an historical perspective. CEPR, London, discussion paper 1319.
O'Rourke, K. H. and Williamson, J. G. 1999. *Globalization and History: The Evolution of a Nineteenth Century Atlantic Economy*. Cambridge, MA.
OECD 2002. *Economic Outlook, 2002/1*. Paris.
Offer, A. 1989. *The First World War: An Agrarian Interpretation*. Oxford.
1993. The British Empire 1870–1914: a waste of money? *Economic History Review* 46: 215–38.
2002. Why has the market sector grown so large in market societies?: the political economy of prudence in the UK, c. 1870–2000. University of Oxford, discussion papers in economic and social history 44.
Ojala, E. M. 1952. *Agriculture and Economic Progress*. Oxford.
Okun, A. M. 1975. *Equality and Efficiency: The Big Tradeoff*. Washington, DC.
Ollerenshaw, P. 1997. The business and politics of banking in Ireland 1900–1943. In Cottrell *et al.* 1997.
Olson, M. 1965. *The Logic of Collective Action*. Cambridge, MA.
1974. The UK and the world market for wheat and other primary products, 1885–1914. *Explorations in Economic History* 11: 352–6.
1982. *The Rise and Decline of Nations: Economic Growth Stagflation and Social Rigidities*. New Haven.
Oman, A. R. 1971. The epidemiological transition: a theory of the epidemiology of population change. *Millbank Memorial Fund Quarterly* 49: 509–38.
Ormerod, P. and Worswick, G. D. N. 1982. Unemployment in interwar Britain. *Journal of Political Economy* 90: 400–9.
Orr, W. 1982. *Deer Forests, Landlords and Crofters*. Edinburgh.
Orwell, George. 1937. *The Road to Wigan Pier*.
Orwin, C. S. and Felton, B. I. 1931. A century of wages and earnings in agriculture. *Journal of the Royal Agricultural Society of England* 92: 231–57.
Overy, R. 1976. *William Morris, Viscount Nuffield*.
Owen, A. D. K. 1933. *A Survey of the Standard of Living in Sheffield*. Sheffield.
Pahl, R. 1990. New rich, old rich, stinking rich? *Social History* 15: 229.
Paish, G. 1914. The export of capital and the cost of living. *The Statist (Supplement)* 79, 14 Feb., i–viii.
Palmer, S. R. 1972. Investors in London shipping 1820–1850. *Maritime History* 2: 42–68.
Parry, R. 1985. Britain: stable aggregates, changing composition. In R. Rose, E. Page, R. Parry, B. G. Peters, A. C. Pignatelli and K.-D. Schmidt, eds., *Public Employment in Western Nations*. Cambridge.
Pavitt, K. and Soete, L. L. 1981. International dynamics of innovation. In H. Giersch, ed., *Emerging Technologies: Consequences for Economic Growth, Structural Change and Employment*. Tübingen.

Payne, P. L. 1967. The emergence of the large-scale company in Great Britain, 1870–1914. *Economic History Review* 20: 519–42.
1979. *Colvilles and the Scottish Steel Industry*. Oxford.
1988. *The Hydro*. Aberdeen.
1990. Entrepreneurship and British economic decline. In Collins and Robbins 1990.
Peacock, A. T. and Wiseman, J. 1967. *The Growth of Public Expenditure in the United Kingdom*, 2nd edn.
Pearce, I. F. 1970. *International Trade*.
Pearce, I. F. and Rowan, D. C. 1966. A framework for research into the real effects of international capital movements. In J. H. Dunning, ed., *International Investment: Selected Readings*. Harmondsworth.
Pearson, R. and Williams, G. 1984. *Political Thought and Public Policy in the Nineteenth Century: An Introduction*.
Peden, G. C. 2002. From cheap government to efficient government: the political economy of public expenditure in the United Kingdom, 1832–1914. In D. N. Winch and P. K. O'Brien, eds., *The Political Economy of British Economic Experience, 1688–1914*. Oxford.
Peebles, H. B. 1987. *Warshipbuilding on the Clyde: Naval Orders and the Prosperity of the Clyde Shipbuilding Industry 1889–1939*. Edinburgh.
Pelling, H. 1987. *A History of British Trade Unionism*, 4th edn.
Pember Reeves, Maud. 1913. *Round about a Pound a Week*.
Perkin, H. 1996. *The Third Revolution: Professional Elites in the Modern World*.
Perren, R. 1970. The landlord and agricultural transformation, 1870–1900. *Agricultural History Review* 18: 36–51. Reprinted in Perry 1973.
1978. *The Meat Trade in Britain, 1840–1914*.
1995. *Agriculture in Depression, 1870–1940*. Cambridge.
2000. Food manufacturing. In Collins 2000b.
Perry, P. J. 1972. Where was the 'great agricultural depression'? A geography of agricultural bankruptcy in late Victorian England and Wales. *Agricultural History Review* 20: 30–45. Reprinted in Perry 1973.
1973. *British Agriculture, 1875–1914*.
Petersen, C. 1995. *Bread and the British Economy c. 1770–1870*. Aldershot.
Phelps-Brown, E. H. and Handfield-Jones, S. J. 1952. The climacteric of the 1890s. *Oxford Economic Papers* 4: 266–307.
Phillips, A. D. M. 1989. *The Underdraining of Farm Land in England During the Nineteenth Century*. Cambridge.
Pilgrim Trust. 1938. *Men without Work: A Report Made to the Pilgrim Trust*. Cambridge
Pindyck, R. S. 1988. Irreversible investment, capacity choice, and the value of the firm. *American Economic Review* 76: 969–85.
Piore, M. J. and Sabel, C. F. 1984. *The Second Industrial Divide: Possibilities for Prosperity*. New York.
Platt, D. C. M. 1973. The national economy and British imperial expansion before 1914. *Journal of Imperial and Commonwealth History* 2: 3–14.
1986. *Britain's Investment Overseas on the Eve of the First World War: The Uses and Abuses of Numbers*.
Political and Economic Planning. 1934. *Report on the British Cotton Industry*.
1939. *Report on the Location of Industry*.
Pollard, S. 1954. Wages and earnings in the Sheffield trades, 1851–1914. *Yorkshire Bulletin of Economic and Social Research* 6: 49–64.
1983. *The Development of the British Economy, 1914–1980*.
1989. *Britain's Prime and Britain's Decline: The British Economy, 1870–1914*.
1994. Entrepreneurship, 1870–1914. In Floud and McCloskey 1994.
Pollard, S. and Robertson, P. 1979. *The British Shipbuilding Industry, 1870–1914*. Cambridge, MA.

Pollins, H. 1957–8. Railway contractors and the finance of railway development in Britain. *Journal of Transport History* 3: 41–51 and 103–10.

Pooley, C. and Turnbull, J. 1998. *Migration and Mobility in Britain since the Eighteenth Century*.

Porter, D. 1986. 'A trusted guide of the investing public': Harry Marks and the *Financial News*. *Business History* 28: 1–17.

Porter J. H. 1970. Wage bargaining under conciliation agreements, 1860–1914. *Economic History Review* 23: 460–75.

Porter, M. E. 1990. *The Competitive Advantage of Nations*.

Prais, S. J. 1995. *Productivity, Education and Training: An International Perspective*. Cambridge.

Prais S. J. and Houthakker, H. 1955. *The Analysis of Family Budgets*. Cambridge.

Pred, A. C. 1977. *City Systems in Advanced Economies*. New York.

Prest, A. R. 1954. *Consumers' Expenditure in the United Kingdom, 1900–1919*. Cambridge.

Price, S. 1981. Riveters' earnings in Clyde shipbuilding 1889–1913. *Scottish Economic and Social History* 1: 42–65.

Prior, A. and Kirby, M. 1993. The Society of Friends and the family firm 1700–1830. Lancaster University, Management School, discussion paper.

Ramsbottom, E. C. 1935. The course of wage rates in the United Kingdom, 1921–1934. *Journal of the Royal Statistical Society* 98: 639–94.

1939. Wage rates in the United Kingdom in 1938. *Journal of the Royal Statistical Society* 102: 289–91.

Raynes, H. E. 1926. The place of ordinary stocks and shares as distinct from fixed interest bearing securities in the investment of life assurance funds. *Journal of the Institute of Actuaries* 59: 21–35.

1937. Equities and fixed-interest stocks during twenty-five years. *Journal of the Institute of Actuaries* 68: 483–94.

Reader, W. J. 1966. *Professional Men: The Rise of the Professional Classes in Nineteenth-Century England*.

Redding, S. 2002. Path dependence, endogenous innovation, and growth. *International Economic Review* 43: 1215–48.

Redford, A. 1964. *Labour Migration in England, 1800–1850*. Manchester, 2nd rev. edn.

Redmond, J. 1984. The sterling overvaluation in 1925: a multilateral approach. *Economic History Review* 37: 520–32.

Reid, G. C. 1987. *Theories of Industrial Organisation*. Oxford.

Report of the Departmental Committee. 1937. *Share-Pushing*. Cmd 5539.

Rew, R. H. 1892a. An inquiry into the statistics of production and consumption of milk and milk products in Great Britain. *Journal of the Royal Statistical Society* 55: 244–86.

1892b. Production and consumption of milk. *Journal of the Royal Agricultural Society of England* 3rd ser. 3: 421–7.

Rew, R. H. 1904. Observations on the production and consumption of meat and dairy products. *Journal of the Royal Statistical Society* 67: 413–27.

Richardson, H. W. 1965. Overcommitment in Britain since 1930. *Oxford Economic Papers* 17: 237–62.

1967. *Economic Recovery in Britain, 1932–1939*.

Riley, J. C. 1994. *Heights, Survival, and Material Comfort: A Comparison of Results*. Indiana University Population Institute for Research and Training, Bloomington, working paper 95–4.

1997. *Sick, not Dead: The Health of British Workingmen during the Mortality Decline*. Baltimore.

2001. *Rising Life Expectancy: A Global History*. Cambridge.

Ringer, F. K. 1979. *Education and Society in Modern Europe*. Bloomington, IN.

Ritschl, A. 1998. Reparation transfers, the Borchardt hypothesis and the great depression in Germany, 1929–32. *European Review of Economic History* 2: 49–72.

Roberts, R. 1971. *The Classic Slum: Salford Life in the First Quarter of the Century*. Manchester.

Roberts, Richard. 1992. Regulatory responses to the rise of the market for corporate control in Britain in the 1950s. *Business History* 34: 183–200.
Robertson, D. J. 1960. *Factory Wage Structures and National Agreements*. Cambridge.
Robinson G. M. 1981. A statistical analysis of agriculture in the Vale of Evesham during the great depression. *Journal of Historical Geography* 7: 37–52.
1983. *West Midlands Farming, 1840s to 1970s*. Cambridge.
Robson, R. 1957. *The Cotton Industry in Britain*.
Roderick, G. W. and Stephens M. D. 1972. *Scientific and Technical Education in Nineteenth Century England*. Newton Abbot.
Rodger, R. 1989a. Crisis and confrontation in Scottish housing 1880–1914. In Rodger 1989b.
Rodger, R., ed. 1989b. *Scottish Housing in the Twentieth Century*. Leicester.
Rodrik, D. 1997. TFPG controversies, institutions and economic performance in East Asia. CEPR, London, discussion paper 1587.
Romer, P. M. 1986. Increasing returns and long-run growth. *Journal of Political Economy* 94: 1002–37.
1990. Endogenous technological change. *Journal of Political Economy*, 98: S71–S102.
Rose, M. B. 1977. The role of family in the provision of capital in Samuel Greg and Co., 1784–1840. *Business History* 19: 37–67.
2000. *Firms, Networks and Business Values*. Cambridge.
Rose, R. and Karran, T. J. 1984. Inertia or incrementalism?: a long-term view of the growth of government. In A. J. Groth and L. L. Wade, eds., *Comparative Resource Allocation: Politics, Performance and Policy Priorities*.
Rosenbaum, S. 1988. 100 years of heights and weights. *Journal of the Royal Statistical Society. Series A (Statistics in Society)*. 151: 276–309.
Rosenberg, N. 1982. *Inside the Black Box: Technology and Economics*. Cambridge.
Ross, D. M. 1990. Banks and industry: some new perspectives on the interwar years. In van Helten and Cassis 1990.
1992. Bank advances and industrial production in the UK: a red herring? In H. Lindgren, P. Cottrell and A. Teichova, eds., *European Industry and Banking, 1920–1939: A Review of Bank–Industry Relations*. Leicester.
1995. Information, collateral and British bank lending in the 1930s. In Cassis *et al*. 1995.
1996a. Commercial banking in a market-oriented financial system: Britain between the wars. *Economic History Review* 49: 314–35.
1996b. The unsatisfied fringe in Britain, 1930s-80s. *Business History* 38: 11–26.
1997. The Macmillan Gap and the British credit market in the 1930s. In Cottrell *et al*. 1997.
Ross, D. M. and Ziegler, D. 2000. Problems of industrial finance between the wars. In C. Buchheim and R. Garside, eds., *After the Slump: Industry and Politics in 1930s Britain and Germany*. Frankfurt am Main.
Rostas, L. 1948. *Comparative Productivity in British and American Industry*. Cambridge.
Rostow, W. W. 1948. *The British Economy in the Nineteenth Century: Essays*. Oxford.
Rothbarth, E. 1946. Causes of the superior efficiency of USA industry as compared with British industry. *Economic Journal* 56: 383–90.
Routh, G. 1965. *Occupation and Pay in Great Britain, 1906–1960*. Cambridge.
1979. *Occupation and Pay in Great Britain 1906–1979*. Glasgow.
Rowe, J. 1953. *Cornwall in the Age of the Industrial Revolution*.
Rowntree, B. S. 1901. *Poverty: A Study of Town Life*.
1941. *Poverty and Progress: A Second Social Survey of York*.
Rowntree, B. S. and Lasker, B. 1911. *Unemployment, a Social Study*.
Royal Commission on Agriculture. 1896. Particulars of the expenditures and outgoings on certain estates in Great Britain. *British Parliamentary Papers*, C. 8125, XVI.
1897. Final report of Her Majesty's commissioners appointed to inquire into the subject of agricultural depression. *British Parliamentary Papers*, C. 8540, XV.

Rubinstein, W. D. 1977. The Victorian middle classes: wealth occupation and geography. *Economic History Review* 30: 602–23.
1981a. *Men of Property: The Very Wealthy in Britain since the Industrial Revolution.*
1981b. New men of wealth and the purchase of land in nineteenth century Britain. *Past and Present* 92: 125–47.
1987. *Elites and the Wealthy in Modern British History*. Brighton.
1994. *Capitalism Culture and Decline in Britain 1750–1990.*
1996. Businessmen into landowners: the question revisited. In N. Harte and R. Quinault, eds., *Land and Society in Britain 1700–1914*. Manchester.
Sandberg, L. 1969. American rings and English mules: the role of economic rationality. *Quarterly Journal of Economics* 63: 25–43.
1974. *Lancashire in Decline*. Columbus, OH.
Sanderson, M. 1972. *The Universities and British Industry, 1850–1970.*
1987. *Educational Opportunity and Social Change in England.*
1988. Technical education and economic decline: 1890–1980s. *Oxford Review of Economic Policy* 41: 38–50.
1999. *Education and Economic Decline in Britain, 1870 to the 1990s*. Cambridge.
Saul, S. B. 1960. *Studies in British Overseas Trade, 1870–1914*. Liverpool.
1968. The engineering industry. In Aldcroft 1968.
1985. *The Myth of the Great Depression*, 2nd edn.
Saville, J. 1957. *Rural Depopulation in England and Wales, 1851–1951.*
1961. Some retarding factors in the British economy before 1914. *Yorkshire Bulletin of Economic and Social Research* 13: 51–60.
1996. *Bank of Scotland: A History 1695–1995*. Edinburgh.
Saxonhouse, G. and Wright, G. 1984. New evidence on the stubborn English mule and the cotton industry, 1878–1920. *Economic History Review* 37: 507–19.
1987. Stubborn mules and vertical integration: the disappearing constraint? *Economic History Review* 40: 87–93.
Sayers, R. S. 1976. *The Bank of England, 1891–1944.*
Schmitz, C. J. 1995. *The Growth of Big Business in the United States and Western Europe*. Cambridge.
Schofield, R. S. 1973. Dimensions of illiteracy, 1750–1850. *Explorations in Economic History* 10: 437–54.
Schremmer, D. E. 1989. Taxation and public finance: Britain, France and Germany. In Mathias and Pollard 1989.
Schulze, R., ed. 1993. *Industrial Regions in Transformation: Historical Roots and Patterns of Regional Structural Change: A European Comparison*. Essen.
Schumann, D. 1999. Buddenbrooks revisited: the firm and the entrepreneurial family in Germany during the nineteenth and early twentieth centuries. In P. L. Robertson, ed., *Authority and Control in Modern Industry: Theoretical and Empirical Perspectives.*
Schumpeter, J. A. 1911. *The Theory of Economic Development.*
1939. *Business Cycles: A Theoretical, Historical and Statistical Analysis of the Capitalist Process*. New York.
Scott, J. and Hughes, M. 1980. *The Anatomy of Scottish Capital: Scottish Companies and Scottish Capital 1900–1979.*
Scott, P. 1999. The efficiency of Britain's 'silly little bobtailed' coal wagons: a comment on Van Vleck. *Journal of Economic History* 59: 1072–80.
2000. The state, interal migration and the growth of new industrial communities in interwar Britain. *English Historical Review* 115: 329–53.
2002. Towards the cult of the equity? Insurance companies and the interwar capital market. *Economic History Review* 55: 78–104.
Scranton, P. 1997. *Endless Novelty: Specialty Production and American Industrialization, 1865–1925*. Princeton, NJ.
Sefton, J. and Weale, M. 1995. *Reconciliation of National Income and Expenditure*. Cambridge.

Sells, Dorothy M. 1923. *The British Trade Boards System.*

1939. *British Wage Boards: A Study in Industrial Democracy.* Washington DC.

Sen, A. 1985. The moral standing of the market. In E. F. Paul, J. Paul and F. D. Miller, eds., *Ethics and Economics.* Oxford.

1987. *The Standard of Living.* Cambridge.

1999. *Development as Freedom.* Oxford.

Shadwell, A. 1909. *Industrial Efficiency: A Comparative Study of Industrial Life in England, Germany and America.*

Shannon, H. A. 1930–3. The first five thousand limited companies and their duration. *Economic History* 2: 396–424.

1932–3. The limited companies of 1866 and 1883. *Economic History Review* 4: 290–316.

Sheail, J. 1993. Public interest and self-interest: the disposal of trade effluent in interwar England. *Twentieth Century British History* 4: 149–70.

1997. Business and the environment: an inter-war perspective on the Federation of British Industries. *Contemporary British History* 11.4: 21–41.

Sheldrake, J. and Vickerstaff, S. 1987. *The History of Industrial Training in Britain.* Aldershot.

Silverman, D. P. 1988. National social economics: the Wirtschaftswunder reconsidered. In Eichengreen and Hatton 1988.

Simon, M. 1967. The pattern of new British portfolio foreign investment, 1865–1914. In J. H. Adler, ed., *Capital Movements and Economic Development.*

Slaven, A. 1977. A shipyard in depression: John Brown's of Clydebank 1919–1938. *Business History* 19: 192–217.

1995. From rationalisation to nationalisation: the capacity problem and strategies for survival in British shipbuilding, 1920–1977. In W. Feldenkircheng, F. Schönert-Röhlk and G. Schulz, eds., *Hans Pohl Liber Amicorum: Wirtschaft Gesellschaft Unternehmen.* Stuttgart.

Slaven, A. and Checkland, S., eds. 1986. *Dictionary of Scottish Business Biography 1860–1960,* I. Aberdeen.

1990. *Dictionary of Scottish Business Biography 1860–1960,* II Aberdeen.

Smiles, Samuel. 1886. *Self-Help,* revised edn. New York.

Smith, A. 1976 [1776], *An Inquiry into the Nature and Causes of the Wealth of Nations.* Oxford.

Smith, Hubert Llewellyn, ed. 1930–5. *The New Survey of London Life and Labour,* 9 vols.

Smout, T. C. 1986. *A Century of the Scottish People, 1830–1950.*

Society of Motor Manufacturers and Traders. 1937. *The Motor Industry of Great Britain.*

Solomou, S. N. 1994. Economic fluctuations, 1870–1913. In Floud and McCloskey 1994.

1996. *Themes in Macroeconomic History: The UK Economy, 1919–1939.* Cambridge.

Solomou, S. N. and Catao, L. 2000. Effective exchange rates, 1879–1913. *European Review of Economic History* 4: 361–82.

Solomou, S. N. and Weale, M. 1991. Balanced estimates of UK GDP, 1870–1913. *Explorations in Economic History* 28: 54–63.

Solow, R. M. 1956. A contribution to the theory of economic growth. *Quarterly Journal of Economics* 70: 65–94.

1960. Investment and technical progress. In K. Arrow, S. Karlin and P. Suppes, eds., *Mathematical Methods in the Social Sciences 1959.* Stanford.

1988. Growth theory and after. *American Economic Review* 78: 307–17.

Soskice, D. 1991. Wage determination: the changing role of institutions in advanced industrialized countries. *Oxford Review of Economic Policy* 6: 36–61.

Southall, H. R. 1986. Regional employment patterns among skilled engineers in Britain, 1851–1911. *Journal of Historical Geography* 12: 268–86.

1988. The origins of the depressed areas: unemployment, growth and regional economic structure in Britain before 1914. *Economic History Review* 41: 236–58.

1991. The tramping artisan revisits: labour mobility and economic distress in early Victorian England. *Economic History Review* 44: 272–96.
Statistisches Bundesamt. *Statistisches Jahrbuch für die Bundesrepublik Deutschland.* Wiesbaden.
Statistisches Reichsamt. *Statistisches Jahrbuch für das Deutsche Reich*. Berlin.
Steckel, Richard H. and Floud, Roderick. 1997. *Health and Welfare during Industrialization*. Chicago.
Stedman Jones, G. 1971. *Outcast London: A Study in the Relationship between Classes in Victorian Society*. Oxford.
Stevenson, J. 1977. *Social Conditions in Britain Between the Wars.*
Stiglitz, J. E. 1998. The role of government in the contemporary world. In V. Tanzi and K.-Y. Chu, eds., *Income Distribution and High-Quality Growth.* Cambridge, MA.
Stiglitz, J. E. and Weiss, A. 1981. Credit rationing in markets with imperfect information. *American Economic Review* 71: 393–410.
Stiglitz, J. E. *et al.* 1989. *The Economic Role of the State*. Oxford.
Stone, I. 1977. British direct and portfolio investment in Latin America before 1914. *Journal of Economic History* 37: 690–722.
1999. *The Global Export of Capital from Great Britain, 1865–1914: A Statistical Survey.* New York.
Stone, R., and Rowe, D. A. 1966. *The Measurement of Consumers' Expenditure and Behaviour in the United Kingdom, 1920–1938*, II. Cambridge.
Stopes, M. C. 1918. *Married Love: A New Contribution to the Solution of Sex Difficulties.* New York.
Streit, C. K. 1949. *Union Now: A Proposal for an Atlantic Federal Union of the Free*. New York.
Sturgess, R. W. 1966. The agricultural revolution on the English clays. *Agricultural History Review* 14: 104–21.
Sugihara, K. 1986. Patterns of Asia's integration into the world economy, 1880–1913. In W. Fischer, R. M. McInnis and J. Schneider, eds., *The Emergence of a World Economy 1500–1914 Part II 1850–1914*, Ninth International Congress of Economic History. Published as Beiträge zur Wirtschafts- und Sozialgeschichte, Band 33: II.
Sull, R. S., Tedlow, R. and Rosenbloom, R. S. 1997. Managerial commitments and technological change in the US tire industry. *Industrial and Corporate Change* 6: 461–500.
Supple, B. 1987. *The History of the British Coal Industry, IV: 1913–1946: The Political Economy of Decline*. Oxford.
Supple, B., ed. 1977. *Essays in British Business History*. Oxford.
Sutherland, G. 1990. Education. In Thompson 1990b.
Svedberg, P. 1978. The portfolio-direct composition of private foreign investment in 1914 revisited. *Economic Journal* 80: 763–77.
Szreter, S. 1984. The genesis of the registrar general's social classification of occupations. *British Journal of Sociology* 35: 522–46.
1988. The importance of social intervention in Britain's mortality decline c. 1850–1914: a re-interpretation of the role of public health. *Social History of Medicine* 1: 1–37.
1996. *Fertility, Class and Gender in Britain, 1860–1940*. Cambridge.
1997. Economic growth, disruption, deprivation, disease, and death: on the importance of the politics of public health for development. *Population and Development Review* 23: 693–728.
Szreter, S. and Hardy, A. 2000. Urban fertility and mortality patterns. In Daunton 2000.
Szreter, S. and Mooney, G. 1998. Urbanization, mortality and the standard of living debate: new estimates of the expectation of life at birth in nineteenth-century British cities. *Economic History Review* 51: 84–112.

Tanzi, V. and Schuknecht, L. 2000. *Public Spending in the 20th Century: A Global Perspective*. Cambridge.

Tawney, R. H. 1915. *The Establishment of Minimum Rates in the Tailoring Industry under the Trade Boards Act of 1909*.

1943. The abolition of economic controls, 1918–1921. *Economic History Review* 1st ser. 13: 1–30.

Taylor, A. M. 2002. A century of current account dynamics. NBER, Cambridge, MA, working paper, 8927. Forthcoming in *Journal of International Money and Finance*.

Taylor, A. M. and Williamson, Jeffrey G. 1997. Convergence in the age of mass migration. *European Review of Economic History* 1: 27–63.

Taylor, D. 1976. The English dairy industry, 1860–1930. *Economic History Review* 29: 585–601.

Teitelbaum, M. S. and Winter, J. M. 1985. *The Fear of Population Decline*. Orlando, FL.

Temin, P. 1966. The relative decline of the British steel industry, 1880–1913. In H. Rosovsky, ed., *Industrialisation in Two Systems: Essays in Honour of Alexander Gerschenkron*. New York.

1989. *Lessons from the Great Depression*. Cambridge, MA.

Thane, P. M. 1990. Government and society in England and Wales, 1750–1914. In Thompson 1990b.

2000. *Old Age in English History*. Oxford.

Thomas, M. 1983. Rearmament and economic recovery in the late 1930s. *Economic History Review* 36: 552–79.

Thomas, M. 1988. Labour market structure and the nature of unemployment in interwar Britain. In Eichengreen and Hatton 1988.

1994. The macro-economics of the inter-war years. In Floud and McCloskey 1994.

Thomas, S. E. 1931. *British Banks and the Finance of Industry*.

Thomas, T. J. 1976. Aspects of UK macroeconomic policy during the interwar period. Unpublished PhD dissertation, University of Cambridge.

Thomas, W. A. 1973. *The Provincial Stock Exchanges*.

1978. *The Finance of British Industry, 1918–1976*.

Thompson, F. M. L. 1959. Agriculture since 1870. *Victoria County History of Wiltshire*, IV.

1963. *English Landed Society in the Nineteenth Century*.

1968. The second agricultural revolution, 1815–80. *Economic History Review* 21: 62–77.

1989. Rural society and agricultural change in nineteenth-century Britain. In G. Grantham and C. S. Leonard, eds., *Agrarian Organization in the Century of Industrialization: Europe, Russia, and North America. Research in Economic History*, Supplement 5.

1990a. Life after death: how successful nineteenth century businessmen disposed of their fortunes. *Economic History Review* 43: 40–61.

1991. An anatomy of English agriculture, 1870–1914. In Holderness and Turner 1991: 211–40.

1992. Stitching it together again. *Economic History Review* 45: 362–74.

1994. Business and landed elites in the nineteenth century. In F. M. L. Thompson, ed., *Landowners, Capitalists and Entrepreneurs*. Oxford.

Thompson, F. M. L., ed. 1990b. *The Cambridge Social History of Britain, 1750–1950*. Cambridge.

Thomson, David. 1984. The decline of social welfare: falling state support for the elderly since early victorian times. *Ageing and Society* 4: 451–82.

Tilly, R. H. 1986. German banking 1850–1914: development assistance for the strong. *Journal of European Economic History* 15: 113–52.

Tolliday, S. 1987. *Business, Banking and Politics: The Case of British Steel, 1918–1939*. Cambridge, MA.

1991. Competition and maturity in the British steel industry, 1870–1914. In E. Abe and Y. Suzuki, eds., *Changing Patterns of International Rivalry: Some Lessons from the Steel Industry*. Tokyo.

Tomlinson, J. D. 1990. *Public Policy and the Economy since 1900*. Oxford.

1994. *Government and the Enterprise since 1900: The Changing Problem of Efficiency*. Oxford.

Toms, J. S. 1998. Growth, profits and technological choice: the case of the Lancashire cotton industry. *Journal of Industrial History* 1: 35–55.

Tout, Herbert. 1938. *The Standard of Living in Bristol*. Bristol.

Trainor, Richard. 2000. The middle class. In Daunton 2000.

Treble, J. G. 1987. Sliding scales and conciliation: risk sharing in the 19th century British coal industry. *Oxford Economic Papers* 39: 679–98.

Treble, J. H. 1978a. The market for unskilled male labour in Glasgow 1891–1914. In I. Macdougall, ed., *Essays in Scottish Labour History*. Edinburgh.

1978b. Unemployment and unemployment policies in Glasgow 1890–1905. In P. M. Thane, ed., *The Origins of British Social Policy*.

1979. *Urban Poverty in Britain 1830–1914*.

1980. The pattern of investment of the Standard Life Assurance Co. 1875–1914. *Business History* 22: 170–88.

Tressell, R. 1955. *The Ragged Trousered Philanthropists*.

Turner, M. E. 1996. *After the Famine*. Cambridge.

2000. Agricultural output, income and productivity. In Collins 2000b.

Turner. M. E., Beckett. J. V. and Afton, B. 1997. *Agricultural Rent in England 1690–1914*. Cambridge.

2001. *Farm Production in England 1700–1914*. Oxford.

Turner. P. and Bowden, S. 1997. Real wages, demand and employment in the UK, 1921–1938: a disaggregated analysis. *Bulletin of Economic Research* 49: 309–25.

Tweedale, G. 2000. *Magic Mineral to Killer Dust; Turner & Newall and the Asbestos Hazard*. Oxford.

Tyack, D. B., ed. 1967. *Turning Points in American Educational History*. Lexington, MA.

United Nations Development Programme. 1990. *Human Development Report*. New York.

United States. 1975. *Historical Statistics of the United States: Colonial Times to 1970*. Washington.

Urquhart, M. C. and Buckley, K. A. H., eds. 1965. *Historical Statistics of Canada*. Toronto.

Usher, D. 1980. *The Measurement of Economic Growth*. New York.

van Antwerp, W. C. 1913. *The Stock Exchange from Within*. New York.

van Ark, B. and Crafts, N., eds. 1996. *Quantitative Aspects of Postwar European Economic Growth*. Cambridge.

van Helten, J. J. and Cassis, Y., eds. 1990. *Capitalism in a Mature Economy: Financial Institutions, Capital Exports and British Industry, 1870–1939*. Aldershot.

Van Vleck, V. N. L. 1997. Delivering coal by road and rail in Britain: the efficiency of the 'silly little bobtailed' coal wagons. *Journal of Economic History* 57: 139–60.

1999. In defense again of 'silly little bobtailed' coal wagons: reply to Peter Scott. *Journal of Economic History* 59: 1081–4.

Veverka, J. 1963. The growth of government expenditure in the United Kingdom since 1790. *Scottish Journal of Political Economy* 10: 111–27.

Von Tunzelmann, G. N. 1982. Structural change and leading sectors in British manufacturing 1907–36. In Kindleberger and di Tella 1982.

Wale, J. 1994. What help have the banks given British industry? Some evidence on bank lending in the Midlands in the late nineteenth century. *Accounting, Business and Financial History* 4: 321–42.

Wall, R. and Winter, J., eds. 1988. *The Upheaval of War: Family, Work and Welfare in Europe, 1914–18*. Cambridge.

Walton, J. R. 1979. Mechanisation in agriculture: a study of the adoption process. In H. S. A. Fox and R. A. Butlin, eds., *Change in the Countryside: Essays on Rural England 1500–1900*.

1999. Varietal innovation and the competitiveness of the British cereals sector, 1760–1930. *Agricultural History Review* 47: 29–57.

Ward, D. 1967. The public schools and industry in Britain after 1870. *Journal of Contemporary History* 2: 37–52.

Wardley, P. 1991. The anatomy of big business: aspects of corporate development in the twentieth century. *Business History* 33: 268–96.

2000. The commercial banking industry and its part in the emergence and consolidation of the corporate economy in Britain before 1940. *Journal of Industrial History* 3: 71–97.

Warner, W. L. and Abegglen, J. C. 1955. *Occupational Mobility in American Business and Industry, 1928–1952*. Minneapolis, MN.

Watson, K. 1995. The new issue market as a source of finance for the UK brewing and iron and steel industries, 1870–1913. In Cassis *et al.* 1995.

1996. Banks and industrial finance: the experience of brewers 1880–1913. *Economic History Review* 49: 58–81.

Webb, Sidney and Webb, Beatrice. 1897. *Industrial Democracy*.

Wehler, H. U. 1970. Bismarck's imperialism 1862–90. *Past and Present* 48: 119–55.

Westall, O. M. 1992. *The Provincial Insurance Company, 1903–1938: Family, Markets and Competitive Growth*. Manchester.

Whiteside, N. and Gillespie, J. A. 1991. Deconstructing unemployment: developments in Britain in the interwar years. *Economic History Review* 44: 665–82.

Wiener, M. J. 1981. *English Culture and the Decline of the Industrial Spirit, 1850–1980*. Cambridge.

Wilkes, A. R. 1980. Adjustments in arable farming after the Napoleonic wars. *Agricultural History Review* 28: 90–103.

Wilkins, Mira. 1988. The free-standing company, 1870–1914: an important type of British foreign direct investment. *Economic History Review* 41: 259–82.

Williams, Alfred. 1915. *Life in a Railway Factory*.

Williams, F. 1935. Insurance companies and investment trusts. In Cole 1935.

Williams, G. 1957. *Recruitment to Skilled Trades*.

1963. *Apprenticeship in Europe: The Lesson for Britain*.

Williams, K. 1981. *From Pauperism to Poverty*.

Williams. N. J. 2000. Housing. In W. H. Fraser and C. H. Lee, eds., *Aberdeen 1800–2000: A New History*. East Linton.

Williamson, J. G. 1981. Urban disamenities, dark satanic mills, and the British standard of living debate. *Journal of Economic History* 41: 75–83.

1984. British mortality and the value of life, 1781–1931. *Population Studies* 38: 157–72.

1990. *Coping with City Growth during the British Industrial Revolution*. Cambridge.

1991. *Inequality, Poverty and History*. Oxford.

1995. The evolution of global labour markets since 1830: background evidence and hypotheses. *Explorations in Economic History* 32: 141–96.

Wilson, C. 1977. Management and policy in large-scale enterprise: Lever Brothers and Unilever, 1918–1938. In Supple 1977.

Wilson, J. F. 1995. *British Business History, 1720–1994*. Manchester.

1997. The finance of municipal capital expenditure in England and Wales, 1870–1914. *Financial History Review* 4: 31–50.

Wilt, A. F. 2001. *Food for War: Agriculture and Rearmament in Britain before the Second World War*. Oxford.

Winstanley, M. 1983. *The Shopkeepers World, 1830–1914*. Manchester.

1994. Concentration and competition in the retail sector c. 1800–1990. In Kirby and Rose 1994.

Winter, J. M. 1979. Infant mortality, maternal mortality and public health in Britain in the 1930s. *Journal of European Economic History* 8: 439–62.

1985. *The Great War and the British People.*

Withers, C. W. J. 1998. *Urban Highlanders: Highland–Lowland Migration and Urban Gaelic Culture 1700–1900.* East Linton.

Wolf, C. 1993. *Markets or Governments: Choosing between Imperfect Alternatives*, 2nd edn. Cambridge, MA.

Wood, George H. 1901. Stationary wage-rates. *Economic Journal* 11: 151–56.

1909. Real wages and the standard of comfort since 1850. *Journal of the Royal Statistical Society* 72: 91–103.

Woods, R. 1985. The effects of population redistribution on the level of mortality in nineteenth-century England and Wales. *Journal of Economic History* 45: 645–51.

1995. *The Population of Britain in the Nineteenth Century.* Cambridge.

2000. *The Demography of Victorian England and Wales.* Cambridge.

Woods, R. and Shelton, N. 1997. *An Atlas of Victorian Mortality.* Liverpool.

Woods, R. and Woodward, J., eds. 1984. *Urban Disease and Mortality in Nineteenth Century England.*

Wordie, J. R. 2000. Perceptions and reality: the effects of the corn laws and their repeal in England, 1815–1906. In J. R. Wordie, ed., *Agriculture and Politics in England, 1815–1939.*

World Bank 1997. *World Development Report, 1997: The State in a Changing World.* Oxford.

Worswick, G. D. N. 1984. The sources of recovery in the UK in the 1930s. *National Institute Economic Review* 110: 85–93.

Wright, G. 1971. An econometric study of cotton production and trade, 1830–60. *Review of Economics and Statistics* 53: 111–20.

1974. Cotton consumption and the post-bellum recovery of the American South. *Journal of Economic History* 34: 610–35.

Wrigley, C. 1987a. The First World War and state intervention in industrial relations, 1914–18. In Wrigley 1987b.

Wrigley, C., ed. 1987b. *A History of British Industrial Relations*, II: *1914–39.* Brighton.

Wrigley, E. A. 1983. The growth of population in eighteenth-century England: a conundrum resolved. *Past and Present* 98: 121–50.

1987. *People, Cities and Wealth.* Oxford.

1988. *Continuity, Chance and Change.* Cambridge.

1998. Explaining the rise in fertility in England in the long eighteenth century. *Economic History Review* 51: 435–64.

Wrigley, E. A. and Schofield, R. S. 1981. *The Population History of England, 1541–1871: A Reconstruction.*

Wrigley, E. A., Davies, R. S., Oeppen, J. E. and Schofield, R. S. 1997. *English Population History from Family Reconstitution 1580–1837.* Cambridge.

Wrigley, J. 1986. Technical training and industry in Elbaum and Lazonick 1986.

Ziegler, D. 1997. The origins of the 'Macmillan gap': comparing Britain and Germany in the early twentieth century. In Cottrell *et al.* 1997.

Index